PERFORMANCE AND PROGRESS

PERFORMANCE AND PROGRESS

Essays on Capitalism, Business, and Society

Edited by

SUBRAMANIAN RANGAN

OXFORD

UNIVERSITY PRESS

OXFORD
UNIVERSITY PRESS

Great Clarendon Street, Oxford, OX2 6DP,
United Kingdom

Oxford University Press is a department of the University of Oxford.
It furthers the University's objective of excellence in research, scholarship,
and education by publishing worldwide. Oxford is a registered trade mark of
Oxford University Press in the UK and in certain other countries

First edition published 2015

Impression: 1

Published in the United States of America by Oxford University Press
198 Madison Avenue, New York, NY 10016, United States of America

British Library Cataloguing in Publication Data
Data available

Library of Congress Control Number: 2015930214

ISBN 978-0-19-874428-3

Printed and bound by
CPI Group (UK) Ltd, Croydon, CR0 4YY

ACKNOWLEDGMENTS

An endeavor like this materializes only upon the willful engagement and encouragement of a large number of individuals and institutions. My home institution INSEAD, whose motto is "business school for the world," provides a solid platform for pioneering at the intersection of relevance and rigor. My chair in "societal progress" was envisioned and endowed by the Abu Dhabi Crown Prince Court. Being appointed first holder of this chair brought me time and confidence to pursue the present work. Independently, it was a substantial grant from the Abu Dhabi Education Council (ADEC) that enabled the organization and assembly of this august group of contributors at the Royal Society in London. I am immensely grateful to Dr. Mugheer and to Dr. Amal for their genuine interest, support, and trust. And last but not least, among institutions, I thank Oxford University Press, and, in particular, David Musson, Clare Kennedy, Rachel Neaum, and Manikandan Chandrasekaran, for taking prompt interest in this work and showing care and attention during its publication.

As for individuals, as far as I can recall, and long before it became fashionable, I have been an adherent of "crowdsourcing." From conception several years ago to inception and implementation this effort has benefitted from the attention, encouragement, input, and support of a large number of individuals (colleagues, former professors, friends, exceptional individuals that I have the good fortune of knowing, and a few great souls that inspired me, as they have others, just through their work and lives).

Though the list below is long, I am afraid that there are more people that have contributed than I might remember. I request their forgiveness for my oversight on this count. Without further ado then I wish to express my heartfelt gratitude for time, encouragement, valuable input, and assistance to (in alphabetical order): Jose Luis Alvarez, John Broome, Stephen Chick, Karel Cool, Catriona Corrigan, Nicholas da Costa, Sherif El Diwany, Martine Durand, Anne Fournier, Doug Frank, Charlotte Fraizy, Catherine Galitzine, Enrico Giovannini, Maria Guadalupe, Dominique Heau, Pekka Hietala, Herminia Ibarra, Ioannis Ioannou, Peter Jadersten, Dipak Jain, Neil Jones, Kevin Kaiser, Charles Mackay, Will Maddux, Sami Mahroum, Jens Meyer, Philipp Meyer-Doyle, Felipe Monteiro, Serguei Nettesine, Jean Claude Noel, Tomasz Obloj, Sophie Peronnet, Michelle Rogan, Filipe Santos, Debra Satz, Florian Schloderer, Metin Sengul, Zeina Sleiman, Hind Talhouk, Andreas Teuber, Heinz Thanheiser, Tim Van Zandt, Theo Vermaelen, and Danqing Wang.

Now, as is often the case in such projects, some people end up playing an especially significant (and sometimes indispensable) role. In this category I wish to mention and express deep personal appreciation to: Rolf Abdon, Ron Adner, Andre Almeida, Phil Anderson, Mike Brimm, Rabih Abouchakra, Frank Brown, Jean Dermine, Aldemir

Drummond, Antonio Fatas, Javier Gimeno, Denis Gromb, Esmond Harmsworth, Alison James, Claude and Tuulikki Janssen, Dr. Mugheer Al Khaili, Robert Lawrence, Miguel Lobo, Ilian Mihov, Dr. Jihad Mohaidat, Michele Plu, Shantanu Prakash, Dr. Amal al Qubaisi, Vikas Tibrewala, Peter Zemsky, and Ming Zeng.

I would be remiss to not explicitly acknowledge the energy I derived from the engagement and encouragement of the distinguished contributors, especially the elders Ken Arrow, Jim March, John Meyer, and Amartya Sen, who came on board graciously to support and contribute to this improbable endeavor. One of them put it this way: this is the sort of idea that is good if it were to happen, but it doesn't usually happen. But this time they made it happen.

I wish to separately underline the contributions of three individuals. The colleague and friend whom I relied on throughout this journey and whose counsel has thoroughly shaped the "dreams and details" has been Gareth Dyas, who twenty years ago recruited me to INSEAD, cherished my training in political economy, and steadfastly encouraged my eclectic interests especially at the intersection of business and society. His wisdom and empathy are sage and have been crucial in terms of minimizing risk. And few nurture aspiration as he does, which has been crucial in terms of minimizing regret. I thank Dana Dyas for steadfast interest, input, and indulgence.

The other person whose contribution has been indispensable is the young philosopher Mike Fuerstein. For someone like me, entirely outside the field of philosophy, it was as challenging as it was important to identify the appropriate scholars to contact for this project. Mike helped navigate this delicate "search and recruit" operation, and, from the acknowledgment of the eminent philosophers themselves, it is clear that he has guided us expertly. The project continues to benefit from his keen mind, able writing, and ready generosity.

In a league apart stands Ebba Hansmeyer without whose conviction and collaboration this project would simply not be. An inherent humanist, Ebba's training in law and work in human rights, her natural engagement with peoples and problems of the world, her belief in the power of ideas and intellectuals, and her selfless and down to earth orientation all sustained and advanced this project in both its design and realization. I am indebted to her (and her family) for incredible sacrifice and support for this project.

A penultimate special category of acknowledgment is to people that were not directly involved in this book, but whose ethos and work have deeply inspired me and shaped my aspirations on this project. They include: Emerson Almeida, Pascal Berend, Henri Claude de Bettignies, Steve Denning, Georges Doriot, John Dewey, Ernst Fehr, Fadi Ghandour, Angel Gurria, Amy Gutmann, Knut Haanaes, Albert Hirschman, Liu Jiren, Abdul Kalam, Chan Kim, Lindsay Levin, Mohamed Mubarak Al Mazrouei, Renee Mauborgne, Henry Mintzberg, Narayana Murthy, Nitin Nohria, Indra Nooyi, Martha Nussbaum, Sandy Ogg, Adam Smith, John Rawls, Hilde and Klaus Schwab, S. D. Shibulal, Jamsetji Tata, Tidjane Thiam, Raymond Vernon, and Sheikh Zayed.

It only remains for me to thank my family, including my loving parents, brother, and sister, my incredibly supportive wife and equipoise life companion, Nalini, and our two children (who've in equal parts been absorbed and amused by this undertaking).

CONTENTS

PART III   BALANCING AND TRADE-OFFS

PART IV   CHOICES AND PREFERENCES

PART V POWER AND TRUST

LIST OF FIGURES

LIST OF TABLES

List of Tables

List of Contributors

Elizabeth Anderson is Arthur F. Thurnau Professor and John Dewey Distinguished University Professor of Philosophy and Women's Studies at the University of Michigan, Ann Arbor. She earned her Ph.D. from Harvard University in 1987 and previously taught at Swarthmore College. She is a Guggenheim Fellow, an ACLS Fellow, a member of the American Academy of Arts and Sciences, and Vice President of the Central Division of the American Philosophical Association. She is the author of *Value in Ethics and Economics* (Harvard UP, 1993), *The Imperative of Integration* (Princeton UP, 2010), and over sixty articles in journals of philosophy, law, and economics. She specializes in moral and political philosophy, social and feminist epistemology, and the philosophy of the social sciences. Her current project is a history of egalitarianism from the Levellers to the present, with a special focus on the organization of the workplace and labor relations, markets, and contracts.

Kwame Anthony Appiah is Professor of Philosophy and Law at New York University. He was born in London, grew up in Ghana, and took both BA and Ph.D. degrees in philosophy at Cambridge University. He has taught in Ghana, France, Britain, and the United States; and has published widely in philosophy as well as in African and African-American literary and cultural studies. Among his books are *The Ethics of Identity and Cosmopolitanism: Ethics in a World of Strangers*, which won the Arthur Ross Award of the Council on Foreign Relations. In 2013 Harvard University Press published his *Lines of Descent: W. E. B. Du Bois and the Emergence of Identity*.

Kenneth J. Arrow is Professor Emeritus of Economics and of Management Science and Engineering at Stanford University, and Senior Fellow of the Stanford Institute for Policy Research and of the Center for Health Policy there. He has taught at Stanford University, Harvard University, and the University of Chicago, and has been a Visiting Professor or Fellow at the Massachusetts Institute of Technology, Churchill College (Cambridge), All Souls College (Oxford), and the University of Sienna. Dr. Arrow graduated from the College of the City of New York (1940) and received an MA (mathematics, 1941) and Ph.D. (economics, 1951) from Columbia University. He is the author of twenty-one books and 279 papers in learned journals or edited volumes. His principal research fields have been social choice, general equilibrium, economics of uncertainty and information, inventory theory, optimal growth with special reference to environmental constraints, health economics, and the economics of innovation. He has received several honors, including the John Bates Clark Medal (American

Economic Association), Nobel Memorial Prize in Economic Science, National Medal of Science, von Neumann Prize, and Medal of the University of Paris. He is especially proud that three students and two close collaborators have won the Nobel Memorial Prize.

David H. Autor is a Professor of Economics at the Massachusetts Institute of Technology Department of Economics, Faculty Research Associate of the National Bureau of Economic Research, Research Affiliate of the Abdul Jameel Latif Poverty Action Lab, and Editor-in-Chief of the *Journal of Economic Perspectives*. Autor is the recipient of an NSF CAREER award for his research on labor market intermediation, the Alfred P. Sloan Foundation Fellowship, the Sherwin Rosen Prize in 2008 for outstanding contributions in the field of Labor Economics, and the John T. Dunlop Outstanding Scholar Award in 2006 given by the Labor and Employment Relations Association. He received the MIT Undergraduate Economics Association Teaching Award in 2005 and the James A. and Ruth Levitan Award for Excellence in Teaching in 2013, awarded by MIT's School of Humanities Arts and Social Sciences. Autor is Co-director of the MIT School Effectiveness and Inequality Initiative (SEII), and Associate Director of the NBER Disability Research Center, funded by the Social Security Administration. He is also a Research Associate of the IZA in Bonn, the IAB in Nuremberg, and the Institute for Research on Poverty at the University of Wisconsin, Madison. Autor received a BA in Psychology from Tufts University in 1989 and a Ph.D. in Public Policy at Harvard University's Kennedy School of Government in 1999.

Jay B. Barney, Presidential Professor of Strategic Management, holds the Pierre Lassonde Chair in Social Entrepreneurship at the David Eccles School of Business at the University of Utah. He holds honorary visiting appointments at Peking University (Beijing), Sun Yat Sen University (Guangzhou), Waikato University (New Zealand), and Brunel University (UK) and has received honorary doctorate degrees (Lund University, Copenhagen Business School, and the Universidad Pontificia Comillas, Madrid). He served on the Executive Committee of the Business Policy and Strategy Division of the Academy, and as President of the Division, was elected a fellow of the Academy of Management and a Fellow of the Strategic Management Society, and received the Irwin Outstanding Educator Award for the Business Policy and Strategy Division of AOM. Professor Barney is currently Senior Editor at the *Strategic Entrepreneurship Journal*. He has published over 100 articles and book chapters and six books. His research focuses on identifying the attributes of firm resources and capabilities that enable firms to gain and sustain a competitive advantage. In addition, he has begun doing research on entrepreneurship and corporate social responsibility, with special emphasis on entrepreneurship among the abject poor.

Julie Battilana is Associate Professor of Business Administration in the Organizational Behavior unit at Harvard Business School. Her research aims to understand whether, and if so, how hybrid organizations can sustainably combine aspects of business and charity and achieve high levels of social and financial performance. She has articles published or forthcoming in *Academy of Management Journal, Organization Science, Management Science, Strategic Organization, Leadership Quarterly, Organization, Research in Organizational Behavior*, and *The Academy of Management Annals*, as well as in handbooks of organizational behavior and strategy. A native of France, Professor Battilana earned a BA in sociology and economics, an MA in political sociology, and an M.Sc. in organizational sociology and public policy from École Normale Supérieure de Cachan. She also holds a degree from HEC Business School, and a joint Ph.D. in organizational behavior from INSEAD and in management and economics from École Normale Supérieure de Cachan.

Bertrand Collomb is Honorary Chairman of Lafarge, a worldwide leader in building materials. He is also a director of Total, DuPont, and ATCO. He is a member of the Institut de France and was chairman of the Académie des sciences morales et politiques. A graduate of the École Polytechnique and the École des Mines in Paris, he also holds a French law degree and a Ph.D. in Management (University of Texas). He founded the Center for Management Research at the École Polytechnique.

From 1966 to 1975, he worked with the French government in various positions. He joined Lafarge in 1975. After several responsibilities in various areas of the group, including CEO of Lafarge Corporation, the North American arm of the group (1985–8), he was appointed chairman and CEO of Lafarge in August 1989. He was Chairman of Lafarge from 2003 to 2007. He led Lafarge to become a global leader, while maintaining a people-oriented culture. He is a proponent of sustainable development, a founding member of WBCSD (World Business Council for Sustainable Development), of which he was the chairman in 2004–5.

Gerald F. Davis received his Ph.D from the Graduate School of Business at Stanford University and taught at Northwestern and Columbia before moving to the University of Michigan, where he is Wilbur K. Pierpont Collegiate Professor of Management and of Sociology. He has published widely in management, sociology, and finance. Recent books include *Social Movements and Organization Theory* (Cambridge University Press, 2005); *Organizations and Organizing* (Pearson Prentice Hall, 2007); *Managed by the Markets: How Finance Reshaped America* (Oxford University Press, 2009); and *Grassroots Social Innovation* (Harvard Business School Press, forthcoming). He is the Editor of *Administrative Science Quarterly* and Co-Director of the Interdisciplinary Committee on Organization Studies (ICOS) at the University of Michigan. Davis's research is broadly concerned with the effects of finance on society.

Robert H. Frank is the HJ Louis Professor of Management and Professor of Economics at Cornell's Johnson School of Management and the co-director of the Paduano Seminar in business ethics at NYU's Stern School of Business. His "Economic View" column appears monthly in *The New York Times*. He is a Distinguished Senior Fellow at Demos. He received his BS in mathematics from Georgia Tech, then taught math and science for two years as a Peace Corps Volunteer in rural Nepal. He holds an MA in statistics and a Ph.D. in economics, both from the University of California at Berkeley. His papers have appeared in the *American Economic Review*, *Econometrica*, *Journal of Political Economy*, and other leading journals. His books, which include *Choosing the Right Pond*, *Passions Within Reason*, *Microeconomics and Behavior*, *Principles of Economics* (with Ben Bernanke), *Luxury Fever*, *What Price the Moral High Ground?*, *Falling Behind*, *The Economic Naturalist*, and *The Darwin Economy*, have been translated into twenty-two languages. *The Winner-Take-All Society*, co-authored with Philip Cook, received a Critic's Choice Award. He is a co-recipient of the 2004 Leontief Prize for Advancing the Frontiers of Economic Thought. He was awarded the Johnson School's Stephen Russell Distinguished teaching award in 2004, 2010, and 2012, and its Apple Distinguished Teaching Award in 2005.

Michael Fuerstein is Assistant Professor of Philosophy at St Olaf College in Northfield, Minnesota. He completed his Ph.D. at Columbia University in 2009 and, following that, held a post-doc at the Center for Cultural Analysis at Rutgers University. His work has appeared in such venues as the *Journal of Political Philosophy*, *Episteme*, and *The Cambridge Dictionary of Philosophy*. His current research focuses on the relationship between democracy and moral progress.

Harrison Hong is the John Scully '66 Professor of Economics and Finance at Princeton University, where he teaches courses in finance in the undergraduate, master and Ph.D. programs. Before joining Princeton in 2002, he was on the faculty of the Graduate School of Business at Stanford University. He received his BA in economics and statistics with highest distinction from the University of California at Berkeley in 1992 and his Ph.D. in economics from MIT in 1997. He is on the editorial board of the *Journal of Finance*. He is a Director of the American Finance Association and a research associate at the National Bureau of Economic Research. In 2009, he was awarded the American Finance Association's Fischer Black Prize, given biennially to the person under 40 who has contributed the most to the theory and practice of finance.

Majid H. Jafar is the CEO of Crescent Petroleum, the Middle East's oldest private oil & gas company, and Vice-Chairman of the Crescent Group of companies which includes interests in port management, logistics, contracting, private equity, and real estate. He is also Managing Director of the Board of Dana Gas (PJSC), the leading publicly listed natural gas company in the Middle East, in which Crescent is the largest shareholder. His previous experience was with Shell International's Exploration & Production and Gas & Power Divisions. In addition to his professional commitments, Majid Jafar currently serves as Chairman of the Middle East-North Africa Business Council and Chairman of the Oil & Gas Independents Community at the World Economic Forum, Co-Chairman of the Business Backs Education campaign launched with the GEMS Foundation, and Vice-Chairman of the Global Energy Initiative (GEI). He is also a Board Member of: the Carnegie Middle East Advisory Council, the Arab

Forum for Environment and Development (AFED), the Higher Colleges of Technology (HCT) Industry Advisory Council, and the Iraq Energy Institute, as well as an active member of: the GCC Board Directors Institute, the Royal Institute for International Affairs (Chatham House), the International Institute for Strategic Studies (IISS), the Young Presidents Organization (YPO), the Young Arab Leaders organization (YAL), and an Accredited Director of the Institute of Directors (IoD Mudara). Majid Jafar attended Eton College and graduated from Cambridge University (Churchill College) with Bachelor and Masters Degrees in Engineering (Fluid Mechanics and Thermodynamics). He also holds an MA (with Distinction) in International Studies and Diplomacy from the University of London's School of Oriental & African Studies (SOAS), and an MBA (with Distinction) from the Harvard Business School.

Philip Kitcher was born in 1947 in London. He received his BA from Cambridge University and his Ph.D. from Princeton. He is currently John Dewey Professor of Philosophy at Columbia University. He has written on topics ranging from the philosophy of mathematics to Joyce's *Finnegans Wake*. Recent books include: *Science in a Democratic Society* (Prometheus Books, 2011), *The Ethical Project* (Harvard University Press, 2011), *Preludes to Pragmatism* (Oxford University Press, 2012), *Deaths in Venice: The Cases of Gustav von Aschenbach* (Columbia University Press, 2013). He has been President of the American Philosophical Association (Pacific Division) and Editor-in-Chief of *Philosophy of Science*. He was the first recipient of the Prometheus Prize, awarded by the American Philosophical Association for work in expanding the frontiers of science and philosophy. He received a Lannan Foundation Notable Book Award for *Living with Darwin*. During 2011–12, he was a Fellow at the Wissenschaftskolleg zu Berlin, where he was partially supported by a prize from the Humboldt Foundation. His Terry Lectures were published as *Life After Faith: The Case for Secular Humanism* (2014).

Inessa Liskovich is an Assistant Professor of finance at the McCombs School of Business, University of Texas at Austin. She received her Ph.D in economics at Princeton University. Prior to beginning her graduate studies she received her BS in economics and in mathematics from MIT in 2009 and then worked as a trader at Goldman Sachs. Her research focuses on empirical corporate finance, covering topics such as corporate governance, corporate social responsibility, and stock market efficiency.

Jack Ma is Executive Chairman, Alibaba Group, People's Republic of China. He obtained a degree in English Language Education at the Hangzhou Teacher's Institute. In 1999 he founded Alibaba and until 2013 was Chairman and Chief Executive Officer. He is a member of the board, SoftBank Corp., one of Alibaba Group's major shareholders and a Japanese telecommunications and internet corporation listed on the Tokyo Stock Exchange; a director at Huayi Brothers Media Corporation, an entertainment group in China listed on the Shenzhen Stock Exchange. He is chair, China Board of Directors, and director, Global Board of Directors, and The Nature Conservancy. He is director of the Breakthrough Prize in Life Sciences Foundation.

James G. March is Professor Emeritus at Stanford University, where he has been on the faculty since 1970. He holds appointments in the Schools of Business and Education and in the Departments of Political Science and Sociology. He received his BA degree from the University of Wisconsin and his MA and Ph.D. from Yale University. He has received honorary doctorates and honorary professorships from several European and North American universities and has been elected to membership in the National Academy of Science, the American Academy of Arts and Sciences, the American Philosophical Society, the National Academy of Public Administration, and the National Academy of Education, as well as several overseas academies. He received the Wilbur Cross Medal from Yale University in 1968, the Academy of Management Award for Scholarly Contributions to Management in 1984, the Walter J. Gores Award for Excellence in Teaching from Stanford University in 1995, the John Gaus Award from the American Political Science Association in 1997, the Distinguished Scholar Award from the Academy of Management in 1999, the Viipuri Award from the Viipuri Society in 2004, the Aaron Wildavsky Award from the Public Policy Society in 2004, and the Herbert Simon Award from Laslo Raik College (Budapest) in 2005. In 1995 he was made a Knight First Class in the Royal Norwegian (Olav V) Order of Merit, and in 1999 he was made a Commander of the Order of the Lion of Finland. He has been a member of the National Science Board (1969–74) and the National Council on Educational Research (1975–8). From 1984 to 1994 he was a member, and from 1991 to 1993 Chair, of the Board of Trustees of the Russell Sage Foundation. He has also been a member of the Board of Directors of Sun Hydraulics Corporation (1989–92 and 1996–2000), the Scandinavian Consortium for Organizational Research (1988–99), and Wally Industries (1996–2001). From 1994 to 2001 he was a member of the Board of the Citigroup Behavioral Sciences Research Council (chair 1994–2000).

He is best known professionally for his writings on decision-making and organizations, including *Organizations, A Behavioral Theory of the Firm, Leadership and Ambiguity, Ambiguity and Choice in Organizations, Decisions and Organizations, Rediscovering Institutions, The Pursuit of Organizational Intelligence, Democratic Governance, A Primer on Decision Making, The Dynamics of Rules, Explorations in Organizations, On Leadership*, and *The Ambiguities of Experience*. He has also written nine books of poetry and two films.

Ramón Mendiola is CEO of Florida Ice & Farm Company, a leading Central American company with three main businesses: beverages & food, retail, and real estate & hotels, with operations in Central America and the United States. Five years ago, he led the company through a breakthrough transformation merging the company business strategy with its sustainability strategy to become a Triple Bottom Line company where its executives' compensation is linked to economic, social, and environmental KPIs. Because of this visionary decision, his company was chosen as one of the Sustainability Champions of the World Economic Forum. Mendiola has a business administration and marketing degree from Babson College and he has an MBA with an emphasis on international business marketing and strategy, from the Kellogg Graduate School of Management at Northwestern University.

John W. Meyer is Professor of Sociology, emeritus, at Stanford. He has contributed to organizational theory, comparative education, and the sociology of education, developing sociological institutional theory. He has studied the national impacts of global society (some papers are collected in *Weltkultur: Wie die westlichen Prinzipien die Welt durchdringen* (Suhrkamp, 2005); a more extensive set is in *World Society: The Writings of John W. Meyer* (Oxford University Press, 2009). One collaborative study examines worldwide science and its national effects (Drori et al., *Science in the Modern World Polity*, Stanford UP, 2003). A more recent collaborative project is on the organizational impact of globalization (Drori et al., eds, *Globalization and Organization*, Oxford University Press, 2006). He now studies the world human rights regime, world curricula in mass and higher education, and the worldwide expansion of formal organization. He is a member of the National Academy of Education, has honorary doctorates from the Stockholm School of Economics and the Universities of Bielefeld and Lucerne, and received the American Sociological Association's section awards for lifetime contributions to the sociology of education, and to the study of globalization.

Susan Neiman is director of the Einstein Forum, an independent public think tank in Potsdam, Germany. Before coming to the Einstein Forum in 2000 Neiman was professor of philosophy at Yale and Tel Aviv University. Born in Atlanta, Georgia, she studied philosophy at Harvard, where she took her Ph.D. with John Rawls, and the Freie Universität Berlin. She is the author of *Slow Fire: Jewish Notes from Berlin, The Unity of Reason: Rereading Kant, Evil in Modern Thought: An Alternative History of Philosophy, Fremde Sehen Anders, Moral Clarity: A Guide for Grownup Idealists*, and *Why Grow Up?* as well as many essays.

Samuel J. Palmisano is the Chairman of the Center for Global Enterprise, a private, non-profit, non-partisan research institution devoted to the study of the contemporary corporation, the management science of the globally integrated enterprise (GIE), global economic trends, and their impact on society. From January 1, 2003, through December 31, 2011, Samuel J. Palmisano was chairman, president, and chief executive officer of IBM. He was chairman of the board from January through September 2012 and served as a senior adviser to IBM until his retirement on December 1, 2012. Under his leadership, IBM achieved record financial performance, transformed itself into a globally integrated enterprise, and introduced its Smarter Planet agenda. Mr Palmisano began his thirty-nine-year career with IBM in 1973 in Baltimore, Maryland. Mr Palmisano is a graduate of the Johns Hopkins University. He was awarded an Honorary Degree of Doctor of Humane Letters from Johns Hopkins University in 2012 and from Rensselaer Polytechnic Institute in 2005. In 2006, he was awarded an Honorary Fellowship from the London Business School. Mr Palmisano has received a number of business awards, including the Atlantic Council's Distinguished Business Leadership Award in 2009 and the inaugural Deming Cup, presented in 2010 by the W. Edwards Deming Center for Quality, Productivity and Competitiveness at Columbia Business School. In 2013 Mr Palmisano was awarded the French Legion of Honor recognizing his successful career at IBM and his personal commitment to French-American friendship. He is also an elected member of the American Academy of Arts and Sciences and served as co-chair of the Council on Competitiveness's National Innovation Initiative.

Philip Pettit is a dual citizen of Ireland and Australia who has spent most of the last twelve years in the United States. He now divides his time between Princeton University, where he is L. S. Rockefeller University Professor of Politics and Human Values, and the Australian National University, where he is Distinguished Professor of Philosophy. His books include *Republicanism* (1997), *The Economy of Esteem* (2004, with G. Brennan); *Group Agency* (2011, with C. List); *On the People's Terms* (2012); and *Just Freedom* (2014). He is a Fellow of the American Academy of Arts and Sciences, the British Academy, and the Royal Irish Academy, as well as the Australian Academies of Humanities and Social Sciences. *Common Minds: Themes from the Philosophy of Philip Pettit*, ed. G. Brennan et al. appeared from Oxford University Press in 2007.

Subramanian Rangan is Professor of Strategy and Management at INSEAD and holds the Abu Dhabi Crown Prince Court Endowed Chair in Societal Progress. In 1998 he won the Academy of International Business's Eldridge Haynes Prize for the best original essay in international business. In 1995 that academy awarded their Best Dissertation Award to his doctoral thesis. In 2010 his research won the Emerald award for Top 50 papers in management. His articles appear in such journals as *Administrative Science Quarterly, Academy of Management Review, Journal of International Business Studies, Strategic Management Journal,* the *Sloan Management Review,* and the *Harvard Business Review.* Professor Rangan is co-author of two books: *Manager in the International Economy,* and *A Prism on Globalization.* He is associate editor of the *Global Strategy Journal;* chair of the World Economic Forum's Global Agenda Council on Emerging Multinationals; and a member of the board of trustees of Fundacao Dom Cabral, a leading business school in Brazil. Professor Rangan is a multiple-time recipient of the Outstanding Teacher award and Dean's Commendation for Excellence in MBA Teaching. He received an MBA from the MIT Sloan School of Management and a Ph.D. from Harvard University.

Mathias Risse is Professor of Philosophy and Public Policy. He works mostly in social and political philosophy and in ethics. His primary research areas are contemporary political philosophy (in particular questions of international justice, distributive justice, and property) and decision theory (in particular, rationality and fairness in group decision-making, an area sometimes called analytical social philosophy). His articles have appeared in journals such as *Ethics; Philosophy and Public Affairs; Nous;* the *Journal of Political Philosophy;* and *Social Choice and Welfare.* Risse studied philosophy, mathematics, and mathematical economics at the University of Bielefeld, the

University of Pittsburgh, the Hebrew University of Jerusalem, and Princeton University. He received his BA, BS, and MS in mathematics from Bielefeld, and his MA and Ph.D. in philosophy from Princeton. Before coming to Harvard he taught in the Department of Philosophy and the Program in Ethics, Politics and Economics at Yale. His books *On Global Justice* and *Global Political Philosophy* were both published in 2012.

David Schmidtz is Kendrick Professor at the University of Arizona. He currently is working on *Markets in Education* with Harry Brighouse for Oxford University Press. Essays of his have been reprinted seventy-one times in ten languages as of 2014. In 2013, he was honored by the University of Arizona for his work as a graduate mentor. His thirteen former doctoral students all occupy faculty positions. In 2014/15, he will be a Phi Beta Kappa Visiting Scholar. He also will be visiting Hamburg University as John Stuart Mill Professor.

Amartya Sen is Thomas W. Lamont University Professor, and Professor of Economics and Philosophy, at Harvard University and was until 2004 the Master of Trinity College, Cambridge. He is also Senior Fellow at the Harvard Society of Fellows. Earlier on he was Professor of Economics at Jadavpur University Calcutta, the Delhi School of Economics, and the London School of Economics, and Drummond Professor of Political Economy at Oxford University. Amartya Sen has served as President of the Econometric Society, the American Economic Association, the Indian Economic Association, and the International Economic Association. He was formerly Honorary President of OXFAM and is now its Honorary Advisor. His research has ranged over social choice theory, economic theory, ethics and political philosophy, welfare economics, theory of measurement, decision theory, development economics, public health, and gender studies. Amartya Sen's books have been translated into more than thirty languages, and include *Choice of Techniques* (1960), *Growth Economics* (1970), *Collective Choice and Social Welfare* (1970), *Choice, Welfare and Measurement* (1982), *Commodities and Capabilities* (1987), *The Standard of Living* (1987), *Development as Freedom* (1999), *Identity and Violence: The Illusion of Destiny* (2006), *The Idea of Justice* (2009), and (jointly with Jean Dreze) *An Uncertain Glory: India and Its Contradictions* (2013). Amartya Sen's awards include Bharat Ratna (India); Commandeur de la Legion d'Honneur (France); the National Humanities Medal (USA); Ordem do Merito Cientifico (Brazil); Honorary Companion of Honour (UK); Aztec Eagle (Mexico); Edinburgh Medal (UK); the George Marshall Award (USA); the Eisenhauer Medal (USA); and the Nobel Prize in Economics.

Jim Hagemann Snabe was appointed co-CEO of SAP in February 2010. In this capacity, and as a member of the SAP Executive Board and Global Managing Board, Snabe focused on developing and executing SAP's strategy, together with Bill McDermott.

Snabe is a member of the Foundation Board of the World Economic Forum; the board of Bang & Olufsen Holding A/S in Denmark; as well as the Danske Bank Group, the largest bank in Denmark. He has also been elected to the supervisory board of Siemens.

In 2013 he and co-CEO Bill McDermott were ranked #2 on Glassdoor.com's listing of the top fifty highest rated CEOs, based on their 99 percent approval rating from employees. Snabe's views about the role which leaders and IT need to play in creating sustainable growth and responsible business strategies have been strongly shaped by his commitment to environmental and humanitarian issues. His management style is influenced by his interest in classical music, inspired by the famous conductor Benjamin Zanders. Snabe received a master's degree in operational research from the Aarhus School of Business in Denmark. He lives with his family in Copenhagen, Denmark.

Valerie Tiberius is Professor of Philosophy at the University of Minnesota, where she has taught since 1998. She earned her BA from the University of Toronto and her MA and Ph.D. from the University of North Carolina at Chapel Hill. Her work explores the ways in which philosophy and psychology can both contribute to the study of well-being and virtue. She is the author of *The Reflective Life: Living Wisely with our Limits* (Oxford University Press, 2008). Her most recent book, *Moral Psychology: A Contemporary Introduction* (Routledge) brings together traditional philosophical and new empirical approaches in order to investigate topics such as moral motivation, moral responsibility, and reasons to be moral. She has also published numerous articles on the topics of practical reasoning, prudential virtues, well-being, and the relationship between positive psychology and ethics, and has received grants from the Templeton Foundation and the National Endowment for the Humanities.

James P. Walsh (Ph.D., Northwestern University) is an Arthur F. Thurnau Professor and the Gerald and Esther Carey Professor of Business Administration at the University of Michigan's Ross School of Business. Jim's research interests lie in the area of corporate governance. Initially doing work framed by the neo-classical model of the firm, he has since expanded his conception of governance to more broadly consider the purposes, accountability, and control of the firm in society. Jim was a founding co-editor of the *Academy of Management Annals*, a Senior Editor and Associate Editor-in-Chief of *Organization Science*, a Consulting Editor for the *Academy of Management Review*, and an Associate Editor for the *Strategic Management Journal*. The current Dean of the Fellows Group of the Academy of Management, he recently completed his service as the Academy's 65th president.

INTRODUCTION

SUBRAMANIAN RANGAN

> Without [human] actions, the world would still be an idea.
>
> (Georges Doriot)

> No matter how many buildings, foundations, schools and hospitals we build, or how many bridges we raise, all these are material entities. The real spirit behind progress is the human spirit...
>
> (Sheikh Zayed)

THE prevailing aspiration of business is performance, while that of society is progress. Capitalism, both the paradigm and practice, sits at the intersection of these dual aspirations. Over the past century, especially relative to the alternatives, capitalism has delivered impressive results on the ground. Still, it now seems uncontroversial that modern capitalism is in some crisis. From grave concerns about climate and fairness to future generations, to trade- and technology-related job concerns, to over-financialization of the economy and business cycles, to declining relative shares in income for labor, to distrust in business and business leaders, we confront a number of acute and chronic dilemmas. To be sure it is not clear how much better one can do, but that is no excuse to eschew effort or forsake hope.

As a student and professor of business strategy for nearly two decades, I have come to appreciate the creativity and efficiency of enterprise. As these anomalies mount, though, it seems no longer tenable to deny that the "paradigm" of capitalism while elegant and powerful seems profoundly incomplete. Enterprise performance without or, worse, at the expense of societal progress is unsatisfactory if not unsustainable. Still, enterprise performance has come to be regarded and taught as an obligation, while societal progress tends to be regarded as a by-product delivered by the magic of the "invisible hand."

To supplement, a convenient if costly division has also been adopted: performance has been placed in the realm of the private sector, while progress has been placed in the realm of the public sector. As the adoption of this set of beliefs has become widespread, the validity of capitalism and, I fear, the role and relevance of its intellectuals is rightly called into question. Regulation is undoubtedly necessary, but in terms of resolution, it alone will be scarcely sufficient or satisfactory.

The time is more than ripe to revisit explicitly how enterprises (and other actors in the economy including executives, employees, investors, customers, and consumers) might integrate performance with progress. While theories of performance are proposed by business scholars with training in economics, finance, operations, psychology, sociology, and such, ideas of progress tend to be explored in the realm of philosophy. Thomas Kuhn observed that "it is . . . particularly in periods of acknowledged crisis that scientists have turned to philosophical analysis as a device for unlocking the riddles of their field." In this spirit, if even a small and suitable group of eminent philosophers and business scholars could come together to discuss, debate, and grapple collaboratively with this set of issues, then we might accelerate the process of filling in some sorely missing moral and conceptual foundations (and also allay the impression of scholars as indifferent intellectuals in this moment of common concern). This is the motivation behind the effort embodied in this volume.

The crux of the challenge I would submit is no longer just with the practice of capitalism, it is rather with the paradigm. Hence the aspiration here is to start to explore the fundamental nature of the preceding dilemmas in a manner that may inform the adaptive evolution of the paradigm of capitalism. Given the expanding reach of enterprise and the deep and growing doubts about its ideal role and practice, such an endeavor seems apropos and urgent.

To be sure, philosophers have theorized about the limits of markets and business scholars about stakeholders and corporate responsibility. Nonetheless, my impression is that important philosophical work in this domain has not found a substantial audience among business scholars. Equally, business scholars goading better practice must fear that bolt-on or ceremonial adoption can scarcely rescue a stressed paradigm. An explicit dialog and sharing among philosophers and business scholars may enlighten and help evolve the paradigm and practice of capitalism.

Spurred by this aspiration, with a kindred spirit and prime collaborator on this effort, Ebba Hansmeyer, we went "recruiting." We sought ten suitable philosophers and ten suitable social scientists. As they came on board, some (especially among the philosophers) implored that the reality of practice ought to ground the debate and discussion. Accordingly, we invited six thoughtful business leaders to join the twenty eminent scholars (philosophers and social scientists) and contribute original essays on the dilemmas of and prospects for modern capitalism. Our hope was that this unique coming together of diverse theorists and practitioners would help vigorously till the terrain, spur the germination of fresh ideas, and eventually nourish better practice.

In April 2014, at the Royal Society in London, we assembled this distinguished group to share and discuss their reflections. To encourage focused and fruitful exchange we outlined five broad themes that would serve as a spine for organizing the sharing and discussion. I nominated two philosophers, two social scientists, and a business leader against each theme. The assignment was meant to provide orientation and the hope was that contributors would bring their own interpretations and variations (which they have). It is the essays by these eminent and accomplished individuals that constitute this volume.

The chapters explore modern capitalism's fraught status at the intersection of business and society. They are addressed in the first instance to students and scholars of social science, especially but not limited to those in business schools around the world. In broad terms, they explore these questions: (i) what's the problem with capitalism?; (ii) is the problem just with the practice or with the very paradigm?; (iii) what is progress and who is responsible for it?; (iv) what evolution is required at the individual, system, and paradigm level so that enterprises and the executives who lead them may better integrate performance with progress?; and (v) in this evolution whither consumers, employees, and investors?

THE FIVE THEMES

The twenty-six essays in this volume are organized around five themes: problem, progress, balancing and trade-offs, choices and preferences, and power and trust. As mentioned above, I assigned each contributor a particular theme and invited reflections oriented to the questions constituting the theme. I also encouraged the authors to interpret and develop variations that reflected their expertise and concerns. In practice, then, the contributions reflect both broader and narrower interpretations. All of the chapters were drafted specifically for this volume, and some of the work reflects a novel direction in the author's thinking. This volume also contains condensed write-ups (ably drafted by Mike Fuerstein) of the discussions on each theme that ensued in London. Below I outline the sets of questions that were shared as prompts for each theme.

Problem

From immoderate consumption to tainted global supply chains, from wrenching financial volatility to dubious audits and ratings, our modern economy provokes concerns. Yet, thanks at least in good part to market-based organization of economic activity, billions have left behind material poverty and are touched by the wonders of innovation. To start at the beginning then, it is important to ask whether there are fundamental problems with the contemporary paradigm and/or practice of capitalism, and, if so, what the nature and scale of these problems is. Which assumptions and which agents in the capitalist arrangement are most problematic? What can we say about purported consequences (e.g. damaging transformation of social relations), their durability, and who is affected? How and to what extent is business enterprise implicated in the problems, causes, and remedies? How implicated are individuals and households (as consumers, employees, investors)? To what extent does capitalism possess self-correcting forces (e.g. competition) to remedy its shortcomings? What about the role and effectiveness of public and private regulation? What can we say about the state of knowledge on this theme and what specific questions merit future research?

Progress

In the context of assessing capitalism and its elements, how might one think about progress? Is progress in this context best thought of in terms of economic development, durable prosperity, well-being, and such? Is progress also properly gauged in broader terms such as justice, liberty, opportunity, trust, respect for rights, and such? To what extent are cross-sectional, intergenerational, gender, and "racial" patterns of distribution constitutive of progress? Is the concept of progress fundamentally a reflection of evolving moral and political aspirations? In this case, should discussions of progress be confined to the public sphere or do they have legitimate relevance in the private sphere? More specifically, to what extent and in what respects should progress be a concern of business enterprise and be compatible with its nature? Who properly decides what the standards of progress should be? What can we say about the state of knowledge on this theme and what specific questions merit future research?

Balancing and Trade-Offs

Enterprises are capable of advancing multiple ends, but they must also allocate resources within a range of constraints and competitive pressures. Sensible balancing and significant trade-offs seem therefore inevitable, particularly when broader ends enter the picture. Uncertainty, incommensurability, disparate preferences, contradictory and incomplete information, not to mention the difficulty of collective action, are among the well-known complexities. Matters are made more challenging with the pace of global competition and offshoring, ubiquitous labor substituting technologies, high-powered incentive contracts, and such. It should come as no surprise then that conventional approaches to addressing these dilemmas (e.g. cost benefit analysis, present value discounting, majority voting) often seem to fall short. For example, how much performance is enough performance? How should we think about the pervasive tensions between the present and the future, efficiency and equity, human beings and other creatures, payoffs and propriety? When might a logic of consequences make way for a logic of appropriateness? When is regulation an appropriate remedy? Should deliberations aim at ideal outcomes or at plausible within-reach outcomes? What can we say about the state of knowledge on this theme and what specific questions merit future research?

Choices and Preferences

Enterprises must feature prominently in assessments of capitalism and its consequences. At the same time it would seem indispensable to explore the motivation
and role of individuals as economic actors (as consumers, as employees, as investors).
At least from the vantage point of a business school, it sometimes appears as if
individuals actively choose means while they passively adopt ends. One executive
paraphrased the concern thus: is my ladder against the right wall? How and when do
individuals apprehend their self-interest? To what extent do we discover versus construct our preferences? What role do ideas and idealism play in this? To what extent do
extrinsic (e.g. marketing, signaling) factors influence the quantity and nature of goods
and services to consume, employment to seek, investments to make? To what extent
do broader notions of meaning, human flourishing, and moral obligations figure in
the process? How do facets of our psychology (e.g. status, envy, empathy) bear on the
prospects for societal progress within a capitalist system? What can we say about
the state of knowledge on this theme and what specific questions merit future research?

Power and Trust

Those who are successful in capitalist systems wield substantial social power through
decisions that affect the welfare of employees, customers, and suppliers. When this
powerful minority (CEOs, business groups, the super-wealthy, financial market actors)
exercises discretion in a predominantly self-serving manner, then trust frays. Governments may willingly step in, but lobbying and corruption often worsen matters. Is
capitalism destined to concentrate power in the hands of a select group of narrow
interests? To what extent is trust important in a modern economy? To what extent are
modern institutional arrangements (including private property and inheritance)
entrenching an unhealthy social and power structure? Is public, political power the
only appropriate check on economic power, or can corporate boards, individuals, and
investors effectively address concerns about their own capacities for social control?
Who pulls and who should pull the relevant levers? What can we say about the state of
knowledge on this theme and what specific questions merit future research?

INTENDED READERSHIP

At business schools worldwide there is a burning and growing need for rigorous
treatment of concerns regarding the paradigm and practice of capitalism. At the
moment the mainstay includes case studies, lectures on ethics, and readings of empirical work purporting to show "doing well by doing good." Understandably, much of the

emphasis remains on making the "business case" for CSR (corporate social responsibility). While the attention to practice is understandable, we need more on the paradigm that is at once relevant, rigorous, and accessible.

The present volume is intended to address this gap and benefit two audiences within business schools: scholars and students. There is a growing interest among scholars in business schools to study, develop, and deepen the corpus of intellectual work on the issue. Yet there seems to be too little theoretical and philosophical grounding in this research and the published work tends to be applied and empirical. The essays in this volume coming from acknowledged authorities and framing issues in a more fundamental manner ought to provide useful and meaningful grounding for future research. This should help elevate both the quality and quantity of future research. The target business scholars work in such areas as strategy, economics, finance, decision science, operations, marketing, entrepreneurship, and organization and leadership.

Business school students too would clearly benefit both at the graduate and undergraduate level. For them it is often unclear why and how a focus on financial results is insufficient (both in terms of means and ends). Perhaps students see too few (non-dogmatic) "big names" associated with concerns on capitalism. In my experience, this hampers curiosity and receptivity, and leads to close-mindedness and pre-judgment. The essays in this volume aim to remedy that and make students more attentive to the debate on capitalism, business, and society, and, in turn, to their future role as enterprise managers and entrepreneurs in integrating performance with progress. It is not often that business school students have the opportunity to hear from seminal theorists about the tenuous assumptions of modern microeconomics and markets, to hear from modern philosophers about the basis and limits of rationality—and comprehend why the world is in "protest," and to reflect on progress or the deep dilemma of trust.

There is a large literature in business ethics that touches on some of these themes, but to my knowledge there is today no volume that attempts to bring together rigor and relevance in such a manner. It is clear to me that we need to go beyond the useful calls for corporate social responsibility and explore not just how to make sustainability robust and profitable, but also how to make profitability and the modern economic system robust and sustainable. A better-adapted paradigm of integrated capitalism will help enrich business school curricula, and better train and equip students to eventually pull practice in the proper direction.

In terms of specific courses, this volume or parts thereof would be apropos in courses pertaining to strategy, economics, marketing, and finance; and in the growing plethora of elective courses on non-market strategy, business ethics, sustainability, social innovation, governance, new business models, bottom of the pyramid, reimagining capitalism, and such. In undergraduate programs this book would be useful for courses on business and society. Chapters of the book, in particular those written by business leaders, would be suitable reading in executive education programs.

I also foresee that chapters of the book will be useful in Ph.D. seminars in management. For instance, Chapter 2 by March on a logic of appropriateness vs a logic of consequences, Chapter 11 by Anderson casting enterprise as a moral (rather than amoral) actor, Chapter 22 by Pettit on trust, Chapter 5 by Meyer on the ecology of "problem factories" and institutionalized reactions, Chapter 20 by Tiberius on the value-full life, Chapter 18 by Hong and Liskovich teasing out agency causes and firm effects, Chapter 24 by Fuerstein explaining the accountability dilemma of markets and better models of governance, and several others could frame and inspire new lines of academic work.

Likewise I foresee that certain chapter (such as those by Arrow, Battilana, Risse, Sen) will be of relevance and interest to graduate and undergraduate students of public policy and government. While contemporary philosophy reflects extensively in abstract terms on questions of social justice, there is little work that addresses such systemic concerns in the specific context of business practice and principles.

In sum, the chapters in this volume have much to recommend. They attempt to address the paradigm not just the practice of capitalism. They are written by a host of eminent contributors who come from philosophy, social science, and practice. The essays explore the supply and the demand side of capitalism. And they suggest key questions for future research.

So What? Looking Back, Looking Forward

Stirring Europe since the sixteenth century, the Renaissance and then the Industrial Revolution were accompanied by a "great transformation" to market organization. The latter has since been conceptualized as a paradigm that we refer to as capitalism. Its evident effectiveness in fueling efficiency, innovation, and material well-being has, despite criticisms and concerns (since at least Adam Smith), brought grudging admiration and adoption. The very idea of *development*, still an unattained and central goal in large parts of the world, is rooted in this relatively modern history.

It would however be an error to conclude, as some may be tempted to, that this epic transformation has run its course and that progress is now accomplished or nearly accomplished. The very idea of *progress* may itself be relatively recent (and not unproblematic). If we may say that progress refers to the audacious aspiration to call out and close the gap between *how our world is* relative to *how our world ought to be*, then it is clear that our journey toward that aspiration, while well begun, is far from completed. Exploring the fundamental nature of this gap in a manner that may inform the intellectual and practical evolution of capitalism is an implicit and unifying aim of the chapters in this volume. While several of them highlight regulation and taxes, none regards government as the proper and sole owner of more effective remedies.

It merits underlining that the essays in this volume are presented in the spirit of opening or continuing rather than closing. The concepts, ideas, and theories of contemporary capitalism emerged over decades and even centuries, and usefully reflecting on and shaping their adaptive evolution will take considerable care and effort, and not a little time.

Another point that merits acknowledging is an understandable impatience, on the part of some, for "action," the end importance of which is not in question. Yet there are good reasons to pursue a more deliberate approach. First, while the broad aspiration to integrate performance and progress may be proper (and perhaps feasible), specific actions in specific cases do not automatically make themselves clear. Good intentions may be necessary but are hardly sufficient for good action. Importantly, actions by a central entity (even an "enlightened" one) are neither feasible nor scalable. The choices and decisions that must precede sensible actions must be made in a decentralized manner. Furthermore, so that even proper actions are not regarded as arbitrary, they have to be justifiable beyond the decision-makers. That is, actions have to be logical against a somewhat publicly defensible standard. What we need to go from intentions to actions are models, methods, and measures of an integrated capitalism. It is this triplet (models, methods, measures) that will constitute a better adapted paradigm of integrated capitalism and make it (i) amenable to decentralized adoption and adaptation, (ii) less arbitrary and more publicly justifiable, and last but not least, (iii) scalable.

As stated at the outset, it is difficult not to marvel at the wonder of the enterprise system. Yet, if we are to better comprehend why the world appears to heave in protest, we must probe the tenuous assumptions of modern microeconomics and markets, and audition philosophers on the basis and limits of modern rationality. Business theory has made great advance as applied social science; incorporating applied philosophy should not be a taboo. The dilemmas we are grappling with are not only techno-economic in nature, but also moral-philosophical. They are not only about decisions, but also about choices. They are not only about peace and prosperity but also propriety. Without proper foundations in fairness, peace and prosperity are fated to remain tentative.

As I opened our meeting at the Royal Society in London in April last year, this is what I confessed: it is conventional for a great teacher to on occasion convene his good students; it is far less conventional for a good student to convene his great teachers. But the circumstances call for unconventional resolve and approach, and that is what we have here. I am confident that like me you too will be enlightened by these thoughtful essays and encouraged that twenty-first-century capitalism may evolve to better integrate performance with progress.

PART I

PROBLEM

CHAPTER 1

....

WHAT'S WRONG WITH CAPITALISM?

....

MAJID H. JAFAR

Abstract

Capitalism as a system for economic organization and resource allocation is suffering a crisis of confidence across many societies worldwide. This has been marked by growing inequality, financial crises, and structural unemployment disproportionally affecting the youth in both the developed and developing world. Above all a sense of unfairness pervades, with a perception that the rules governing the way the system is applied are disproportionately being set by the better off and for their own benefit, whether corporates or wealthier individuals. What compounds this crisis in many ways is a sense since the Cold War that western capitalism it is the only acceptable form of economic system, with little or no debate in the public or political discourse, which has itself come to be dominated by the money of special-interest groups. We see mass protest movements across the world, and a weakening of the political center in favor of more extreme political currents.

Fissures in society have been widening between the investor class enjoying growing returns on capital and the wage-earning class suffering declining returns from their labor. And increased financialization of the economy means the traditional economic theories based on production in a classical sense are increasingly irrelevant to the modern economy. The sense of injustice which has grown from decades of growing inequality puts at risk the stability and sustainability of the system and its acceptance, as well as causing an erosion of societal trust and the very institutions needed to sustain the capitalist system.

FUNDAMENTAL ISSUES WITH THE CONTEMPORARY PARADIGM AND PRACTICE OF CAPITALISM

....

The decree had the opposite effect since when the capitalists received payments they hoarded it to buy land. These extensive transactions reduced prices. But large-scale debtors found it difficult to sell; so many of them were ejected from their properties, and lost not only their estates but their rank and reputation. Then [Obama] came to the rescue. He distributed [US$75 billion] among especially established banks, for interest-free three year state loans, against the security of double the value in landed property. Credit was thus restored; and gradually private lenders reappeared. (From Tacitus, *Annals*, bk 6, quoted in Milanovic 2010: 208)

What appears here to be a narrative from 2009 is in fact from two millennia earlier in AD 33 (replace "Obama" with Emperor Tiberius, and the $75 billion was actually its equivalent at the time of 0.5 percent of GDP, or 100 million Roman sesterces). The similarities otherwise are striking, which tells us that crises of performance of, and confidence in, the economic system, accompanied by systemic harm caused to many of the players in the system, are not a recent phenomenon. It also tells us that capitalism as a system of markets to allocate resources driven by motives of profit and wealth generation are as old as the civilization of mankind, though more recent developments such as the industrial revolution and the global financial revolution have accelerated both its scope and scale, with the end of the Cold War giving an apparent ideological boost to free market enterprise through the collapse and discrediting of its main perceived alternative.

Government bailouts are also nothing new—the United States Government has been forced to engage in such actions almost from that nation's birth, with the Panic of 1792, and at least six times since. Yet beneath the headlines of financial crises and unsustainable debt levels risking collapse of both banks and countries, there are some chronic trends of widening inequality and eroding trust in the system that may threaten long-term sustainability.

Capitalism can be a great creative force but it can be a destructive force. It is not immoral but it is amoral, we need to give it some instructions. (Bono of U2, speaking at the World Economic Forum in Davos in 2014)

In one sense capitalism is akin to a car. The engine that drives it is the markets. Different nations may choose different cars as a societal choice, depending on their preference for size, speed, efficiency, tradition, aesthetics, and so on. But in the end it is a vehicle—a means of getting you from where you are to your intended destination. Societies and the governments that represent them are the drivers of the cars, governed by necessary rules and regulations that continue to evolve as the road network we navigate increases in size, scale, and complexity. The road markings and traffic laws that regulate the system are just as important as ensuring the driver isn't intoxicated and not in control of the vehicle, which many would argue is exactly what happened with the global financial and then economic crisis in 2008.

The clash of ideas between capitalism and socialism or communism appeared to come to an end at the end of the Cold War, with a celebrated "End of History" (Fukuyama) and a triumphalist celebration of the supposedly superior values of freedom which prevailed—of free markets married to free political systems re-enforcing one another. So much so that the 1990s saw the Washington Consensus imposed on countries across the world with assumptions that it was just the rules of the game that mattered and not the fitness of the players or the condition of the playing surface. The commanding heights of the former Soviet economy were transferred overnight into private hands, with a destruction of the social fabric and contract, a collapse of economic output which took two decades to recover, and millions pushed into poverty.

A serious risk to the capitalist system also comes from the interplay between money and politics, where democratic systems become hijacked by wealthy individuals or corporations, who in turn dictate the legislative and regulatory agenda to suit their own interests. To go back to the car metaphor, this is a dangerous pollutant in the fuel of the car. In most developing countries, money buying power and influence would be termed corruption, but in many of the more advanced economies it takes place on a much bigger scale but in a regulated and professional framework of lobbyists, lawyers, media campaigns, campaign finance, and research funding.

The Purpose of an Economic System—Confusing Moral Aims with Amoral Methods

In analyzing the question, "what is wrong with capitalism," we are seemingly attempting to apply a subjective normative frame of reference to an objective mechanistic system of economic resource allocation.

To commence analysis of the problems of capitalism as applied today, we must start with inquiring what is actually the purpose of capitalism or indeed any economic system? For how are we to measure the performance without a defined objective? I shall posit therefore that the purpose of capitalism, or any economic system, is to set the conditions to allow the sustained enhancement of the standards of living and well-being of the people in a society.

By that measure there is clearly a sense in many sectors of society and in many nations today that the purpose is no longer being fulfilled. And the effect goes beyond growth cycles and affects the basic social contracts and confidence that underpins the system. Wage-earning skilled workers in much if not all of the developed world are no longer seeing growing real earnings and in fact in many countries are seeing them decline in absolute relative terms, aside from their relative decline in comparison to the wealthy asset-owning "capitalist" class. While in developing countries we see hundreds of millions in countries like China and India escaping poverty and entering the middle class thanks to capitalism, leading to lower inequality on a global scale, even though in the case of China this takes place in a state-dominated economy without the western liberal democracy that was thought to be a sine qua non for the capitalist system to properly function in a country of any sizeable population.

One of the most glaring apparent problems with the current system or at least its application is the growing over-emphasis of mass consumption and materialism, whereby standards of living and even overall well-being are increasingly narrowly defined in terms of acquiring of goods and services driven by not an actual but rather a perceived utility that is increasingly defined by mass global advertising and trends. And the brands themselves are global to the point of conformity across continents, threatening both culture and societal structures and their value systems.

Globalization combined with advancing technology has enabled rapid rises in productivity and economic growth without the commensurate labor utilization, leading to wage repression in many countries and the lesser skilled workers (or those whose skills are outdated) getting squeezed down the socio-economic ladder in a seemingly permanent decline that erodes trust in the capitalist system. And simultaneously those in the societies at the top who are investors and asset owners have continued to do well, even during the worst of the economic downturn.

Inequality rather than inflation or headline employment has become the critical phenomenon defining governments' policy priorities almost worldwide, although in fact it is simply those with relative disadvantage who have suffered, while those with an advantage have prospered. In general, the worst off over the last three decades have been the working and middle class in the western developed (OECD) economies, many of which have seen declining real incomes, and also the poorest in the lesser developed economies (LDCs) such as sub-Saharan Africa, who have had flat real incomes. The wealthiest "investor" class in the OECD have done well, while many workers and professionals in major fast-growing developing economies have seen rapid rises in income thanks to capitalism and globalization.

Yet even in some of the fastest growing economies, rising Gini coefficients have led to rising crime and societal unrest. Most fundamentally, this failure to achieve *inclusive* growth, as it has come to be known, threatens the basic sense of fairness required for system sustainability and potentially also the economic growth potential according to more recent studies which dispute the "trickle down" theories.

Worsening socio-economic mobility, whether real or even perceived, can harm the incentives and overall competitiveness so crucial for proper system functioning. And there is evidence that overall societal consumption and investment patterns are negatively impacted by an increasing concentration of wealth, in a manner which weakens sustainable growth prospects for an economy.

Re-enforcing this trend, we see rising "financialization" where the dominance of returns on financial investments, whether through leverage or capital market investments, has overshadowed traditional industrial production that formed the basis of most economic theory. Deregulation, including the tearing down of the wall between investment banking and commercial banking, has exposed the whole economy to the higher risks of the fast-moving financial system. And the higher financial returns achieved are also attracting much of the best talent that might otherwise be more "productively" engaged in the economy, which in itself threatens innovation, new company creation, and long-term competitiveness.

It was of course this phenomenon which led to the huge surpluses of liquidity from wealthy individuals and corporations being cycled through complex products beyond the grasp and sophistication of most regulators, and feeding the frenzy of cheap consumer debt at the bottom of the socio-economic ladder. This was further spurred on in many countries by the political drive to encourage home ownership at any level, and the resulting virtual wealth from rising house prices encouraging further unsustainable consumer debt in a vicious circle until the bubble burst.

But to blame the crisis on sub-prime mortgages is in many ways confusing the symptom with the cause. At its heart it was caused by rising income inequality, leading to a concentration of disposable funds at the top being leveraged to feed unsustainable consumption and debt lower down the ladder.

Of course the global financial crisis and subsequent fall-out over the past five years is neither unusual nor historically unique, as systemic risks and the emotions of markets caused by the herd mentality are a noted and some would say necessary characteristic of the capitalist system. But the perception of most government responses as felt by most of the population—quick to save the bankers and speculators who caused the crisis, while slow to help the struggling people at the bottom—has further eroded sense of equity and confidence in the system.

We also seen increased short-termism in the allocation of capital across the system. Rather than the stewardship of true investors seeking value over the long term in line with the company's best interests, we have the rise of day trading, program trading, and high-frequency trading by computers, leading to disconnect between supposed investors and the companies or products in which they are supposed to invest, and short-term financial returns with smaller margins over increasing volume of trade replacing any concern for production or growth in the underlying business. This has also increased volatility and instability of markets, with an increasing number of one-day crashes attributed to computer glitches rather than even negative market sentiment. Even when investors are more long-term, they are usually large pension funds or mutual funds who are acting as asset manager agents and aggregators on behalf of the ultimate investors, who are so far removed from the investments as to have no idea where their savings are invested.

When it comes to labor allocation the traditional models of lifetime secure employment with reciprocal loyalty between firm and employee and a long-term career have long since vanished, being replaced by frequent changes with short-term stints with both firm and staff looking for short-term financial gain, and globalization pushing multinationals to look abroad for the lowest labor costs with the most flexible regulations. These trends change the traditional paradigm of resource allocation and the nature of capitalism as applied and though they may enhance the efficiency of markets, they are also leading to increased volatility, job insecurity, erosion of social bonds and values, and a deficit of confidence and trust in the system itself.

Looking beyond just the developed world and taking a global perspective, we see growing discontent and even rejection by many developing countries of how globalization and capitalism are being internationally applied, particularly when it comes to double standards in trade policy. The economic hegemon in each of the past few centuries—Britain in the nineteenth, the United States in the twentieth, and China so far in the twenty-first—has in each case achieved dominance and sustained growth through high tariffs and state nurturing of local industry, massive and widespread protectionism, monopolistic behavior, and "imperialist" capitalism—the very opposite of the western prescription doled out to the developing world. Even today, the EU and the US spend massive amounts on subsidizing their agricultural sectors—the very industry upon which 70 percent of the poorest workers on the planet rely—while insisting that the developing countries lower their barriers to first-world capital and enforce their intellectual property rights, but refuse to allow immigration of their labor back into the developed world. Market capitalism on a global scale becomes very one-sided and discredited when these double standards ignore competitiveness at the expense of the poorest and middle-income countries.

Another enduring phenomenon since the last crisis worldwide is the structural unemployment—particularly badly affecting the youth population in many regions of the world. This has led to increasing fears of a "jobless recovery" with a "lost generation" in many economies, and fears that long-term unemployment in the new generation will permanently stifle long-term growth potential, while also inflict-ing major societal strains and tensions between the generations, with protected older workers in the job market crowding out their own children who are trying to get ahead.

In my own region of the Middle East, youth unemployment has been a chronic problem for some years, with rigid markets, poor education systems, and inadequate growth relative to population increases all contributing causes. All the polls in fact showed that this phenomenon was the major driver behind the Arab uprisings since 2011 (compounded by other economic phenomena such as food price rises in places like Egypt, and a crop drought in Syria), and yet almost all the focus by global and local media and politicians has been on constitutions, elections, and the political processes, with little done to address the core underlying economic causes, which have been worsened by the consequences.

This has led to further frustration with instability and demonstrations or even secondary revolutions in some cases, and a perpetual vicious cycle of political instabil-ity and a worsening the economic outlook feeding each other. This must be broken, for only through productive employment of the new generation can the Middle East and other affected regions achieve sustainable prosperity and stability. The flipside of this threat is also therefore a massive opportunity if the potential of this labor force caused by the youth bulge can be productively unlocked.

In 1942 Schumpeter presciently stated that capitalism's success tends to undermine the social institutions that protected and nurtured it, and some seven decades later that still summarizes well the crux of the problem. The very profit motive which spurs innovation, advancement, and increasing incomes to a society can over time and if the system is left unchecked lead to concentration of wealth and growing inequality, rent-seeking cronyism or monopolistic behavior rather than innovation, and a weakening or hijacking of the political and regulatory system to protect special interest groups at the expense of the wider community.

In this sense capitalism is like some ravenous beast which must be constantly tamed and controlled to keep its worst traits in check, but without extinguishing its positive creative essence. This requires constant scrutiny and examination of the basic assumptions of the system as applied, to correct flaws and take account of changing contexts. It also requires strong (though not large) government acting as regulator and ensuring redistributive policies and effective provision of public goods, as well as enabling the investment environment and infrastructure provision which are all critical to underpin capitalism and long-term competitiveness of an economy.

Finally the application of capitalism cannot be removed from the particular normative context that stems from both culture and history. Just as the citizens of the United States may tolerate higher inequality and even extreme poverty, providing the sense of economic opportunity and upward mobility prevails, so the citizens of the Scandinavian countries will tolerate very high taxation in order to enjoy a more equal society with social justice and full provision of services. What is tolerated or accepted by citizens of one society may seem intolerable or unjust to the citizens of another. But while concepts of fairness and sense of justice are therefore necessarily contextually dependent, there is nevertheless a general sense today that, with so many trends in apparently the wrong direction, a revisit of some basic assumptions and approaches in the current application of capitalism is required.

TESTING OUR ASSUMPTIONS

Despite the passage of centuries, when it boils down to it, economic system thinking around markets is still founded upon the basic assumptions of Adam Smith's *Wealth of Nations*, and faith in the invisible hand of unregulated enterprise capitalism, many or most of which are simply false in the real world, even more so today than in 1776. They take as the basic agent the self-interested rational individual, without regard for reciprocity, social values, or morality. They also assume perfect information and an efficient market mechanism, and perfect competition, none of which have ever existed. There is debate today whether the modern age in which we live with its greater complexity and globalization is moving reality closer to or further from these classical assumptions.

Apart from regular scrutiny of the basic economic assumptions which underpin the functioning of the capitalist system, we have to question the nature of the free markets espoused by the capitalist system. Of course there is no such thing as a free market in the real world, but what appears to be increasing freedom or deregulation of markets in the economic sense is actually characterized by increased political intervention through legislation and regulations which are hijacked by special interests. In this sense the assumption of objective disinterested regulation is increasingly flawed. We have witnessed after the financial crisis the disproportionate financial bailouts given to banks and large corporations while the average homeowner lost his home and pension. The financial crisis has shaken confidence in the political system across the developed world, particularly when contrasted with the seemingly constant rise of China with a very different political system.

We see societal blame of the "market fundamentalism" that has dominated the agenda since the end of the Cold War. The idea that markets will self-correct if left to the self-interested rational behavior of individual market participants has been discredited, and is certainly not relied upon to ensure greater well-being of the majority.

The societal goal of equal opportunity—the idea that with a good education and hard work you can get ahead in life—has been significantly eroded as well, with declining mobility going hand in hand with increasing inequality in many developed economies. This further damages perceptions of justice and fairness, undermining both capitalism and faith in the political system.

The trickle-down economics which was the basis for increasing tax breaks for the wealthy and corporations has also been eroded, as standards of living further down the ladder have not caught up and it has become increasingly clear that the beneficiaries were the wealthy. The bank bailouts were justified on the basis that the banks would start lending again to increase credit in the system but this response was sluggish. All the public sees is the banks going back to their old ways and paying out seven-figure bonuses while average household income declines.

The assumption that rising inequality is a normal and perhaps necessary attribute of successful market capitalism has also come under fire, including in the academic world. The traditional view was that the incentive of larger financial rewards was required to spur the risk-taking which is the bedrock of entrepreneurship and innovation, and that there is in fact a trade-off between equality and market efficiency. Today there are various theories and studies questioning the impact of inequality on sustainability of economic growth. Whereas the exact causal relationship is unclear, there is certainly a demonstrable correlation between high inequality (Gini coefficient) and lower growth in income per capita.

A properly functioning market-based economy also assumes equality before the law and objective legislation and regulation. Yet with the increasing complexity of national tax legislation and commercial legislation, the wealthy incumbents of market power have a distinct and increasing advantage, both in influencing regulation and legislation through political influence with campaign finance and lobbyists, and in the actual implementation and compliance, through expensive lawyers, accountants, and tax advisors.

In the same vein, there has been increasing disquiet about the issue of tax evasion. Wealthy individuals have long been able to shield their income and wealth through efficient tax planning, and therefore pay a much lower percentage of income than middle-class households. But now there has been the realization that major global corporations and household brands, like Starbucks, Apple, Microsoft, and Amazon, have been paying next to no taxes thanks to offshore optimized tax structures. When their customers are forced to pay taxes on both their income and then often on the purchases they make from these companies, while the companies themselves and their wealthier investors pay next to nothing in comparison, it is easy to see how this further erodes faith in the system, and politicians in many countries have spoken out against the trend, though actual enforcement in an increasingly globalized world is another challenge altogether. Profit-seeking corporations are of course necessary actors in the market system, but the assumption was that they were bound by national economies and playing by the rules, neither of which may apply any more to the largest and most influential corporates in global capitalism.

RISKS AND CONSEQUENCES

Many of these trends do not bode well for the future of the capitalist market system and even the political systems which underpin it. There is a real risk that the basic social contract and the trust in societies have been eroded. A good education and hard work no longer necessarily provide a stable job and a decent living. GDP growth no longer means that everybody gets better off. In fact GDP per capita is increasingly criticized as a measure of changes to economic well-being and median household incomes might be a better indicator. For example, according to the IMF, since 1980 US GDP per capita has increased by 67 percent while median household income has increased by just 15 percent. If we exclude the 1980s and start in 1989, GDP per capita has increased by 34 percent while median household real incomes have actually fallen by 1 percent, meaning the typical US household is actually *worse off* in real terms than twenty-five years ago (US Census Bureau).

Then we compare this to the steep rise in executive compensation, where CEOs in the United States are now getting paid 300 times the average worker (or 100 times in supposedly socialist France), versus just twenty times in the early 1980s. And this is not because of added value but rather bargaining power—the collective bargaining power of the workforce was destroyed with the unions, whereas CEOs appoint compensation committees and external consultants to continuously justify higher competitive packages for themselves in comparison with their peers.

This harms the sense of fairness, equity, and justice, and we see a commensurate plummeting in trust in public institutions and politicians in opinion polls in almost every country, with lower voter turnouts, sharp falls in party membership, and increasing demonstrations and anti-establishment action groups, from "Stop Wall Street" in the US, to the demonstrations in Brazil, Turkey, across southern Europe, North Africa, and many other countries. Even in the successful economies of China and India, where hundreds of millions have escaped poverty in recent decades, the rise in inequality and crony capitalism with political connections has caused increased discontent and may threaten the sustainability of the capitalist experiment.

The increased focus on mass consumption and accumulation brought about by the capitalist system, combined with globalization and the power of global brands, represents a clear threat to local culture and societal values across the world, as well as weakening the social cohesion which is necessary for the long-term sustainability and success of the capitalist system.

THE ROLE OF BUSINESS

Companies of all sizes and nationalities are of course critical players in the market system. Seeking profit, leading innovation, productively employing and developing the workforce, and increasingly investing in social goods as well, they play a big and mostly positive role in the global economic system. Multinationals corporations in particular, many with valuations higher than most national GDPs, are extremely powerful influencers in local economies, dictating tastes and global trends, while making a large impact on developing economies in particular. Their influence can of course be malign as well, and their political power can threaten national governments.

We also see a growing trend of social investing and philanthropic engagement by corporations and wealthy individuals to tackle societal and global issues such as healthcare, the environment, education, and development. There are of course those skeptics that see this trend as but a PR smokescreen to shield companies from criticism, while free market defenders believe such actions are improper for companies who should seek profit and leave the altruism to their shareholders after dividends have been distributed. This of course highlights the debate on the role of corporations today—and whether it is just shareholders or the wider set of stakeholders (including governments, employees, customers, and society at large) whose interests should be considered in taking company decisions.

Yet on a basic level corporations are but the players in the game and will play the game to the best of their ability. A crude summary of the situation today might be that the players are getting stronger while the rules are getting weaker or not keeping up. And it is therefore the rules of the game and their enforcement that require our greatest scrutiny and constant attention, including regular renewal as changing times and the evolving context require. Imagine a football game with an inadequate rule-book, no lines on the pitch, and no referee—one wouldn't blame the players for the messy and ugly game that would likely ensue.

One is reminded of the period at the turn of the twentieth century and the anti-trust backlash against the monopolist robber barons who were stifling competition and gouging on prices, though without nationalizing or ending their operations—merely rebalancing the system so that capitalism could proceed in a positive sense of innovation and further productive enterprise and away from its tendency towards rent-seeking monopoly. It is time now for a similar renewal and rebalancing of capitalism to better ensure its survival and success.

THE MULTIPLE ROLES PLAYED BY INDIVIDUALS

Individuals in society play a number of different roles. Market capitalism has created a society of consumers almost universally across the globe. And their tastes are in turn influenced by an advertising industry that has grown to in excess of half a trillion dollars in spending annually worldwide. Quality of life and well-being has become increasingly measured by external material wealth and purchasing power, at the expense of spiritual or social rewards. And political participation had also declined, though by some measures narrower forms of activism for specific causes or objectives may be on the rise, assisted by new forms of technology-enabled social communication and organization.

In addition individuals are employees of corporations, though with increased global competition in the workforce and we see the "commoditization of labor." This is of course accelerated by the use of technology and globalization, with firms seeking lowest costs and highest productivity. Yet whereas in the past this phenomenon was thought restricted to blue-collar workers, we see now with the latest wave and the internet revolution that the phenomenon has spread to impact white-collar workers even harder in many developed economies. Downsizing and outsourcing have become highly controversial political issues, though with seemingly little ability to prevent what are natural trends in a global capitalist system. In the meantime the rise of the East with millions of graduates in the right subjects and growing populations is in contrast to the West's largely ageing populations with high-cost workers and declining education standards. This highlights the continuous requirement to scale up in terms of skills and innovation capacity in order to compete in a global marketplace for labor and production, though it is easier said than done, and millions are suffering during the transition, even if it can be achieved.

The role of individuals as investors is also important, and in some ways at odds with their role as consumers. Indeed savings and economic investment need to be enhanced in most western economies, where GDP has become too dependent on consumption fueled by debt. In the United States 70 percent of GDP comes from household consumption, double that of China. And China sees 50 percent of its GDP from investment. There are of course many Chinese policy-makers today who feel that a rebalancing may be required for their economy in the opposite direction, and to encourage greater domestic consumer spending to reduce the dependence on exports, but it is clear that in many developed economies the pendulum has swung too far in a consumption-driven economy.

As investors in capital markets, citizens across the world have increased their participation in stock market investments, with 20–40 percent participation in most developed economies compared with a small minority a few decades ago. And even more are indirect investors through pension funds and employee savings schemes. All this gives a sense of ownership and a stake in the economy beyond that of just wage-earner. But combined with increasingly high levels of household debt, it also leads to higher volatility and risk when considering the incomes and savings of average households.

This was experienced with devastating effect during the recent financial crisis when millions saw their jobs lost (with the loss of health insurance in the US), their homes repossessed, and the value of their pensions disappear, sometimes all at once. Encouraging more homeowners and capital markets investors may be an admirable political objective in a rising economy, but can have terrible consequences if it is debt-enabled and the economic tide turns, with little government support to cushion the fall for individuals and homeowners.

SELF-CORRECTING FORCES AND
THE NEED FOR REGULATION

Despite the classical economic assumption of self-correcting forces and the "invisible hand" steadying the free market system, we see that many of the problems described in this chapter are not simply classically economic in nature, but cross into the realm of normative economics, sociology, and politics. Even those problems that are economic need to be analyzed in the imperfect framework of the market imperfections prevailing, rather than the free market model assuming perfect competition. Few markets in practice appear to have innate self-correcting mechanisms, and therefore external intervention is needed in the form of suitable regulation to either restrict certain undermining behaviors or to create incentives for better enforcing behaviors of a successful capitalist system—always with the stated purpose in mind of allowing the sustained enhancement of the standards of living and well-being.

First, we see a natural tendency towards monopolistic and rent-seeking behavior at the firm level, and protectionist tendencies at the national level, both exacerbated by the weaker economic climate. This in turn stifles competition, innovation, and entrepreneurship, and amplifies the concentration of wealth and rising inequality. The wealthy incumbents are further able to influence the political and regulatory system in their favor to protect the incumbency, and a vicious cycle emerges. To break this cycle requires courageous and disinterested political leadership to strengthen and rigorously enforce adequate competition laws, and this time on a global level to account for transnational corporations and trade. But of course such political will is difficult to realize when the incumbent beneficiaries of the status quo wield such enormous influence over government policies through supporting lobby groups, academic institutions, and think tanks to inform opinion in their favor.

It is also particularly hard to break out of the re-enforcing nature of politics and regulation benefitting the wealthy when you have loose campaign finance regulation and no limits on political advertising, which is particularly acute in the United States but also a rising trend in many other countries. And even in China, absent western democracy, we see the link between power and money growing to a level which may threaten the economic miracle, with over one-third of all Chinese billionaires now senior national party officials, and many more with close political affiliations. Whether it's the powerful extracting the money as in much of the developing world, or the money buying the political influence in much of the developed world (albeit in a legally sanctioned manner), this "corruption" (whether legal or illegal) of the political and regulatory process becomes self-reinforcing and undermines the free market system.

Weakening these links between money and political influence requires a whole host of seemingly obvious measures that are also of course very difficult to enforce, given that to do so would require the acquiescence again of the incumbent dominant actors, absent an overwhelming groundswell of public opinion. In the United States and other developed economies, campaign finance reform, reverse of gerrymandering, better transparency and control of political lobbying, and secret balloting in legislative votes, at least at committee level, may all help shield the regulatory and legislative process from the moneyed special interests. And in developing countries, anti-trust legislation, and stronger anti-corruption laws with international monitoring and enforcement, would better enhance investment and competitiveness in the economies.

The issue of rising inequality again seems to have no self-correcting mechanism, and requires redistributive government policies to reverse it, particularly in an economic downturn. But the challenge lies in doing this in an economically productive manner and not one that rewards inactivity. The flip-side is also true of course—tax breaks for corporations and wealthy individuals may only work to spur growth when they are made conditional upon further investment, particularly in physical capital and productive long-term output, rather than short-term financial returns.

The rapid financialization of the global economy again has no apparent self-correcting mechanism, with higher returns and leverage creating faster growth of the sector and increased short-termism, volatility, and vulnerability. Also financial capital may be crowding out physical capital so critical to the long-term health of the economy. Despite the furore in the aftermath of the financial crisis and the blame attributed to this phenomenon, virtually nothing has been done to change the situation.

Many reasonable responses have been suggested, such as a reinstatement of the separation between investment and commercial banking, and measures to effectively reduce the devastating impact and speed of short-term financial flows, such as a tax on financial transactions (Tobin tax), regulation of the derivatives market, increasing margin requirements, and in developing countries allowing some regulations to control capital market flows and speculation. Yet in practice the previous free market consensus and prescription has remained largely intact, and the likelihood of financial sector reform appears ever more remote as the global economy seemingly sluggishly recovers and world attention focuses on the latest headline of conflict or crisis.

In terms of the consumption–investment balance, the culture of debt-fueled consumption will take time to reverse and will require both regulation of debt-providers to stem the easy debt provision to those most at risk, and better incentives to encourage higher savings and investment.

The squeezing out of blue- and white-collar workers in many countries from the global labor market will require better skills retraining and education provision, including a focus on vocational skills and more graduates in science and engineering, with stronger standards in public education from the earliest years onward. Affordable universal healthcare provision is an important policy objective for all countries, improving both productivity and the standard of living.

Improving socio-economic mobility and breaking the barriers between segments of society again requires high standards of public education first and foremost, as well standardized testing and a goal of needs-blind admissions at leading universities, with public scholarships for the best and brightest, particularly in the developing world.

Strengthening the environment for entrepreneurship and small-firm growth requires better access to funding, which may require regulatory incentives to banks ending to start-ups and SMEs. In addition bankruptcy laws are still absent in much of the developing world, and bureaucratic red-tape and the costs of establishing a business are prohibitive except for the well-off. And the hurdle for capital markets access is so high in many markets now that they are accessible to only well-established and larger firms, though crowd-funding and other technology-driven innovations are attempting to plug the gap.

Structural unemployment and lack of economic opportunities for the youth are a prevalent feature in many regions of the world and are particularly evident in southern Europe, the Middle East, and Africa, though this is also a challenge in North and South America and northern Europe. This is usually caused by the combination of insufficient growth, rigid labor markets, and a skills mismatch between what the education system provides and what the labor market requires. Higher investment in infrastructure to enhance short-term employment and longer term productivity and competitiveness could be enabled through global infrastructure funds and enabling national legislation.

In addition labor markets need to be reformed to make it easier for young people to get on the ladder, rather than just protecting those already on it. And stronger ties between the private sector and education provision need to be established in many of the most affected regions, with incentives for firms to provide mentorship and training programs both pre- and post-graduation.

Trust and faith in politics and institutions needs to be restored in order for the capitalist system to continue to be supported. For this aim, it may be required to turn the emphasis away from more "open-ness" and "democracy" and toward better institution building, professionalism, and accountability. It is telling for instance that in many countries trust in and popularity of elected politicians has plummeted in recent times, while respect for and trust in unelected established institutions, such as the judiciary, the central bank, the armed forces, or religious establishments, has held up much better. The fierceness of the twenty-four-hour media cycle, with its scandal seeking, has in many ways undermined public confidence in politicians, and the tribalism or zero sum game politics in some countries has been an obstacle to progress and effective governance. Stronger independent or cross-party institutions and regulators can have a role to play in addressing this, as well as scrutiny of the policies and outcomes of government, without allowing as much external interference in the process.

GAPS IN KNOWLEDGE AND FUTURE RESEARCH

With a seemingly whole host of things wrong with capitalism today, we should step back and recognize that, despite these apparent faults in its current application and performance in many countries, it has on the whole performed extremely successfully in enhancing incomes and standards of living over the course of human history and over the last few centuries in particular. And the last few decades have seen the exciting and rapid spread of these benefits to many parts of the developing world, with hundreds of millions of people leaving poverty and entering a global marketplace of choice and higher utility. So what we are really seeking to address is how and where the system may have gone wrong, or gone too far, or gotten stuck, resulting in sub-optimal outcomes in a normative and not just an economic sense. And in examining these issues knowledge and better understanding is always the first step in addressing them.

A first line of inquiry is into the topic of inequality. This one simple word can open up a myriad of research topics, spanning the fields of economics and econometrics, philosophy, psychology, sociology, development studies, and management studies to name a few. In the modern context in particular, the relation between rising inequality and future growth potential is an area that is already receiving more attention. There are the classical economic consequences in terms of differences in propensity to consume or save between poorer and the better-off; also the potential negative impacts on productivity, with lower worker motivation due to lower social mobility, poorer healthcare, higher crime rates, and so on. But there is also the interesting question of how rising inequality weakens trust and societal cohesion, thereby undermining the capitalist system itself over time.

The topic of corruption—not just in the limited sense of bribery or fraud but in the wider sense of corruption of the system through the interplay of money and power—is one that certainly merits more in-depth analysis. Empirical studies showing how the increased influence of lobbying and special interests have affected inequality and harmed the general consumer are one place to start in the developed world (though it is not surprising they have struggled to find funding). Costs of corruption to a developing economy and the negative consequences on attracting investment are an important area of analysis for much of the world. But solutions are needed to tackle the incentives at the root cause of corruption, including bureaucracy and weak legal systems and media. The use of technology to streamline public service delivery and disintermediate the government official (e-government) is one area that has potential to significantly reduce corruption.

In the area of anti-trust and competition policy, the focus has so far mostly been about enforcement within the US, or within the EU. But much more needs to be done to develop updated standards, laws, and regulations more relevant to a globalized system of trade and investment, given the prevalence and dominance of multinationals in many sectors. And in addition, guidelines on best practices in the implementation of domestic competition laws need to be developed for use by developing countries, in order to spare them the same arduous journey through the process taken by the United States and others.

The topic of financial sector reform is clearly one that garnered a lot of interest when the financial crisis first struck in 2008, yet it seems to have largely passed unaddressed. A deeper dive into the psychology of incentives of individual market decisions, a broader historical analysis of lessons learned from previous crises, more research into the topic of market confidence and the effects of volatility on growth trajectory, are all possible lines of further inquiry. Also beneficial might be studies into how the rise of financialization has impacted societal values and inequality.

In assessing patterns of consumption and investment it would be interesting to study the cultural dynamics around propensity to save or consume, whether these can be easily taught or changed over time, and what relation they may have to the national stage of economic development. The interplay between these metrics and rate of growth and inequality are also of interest.

In tackling youth unemployment, further analysis on what short-term training and skills provision best enhances productivity and employability would be of high value; also on the long-term effects on motivation, entrepreneurship, and trust of extended periods of unemployment for young people, not to mention the effects on political stability. Optimum labor market reforms in the developing world to tackle this challenge is another topic that could benefit from rigorous empirical research. And on the investment side, the sectors and types of infrastructure spending that can most rapidly enhance employment for the young need better understanding.

Finally, the study of institutional structures and their role on market and economic development is certainly a field worthy of deeper research and understanding, not just from a sociological or political perspective but from an economic one in particular. One aspect that always seems taken for granted in economic and political discourse in the western world is the vital yet complex institutional framework that underpins the capitalist market system. Not understanding their role and evolution is dangerous enough in developed economies, but even more so for countries in the developing world, particularly when they are attempting to digest and implement supposedly optimum market-based policies with little or none of the required institutional framework to support them.

For many of these topics the most interesting areas of further research are on the boundaries between the traditional academic disciplines, since those are the areas where many of the required solutions may lie to solve the complex challenges of the real world.

BIBLIOGRAPHY

Chang, Ha-Joon (2010). *23 Things They Don't Tell You about Capitalism*. Harmondsworth: Penguin Books.

Eagleton, Terry (2011). *Why Marx was Right*. London: Yale University Press.

Harvey, David (2010). *The Enigma of Capital and the Crises of Capitalism*. London: Profile Books.

Milanovic, Branko (2010). *The Haves and the Have-Nots*. New York: Basic Books.

Schumpeter, Joseph A. (2011). *Capitalism, Socialism and Democracy*. Reprint. Eastford, CT: Martino Publishing Mansfield Centre.

Stiglitz, Joseph (2010). *Freefall*. Harmondsworth: Penguin Books.

Stiglitz, Joseph (2013). *The Price of Inequality*. Harmondsworth: Penguin Books.

CHAPTER 2

....

DO THE MISTAKES LIE IN
DECISION-MAKERS OR
IN ECONOMICS?

....

JAMES G. MARCH

Abstract

Micro-economic analysis and its various derivatives seek to provide partial answers to two distinct questions. How *should* an intelligent actor choose among available alternatives? How *do* presumably intelligent actors choose among available alternatives? The two questions are distinct, but they are intertwined. Insofar as an answer to the first is widely shared and obeyed, it becomes the answer to the second. Insofar as the two questions yield different answers, as they often do in observations of economic actors, the disparity can be seen as revealing some mix of lack of intelligence on the part of actors and inadequate specification of the nature of intelligence on the part of their advisors and their theories. One persistent issue is: Do the mistakes lie in the decision makers or in economics? A full answer to that question involves an exploration of the use of rules by human actors and the role of value torment in the making of choices.

DECISION THEORY INTELLIGENCE
....

At least for the last century, most of economics has assumed that intelligent action is defined by decision theory (Raiffa 1968) and that competitive selection assures that surviving actors will make choices in the way that decision theory asserts they should. In conventional decision theory, intelligence is defined as making trade-offs among alternative goods so as to maximize long-run expected subjective utility. It reflects a refinement on classical admonitions to pursue pleasure and avoid pain.

Although the basic ideas of decision theory dominate economic thought, they are not without their skeptics. The skeptics note that the focus on choice among available alternatives ignores the processes by which alternatives become available, processes that may have a greater impact on decisions than the choice among them. The skeptics also note that the bulk of empirical studies of actual decision-making reveal extensive use of rules (Cyert and March 1963; Kratochwil 1989), heuristics (Hutchinson and Gigerenzer 2005), and the logic of appropriateness (March and Olsen 2006). The logic of appropriateness associates action with an identity and a definition of the situation. At least explicitly, it does not involve anticipation of consequences but a process of matching rules linked to an identity with a situation. These include many rules that are collected formally in standard operating procedures, as well as many that are less formally encoded but clearly present. The ubiquity of rules as a basis for making decisions is a conspicuous feature of modern life (March and Simon 1958; Mills and Murgatroyd 1991), and their processes of change a vital part of understanding organizations (March et al. 2000). An obvious question is how such procedures for making choices survive if the procedures of decision theory are superior.

INTERPRETING DEVIATIONS FROM DECISION THEORY INTELLIGENCE

Most empirical studies of individuals and firms seem to indicate that decision theory captures some elements of choice behavior but that it is an inadequate general portrayal of either the processes of choice or of the choices made (Witte and Zimmerman 1986; Hodgkinson and Starbuck 2008). For example, decision theory correctly predicts that most of the time, though sometimes after some time and with some qualifications, prices will increase with increases in demand and decrease with decreases in demand; but the processes of price determination seem explicitly more linked to costs and routines associated with them than to calculations of marginal returns (Cyert and March 1963). Similarly, studies of individuals show them persistently violating the dicta of decision theory, both in decision procedures and in choices made, though less so when they have been indoctrinated in business schools to make decisions by maximizing present value (Tversky and Kahneman 1974; Kahneman et al. 1982; Schoemaker 1982).

Within the standard formulations of most economics, this history suggests that human decision-making is often filled with correctable errors (Kahneman 2011), including the possibility of irrational persistence in mistakes (Einhorn and Hogarth 1978). This possibility is one factor in the extensive use of decision consultants in modern business. Very large numbers of consultants and academics search for ways to improve business decision-making by attaching it more effectively to decision theory consequentialism. There is little doubt that the past seventy-five years have seen considerable modification of business procedures to reflect this effort, and the results have improved the decision intelligence of management.

The dominant intellectual view reflected in most economics is, however, implicitly (but not always explicitly) at variance with the presumption of extensive defective intelligence on the part of economic actors. The dominant view postulates that the natural processes of competitive selection will expose and eliminate any mistakes that humans make or eliminate the humans who make them (Friedman 1953). As a result, most of economic theory uses a theory of how decisions should be made as a theory of how they are made, thereby characterizing empirical studies of actual decision behavior as exposing minor transient errors that are anomalies, or at least will not persist. If this is to be taken literally, it leaves little room for management consultants or operations research except as instruments of selection. In a similar spirit, there is a tendency in economic treatments of rules to imagine that any rules that are followed by economic actors are the outcomes of some long-run evolutionary processes that favor optimal procedures, thus that rule-following is a form of optimization (North 1990).

THE LIMITATIONS OF ADAPTATION

The notion that superior ideas, rules, and species ultimately come to dominate inferior ones is a fundamental dictum of theories of progress. However, if the time involved is some number of millennia, the ultimate outcome of a process may be of less interest than its shorter run path. Moreover, to be meaningful, such a notion requires that "fitness" is not defined tautologically by survival but exists as an observable property of rules. Defining a set of mechanisms by which the triumph of superiority is assured has proven difficult. For example, the rise to evolutionary dominance of the human species can be seen as an outcome of an evolutionary process, but the outcome seems to be neither a necessary nor a stable one. Most species that have ever existed no longer do.

Modern explorations of adaptive processes have identified numerous examples of adaptive processes that have multiple stable equilibria and frequently exhibit less than optimal outcomes (McNamara and Houston 1982; Kauffman 1989, 1993; Selten 1991; Gimeno et al. 1997; Gary et al. 2008). Insofar as procedures that associate action with identities and particular situations come to be more common than procedures that associate action with expected consequences, it is possible that the processes of choice evolution disadvantage the procedures of decision theory, despite their superiority. Decision theory rules may have features that make them more difficult to replicate than more traditional rules. For example, they normally involve some elements of technical skills that require separating the calculations from the actions they discover or anoint. Such a separation involves a level of trust between a calculator and an actor that is hard to maintain, partly because as the trust level rises the opportunity for manipulation by the calculator also rises. As a result, in order for decision theory rules to become dominant, the evolutionary process must not only favor the rules of decision theory but also the rules of organizational behavior essential to them.

POSSIBLE ADVANTAGES OF RULE-FOLLOWING

Except by definition, evolutionary processes do not assure optimization. As noted, it is possible that the processes of evolution favor rule-based procedures over decision theory procedures despite the superiority of the latter. There is, however, an alternative speculation. It is possible that the observed actual procedures of human decision-making, evolved over thousands of years, show intelligence in their deviation from the analytics of decision theory. The possibility that intelligence may follow from something other than instrumental decision theory is a familiar theme in social science. Max Weber (Kalberg 1980) distinguished four varieties of "rationality" in human behavior: practical, means-end rationality; theoretical rationality; substantive rationality; and traditional (formal, rule-based) rationality.

It is a possibility, by no means a certainty, that rules that associate action with particular situations and identities are superior in some specifiable ways to rules that associate action with expected consequences. Thus, it is possible that decision theory with its logic of consequences may be less intelligent than is presumed, and the logic of appropriateness more intelligent. By this speculation, the precepts of decision theory are often shunned by human actors because humans and human institutions have learned that the precepts are incomplete or erroneous instruments of intelligence.

Decision theory conceptions of intelligence are built on classical economic notions of exchange. The idea is that values can be reduced to a well-defined metric (ordinarily captured by subjective revealed utility) that permits the specification of trade-offs among them. The nature of that utility function is revealed by examining the choices made, but whether it is otherwise observable is in dispute.

Critics have noted several major potential flaws of conventional decision theory (Halpern and Stern 1998), of which three may be illustrative. The first is that the estimates of the future that the procedure requires are not only subject to substantial random error but also are prone to systematic bias (Lord et al. 1979; Ross and Sicoly 1979; Kahneman et al. 1982; Rabin and Schrag 1999; Kosnik 2008). For example, human decision-makers rarely estimate extremely low probability events correctly, either considerably overestimating or considerably underestimating their likelihoods. They systematically underestimate the likelihood of events they have never experienced and of outcomes that they have not imagined. They systematically exclude alternatives different from the ones conventional to their experience. Estimates of the future are disturbingly affected by desires, as are the realizations.

A second domain of major potential flaws is the decision theory procedure for dealing with preferences. The conventional decision theory definition of intelligence has at least three major inconsistencies with observed preferences of individuals and organizations (March 1978). First, the subjective utilities involved in decision theory are assumed to reflect preferences that are stable so that what is desired now will also be desired when the consequences of action are realized. Unfortunately, human preferences appear to change often. Second, the subjective utilities involved are assumed to be known in advance and exogenous to the choice. Unfortunately, human preferences seem to develop in the course of taking action and experiencing its consequences (Greber and Jackson 1993). Third, the subjective utilities involved are assumed to be consistent. Unfortunately, human preferences seem often to be strikingly inconsistent. Faced with these complications, the priests of decision theory typically undertake to remove them by making the preferences of their acolytes stable, exogenous, and consistent, and deriving "optimal" choices from them. Unfortunately, the decisions so derived often turn out to be more clever than wise. They incompletely define the situation or the preferences (March 2006).

A third domain of major potential flaws is the tendency to overlook the ways in which the environment consists in part of strategic actors who are simultaneously anticipating the decisions derived from anticipating them (von Neumann and Morgenstern, 1944; Shubik 1959; Harsanyi 1977). Decision-makers routinely try to anticipate the decisions made by other actors, who are simultaneously trying to anticipate their anticipators.

To a lesser extent, students of decision-making have also tried to assess the weaknesses of rules. In particular, they note that the mechanisms for making rules consistent are weak. Individuals typically have multiple identities, each with a different set of rules. The differences among the imperatives of different identities are obscured by mechanisms of attention that discourage the simultaneous evocation of multiple identities; but the result is that rule-following appears to be an imperfect instrument for consistent action over time, an imperfection that is manifest in the continuing efforts of courts to make laws and rules consistent.

Nevertheless, the extensive use of the logic of appropriateness by humans suggests that there may be something intelligent about the use of rules, although there is little agreement on the elements of intelligence that are found in rules. When we ask "What is intelligent about the use of rules, identities, and the logic of appropriateness?," we discover the question is a disturbingly difficult one. It seems too narrow a question if it reduces to: how can we rationalize rules within the dicta of decision theory? On the other hand, it is hard to see any other idea of intelligence that gathers much contemporary support.

One obvious possible rationalization of rules within an economics tradition focuses on the cost advantages of rules. Rules reduce computation and communication costs. We summarize a great deal of computation and experience in the simple rule: eat three meals a day. In many areas of business, rather complicated analyses are summarized in terms of simple rules. They save time and reduce errors of implementation. This rationalization is eminently reasonable, but it does not exhaust the possibilities. One possibility is that a personal struggle with contradictions will resolve the conflicts better than simply specifying trade-offs. How this can be true is not obvious, but one possible direction to explore is the possibility that a trade-off framework resolves the issues too fast, that contradiction stimulates delay and search.

On the other hand, the intelligence of rules may lie less in how they facilitate consequential choices than in how they address a different set of problems, in particular, how they allow adjustment to variations over time in attention to multiple, conflicting values. The values that drive humans are not continuously salient. On the surface at least, the adaptation of a human organism seems to depend heavily on the allocation of attention and the mobilization of response to a sequence of problems (Cyert and March 1963). The inefficiencies involved in considering objectives and situations sequentially, rather than simultaneously, may be outweighed by the motivational and cognitive advantages of focus. It is widely understood that attempting to solve the full future unfolding of problems is counter-productive, partly because the unfolding of those problems is subject to innumerable factors.

The organizations literature contains somewhat parallel arguments on the organizational level. It has frequently been observed that organizations attend to goals sequentially, rather than simultaneously, thus avoiding explicit confrontation of conflicting goals by attention procedures that tend to focus on a small subset of goals (Cyert and March 1963). The underlying desirability of such procedures is found in the way their own limited attention restricts the capability of coalition members to attend continuously to their individual concerns. The organization maintains a coalition by attending to potentially conflicting coalition members sequentially rather than simultaneously, and taking advantage of attention limitations among those members.

THE SOCIAL FUNCTIONS OF DECISION-MAKING

As has been observed frequently by students of decision-making, decision processes have important outcomes in addition to the decisions they generate (March and Olsen 1976, 1989, 1995). In particular, decision processes provide an arena for shaping social values and educating the individual. In this respect, rule-based choices can be contrasted with choices based on decision theory. Decision theory produces resolution and thereby reduces the values involved to exchangeable items. Rules produce torment over value conflict and thereby reinforce the importance of the values involved. In the short run, the difference may be slight; but in the long run, decision theory tends to erode values by focusing explicitly on their trade-offs and reducing the angst associated with violating them.

Things that are "priceless" will sometimes have to be sacrificed, and conscious decision trade-offs allow their sacrifice to be experienced without the profound anguish that helps sustain the values. In many areas of strongly held values, therefore, the proposition that "everything has a price" is viewed as demeaning to human dignity; and the notion that a market for dignity determines the value of dignity is condemned. If a mother calculates expected value in making a decision about which child to sacrifice, she undermines the force of the moral precepts that exhort her to defend her children. The point is not that angst, in itself, is a good thing, but that the calculation of trade-offs, regardless of its outcome, reduces the commitment to things that are strongly valued. The public confession of sin and abject petition for forgiveness appears to be valued more than the determination of exchange values and the exchange of money for indulgences.

Compelling rules are not only premises of action; their contradiction is also a basis for social and individual discourse over virtue. Such discourse seeks less to reconcile differences among values than to reinforce their importance. The problem of retaining commitment to conflicting values is a foundational problem of sound education and personal development. Johan Wolfgang Goethe's masterful novel, *Wilhelm Meister's Lehrjahre* (Goethe 1795–6), portrays the maturation of a young man as he wrestles with the confusions of doing and being good. The hero tries to resolve the contradictions of youth, less by calculating trade-offs than by anguishing over the demands of hormones and the precepts of relationships. His resolutions are incomplete with residual elements of contradiction, and they exhibit a persistent effort to find a life that embraces contradictory values wholeheartedly enough to discover ways of maintaining them, rather than simply determining their exchange rates.

THE LIMITS OF ECONOMICS

Economics is a discipline addressed to making trade-offs among well-defined, exchangeable goods in terms of clear, consistent preferences. Indeed, it is sometimes said that economics is the study of goods that have exchange value, goods that have a market price. Such a definition of economics has considerable merit, but it excludes from the field the study of decisions involving things about which human typically care a good deal, choices that evoke deep sentiments of revulsion or ecstasy. In such domains, the educational value of debates over the issues may be greater than any improvement in the quality of the decision per se.

Consider, for example, the efforts to discover and discuss the value of a human life as implicit in decisions involving the possibility of mortal consequences. Humans often make decisions that involve risks to life. It is well-known that determining the value revealed by choices involving life or death yields implicit trade-off values that vary widely among different choices (Blomquist 2001; Viscusi and Aldy 2003; Viscusi 2004). By such criteria, humans are characteristically hopelessly inconsistent in making life and death decisions. Moreover, individuals will debate issues of life or death at great length without showing any inclination to inform the debate by decision theory calculations of revealed value. The values involved are too precious to be calibrated. The debate is more significant than its outcome.

A decision theorist might reasonably say that, since one necessarily defines implicit trade-offs in making decisions, the decisions can be improved by rendering those trade-offs explicit. A rule-follower might reasonably respond that it is better to suffer the anguish of contradictory values underlying rules and the implicit inconsistency exhibited in a set of specific resolutions than to make decisions based on explicit trade-offs that moderate the anguish. Perhaps it is no accident that describing a decision-maker as "coldly calculating" is normally criticism, not praise.

In the end, intelligence, or virtue, is a product of action. It depends on appropriate choices. Appropriate choices depend on an apparatus of choice and a foundation of values. By focusing on the apparatus of choice, economics has explicitly ignored problems with values. The limitation of attention to choice has a defensible foundation. There are many reasons to distinguish economics from religion (Becker and Stigler 1977). However, in this case, the forbearance is potentially misleading. Economic and political institutions and practices are not only part of the apparatus of social choice; they are also part of the social elaboration of value. It seems possible that rules, logics of appropriateness, and anguish may underlie the social debates without end by which a society both builds values and changes them with neither explicit specification of trade-offs nor conclusiveness. Perhaps a good society debates its contradictory desires not to resolve the contradictions but to reinforce the values that conflict. It suffers the pain of choice with anguish over the losses produced by choice rather than pride over its rationality. Such a possibility undoubtedly glorifies human resistance to decision theory, but it is a reminder that cleverness is inclined to scorn the longer run processes of social life that wisdom embraces.

Do the Mistakes Lie in Decision-Makers or in Economics?

Adaptive processes make mistakes. The rules for making decisions evolved from years of experience by human actors and human institutions can be imperfect (March 2010). One responsibility of scholarship is to expose and correct the imperfections in established human practices, including the rules that organize the making of choices; and one of the glories of modern scholarship is the development of decision theory into an instrument of human improvement.

The successes, however, conceal an array of weaknesses. In particular, treating value inconsistency as an invitation to specifying explicit trade-offs among values makes the values recognized by decision-makers less compelling. It undermines the endless anguish and inter-personal and intra-personal struggles over multiple compelling demands that typify human decision-making. This anguish and struggle stimulate the discourse and argument that maintain primary values in the face of efforts to reduce them to the lesser status of exchangeable goods.

Acknowledgment

I am grateful for the thoughtful comments and continuing colleagueship of Johan P. Olsen.

REFERENCES

Becker, G. S., and G. J. Stigler (1977). De gustibus non est disputandum. *American Economic Review*, 67: 76–90.

Blomquist, G. (2001): Economics of Value of Life. In N. J. Smelser and P. B. Baltes (eds), *The International Encyclopedia of the Social and Behavioral Science*. New York: Pergamon of Elsevier Science, xxiv. 16132–9.

Cyert, R. M., and J. G. March (1963). *A Behavioral Theory of the Firm*. Englewood Cliffs, NJ: Prentice-Hall. 2nd edn Oxford: Basil Blackwell, 1992.

Einhorn, H., and R. Hogarth (1978). Confidence in Judgment: Persistence in the Illusion of Validity. *Psychological Review*, 85: 395–416.

Friedman, M. (1953). *Essays in Positive Economics*. Chicago: Chicago University Press.

Gary, M. S., G. Dosi, and D. Lovallo (2008). Boom and Bust Behavior: On the Persistence of Strategic Decision Biases. In G. P. Hodgkinson and W. H. Starbuck (eds), *The Oxford Handbook of Organizational Decision Making*. Oxford: Oxford University Press, 33–55.

Gimeno, J., T. B. Folta, A. C. Cooper, and C. Y. Woo (1997). Survival of the Fittest? Entrepreneurial Human Capital and the Persistence of Underperforming Firms. *Administrative Science Quarterly*, 42: 750–83.

Goethe, Johan Wolfgang von (1795–6). *Wilhelm Meisters Lehrjahre*. Berlin: Johan Friedrich Unger.

Greber, E. R., and J. E. Jackson (1993). Endogenous Preferences and the Study of Institutions. *American Political Science Review*, 87: 639–56.

Halpern, J., and R. N. Stern, eds. (1998). *Debating Rationality: Nonrational Aspects of Organizational Decision Making*. Ithaca, NY: Cornell University Press.

Harsanyi, J. C. (1977). *Rational Behavior and Bargaining Equilibrium in Games and Social Situations*. Cambridge: Cambridge University Press.

Hodgkinson, G. P., and W. H. Starbuck, eds. (2008). *The Oxford Handbook of Organizational Decision Making*. Oxford: Oxford University Press.

Hutchinson, J. M. C., and G. Gigerenzer (2005). Simple Heuristics and Rules of Thumb: Where Psychologists and Behavioural Biologists Might Meet. *Behavioural Processes*, 69: 97–124.

Kahneman, D. (2011). *Thinking, Fast and Slow*. New York: Farrar, Straus, & Giroux.

Kahneman, D., P. Slovic, and A. Tversky (1982). *Judgment under Uncertainty: Heuristics and Biases*. Cambridge: Cambridge University Press.

Kalberg, S. (1980). Max Weber's Types of Rationality: Cornerstones for the Analysis of Rationalization Processes in History. *American Journal of Sociology*, 85: 1145–79.

Kauffman, S. (1989). Adaptation on Rugged Fitness Landscapes. In E. Stein (ed.), *Lectures in the Sciences of Complexity*. Reading, MA: Addison-Wesley, 527–618.

Kauffman, S. A. (1993). *The Origins of Order: Self-Organization and Selection in Evolution*. Oxford: Oxford University Press.

Kosnik, L.-R. D. (2008). Refusing to Budge: A Confirmatory Bias in Decision Making. *Mind and Society*, 7: 193–214.

Kratochwil, F. V. (1989). *Rules, Norms and Decisions: On the Conditions of Practical and Legal Reasoning in International Relations and Domestic Affairs*. Cambridge: Cambridge University Press.

Lord, C., M. R. Lepper, and L. Ross (1979). Biased Assimilation and Attitude Polarization: The Effects of Prior Theories on Subsequently Considered Evidence. *Journal of Personality and Social Psychology*, 37: 2098–110.

McNamara, J. M., and A. I. Houston (1982). Short-Term Behavior and Life-Time Fitness. In D. J. McFarland (ed.), *Functional Ontogeny*. London: Pitman, 60–87.

March, J. G. (1978). Bounded Rationality, Ambiguity, and the Engineering of Choice. *Bell Journal of Economics*, 9: 587–608.

March, J. G. (2006). Rationality, Foolishness, and Adaptive Intelligence. *Strategic Management Journal*, 27: 201–14.

March, J. G. (2010). *The Ambiguities of Experience*. Ithaca, NY: Cornell University Press.

March, J. G. (2014). The Two Projects of Micro Economics. *Industrial and Corporate Change*, 23: 609–12.

March, J. G., and H. A. Simon (1958). *Organizations*. New York: Wiley.

March, J. G., and J. P. Olsen (1976). *Ambiguity and Choice*. Oslo: Universitetsforlaget.

March, J. G., and J. P. Olsen (1989). *Rediscovering Institutions: The Organizational Basis of Politics*. New York: Free Press.

March, J. G., and J. P. Olsen (1995). *Democratic Governance*. New York: Free Press.

March, J. G., and J. P. Olsen (2006). The Logic of Appropriateness. In M. Moran, M. Rein, and R. E. Goodin (eds), *The Oxford Handbook of Public Policy*. Oxford: Oxford University Press, 689–708.

March, J. G., M. Schulz, and X. Zhou (2000). *The Dynamics of Rules: Change in Written Organizational Codes*. Stanford, CA: Stanford University Press.

Miller, D. T., and Ross, M. (1975). Self-Serving Biases in the Attribution of Causality. *Psychological Bulletin*, 82: 213–25.

Mills, A. J., and S. J. Murgatroyd (1991). *Organizational Rules: A Framework for Understanding Organizational Action*. Philadelphia: Open University Press.

North, D. C. (1990). *Institutions, Institutional Change and Economic Performance*. Cambridge: Cambridge University Press.

Rabin, M., and J. L. Schrag (1999). First Impressions Matter: A Model of Confirmatory Bias. *Quarterly Journal of Economics*, 114: 37–82.

Raiffa, H. (1968). *Decision Analysis*. Reading, MA: Addison-Wesley.

Ross, M., and F. Sicoly (1979). Egocentric biases in availability and attribution. *Journal of Personality and Social Psychology*, 37: 322–36.

Schoemaker, P. J. H. (1982). The Expected Utility Model: Its Variants, Purposes, Evidence and Limitations. *Journal of Economic Literature*, 20: 529–63.

Selten, R. (1991). Evolution, Learning and Economic Behavior. *Games and Economic Behavior*, 3: 3–24.

Shubik, M. (1959). *Oligopoly, Competition, and the Theory of Games*. New York: Wiley.

Tversky, A., and Kahneman, D. (1974). Judgment under Uncertainty: Heuristics and Biases. *Science*, 185: 1124–31.

Viscusi, W. K. (2004). The Value of Life: Estimates with Risks by Occupation and Industry *Economic Inquiry*, 42: 29–48.

Viscusi, K., and J. E. Aldy (2003). The Value of a Statistical Life: A Critical Review of Market Estimates throughout the World. *Journal of Risk and Uncertainty*, 27: 5–76.

Von Neumann, J., and O. Morgenstern (1944). *The Theory of Games and Economic Behavior*. Princeton: Princeton University Press.

Weary, F. (1979). Self-Serving Attributional Biases: Perceptional or Response Distortions. *Journal of Personality and Social Psychology*, 37: 1418–20.

Witte, E., and H.-J. Zimmerman, eds. (1986). *Empirical Research on Organizational Decision Making*. Amsterdam: Elsevier.

....

CHAPTER 3

SOME FAILURES OF
THE ECONOMY

....

KENNETH J. ARROW

Abstract

This chapter lays out some of the ways in which the current capitalist market economy fails to achieve some human needs and its own full potential. It is not intended to be comprehensive. For one, it ignores the problems of inequality of income and wealth, which would require a long consideration on its own. The chapter reviews the strengths of the market system and then discusses information incompleteness and asymmetry, limitations of the price system in market clearing, and especially externalities. Climate, the financial industry, and the business cycle are mentioned as instances of problems that the market system is yet to address satisfactorily.

INTRODUCTION

....

In this chapter, I will be emphasizing the directions and, to some extent, the degree to which the economic system falls short of its potential for benefitting the human enterprise. It is important to keep in mind the extent to which our present economic system, a market system based on private property and trade, with strong admixtures of political regulation and less formal social controls, has been beneficial. Certainly as regards what are ordinarily regarded as tradable goods, today's abundance cannot be gainsaid.

It must also be observed that even in economic systems that one would not describe as capitalist, markets have played a major role. Of course, objections to markets and to capitalism are equally ancient. One is that the accumulation of goods is itself bad; more mildly, the desire to accumulate goods leads, it is held, to unethical behavior or to the degradation of social and family ties. The desire for money in the abstract is a further step in moving away from directly human ends; it is demand for command over goods rather than the goods themselves and can, it is held, distort true human relations (as in George Eliot's novel, *Silas Marner*).

These arguments are hard to assess, and there is a contrary viewpoint that commerce is a civilizing influence that increases concern for others. The discussions on this point in the eighteenth century are to be found in A. Hirschman (1977); for a modern analysis, which finds other-regardingness, measured by playing appropriate games, to be higher in more market-oriented economies, see Bowles et al. (2005). In this note, I will emphasize more the failures of the economic system within the economic world. However, I will raise some of the ethical questions that arise because of the actual nature of the economy.

One more preliminary remark: an essential element of the human being as a biological entity is the importance of cooperative behavior. Though cooperation occurs in many other species, it is clear that the evolutionary success of *Homo sapiens* is due at least in great part to social behavior. The market is one form in which this cooperation takes place. This is somewhat odd, since the market mimics Hobbes's war of each against all, yet it is a way to achieve cooperation in a way that reduces the frictions in the process.

The evolutionary success of *Homo sapiens* is indeed a potential danger to its long-run future. Yet the values for cooperation supply one of the hopes for controlling this danger.

COMPLEX ADAPTIVE SYSTEMS: ADAPTING TO WHAT?

The economy is an example of what has come to be known as a complex adaptive system (CAS). An interacting system is composed of parts, each of which has an internal structure. Each part is "adapting," which may be interpreted as seeking to maximize some objective. However, the activities of each part affect the performance of the other parts.

The prototype of a CAS is the evolution of living entities. It is a tautology that each species survives by its fitness. But the success, in this sense, of one species may be at the expense of other species. They may compete for the same scarce resources; one may be the prey of the other. It is also possible that two species may be complementary, in many different ways. One, for example, is that species A preys on species B which, in turn, preys on species C. Then species A and C are complementary. These relations have been termed, "co-evolution." (It turns out that similar ideas have also been of great use in studying some complex systems in physics.)

The very term, "adaptation," hints at a valuation. Indeed, in biological language, teleological terms abound. One refers to "successful" and "unsuccessful" species and genetic mutations. In principle, this terminology could be eliminated, and all biological processes described in mechanistic and causal terms. But the usage suggests a value by which systems can be judged. At the very least, the "success" or "value" to be ascribed to the system is governed in some way by the values or successes of the individual parts.

The Economy as a Complex System: How do we Evaluate its Performance?

By any description, the economy is certainly to be considered a complex adaptive system. Firms and households are striving to improve their lots, increasing profits in the case of firms, increasing some measure of preference ("utility") for households. Since profits increase the incomes of the owners of the firms, the ultimate criteria for the values ascribed to the parts of the system are the household utilities. Hence, the evaluation of the entire system should be at least compatible with the condition that economists have named, "Pareto optimality," after the economist who first formulated it: one outcome of the system is better than another if every household is made better off in the first than in the second.

In an oversimplified account of the economy, all economic transactions are mediated by prices, whose levels are determined by the condition supplies equal demands on all markets (more exactly, that supply is at least equal to demand on all markets and that price is zero on any market where supply exceeds demand). Then it can be shown that the competitive market (when each economic agent is so small that it cannot, by itself, change prices) yields a Pareto-optimal outcome. This is a modern version of Adam Smith's reference to the "invisible hand" by which the individual entrepreneur, only aiming to increase his or her own profit, is led to achieve the social good.

The problems of the economy arise, for the most part, from its failure to satisfy the conditions of the ideal standard model. We therefore need some criterion for evaluating alternative outcomes that do not arise from the competitive equilibrium. The spirit behind the definition of Pareto optimality suggests that the outcomes of, for example, two alternative policies could be compared by saying that policy A is better than policy B when every individual has a higher utility under A than under B. This criterion is hardly debatable but also clearly not very useful. If most individuals are better off under A than under B but a few are better off under B than under A, the criterion gives no answer.

There are clearly many cases when a reasonable judge would have a clear judgment not reachable by the Pareto ordering just described. I can only say the formal theory by which individual valuations are combined into a social valuation has met with many as yet unsurmounted obstacles. This statement seems to hold even if interpersonal comparisons of utility are taken as known, so the problem goes beyond the issues raised in my study (1951), for example, if individual have differing probability assessments or differing rates of pure time preference.

Nevertheless, the social orientation of *Homo sapiens* implies that there will be some convergence of values across humans. Philosophers have tended to assume this takes the form of saying that, in some sense, a genuinely moral judgment must be independent of the individual holding it, an idea expressed in different ways in Kant's categorical imperative, Bentham's and Sidgwick's utilitarianism, Hare's rule, or Adam Smith's "impartial spectator."

The Case for the Success of the Economy

Obviously, the history of capitalism has been marked by a relatively extraordinary growth in the availability of economic goods, not matched by any system that has lesser dependence on the market. In a predominantly agricultural economy, food and clothing can be supplied locally through feudal or peasant economic systems. But there was always a need for trade over considerable distances in metals and stones as well as specialized food inputs, such as salt or spices. When Cortez embarked on the conquest of Mexico, he encountered a large market distinguishable from those he was accustomed to in Spain only by the greater variety of the goods offered.

Even in prehistoric times, we have evidence of obsidian, for knives, used in areas several hundred miles from their source. Similarly, amber, obtainable only in the areas around the Baltic Sea, is found in prehistoric Greece. Even at the height of the classical period in Athens, Herodotus, certainly as well informed about geography as anyone in his time, did not know the ultimate source of the tin used to alloy copper to make bronze. He knew only that the Greek colonists in what we now know as Marseilles bought the tin from Gallic merchants who rafted it down the Rhone. Here is a perfect picture of a market system; the purchaser need only know from whom he or she is dealing. The relations in this chain are strictly commercial and so governed by the market. There are no personal or authoritative elements in this allocative process. In fact, we now know the tin came from Britain, an island whose very existence was unknown to the Greeks, the ultimate purchasers.

No stronger evaluation of the productive role of the capitalist market can be found than that of Marx and Engels, in *The Communist Manifesto* (1848):

> The bourgeoisie, during its rule of scarce one hundred years, has created more massive and more colossal productive forces than have all preceding generations together. Subjection of Nature's forces to man, machinery, application of chemistry to industry and agriculture, steam-navigation, railways, electric telegraphs, clearing of whole continents for cultivation, canalisation of rivers, whole populations conjured out of the ground—what earlier century had even a presentiment that such productive forces slumbered in the lap of social labour?

To be clear, I am not of the opinion that the extraordinary explosion in productive power that began in England in the late eighteenth century and then spread to Europe and the United States and now to the entire globe, is entirely due to the capitalist system. The development of science and the scientific attitude certainly made a profound difference from previous periods of development, and I see no evidence that capitalism is especially favorable to science. But it is certainly true that the use of science to increase productivity is greatly promoted by economic incentives and the decentralized structure of economic decision-making implicit in a system of markets and individually-motivated investment.

INCREASING RETURNS AND ECONOMIC PERFORMANCE

The microeconomic tradition has emphasized the presence of increasing returns as a source of inefficiency. Either there is an undersupply of a good produced under these circumstances or a monopoly emerges. Historically, this problem has been addressed by anti-monopoly legislation and regulation, which has now spread from its origin in the United States to become standard in Europe.

However, there is a counter-argument, that monopoly profits are a necessary reward for innovation. From a fundamental point of view, the problem is that information (e.g. new knowledge needed for innovation) is an input which automatically creates increasing returns. Since most of the discussion about the welfare implications of increasing returns is very well known, I will turn to examining the economics of information in some more detail.

INFORMATION AND THE ECONOMY: THE GOOD AND THE BAD

The economic system depends on information; it also generates information. Firms depend on knowledge of production processes. Indeed, it is generally accepted that, in the long run, the growth in the quantities of economic goods is mainly due to increase in knowledge, i.e. technological progress. (The key papers are those of Abramovitz (1956) and Solow (1957).) The original formulation assumed that the knowledge is accumulated by processes exogenous to the economic system, a by-product of the development of science. More modern thought emphasizes the role of the economic system in motivating and inducing the expenditure of resources in the process of innovation, though there is undoubtedly scientific development induced by curiosity which turns out to have productive implications. These implications, however, require incentives to be drawn in actuality. The move from the scientific understanding of the molecular nature of polymers (such as rubber) to the development of synthetic fabrics required considerable investment in research and development by the chemical industry.

To create the incentives for development of new products and of new processes for making existing products, an institution departing considerably from the simple market model was needed. This was the patent system. The creator of new knowledge was rewarded with a property right. But the property is very different from more customary forms of property. If I own land, I can sell it; but once I sell it, I no longer have it. Similarly, if I produce something, I own it. I can sell it or hold on to it, but

I cannot do both. But intellectual property is different. I can sell it, but I still possess it. Technological information is a commodity, in the broad sense that it is valuable to the user and, usually, is costly to produce. But it does not satisfy the conservation properties that we ascribe to commodities.

The role of information in the economy is not confined to the technological. A buyer wants certain qualities in the commodities purchased. However, they may not be self-evident. This is certainly clear in the case of complex machinery, such as automobiles or computers, much more commonly today than in the past.

Another, very important, example is that of professions, such as medicine or law. Essentially, what a professional supplies is knowledge. Since knowledge can be used over and over again, it is economical to have a small number of individuals with that knowledge, which can be used for many different clients, instead of having each client acquire the information when needed. But then the dealing between the professional and the client is one where the two parties have different degrees of knowledge. In particular, the client is in no position to check on the quality of the service supplied or the degree of effort.

The set of situations in which different parties to a transaction have differing information is much more extensive than these examples, but one more is certainly of great importance: financial transactions. The economic status of the borrower is obviously of great importance to the lender. Even as something as apparently simple as a sale of common stocks may be motivated by differing knowledge sets of buyers and sellers. With the hypertrophic growth of the financial sector, this consideration is hardly negligible.

The implications of what has been called *asymmetric information* are very profound. In the first place, the impersonality of conventional markets, with prices the same for all, is supplemented by additional incentives to minimize the possibility of exploitation of informational advantages. Personal examination of individual cases, as in bank loans, has to be added.

Even more fundamentally, many markets that would seem to be desirable cannot be formed. If there were a full market economy, there would be markets for goods to be delivered in the future. In this way, the amount of investment today could be chosen optimally (given the prices for delivery today and in the future). As I have suggested, there will be uncertainty about the factors governing future supply and demand and therefore about the equilibrium prices. This could in theory be met by having markets contingent on the realization of the uncertainties. But if the different parties have different information, they may not be able to agree on what uncertainties have been realized. Hence, the futures markets will not emerge, and, of course, futures markets in manufactured goods or in services do not exist. (There is a limited set of futures markets for limited periods in agricultural goods and in minerals.)

The absence of futures markets for goods is partly compensated for by the existence of credit instruments, payable in the future, sometimes conditionally on outcomes (common stocks, even bonds and other loans, when one considers the possibility of bankruptcy). Because they are striving to overcome the problems of asymmetric information, they can and increasingly do take on very complex forms. Further, to a considerable extent, the transactions leading to the issuance of these credit instruments cannot be said to constitute markets. Loans (e.g. mortgages) are individual transactions, and their prices may vary from one to another. These are not prices in the sense understood in standard economic theory or in the defenses of the market system, and they do not therefore convey the information that prices are supposed to convey.

To sum up, the existence of asymmetric information implies that the market structure that should support the allocation of resources is very incomplete. One implication is that the arguments for the Pareto optimality of market outcomes fail. Another is that the failure of the markets increases the need for information and leads it to an even more complicated form. In particular, investments without knowledge of future prices must require forecasts of the behavior of future markets.

But how future markets will behave depends in part on the investment behavior of others today, and that in turn depends on their forecasts. Hence, the forecasts are mutually dependent. However, in the absence of markets, there is no simple mechanism to make them coherent. This is an issue that was raised in the 1930s both by Keynes (1936) and by Morgenstern (1935).

THE FAILURES OF THE PRICE SYSTEM

The ideal of universal marketization is clearly not achieved and is not achievable. Hence, we already know that the outcome will in general not be efficient.

The asymmetry of information is not the only cause of market failure. I have spent much space on this topic because it is not as well recognized as others. Much the best recognized, especially since the classical work of A. C. Pigou (1920), is the notion of an externality, an action by one party that affects the welfare of another and is not mediated by a market or other voluntary agreement. Air pollution has been the standard example. One cannot conceive of a market in which a potential polluter could buy pollution rights from all the potential pollutees. The polluter cannot direct the pollution to just those from whom he or she has bought rights.

Air and water pollution are classical and important examples of externalities. Flood control and irrigation are somewhat more complex examples, which we will not analyze here. The market failure has been recognized in practice by the role of government intervention both by regulation and by public supply of the relevant goods. To help create some degree of efficiency, the tool of benefit cost analysis has been developed. It has raised many problems in design; these are indeed the problems of evaluating the outcomes in a complex adaptive system. The government has its own difficulties in acquiring and using information. Even more seriously the decisions are made by a political process, as they must be in a governmental setup, and the calculated outcomes of benefit cost analyses are simply one input among many in the process.

An externality of overwhelming proportions is that of climate change. It is very large in its potential consequences. It is also very large in extent in space and in time. Indeed, greenhouse gases, once emitted, travel all over the Earth within a day. Further, once in the atmosphere, they remain there for centuries.

Climate change exemplifies another issue in the workings of the economic system. The market system's thrust to efficiency depends, as I have already said several times, on burdens being accepted voluntarily in return for a compensatory benefit. But an emission of carbon dioxide creates an adverse effect on those one or two hundred years in the future; the latter cannot voluntarily make a trade since they don't exist today. This effect is partly offset by individuals' making provisions for their own offspring, who in turn will provide for their offspring.

The obligation on society to provide for the future in a way that does not permit for return compensation is not confined to climate change. Education is an obligation of the present generation to those certainly not yet in a position to make a return payment or even to commit to one. Yet there is considerable evidence that even childless individuals vote for providing education.

Let me list some of the concrete problems that the market system fails to meet. Most conspicuous is the repeated failure of markets to achieve even short-run efficiency, the business cycle. The emergence of a full-bodied capitalist system was followed immediately by the emergence of a new phenomenon in the world's economy: a failure of markets to clear, unemployment, business failures, interruptions in the flow of credit. Certainly, a recession of very modern form occurred in the United States and Great Britain in 1819, and the nineteenth and twentieth centuries were marked by repeated severe depressions and milder recessions. Notice these are periods in which even the markets that exist do not clear. There is excess supply on the labor market and clearly also on most product markets; the productive capacity is there but not the demand. At an early stage, Sismondi (1819) was already concerned with the balance between production and consumption and urged the need for government intervention.

The treatment of externalities and the use of public works (highways, dams, irrigation systems) and regulation (e.g. of road or air travel) for that purpose suffer, as already indicated, from the difficulties of benefit cost analysis and the limits to its acceptability. It is easy to find examples of different government programs in the United States where the valuation of a given social effect (e.g. the saving of life) differs very considerably from one program to another, a clear violation of rationality.

A major allocation issue in all countries but especially in those of higher incomes is the amount and direction of resources to medical care. I have already sketched some reasons that medical service markets cannot work well by themselves; the difficulties are compounded by the recognition of the importance of uncertainty in incidence, diagnosis, and outcome, to be met by some form of insurance. All high-income countries, even the United States, have provided some form of government-provided insurance (in the United States, over 50 percent of all medical costs are paid for by the Federal government). Yet the continuing political conflicts show that the current situation is far from fully acceptable to many.

A very serious issue, in my judgment, is the extraordinary growth of the financial industry. The financial industry, in a way, does not produce anything. It just facilitates economic transactions, putting borrowers and lenders together. It is not unreasonable to suppose that this is a costly activity and will earn some reward. In fact, the profits of the financial industry are 30 percent of all profits (computed from US Bureau of Economic Analysis, NIPA Table 6.16, <http://www.bea.gov/national/nipaweb>), far bigger than might be supposed if credit markets clear with just a little help. It is certainly at least possible that the diffuse nature of information has spawned a wasteful activity, one which seems in fact to have been the source of negative rather than positive effects on the economy.

There is one very serious problem that I will not address in detail but must mention for completeness. It is the rapidly growing inequality in income and wealth in many countries. Personally, I regard inequality as a negative and extreme inequality as a serious offense. Certainly, however we may judge inequality at the upper end, serious poverty in a country as rich as the United States or the United Kingdom is an offense in my eyes. Yet I am struck by the apparent fact that general public opinion does not seem to share my views. Candidates do not seem to get votes by asking for higher income tax rates in the upper brackets. A rather pure test was an initiative (hence, not contaminated by legislative politics) in California to repeal the state tax on estates. Because of the exemption limit, only 7 percent of all estates paid any tax. Nevertheless, the initiative passed. Evidently, a majority of voters identified with the rich or assumed that they would enter their ranks.

THE SOCIAL, POLITICAL, AND ETHICAL NECESSITIES FOR GOOD PERFORMANCE

To the extent that differences in information are a major source of failure in the economic system, one remedy is making public reliable information. In the presence of asymmetries in information, it can pay to present false statements on the profitability of corporations, on the qualities of goods, and on the risks underlying securities and other credit instruments. The problems are compounded by the fact that there are asymmetries of information within financial and other firms, so that they create incentive schemes, with payment conditional on some presumed measure of performance. These incentives, almost necessarily short-run in nature, may however induce behavior profitable to the firm but inimical to those with whom the firm is dealing, either as customers or as stockholders or creditors.

There has been a long tendency to require by law higher standards of truth-telling. Already in the period of the New Deal, laws were enacted to require truth in advertising (probably increasing its value) and in corporate financial statements. More has been done, particularly with regard to financial institutions, in recent years. Legal penalties are added to the other incentive mechanisms.

Similar problems have arisen with regard to medical care and also to the relation among physicians, patients, and health insurance carriers (public and private). Here, there have been monetary incentives to avoid overcharging, and malpractice suits to regulate quality. But in this case, society relies on ethical codes and training to create an internal motivation, no doubt made possible by the pro-social inclinations embodied in us by evolution.

Much has been made of greed as a motive. It is listed by the Catholic Church as one of the seven cardinal sins, and the Church's view is hardly unique. The role of greed in a market system is a little paradoxical. On the one hand, the market is a social system, designed to achieve cooperation in a complicated society. On the other hand, it mimics the most individualistic example of the "war of each against all." In that system, greed is a way of achieving efficiency in production and consumption. As I noted in my introductory remarks, so long as market-clearing prices govern the economic system, it is correct that optimization (i.e. greed) is socially advantageous. It is especially in the presence of market failure for whatever reason that greed becomes a social obstacle.

The government, in some form or another, is the most common locus for remediation of the economic system. The government is indispensable even to the workings of an ideal market economy. It is needed to enforce contracts and to protect property against theft in all its forms. As already indicated, with some imperfections, it plays a much more prominent role in trying to insure some degree of equality in knowledge. It plays a role through taxes and expenditures and through intervening in the supply of credit and money in minimizing to some extent the fluctuations to which a capitalist economy is subject. It has played a major role in supplying the public goods that the market cannot well supply. More recently, the responsibility for medical care and insurance has become increasingly large relative to the economy. It is not therefore surprising that the proportion of the national income that is directed by the government is much greater in modern times than in the nineteenth century.

REFERENCES

Abramovitz, M. (1956). Resource and Output Trends in the United States since 1870. *American Economic Review*, 46: 5–23.

Arrow, K. J. (1951). *Social Choice and Individual Values* (1st edn). New York: Wiley.

Bowles, S., R. Boyd, E. Fehr, and H. Gintis (2005). *Moral Sentiments and Material Interests: The Foundations of Cooperation in Economic Life*. Cambridge, MA: MIT Press.

Hirschman, A. O. (1977). *The Passions and the Interests: Political Arguments for Capitalism Before its Triumph*. Princeton: Princeton University Press.

Keynes, J. M. (1936). *The General Theory of Employment, Interest and Money*. London: Macmillan.

Marx, K., and F. Engels (1848). *The Communist Manifesto*. London.

Morgenstern, O. (1935). Vollkommene Voraussicht und wirtschaftliches Gleichgewicht. *Zeitschrift für Nationalökonomie*, 6: 337–57.

Pigou, A. C. (1920). *The Economics of Welfare*. London: Macmillan.

Sismondi, J. C. L. de (1819). *Nouveaux principes d'économie politique*. Paris.

Solow, R. M. (1957). Technical Change and the Aggregate Production Function. *Review of Economic and Statistics*, 39: 312–20.

CHAPTER 4

....

CORRUPTION

What Really *Should Not Be For Sale*

....

DAVID SCHMIDTZ

Abstract

Adam Smith explained how market society liberates human beings both from starvation and from servility. However, to have a rule of law framework within which markets can operate, officials are required, and must exercise oversight. Officials must not only enforce rules, but interpret them, amend them, and so on. They accordingly have power and a measure of discretion. The trouble is that this power of oversight is precisely what crony capitalists are buying and selling, and this is the ultimate source of market corruption. Officials are subject to vices: not only greed but officiousness as well. To be uncorrupt is an achievement, not simply a decision, and involves walking a fine line between the vice of selling services that are not theirs to sell, and the vice of withholding services that are not theirs to withhold. A market society's best hope for limiting corruption is to preserve and enhance forms of power that are relatively resistant to corruption, such as the essentially dispersed power of buyers and sellers to vote with their feet.

I played football in high school. Then I coached. After that, I served as a referee. Our responsibility as referees was to interpret and apply the rules. With responsibility came power. With power came a measure of discretion. Our calls could determine a game's outcome. And yet, it was not our place to *prefer* a particular outcome. Favoring a team would have been corrupt. Nor had we any right to prefer games ending in a *tie*. That too would have been corrupt—incompatible with the unobtrusive impartiality that defines successful refereeing. We had a duty not to aim for *any* outcome, not even an equal one.

This chapter works toward an anatomy of corruption. The first section discusses the corrupting influence of concentrated as opposed to dispersed power. The following section argues that, although greed may be the paradigmatically rotten motive, it is but one among several corrupting vices. One general cost of rotten motives, that section concludes, is a loss of self-awareness. It is next argued that this loss of self-awareness can afflict organizations as well as individual persons, and for an oddly similar reason: the downfall of many an institution involves internal corruption that leads to a loss of any sense of mission on the part of the organization, such that a corporation qua *agent* falls apart. The section after that argues that there is a wrong way of striving to avoid this loss of self-awareness and maintain unified corporate agency: namely, by grasping for ever more concentrated top-down power. In general, nothing good comes from concentrating power at the top, because it treats as spectators or pawns those agents on the ground who need to play, and play well, if a society is to prosper. The chapter closes by articulating an implicit contrast between goals of justice and of conflict resolution. We have compelling reason to treat the latter, not the former, as the first virtue of social institutions. Otherwise, in the name of justice, we systematically give our leaders more power than we properly can afford.

CONCENTRATED POWER: THE CURE
THAT *IS* THE DISEASE

Which social arrangements have a history of fostering progress and prosperity? One quick answer, falsely attributed to Adam Smith, holds that we are guided as if by an invisible hand to do what builds the wealth of nations. A more sober answer, closer to what Smith said and believed, is that, *if* we have the right framework of rules—plus decent officiating—steering us away from buying and selling monopoly privileges and toward being valuable to the people around us, we indeed will be part of the engine that drives human progress and the wealth of nations.[1]

However, to have a rule of law framework within which markets can grow a healthy nation, officials must exercise oversight. Officials not only enforce rules, but must also interpret, amend, and so on. Smith saw this, and perceived a further, chronically tragic reality: namely, this power to oversee markets is precisely what crony capitalists are buying and selling.

Smith's observation changes everything. In academic philosophy, theorizing about justice has a history of starting by asking us to imagine how a pie would ideally be sliced. *Could this be a bias?* There is of course another place to start, namely by

---

[1] If we want to see evidence of progress, we look where progress is. If we want to fail to see evidence, we look where evidence isn't. Diphtheria vaccine ended a disease that killed mind-boggling numbers of people. Today we don't remember there even was such a thing. Was that progress? What is the appropriate response when we *don't want to know*? Many people assume income inequality is rising and further assume that rising income inequality is bad for the poor. We should want to know whether the latter assumption is true, and if it is, then that gives us reason to care whether the former assumption is true. I am grateful to Amartya Sen for asking (in conversation): gaps in *income* are rising but gaps in *life expectancy* are closing, so while the 5 percent manifestly resents being left behind by the 1 percent, where are the dimensions of rising inequality that matter to *poor* people? Where are the dimensions of rising inequality that are causing life expectancies of poor people to fall?

acknowledging what it takes to bring pie to the table and reflecting on what it takes to respect those who brought it, and convince them that bringing the pie is self-affirming rather than degrading.

Yet a third place to start is with a premise that power (i.e. power to slice the pie) corrupts. Imagine concentrated power in the hands of the worst ruler in living memory. Assume what you know to be true: namely, concentrated political power actually does fall into the hands of people like that. This suggests a preliminary conclusion. When formulating theories about what is politically ideal, we should ask, "Ideally, how much power would be wielded by people like *that*?" and not, "Ideally, how much power would be wielded by ideal rulers?"

Which of these two questions about power is a genuine question about the human condition? Can political philosophy answer the one that *needs* answering? Why isn't it trying?

Concentrating Power

Robert Frank expresses bafflement over why anyone would reject modest redistribution from rich to poor.[2] I assume for argument's sake that no one does. However, if we grasp the import of the premise that power corrupts, we see why people who honestly embrace redistribution from rich to poor are wary of *creating the power* to redistribute from rich to poor.

Everyone should deplore the creation of such power when it will be used to redistribute not from rich to poor but from poor to rich (more precisely, from those who have less control over the political process to rich cronies who have more). We want officials to have power to pursue our agenda, but wanting this too much has made us gullible. What should we infer from the premise that officials, when given such power, use it to pursue their own agenda, not ours? I infer this: we should be skeptical of conceptions of justice that make it seem like we should invest enormous power in the sort of people who most *covet* enormous power.

Power to ensure what we call justice is power to inflict a gusher of injustice. There is no use lamenting that valuable commodities are bought and sold, and that power is a valuable commodity. What is disconcerting is that power's corrosiveness is proportionate to scale. More power commands a higher price, notwithstanding cosmetic tweaks to campaign finance laws. There is absolutely no mystery why candidates would spend ever more on campaigns. It is not because regulators are becoming more lax. It is because the prize is getting bigger.[3]

---

[2] In his opening comment on a presentation of this chapter, Apr. 2014.

[3] Some say transparency is the solution. Perhaps, but we might also see transparency as a hard-won achievement, not a policy instrument—an effect of beating corruption rather than a weapon with which we fight.

The bigger the prize, the richer and more unscrupulous one will need to be to compete for it. The process by which people gain political appointment will systematically tend, and *increasingly* tend, to select the wrong person for the job.

If you want politicians to be "not for sale" then you have to reduce the value of whatever power is up for grabs. You have to reduce the incentive of politicians who *are* for sale to do whatever it takes to acquire power.

The truism that power corrupts implies that randomly selected officers would be corruptible. Yet, the truism is misleading, insofar as the more realistic worry is far worse than this. Namely, the process of selecting officers is not random. We *select* for corruption. It is not a randomly selected fox but the most ravenous fox that tends to get the job of overseeing the henhouse. Political debate then degenerates into something so shameful that it is terrifying: a question of which hens can entice the fox to devour the other hens first.

Some candidates may be noble, but we won't be able to sort them out simply by listening to their speeches. Bought politicians keep the names of their buyers out of the news. They all make speeches denouncing corruption, but when *bought* politicians name names, they target not *their* buyers, but the chief *rivals* of their buyers. Majid Jafar suggests that, in underdeveloped nations, power buys money, whereas in developed nations, money buys power.[4] Where power buys money, the most corrupt lives are studies in ostentatious opulence. By contrast, where money buys power, corruption is clandestine.

Is there an Alternative?

Does that leave political philosophy at a loss? The argument so far is that concentrated power to ram through what we call justice is not a kind of power that merits our endorsement in the actual corruptible world. So, what else is there? Is there any power that is not a license to dominate, subjugate, or otherwise treat subjects of that power like pawns? Is there any power that would not corrupt?

I see one decent—if neither original nor fully satisfactory—answer. Powers that define liberal equal citizenship (rights to say no, rights to exit, constitutional limits on executive power) are as innocuous as power can be. These are the powers that *limit* rather than extend the reach of those who treat us as pawns. Arguably, these are powers worth endorsing. Such power as they embody is inherently dispersed rather than concentrated.

The constitutional part of constitutional democracy is the part that enshrines these powers. Therefore, the constitutional part of democracy is also the liberal part, when there is a liberal part. Democracy is premised on a core of individual rights not subject to the whim of a shifting majority. Insofar as you want democracy, you want constitutional democracy so that, for example, legislators can't *vote* on whether you have a vote, and demagogues cannot divide and conquer a population by sequentially

[4] In conversation at the Royal Society of London, Apr. 2014.

targeting one minority after another. You *bind* legislators because you don't want legislatures to be where the action is. Living in a free country involves letting the rules settle down and become a framework of mutual expectations around which real players make plans and in which real players make the moves that ultimately lift their communities to the next stage of human progress. To the extent that legislators become players, citizens become spectators to decisions that shape their lives. The right to say no to that logic is as liberal a right as there is.

Montesquieu and America's founders concluded that dispersed power was less corrupting than concentrated power. They sought to create a system of divided sovereignty, backed up by a free press, so that no ruler would rule with impunity simply by executive order. The idea was functional enough to blow the ceiling off the human condition as we knew it in the early 1700s.

However, there is a factual limit on how concentrated power can be. As a hierarchy grows, it adds layers of internal complexity, resulting in a proliferation of corruptible middle managers and local politicians along with decreasing ability to gather enough information to effectively monitor local circumstances from the hierarchical top. Human social organization being what it is, concentrating power at the top entails delegating executive power to operatives on the ground.

This suggests an intriguing (if confusing) possibility, namely that corruptibility is as much a function of power's dispersal as of power's concentration.[5] Yet, if we view the hierarchy from the bottom—from the perspective of the vulnerable—the fact remains: where discretionary decision-making power is concentrated, that is where we find the threat, regardless of whether such power has been delegated. A node of discretionary power may exist by virtue of power being delegated from the top, but to the people below, the danger posed by that node is still a function of power concentrated in that node. *Delegated* power is not quite what Montesquieu and America's founders had in mind when they championed dispersed power. They sought a distribution of power that (among other things) would make everyone accountable.

Note also that, while size matters, it takes only two, one principal and one agent, to make a *principal-agent* problem. Thus, organizations can be corruptible without being vast. Expanding the parts of an organization from one to two, with the second part having a degree of power, responsibility, and discretion, creates the possibility of corruption. Possibilities multiply as each link is added. The whole loses its ability to self-monitor its own motives, and becomes internally opaque, as delegating decision-making power disperses *motives* that drive decisions.[6]

---

[5] I thank Jacob Levy for the observation.

[6] Needed regulations become more complex over time, in part because new regulations will need to fit into an existing regulatory environment that is itself increasingly complex. As this happens, it becomes increasingly true that the only people who know enough to design, interpret, and apply regulations will be the very people whom the regulations are supposed to regulate. Thus, bankers write banking reforms, insurance companies write health insurance reforms, and so on. Such regulators have a history of responding exactly as one would expect, by designing regulations that reduce consumer access to alternative providers.

BEYOND MONEY

Organizations employ officials to speak and make decisions on their behalf. The most widely recognized corruption consists of officials treating their fiduciary authority as a service to buy and sell for personal gain (Schwartz 2004: 173). Officials often are tasked with making it easier to transact with organizations that they represent, but when corrupt officials regard their authority as a service that they are at liberty to sell for personal gain, they treat themselves as *licensed* to make it harder. When they take bribes for approving transactions they ought to approve, transaction costs do in fact rise. Or, when they take bribes for approving transactions they should *not* approve (say, granting a license to dump toxic waste in the middle of an ordinary neighborhood), *external* costs (that they may be responsible for minimizing) can skyrocket instead.

Corruption involves, let's say, being entrusted with power for particular purposes, then using that power for other purposes. It is a kind of principal-agent problem. Note: this rough characterization of corruption does not entail that we always want to stop it. An opportunistic Nazi prison guard who, *to make money*, takes bribes to let victims escape is handling an evil responsibility in a corrupt way. Note, further, that a Nazi guard who lets victims escape *to resist evil* is not corrupt. Corruption presupposes motive—*rotten* motive. The paradigm is seeking payment where one freely accepted fiduciary duties that preclude seeking payment.

Although paradigmatically rotten, however, greed is but one species in the genus of corrupting motives.[7] For example, there is something corrupt about students who cheat on exams. Cheaters normally are seeking personal gain of a kind, but even this more generic idea of seeking gain does not seem strictly necessary. Petty tyrants sometimes say, "rules are rules" and there is nothing they can do, when in fact their job is to *get things done*, which includes granting exceptions as required by circumstances not anticipated by those who made the rules. Petty tyrants officiously withholding what isn't theirs to withhold is as corrupt as selling what isn't theirs to sell. Sometimes the motivation is downright hostile. Imagine county officials going the extra mile to make it gratuitously difficult for minorities to register to vote. More often, the motivation is simple cowardice. They suppose the most blameless thing they can do is hide behind the rules, when their job is not to avoid blame but, again, to get things done.

Or sometimes a vacuum of reason can be more corrupting than spurious reason; some officials are dead to the honor of being good at their jobs. They show up in appearance only, aiming only to collect a paycheck or kill time. They do not even aim to get the job done so much as to be in compliance with job requirements. They may bear no ill will, but they are of no use.

---

[7] Shelley Burtt says an account of corruption addresses four questions (paraphrasing): What gets corrupted? What does the corrupting? What is the damage? What can limit the damage? (Burtt 2004: 109).

Another form of corruption, likewise not involving greed, is manifest when junior colleagues evaluate every decision (to go to lunch, serve on a committee, write a book, help a student, *or represent themselves as committed to scholarship*) as a means to the end of getting tenure. Professors thus obsessed generally should not get tenure. They tend to fall apart when they do. They aim to be in compliance with requirements for tenure, which is rotten insofar as deserving tenure requires treating tenure as means, not as end. The honest end is to be the kind of scholar who sees the herd for what it is and tells the truth no matter what.

While using public office for private gain may be a paradigm of corruption, it is not a definition. Corruption can be a child of greed, to be sure, but also of other vices, including apathy, officiousness, and cowardice. Among the corrupt, self-deception will be the rule rather than the exception. Upon being caught, their first reaction will be to say, and to convince themselves, that everyone does it.

Corruption Compromises Self-Awareness

A closely related risk of corruption goes with our need to find *kindred* souls—people with whom we can reach a concurrence of sentiment (Otteson 2002: 207). Because this desire runs so deep, it corrupts in the following way. We tend not to notice how we adjust our attitudes to fit those of people around us. Adjusting subconsciously makes us more vulnerable to social pressure.[8] If we *notice* ourselves "going along to get along" then we can resist, or at least be cynical. But if we do not even notice ourselves adjusting as needed so as to be agreeable company, our ability to master this threat to our autonomy is compromised. It is human nature that we do almost anything to avoid being outcasts. Thus, when colleagues insinuate that they are willing and able to bully us, it is only human to voice no resistance. We then grasp at reasons to agree, however flimsy, so as to make the depth of our capitulation less humiliating (Haidt 2012). Social pressures warp minds.[9] To let oneself be corrupted by such pressure is to let oneself become a self that one cannot afford to examine too closely—a self unworthy of esteem.

Finally, administrators are prone to cowardice. Finding that one of their faculty is a sexual predator, a plagiarist, vicious to students with contrary opinions or to colleagues who make them feel small, college administrators freeze, hoping to avoid scandal. If we

---

[8] Thus, Smith acknowledges, circumstances in the "earliest period of society" conspired to make infanticide pardonable, but later it was condoned even by Plato and Aristotle, for no better reason than because it was "commonly done." A brooding Smith worries that "When custom can give sanction to so dreadful a violation of humanity, we may well imagine there is scarce any particular practice so gross which it cannot authorize." See Smith (1790/1984: V.2.15).

[9] To Smith, wanting to be validated by others can drive our maturation through a certain stage, but we must outgrow that drive. To care too much about validation is to be controlled by the hoped-for source of validation.

treat being uncorrupt as a virtuous mean between extremes of vice, then passively silent cowardice at one extreme can be more lethal to a community than active greed at the other.

A corrupt person *needs* to be less self-aware and less reflective, for accurate self-perception becomes unaffordable. When one looks inward, there is, in a way, not enough there to be worth being aware of. Here too, then, at this more personal level, cowardice under pressure is as corrupting as raw greed, and even more deeply shattering.

AGENCY IS AN ACHIEVEMENT

Internal transparency is a prerequisite of agency, and corruption compromises transparency. I once heard an interview on National Public Radio. The guest was developing tools for screening job candidates. One of the guest's survey questions was, "If I had an opportunity to steal $20,000 from my company with no chance of being caught, I would steal the money. True or false?" NPR's interviewer said, isn't that question a waste of time? Every applicant says False, so why bother? The guest replied that, on the contrary, about 20 percent of applicants say they would steal the money. NPR's interviewer, astounded, asked how an applicant could be so crazy. The guest answered (paraphrasing from memory), "All I know is that 20% say they would steal the money. My speculation, for what it is worth, is that applicants realize that the survey is testing their honesty, but then guess that they show that they are *relatively* honest by admitting what to them seems obvious: like everyone else, they would steal the money."

I regard the guest's theory as an implicit theory of corruption's ultimate price. As corrupt behavior warps perception, you reach a point where you are so far from being honest that you no longer have a clue what honesty would be like. When you can't remember what honesty is like, you can't remember how to fake it either. You are falling apart. Internal transparency, and the possibility of self-awareness that goes with it, is an achievement, not just a decision.

Compromised Group Agency

This undermining of agency[10] can be understood as a danger to organizations as well as to individuals. Suppose your job involves balancing your unit's budget, and one of your balancing tools involves collecting fees from other units within the organization. You may wake up some day to find that your job, as an administrator in your unit, is to

---

[10] Philip Pettit believes there is such a thing as group agency. Obviously, Pettit's perspective is controversial, yet it does give us an intriguing vocabulary for talking about corruption within organizations. I thank Pettit for conversations at the Royal Society and at a Chapel Hill workshop honoring our friend Geoff Brennan.

cannibalize other units. You need not be a monster to find yourself in such a position. It may happen as a consequence of your bosses restructuring your responsibilities. They need not be at fault either. They may be under orders to impose fiscal accountability and discipline, as part of an effort to *combat* corruption.

When Plato wrote about justice in the polis as a "writ large" model of justice in the individual soul, he was treating the paradigm of injustice as an individual soul divided against itself. Plato's discussion may be archaic in some ways. And yet, the word "corrupt" does, after all, carry with it connotations of being rotten, in a state of decomposition. This rendering seems natural from a virtue-theoretic perspective. What makes a tyrant unjust is what makes a tyrant corrupt: the tyrant's soul is decomposing, falling apart, losing its unifying purposiveness.

We need not entirely trust Plato's analogy. However, consider how it illuminates the corruption of organizations. When an official accepts bribes under the table, the agency for which the official works becomes less transparent to itself. The agency is a soul out of touch with itself. Its left hand does not know what its right hand is doing. The right hand does not even *want* the left hand to know. Such loss of self-awareness is compromised agency.

Weakness of will compromises human agency. Specifically, it compromises the potential to be an agent with a unified purpose. A corrupted agent's soul is divided against itself. *Corporate* agency likewise is a kind of agency that comes apart under the toxic influence of corruption. For example, perhaps your provost counts on faculty to distinguish between the letter of their contract and the spirit of their actual role. If faculty understand the difference, and care about the spirit, all is well. If not, the organization will break down. The college will come to lack both appearance and reality of being on a mission.

As the organization comes to lack intention, it stops resembling an agent. Thus, some organizations are usefully seen as agents. Others may once have seemed more like agents but now are corrupted; we no longer have reason to call them agents. Notice: where we have no reason to call *x* an *agent*, we have no reason (linguistic habit aside) to call *x* an *organization* either. What *x* is, literally, is a dysfunctional mess.

Mission-driven firms are the exception rather than the rule. Mission-driven people are likewise exceptional. Not all missions are good, but regardless, the point is that being mission-driven is an achievement, not something to take for granted.

Finally, there are times when officials exercising discretionary power cannot simply follow the rules, because they have no uncontroversial interpretation of the letter or the spirit of the law. Suppose you are a compliance officer administering a grant, and the grantee asks you to look the other way while the grantee uses the money for a purpose other than the purpose for which the grant was given. Suppose the grantee is asking permission for a manifestly smarter purpose than the purpose for which the grant was given. Fill in the details to make the case as compelling as you like. The risk of emerging from that situation as more or less corrupt is real whichever way you decide—lazy and irresponsible if you go one way, a pompous bureaucrat if you go the other. Having fiduciary responsibility along with discretionary power, and remaining uncorrupted over time, is not a simple thing.

No Man is an Island

Rawls's *Theory of Justice* starts by observing that society is a cooperative venture for mutual advantage. That simplification sets aside a world of detail. Moreover, in some ways Rawls was articulating aspiration as much as observation. Cooperative ventures for mutual advantage are an ideal. Real societies are always more than that, and sometimes less. Even so, Rawls was right. Communities essentially are cooperative ventures for mutual advantage.

Another word for cooperation—natural to an economist, less so to a philosopher—is trade. Trade is cooperation. Cooperation is community. Among the most basic economic insights is that there are gains from trade. If any insight is more basic than that, perhaps it is the idea that gains require explanation. There is a reason why we live as well as we do. To say "no man is an island" is to say that, without trade, we would at best live and die like any other large mammal. Prosperity is not our natural state. Burgeoning wealth requires explanation. What explains the explosion of wealth since Adam Smith's time is the explosion of trade since Adam Smith's time.

Trade is not only positive-sum but win-win. Everyone can win, and in some communities it is a close approximation of observable reality that everyone does. It is not only an elite whose life expectancy nearly doubled over the course of the twentieth century. No group was more notoriously left behind than African-Americans, and yet, between 1900 and 2010, African-American life expectancy went from 33 to 75 years.[11] That isn't to say everyone did *well*. In the earlier years of that era, staggering numbers of children (staggering to us, that is) died before reaching the age of 5. Yet they were not born losers. At any point, everyone had better prospects than if they had been born a century earlier.

The expanding freedom of ordinary people to contract with persons other than their lord was transforming Europe's economy in Adam Smith's time.[12] Under feudalism, if you are born a serf, you are entitled to your lord's protection. However, you also lack rights that today we take for granted. You live where your lord tells you to live. You grow what your lord tells you to grow. Most shocking of all: you sell your harvest to the lord *at a price of the lord's choosing*. If you want to leave, you ask permission. When you meet your lord, you bow.

As market society supplanted this system, the effect was liberating for all, especially the poor. Your dependence on a particular lord's mercy is replaced by autonomous interdependence in a loose-knit but functional community of customers and suppliers (Smith 1776/1981: III.iii). If you choose to work for an employer instead of launching a business of your own, then you delegate to your employer many key decisions along with much of the risk that comes with those decisions. You remain a free agent in the

---

[11] See <http://www.cdc.gov/nchs/data/hus/2012/018.pdf>.

[12] The next five paragraphs are a synopsis of Schmidtz (2015).

pivotal sense that, when you decide to leave, you will not need permission. Even as an employee, you are in crucial ways a partner, not a mere possession. You won't necessarily *prefer* being a partner to being a serf. You may feel insecure. But you will be free.

As Hanley sees it, "this fascination with and gratitude for the harnessing of the powers of the strong for the relief of the weak is the fundamental fact uniting Smith's seemingly separate defenses of both commercial society and his specific vision of virtue." Commercial societies "promote not only universal opulence but also a universal freedom of which the weak are the principal beneficiaries" (Hanley 2009: 19). The crucial bottom line: when people achieve freedom in commercial society, such freedom will involve *depending* on many, yet being at the *mercy* of none.

Smith wondered how internally stable a liberal community could be in the face of a tendency for its political infrastructure to decay into crony capitalism: mercantilists lobbying for subsidies for exporters, protectionists lobbying for tariffs or other trade barriers to choke off competition from importers, and monopolists who pay kings for a license to be free from competition altogether. Partnerships between big business and big government culminate in big subsidies. These ways of compromising freedom are sold to voters as protection for the middle class, but their hidden purpose almost always is to transfer wealth and power from ordinary citizens to well-connected elites. As a result, an ordinary citizen's pivotal relationships are not with free and equal trading partners but with bureaucrats: people whose grip on our community is so tight that we cannot walk away from such terms of engagement as they unilaterally propose. Thus, we reinvent feudalism. We are at the mercy of lords. Corrupt officials manipulate us and in various ways torture us even when they do not actually impoverish us. Corruption makes us less free, not only less wealthy.

I conjectured earlier that the least corruptible forms of power are the least concentrated. They are variations on our liberty as equal citizens to walk away from a bad deal, to say no, to *vote with our feet*. These are liberties that separate liberal from feudal societies. Having an effective right to exit a relationship limits how corrupt your partner can be.

Beyond Men of System

As Smith understood, the market for monopoly power—kings selling monopoly licenses to raise funding for mercenaries to fight their wars—has a singularly unhappy logic. Namely, kings adopt policies systematically favoring merchants who have lost their economic edge, because inferior competitors are the ones who have something to gain from and who thus are willing to pay for barriers to competition. The ease of transferring external goods from one citizen to another[13] is thus a foundation of both

---

[13] Noted by David Hume, *Treatise of Human Nature*, 3.2.2.16.

the promise and the downfall of capitalism. Easy transfer makes piracy possible, and the political process enables crony capitalists to enlist kings to bureaucratize piracy and thereby make it seem normal.

Exacerbating crony capitalism's perils is the ubiquitous threat posed by "men of system." As Samuel Fleischacker says, "the limitations Smith describes on what anyone can know about their society should give pause to those who are confident that governments can carry out even the task of protecting freedom successfully. Taken together with his scepticism about the judiciousness, decency, and impartiality of those who go into politics, this is what gives punch to the libertarian reading of Smith." (2004: 235).[14] One of Smith's insights is that a "man of system"

> seems to imagine that he can arrange the different members of a great society with as much ease as the hand arranges the different pieces upon a chess-board. He does not consider that the pieces upon the chess-board have no other principle of motion besides that which the hand impresses upon them; but that, in the great chess-board of human society, every single piece has a principle of motion of its own, altogether different from that which the legislature might chuse to impress upon it. (Smith 1790/1984: VI.ii.42)

A "man of system" moves pawns in pursuit of his goals. Pawns, however, respond as if they had minds of their own, which, after all, they do. Irritated by the pawns' contrarian response, men of system adjust, now seeking more to dominate than to help pawns. These bureaucrats are corrupted and rendered negligent by their own petulance, without ever dreaming of anything so bold as selling public power for private gain.

Consequently, there is a disconnect between what benevolent people seek and what men of system deliver. Again, however, as Smith understood, we face a conundrum. If our community is to achieve a rule of law, there has to be some officiating. Referees have to understand constraints within which the game of trade is to be played. Where referees succeed in taking nonconsensual and fraudulent transfers off the table, players learn to pursue their interests in mutually advantageous ways—positive for everyone *involved* in a trade and at least not a negative for anyone *affected* by it.

As with sports, if the game inspires, it will be by virtue of what comes from letting the players play. Letting the players play is not the same as giving up. Asking whether players should aspire to be more than players is not the same as asking whether referees should aspire to be more than referees. One worry is that referees aspiring to do more could leave *players* aspiring to do less. When *referees* become *players*, players become *spectators*.

Again, power we give officials to push *our* agenda is power to push *their* agenda. If officials push their agenda aggressively, then other players are relegated to sidelines waiting to see how it all plays out. Eventually, the richest spectators tire of watching

---

[14] See also Fleischacker (2004: 233) on the delusions of the sovereign and the folly of the statesman who fancies himself fit to exercise the power to impose a central plan. See also Smith 1776/1981: IV.ii.10 and IV.ix.51.

from the sidelines and get into the legislative game in the only way they can: by buying and selling referees who have turned themselves into the game's most valuable players.

Obviously, this is a logic to be avoided, even if our need for officiating renders the logic impossible to avoid altogether. The logic of a healthy society is a logic of coordination rather than a logic of unified agency. A healthy society is in that respect unlike many of the organizations thriving within it. In a healthy society, people's movements constitute a flow of traffic that moves smoothly, not by virtue of people reaching consensus on what their destinations should be, but by virtue of people reaching consensus on who has the right of way.

CONFLICT AND JUSTICE

We all have been taught to think that when we do abstract theory, "justice is the first virtue of institutions" (Rawls 1999: 3), from which we infer that our first task is to articulate principles of justice.[15] Benjamin Barber expresses the problem in a stinging remark about Rawls's writing: "When political terms do occasionally appear, they appear in startlingly naïve and abstract ways, as if Rawls not only believed that a theory of justice must condition political reality, but that political reality could be regarded as little more than a precipitate of the theory of justice." (Barber 1989: 310).

Robert Paul Wolff's criticism is equally sharp.

> Rawls seems to have no conception of the generation, deployment, limitations, or problems of political power. In a word, he has no theory of the state. When one reflects that *A Theory of Justice* is, before all else, an argument for substantial redistributions of income and wealth, it is astonishing that Rawls pays so little attention to the institutional arrangements by means of which the redistribution is to be carried out. One need not know many of the basic facts of society to recognize that it would require very considerable political power to enforce the sorts of wage rates, tax policies, transfer payments, and job regulation called for by the difference principle. The men and women who apply the principle, make the calculations, and issue the redistribution orders will be the most powerful persons in the society, be they econometricians, elected representatives, or philosopher-kings. How are they to acquire this power? How will they protect and enlarge it once they have it? Whose interests will they serve? (1977: 202)

In practice, officials who make our basic structures work have to begin with resolving and avoiding conflict, not with justice. While theorists treat justice as more foundational than conflict-resolving rules of practice, practitioners have no choice but to do the opposite. Thus, when practitioners ignore our theorizing about what *would be* ideal (but for the fact that that it only solves the problem in our misleading model), they are

---

[15] Bernard Williams (2005) sees the same thing, and laments it.

doing the right thing. They know that what we learned in our philosophy classes is somehow badly mistaken.

The kind of questions that judges actually need to answer are questions such as, "Is flying over someone's ranch at a height of 10,000 feet a form of trespass, or a way of peacefully minding your own business?" Or, "Is drilling for oil underneath your land a form of trespass, or a way of peacefully minding your own business?" Some of these questions have no answers until judges sort out what will help current and potential litigants in particular circumstances to stay out of court and get on with their lives. After judges settle a dispute, citizens go forward with legitimate mutual expectations about what to count as their due. Judges get it right when they actually settle it—when they establish expectations that everyone can live with and thereby minimize the need for future intervention by corruptible public officials. Judges know this. They cannot settle for expressing personal convictions about fairness. They have to settle disputes.

We are trained to think that, in the name of justice, it would be *ideal* if the world were to magically be remade in accordance with our vision. We are supposed to inspire those who do hold power to so remake the world. They are supposed to listen. They are supposed to accept that our theory cannot be reasonably rejected, and get ready to make a difference.

And yet, a mandate to pursue justice *tout court* is, after all, not remotely the same as a mandate to pursue a vision with which not everyone agrees. There would be something maniacal in thinking that one's vision of justice just is justice, and something insufferable—adding insult to injury—in thinking that one has a vision that cannot reasonably be rejected. Moreover, imagine thinking that our vision itself licenses us to ram it through at other people's expense. Whatever else we know about our vision, knowing that much should be enough to tell us that what we are envisioning is something other than justice. In the arena of politics, the problem is compounded: first, power to ram through justice is power to ram through injustice. Second, the process by which a candidate acquires power is perverse in the sense that power is more valuable to those who would use it for corrupt ends. Therefore, anyone who truly cares about justice avoids creating concentrated power in the first place, and avoids conceiving of justice in such a way that justice so conceived offers the appearance of an excuse for those too eager to create manifestly corruptible concentrated power.

The first virtue of social institutions is to establish a rule of law that keeps the peace well enough to create conditions for cooperation: conditions that enable society to be, in the most rudimentary and non-theory-laden sense, a cooperative venture for mutual advantage. Without that first virtue, we are heading for misery. However, that first virtue rules out creating the power to ram through a thick conception of justice, which in turn should lead us to suspect that no *thick* conception of justice is a *true* conception. Thick justice is an imposter. Underneath the fine disguise is a gnawing hunger for the power to impose a vision of how things ought to be.

If we settle for conflict resolution—for having a forum for airing grievances as they arise—then we remain vulnerable to corruption, but there is less scope for corruptible discretion. Instead of judges having a license to pursue a *vision*, they have a license to find out what litigants can live with. They have a license to find out what real people whose futures genuinely hang in the balance can regard as preferable to treating a conflict as unresolved. Judges are constrained by a need to converge on a result that leaves litigants feeling like they had a say, and were given terms of peace preferable to where they were heading before those terms were set.

In summary, when corruption is a problem, it tends to take the form of a principal-agent problem. Inevitably, there will be officials, and official responsibilities, and officials with the power and discretion to take on those responsibilities. That measure of power and discretion will invite officials to use power for purposes other than the purposes for which power was given.

Regarding the prospects for maintaining a rule of law, the least corrupt system in the long run minimizes reliance on powerful officials, thereby minimizing the concentration of what corrupts—namely power—in corruptible officials. Thus, one key question for a legal system is: does the rule of law embodied in this system minimize the need for ongoing tinkering? The power to tinker will be a supremely valuable commodity, and sooner or later those who possess that power will be corrupt. The least corruptible forms of power are the most dispersed forms, and above all the power to vote with one's feet.

Our theorizing must reflect what it takes for people to be better off with (what we call) justice than without it. Our theorizing must begin by reflecting on what it takes for people to live in peace, which means reflecting on what it takes to resolve and avoid conflict. Unless our theorizing about justice is theorizing about what people are better off with than without, officials whose job is to settle disputes on the ground will be morally required to ignore us.

Finally, theorizing about justice that sets aside whether alleged requirements of justice can be satisfied without inviting wholesale corruption is not merely in need of some adjustment downstream, prior to practical application. That sort of theorizing sets aside what matters when it comes to figuring out terms of engagement that enable us to sustain flourishing lives together, thereby setting aside anything we have any good reason to regard as justice.

ACKNOWLEDGMENTS

Work on this chapter was supported by a grant from the John Templeton Foundation. The opinions expressed here are mine and do not necessarily reflect the views of the Templeton Foundation. I'm also grateful to the Property and Environment Research Center in Bozeman for welcoming me as Julian Simon Fellow in the summers of 2012 and 2013, and to the Earhart Foundation for support in the fall of 2013.

I am immensely grateful to Subramanian Rangan, Ebba Hansmeyer, and fellow participants at the Royal Society of London for encouraging feedback, especially Rabih Abouchakra, Elizabeth Anderson, Anthony Appiah, Kenneth Arrow, Robert Frank, Michael Fuerstein, Majid Jafar, Mugheer Al Khaili, Philip Kitcher, Jihad Mohaidat, and Amartya Sen. For helpful feedback at a workshop in Prague, I thank Ralph Bader, David Boonin, Jacob Levy, Carmen Pavel, Guido Pincione, Hillel Steiner, and Steve Wall. Thanks also to Andrew J. Cohen.

REFERENCES

Barber, Benjamin (1989). *The Conquest of Politics*. Princeton: Princeton University Press.

Burtt, Shelley (2004). Ideals of Corruption in 18th Century England. In W. Heffernan and J. Kleinig (eds), *Private and Public Corruption*. Lanham: Rowman & Littlefield, 101–23.

Fleischacker, Samuel (2004). *On Adam Smith's Wealth of Nations*. Princeton: Princeton Press.

Hanley, Ryan Patrick (2009). *Adam Smith and the Character of Virtue*. New York: Cambridge University Press.

Otteson, James R. (2002). *Adam Smith's Marketplace of Life*. New York: Cambridge.

Rawls, John (1971/1999). *A Theory of Justice*. Cambridge, MA: Harvard University Press.

Schmidtz, David (2015). Adam Smith on Freedom. In R. Hanley (ed.), *Princeton Guide to Adam Smith*. Princeton: Princeton University Press.

Schwartz, Adina (2004). A Market in Liberty: Corruption, Cooperation, and the Federal Criminal Justice System. In W. Heffernan and J. Kleinig (eds), *Private and Public Corruption*. Lanham: Rowman & Littlefield, 173–223.

Smith, Adam (1776/1981). *Wealth of Nations*. Indianapolis: Liberty Fund.

Smith, Adam (1790/1984). *Theory of Moral Sentiments*. Indianapolis: Liberty Fund.

Williams, Bernard (2005). *In the Beginning was the Deed*. Princeton: Princeton University Press.

Wolff, Robert Paul (1977). *Understanding Rawls: A Reconstruction and a Critique*. Princeton: Princeton University Press.

CHAPTER 5

SOCIAL CONTROL IN A STATELESS WORLD SOCIETY

Confronting and Constructing Social Problems

JOHN W. MEYER

Abstract

Regulating global capitalism is part of a more general problem of regulating all sorts of interdependencies—economic, political, military, social, and cultural—in a globalizing world without a superordinate state. The extraordinary expansions of science, individual human rights principles, and relatively common systems of extended education have facilitated a great expansion of global social movements, globalized professions, international nongovernmental organizations, international intergovernmental organizations, and of course multinational capitalist firms. Associated with this is a movement for global social responsibility. This structure clearly works to regulate interdependencies, but is not adequate to the problem. The global movements and organizations are not integrated, and their expansion may globalize all sorts of conflicts. Finally, many of the global organizations and professions gain by discovering and furthering new problems and issues.

INTRODUCTION

Since World War II, the interdependence of societies around the world has increased on many dimensions: economic, certainly, but also military, political, ecological, social, and cultural. There is an even greater increase, and spread around the world, in social perceptions of the interdependencies involved. It is now easy for people to see their local circumstances as affected by distant forces—cultural threats (such as the legitimization of homosexuality), economic threats (the export or import of jobs and workers), or ecological crises (global warming).

Throughout modern history, the management of interdependence and its threats has generally been assigned to the charismatic national states (with monopolies over mortal violence). With actual and perceived global interdependence, this solution has broken down. There is nothing like a world state. And the national states that do exist have lost much of their charisma (though not their organizational power and responsibility) as the post-war period has gone on.

Thus there are great and increasing gaps between expanding interdependencies, with the various problems they are seen to create, and the capacity of established institutions to deal with them at a global level. Dramatic efforts arise to fill these gaps, with great social movements and much social change. Enormously expanded—and globalized—sciences and social sciences provide bases for regulation in natural rather than positive law. Human social life is reconceptualized around principles of universal individual human rights, with empowered, entitled, and responsible persons, often professionalized, now seen as "actors" on the world stage. And the new human is melded to the new knowledge system in what is now a global system of education that has enormously expanded everywhere.

Under these conditions, an explosion of social mobilization and social organizing appears at every level from world society down to local communities, attempting to control and respond to the new interdependencies. Social, economic, political, and cultural groups mobilize, and take on the forms of large-scale rationalized formal organizations. Since there is no real central coordination, a great deal of conflict and inconsistency is involved: the competition intensifies the level and scale of formal organizing. One group's problem (e.g. the breakdown of religious control) is another group's solution (individual freedom).

So the resultant world society is a very open, and quite liberal, one. It is organized to solve problems, but also to create and perceive them. The empowered and problem-solving actors, now organized at supra-national levels, can easily find disorder and injustice everywhere. In a very diverse and unequal world, it is very easy to see problems, and world society is filled with people and structures designed to do just that.

In this chapter, I discuss the points just outlined. The first section elaborates the background conditions of the post-war period. The second section reviews the massive resultant social control efforts, and the third, their consequences for social organization. A fourth, dialectical, section considers the ways in which the institutions built to provide social control also support further mobilization, and extensions of perceived problems of order.

A Note on Labels

This is much variation on what world society is called. This is intensified by the absence of a central world state. Labels are of some consequence, as they call attention to varying causal forces, and therefore to variations in perceived problems and resolutions. Some fashionable terms, like "earth" or "biosphere," focus on ecosystemic dimensions. Others, like "the human race" or "humanity," emphasize the distinctive normative standing of the human individual. "World society" gives this a social organizational aspect.

More specific conceptions focus on specific institutions, with implied causal and normative structures. "World polity" evokes one set of considerations, "the human family" another, "the world economy" still another. Some usages (e.g. following Wallerstein 1974) have it as "world capitalism," which creates two problems. First, it gives a peculiar picture of the world and its problems as especially economic in character: given the expanded and vacuous definition of what the economic is in modern social science (e.g. "Knowledge Economy"), this lacks clarity. Second, even given a focus on the modern vaguely defined "economy," treating this economy as having "capitalism" as its defining component is very unrealistic (see Appiah, Chapter 6).

The Structural Setting of Perceived World Problems

The decades since 1945 have been marked by rapid increases in interdependence on a great many fronts, by the continuing absence of any real state-like structures in the world, and by declines in the faith in the capacity and authority of the national states to manage the world.

Expansion and Interdependence

Globalization has, quite reasonably, become a watchword in descriptions of world society. It describes both expansion and integration across many dimensions in world society. Most obvious, and often discussed, there is enormous expansion in material production and exchange. But just as fundamental, there is the expanded structuration of the world as a political and military system, fueled by the Cold War and by threats of nuclear conflict. And there is expanded and globalized transportation and communication.

Interdependence and expansion in reality were accompanied by an expanding cultural awareness and codification, by turns hopeful and fearful, of these phenomena. On the one hand, global threats—economic, political, cultural, and ecological—became more and more apparent. On the other hand, conceptions that the world is one place and one society strengthened (a view taken for granted in the chapters in this volume). So common data and measurement schemes arose, characterizing many dimensions of social life. For instance, all countries (after the decline of Communism) acquired a common measure of development and fundamental value, with the GDP/capita, and all were generally expected to try to achieve secular salvation by increasing it. And of course, such statistics are measured in currencies that are increasingly intertranslatable.

Overall values, thus, are assessed on a common scale. But so are the particular values associated with specific institutions. Health care and life expectancy, educational attainment and achievements, organizational transparency and corruption, ecological footprints—all can be assessed and compared on common bases. This means, as we discuss below, that issues on any of these fronts become global social problems: one can no longer assume that people on another continent have different needs, or place different valuation on life and health.

The old resolution to such problems—the assertion of national uniqueness because of race, religion, or history—is less and less available. It did not look good in the world of 1945. Most strikingly, whole stabilizing edifices of caste and empire were destroyed, and in the Atlantic Charter, racist America and imperialist Britain joined hands in the celebration of higher and more universalized values.

A Stateless World Society

For centuries, modernizing intellectuals have seen the value, and indeed necessity, of some sort of supra-national organizational structure to manage order given expanding interdependence. The world of conflicting national states, despite much theorizing and legitimating (e.g. in the field of international relations), never has seemed adequate, and the suspicion has always been that the Western world has been immersed in a long interstitial "period of warring states." This suspicion was greatly encouraged by the events of the first half of the twentieth century.

The First World War produced the rather tame League of Nations, but killed off the more optimistic visions of the turn of the century: Esperanto, for instance, never recovered its strength (Kim 1999). But the Westphalian conception of fairly murderous national states had one more cycle in it. The resultant second war produced the United Nations system of structures, and two great ideologically based supra-national blocs. And eventually, it produced a European political order, along with weaker reflections in other world regions.

All these structures work to manage interdependencies in the world. None of them have the authority and power of the old national state. There are regional and world courts, but they provide little recourse. For the resolution of no great social problem in an interdependent world are these structures perceived as remotely adequate. The magic of the authoritative state, of Carlus Magnus, of the universal empire, does not attach to the World Health Organization.

As an indicator, we can imagine the understanding of a typical secondary school graduate in the world. What names and faces of central elites would this pupil recognize? Probably the head of the local state, and maybe the American or Russian chief executive. Probably the head of no supra-national organization.

The Lowered Legitimacy of the National State

The first half of the twentieth century did not make the absolutely sovereign national state look good. Increasing interdependence make it look inadequate, and often destructive, supra-nationally. In an integrated and interdependent world, with increasingly elaborated standards of proper political, social, cultural, and economic life, the state was increasingly assessed in terms of its internal functioning by global standards. And in these assessments, the notion that a state is a "failed state" came into more frequent use.

In the earlier period of high nationalism, massive supports for the nation state's monopoly of legitimate violence existed. Millions of people agreed to try to die or kill for the nation state, and in much of the world this principle was ensconced in laws supporting universal conscription. There was, indeed, a good deal of celebration of inter-state war, and depictions of such wars were very prominent in the textbooks constituting national history and society (Bromley et al. 2011).

As social organizations, of course, national states survive and expand. The point is they have much less of a monopoly over the drama of problem-solving public action, especially confronting problems seen as global. They become less and less foci of adequate answers to the problems of the world. They lose actual and depicted control over the great matters of the environment, human rights and welfare, economic growth and interdependence, and indeed social order.

THE CULTURAL CONSTRUCTION OF GLOBAL SOCIAL ORDER

In the post-war decades, dramatic efforts have been made to construct an orderly world society without a central state. Extraordinary social and cultural changes have been involved, producing a very differently structured world society. Driven by the actualities and perceptions of massive social problems, the sociocultural order of the twenty-first century is transformed from the one of the mid-twentieth century.

We can understand many of the changes through the lens produced by the great social theorist of order in stateless societies: Tocqueville. In *Democracy in America* (1836 [1969]) he reports to the state-burdened Europeans on how a democratic society can function without much of a national state. And without collapsing into anarchy. The keys are the religious and educational socialization of the citizens (not the king and his ministers), and their incorporation into endless rounds of participatory association. These ideas and observations, ever since, have been the stock in trade of theorists of the liberal society: they are celebrated by Dewey (1944 [1996]), Mead (1964), and in our own time by people like Robert Putnam (2000) And they are seen as a foundation for a new world order—a world civil society.

Critics have the same model in mind, but with a much more negative tone. Until the recent period of American hegemony, intellectual critics like Mencken (1922) and Lewis (1922) saw the putative American democracy as a sea of conformist babbitry: to get real fresh air, the intellectuals and artists understood, one had to go to Paris. In the current period, the same skepticism about the McDonaldization of the world obtains (Ritzer 2002).

In any event, Tocqueville's analysis provides a rough guide to three great worldwide sociocultural changes in the period since World War II. There is the rationalized reconstruction of nature and science through scientific and scientistic doctrines. There is the reconstruction of human activity as "action" of the empowered but responsible individual. And there is the melding of the human individual with the rationalized knowledge system through education, which has exploded worldwide.

Scientization

In the absence of a global political order that could support much positive law, natural law doctrines—though not rooted in what is conventionally seen as religion—have expanded exponentially, and have acquired much authority worldwide. This conception of science as supporting global order (i.e. social control) was built into the founding of UNESCO (nee UNECO, as the S came later).

It is commonly noted that science has expanded on many different dimensions, though explanatory analyses of why this has happened are much weaker (Drori et al. 2003). First, the amount of scientific activity has grown dramatically. Second, the growth has been worldwide in character—and a full range of sciences can be found in essentially every country, most commonly in the universities which have spread everywhere. Third, the substantive range over which the sciences assume an authoritative posture has grown enormously.

To illustrate this last point, we consider the ubiquitous phenomenon of childhood. This was the focus of very limited scientific attention a century ago: Stanford University had two courses mentioning the word (one in the law school, discussing inheritance, the other a single course in the education school). After the World War II, courses skyrocketed, and twenty-two different departments had relevant instruction. Most of these are rooted in scientific analysis (e.g. medicine, psychology, sociology).

Of course, the explosion of rationalized analyses of childhood provides support for collective social action on behalf of childhood extending around the world: states make laws, internal organizations advocate them, and international professional and organizational structures demand them. A world polity of childhood results, since scientization means that common and universal principles of various sorts apply everywhere.

The whole global system of organizations and discourse attempting to address the world's problems rests heavily on the assumptions, conceptions, and observations of the sciences: the scientists themselves are often backstage, but their culture and their particular professional organizations and associations are ever-present.

Aside from scientific expansion in scale, the really dramatic change in the whole period involved the expansion of the recognized social authority of science. Science as supporting progress (e.g. innovation, entrepreneurship); science as supporting justice (e.g. studies of inequality); science as adjudicating relations with the physical environment; and so on. To illustrate the point, we show in Figure 5.1 (taken from Drori et al. 2003), growth of authoritative scientific institutions in the world. For example, in 1950, almost no countries had a national Ministry concerned principally with science: a few decades later, such ministries were very widespread. Other indicators of national and global scientific authority followed similar paths.

The problems that seemed most pressing in the post-war period were very often issues of social organization and welfare—only later were crises of the natural environment made more central. Important issues related to the chaotic and impoverished conditions of the Third World; all sorts of national and ethnic conflicts worldwide; and continuing conflicts over justice between classes, regions, ethnic groups, and so on. To help pacify these, the greatest expansions of the sciences in the period were in social rather than natural fields. Frank and Gabler (2006), working with data on many universities around the world, show high rates of growth—even relative to the rapidly expanding university system—in all the social sciences through the twentieth century. The social sciences were only marginally present in the universities of the early twentieth century, and become quite central after the World War II.

To illustrate the matter, Figure 5.2 (taken from Drori and Moon 2006) reports average higher educational enrollments in various academic fields across the countries

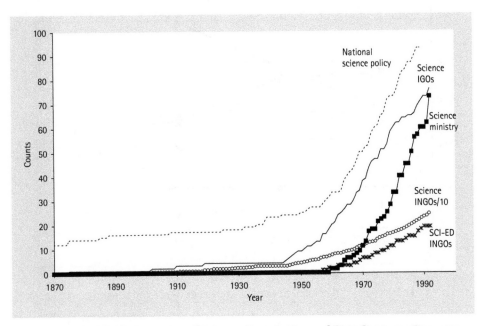

FIGURE 5.1. Worldwide Expansion of Science: Organization and State Stucture, 1870–1995
(Drori et al. 2003)

of the world since 1965. Enrollments exploded during the period, but the figure controls this by reporting percentages. Strikingly, the various natural sciences (e.g. engineering) show relative stability over time. The social sciences expand dramatically. And they replace the once-dominant humanities.

Of course, this all makes sense if we think of the massive cultural effort to provide common rules of social life and order on a worldwide scale. The humanities, often rooted in particular cultural understandings, provide weak grounds—and famously, they supported a great deal of what is now called cultural imperialism in the period between the Enlightenment and World War II. They directly and indirectly celebrated the special status and privilege of the West—racially, historically, religiously, and culturally.

For example, the missionaries, on confronting patterns of female circumcision, commonly took issue with them, operating basically on religious and cultural grounds. They had some success, but not very much. In the post-war period, vastly greater legitimacy is carried by great governmental and non-governmental international organizations carrying the authority of the natural sciences (e.g. medicine) and the social sciences (e.g. human rights) (Boyle 2002).

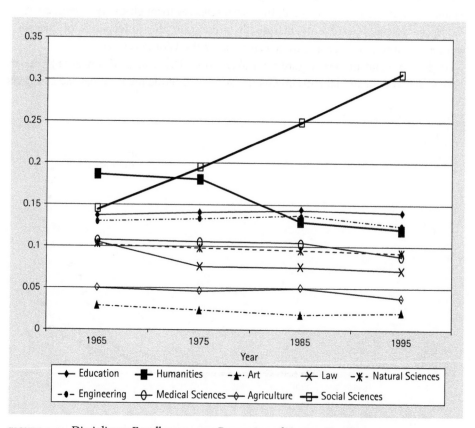

FIGURE 5.2. Disciplinary Enrollment—as a Proportion of Tertiary Enrollment

(Drori/Moon 2006)

The Entitled and Empowered Human Individual

As has often been noted, the expansion of scientific rationalization consequent on the Enlightenment was closely accompanied by a dramatic cultural enlargement of the social space accorded the human as central actor on the sociocultural stage. Many resultant institutional enactments of this status—democracy, the free economy, weakened traditional and familial authority, and the open religious and cultural systems—are much celebrated: Toulmin (1989) and many conservatives take a dimmer view. The phenomenon is an overpowering reality, constitutive of modernity. Disputes center on causal ordering: some, following Polanyi (1944) treat human empowerment as a social defense against the Leviathan of an onrushing economic expansion. Others, sometimes citing Weber (1930), treat the individualism as causal. It's probably most reasonable to see both transformations as part of a more general expansionist one.

The human empowerment movements flowing from the Enlightenment located the expanded charisma in several different locations. Perhaps the key actor was the nation state, and much political theory of modernity celebrated this putative result of Westphalia as a sort of divine intervention. Or perhaps it was the individual human person, endowed with standing in various liberalisms. (And there were various corporatist resolutions emphasizing society rather than the individual or the state as the nationalist locus of authority: see Jepperson 2002 for a useful typology.)

World War II changed the balance here. In 1945, statisms and corporatisms were strikingly delegitimated; and the subsequent Cold War conflict intensified the individualism involved. (It probably helped that the radically liberal United States was the main power left standing.)

Individualisms thus expanded rapidly through the whole subsequent period. Two phases are commonly distinguished (e.g. Ruggie 2008). For two or three decades, social progress and order were thought to result from the expansion of a disciplined national state reflecting the needs and perhaps choices of the people, and an orgy of state planning resulted (Hwang 2006). As the competition from Communism weakened, this broke down, and a more extreme set of well-known neo-liberal individualisms resulted.

But throughout the period, there was an enormous growth of global principles of human rights (Lauren 2003; Stacy 2009). There is a long earlier history, but the movement really took off with the formation of the United Nations and its Declaration of Human Rights. The resulting decades showed very rapid expansion. Elliott (2008), for instance, simply counts the number of international instruments (treaties and the like) asserting general human rights. His results are tabulated in Figure 5.3, which shows the extraordinary growth involved.

The expanded assertion of human rights is by no means the whole story. Yes, there were more and stronger assertions. But also these assertions covered an ever-expanding set of persons and groups defined by their membership in the human race, not their national citizenship—people in general, women, children, the aged, indigenous peoples, workers, disabled people, immigrants, minorities, gay and lesbian people. Further, the set

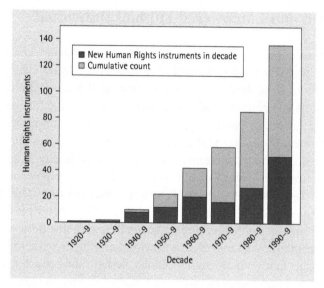

FIGURE 5.3. International Human Rights Instruments: Cumulative Number of Rights, Freedoms, and Entitlements Declared over Time

(Elliott 2008)

of basic human rights constantly expanded, far beyond Marshall's (1964) scheme of civil, political, and social rights. Rights to education, employment, health care, basic income, and safety appear. And there is a great expansion of the rights domains to include personal and cultural matters—the rights to choose one's mate, religion, language, and culture, and to migrate to places of one's choosing.

In the same way that the expansion of the nation-state system in the modern period involved the enhanced right of the state to demand complete loyalty, the subsequent expansion of the human rights regime transformed the possibilities of individuals. In both cases, of course, massive decoupling meant that principled rights and powers were commonly not carried out in practice. But in the current regime, the collective assertion of the primordiality of the individual as a fundamental ontological matter has been breath-taking.

And not simply primordiality. The most important expansion of human rights doctrines in the post-war period has been in the principled *empowerment* of the individual. The individual has the legitimate capacity to act, for the self and for other principles. Indeed, in much modern social and cultural and legal theory, the individual's legitimate choices and actions (and responsibilities) are seen as constituting the social universe (Meyer and Jepperson 2000). In economy, polity, culture, and social life, everything is to result from the choices and actions of individual persons. To illustrate this, we can again cite Elliott's work. He tabulates the variety of human groups and individuals that are, in the various international instruments he analyzes, empowered to act on their own (and others') rights. His list is most impressive: the depicted human individual is no longer dependent on the kindness of state, church, landowner, and even social community: he can, and should, defend his own rights, and those of all others.

Thus, an important feature of the human rights regime is its celebration of the perceived capacity of human individuals to take action—and to take action legitimated by a whole global order. The implication is that the properly socialized and empowered human person is capable of behaving in ways that will support peace and justice and order on a worldwide scale. The assumptions here are striking: each human person has within himself a set of actual or potential qualities that can and should and perhaps will support world order. At a minimum, some sort of universalism is involved—and rationality, such that individuals' activities can be coordinated in terms of the laws of nature. All these assumptions, of course, require much social institutional support: absent an authoritative world religion in the post-war world, education has expanded beyond all expectations.

Education

Given the problems of stateless order in Tocqueville's America, it is not surprising that education became a main institutional focus throughout its formative century and more: the country was a leader in the expansion of mass education (Meyer et al. 1979). In the individualist context, education was seen as a main instrument by which the empowered individual could be melded with a more universal political (and religious) culture and identity: a rational actor, as it were. The focus of education was by no means primarily on the economic capacities of the individual—the point was to create a person inclined and capable of participating in orderly collective action, or in other words a responsible and effective citizen.

As education expanded there was a good deal of resistance from more traditional social structures. Landowners did not necessarily want more schooled peasants, nor did traditional religious and political authorities. And the peasants themselves were often reluctant to surrender their children to schooled loyalties to nations and states and empires. Over several centuries, the resistance abated, and more and more social and cultural supports for educational expansion were institutionalized.

Thus, the long historical process of the growth of mass education expanded greatly after the World War II (Meyer et al. 1992b). New countries entered this order and immediately acquired mass educational systems: the rate at which they did so increased greatly. Countries within the order already had some mass education, but rates of growth in it doubled. If, in 1950, less than half the world's children were enrolled in primary schools, by 2000 it was well over 90 percent. Further, problems in enrolling children (e.g. female children) came to be seen as major social problems, and an Education for All movement established universal schooling as a global norm to be supported by global forces (Chabbott 2003).

The most striking expansion occurs with higher education, which expands in every part of the world, as indicated in Figure 5.4 (Schofer and Meyer 2005). At present, something over a fifth of a cohort of humans is enrolled in higher education—and probably between a quarter and a third receive some of its blessings. So there are more university students in, say, Kazakhstan than there were in the whole world in 1900.

The expansion of higher education is especially striking because it ran against much normative resistance. It was a major element in the midcentury theories of development that higher education should be limited to that needed in the occupational and professional labor force—anything more would be inefficient and destructive, creating "revolutions of rising expectations" (Huntington 1968). The literature of the period captures the idea: *The Diploma Disease* (Dore 1976); *The Overeducated American* (Freeman 1976), *The Great Training Robbery* (Berg 1970), and so on. A few decades later, expanded and improved higher education was seen as an essential component of a country's ability to enter into the great global Knowledge Society.

Precisely because expanded education is understood not as a functional enterprise for some occupations, but as a cultural and social control system for the whole world, rates of expansion are little related to local or national economic resources and exigencies—they are more affected by national linkages to the great world society than by local factors (Schofer and Meyer 2005). In the same way, as already noted, the university systems of the world stress, in their curricula, the universalized notions of the sciences and social sciences, not the more particularized ones of the humanities.

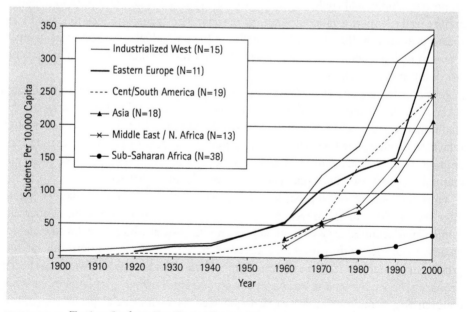

FIGURE 5.4. Tertiary Students Per Capita, Regional Averages, 1900–2000

(Schofer and Meyer 2005)

The point is that the educational systems of the world, to an astonishing degree, carry the same cultural materials to the world's population (e.g. Meyer et al. 1992a; Frank and Gabler 2006). They create great masses of people schooled in common, and by and large rather universalistic, cultural materials. The field of economics, for instance, varies across countries, but not very much (Fourcade 2010). It is striking that a world with such extreme inequalities and "cultural" differences constructs a common and universalistic cultural frame—and it reflects the great exigencies of social control in a globalized world that it is so.

Summary: The Rise of the Actor

The sections above review fundamental cultural forms of the interdependent but stateless contemporary world society. Sweeping scientific rationalization tames nature and society, rendering legitimately justified action proper and necessary—and standardized on a universal basis. The entitlement of equal human persons across many social domains provides baseline standards and goals for proper social action and societal development; and the empowerment of these persons legitimates their capacities to act.

The universalized knowledge system and the empowered actor are conjoined in a massive worldwide system of education, which creates a global population with relatively standardized identities and cultural frames. The effort, obviously, has been to create an integrated social control system, and is supported by the widest variety of interests and ideologies.

The notion of national and world societies as filled with empowered and schooled persons works its way into the assumptions and analyses of the social scientists. In the same way that an earlier generation of analysts shifted from anthropological discussions of tribesmen and peasants, and developed sociological and economic conceptions of persons, citizens, and individuals, contemporary social scientists believe they are studying something better than persons. They have promoted these people into a new category: the term "actor" is more and more commonly employed in leading social science journals (Hwang and Colyvas 2013).

PROBLEM-SOLVING ACTIVISM AND ORGANIZATION IN THE GLOBAL ORDER

The global cultural transformations and constructions we have reviewed reflect enormous efforts to bring integrated order into world society. They do this directly by providing rationalized bases for common and collective action, and by empowering and schooling the participants involved in a cultural order vastly more homogeneous than the diversities of prior cultural systems. We live in a world in which professionals and elites coming from radically different contexts can discuss and deal with common identities and with common rules. They may already know each other from the universities or business schools in which they have acquired these frameworks.

Integration is facilitated indirectly through the social structures that embody the new principles. The contemporary world is filled with legitimated activism. New social movements in great number are facilitated by the new global culture, which not only supplies universalistic principles for action, but also reconstitutes the identities of persons so that they can act in common and are empowered to do so.

Many of the movements involved are simply discursive structures through which people communicate their common goals, problems, and proposed social changes. Others are pools of collective activity, reaching sometimes to violence.

Beyond less formalized social movements, the modern system generates, as Tocquevillian systems do, massive amounts of formal organization, reaching to the global level (Meyer and Bromley 2013). Organizations appear in every sort of national society, and in large numbers at supra-societal regional and global levels.

Social Activist Orientations and Action

The contemporary global cultural system supports the activism of individual and groups. They are empowered to act, and are provided with frameworks that make problem-solving action appear to be reasonable and proper. The schooling systems of the world increasingly transmit such principles, even in mass education. Table 5.1 reports results from a cross-national survey of hundreds of secondary school social science textbooks (Bromley et al. 2011). The issue is the extent to which students are

Table 5.1. Changes in Student–Centrism in Social Science Textbooks (Bromley et al. 2011)

Indicators of Student Centrism (means)	1970–84 (n=97)	1985–94 (n=155)		1995–2008 (n=213)	
Pictures, esp. Child-Friendly (0–3)	1.21	1.47	**	1.98	****
Assignments for Students (0–2)	1.27	1.5	**	1.85	****
Projects for Students (0–2)	0.20	0.43	***	0.64	***
Role-Playing for Students (0–2)	0.12	0.24	**	0.44	****
Open-Ended Questions for Students (0–3)	1.22	1.53	**	1.99	****
Text in Expanding Environments Format (0–3)	0.33	0.32		0.61	****
Amount Children Discussed in Text (0–5)	0.82	0.88		1.20	**
Mentions Children's Rights (0–1)	0.23	0.14		0.28	****

**** p<0.001, *** p<0.01, ** p<0.05, * p<0.1, one-tailed tests

supposed to take a positive participatory orientation to the society whose history and structure they are to study. The table shows a striking increase in such orientations, over the thirty-odd years of the survey. The students are to be much more than passive learners: the book should interest them, and they should form (perhaps diverse) opinions, and even engage in role-playing about historical questions once presented.

And, indeed, people around the world now have opinions and what they take to be knowledge on great common questions. And these can be surveyed in a way that was not possible a half-century ago. Lerner (1958) reported the problem—for example, a Bedouin who complained when asked questions about national public policy, and wondered why he was not asked about camels, on which he was well-informed. Surveys can be and are now conducted in well over one hundred countries, and it is reasonable to discuss a literal "world opinion" on many questions. Naturally, levels of articulated opinion are much higher among schooled people.

Of course, it is characteristic of modern opinion research, and the circumstances that facilitate it, that over a great range of issues, common questions can be asked of people everywhere. So several international bodies each routinely survey people in several dozens of countries—The Eurobarometer, the International Social Survey Program, and the World Values Survey among them. People will now opine on the broadest range of problems and issues (Jepperson 2002)—environmental damage, gender roles, welfare policies, the virtues of democracy, inequalities, and so on. And their opinions are no longer bounded to the specifics of their local or national setting. They will produce judgments intended to be applicable to the whole world, exactly as social scientists do.

Shared concerns and opinions, of course, make possible more aggressive positive collective action. And it is well-known that the contemporary world is filled with such action. Any problem that comes to light supports a whole penumbra of mobilizations, so there are worldwide movements about all sorts of human rights, about a wide variety of environmental problems, and about corruption and injustice everywhere.

It is all rather poorly mapped, partly because of the informal nature of many of the activities, and partly because social scientists and their publics attend to activities that produce troubles, conflicts, and engage in direct oppositions. So a protest by an ethnic group gets attention, but a whole new ideological wave in the field of economics does not, and nor does a sweeping new fashion of organizing in the business world. One can see the multifaceted International Standards Organization as a beehive of social movements—collective action perceiving and solving one or another social problem.

In fact, a proper description and assessment of the full range of mobilization of opinion and action in the modern world shows that mobilization is a feature of the schooled populations and is oriented for better or worse to great globalized collective goods. The people who flew airplanes into the World Trade Center, for instance, were generally highly educated, and acted with a religiously inspired vision of a great world society. As almost always, in an expanding world society, the great conflicts are not between modernity and tradition, but between competing modernities—and both Communism and the current Islamic mobilizations, supported by schooled people with strong senses of empowerment, have in the main precisely that character. As we discuss in the next section, a world society filled with mobilized problem-perceivers and problem-solvers is likely to have a great deal of conflict, which poses a new set of problems to be solved.

It should be noted that social mobilizations, in a globalized world, often occur in global waves. But local reflections of these waves are common and, in the Third World, dominant. Robertson (1992) coined the term "glocalization" to describe the phenomenon. As local people see themselves in light of great global norms and principles, all sorts of formerly impossible mobilizations become likely. Young women informed about global realities, for example, take action, expecting educational and occupational prospects that would never have been activated locally.

The Ubiquity of Organization

A rationalistic culture and empowered and schooled populations of actors combine to produce a great expansion of formalized rational organization worldwide (Meyer and Bromley 2013). The cultural conditions facilitate this, and local mobilizations help produce it: successful social movements become organizations. A whole array of intervening institutions make it available and necessary—legal requirements (e.g., for safety specialists) and the very widespread professionalism generated by expanding higher education (e.g. human resources specialists, planners, and strategists). So traditional staid public bureaucracies supported by the sovereignty of the state, under the pressures of the New Public Management movements, become autonomous and accountable formal organizations. Old-style family firms, subject to the sovereignty of the owner, move in the same direction. And a whole host of traditional professional and religious institutions are pressed to be rationalized decision-making organizations. CEOs and strategic plans appear in hospitals, schools, universities, charitable enterprises, religious orders and denominations, and a range of other structures: they all become "non-profit organizations."

A great expansion in numbers and scale of organization occurs in essentially every national society. The breakdown of Communism produced a huge wave in the East. But the failures of World War II, and American domination, generated a long-lasting similar wave in Western Europe (Djelic 1998).

Organization, in modern usage, means something different from traditionally modern structures like bureaucracies. Organizations are created by empowered human actors, not sovereign elites and professions, and are themselves endowed with sovereign responsibilities (Brunsson and Sahlin-Andersson 2000). They are collective actors, not inert servants of external sovereigns (like the state).

So organizations expand in every national society, but the growth is especially striking at the supra-national level, where it has exploded. The Union of International Associations has tried, for over a century, to keep counts of these. Figure 5.5 shows the

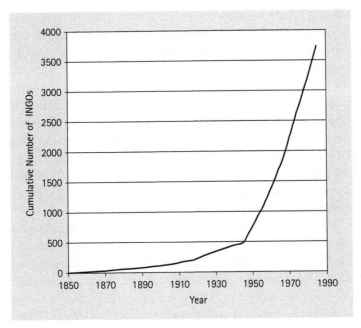

FIGURE 5.5. Cumulative Number of International Nongovernmental Associations, 1850–1986

(*Source*: UIA)

Note: Data prior to 1945 estimated based on founding dates from 1989 UIA Yearbook

growth of one main category of these organizations: international non-governmental organizations (INGOs)—organizations with participation from multiple countries. Some of these organizations are regional (as with structures associated with the European Union), but may try to cover the globe.

The figure shows an astonishing amount of growth, most of it after the World War II. Boli and Thomas (1999) and their colleagues analyze these data in various ways. Most of the organizations are devoted to one or another sort of world problem-solving: religious and educational and scientific and professional structures. And they cover essentially every problem known to globalized humankind. This one works on protecting wildlife, that one the rights of women, and over there associations promoting common measures and metrics.

It is obvious that contemporary cultural conditions, as well as technical ones in communications systems, facilitate organization-building. People in multiple countries, schooled in institutions that are at bottom quite similar, and empowered with professional standing in the same categories, build these structures with great ease. Something that was difficult in earlier periods—finding commonalities across great boundaries—has become absurdly easy in our own time.

What has happened is that a great many people have become much more than citizens of local and national society—they have become legitimated actors, and have their actorhood in common with people with some common interests everywhere. And the structures they create are now actors, too, rather than more inert social forms. All this can occur in multiple layers: many of the INGOs of importance in the world are themselves assemblies of organizational rather than individual actors: Ahrne and Brunsson (2008) call them "meta-organizations."

Many of the most important organizations created in the post-war period have been international governmental organizations (IGOs). With the continuing loss of primordiality of the nation state, these structures too have become more and more like actors too—and actors with much in common with all other actors. So the rate at which they form IGOs has dramatically increased over the period. A very rare social form in an earlier period has become a conventional one now: there are hundreds of them. The Union of International Association reports on them too, showing a pattern of change directly paralleling the growth of INGOs.

Famously, the world of profit-making business experiences exactly the same organizational expansion and reconstruction. Trade increases during the period, but not on a dramatic scale. But during the post-war period, and especially the neo-liberal period of recent decades, global activity increasingly occurs within international business organizations—multinational firms. This was a very rare form of economic organization in 1950, and has become very widespread. A number of counts of these firms have been assembled, all showing the same explosive trend. We display one of them in Figure 5.6, taken from Gabel and Bruner (2003) which shows an explosion from almost nothing to numbers in the tens of thousands.

The literature on business organization of the eighteenth century—Adam Smith and his colleagues—was generally very skeptical about the virtues of what we now call

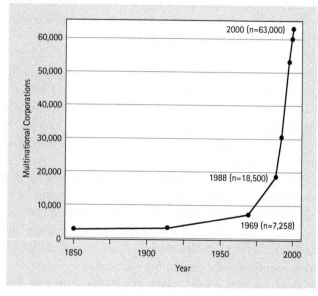

FIGURE **5.6.** Number of Multinational Corporations, 1850–2000

(Gabel and Bruner 2003)

expanded formal organization. It was generally thought, and much experience confirmed the idea, that turning a business over to employed managers essentially invited them to steal from the owners. With modernization during the nineteenth century, it slowly became clear that impersonal formal organization could be made to work. But the idea of doing this across great national and cultural boundaries seemed of dubious value. Even after the World War II, it was generally thought that such cultural boundaries posed great difficulties for transnational organizational construction. All this has now changed: business schools and consultants can provide instruction in the cultural particularities around the world. Indeed the schools have international student bodies; and the consulting firms themselves function worldwide, providing very similar advice with only minimal local adaptation everywhere.

So just as with the non-profits and their INGOs, and the government agencies and their IGOs, the world is now filled with massive numbers of multinational firms in an extraordinary organizational revolution.

Legitimating and Controlling International Capitalism

One great criticism of large-scale organization, as noted above, is that it puts resources in the hands of people who may not live up to their responsibilities. Managers will steal from owners. This can be seen as a problem with the INGOs and IGOs, too. And the modern assumption is that, with effective informational controls, and with schooled and responsible individuals-cum-actors, order will be maintained.

But international economic organization has a problem over and above that of the IGOs and INGOs, which are generally explicitly structured around common and legitimated collective goods. In an earlier period, of course, some IGOs could be structured as competitive military threats to others; and there was a good deal of suspicion that INGOs (e.g. religious ones) were pursuing perverse goals. There was a fear, in other words, that organization amounted to conspiracy.

With economic organization, explicitly organized around private profit and capital accumulation, fears along these lines have generally been overwhelming (see the concerns on the issue in many chapters in this volume—by Pettit, Anderson, Fuerstein, Jafar, Mendiola, and others). And capitalist firms have always faced a problem of legitimacy that other structures face only in more limited ways. There is, of course, a very long literature on the various ways the capitalists, the long-distance traders, and the large economic combines, have been legitimated or suppressed in various political contexts. In the medieval West, they tried to maintain close relations with the Church and did their business between the arches of the cathedral. In Tocqueville's America, they engaged in massive displays of conformity large and small. But overall, historically, a major support has been the long development through Western history of liberalism—models of society treating individuals, and sometimes organized actors, as creating collective goods through the exercise of more or less enlightened self-interest in marketplaces, thus legitimating private action as almost by definition in the long run public good (see Chapter 12 by Barney).

All these problems are intensified with the construction of very large-scale private actors, which raises the fear of monopolies no longer under the effective control of markets. Throughout modern history, expanded economic organization is everywhere seen as requiring some sort of state action. Corporatist systems build regulations into treaties between states and corporate bodies. More liberal ones create state regulation. Of course socialist ones collectivize the large-scale economic structures. In all cases, the nation state becomes a central participant.

With the rise of large-scale international economic structures, all these problems come to a head. In this case, there is obviously no state to do the balancing, the regulating, or the incorporating. The legitimacy problem seems overwhelming.

In the post-war period, scandal involving large-scale international economic organization has been endemic. Here an oil company despoils the environment. There extremely exploitive labor control violates the rights of children. And yonder, great companies corrupt weak states with bribes, with raw political and market power, and with extremes of information distortion. In most of the Third World, local regulation is a weak reed struggling against the great capitalist organizations.

Of course, there are scandals involving smaller economic structures, too (including state capitalisms). Small gold-mining operations destroy landscapes. Uncontrolled decentralized lumbering destroys forests. The little business people create informal versions of slave labor, and through petty corruption violate all reasonable control. The self-interest of small actors, projected on the stage of world markets in a stateless globe, can be extremely destructive of human social order. But the scandals that do good business in the scandal markets of the great media have tended to be those in which self-interest is linked to large-scale powerful organizational structures that are seen to dominate the world economy.

In the early post-war period, the discursive solution was to locate blame for scandals on the national states that were the primary locations of the big multinationals. In this way, corporate misconduct in Chile, Guatemala, Iran, India, and many other places could be seen as the responsibility of particular core national states, most often the United States. This solution became less and less tenable or convincing as the decades passed. Thus few people now would think of blaming the United Kingdom for the recent scandalous environmental destruction by British Petroleum, or the United States for the sins of Chevron or Texaco. Increasingly, it became clear that the great multinationals themselves are autonomous organizations and must be held accountable.

As a result, a huge global field, now called Corporate Social Responsibility (CSR) has arisen (see the discussions in this volume by Anderson, Battilana, or Hong and Liskovichy). Mainly starting with limited efforts of limited success in the 1970s (e.g. the Sullivan Principles concerned with investment in apartheid-ridden South Africa), an increasing range of structures and discourses developed. There were social movements (Soule 2009), non-governmental organizations, and the intergovernmental organizations (principally related to the United Nations) of increasing number and

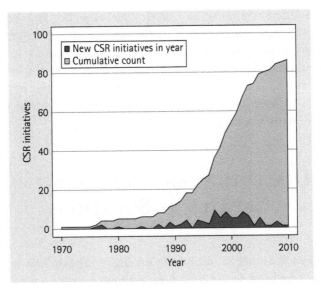

FIGURE 5.7. Corporate Social Responsibility Initiatives, 1970–2010

(Visser et al. 2010)

Note: One initiative started in 1948, but the next initiative is not established
until 1976. The timeframe starts in 1970 to ease visual representation.

force. Increasingly, the great business organizations, especially those with supra-
national bases and functions, joined in, subscribing to related organizations and
principles (see Chapter 15 by Snabe and Chapter 17 by Mendiola; and the related
comments by Collomb).

Figure 5.7 shows a simple count of the extraordinary rise of CSR initiatives (taken
from Visser et al. 2010)—organizations of some sort providing or supporting standards
of conduct for organizations (principally, but not always, business organizations).
There are many of these, some particular to specific industries, others much more
general. Massive numbers of organizations join or subscribe to them (Meyer et al.
2015).

Over and above the specific structures noted here lies a whole field of supportive
arrangements (Meyer et al. 2015). Public rankings arise to discipline firms along the
various dimensions of CSR. Business schools and universities incorporate CSR training
in their programs: indeed one can get a degree in the field. CSR people are professionalized, and participate in the expected range of training programs and conferences.
Large corporations not only join CSR initiatives, but internalize the external threats
and pressures involved, creating CSR offices. And in the environment, a huge array of
consulting services arises, so that there are now thousands of people and organizations
offering services to help companies (and other structures) to engage in CSR-correct
policy and sometimes practice. Of course, many media get involved, generating a huge
array of publications.

The key observation here is that, in a stateless global society, large organizations are to transcend their status as interested parties and become complete and properly responsible social actors. This is exactly analogous to the processes that went on in Tocqueville's America, in which all sorts of organizations, not only the famous American "individual," assumed the posture of citizen. And they were pressed from all sides to do so. In America, leaders of such enterprises were careful to go to church. Now they go to Davos, but it's pretty much the same thing.

DIALECTICS, AND THE PROBLEMS
CREATED BY SOLUTIONS

We have reviewed the range of institutions arising in the post-war world to manage the increasing interdependencies involved without a proper state, and with the decreasing charisma of the old national states. Absent much capacity to generate positive law, global society is filled with the laws of science and social science thought to be applicable everywhere. Without the strong motor of the national state, global society greatly enlarges the perceived standing and capacity of the individual person. And the empowered individual is mapped onto the scientized laws of nature through an enormously expanded and globalized educational system, so that in principle massive numbers of humans are turned from ordinary persons into real social actors.

An explosion of globalized social participation results. Individuals and groups opine on great social questions (e.g. should we attempt the re-re-conquest of Granada?). Associations form on a massive scale. They turn into formal organizations—dynamic and empowered actors in the modern scheme. And all these things happen on a supra-national scale.

All these changes greatly expand human problem-solving capacity. Individuals, associations, and organizations work at the widest range of problems. They press to solve environmental problems such as deforestation to an extent previously unthinkable. They define and try to resolve fundamental problems of human rights and human welfare, formulating for instance strong doctrines of the Education for All movement. They create universal standards of transparency and accountability in social life, supporting for example principles of democracy in social life and opposition to corruption in the business world. They attempt to do all these things on a dramatically supra-national scale: creating global standards for multicultural respect for diversity and peaceful mechanisms for resolving conflicts.

We leave aside the question—much discussed in the widest range of tones, and central to the discussions in this volume (e.g. the chapters by Pettit, Jafar, or Neiman)—of whether all this social material in fact resolves major issues of interdependence in the world. We can take little comfort in history: the wonders of Tocquevillian America ended in a destructive Civil War, and the one-world ideas and institutions of the turn of the twentieth century collapsed in 1914.

But our point here is that in several ways the structural and discursive problem-solving constructions of the contemporary world society themselves constantly expand the range of real and perceived social problems. The Tocquevillian world is dynamic, resolving problems and conflicts at the cost of creating more: recent decades have seen an explosion in the range of problems produced.

Contestations

Global organizational and discursive space is, as we have stressed, filled with legitimated groups and ideas promoting resolutions to actual and perceived problems. Standardizing scientistic, human rights, and educational ideologies helps in creating some consistency between the various contenting forces, but not very much, and there is no overarching administrative or judicial system to resolve the problems.

So demands for increased production and efficiency run up against human rights and environmental claims. All these pressures have expanded legitimacy in the contemporary world, and expanded organization and capacities for action. Similarly, concerns for human equality run up against advocates of free exchange and markets.

Further, the expansion in legitimated human rights to cultural, religious, and linguistic choice, produce mobilizations—sometimes at the world level—of contending and inconsistent ideologies. People are entitled to their cultures, and on universalistic principles: so a culture supporting the rights of homosexual people runs up another culture prohibiting these rights. Sometimes the cultural claims involve overlapping rights to territory and resources, so the rights of increasingly organized (and sovereign) indigenous peoples come up against standardized cultures of national states (Cole 2011).

Thus a world that is increasingly organized is filled with organizational mechanisms for problem-solving, but also with scaled-up capacities for massive conflicts, sometimes on a global scale. These conflicts commonly transcend the capacities of any national state, or combination of national states, to suppress them. And the legitimacy of the national state's putative monopoly over violence steadily declines in the wake of increased intra-state, but also supra-state, conflict. So an environmental group, organized supra-nationally, attacks the whaling vessels from multiple national states. Issues about the status of women or children come to be organized at global levels, producing wide-ranging conflicts among legitimated contending forces. An obscure book or article published without contention in one locale can generate massive riots in multiple other locales. All the participants involved can make legitimated claims for their rights to participate, and their substantive agendas.

Problem-Creating Capacity

The advocacy structures that arise, increasingly at a global level, are also structures with the legitimated capacity to discover, develop, or recognize new social problems. This is most transparent with the world's huge system of universities and research institutes, filled with basic and applied natural and social scientists. For these people, and their organizations and professions, problem discovery is a highly rewarded enterprise, leading to honors, prestige, and material resources. A world which puts such positive value on "entrepreneurship," "innovation," and "creativity"—all formerly suspect human qualities—is a dynamic world of social and intellectual problem creation as well as problem-solving capacity.

Thus the medical researchers who discover and analyze a new disease—the Carpal-Tunnel syndrome might be an example—are generally highly rewarded on multiple fronts. But the net consequence of their efforts is to turn a former unfortunate human condition into problem and a cost for society. The same can be said of the researchers who discover new pollutants in the air or water, often producing great costs for industrial production.

Similarly, the medical or social scientists who analyze inequalities can discover and analyze disabling conditions, requiring enormously expensive medical, educational, or social therapies to repair. Analyses of the world trading systems, for instance, can reveal massive inequalities in the management of labor in the world's peripheries, can analyze these formerly considered natural differences as injustices, and can promote costly revisions.

Thus the expansion of problem-solving sciences is also the rise of problem-creating ones. The expansion of legitimated human rights functions similarly, ever enlarging the zones of social life subject to norms of equality. The educational systems that carry both create cultural and material rewards for the expansion of analyzed social problems and costs.

CONCLUSION

The post-war world has seen great increases in actual and perceived global inter-dependence on many different political, social, economic, and cultural fronts. The more recent neo-liberal period has intensified the perceptions, and probably the realities involved. And an old solution—the formation of larger and larger scaled states or empire—was not really available, even in Europe. Further, a second old imagined solution via theories of balances of power in anarchy was implausible, in part because the old primordial national-state model had lost much legitimacy in a half-century of disaster.

So the main effort has employed still a third, Tocquevillian, solution: to construct, discipline, empower, and control subunits. This has involved the massive expansion of scientistic cultural ideologies covering all of natural, social, and personal life with standardizing and universalizing principles. It has involved a similarly expanded conception of empowered and universalized human beings. And it has involved the explosion of an institutional system of education designed to remove all persons from the particularities of family and community and traditional culture into the sunlit world of universal identities and truths. If ordinary humans in their tribes engaged in endless conflict, turning them into citizens and persons shifted the conflicts to national levels: in the globalized world, they can in principle conflict or cooperate everywhere.

An enormous array of mobilizations and organizational expansions is consequent on these cultural changes. For every problem, social movements and their ideologies develop resolutions, and ultimately great organizational systems develop on a world scale. Public agencies expand as organizations more than bureaucracies: the non-state public world turns schools and hospitals and churches into large-scale non-profit organizations. Both changes occur on a world scale, as does the reorganization of the expanding world economy with the rise of massive new multinationals.

In this last case, the special problem arises that the large economic organizations have monopoly qualities, and are conspicuously dedicated to private profit. The attempted solution has involved the construction of a whole social control regime turning the private multinationals into citizens of a world economy and society. As in liberal systems everywhere, the ideas are that good corporate citizenship is (a) economically sensible, or (b) a necessary trade-off for legitimacy (see Chapter 26 by Collomb or Chapter 12 by Barney).

A final consequence of this mobilized world is that the empowered subunit actors work to create problems, not only to solve them. They contend with each other over myriad inconsistencies and conflicts of interest, all intensified by their very legitimation. And they work to elaborate the logics that create and sustain them: the scientists and advocates of human rights gain honor by discovering new problems, and the organizational structures naturally develop their agendas. Everybody can gain something from the development of new problems.

Future research can develop and correct the lines of thought put forward here, which rest on rather limited data. The changes we observe are extreme, and for that reason our descriptions are rather convincing. But we clearly cannot pin down the extent to which institutions creating standard models around the world (e.g. in knowledge systems, education, organizational forms, or conceptions of human rights) in fact create on the ground conforming practical social realities. And available research does not permit us to confidently answer crucial questions about the success of the social forces involved in actually controlling the behavior of great multinational organizations—we know that they subscribe formally to the institutions of the CSR system, for example, but know much less about the impact such subscriptions have on practices in crucial areas such as the environment or human rights. We also have limited understanding of the operation and development of the powerful forces of conflict built into the globalization process, and future events as well as future research on them will undoubtedly be instructive, if not humiliating.

ACKNOWLEDGMENTS

I am indebted to the work of many collaborators, as cited here. The chapter reflects research supported by the Spencer and National Research (Korea) Foundations, some of which appears in Meyer et al. (2015), Meyer and Bromley (2013), and Meyer (2009).

REFERENCES

Ahrne, Göran, and Nils Brunsson (2008). *Meta-organizations* (2008). Cheltenham: Edward Elgar.

Berg, Ivar E. (1970). *Education and Jobs: The Great Training Robbery*. New York: Praeger Publishers.

Boli, John, and George M. Thomas, eds (1999). *Constructing World Culture: International Nongovernmental Organizations since 1875*. Stanford, CA: Stanford University Press.

Boyle, Elizabeth H. (2002). *Female Genital Cutting: Cultural Conflict in the Global Community*. Baltimore, MD: Johns Hopkins University Press.

Bromley, Patricia, John W. Meyer, and Francisco O. Ramirez (2011). Student-Centeredness in Social Science Textbooks: Cross-National Analyses, 1970–2005. *Social Forces*, 90(2): 547–70.

Brunsson, Nils, and Karin Sahlin-Andersson (2000). Constructing Organizations: The Example of Public Sector Reform. *Organization Studies*, 21(4): 721–46.

Chabbott, Colette (2003). *Constructing Education for Development: International Organizations and Education for All*. New York: Routledge Falmer.

Cole, Wade (2011). *Uncommon Schools: The Global Rise of Postsecondary Institutions for Indigenous Peoples*. Stanford, CA: Stanford University Press.

Dewey, John (1944 [1996]). *Democracy and Education: An Introduction to the Philosophy of Education*. New York: Free Press.

Djelic, Marie-Laure (1998). *Exporting the American Model: The Post-War Transformation of European Business*. Oxford: Oxford University Press.

Dore, Ronald P. (1976). *The Diploma Disease: Education, Qualification, and Development*. Berkeley, CA: University of California Press.

Drori, Gili, John W. Meyer, Francisco Ramirez, and Evan Schofer (2003). *Science in the Modern World Polity: Institutionalización and Globalizatión*. Stanford, CA: Stanford University Press, 2003.

Drori, Gili, and Hyeyoung Moon (2006). The Changing Nature of Tertiary Education: Cross-National Trends in Disciplinary Enrollment, 1965–1995. In D. Baker and A. Wiseman (eds), *The Impact of Comparative Education Research on Institutional Theory*. Amsterdam: Elsevier Science, 157–86.

Elliott, Michael A. (2008). A Cult of the Individual for a Global Society: The Development and Worldwide Expansion of Human Rights Ideology. Doctoral dissertation, Emory University.

Fourcade, M. (2010). *Economists and Societies: Discipline and Profession in the United States, Britain, and France, 1890s to 1990s*. Princeton: Princeton University Press.

Frank, David John, and Jay Gabler (2006). *Reconstructing the University: Worldwide Shifts in Academia in the Twentieth Century*. Stanford, CA: Stanford University Press.

Freeman, Richard B. (1976). *The Overeducated American*. New York: Academic Press.

Gabel, Menard, and Henry Bruner (2003). *Global Inc.: An Atlas of the Multinational Corporation*. New York: New Press.

Huntington, Samuel (1968). *Political Order in Changing Societies*. New Haven: Yale University Press.

Hwang, Hokyu (2006). Planning Development: Globalization and the Shifting Locus of Planning. In G. Drori, J. W. Meyer, and H. Hwang (eds), *Globalization and Organization*. Oxford: Oxford University Press, 69–90.

Hwang, Hokyu, and Jeanette. Colyvas (2013). Actors, Actors! Actors? The Proliferation of the Actor and its Consequences. Paper presented at the European Group for Organization Studies Annual Meeting. Montreal, Canada.

Jepperson, Ronald (2002). Political Modernities: Disentangling Two Underlying Dimensions of Institutional Differentiation. *Sociological Theory*, 20(1): 61–85.

Kim, Young S. (1999). Constructing a Global Identity: The Role of Esperanto. In J. Boli and G. Thomas (eds), *Constructing World Culture*. Stanford, CA: Stanford University Press, 127–48.

Lauren, Paul (2003). *The Evolution of International Human Rights*. 2nd edn. Philadelphia: University of Pennsylvania Press.

Lerner, Daniel (1958). *The Passing of Traditional Society*. Glencoe, IL: Free Press.

Lewis, Sinclair (1922). *Babbitt*. New York, Harcourt, Brace & Co.

Marshall, Thomas H. (1964). *Class, Citizenship, and Social Development*. Garden City, NY: Doubleday.

Mead, George Herbert (1964). *The Social Psychology of George Herbert Mead*. Ed. with an introduction by Anselm Strauss. Chicago, IL: University of Chicago Press.

Mencken, H. L. (1922). *Prejudices*. New York: Knopf.

Meyer, John W. (2009). Reflections: Institutional Theory and World Society. In *World Society: The Writings of John W. Meyer*, ed. G. Krücken and G. Drori. Oxford: Oxford University Press, 36–63.

Meyer, John W., and Patricia Bromley (2013). The Worldwide Expansion of "Organization." *Sociological Theory*, 31(4): 343–65.

Meyer, John W., and Ronald Jepperson (2000). The "Actors" of Modern Society: The Cultural Construction of Social Agency. *Sociological Theory*, 18(1): 100–20.

Meyer, John W., David Tyack, Joane Nagel, and Audri Gordon (1979). Public Education as Nation-Building in America: Enrollments and Bureaucratization in the American States, 1870–1930. *American Journal of Sociology*, 85(3): 591–613.

Meyer, John W., David Kamens, and Aaron Benavot, with Yun-Kyung Cha and Suk-Ying Wong (1992a). *School Knowledge for the Masses: World Models and National Curricula in the Twentieth Century*. London: Falmer.

Meyer, John W., Francisco Ramirez, and Yasemin Soysal (1992b). World Expansion of Mass Education, 1870–1970. *Sociology of Education*, 65(2): 128–49.

Meyer, John W., Shawn Pope, and Andrew Isaacson (2015). Legitimating the Transnational Corporation in a Stateless World Society. In K. Tsutsui and A. Lim (eds), *Corporate Social Responsibility in a Globalizing World*. Cambridge: Cambridge University Press.

Polanyi, Karl (1944). *The Great Transformation*. New York: Farrar & Rinehart.

Putnam, Robert D. (2000). *Bowling Alone: The Collapse and Revival of American Community*. New York: Simon & Schuster.

Ritzer, George, ed. (2002). *McDonaldization: The Reader*. Thousand Oaks, CA: Pine Forge Press.

Robertson, Roland (1992). *Globalization: Social Theory and Global Culture*. London: SAGE.

Ruggie, John G., ed. (2008). *Embedding Global Markets*. Aldershot: Ashgate.

Schofer, Evan, and John W. Meyer (2005). The World-Wide Expansion of Higher Education in the Twentieth Century. *American Sociological Review*, 70(6): 898–920.

Soule, Sarah A. (2009). *Contention and Corporate Social Responsibility*. Cambridge: Cambridge University Press.

Stacy, Helen (2009). *Human Rights for the Twenty-First Century*. Stanford, CA: Stanford University Press.

Tocqueville, Alexis de (1836 [1969]). *Democracy in America*, ed. J. P. Maier, tr. G. Lawrence. Garden City, NY: Anchor Books.

Toulmin, Stephen (1989). *Cosmopolis*. New York: Free Press.

Union of International Associations (1989, and various years). *Yearbook of International Organizations*. Munich: Saur.

Visser, W., D. Matten, M. Pohl, and N. Tolhurst (2010). *The A to Z of Corporate Social Responsibility*. London: Wiley.

Wallerstein, Immanuel (1974). The Rise and Future Demise of the World Capitalist System: Concepts for Comparative Analysis. *Comparative Studies in Society and History*, 16(4): 387–41.

Weber, Max (1930). *The Protestant Ethic and the Spirit of Capitalism*. London: G. Allen & Unwin.

PROBLEM: DISCUSSION SUMMARY

THE first theme of the assembly—"Problem"—is covered in five chapters devoted to achieving some clarity about the presence, nature, and extent of problems related to modern capitalism. Their general premise is that the aims and practice of business enterprise have become decoupled in some important respects from the notion of societal progress. The chapters explore this decoupling on both conceptual and practical levels. This short writeup summarizes the discussions that took place around those five papers.

On a note of clarification, both Autor and Sen observed that the very notion of "capitalism"—around which much of the discussion revolved—was itself ambiguously defined. Autour pointed out that all countries are mixtures of capitalist and socialist institutions and that it might be better to speak of "market-focused economies" instead. Likewise, Sen observed that the notion of "capitalism" has a diversity of meanings, some more closely associated with the distinctive economic mechanisms of the system, and others more closely associated with its values and social consequences.

As Pettit noted at one point, a certain "fault line" ran through much of the discussion, dividing a focus on the rules which govern the system from a focus on the "players" who operate within that system. In his chapter, for example, Jafar points out the way in which the bad behavior of businesses follows in a kind of natural way from inadequacies of the laws, regulations, and institutions that govern business practice. If one plays a game in which the rules are ambiguous, inadequate, and enforced inconsistently, then playing the game successfully almost seems to require exploitation of every regulatory gap.

This perspective is consistent with Arrow's suggestion that the market mimics in certain respects Hobbes's "war of all against all." That is, if we treat the market as a kind of prisoner's dilemma populated by self-interested agents, then the exploitation of limitations in rules and enforcement becomes essential to competing effectively as a business.

In response to Jafar's essay, Fuerstein asked about the role of businesses' moral dispositions and temperament in explaining the failures of capitalism, thus highlighting the correlative role of the system's players within a framework of rules. Much of the discussion throughout the session focused on the importance of a moral or professional ethos within the business community.

Arrow's presentation of his essay focused on the particularly significant role that information asymmetries play in generating the need for morality in economic transactions. In an idealized competitive market (an "Arrow-Debreu world"), Arrow noted, the freedom to buy and sell leads to mutual advantage as prices reflect all relevant information and parties get what they want and expect from transactions. When some parties have more information than others, however, opportunities for exploitation arise. Exploitation might take the classic form of selling a "lemon," but can also arise from the escalating complexity of market transactions. The performance of financial services firms, for example, is a function of an enormously complex and interactive range of factors extending into the future. Without adequate indicators of such future performance, it is easy for firms to exploit the consumer's limited perspective for their own gain. Ethics under such circumstances becomes a "control factor" that supplements the price signal to limit exploitative behavior.

In response to Arrow, Snabe observed the vital role that technology might play in mitigating information asymmetries. "What if," Snabe asked, "in the future there is full transparency at zero cost?" Thus, Snabe suggested, future patients might go to the doctor armed with knowledge from "the cloud" of what sort of cure is appropriate for what disease, etc.

How we think about ethics in the market context depends significantly on how we characterize the basic motivations of market actors. In this respect, Schmidtz observed (both in his essay and discussion) that Adam Smith's classical take on capitalism has been egregiously misrepresented. Whereas conventional views of Smith suggest that he views egoistic gain as the driving motivation of economic actors, Schmidtz suggested that "Smithian self-esteem" derives, not from gaining at the expense of others, but rather from the satisfaction taken in being valuable to others around us.

Anderson picked up on these ideas in her response to Arrow's reference to Hobbes. While regulation and enforcement have a crucial role to play in aligning the incentives of egoistic actors with the social good, Anderson observed that the model of Smithian self-esteem underlines the central role of a moral or professional ethos in market transactions. On the vital question of how to cultivate such an ethos, she noted a perverse dynamic in which "in the effort to incentivize everything, we actually drive out motivation according to professional standards," i.e. we undermine social structures that might cultivate and take advantage of Smithian desires to be valuable to others.

So, concerning the "players" within the capitalist system, there was a fairly strong consensus among the group that a substantial part of the problem with contemporary capitalism concerned the tendency to valorize selfishness as a kind of self-sufficient motivation, and to design institutions around that assumption. Importantly, there also seemed to be a reasonable consensus that selfishness was not an immutable feature of human nature in economic transactions. Aspiring to a moral ethos of market interactions was, the group seemed to agree, a necessary and viable objective.

Reflection on the rules of the game, or the systemic, institutional constraints on markets and businesses, introduced a number of distinct worries. While there was reasonable convergence on the general idea that governments had an essential role to play in promoting the pro-social functions of business activity, a number of participants raised significant questions about the power and efficacy of governments in this context.

As Collomb observed, one of the dominant problems that we confront in designing an adequate regulatory framework is that capitalism is now a thoroughly global phenomenon. As a result, we seem to need a global framework for the design and enforcement of any rules. And yet the prospects of achieving a robust and viable framework of that kind seem rather dim. For Collomb, this observation pushes us back in the direction of ethics and civil society rather than governmental solutions. Perhaps, for example, we should be thinking more seriously about the role that business schools play in shaping the moral worldview of actors within the business world, or what Battilana later referred to as a "socialization of professionals."

While Schmidtz acknowledged an important role for governments, he raised grave worries about the tendency of centralized power to undermine the mechanisms of human prosperity. As he put it, the power to oversee the market also introduces the prospects of crony capitalism, i.e. the buying and selling of "monopoly privileges." In light of those prospects, we ought to take seriously the possibility that "we may be talking here about problems that don't have solutions." Following up on Schmidtz, Jafar observed the recurrent tendency for powerful economic players to use their advantages to distort the rules of the system in their favor via political means.

One aspect of Schmidtz's skepticism about government intervention concerned the objections to wealth redistribution articulated in his essay. In response, Frank pointed to the necessary role of progressive taxation, broadly conceived, in any viable model of government. While much of the discussion up to that point had focused on the "rules" as regulations, Frank's claim pointed to the way in which rules function not only to constrain transactions, but also to modify or constrain the results of those transactions. Building on Frank, both Anderson and Sen pointed out that much of what was typically characterized as "redistribution" was actually investment in the future, specifically in the form of children's capacities via education, nutrition, and health care. In light of Jafar's observations about political corruption, Sen observed, so-called "redistribution" is often better conceived as a kind of investment in the prospects of democracy itself.

Several participants pushed the group to think beyond governmental institutions in reflecting on the functioning of the capitalist system. In his essay, Meyer offers a picture of a world increasingly populated, and defined by, a diverse range of non-governmental organizations: scientific organizations, universities, professional associations, social movements, charities, etc. On Meyer's view, such organizations have increasingly supplanted the role of governments, resulting in a kind of spiraling complexity that proliferates new problems as much as it solves old ones.

For Meyer, this point raises skepticism about the very questions of injustice under consideration at the assembly: was the perception of a "problem" simply an artifact of a massive increase in professional problem-solvers? But it also suggests that we live in a world which is, in some sense, increasingly beyond the control of central institutions. In response Pettit observed that, in spite of the proliferation of non-governmental organizations, governments have played a profound role in shaping the development of human rights, education, and science, among many other things. The crucial worry, Pettit suggested, is the increasing power of one specific kind of non-governmental organization, namely large corporations.

Following up on Pettit, Davis noted the peculiar manner in which corporate actors now shop around among states for the distinctive policies and regulations that suit them. As Davis put it, "the state is like a bespoke tailor and . . . corporations are there to get the policies that they want." In this respect, corporations are exploiting the globalization of business to free themselves from the constraints of governmental entities.

PART II

PROGRESS

CHAPTER 6

CAPITALISM AND HUMAN PROGRESS

KWAME ANTHONY APPIAH

Tous les jours à tous points de vue je vais de mieux en mieux.

(Émile Coué)

Abstract

This chapter discusses the relationship between capitalism and progress and ends with a discussion of three mechanisms for reducing some of the problems associated with markets. A familiar argument says that markets must advance progress under ideal conditions because they guarantee Pareto optimality. It is shown here that for a variety of reasons—among them the incommensurability of values, the incommensurability of persons, and the fact that history matters—Pareto optimality is neither necessary nor sufficient for progress. Capitalism—understood as the pervasive use of markets—appears, under modern conditions, to lead to greater material inequality, but what is problematic is (a) the absolute lack of certain basic resources and (b) the social and political inequalities associated with great differences in wealth. These last can be mitigated by the familiar state mechanisms of law regulation and tax incentives, but also by professional business norms sustained by a concern for one's honor.

METHODOLOGICAL PRELIMINARIES 1: PROGRESS

Intellectuals in the North Atlantic world are prone to make certain assumptions about how to assess the general state of society. One is a sort of methodological individualism: the overall worth of a state of society is a function of the worth of the lives of its individual members. Fix the worth of the individual lives, measure their individual welfares, and you will have fixed the worth of the total social state, what

I will call the social welfare. This technical thought about the measure of welfare is embedded in a wider substantive picture. On that picture, social arrangements are good because of their consequences for individuals and for no other reason: social good is explained by individual good and so social good supervenes on individual well-being. Because societies exist in order to advance the welfare of individuals, theories of contract in a state of nature seem like a reasonable basis for justifying social arrangements. If all of us are to agree rationally to an arrangement it must aim to make things better for each of us, better, that is, than they would be with no social institutions at all. Convinced of this, you would have a natural way of identifying progress. Progress occurs when (and only when) the social welfare, conceived of in this individualist way, increases. And, given a second widespread assumption—that we should aim to increase social welfare where we can—we ought to seek progress.

I hope all this strikes you as commonsensical—because that makes it more interesting that there are so many problems with this package of ideas. Notice, first, however, that this methodological individualism does not entail that every improvement in the state of one person that costs nothing to anyone else increases the social welfare. This methodological individualism does not, that is, entail, in the technical jargon, that every Pareto improvement is an improvement. If equality matters, to give one example, increasing my material welfare while leaving everybody else's the same may not be progress if I already have a lot more than everybody else. So methodological individualism is consistent with a concern for the *shape of distributions* in a way that Pareto efficiency ignores. If justice matters, to give a second example, and some principles of justice are what Robert Nozick called "historical principles," then I may make things worse overall by giving someone what they're not entitled to, even if it is at no cost to others (Nozick 1974: 153–5). Pareto improvements in distributions of welfare are not sufficient to increase social welfare.

Nor, even more obviously, does methodological individualism entail that every improvement is a Pareto improvement. So Pareto improvements in distributions of welfare are not necessary for increasing social welfare, either. If contracts matter, perhaps things would be better if John had what Mary has, because she owes it to him. Here we get social improvement without a Pareto improvement. If justice matters, an allocation that reduces my material welfare as a punishment for a wrong I have committed may be preferable to leaving things as they are, even if that does no one else any good. Here Pareto deterioration may increase social welfare. So, on reasonable assumptions, if you want to maximize social welfare, Pareto efficiency can't be your aim.

As a result, arguments that show that markets of certain idealized kinds tend towards Pareto efficiency, producing distributions that can only improve the material welfare of some at the expense of the welfare of others, offer no guarantee that such markets improve material social welfare, understood in this widespread individualist way. (One argument of this form is any proof of the first of the so-called fundamental theorems of welfare economics.) And that is not—or not just—because the models are idealized, but also because Pareto efficiency is, as we have seen, neither necessary nor sufficient to justify a distribution of goods or of welfare. So the fact that a policy does *not* guarantee a Pareto improvement is, by itself, not an argument *against* it; and the fact that it *does* is not, by itself, a decisive argument *for* it.

Here is another reason for skepticism about the significance of these arguments: they attend only to distributions between actual persons, and so give no weight to the consequences of current distributions of goods for the lives of those who do not yet exist or for our obligations to those who no longer exist. They are, in short, strongly anchored in the present. Even if you did not grow up (as I did) in a society where the ancestors were very much before our minds, you can think that we owe them more consideration than that. And we all now see that we must take some care for future generations, even though it is controversial how we should weigh the interests of people who do not yet exist.

Methodological individualist arguments tend also to be anchored in the actual world and its distributions. But surely there are reasons to favor social arrangements in which what we have we have more securely rather than less. And that is a question not just about my actual welfare but also about what my welfare would have been in certain counterfactual circumstances. It might be better not just that we each have a certain bundle of goods but that we have them securely, so that we would continue to have them over a wide range of possible circumstances. Progress might be thought to require greater security of this sort, which won't show up if we look only at the current distribution of goods. Such arguments are, then, not just too anchored in the present but too anchored in the actual as well.

Once you move away from defining individual improvements in material terms alone, you might think that things can get better for a person in a number of incommensurable dimensions, and, since many changes in the world increase individual welfare in one dimension while reducing it in others, things generally get both better and worse for individuals over time, and individual welfare doesn't have a single ordinal ranking. Rather individual overall welfare is measured by an n-tuple of rankings. If that is right, then, there is a variety of ways of applying the individualist idea. One would be just to assume that there is a function from individual welfare in each of the n dimensions to a social ranking in *that* dimension. That would make the social welfare itself an ordered n-tuple of rankings, so that many changes would involve both improvement and decline, and we wouldn't be able to identify overall progress. But, in any case, it is not obvious that this will be possible in general, since there may be no way to aggregate the individual dimensions, as we know there is no uncontroversial way to aggregate individual ordinal utilities.

So, even if methodological individualism were correct, it wouldn't help us in deciding whether things were progressing generally. We have already seen three reasons why this might be. One—call this "incommensurability of goods"—is that human welfare has many incommensurable dimensions and nothing guarantees they will move in lockstep. A second—call this "incommensurability of persons"—is that things generally get better for some and worse for others even in a single dimension and we have no general way of telling whether or not this results in an overall improvement. And the third—call it "history matters"—is that whether things are progressing depends in part not just on who has what but on how they got it or what effects current practices will have on those yet unborn.

In fact, however, I doubt that this methodological individualism is correct. Let me offer two entirely different sorts of consideration.

First: I live in New York, a city with a rich and vibrant literary and artistic life. This cultural wealth seems to me a good thing; it contributes to the social welfare. But it is far from clear—I learned this from Andrew Huddleston (Huddleston, 2012)—that what is good about it is just that many of us individually draw something worthwhile from it. You do not have to be a Nietzschean to think that the value of a culture is not some aggregate of the value of its contributions to the individuals who participate in it. The value of culture may be non-aggregative. And in asking oneself whether we are progressing, the value of our culture is one of the things that surely matters a very great deal.

Second: I take it that your social identity, while it is an important fact about you which helps shape your welfare, is not itself an aspect of your welfare. It may help determine what is good for you—it way be what Ronald Dworkin dubbed a parameter of your welfare—but it is not itself a good you possess (Dworkin 2000: 260–3). Suppose that is true. Then methodological individualism entails that we should be indifferent to the choice between two distributions of goods, one of which allocates the best bundles to people of one identity and another which distributes them in such a way that the average bundle for people of one identity is the same as the average bundle for every other. This does not seem to me to be obvious: in fact, I doubt it is even true—and not just because group differences may lead to other bad consequences, such as low trust or envy, which are bad for individuals. Some features of progress have to do with distributions not between individuals but between groups: groups matter.

So we cannot settle questions about progress by considering only the actual distribution of material goods among current individuals. Cultural value is emergent not aggregative. Human beings and their goods are incommensurable. History and groups matter. These are some of the reasons I think it is hard to figure out what progress is and therefore how individuals or corporations or political or economic institutions can advance it. And if it is hard to answer these questions about the nature of progress, how should we think about what these various social agents should aim to do?

One possibility for corporations would just be to impose certain legal obligations on them and permit them to maximize profit subject to those legal constraints. But given the difficulty of identifying what contributes to progress—and given that legal requirements backed by penalties must, as a matter of justice, be determinate enough that one can follow them—it isn't obvious that we can identify a set of legal obligations respect for which will contribute to progress. A better, more modest, and more practical strategy, I think, is to identify features of the economy that are generally bad for people and instruct corporations and individual economic agents to avoid them; and identify things that are generally good for people and urge them to advance those. I shall return to this strategy in a moment.

METHODOLOGICAL PRELIMINARIES 2:
CAPITALISM

If it is hard to define progress, it is not so easy to define capitalism. In all the important economies in the world today large sectors of industry, commerce, and the means of production are in private hands, so that the intellectual contest between defenses of private property and the older socialist ideal in which production and its means are largely held and managed by the state—i.e. by public officials—is largely over. The debates now are about what aspects of production and distribution should be owned by the state, and how the state should seek to regulate private ownership. And, as a result, many of the major economic decisions in the world today are taken by non-state actors, in particular, by individuals acting for large corporations, many—though not all—of which are technically owned by shareholders who can buy and sell their stock in public markets.

But it is worth insisting that many of the means of production are, in fact, held by states, even in the USA, which is the state most strongly associated with a commitment to global capitalism. The highways and railways and public lands, for example, are means of production, large sections of which are owned by states and the Federal government. The lands on which many farmers graze their cattle in the American West are publicly owned. So those rugged individualists the cattle ranchers depend on the Federal government for their means of production. The US Forest Service manages about one-twelfth of the land in the continental United States for the Federal government (US Forest Service 2008). The Crown Estates in England own more than 350,000 acres of agricultural land and forests, more than half the foreshore, and the seabed out to the twelve-nautical-mile-limit (Crown Estate 2014a, b, c); the Forestry Commission manages nearly 2 million acres more (Forestry Commission 2014). And that is far from being all the public land there is in England.

The state's involvement in the economy extends way beyond ownership of some of the means of production. There are, for example, many industries whose goods and markets are heavily regulated by the state. Public utilities and insurance companies in New York or California may only raise prices with the consent of insurance and utilities commissions. And it is not just prices but the actual services they offer that are legally constrained. Health and car and home insurance companies, for example, may not offer different policies to people of different races. And public accommodations—hotels, restaurants, and bars—must not deny entry to people in a long list of protected categories. Finally, the business of public corporations is highly regulated, too. Under certain circumstances, in many states, they must recognize trades unions. They must publish accounts and have public meetings of stockholders. If they are banks, they must meet all sorts of liquidity requirements. And they are required, like all legal persons, but often to a greater degree, not to damage the environment in certain specific ways. The private economy depends on all sorts of public activity.

The point is not new and nor is the practice: capitalism, however far back you trace its origins, depends on law and legal regulation, since the financial capital that allows the creation of enterprises is secured by enforceable legal agreements. Corporations, with their privileges and immunities, are created by law. And it seems obvious that, in the design of corporations, states reasonably consult some notion of the public good.

So, in case there is anyone left who is in doubt about this, let me insist that if the economic system of the United States or Great Britain is capitalist, then capitalism is an economic form that requires active state regulation and is compatible with extensive public ownership of land and other developed means of production. Without the vast apparatus of national commercial and administrative law, modern capitalism would be impossible.

This fact is especially important when we come to thinking about the behavior of modern multinational corporations: they may be big enough to be able to out-run the regulatory capacities of weaker states, and they may also use the political might of the states where they are domiciled to put pressure on states where they do business. Collaboration among states in the service of the general good is necessary if these MNCs are not to escape necessary forms of regulation. And here the fact that the general good is so hard to define is an obstacle to coming to agreement.

CAPITALISM AND PROGRESS: POVERTY AND INEQUALITY

Even under Soviet or Maoist state socialism, there were markets. People received wages and bought food and paid for housing and clothing, entertainment, books, records, and the like. But the former state socialist societies did not use markets with the same gusto as they now do to organize production and trade. In China the release of the energies of the market—along, no doubt, with many other changes in social organization—has taken hundreds of millions of people out of poverty and created, as we all know, a vast new middle class, whose production and consumption are shaping the global economy. At the same time, the effects of this new development are somewhat uneven, and the increase in the proportion of those who live well above subsistence has come along with an increase in measures of inequality. Until the late 1980s the Chinese Gini coefficient was under 30; now it is over 40. There has been a similar shift over the same period, as the Soviet Union became the Russia Federation (Alexeev and Gaddy 1993, OECD 2014a: 111).

It's important though that inequalities in income created by the market do not determine overall levels of economic inequality on their own. As John Cassidy pointed out in 2013 in his *New Yorker* blog, pre-tax inequality in the United States (with a Gini coefficient of 0.57) is the same as in the Netherlands, Denmark, and Sweden: it is differences in public policy that account for the effective differences in their overall levels of inequality. After taxes and transfers, US inequality is at 0.42, that in the three North

European countries is at 0.33 (Cassidy 2013). In 2010 in the OECD only Chile, Mexico, and Turkey were less equal than the United States, only Iceland, Slovenia, and Norway were more equal than Denmark (and the differences were marginal) (OECD 2014b).

So even if you think that high degrees of inequality are either intrinsically or consequentially bad, you can still think the extension of capitalist markets around the world has been a good thing for welfare, provided their inegalitarian consequences can be moderated by some combination of taxes on the rich and transfers to the poor. That they *can* be is demonstrated by the difference between the Scandinavian countries and the United States.

Social Norms

But why are more equalizing social policies in place in Denmark than in the United States? One obvious answer is that material inequality is less acceptable in Scandinavia: there is a normative difference between the cultures that shape the different political systems. Similar observations surely explain part of the growth in inequality over time in the United States: in 1965 the CEOs of the 350 highest-revenue public companies earned about twenty times the average person who worked for them; in 2011 the ratio was more than 200 to 1 (Mishel and Sabadish, 2012). A CEO who had demanded a salary that was 200 times that of a typical worker in 1965 would have been thought by his board and his shareholders to be simply crazy. It would also have been seen as greedy to ask for that much money: and greed of that sort would have lost you the respect of your peers. Clearly this is no longer the case. Some people criticize the emoluments of some business leaders; but there is no evidence that they or most others find something shameful in these compensation packages. Indeed, judging by their occasional public pronouncements, most of them think their rewards are just.

It's perhaps worth observing that, though these changes have happened under capitalism, they are not reflections of the increasing power of the owners of capital. Far from it. Many of the new super-rich are people who are gaining increased rates of return on their human capital: David Beckham, Angelina Jolie, and Lloyd Blankfein, each has extracted a large return from those who provide the capital that is needed to pursue their labor. As Malcolm Gladwell has pointed out, the massive salaries of movie and sports stars, like the massive emoluments of CEOs, are new in the American economy. "In the postwar years, corporate lawyers, Wall Street investment bankers, Fortune 500 executives, all-star professional athletes, and the like made a fraction of what they earn today." Then, in the 1970s, as he says,

> the world changed. Taxes began to fall. The salaries paid to high-level professionals—"talent"—started to rise. Baseball players became multimillionaires. C.E.O.s got private jets. The lawyers at Cravath, Swaine & Moore who once despaired of their economic future began saving money in substantial amounts, building country

homes and gardens for themselves like their fathers and grandfathers did, and planning extensive European holidays. In the nineteen-seventies, against all expectations, the salaryman rose from the dead. (Gladwell, 2010)

Interesting as this change is, it is worth asking whether or why it might be something to worry about. Modern liberal political theory, in the form developed by John Rawls, begins with the thought that differences in material goods need justifying: and Rawls thought, with many liberals, that what justified them was the necessity of incentive effects to produce greater wealth. Provided economic inequality benefitted the worst off, he thought, it was justifiable. It would, after all, be irrational for the poor to want to have less in order to reduce inequality. I start in a different place. My own view is that there is nothing wrong with material inequality as such. I am, in an unattractive formula, a "sufficientarian." It matters that everyone has enough for a decent life. It also matters—but this is a separate issue—that access to a greater share of goods is not denied people on the basis of race, gender, and other factors irrelevant to their capacity to do the job. What matters is equality of opportunity and the material basis for a decent life: material inequality, in se, is not a problem.

The consequences of material inequality fairly earned that do matter are extrinsic. They are of two kinds. Some are absolute: not having enough to eat, or a chance at meaningful work, or love and friendship, or what John Rawls called "the social bases of self-respect." None of these problems would be made more acceptable by reducing the quality of life of the rich, unless that reduction led to an absolute increase in what was available for the worst off. But some of the consequences of inequality are relative: there are many positional goods whose value to those who consume them is a function of the fact that others have less or none of them. These cannot be equally distributed. "Caviare for the general," in Hamlet's phrase, ceases to be a status good.

In the first instance what matters in the global patterns of distribution of goods today is that too many people do not have the absolute non-positional goods that are essential to a decent human life. Provided everybody had the baseline level of these goods, the level necessary for a chance at a decent human life, I don't, as I say, think it would matter normatively in itself that some had more goods, including positional goods, than others (provided, as I said, that they were fairly acquired). It might be better if everyone had more, but I don't think it's anybody's obligation to make that happen.

But it does matter that inequality of material goods can cause inequalities in other respects: for, unlike material goods, our access to the rights of citizenship and to political participation *are* things that we ought to have equally. And material inequalities, especially massive ones, even where they pose no problem in themselves because they are fairly arrived at, can lead to political inequalities that do matter.

Furthermore, if relatively high wealth comes to be regarded as a condition for having social respect, then something needs to be done to change the attitudes that make this true. And one thing that might help here is to have a society, like Sweden or Denmark or the Netherlands, that has less sharp gradients in wealth. So, if capitalism is going to produce large inequalities of income and wealth—and the evidence shows that it will—special care needs to be taken to keep track of the political and social effects of these inequalities. If the very rich want to remain very rich, it must be at the price of not being able to buy more than their fair share—their equal share—of political goods.

But there are also potential economic downsides to material inequalities. Whether or not you think the sorts of salaries earned by top CEOs are shameful—and, as with many matters of what is regarded as honorable or dishonorable, there are big cultural differences across space and time in attitudes on this question—there would be economic reasons to worry about the growing inequality if it had further bad economic effects: and there is a recent literature that argues that some kinds of inequality are more harmful to growth than others. Some inequalities in income derive from what you can call different returns to effort. But some inequality is the result of inequality of opportunity, which is roughly, as a World Bank blog puts it, "the share of overall inequality that is explained by pre-determined circumstances—things like race, gender, family background, place of birth, etc." (Ferreira 2012); and Gustavo Marrero and Juan Rodríguez have argued using comparative data from different American states that there is "robust support for a negative relationship between inequality of opportunity and growth, and a positive relationship between inequality of returns to effort and growth" (Marrero and Rodríguez 2010). This combines with the fact—which I mentioned in discussing political inequality a little while ago—that equality of opportunity seems to be intrinsically a good thing, to give us very strong reasons to seek to secure it. And there is debate among economists at the moment about whether the advantages that the very rich can secure for their children—in a world where there are significant differences between the average quality of public and private education, for example—mean that we have less equality of opportunity in the United States than in the past. The historical question is interesting but not, I think, all that important: for there is surely no doubt that there are now mechanisms in place in the United States educational system (as in that of Britain) that are meant to allow rich parents—and a few talented beneficiaries of private largesse—to secure for their children a huge advantage in the competition for material rewards; and it is not, on any reasonable construction, an advantage that that those children have earned. About this form of inequality, which generates inequality of opportunity—it seems evident that something needs to be done.

INSTITUTIONAL RESPONSIBILITIES

Capitalism has created great amounts of wealth and many people—far beyond the famous 1 percent—have benefitted from it. Hundreds of millions of the new middle classes in China have benefitted from the globalization of their country's trade and the opening of internal markets. In India new technologies managed by private corporations have created new layers of wealth. One can add Brazil and Indonesia and Russia—the list is long. Capital has funded innovation and created goods that were unimagined a generation ago. And the Gini coefficients of the countries that have created the new global middle class—from Norway to China to Brazil—are quite various. Nevertheless, despite the occasional setbacks like the Great Recession of 2008, it is hard to see why one should regret this development.

On the other hand, it has been achieved at the cost of increases in inequality in many places over the last two decades, with great costs to the environment that will create challenges for the welfare of future generations, and with unsustainable levels of consumption. We are living as if we had a bigger planet than we actually have. And at some point there will be too many of us. We have known for a long time that capitalism needs careful mechanisms to manage the negative externalities of many forms of production and of consumption. You cannot allow producers to impose costs on the health of their neighbors—in the form of pollution—unless you create mechanisms by which those costs can be paid. Markets can be a useful mechanism here, too, of course, as can criminal and civil and administrative law. But like intellectual property, rights to pollute are a form of property that depends very heavily on institutions that are likely to have to be managed by the state and will, in any case, have to be the creatures of carefully crafted legal regimes. They will be, like patents and copyrights, the product of extensive public–private collaboration. And there will be the consequent risks of private capture of the public regulators, and private corruption (which is associated with practices like lobbying in Washington) of the political processes that set their terms.

If we give credit to capitalists and to the great corporations that are the major international actors in the global economy for the new levels of wealth—for the fact that we have taken so many out of extreme poverty in the last few decades—what responsibilities should we give them for the less attractive consequences of the new global economic regime?

It is here that I want to return to the proposal I mentioned earlier: that we should identify features of the economy that are generally bad for people and motivate corporations and individual economic agents to avoid them; and identify things that are generally good for people and urge them to advance those. And here I want to identify the three major mechanisms by which this can be done and exemplify the forms of incentive and disincentive that they can generate. Others may have more substantive ideas about the aims at which these mechanisms should be directed: I want to draw attention to the full range of the available mechanisms.

LAW, MONEY, HONOR

Corporations are rightly governed by reasonable environmental laws. The penalties for breaches of these laws should obviously be set in such a way that individual companies cannot compete by imposing unreasonable negative externalities on others, and industries produce collectively a manageable amount of pollution. To achieve that you may have to combine fines for corporations with criminal penalties for their officers; but you will also need active policing. Corporations are probably more likely than private individuals to do the accounting of the likely costs of their breaches of law; but the expected cost of a breach is a function both of the size of the penalty and of the probability of being caught. With no inspections, many forms of pollution may go undetected for a very long time. And the interests of the officers and the corporation are not aligned here: the officers will want to maximize returns on their watch and it will be rational for them to ignore costs that will have to be paid after they have departed, while the corporation will want to take time-discounted future costs into account. That is one reason why criminal penalties for some breaches might seem to be a good idea: they mean that you cannot escape the consequences of bad behavior by changing your job.

A second form of shaping of the behavior of corporations is going to be not through legal penalties, whether financial or criminal, but through economic incentives. Tax regimes can allow corporations to take risks that would be irrational if their costs and rewards were not shifted. Governments, for example, can make some lines of research worth investing in by promising to buy certain quantities of goods—like malaria vaccines or missiles—that meet certain specifications once they exist. Reducing taxes on profits in zones of high employment can make it rational for companies to create jobs in places where they are needed. While the structure of the US tax code is too much the result of lobbying by corporations for perks they do not need, there is nothing intrinsically troubling about practices like these.

These points are obvious: the role of legal regulation, civil and criminal penalties, and tax and other incentives in shaping the behavior of corporations is well under-stood, as are the risks that the legal framework will be corrupted, whether in the legislative or in the judicial or in the executive branches of the government. There is also a widespread appreciation that some forms of legal regulation are necessary because of informational asymmetries and other problems that undermine the effective working of markets. But I want to end by saying a little more about a third force shaping the behavior of corporations and their officers, one that is less commonly appreciated and understood, and that is what Philip Pettit and Geoffrey Brennan have dubbed the "economy of esteem" (Brennan and Pettit 2005).

HONOR WORLDS

The workings of esteem—and more generally of honor and shame—as modes of social regulation are not as widely appreciated as the role of the law and the economy. Honor has many subtleties, which I won't be able to explore here. But the basic workings of honor can be summarized quickly.

First of all, honor gives someone an entitlement to respect. But you can lose that right, if you breach the codes that govern it. And losing honor leads, in those who care about their honor, to shame. Shame is the feeling appropriate to your own dishonorable behavior; the appropriate response from others is, first, to cease to respect you and, then, actively to treat you with disrespect. Second: your honor is always your honor as a person of some social identity. Identity actually matters to honor in two quite distinct ways. First, you may share in the honor of those whose identity you share. We may both gain and lose honor in part because of the successes and failures of those with whom we share an identity. But identity matters in a second way because it determines what the codes of honor require of you.

To be respected is, of course, to be respected by somebody. Usually, honor does not seek the respect of people in general; it requires the respect of some particular social group, what I shall call an *honor world*, a group of people who acknowledge the same codes. In an honor world some people are defined as your *honor peers*, because the codes make the same demands of you as of them.

But finally, while it is crucial to recognize that honor is an entitlement to respect, a person of honor cares not (or, at least, not only) about being respected, but about being *worthy* of respect. For the honorable person, honor itself is the thing that matters, not honor's rewards. It is something you care about for its own sake. You want respect, but only the respect you are entitled to. A final schema, then: an honorable person wants to do what is worthy of respect according to the honor code, but doesn't conform to the code of honor simply in order to get respect from the honor world (and the consequent social rewards).

Now here's my main point: honor can be especially useful in shaping the behavior of people in specific social roles, such as the officers of corporations. When it comes to sustaining and disciplining such social roles, a particular kind of respect—peer esteem for those who achieve excellence—plays a critical role. It helps maintain demanding norms of behavior. As Geoffrey Brennan and Philip Pettit have pointed out, esteem, as a way of shaping our behavior, is, in effect, policed by everybody in the honor world. The reason is simple: people in an honor world automatically regard those who meet its codes with respect and those who breach them with contempt. Because these responses are automatic, the system is, in effect, extremely cheap to maintain. It only requires us to respond in ways we are naturally inclined to respond anyway.

Suppose, instead, you wanted to achieve the same effects through the formal mechanism of the law. Then you'd have to give new police and sentencing powers to particular people, which would produce new worries. You'd face the old Latin question: *Quis custodiet ipsos custodes?* Who will guard the guards? One attractive feature of the economy of esteem is that all of us are its guards. No individual has the focused power to apply the incentives of esteem that a police officer has when she arrests you, or a judge does in deciding a sentence (Brennan and Pettit, 2005: 260).

Consider the code of military honor. It calls on people as soldiers (or as marines, or officers, . . . there is a variety of relevant identities) and, of course, we now know, as Americans or Englishmen or Pakistanis; and while soldiers may feel shame or pride when their regiment or their platoon does badly or well, fundamentally it matters to them that they themselves should follow the military's codes of honor.

It is worth asking why it is that honor is needed here. We could, after all, use the law all by itself to guide our armies; military discipline makes easy use of all sorts of punishments. And mercenaries can be motivated by money. So, why aren't these ordinary forms of social regulation—the market and the law—enough to manage an army, as they are enough to manage, say, such other state functions as the maintenance of the highways?

Well, first of all, both these other forms of regulation require surveillance. If we are to be able to pay you your bonus or punish you for your offenses, someone has to be able to find out what you have done. But when the battle is hardest, the fog of war obscures everything. If the aim of a soldier were just to get his bonus or escape the brig, he would have no incentive to behave well at the very moment when we most require it. Of course, we could devote large amounts of expensive effort to this sort of surveillance— we could equip each soldier with a device that monitored his every act—but that would have psychological and moral costs as well as significant financial ones. By contrast, honor, which is grounded in the individual soldier's own sense of honor (and that of his or her peers), can be effective without extensive surveillance; and, unlike a system of law or a market contract, anyone who is around and belongs to the honor world will be an effective enforcer of it, so that the cost of enforcement of honor is actually quite low, and we won't have to worry about guarding its guardians.

There's another reason for favoring honor over law as a mechanism for motivating soldiers. The sorts of sacrifice that are most useful in warfare need people to take risks that require them to do things that are, in the jargon, supererogatory: they are acts that are morally desirable but which ask too much of us to be morally required. To punish someone for failing to do something that they have no duty to do is morally wrong. Since it is normally permissible, however, to offer a financial reward for doing what is supererogatory, that might lead you to think that the right way to regulate military behavior, if you could solve the problem of the fog of war, would be by financial incentives.

Once we have a set of shared codes about military honor, though, we also have commitments that make us think of money as the wrong idiom for rewarding military prowess: it is symbolically inappropriate. We don't give soldiers bonuses for bravery, we give them medals; and, more important, we honor them. We give them the respect we know they deserve. I have been arguing that we live not after honor but with new forms of honor. Still, our modern standing armies have kept in place a world of military honor many of whose loyalties and sentiments I suspect Wellington would have recognized; as would, indeed, Homer's Achilles or Shakespeare's Duke of Bourbon, who—realizing at Agincourt that the day is lost—cries out: "Shame and eternal shame, nothing but shame, / Let's die in honor!" (*Henry V*, Act IV, Sc. 5). Soldiers who think like that make formidable opponents.

These reflections on why honor is such an effective and powerful way of motivating soldiers suggest that there may be analogous arguments to be made for other professions. Bankers and corporate officers, for example, all do many things where it is very hard or expensive for outsiders to keep an eye on how conscientious they are being. We have every reason to hope that they will do more than can be required of them by their contracts of employment. And, as we saw in the crises in the American economy in the first decade of this millennium, the behavior of individual bankers seeking to make profits can, in the aggregate, impose large costs on all of us.

And the key point here is that a sense of honor—and the correlative need to avoid shame—when it works, does a better job than regulation and the threat of sanctions on its own, or the market and the promise of profit alone, in shaping the behavior of business people to reduce these costs. We need regulation; and the market incentivizes many useful things and disincentivizes many things we would rather not see. But if the makers of markets don't care about whether they are worthy of respect, we can be pretty confident that they will find ways, some of them dishonest, around regulation. You can't make a perfect regulatory system and you can't implement one perfectly. And the major disincentives to dishonesty are two: that, once you're caught at it, you will cease to have the trust essential to do business; and that you cannot live with the sense of yourself as *that* kind of person. And, as I say, that means that, in a business culture of honorable men and women, the costs of this system of regulation of behavior are pretty low.

I'm not an economist or a psychologist, and to understand how we should shape professional norms requires the sorts of reflection on the design of institutions that economists have made their professional study and the sort of knowledge of social psychology that also goes into that design. But it is a noticeable fact of recent history that in many professional domains the consolations of money have, to some extent, shouldered aside those of esteem. Sometimes the two currencies have reached an unappealing compact. The surgeon Atul Gawande has argued, in reviewing the evidence about the rising costs of health care in the United States, that there are medical communities in which the values of entrepreneurship—hard work and innovation in the service of expanding profits—have overtaken the traditional guild values of the Hippocratic Oath. When this happens, esteem grows aligned with money, to the detriment, as he argues, of health (Gawande 2009). So in the business of health care a purely market psychology is less effective than one that combines markets with structures of professional honor in producing progress. As I argue in *The Honor Code*, honor is a hugely important social resource (Appiah, 2011).

Envoi

Not long ago I was at a dinner with the CEO of a well-known German company based in Hamburg. He discovered I was an academic and we started talking about the Hamburg School of Business Administration, with which he was associated. The School, it turns out, has a degree that it calls the MA in "Business Administration and Honorable Leadership," a program sponsored by the Versammlung Eines Ehrbaren Kaufmanns zu Hamburg (the Hamburg Association of Honorable Merchants), whose history goes back to the early sixteenth century. Its members are committed, as you can learn from their website, both to operating honorably themselves and to "maintaining the conditions for honorable dealing in their enterprises" (VEEK 2014).[1] They think that capitalism will contribute the most to human progress, however we define it, if it is run by honorable men and women who seek to lead those who work for them to behave honorably too. I think they are right.

References

Alexeev, M., and Gaddy, C. (1993). Income Distribution in the USSR in the 1980s *Review of Income and Wealth*, 39(1): 23–36.

Appiah, K. (2011). *The Honor Code*. New York: W. W. Norton.

Brennan, G., and P. Pettit (2005). *The Economy of Esteem*. New York: Oxford University Press.

Cassidy, J. (2013). American Inequality in Six Charts. *The New Yorker*, Nov. <www.newyorker.com/online/blogs/johncassidy/2013/11/inequality-and-growth-what-do-we-know.html> [Accessed Apr. 2014].

Crown Estate (2014a). *Agriculture*. <www.thecrownestate.co.uk/rural/agriculture> [Accessed Apr. 2014].

Crown Estate (2014b). *Forestry*. <www.thecrownestate.co.uk/rural/forestry> [Accessed Apr. 2014].

Crown Estate (2014c). *Coastal*. <www.thecrownestate.co.uk/coastal> [Accessed Apr. 2014].

Dworkin, R. (2000). *Sovereign Virtue: The Theory and Practice of Equality*. Cambridge, MA: Harvard University Press.

Ferreira, F. (2012). Rising Inequality in the United States: Lessons from Developing Countries. Development Impact, World Bank blog, Jan. 25. <http://blogs.worldbank.org//impactevaluations/rising-inequality-in-the-united-states-lessons-from-developing-countries> [Accessed Apr. 2014].

Forestry Commission (2014). Britain's Forest Area Hits Almost 3m Hectares. <www.forestry.gov.uk/newsrele.nsf/WebNewsReleases/7C3602A5E6059A6480257C890060DA7D> [Accessed Apr. 2014].

Gawande, A. (2009). The Cost Conundrum: What a Texas Town Can Teach us about Health Care. *The New Yorker*, June 1. <www.newyorker.com/reporting/2009/06/01/090601fa_fact_gawande> [Accessed Apr. 2014].

Gladwell, M. (2010). Talent Grab. *The New Yorker*. Oct. 11. <http://gladwell.com/talent-grab> [Accessed Apr. 2014].

Huddleston, A. (2012). Nietzsche on the Decadence and Flourishing of Culture. Ph.D. thesis, Princeton University.

Marrero, G., and J. Rodríguez (2010). Inequality of Opportunity and Growth. *ECINEQ, Society for the Study of Economic Inequality*, 2010–154, Feb. <www.ecineq.org/milano/WP/ECINEQ2010-154.pdf> [Accessed Apr. 2014].

---

[1] "Wir sind ein Zusammenschluss von Hamburger Kaufleuten, die sich den Werten des Ehrbaren Kaufmanns verpflichtet fühlen und in ihren Unternehmen die Bedingungen für ehrbares Handeln pflegen."

Mishel, L., and N. Sabadish (2012). CEO Pay and the Top 1%: How Executive Compensation and Financial-Sector Pay have Fueled Income Inequality. Economic Policy Institute, May 2. <www.epi.org/publication/ib331-ceo-pay-top-1-percent> [Accessed Apr. 2014].

Nozick, R. (1974). *Anarchy, State and Utopia*. New York: Basic Books.

OECD (2014a). *OECD Social Indicators: Society at a Glance 2014*. <http://dx.doi.org/10.1787/soc_glance-2014-en> [Accessed Apr. 2014].

OECD (2014b). *United States: Tackling High Inequalities, Creating Opportunities for All*. <www.oecd.org/unitedstates/Tackling-high-inequalities.pdf> [Accessed Apr. 2014].

US Forest Service (2008). Table 4: Areas by State. <www.fs.fed.us/land/staff/lar/2007/TABLE_4.htm> [Accessed Apr. 2014].

VEEK (Versammlung Eines Ehrbaren Kaufmanns zu Hamburg). (2014). Herzlich Willkommen bei der Versammlung Eines Ehrbaren Kaufmanns zu Hamburg e.V. <www.veek-hamburg.de> [Accessed Apr. 2014].

CHAPTER 7

....

ON PROGRESS

....

PHILIP KITCHER

Abstract

This chapter offers a general approach to the concept of progress, illustrating it by two examples. The first focuses on the least controversial instance of progress, in the domain of the natural sciences. The second considers the notion of ethical progress, a notion viewed as fundamental to the understanding of social progress. At the heart of my approach is a distinction between the ambitious idea of teleological progress, and a more modest concept of pragmatic progress. The last two sections turn to the concept of social progress, identifying the spread of capacities for an autonomously chosen valuable life as the key. Standard economic measures of progress are often poor guides to social progress in my sense, and there are serious questions about whether contemporary socio-economic institutions are antipathetic to social progress.

INTRODUCTION

....

Confident claims about human progress meet two kinds of skepticism. The more straightforward of these challenges the measures used in making judgments about progress. So, for example, when those judgments rest on data about increasing productivity (either within a nation or worldwide) or about a consistent rise in wages, critics deny that the cited figures correspond to the determinants of *real* progress. This first form of skepticism thus accepts the concept of human progress, but charges that the economic measures supposed to signal progress fail to do so. A more radical response is to question the coherence of the target concept.

Talk of human progress can be criticized on a number of grounds. It can be interpreted as committed to a form of perfectionism that has been exposed, since the days of Enlightenment optimism, as a utopian fantasy. Alternatively, it may be understood as necessarily embedded in some theory of history as goal-directed, in which progress consists in proximity to some alleged end, the realization of Spirit or the withering away of the state (for example). Or it may simply and prosaically be viewed as a quixotic attempt to find some common measure for a wide variety of valuable properties that turn out to be incommensurable.

In my judgment, we shall not make much progress with progress unless we address both types of skepticism. An adequate response to the first—our main concern—requires recognizing differences in concepts of progress that are best identified by considering the second challenge. So my strategy in the following sections will be indirect. I shall start by using familiar worries about the coherence of the notion of progress to bring out some complexities of the concept (in a past idiom, I'll be concerned with the "logic of progress talk"). I'll then use the least controversial application of the concept—namely in discussions of the natural sciences—to provide a model for understanding progress. That model will be extended into the domain of everyday human affairs by articulating an account of ethical progress. With these two examples at our disposal, I'll take up the possibility of a general concept of human progress and of better measures than those adduced in the economic discussions that prompt the first sort of skepticism.

PRELIMINARIES

To make a judgment of progress is to consider two temporally distinct states of some system and to claim that the later is superior to the earlier. The judgment is quantitative when the states are assigned numerical representations of their value and superiority is taken to consist in having a representation with a greater number. In principle, we can make such judgments about many types of system—the theory of the chemical bond, the Catholic Church, the workforce of a nation. Even when the judgments are not quantitative they typically depend on other mathematical concepts: we might recognize a child's progress in a given domain by seeing that she can now do all the things she used to be able to do and more besides (the old set of her accomplishments is a proper subset of the current one).

I'll say that a notion of progress is *global* just in case it admits of comparison between any two states of the system. Casual use of "progress" often assumes globality, and this sometimes gives rise to debates about the application of the concept. So, for example, biologists often deny that Darwinian evolution is progressive (Gould 1989); others take improved adaptation as a mark of progress (Nitecki 1988); the dispute can be dissolved by recognizing the possibility of making comparisons between temporally proximal states of a lineage but not of all states—thus allowing for the judgment of progress among the *Equidae*, but not for rating the progress of mammals with respect to ants or archebacteria. A notion of progress is *local* just in case it licenses comparisons of some pairs of temporally adjacent states.[1] The notion is *locally complete* just in case it permits comparison of *any* two temporally adjacent states.

---

[1] I'm assuming that the time period under consideration is divided into a discrete set of states, so that it makes sense to identify a successor relation among the states.

Does local completeness entail globality? I'm inclined to think not. Consider the evolutionary example. If you think of populations of organisms as situated in fitness landscapes, it's easy to identify evolutionary progress: it consists in marching uphill to states of higher average fitness. For widely separated populations, however, even if one is a direct descendant of the other, the environmental changes correspond to location in very different regions of the landscape—the populations are no longer on the same hill. This case brings home the fact that, over time, the measures underlying a quantitative concept of progress may gradually shift, and that, in consequence, the relation of local progressiveness isn't transitive. Without transitivity, the inference from local completeness to globality doesn't go through. This point is important in understanding the example of human progress.

Another useful division is between *teleological* and *pragmatic* concepts of progress. A notion counts as teleological just in case it assesses the relation between states by considering their distance from some goal state: in traveling, we make progress by decreasing the distance to the destination. Yet there are other, non-teleological, notions of progress, prominent in such areas as technology and medicine. Here, we make progress—pragmatic progress—by overcoming problems. Transportation technology progresses by solving the problems that prevent people from moving—quickly, safely, and comfortably—from place to place; medicine progresses by finding ways of curing, treating, or palliating the diseases that afflict us. In neither case is there any ideal final state, the perfect system of transportation or the Platonic ideal of human health.

You might wonder if the pragmatic idea of progress as problem-solving collapses into a teleological concept, in that the identification of a situation as problematic already presupposes a goal, to wit the goal of finding a solution. Now that generic "goal" might cover any number of incompatible alternatives, many of which could not be ranked with respect to one another. Further, as in the evolutionary case, the solution is local. Once it has been achieved, people attempting to improve the system move on to address new difficulties, some of them perhaps generated by the solution itself. The goal is not some final state against which all successive stages are to be measured. Insofar as there are general considerations that count in assessing progress, ideals of successful transportation or of health, they serve as tools for diagnosing current problems and assessing rival solution. In Dewey's terminology (1925), they are "ends-in-view," susceptible to reshaping in the context of the solutions achieved, and thus allowing for the shift in the variables measured that undermines the transitivity of local comparisons.

In considering human life and human society, teleological notions of progress are, quite reasonably, out of fashion—we find it hard to believe in any of the "grand narratives" of the philosophical historians of the past. Yet the rejection of teleological accounts of human progress doesn't cancel all possibilities of discussing improvement in human life and human society. The pragmatic notion of progress, recognizable in connection with technology and medicine, yields promising ways of approaching such discussions. If we look for a notion of human progress it should be pragmatic and local, probably locally complete (at least for significant temporal periods), but not necessarily global.

Natural Science

If there is any domain in which the concept of progress seems at home, it is that of the natural sciences. It seems hard to deny that genetics has made spectacular progress since 1900. Progress in science is often contrasted with the allegedly more haphazard development of the arts: the molecular genetics of 2014 is superior to that practiced at the time of the rediscovery of Mendel's ideas (1900) in a way that the painting of 2014 isn't better than the painting of the turn of the twentieth century. Interestingly, there's a subtle bias in the way the comparison is made: in identifying the state of genetics in 2014, we tacitly include all the achievements of the previous 113 years, while in the artistic comparison we look at the paintings produced in two different calendar years (1900 and 2014). If we thought explicitly of the "science available" at a time, and, similarly, focused on the "art available," we'd see *both* domains as accumulating a collection of resources—for investigators, people curious about nature, policy-makers, and viewers—and it would be arguable that in *both* instances the accumulation affords richer opportunities to those who come later. This point will be important as we proceed.

The simplest model of scientific progress is teleological: there's a complete truth about nature, and progress consists in grasping more of it. With respect to natural science as a whole, we can envisage *Nature's Book*, the final and complete text, and suppose that natural science makes progress through achieving partial texts that contain more and more of the sentences in the book and less and less sentences that do not belong to it. Individual sciences, like genetics, are associated with chapters of the book, and the same pattern holds with respect to them.

This teleological conception has been in trouble for over fifty years, since Thomas Kuhn published a landmark monograph (Kuhn 1962). Kuhn's explorations of the history of the sciences, particularly of those moments at which large change occur, undermined any idea of simple accumulation. Kuhn argued that scientific revolutions change the vocabulary of the sciences and that they discard both apparently successful problem solutions and the questions those answers addressed. His conclusions about particular instances of conceptual change and loss of previously valued achievements led him to question the applicability of any notion of truth in terms of correspondence to nature, effectively undermining the thought of privileged sentences belonging to nature's book. In the final chapter of his monograph, moved by the conviction he found hard to displace that there is *some* sense in which the sciences make progress, he gestured towards an analogy with evolutionary biology and a pragmatic conception of progress (incompletely developed).

In response to Kuhn's concerns, many philosophers—moved by the concern to rehabilitate the notion of scientific progress—attempted to substitute a better teleological conception.[2] So, for example, in my (1993), I proposed that there were many

---

[2] Although not all responses were along teleological lines. In his (1977) and (1984), Larry Laudan began to develop a pragmatic conception of scientific progress. Although I believe that many of the

dimensions of scientific progress, including conceptual progress (refashioning language so that it fits better with the divisions intrinsic to nature), explanatory progress (identifying the objective dependencies in nature), finding significant questions (those that arise from the explanatory schemata that mirror the objective dependencies), and accumulating true answers to significant questions. Part of this account still seems to me to be correct, in its emphasis on multiple dimensions of scientific progress (with the resultant possibility that a transition in some area of inquiry might be progressive along some dimensions and not along others) and in its commitment to a (modest) notion of truth as correspondence.[3] It is, however, wrongheaded in its confidence about divisions and dependencies in nature, which yield some language that is "nature's own," mistaken too in supposing some complete system of truths about the cosmos, the entirely fictional "Book of Nature." Like some prominent scientists, philosophers dream far too easily of a "final theory."

Contemporary science is a patchwork of areas that address many different questions, and that do not fit easily together (Cartwright 1999; Dupre 1993; Kitcher 2001). For any region of space-time, there are at least continuum-many facts about that region and continuum-many languages in which those facts could be represented. Even if the notion of a "complete description" of the universe is coherent (which seems highly dubious), there's no possibility—even in principle—that human beings could ever arrive at it. Champions of a "final theory" do not, of course, think that scientific investigation should provide some haphazard list of "all the truths" about nature. Inspired by the economies of axiomatization, they imagine some manageable set of fundamental principles from which, with the help of some (infinite) set of initial and boundary conditions, the whole truth could be derived. Not only is the required set of conditions both too vast for human comprehension, but the axiomatic project presupposes a commitment to reductionism that is dramatically violated in contemporary scientific practice. We cannot, even in principle, derive the guiding (approximative) generalizations of genetics from biochemistry, and nor would our explanatory purposes be served by our doing so (Kitcher 1984); in this instance, the troubles are apparent, for the sciences supposed to stand in the reduction relation are both well-developed—but we can expect similar difficulties to pervade other areas. Furthermore, the central conception of highly general laws—fundamental principles—rests on an unwarranted extrapolation from much more limited exercises in model-building (Cartwright 1999). It's not just that we don't *have* a "final theory," but that the contemporary sciences expose systematic obstacles to our *ever having* one.

What research communities settle for in practice is a piecemeal attempt to answer questions that matter to us, producing conclusions that are "true enough" (Elgin 2004)

criticisms leveled in my (1993) against Laudan's approach retain their force, I now think that I underappreciated his guiding conception. The account of progress articulated here, originally introduced in my (2001) and extended in subsequent writings (e.g. 2012), embodies ideas Laudan had grasped much earlier (and which I regret having not appreciated earlier).

[3] For defense of correspondence truth, see Kitcher 2012: chs 3–5.

for our purposes. "Settling" is, however, too uncomplimentary—work of this sort is as valuable as human activities get. Scientific progress is relativized to a notion of significance: the sciences advance by providing solutions to significant problems, some of them demanding devices for intervention in nature, others requiring predictions of future events or explanatory accounts. The criteria of significance are ours, not "nature's own," and they evolve with the changing conditions of human life. To make a judgment about the significance of a problem is to adopt a stance about what matters to a group of people, living at some particular place and time.

Let me note immediately the possibility of differentiating the judgments of significance that are actually made from those that ought to be made. Practices of commending particular projects or particular problems are subject to critical judgment. Are they worthy of our attention? Or do they stem from a myopic or parochial perspective? I'll take up this possibility of a normative notion of significance shortly, but, before I do so, it's important to recognize that, once progress is relativized to significance and significance grounded in the broader framework of human life, the standard ways of talking about scientific progress, by adverting to what is "on the books" involve an obvious abstraction. Simply to compare the accumulation of what the experts know at different times is to ignore the connection of their knowledge to the convictions of a public whose needs and aspirations ultimately underlie the singling out of the bits and pieces of expert knowledge as significant. When the sciences are seen as socially embedded, their progress consists not only in the fact that some small subgroup comes to acquire solutions to the problems that a larger population would count as significant, but that these solutions are distributed to the people who need them. A field of science might make progress in the abstract by accumulating answers to socially important questions, but the answers might never reach the vast majority of those who would potentially benefit from them. There might even be circumstances under which the ability of the expert community to identify such answers initiated social processes that interfered with their translation into public policy—imagine that the answers are unpopular with powerful figures in society, who then take steps to ensure that media discussion of them is so confusing that most people do not believe them, thereby undermining the credibility of the experts and preventing measures that would alleviate or forestall serious threats to the interests of the vast majority. Perhaps this exercise does not even require much imagination.

The simplest questions about scientific progress ask whether later practices within a scientific field provide additional solutions to significant problems, where the concept of significance is generated by the projects some people actually have. A more socially oriented judgment of scientific progress proceeds by recognizing that the additional solutions are translated into activities that actually advance the projects in question. Adding an ethical dimension, a richer conception of scientific progress would focus on whether the problems solved are the ones that ought to have been addressed under those particular circumstances, and whether the achievement of the solutions makes those solutions available in an ethically justifiable distribution. The oft-drawn contrast between science and art furnishes a useful analogy: we might ask if the art of the world is accumulating new paintings that will appeal to actual aesthetic sensibilities; whether, if so, the paintings are available to those who would gain from seeing them; and whether the paintings are genuinely valuable and open to public appreciation in ways that are fair.

It's now possible to understand why scientific progress has seemed so obvious, and why, nonetheless, there are critical voices that challenge the idea. In the simplest sense, scientific progress is evident in many domains, as researchers answer questions that they identify as significant and that, given sufficient instruction and explanation, many people would agree to be worth posing. Yet there are sometimes reasons to worry that actual judgments of significance are parochial (as in the focus of biomedicine on minor ailments of affluent people, while infectious diseases that afflict millions of the world's poor receive only slight attention) and that the distribution of benefits is skewed or even blocked (as in the translation of findings about climate change and about potential energy sources). A deeper criticism would charge that the embedding of science within other institutions distorts the formation of personal projects, so that people routinely come to draw from a limited menu of options and never identify the forms of human life that, under different circumstances, they would recognize as far richer and more valuable for them. Even if the practice of science absorbs a notion of significance that is not parochial, that notion inherits a truncated version of what human lives can be. To see matters in this way is not necessarily to endorse the charges raised against the "evils of technoscience," but it is to recognize that those charges are intelligible and cannot be dismissed out of hand.

The moral of the story so far is that, even in what seems to be the clearest instance, the concept of progress is complex and has social and ethical dimensions.

ETHICAL PROGRESS

My discussion of scientific progress presupposes the possibility of assessing science from a normative perspective. Some human projects are worthwhile and, consequently, the questions they generate are not only actually judged as significant but really so; some distributions of scientifically achieved benefits are fair, and not merely accepted as just. That presupposition often alarms people, inspiring them to ask "But who has the right to make these judgments?" Their suspicions are not allayed when ethicists write of a "moral point of view" and of "objective values" supposedly accessible through "intuitions" about contrived cases.[4] In many philosophical discussions, objective normative assessment is assumed to be grounded in a prior realm of ethical truth. Ethical inquiry progresses as investigators identify more and more parts of this realm. So, by

---

[4] Contemporary moral philosophy contains a large number of discussions that take for granted the type of position I briefly characterize here. For an especially forthright (and admirably open) presentation, see Parfit 2011.

analogy with the book of nature, there is a book of values, and we make progress by recognizing and accepting more and more of its sentences.

In my judgment, the "dream of a final theory" is even less plausible in the case of ethics than in the instance of natural science. Like Dewey, I view ethics as a human venture, one that is never completed and that has no final goal. We can, I propose, make sense of ethical progress, but the type of progress at stake here is not teleological but pragmatic. It is progress *from*, not progress *to*.[5] The concept of ethical progress supports a perspective from which the significance of problems and the fairness of distributions can be assessed, and supplies an answer to the worry about who is capable of rendering those types of judgment.

Fully to defend this position would require far more space than I have, and I shall settle for a compressed version of an account I develop elsewhere (Kitcher 2011). There is no prior ethical reality that human beings attempt to fathom. Rather, ethics is an invention. For all that, it is not made up *arbitrarily* nor is it the creation of a *single individual*. The ethical project is a collective enterprise, sparked initially by a prevalent feature of our condition as a particular type of evolved social primate. Like many other primate species (including the two species—chimpanzees and bonobos—most closely related to us), we have evolved to be social, with adaptations that incline us not only to *want* to live among others, but to *need* to do so (Churchland 2011; Tomasello 2009). The special sorts of societies in which our hominin ancestors evolved to live, with a range of ages of both sexes, required an ability to identify and to respond to the desires and plans of others, exemplified in sporadic acts of cooperation. Yet the capacity is limited and the cooperation consequently only sporadic. Our evolutionary history equipped us to live together, but not to live together easily or stably.

In terms of their size and their range of cooperative ventures, the societies in which people have lived, today and in the recorded past, are an extraordinary achievement. That achievement rests on a historical process through which people have come to supplement their limited capacities for mutual responsiveness with something quite novel—a collectively planned patterning of their social interactions that would reduce the frequency with which group members would fail to take into account the wishes of those around them, thereby increasing the chances of cooperation and decreasing the number of occasions on which the group threatened to fall into violent conflict. Like our close evolutionary relatives (de Waal 2013) our hominin ancestors had some ability to inhibit their behavior in response to a perception of likely outcomes. That ability has been combined with a social practice of singling out some patterns of conduct as to be avoided, others as required. In the fashion of those contemporary people whose lives most resemble those of our ancestors—the surviving hunter-gatherers—the shape of ethical life was fashioned in group discussions in which all mature members participated on roughly equal terms (Boehm 1999, 2012).

---

[5] Here I see myself as in agreement with Amartya Sen (2009). But perhaps he would disavow the kinship.

The origins of the ethical project were almost certainly crude and simple: rules to enjoin sharing and to forbid initiating violence; compliance was promoted by the threat of punishment. Yet, between these primitive beginnings, at least 50,000 years before the present, and the ethical life recorded in the first written documents, many important things happened. Other emotions besides fear were recruited to support conformity to the agreed-on rules. The framework of rules itself was vastly extended, to encompass many areas of human life, to articulate roles and institutions, and even to apply it to outsiders, at least in some contexts. These developments are visible in the emergence of art, of burial customs, of trade with neighbors, of occasions on which groups coalesce for short periods, of increasing group size in the late Paleolithic, of the domestication of plants and animals and the construction of large permanent settlements (the first cities with more than a thousand inhabitants are at least 8,000 years old). Stable patterns of cooperation extended the repertoire of human desires and emotions, providing a conceptualization of human life and its possibilities that emerges in early written documents. All this, I suggest, is a matter of gradual evolution, as our ancestors struggled to resolve the fundamental problem posed by our limited responsiveness to those among whom we must live, and tackled the derivative problems generated by partial solutions to it. In the course of that evolution, some features of the earliest stages of the ethical project were lost. Collective decision-making about how to live together was displaced by reliance on experts, and the emphasis on equality gave way to a structured hierarchy of roles.

The short answer to those who worry about "who judges" is that we all did once—and that we all should now. Ethics is a social invention, prompted by the difficulties of living together, and the straightforward solution to the root problem, the problem of limited responsiveness, is to do just what our ancestors did: bring all the affected parties together in the "cool hour," sort out the facts of the situation, and proceed to a conversation in which all attempt to reach an agreement with which everyone can live. In the contemporary world, the problem of limited responsiveness to others has not exactly gone away, although the societies in which we now live are larger and much more diverse, and the range of causal influences on the lives of others is enormously amplified. We cannot, of course, simply scale up the ancestral solution, for that would not only produce a cacophony of voices but also fail to recognize the fact that most of those whose lives are affected by the choices made are not yet born. Yet, in the pragmatic spirit of problem-solving, it is possible to recognize deficiencies in the ways our ethical discussions proceed, and to try to correct for them. The conversations we have might abandon the myth of ethical authorities, people entitled to pronounce the last word; they might endeavor to achieve greater representation of those affected, to eradicate appeals to premises that can be identified as erroneous, and to aim at a form of mutual engagement that is dissatisfied so long as others cannot accept the proposed solution.

Viewing the ethical project in this way yields a concept of ethical progress. That concept is pragmatic: we make progress by problem-solving, and the problem that generates the enterprise and that remains for us is that of our limited responsiveness.

The concept is also local. We can make sense of a transition from one state of ethical practice to a subsequent state as progressive, through seeing the later state as resolving a problem present in the earlier state. It's not locally complete, even for relatively short periods of time, since there are sometimes stages at which gains in solving some problems are accompanied by losses in solving others; perhaps some of those can be subsumed under the notion of progress by supposing that an ideal collective discussion would agree on issues about the relative priority of the problems involved, but I doubt that this will always be the case. The notion of ethical progress is surely not global.

The normal form of the problem situation is one in which some individual, or group of individuals, encounters a difficulty in the pursuit of some goal. Any ideal discussion must explore the place of that goal within the lives of the parties affected, and must conclude that, when full factual clarity and full mutual engagement ascribes to that goal an important place within an endorsable human project, there is a genuine lack that must be addressed. If identifiable errors have been expunged, and concern for all involved reveals a threat to a life that someone has validly chosen, ideal discussants must conclude that there is real deprivation. At the center of the ethical project, as we have inherited it, is the notion of a human life and its possibilities, and the ways in which those possibilities are curtailed, often very narrowly confined, by the circumstances in which many people live.[6]

As in the case of science, we can conceive of progress in ethics abstractly, in terms of the modification of the codes accepted within particular societies. Our ancestors made progress when they decided that the prohibition against violence applied not only within the local band but also in some interactions with the neighbors; the societies of Mesopotamia made progress when they no longer permitted the death of a murderer's child to serve as penalty for the killing of another person's child; slave-owning societies have made progress when they have repudiated the practice; societies that have sharply differentiated the roles of the sexes have made progress when they have offered a more inclusive set of opportunities to all; in my lifetime, many societies have made progress by abandoning the idea that sexual relations among people of the same sex should be condemned or mocked. In all these instances, problems in human responsiveness to others have been overcome and limitations on human lives have been removed—at least at the level of the ethical ideals and precepts promulgated within a society and passed down to younger generations. Nevertheless, what occurs at the level of the official code may not be translated into behavior.

In a richer sense, societies make ethical progress when they not only amend their codes to address antecedent problems but also exemplify the solutions in subsequent conduct. The recognition officially extended to the emancipated slaves in the aftermath of the American Civil War was (to understate) incompletely realized in the attitudes and actions of the vast majority of the citizens for many decades; the Civil Rights movement surely brought important further progress, although it's worth reflecting on

---

[6] Here again, the approach I propose converges on Sen's recognition of capability-deprivation as a central concept in thinking about ethics and social policy (see his 1999 and 2009).

whether, even today, the United States, or any other society, has even approximated in practice what is preached in its "fundamental principles" with respect to the irrelevance of some historically salient human differences. The richer notion of ethical progress demands that the problems not merely be solved in the official declarations but also "on the ground," in conduct towards those whose limitations have been officially addressed that realizes the theoretical solution.

This section began with a popular worry, to the effect that certain types of judgment—about the worth of particular projects and the fairness of distributions— raise awkward questions about who is entitled to judge. Those concerns are answered by abandoning the fiction that some select group of "experts" are able to limn the features of a realm of values, in favor of the thought that authority is collective. In practice, judgments often rely on the version of the ethical project that a society (or the human community) has accepted, but they are always subject to critique and appraisal in light of a well-informed and mutually engaged deliberation that embodies a wider set of human perspectives.[7] Although we cannot take stock as our pioneering ancestors did, when they worked out the first simple rules for living together, we can constantly endeavor to improve the patterns and principles handed down to us through conversations that better approximate their discussions "in the cool hour."

SOCIAL PROGRESS

Standard economic indices of social progress are attractive because they "operationalize" a concept whose cloudiness threatens to plunge those who use it into sterile controversies. Perhaps there is a general correlation between such measures as GDP or average real wages and more important facets of human lives like material well-being, but it is a familiar fact that aggregation and averaging are at best blunt indicators of social progress. The GDP of a nation may increase while the distribution of the resources becomes ever more skewed toward a small group of individuals; average real wages may rise because those who already make the most receive monstrously large rewards while those at the bottom of the pay scale experience further reductions. Sensitivity to the importance of distribution prompts some people to impose a Pareto constraint on progress: a nation makes social progress only if the real wages of all its citizens are greater than or equal to their previous value, with the inequality holding strictly in some cases. Proposals of this sort are vulnerable on two counts: first, they fail to apply to vast numbers of transitions whose progressiveness we might want to

---

[7] As Jay Barney pointed out in discussion, there is considerable idealization involved here. But it's important to note that the ideal doesn't function as a goal to be realized, but (as I noted earlier in reference to Dewey's "ends-in-view") as a diagnostic instrument. It draws our attention to places at which deliberation is parochial or ill-informed or oblivious to the aspirations of other discussants, and it should inspire us to correct these features of the deliberative situation.

evaluate (e.g. episodes in which the fabulously rich experience a slight diminution of their wealth and the income of everyone else increases, with those who are poorest gaining most);[8] second, even though they might be more closely correlated with important features of human lives, it's easy to envisage circumstances under which the non-economic costs imposed on the citizens outweigh the economic gains.

I suggest, therefore, abandoning the "operational" measures and conceiving social progress as improving both the level and distribution of human welfare. To combat the charge of inevitable vagueness, I'll draw on ideas supplied by Mill and Dewey: I'll dub my concept of social progress "MD-progress."[9] At some stages of human history, human welfare is advanced by providing the material resources that sustain life from day to day: food, water, medicines, shelter, and so forth. For much of the human population, even today, those resources are not reliably available. Social progress would be made by transitions in which their chances of being supplied were increased—and in cases like these, it is often quite reasonable to use economic measures as proxies.

Mill's conception of human welfare recognizes the importance of material resources in what he calls the "puerile condition of mankind," and, consequently, the plausibility of Benthamite utilitarianism as a guide to decision-making at certain historical stages. He appreciates the fact that, for those fortunate enough to be released from concerns about the basic material resources, other dimensions of welfare come into prominence—and he looks forward to a world in which their aspirations can be shared by all members of our species. Following Kant and Wilhelm von Humboldt he emphasizes autonomous choice, seeing the worthwhile life as requiring the possibility of finding your own pattern for it, your own project that selects some ends as particularly worthy of pursuit: "The only freedom which deserves the name, is that of pursuing our own good in our own way, so long as we do not attempt to deprive others of theirs or impede their efforts to attain it" (Mill 1859/1958: 17).

Mill's account of welfare sometimes inspires people to divide human lives into a period of choice and a period of pursuit—as if people first moved to some adolescent or young adult epiphany in which they decided what they wanted to make of themselves, and then spent the subsequent years on the selected course. I'll follow Dewey (especially 1915) in thinking of choice and pursuit as co-evolving throughout the period of our existence. However we think of it, self-fashioning has preconditions. You can't choose your own good if the structure of your life is thrust upon you, fixed by your class or caste or race. Nor, even if those constraints are lifted, can you succeed unless you are acquainted with a range of genuine options, given some opportunities to understand what those options would be like, allowed the chance to develop your own individual talents and to become aware of what you can and can't do. To take the Enlightenment ideal of autonomy seriously is to appreciate the need for a very specific form of

---

[8] In discussion, Amartya Sen eloquently pointed out the absurdity of thinking that no comparisons are possible when the Pareto condition is violated.
[9] Similar ideas are also developed by Sen, so it might be more apt to name it "MDS-progress."

education, one that is wide-ranging in its exploration of human possibilities and one whose pace allows time for the unfolding of talent and for reflection on the directions in which your own embryonic talents point. In the history of our species, a tiny number of people have enjoyed that kind of education. As critics of "liberal education" sometimes point out, it is economically inefficient and ill-suited to produce a workforce that will compete under conditions of global capitalism.[10]

The emphasis on autonomy is sometimes seen as a particular feature of Western conceptions of the worthwhile life, one that has dangerous implications for other values (values not given sufficient weight in the ethical discussions of the West). To insist on the individual's opportunities for self-fashioning is, critics claim, to overlook the value of being part of a community, to be involved in cooperation with others and to see yourself as continuing the traditions of the community to which you belong. Now there is clearly something correct about the critics' protest. Just as the ideal of autonomy is moved by horror at the thought that the pattern of your life is stamped on you at birth, that you will live in a specific way because you are female, or of a particular race or caste, or because your family practices a certain religion, so too the critics react to a readily comprehensible fear—they are appalled by the idea of the deracinated individual, adrift in the world and at home nowhere. When these polar dystopian visions are clearly in view, it becomes evident that they don't exhaust the possibilities. In forming our life projects, it matters to us that they matter to others. What we do should have an impact on other lives, typically because we work with others on some joint project, espoused by all, within which we can see ourselves as making a genuine contribution, occasionally because, through our lone efforts, we make a positive difference to other human lives. To be deprived of the sense that your life will have made some difference is a terrible thing, and people are usually sustained by the explicit recognition of their efforts. Mutual recognition is an important part of human life (Honneth 1991), and it requires a web of connections that constitutes a community. The ideal choice, made possible by the ideal education, involves more than simply recognizing abstract options, understanding your own talents and limitations, and finding what seems the best match: it must also hold out the possibility of your pursuing important things in coordination with others who share your goals, or at least the conviction that your solitary efforts will result in achievements, whose value others will come to appreciate.

Let me now draw these various ideas together by offering an explicit account of MD-progress. A society S makes MD-progress just in case, for each member of S, in the subsequent state each of the dimensions of welfare attains at least as high a value as in the preceding state, with the inequality holding strictly for some members with respect to some dimensions. The dimensions of welfare include reliable access to basic material resources (food, water, shelter, protection against disease, protection from violence), as well as the "higher" dimensions of opportunities for autonomous choice, for participation in community, and for mutual recognition. Those "higher" dimensions are

---

[10] For an exposition of the difficulties, see my "Education, Democracy and Capitalism" (ch. 15 of Kitcher 2012).

typically achieved by constructing or reconstructing important social institutions, such as systems of education, or agencies that promote community or that regulate work and working conditions.

Does this approach to progress fall victim to the worries about applying Pareto conditions, worries that beset economic indices of social progress? The question is hard to answer definitively, but I'm inclined to think it doesn't. Pragmatists ought to ask what the point of a concept of social progress is. In my judgment, the concept should guide us in our policy-making—it ought to be oriented toward action in the future, rather than toward retrospective judgments about the actual course of history. While it may be true that many past social transitions involve a mixture of gains and losses for the dimensions of welfare I've listed, they could often have preserved the gains without incurring the losses—and, as we envisage similar changes, we can strive for those better possibilities. As we think about improving reliable access to basic resources, we don't have to make access less reliable for those whose needs are already addressed; as we think about providing better education for children with inadequate schools, we don't have to subtract necessary features of those schools that currently work well. Unlike the distribution of wealth, the distribution of the determinants of welfare needn't be zero-sum.

MD-progress offers us an ideal, one that might make sense at a particular historical stage (our phase of the ethical project). As I suggested earlier, the purpose of ideals is to serve as "ends-in-view" that promote the diagnosis of problems in our current situation. To survey the ideal of autonomous choice and pursuit of "one's own good" and to try to integrate it with the value of belonging to a community isn't to gesture toward some future human utopia in which social perfection is attained. Like the richer concepts of scientific progress and the concepts of ethical progress, the notion of social progress is pragmatic and local. To make social progress is to solve problems, and the canvassing of thoughts about the worth of human lives, of ideals of autonomy and of community, provides the matrix for discerning those problems.

The major obstacles to social progress in our species today arise from two main sources: the dominance of ideologies (particularly religious ideologies) in different societies, and the profoundly unequal distribution of wealth. For present purposes, I'll ignore the former.[11] I'll conclude by raising some questions about the latter.

[11] The clash between autonomy and community results from the contingent fact that, in a large number of contemporary societies, many people can only continue to belong to their natal community if they acquiesce in a pattern of life prescribed for them, and there are no alternative communities they might join (or none that are free from similar prescriptions). One of the most persuasive parts of Richard Dawkins's (over-zealous) campaign for atheism is his recognition of the extent to which many human lives are limited by relentless pressures from the family (often a considerably extended family) to conform to the received doctrines of a particular religion (Dawkins 2006). If a discussion of child-rearing and of education were guided by the commitment to mutual engagement and to the eradication of identifiable errors, it would be impossible to justify any practice of forcibly limiting the options for the young. Yet any global campaign to remove the ethically indefensible invasion of autonomy that Dawkins correctly perceives in many programs of religious indoctrination, or more generally to eliminate the coercive imposition of other types of ideology, will demand a form of social activism that is hard to

QUESTIONS

The concept of MD-progress might be applied at various scales. So we might look at social progress within particular nations, or even within particular local communities. Or our target might be the entire human population. This raises a first and obvious question. Is a judgment of progress undercut if the transition assessed as progressive for some group S fails to be progressive with respect to a more inclusive group S^+, because members of a subgroup of S^+ experience a decrease along some dimension of welfare? To answer the question affirmatively is to endorse the *Cosmopolitan Stance*: social progress for humanity as a whole is a precondition of social progress in any more limited group.

As I'll now suggest, this question leads to further issues. In particular, it generates concerns that MD-progress can only be achieved if some of the conditions of contemporary capitalism are amended. In other words, treating MD-progress as a diagnostic ideal is not simply discarding standard economic indices in terms of something more fundamental, but introducing a new standard at odds with current economic arrangements.

Among the most obvious ways to make MD-progress are transfers of resources from affluent nations to address the basic needs of the world's poor.[12] Suppose that sufficient wealth were transferred from the affluent world to alleviate the problems of "basic deprivation": providing for reliable sources of food, clean water, construction of settlements adequate for shelter, instituting systems of medical care and public health that protected people against the diseases that citizens of rich nations no longer have to fear, and setting in place ways of defending against predation and violence (this last, of course, requiring overcoming difficulties of local politics, difficulties that may often prove intractable). The result would be a more egalitarian world, one in which the opportunities available to the poor would be increased. On the face of it, that increase of opportunities would threaten the citizens of the wealthier nations, since the people whose lives were improved would constitute a potential workforce likely to be able to supply cheap labor to multinational corporations. Under the conditions of global capitalism it thus seems that the governments of wealthy nations have a responsibility not to undertake the envisaged forms of MD-progress, unless their aid comes with strings attached—perhaps by supplying the agriculture of drought-prone regions with genetically modified crops, unable to be harvested for seed and requiring the farmers constantly to pay tribute to their suppliers (funds that can then be used to offset the

---

imagine—and exploring possible solutions to this deep problem would lead far away from the economic questions that centrally concern us.

[12] In discussion, Jim Snabe proposed giving higher priority to the most basic needs of people, needs that still go unfulfilled in various parts of the world. I suggest that we always think more holistically, and that we guard against interventional policies that introduce obstacles for future attempts to achieve the further goals (e.g. access to education that enhances autonomy).

higher wages demanded of workers in the affluent nations). Perhaps there are other ways in which global economic competition can be adapted to allow for the transfers that would amend the most basic forms of deprivation.

Effectively, adopting the Cosmopolitan Stance and retaining the conditions of global capitalism undermines the status of apparently progressive transitions as MD-progressive. One reaction would be to declare that the Cosmopolitan Stance is utopian and to insist on a more pragmatic approach. Yet, even allowing for MD-progress that is exempt from the requirement that progressiveness be preserved as more inclusive groups are considered, difficulties still emerge.

Conflicts with the constraints of contemporary capitalism arise in three spheres. First *education*: a precondition for the autonomous choice of "one's own good" is the ability to recognize a range of options and to appraise them in light of an understanding of one's individual talents and limitations; in a just society, access to an education of this sort should be fairly distributed. Second *work*: since work typically occupies a significant portion of a person's life, the presupposition of engaging in activities with others or that make a difference to the lives of others is not easily satisfied unless the workplace provides some reflectively sustainable sense of contributing to an enterprise that can be endorsed as valuable. Third *community*: if, as I've suggested, an important dimension of valuable lives results from the ability to participate in cooperative actions to reach shared goals, worthwhile lives require the preservation of structures that can foster deliberation about goals and efforts to attain them. In all three spheres there are apparent opportunities for MD-progress.

Plainly the educational systems of affluent nations differ in their capacity to foster autonomous choice. But, as things currently stand, only a tiny minority of the world's children enjoy the chance to reflect seriously on what they might wish to become. Liberal education is under increasing pressure to conform to the conditions of global competition, and its defenders rightly see themselves as fighting a rearguard action (Nussbaum 2010; Delbanco 2012). In each of the most affluent nations, it's not hard to envisage incremental measures that would have non-negligible chances of promoting MD-progress—but those measures are typically subordinated to other, apparently more pressing, demands. Yet, even if they were carried through, the social progress achieved would almost certainly be accompanied by a decline in the economic fortunes of the nation, and a corresponding reduction in the resources available to promote the welfare of the citizens. To the extent that education is conceived as advancing Mill's "only freedom worthy of the name," it subtracts from the inculcation of the information and the acquisition of the skills necessary to achieve a competitive workforce in the contemporary world. This trade-off doesn't assume that the successful workers of coming generations are those who have been efficiently trained in a narrow set of technical skills—very probably, an economically effective education ought to cultivate some degree of intellectual flexibility—but that the demands to master the range of subjects most central to technological development and innovation are sufficiently different from those of a Millian education to penalize any nation that invests heavily in the "autonomous self-fashioning" of its citizens. Millian education is a luxury economically competitive nations cannot afford.[13]

Similar troubles arise with respect to the other two spheres. The capacity of seeing yourself as engaging in meaningful work depends on being able to judge that your own individual contribution makes a difference to an enterprise whose goal you can validate. If the products and goals of ventures are shaped to the demand of potential consumers, and if those consumers form their preferences by substituting ends largely shaped by external influences—suppliers who compete to persuade potential buyers of the need for their goods—it will often be hard for workers, especially those who think about what they are doing, to endorse the venture to which they contribute their labor. They will see themselves as "just in it for the money." More fundamentally, the pressures to produce efficiently point in the direction of rendering workers intersubstitutable, insofar as that can be achieved. To the extent that production can be partitioned into a sequence of tasks, allowing for novices to replace experienced workers with little or no loss of time or function, it will be profitable to do so. As Adam Smith foresaw, towards the end of a long book, the resultant situation is one in which the worker becomes a mere cog, a being whose "torpor" constitutes a significant reduction of his humanity. Understandably, perhaps, Smith was not inclined to return to his opening chapter, and revise everything that followed. Marx, however, taking notes on political economy, saw the point clearly—and wrote of "alienated labor."

Perhaps the most fundamental clash between the idea of autonomous self-fashioning emerges from the submersion of individual choices in a sea of suggestions, each designed to increase demand for some product. Effectively, any ability for groups of people to collect together and reflect on goals they might jointly pursue is diminished by an insistence on consumption, far beyond human needs or even our reflective wants. The result is not only enormous wastage of resources, but also a reorientation of human aspirations toward the accumulation of material goods. Communities do still form, sparked by political causes or fostered by religious teachings that remind people that the ones who die with the most toys are not, perhaps, the ones who have won. As education fails to prompt reflections that might lead to self-fashioning, as work proves unsatisfying, the way is prepared for adult citizens whose aspirations are bounded by the horizons of accumulating "assets," crowding out the possibility of achieving the rewards of community. Dewey's (1927) lament of the "loss of the public" is echoed in Robert Putnam's study of how Americans are reduced to "bowling alone."

There are thus, I believe, three major types of apparently socially progressive transitions, in which affluent nations might engage in a pragmatic and piecemeal fashion, for which doing so would require resisting the pressures of contemporary capitalism.

Conceived as MD-progress, social progress consists in solving problems, and the problems center on deprivations that affect "the only freedom worthy of the name."

---

[13] This line of argument is developed in more detail in Kitcher 2012: ch. 15.

Initially, we might think that the Pareto condition embedded in MD-progress is relatively easy to satisfy, that there are many ways to increase Millian freedom of some people without compromising the Millian freedom of others. If I am right, however, even when you back away from the Cosmopolitan Stance, settling for a more pragmatic approach, seemingly obvious instances of MD-progress clash with the constraints of contemporary capitalism. A major question for my approach is whether this seeming conflict is genuine.

Assuming that my analysis is correct, what is the moral? Should we simply reconcile ourselves to giving up an apparently attractive conception of human welfare and of social progress? Or should we think more critically about the conditions of capitalism, and about the proper uses of markets? Do we need new types of economic analysis that combine the rightly prized mathematical techniques with the older practice of embedding economic agents within an ethical/political framework? (Was the transition from classical political economy to the economics of Marshall, Walras, and their successors an instance of Kuhn's picture of scientific revolutions—gains of one sort accompanied by losses in other respects?)

Hanging above all this is a specific question, one I do not have space to elaborate here. Can we avoid the Cosmopolitan Stance in a world in which pan-human cooperation is urgently needed if our descendants are to have a reasonable chance of enjoying the preconditions for the kind of welfare envisaged by Mill and Dewey? Anthropogenic climate change threatens to undermine much of the MD-progress we have made, even to return vast segments of the human population to Mill's "puerile condition." Are there any possible measures, compatible with contemporary capitalism, that will enable us to achieve the level of global cooperation required to keep our planet's climate within manageable bounds?

Acknowledgments

Many thanks to Subi Rangan for his helpful suggestions about an earlier draft. I am also grateful to all those who participated in the meeting in London, for illuminating the issues with which we are all concerned.

References

Boehm, Christopher (1999). *Hierarchy in the Forest*. Cambridge, MA: Harvard University Press.
Boehm, Christopher (2012). *Moral Origins*. New York: Basic Books.
Cartwright, Nancy (1999). *The Dappled World*. Cambridge: Cambridge University Press.
Churchland, Patricia (2011). *Braintrust*. Princeton: Princeton University Press.
Dawkins, Richard (2006). *The God Delusion*. New York: Bantam Books.
Delbanco, Andrew (2012). *College*. Princeton: Princeton University Press.

De Waal, Frans (2013). *The Bonobo and the Atheist*. New York: Norton.

Dewey, John (1915). *Democracy and Education*. Carbondale, IL: University of Southern Illinois Press.

Dewey, John (1925). *Experience and Nature*. Carbondale, IL: University of Southern Illinois Press.

Dewey, John (1927). *The Public and its Problems*. Carbondale, IL: University of Southern Illinois Press.

Dupré, John (1993). *The Disorder of Things*. Cambridge, MA: Harvard University Press.

Elgin, Catherine (2004). True Enough. *Philosophical Issues*, 14: 113–31.

Gould, Stephen Jay (1989). *Wonderful Life*. New York: Norton.

Honneth, Axel (1991). *Kampf um Anerkennung*. Frankfurt: Suhrkamp.

Kitcher, Philip (1984). 1953 and All That: A Tale of Two Sciences. *Philosophical Review*, 93: 335–73.

Kitcher, Philip (1993). *The Advancement of Science*. New York: Oxford University Press.

Kitcher, Philip (2001). *Science, Truth, and Democracy*. New York: Oxford University Press.

Kitcher, Philip (2011). *The Ethical Project*. Cambridge, MA: Harvard University Press.

Kitcher, Philip (2012). *Preludes to Pragmatism*. New York: Oxford University Press.

Kitcher, Philip (2014). *Life After Faith*. New Haven: Yale University Press.

Kuhn, Thomas S. (1962). *The Structure of Scientific Revolutions*. Chicago: University of Chicago Press.

Laudan, Larry (1977). *Progress and its Problems*. Berkeley, CA: University of California Press.

Laudan, Larry (1984). *Science and Values*. Berkeley, CA: University of California Press.

Mill, John Stuart (1859 [1958]). *On Liberty and Other Essays*. Oxford: Oxford University Press, World's Classics.

Nitecki, Matthew, ed. (1988). *Evolutionary Progress*. Chicago: University of Chicago Press.

Nussbaum, Martha (2010). *Not for Profit*. Princeton: Princeton University Press.

Parfit, Derek (2011). *On What Matters*. 2 vols. Oxford: Oxford University Press.

Putnam, Robert (2000). *Bowling Alone*. New York: Simon & Schuster.

Sen, Amartya (1999). *Development as Freedom*. New York: Anchor Books.

Sen, Amartya (2009). *The Idea of Justice*. Cambridge, MA: Harvard University Press.

Tomasello, Michael (2009). *Why We Cooperate*. Cambridge, MA: MIT Press.

CHAPTER 8

FREEDOM, RESPONSIBILITY, AND KEEPING (OUR) HOPE ALIVE

JAMES P. WALSH

Abstract

What is progress? Exploring the nuances of marathon running and access to improved sanitation, I conclude that progress is defined by our freedom to be and by our responsibility to help the vulnerable among us. It is embodied at different levels—in the hearts, minds, and behaviors of individuals and in the institutions that enable and safeguard that freedom and responsibility. At a fundamental level, hope embodies progress. What is the scholar's role in a world of hope and hopelessness? If we live with integrity, I argue that we become something of a role model for freedom. And if we cultivate our students' imaginations and talents and, at the same time, remind them of their responsibilities, we work to safeguard humanity's future. Truth be told, we are all vulnerable. With faith as hope's companion, I close by asking us to consider the faith that sustains us.

I am pleased to be a part of this inaugural assembly. I can think of no worthier undertaking than to gather a group like this to consider the state of the world, its future, and even our role as scholars in enabling a better world. While I have no particular expertise on the subject of progress, with reflection, I discovered that the idea orients much of my life. What follows then is an idiosyncratic meditation on the nature of progress and its place in our lives. To begin, we need to grapple with the most basic question: what is progress?

EVIDENCE

It is difficult to escape the idea that progress is to be understood as some kind of measurable improvement over time. As a life-long runner, my thoughts first turned to

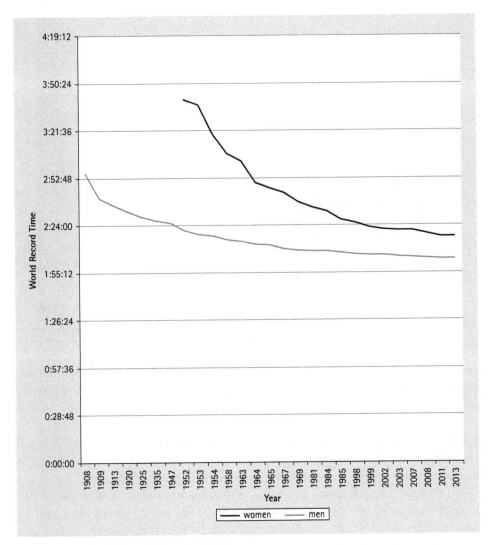

FIGURE **8.1.** World Record Marathon Times

the marathon. Figure 8.1 captures the evolution in male and female world record times from 1908 (male) and 1926 (female) to the present.[1]

We see that the record time dropped markedly over the years. Kenya's Wilson Kipsang recently ran the 2013 Berlin Marathon in 2 hours 3 minutes and 23 seconds. The current women's mark was set ten years earlier by the United Kingdom's Paula Radcliffe. She ran the 2003 London Marathon in 2 hours 15 minutes and 25 seconds. And while the men's record time is faster than the women's record, we see that the rate of progress for women outpaces that for the men (with a roughly 60 percent improvement over 61 years,

---

[1] If multiple records were set in a given year, I pictured the fastest time of the year.

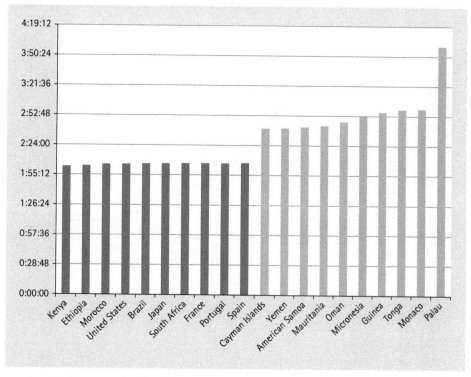

FIGURE **8.2.** The Ten Fastest and Slowest Countries

compared to about a 30 percent improvement for males over 105 years). What is progress? Is it an absolute appreciation of the current record time or an admiration for its rate of improvement? Either way, we see evidence of progress here.

But there are complications. As we look at world records, we look at progress at the level of the human species. Countries matter too. How do the record times vary by country? Figure 8.2 captures the fastest times run by men from the ten "fastest" and "slowest" nations in the world.[2]

Here we see that progress may not be equally experienced. While the record times among those from the top ten nations differ by less than 3 percent, the fastest time recorded by a citizen from Palau is almost 95 percent slower than a Kenyan citizen's best time—and almost 50 percent slower that the Cayman Islands' best. Perhaps we should appreciate any evidence of progress against deeper ideas of progress, such as how the fruits of global progress are shared.

And if we really want to consider how well progress is shared, we need to appraise individual experience. Figure 8.3 captures my own twelve marathon times. While I am

---

[2] These nations are the countries with the fastest and slowest marathon records among the counties that are also followed by the World Bank—and looking ahead, among the countries where we have full information about the quality of their sanitation infrastructure (see Figure 8.4).

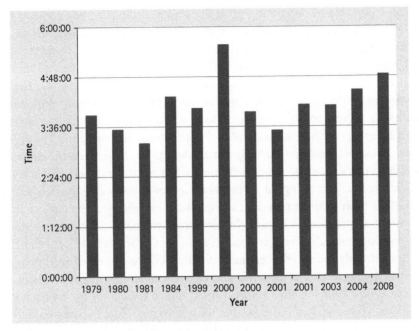

FIGURE 8.3. My Marathon Experiences

an American, and hail from a country that sports a current national record that is just 1.8 percent slower than the world record, my own best time is 56 percent slower than this current record. I ran the 1981 Toledo Heart Watcher's Marathon in 3:12:07 (50 percent slower than the record at the time). While this performance is not fast by current world standards, had I run that race in the early Olympic Games, I would have won the 1900 Bronze Medal in Paris and the 1904 Gold Medal in St Louis. Perhaps the fact that an unremarkable graduate student could run an earlier Olympic medal-winning time is itself a form of progress. Still, my experience tells me that we need to be alert to lived experience, in settings marked and unmarked by omnibus progress. The fact that one American can run a marathon in 2 hours and 5 minutes is obliquely related, at best, to any other American's ability to run a marathon. This look at marathon running at multiple levels of analysis reminds us that it is no simple task to appraise the experience of progress.

It is also no easy task to accurately measure progress. My experience with measurement technology illustrates the point. My first official time of 3:52:59 in the 1979 New York City Marathon does not reflect the actual time it took me to run those 26.2 miles. It is a "gun time," the time that elapsed between the sound of the starter's gun and the moment I crossed the finish line. The problem is that with so many runners at the start of that race (thousands of us stood cheek-by-jowl on the Verrazano-Narrows Bridge that October morning), it took me about 15 or 20 minutes to begin running that day. I had a very different experience in Milwaukee seven months later. Conditions changed. My 3:32:04 time that day is accurate. With just hundreds of people running that race, I was able to begin running at the sound of the gun. Fast forward twenty years. My 2001 Chicago Marathon experience was very much akin to my 1979 experience. 37,500 runners registered to run the race that day. Nevertheless, my 3:30:08 time that day is very accurate. It is my "chip time." Each runner these days attaches a sensor to his or her shoe; a mat at the start and finish (and at various points along the way) picks up its unique signal as the runner passes over it. With everyone (regardless of ability) no longer straining to be as close to the starting line as possible, people queue up according to their ability. Faster runners line up in front of the slower runners. Just about everyone starts to run at their ability level when the starter's gun sounds. A runner's race with time begins only when he or she crosses that special mat at the starting line. Technological progress has improved our ability to assess a runner's performance. Such progress reminds us to question the validity of any data we compile.

And even if progress is accurately measured, we need to appreciate the lived conditions under which it is appraised. Flynn (2012), for example, revealed that IQ levels have steadily increased over time. Whether due to improved nutrition, health care, education, or even the demands and consequences of living in a possibly more complex day-to-day living environment, an IQ of 100 today may not be equivalent to an IQ of 100 years ago. It is not clear that today's average New Yorker would thrive as something of a wunderkind if transported back in time to New York in 1914. Relatedly, we know intuitively that running a 3 hour marathon at age 30 is somehow "not the same" as running a 3 hour marathon at age 50. Running the 2001 Chicago Marathon in 3:30:08, I ran my second fastest race twenty years after running my fastest. An age-equivalent calculation, however, tells us that this time for a 48-year old man is equivalent to a 3:10:24 for a 28-year old man. Perhaps 3:30:08 is 1 minute and 43 seconds "faster" than 3:12:07.[3] It is by no means a straightforward task to appreciate the nature of progress.

BEYOND RUNNING

Measurement difficulties notwithstanding, we need to consider what domains of humanity are worthy of measurement. As we have seen, the measurement issues are tricky. We cannot ignore them as we collect our own data or interpret others' data. That said, these issues can almost always be addressed in some fashion. Does all progress matter? The "What?" question may be more important to consider than the "How?" question. Let's pause for a minute. Subi Rangan cares deeply about the state of the world, imagines a gathering such as this to consider its future, and kindly invites me to contribute. And what do I do? I gather all manner of marathon statistics and reminisce about my running past. With this kind of talk, many might wonder why

[3] <http://www.marathonguide.com/fitnesscalcs/ageequivalent.cfm>.

I am invited to join the group. After all, who really cares about how fast a human can run 26.2 miles (42 kilometers)? While we may all care about progress, few may care about the marathon.

How can we think about what matters most? Perhaps we should begin by considering our universally affirmed aspirations for humanity. Let's take the 1948 United Nations Declaration of Human Rights as a point of departure. Its thirty articles serve as a yardstick to evaluate the state of the world. Consider Article 25:

> (1) Everyone has the right to a standard of living adequate for the health and well-being of himself and of his family, including food, clothing, housing and medical care and necessary social services, and the right to security in the event of unemployment, sickness, disability, widowhood, old age or other lack of livelihood in circumstances beyond his control.
> (2) Motherhood and childhood are entitled to special care and assistance. All children, whether born in or out of wedlock, shall enjoy the same social protection.

The challenge of appraising progress in the world of marathon running pales in comparison to how we might best appraise progress in these more complex domains. Article 25's two sentences belie a host of measurement challenges. Undaunted, the World Bank compiles data that speak to these aspirations. Following the same countries that we followed in Figure 8.2, Figure 8.4 captures the twenty-two-year trend in countries' access to improved sanitation (defined as the percentage of the population with access to such improved sanitation facilities as a piped sewer system, a septic tank, a pit latrine, a ventilated improved pit latrine, a pit latrine with slab, or a composting toilet).[4] No one would dispute that clean sanitation facilities are essential to human health and well-being.

We see good news and bad news in these data. The good news is that we have witnessed a 33.4 percent increase in the worldwide availability of improved sanitation. In 1990 47.6 percent of the world's peoples enjoyed such access; that percentage increased to 63.7 in 2011. The bad news is that over 2.5 billion people still did not have access to a clean toilet in 2011. While I cannot imagine that anyone cares about the relationship between a nation's best marathon time and the percent of its population with access to improved sanitation, we see that the world's two fastest countries, Kenya and Ethiopia, reveal two of the poorest levels of access to healthy sanitation (with 2011 figures of 29.4 and 20.7 percent).[5] On the other hand, 100 percent of the population in the two slowest countries, Palau and Monaco, has such access. That simple fact reminds us that variance matters—progress of different kinds may be shared differently around the world.

Exploring the kinds of statistics that we did with the marathon, we see that Ethiopia, for all its troubles with sanitation, revealed a very impressive 800 percent improvement

---

[4] <http://data.worldbank.org/indicator/SH.STA.ACSN>.
[5] The correlation between the 2011 sanitation statistic and the men's national marathon record (for 197 countries and territories) is actually -0.18. The experiences of Kenya and Ethiopia notwithstanding, countries whose citizens enjoy access to decent sanitation are somewhat more likely to produce faster marathon runners.

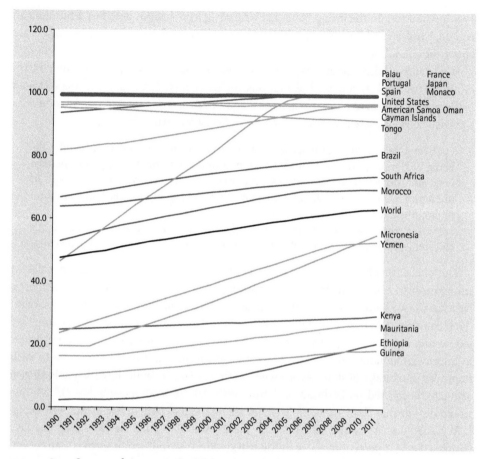

FIGURE 8.4. Improved Access to Sanitation: 1990–2011

over those 22 years (moving from 2.3 percent to 20.7 percent). Palau sets another exemplary world standard. While its sanitation "only" improved by 93.6 percent, it reached a level of 100 percent in 2007 (and sustained it). Tonga reminds us, however, that progress is by no means guaranteed. Their sanitation picture worsened a bit over time. Whereas 95.4 percent of its citizens enjoyed healthy sanitation facilities in 1990, only 91.5 percent did so twenty-two years later. Said differently, the number of Tongans living with substandard sanitation facilities moved from 4,764 in 1990 to 8,887 in 2011 (the population increased from 103,557 to 104,554 in that same time period).

And while the individual experience of living in unsafe and unhygienic conditions is largely invisible to Americans and Europeans, with very little effort, we can appreciate how others live. Anthropologists (Goldstein 2013), journalists (Boo 2012), and film-makers (Volkers 2011) bring their lives to us in compelling fashion. While to be sure, people are able to find joy and meaning in most any circumstance, we know that people struggle in this world.

REFLECTIONS

What can we learn from this brief look at the evidence for progress in the worlds of running and sanitation? Two things. First, the level of analysis matters. While we should certainly appreciate progress at the level of the human species, we should never forget to examine individuals' lived experiences.[6] To know that the men's world record for the marathon improved by say 30 percent in 100 years may be important but it says little about the lived experience of one person's attempt to better his or her time (or even an attempt to run this distance in the first place). And to know that world's access to improved sanitation improved by 33 percent in a recent twenty-two-year period says little about the life experience of someone still struggling to live in an unhygienic condition, be that one of the 81.5 percent of Guinea's citizens who do or one of the "just" 0.4 percent of the US citizens who do.[7] And second, we know that in an effort to appreciate progress, a look at running is somehow qualitatively different from an examination of access to sanitation. This second point is crucial. Just how do these two examples differ and does that difference matter?

March (2003) reminds us that human behavior is often seen in one of two ways. One reflects what he calls a logic of consequences, where action is inspired by anticipations, incentives, and desires. The other is rooted in what it means to be human in some essential sense, "It is a tradition that speaks of self-conceptions, identities and proper behavior rather than expectations, incentives and desires" (2003: 206). He refers to this as a logic of appropriateness. To be sure, we can track progress in world, national, and personal records but as we do, it might feel either wrongheaded ("Who cares about running?") or just plain wrong ("Who cares about running fast?"). These two reactions tell us that running is not so much about consequences as it is about "appropriateness" in March's human sense.

To focus on speed per se is also "wrong" because we rarely run in an anticipation of prize money or records. We run because we are human. In fact, running may be the one of purest of human activities. We began running as hunter-gathers on Africa's plains and have not stopped. Yes, we used to run for food, just as today we may run for good health. And yes, we can run for speed and the glory of standing on a winner's podium but, at a fundamental level, we run because we can. Again, we run because we are human. A runner who reads that last sentence knows exactly what I mean. Speaking to a non-runner, we strain to find words of explanation. Non-runners have no idea that running is about freedom and discipline, self-awareness and self-discovery, character, inner peace, and more. It is about a kind of inchoate

---

[6] Of course, we can investigate progress at any level of aggregation that interests us (i.e. perhaps investigating country, community, and family differences).

[7] Remember that 0.4% of 311,582,564 is 1,246,330. Seen in this light, the magnitude of America's sanitation problem is shocking.

fusion between body, mind, and soul. Sheehan (1978: 117) captured the challenge of articulation:

> But what matters whether we can be understood by someone else? By someone who is not a runner? Not certainly to induce them to try it themselves. But rather to encourage them to seek their own art, to become their own artists. To listen for that inner way of being in this world. To what they must be.

Running is about being. Running exemplifies the logic of appropriateness.[8]

And what of improved sanitation? Bringing hygienic sanitation facilities to everyone in the world is a noble aspiration. It accords with our universal conception of human rights. Setting targets, working toward them, and measuring progress against those targets feels worthy of our attention, time, and talents. With some reflection, we can see that running and sanitation are more alike than they are different. To run is human, just as to enjoy clean sanitation is human. They both embody a logic of appropriateness. Indeed, their difference and yet essential similarity point to a fundamental truth about progress.

PROGRESS

To improve the sanitation facilities of the world's poor and vulnerable is as deeply human as it is to run. Corballis (2011) argues that our recursive mind distinguishes us from the other members of the animal kingdom. We are self-reflective. We think about our thinking. And importantly, we have the ability to take the perspective of others. We are empathetic. With empathy comes the ability, and yes inclination, to care for others, especially those who are helpless. Pinker (2011) argues that violence among the human species began to decline with the invention of the printing press. The interior lives of others were made available to others at scale and with that came empathy, and with empathy, our indifference to others' suffering—and so, violence—began to ebb. In March's terms, it is as appropriate to run as it is to care for others.

---

[8] While I ran many marathons at a pace that would leave me satisfied at the end that I did my best, this was not always so. I ran my first marathon very cautiously. Never having run more than 18 miles—and fearful of what "hitting the wall" might do to me—I ran very conservatively for the first 20 miles that day. Each race has its own story. For example, I ran the Chicago Marathon in October 2000 in 5 hours and 34 minutes; seven weeks later, I ran the Dallas Marathon an hour and a half faster. The difference is that I ran with my brother that day in Chicago, accompanying him on his first marathon. That day was all about love, not speed. I ran the Chicago Marathon in 3 hours and 30 minutes in 2001; four weeks later, I ran the New York City Marathon in 4 hours and 6 minutes. I escorted a disabled person through the streets of New York that day. Speed also meant nothing to me that day. I only trained with real discipline and focus to run at my absolute limit once in my life—for the 2001 Chicago Marathon. My goal was to qualify for the Boston Marathon (for what it is worth, I made it with 51 seconds to spare). Yes, speed can matter. I ran as fast as I could that day just to see if I could (embodying a logic of appropriateness) and yes, I ran in a very determined attempt to enter the Boston Marathon (embodying a logic of consequences). Still, there is so much more to running a marathon than running it fast.

This look at running and sanitation points the way to a two-fold conception of progress. Progress is defined both by our freedom to be and by our responsibility to help others who are vulnerable, infirm, or helpless. As such, progress is fundamental to human life. It is embodied in our unrestrained ability to become our own artists (to run if that calls us) and it is embodied in our commitment to help the vulnerable among us (the UN Declaration of Human Rights enshrines such an aspiration). In words that every American schoolchild understands, progress is embodied in the pursuit of liberty and justice for all. And it is embodied at different levels of analysis—in the hearts, minds, and behaviors of individuals and in the institutions that enable and safeguard their liberties and ensure justice.[9]

Hope and Hopelessness

Seeing that progress is about both our ability to be free and our responsibility to help the helpless, we see that, at a very fundamental level, progress is all about hope—for ourselves as individuals and for us as people. Our hope for a better world actually embodies progress. Indeed, the thought of it enables us to live with confidence and security.

Our conversation about the evolution of capitalism in this assembly begins with a consideration of society's problems and then moves immediately to consider the nature of progress. Embedding our consideration of problem in a conversation about progress reflects its own kind of hope. I wonder if society's attention to progress might wax and wane with the state of the world. To this end, I turned to *The New York Times* for insight. Figure 8.5 captures the results of a bibliometric analysis that captures the percentage of articles published each year that mention the word "progress." Using the ProQuest Historical Newspaper database, I analyzed the years between 1890 and 2008. A polynomial trend line shows us that conversations about progress bottomed out around the Great Depression, World War II, and the Korean War. This might have been a particularly hopeless time for *The New York Times'* readers. Figure 8.6 suggests that this may be so. This same bibliometric analysis, focused this time on the world "hope," shows us that mentions of hope bottomed out in this time period too. Indeed, the correlation between the percentage of annual articles that mention the word "progress" and "hope" is 0.49. Hope embodies progress.

Students of progress and hope might be pleased to see the upward trend lines in both of these two figures. Those positive slopes may reflect a kind of optimism about our future. They might also reflect a longing for optimism, however. Absent further study, we do not know if a great percentage of articles reflect a hunger for hope or its presence.

---

[9] To see progress as embodying both freedom and responsibility is broadly consistent with Sen's (1999) view of the importance of freedom. Indeed, freedom enables our ability to take responsibility for the vulnerable and in so doing, ultimately enables their freedom to be. These people can then take responsibility for others, enabling their freedom to be. A virtuous cycle is thus sparked and sustained.

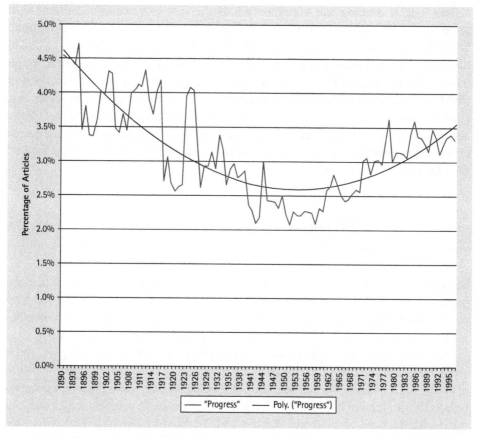

FIGURE 8.5. Percentage of Articles in *The New York Times* that Mention the Word "Progress"

Still the fact of the swings themselves tells us that we may live in times of hope and hopelessness. How are we to live when hope about the human condition fails us, when hope gives way to hopelessness? And what is the scholar's role in such a world of hope and hopelessness?

KEEPING HOPE ALIVE

The scholar is crucial to keeping hope alive. Perhaps Whitehead (1929: 93) saw our role most clearly when he observed, "The justification for a university is that it preserves the connection between knowledge and the zest for life, by uniting the young and the old in the imaginative consideration of learning." Foreshadowing March's (2003) retirement address, he went on to say, "The learned and imaginative life is a way of living and not an article of commerce" (p. 97). At our best, scholars live a life expressed by the logic of appropriateness. We exercise the freedoms that define the first pillar of progress—we

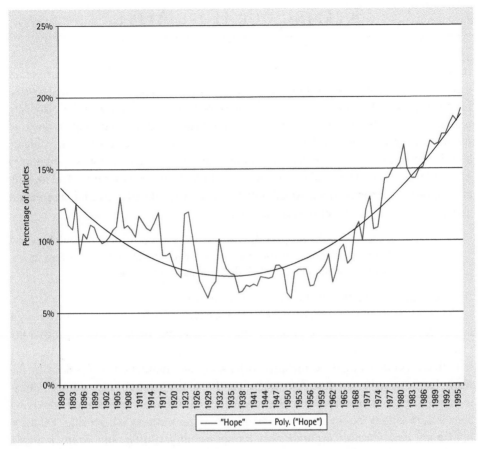

FIGURE 8.6. Percentage of Articles in *The New York Times* that Mention the Word "Hope"

imaginatively pursue knowledge and share this calling with others, especially the young. If we live our lives with integrity, we can become something of a role model for freedom.

And just as we are doing here in this assembly, our job is to identify the problems that bedevil us. Having done so, we then help others develop their talents and encourage them to try to solve them. By cultivating our students' imaginations and talents and, at the same time, reminding them of their responsibilities to the vulnerable and weak, we work to safeguard humanity's future. In this way, we help to build the second pillar of progress. With this role in society, it is no surprise to see that we are one of just three professions that, by custom, don robes (we join the clergy and justices in this practice).[10] If scholars are so important to society and its hopes, then how do we keep our own hopes alive?

[10] I am certainly not arguing that we alone (or that we and members of the clergy and the judiciary alone) work to safeguard humanity's future. Humankind safeguards its future. Still, I believe that society grants us a sacred trust. Our work matters.

Keeping our Hope Alive

It turns out that this is a timely question. Walsh (2011) chronicled the contemporary forces at play in the academy, forces that leave many research scholars oriented toward producing research scholarship in much the same way that a factory worker, laboring under a piece-rate control system, might produce widgets.[11] Turning to look at teaching, Edmondson (2013) worries that vocational pressure, pressure on students and faculty alike, works to undermine contemporary education. Sadly, we sometimes hear colleagues say, "I pretend to teach and my students pretend to learn." And looking at even deeper currents in our world, Rorty (1999: 263) offered a bracing observation about life in the academy at the century's end:

> Whereas intellectuals of the nineteenth century undertook to replace metaphysical comfort with historical hope, intellectuals at the end of this century, feeling let down by history, are experiencing self-indulgent, pathetic hopelessness.

If these observers are even half correct, we are in trouble. What to do?

One way forward is to work on projects that directly inform progress. If the freedom to be who we are is a pillar of progress, then we can contemplate and investigate the factors and forces that inhibit such freedom (at any level of analysis). As a business school professor, I might be inclined to look at the attenuation of freedom in the workplace and so, investigate discrimination (Desai et al. 2014), toxic work environments (Frost 2007), or corruption (Svennson 2005). If I wanted to look at other-serving behavior, I might be inclined to investigate organizational citizenship behavior (Chiaburu et al. 2011), corporate social responsibility (Porter and Kramer 2006), benefit corporations (Reiser 2011), or social entrepreneurship (Santos 2012). And if hope itself embodies progress, then I might even investigate the nature of hope in organizational life (Branzei 2012; Carlson et al. 2012; Ludema et al. 1997). Whether or not the research scholar is mired in a funk of pathetic hopelessness, such work would contribute to the world and maybe even lift that scholar's spirits.

Teaching is more complicated. The teacher's spirits always matter. Parker (2007: 10) knows this better than most, "Good teaching cannot be reduced to technique; good teaching comes from the identity and integrity of the teacher." While our research projects may help to lift our spirits, life in the classroom is more difficult. Enter the room feeling hopeless and you will likely leave feeling even more hopeless. Again, Parker (2007: 2-3) identifies the heart of the problem:

> Teaching, like any truly human activity, emerges from one's inwardness, for better or worse. As I teach, I project the conditions of my soul onto my students, my subject, and our way of being together. The entanglements I experience in the

---

[11] Research scholars increasingly work under—or work in spite of—control systems that offer high-powered incentives for publication in well-regarded international journals (Franzoni et al., 2011).

classroom are often no more or less than the convolutions in my inner life. Viewed from this angle, teaching holds a mirror to the soul. If I am willing to look in the mirror and not run from what I see, I have a chance to gain self-knowledge—and knowing myself is as crucial to good teaching as knowing my students and my subject.

Like it or not, our interior lives are always on display. Mix Whitehead's high aspirations with Rorty's somber reflections and we are left with an unsettling question: do we want our children, filled with their zest for life, to encounter teachers who are mired in a state of self-indulgent, pathetic hopelessness? While we may warm to the thought that we scholars can help to keep humanity's hopes alive, we may shiver at the thought that our inner lives are always on display and matter so much.

FAITH

Each of us is faced with the challenge of finding hope in a world that offers plenty of cause for hopelessness. Without hope, we risk falling into a state of despair and depression, unable to live with vitality and resilience. We would then be no one's role model. Some appear to be born with an optimistic orientation to life (Scheier and Carver 1992), but many struggle to sustain it (Seligman 2006).[12] The phrase "Keep the faith" comes to mind. It may very well be that faith is hope's companion. Religious writings often connect faith and hope. For example, we read in the Bible that "faith is confidence in what we hope for and assurance about what we do not see" (Hebrews 11: 1). What is the wellspring of such confidence and assurance? That is a question for each of us to ponder.

Perhaps the "metaphysical comfort" that Rorty tells us was rejected by so many intellectuals in the nineteenth century still holds promise. After all, there is some evidence to suggest that those who heartily believe in God are more optimistic and hopeful than those who do not (Sethi and Seligman 1993). While there are scholars in our midst who do believe, and say so out loud (cf. Sandelands 2003, 2015), most probably do not. A 2013 Harris poll tells us that there is a negative relationship between education level and a belief in God. Just 37 percent of those with a postgraduate education believe; 48, 55, and 60 percent of those with a college degree, some college, and a high school education or less, respectively, believe.[13] Clarke (2003: 165), an

---

[12] While hope and optimism may be close cousins, Carlson et al. (2012) pointed out their differences. Hope may embody more a sense of openness to unknown possibilities in unarticulated worlds, while optimism may be rooted in an expectation that those possibilities are within reach. As such, scholars, those dispositionally inclined to challenge ideas, their assumptions, boundary conditions, unintended consequences, and the like, may live more comfortably in a world of hope while entrepreneurs and innovators, those who imagine a better world and lead organizations to create it, may dwell more in the world of optimism.

[13] <http://www.harrisinteractive.com/vault/Harris%20Poll%2097%20-%20Beliefs_12.16.2013.pdf>.

expert in treating depression, observed that "most so-called 'intellectuals' cringe at the words 'faith' and hope.'" Still, we are free to select our role models. Nicoli (2002), for example, chronicled the lives of two intellectual giants, C. S. Lewis and Sigmund Freud, and their very different attachments to God. In his popular seminar, Professor Nicoli has asked a generation of Harvard students to examine their lives for clues about how we may best live. Of course, we are free to embrace or reject the many extant notions of God. We can certainly fashion our own ideas. As we go forward, we might learn from the choices others make.

David Foster Wallace comes to mind. He was the brilliant and much lauded writer who struggled with such questions. Clinically depressed, he took his life three years after offering his best counsel to the next generation. Speaking to the importance of the metaphysical at Kenyon College, he spoke of taking a leap to faith.[14] Likely with a very clear eye on his own struggles, he asked us to examine what he called our default settings. He suggests that a turn to God or the metaphysical would serve us well. I will quote him at length here. Perhaps his words will offer some hope for the hopeless.

> You get to decide what to worship . . . . In the day-to-day trenches of adult life, there is actually no such thing as atheism. There is no such thing as not worshipping. Everybody worships. The only choice we get is what to worship. And the compelling reason for maybe choosing some sort of god or spiritual-type thing to worship—be it JC or Allah, be it YHWH or the Wiccan Mother Goddess, or the Four Noble Truths, or some inviolable set of ethical principles—is that pretty much anything else you worship will eat you alive. If you worship money and things, if they are where you tap real meaning in life, then you will never have enough, never feel you have enough. It's the truth. Worship your body and beauty and sexual allure and you will always feel ugly. And when time and age start showing, you will die a million deaths before they finally grieve you. On one level, we all know this stuff already. It's been codified as myths, proverbs, clichés, epigrams, parables; the skeleton of every great story. The whole trick is keeping the truth up front in daily consciousness.
>
> Worship power, you will end up feeling weak and afraid, and you will need ever more power over others to numb you to your own fear. Worship your intellect, being seen as smart, you will end up feeling stupid, a fraud, always on the verge of being found out. But the insidious thing about these forms of worship is not that they're evil or sinful, it's that they're unconscious. They are default settings.
>
> They're the kind of worship you just gradually slip into, day after day, getting more and more selective about what you see and how you measure value without ever being fully aware that that's what you're doing.

Progress is defined by our freedom to be and by our responsibility to care for the vulnerable. David Foster Wallace begged us to pay attention. His life and death reminds

---

[14] His 2005 Kenyon College commencement address is recognized as one of the best ever. Those accolades are summarized in a Kenyon College alumni bulletin: <http://bulletin.kenyon.edu/x4276.xml>. The address itself is available here: <http://moreintelligentlife.com/story/david-foster-wallace-in-his-own-words>.

us that we are all vulnerable. As people who are called to do so much to inspire and ensure progress, we scholars have been granted manifest freedoms and deep responsibilities. Still, life is complicated. Perpetually pursue those freedoms and we may ignore the vulnerable; tend to the vulnerable with all our being and we may lose that being. We cannot forget to take care of ourselves...and each other. In the end, two questions orient so much of who we are and what we do. One, what are our hopes for humanity? And two, what are our pillars of faith? The answers matter. They matter to us as individuals. They matter to our students, those who count on us to be our best and to do our best. And if I am right to think that scholars do much to embody and ensure progress, they matter to the world.

Acknowledgments

I want to thank Oana Branzei, Tom Donaldson, Jane Dutton, Ed Freeman, Ira Fried, Subi Rangan, Lance Sandelands, and my colleagues at the inaugural assembly for their conversations about this chapter, and Sara Hess and Kan Yu for their help collecting the hope and progress data.

References

Boo, K. (2012). *Behind the Beautiful Forevers: Life, Death, and Hope in a Mumbai Undercity.* New York: Random House.

Branzei, O. (2012). Social Change Agency Under Adversity: How Relational Processes (Re)Produce Hope in Hopeless Settings. In K. Golden-Biddle and Jane E. Dutton (eds), *Using a Positive Lens to Explore Social Change in Organizations.* New York: Routledge, 21–47.

Carlson, A., A. L. Hagen, and T. F. Mortensen (2012). Imagining Hope in Organizations: From Individual Goal-Attainment to Horizons of Relational Possibility. In K. S. Cameron and G. M. Spreitzer (eds), *The Oxford Handbook of Positive Organizational Scholarship.* New York: Oxford University Press, 288–303.

Chiaburu, D. S., I.-S. Oh, C. M. Berry, N. Li, and R. G. Gardner (2011). The Five-Factor Model of Personality Traits and Organizational Citizenship Behaviors: A Meta-Analysis. *Journal of Applied Psychology*, 96: 1140–66.

Clarke, D. (2003). Faith and Hope. *Australasian Psychiatry*, 11: 164–8.

Corballis, M. C. (2011). *The Recursive Mind: The Origins of Human Language, Thought, and Civilization.* Princeton: Princeton University Press.

Desai, S. D., D. Chugh, and A. P. Brief (2014). Marriage Structure and Resistance to the Gender Revolution in the Workplace. *Administrative Science Quarterly*, 59(2): 330–65.

Edmondson, M. (2013). *Why Teach? In Defense of a Real Education.* New York: Bloomsbury.

Flynn, J. R. (2012). *Are we Getting Smarter? Rising IQ in the Twenty-First Century.* Cambridge: Cambridge University Press.

Franzoni, C., G. Scellato, and P. Stephan (2011). Changing Incentives to Publish. *Science*, 333: 702–3.

Frost, P. J. (2007). *Toxic Emotions and Work and What you Can Do about Them*. Boston: Harvard Business Press.

Goldstein, D. M. (2003). *Laughter Out of Place: Race, Class, Violence, and Sexuality in a Rio Shantytown*. Berkeley, CA: University of California Press.

Ludema, J. D., T. B. Wilmot, and S. Srivastava (1997). Organizational Hope: Reaffirming the Constructive Task of Social and Organizational Inquiry. *Human Relations*, 50: 1015–52.

March, J. G. (2003). A Scholar's Quest. *Journal of Management Inquiry*, 12: 205–7.

Nicoli, A. M. (2002). *The Question of God: C. S. Lewis and Sigmund Freud Debate God, Love, Sex, and the Meaning of Life*. New York: Free Press.

Parker, P. J. (2007). *The Courage to Teach: Exploring the Inner Landscape of a Teacher's Life*. San Francisco: Jossey-Bass.

Pinker, S. (2011). *The Better Nature of our Angels: Why Violence has Declined*. New York: Penguin Group.

Porter, M. E., and M. R. Kramer (2006). Strategy and Society: The Link between Competitive Advantage and Corporate Social Responsibility. *Harvard Business Review*, 84: 78–92.

Reiser, D. B. (2011). Benefit Corporations: A Sustainable Form of Organization? *Wake Forest Law Review*, 46: 591–625.

Rorty, R. (1999). *Philosophy and Social Hope*. London: Penguin Books.

Sandelands, L. E. (2003). The Argument for God from Organization Studies. *Journal of Management Inquiry*, 12: 168–77.

Sandelands, L. E. (2015). On Taking People Seriously: An Apology, to my Students Especially. *Journal of Business Ethics*, 126: 603–11.

Santos, F. M. (2012). A Positive Theory of Social Entrepreneurship. *Journal of Business Ethics*, 111: 335–51.

Scheier, M. F., and C. S. Carver (1992). Effects of Optimism on Psychological and Physical Well-Being: Theoretical Overview and Empirical Update. *Cognitive Therapy and Research*, 16: 201–28.

Seligman, M. E. P. (2006). *Learned Optimism: How to Change your Mind and your Life*. New York: Vintage Books.

Sen, A. (1999). *Development as Freedom*. New York: Anchor Books.

Sethi, S., and M. S. Seligman (1993). Optimism and Fundamentalism. *Psychological Science*, 4: 256–9.

Sheehan, G. (1978). *Running and Being*. New York: Rodale.

Svennson, J. (2005). Eight Questions about Corruption. *Journal of Economic Perspectives*, 19: 19–42.

Volkers, M. (2011). *The Fourth World: Real People. Real Slums. Real Stories*. Sioux Center, IA: Prairie Grass Productions <www.fourthworldfilm.com>.

Walsh, J. P. (2011). Embracing the Sacred in our Secular Scholarly World. *Academy of Management Review*, 36: 215–34.

Whitehead, A. N. (1929/1967). The Aims of Education and Other Essays. New York: Free Press.

CHAPTER 9

....

PROGRESS AND PUBLIC
REASONING

....

AMARTYA SEN

Abstract

Central to the exercise of evaluation of progress is the conception of human beings. The importance of greater fulfillment of people's needs has been rightly emphasized by a number of leading thinkers. And yet the idea can be further enriched by invoking a fuller concept of humanity. People do have *needs*, but they also have *values*, and in particular, cherish their ability to choose, act, argue, agree, or disagree—and most importantly, reason alone and reason with others. The world tends to progress not just by expanding the achievement of pre-identified needs, or by expanding the fulfillment of antecedent values, but also by progressive assessment—and reassessment—of the values we can defend and the reasons that we can give in support of our priorities: old and new. It is in the interplay of reason and accomplishment that the idea of progress has to find its sustainable home.

1

....

"All men are philosophers," wrote Antonio Gramsci, in an essay on "The Study of Philosophy." He went on to elaborate: "it is essential to destroy the widespread prejudice that philosophy is a strange and difficult thing just because it is the specific intellectual activity of a particular category of specialists or of professional and systematic philosophers." Gramsci's own approach to philosophy, developed around 1920, was based on his argument that the use of language itself involves a philosophical discipline, since a language reflects "a totality of determined notions and concepts and not just of words grammatically devoid of content." He argued that people constantly participate in pursuing philosophy through their use of ordinary language and through following its rules. The idea of progress has to be situated within a framework of communication among people.

I have discussed elsewhere (Sen 2003) how this understanding of philosophy (which Piero Sraffa, a leading economist, shared with Gramsci) would play a big part in some momentous conversations between Sraffa and Ludwig Wittgenstein. And those conversations, in turn, would greatly help the founding of what came to be known as "ordinary language philosophy," led by the later Wittgenstein of *Philosophical Investigations*. The similarities between Gramsci's ideas and those of Wittgenstein on "rule following" in the use of language as a central philosophical exercise are certainly very striking.

Wittgenstein was profoundly influenced by the arguments he had with Sraffa. After absorbing Sraffa's critique of Wittgenstein's earlier work, *Tractatus*, Wittgenstein felt "like a tree from which all branches have been cut" (as Wittgenstein himself told another distinguished philosopher, Henrik von Wright). The new direction in Wittgenstein's thinking had a profound influence on Anglo-American philosophy in the second half of the twentieth century.

The role of language and communication is very worth recollecting in this carefully planned seminar, in which philosophers and social scientists have been placed together to investigate the problems that the contemporary world faces. This is not because ordinary language philosophy is the only kind of philosophy worth pursuing—that is very far from the case (as both Gramsci and Wittgenstein knew). But the importance of language and communication must have a place as we examine the challenges and prospects of the contemporary world, (1) following a set of rules of communication that we can share (and with the help of which we can understand each other), and (2) expressing our respective views that we may or may not share (at least initially).

2

In coming to grips with the idea of progress (the topic assigned to me), we have to take note of different views on how progress should be judged and how we can subject the respective claims to critical arguments and public scrutiny. Our discussions—disputations as well as approvals—must involve something of a shared discipline, including, presumably, an interest in the objectivity of our perspectives. It has been argued, with considerable plausibility, that valuational objectivity has a fundamental connection with the ability of a claim to stand up to contrary arguments in public discussion, in a way that the reasonableness of the claim is clear to others. Indeed, as John Rawls, perhaps the leading moral and political philosopher of our time, has argued:

> To say that a political conviction is objective is to say that there are reasons, specified by a reasonable and mutually recognizable political conception (satisfying those essentials), sufficient to convince all reasonable persons that it is reasonable. (Rawls 1993: 110, 119; see also Rawls 2001)

The "survival" of valuational claims—against counter-arguments—in unobstructed discussion among reasonable people (people who are ready to listen to reasoning rather than confronting each other with fisticuffs) can indeed be seen to be at least one way, indeed a cogent way, of assessing the objective standing of such claims.

Before I proceed further, I should make a few clarificatory remarks. First, even though I am following John Rawls in seeing objectivity in normative evaluation as a critical interactive exercise among people, I would not like to restrict the domain of this exercise within the boundaries of a nation (in the way Rawls is tempted to do, particularly in his exposition of "justice as fairness"). Rather, taking a leaf from Adam Smith's *Theory of Moral Sentiments* (1790/2009), I will treat critical evaluation across borders to be crucially important for the idea of normative objectivity.

Second, there need not be any complete agreement on what should be valued and to what extent, even after critical scrutiny, but informed scrutiny and exchange of views is likely to lead to quite extensive agreement on particular rankings, and these partial orderings are of particular use in the evaluation of progress. I shall have more to say on this presently, but I have also discussed these issues in my book *The Idea of Justice* (2009).

Third, the partial agreements to which we can be led by reasoned scrutiny may well progress over time. If there was an emerging consensus on the unacceptability of slavery that became prominent and powerful in the eighteenth and nineteenth centuries, it would be wrong to assume that such an agreement existed in earlier times as well. The consensus that is emerging today, if rather slowly, on the unacceptability of the continuation of illiteracy, abject poverty, and the absence of medical attention for a great many people in the world was not present in that form in earlier centuries. The reach of our reasoning can expand just as our appreciation of science can also tend to grow.

3

Any serious discussion on the criteria of progress has to go into a number of empirical issues, involving practical connections, in particular, the role of institutions, their working, and their consequences. I shall try to take on such issues presently, but before that it may be important to comment briefly on two basic conceptual distinctions in the way we try to assess progress.

The first contrast, which I have presented in *The Idea of Justice*, relates to two different conceptions of justice, entailing two quite distinct ways of seeing progress. Two words—*niti* and *nyaya*—both of which stand for justice in classical Sanskrit, help us to differentiate between these two separate concentrations. Among the principal uses of the term *niti* in Sanskrit are organizational propriety and behavioral correctness. In contrast with *niti*, the term *nyaya* stands for a more comprehensive concept of realized justice that must take note of what actually happens. In the perspective of *nyaya*, the roles of institutions, rules, and organization, important as they are, have to be assessed in the broader and more inclusive light of the world that in fact emerges through the interactions among people, in specific settings of institutions and rules (rather than focusing on the institutions and rules themselves).

To illustrate, early Indian legal theorists talked disparagingly of what they called *matsyanyaya*, "justice in the world of fish," where a big fish can freely devour a small fish. We are warned that avoiding *matsyanyaya* must be an overwhelming priority, and it is crucial to make sure that the "justice of fish" is not allowed to invade the world of human beings. The central recognition here is that the realization of justice in the sense of *nyaya* is not just a matter of having good institutions and good rules, but of judging the societies themselves. No matter how perfect the rules of behavior and proposed organizations may look, if the world emanating from such a setting still allows a big fish to devour a small fish at will, then that is a patent violation of human justice in the sense of *nyaya*.

To illustrate, consider the famous claim by Ferdinand I, the Holy Roman Emperor, in the sixteenth century: "Fiat justitia et pereat mundus," which can be translated as: "Let justice be done, though the world perish." This severe maxim could figure as a *niti*—a very austere *niti*—that is advocated by some (indeed Emperor Ferdinand did just that), but it would be hard to accommodate a total catastrophe as an example of a just world, when we understand justice in the broader form of *nyaya*. If indeed the world does perish, there would be nothing much to admire in that accomplishment, even though the stern and severe *niti* leading to this extreme result could conceivably be defended. I have argued in *The Idea of Justice* that we have reason to judge progress as the enhancement of *nyaya* in the world, rather than concentrating only on *niti*.

The second distinction concerns the contrast between (1) ranking—to the extent we can—the extents of injustice in different states in the world, or (to put it more positively) ordering the respective achievements of justice, and (2) seeking perfect justice (with little interest in ranking alternative states which are all likely to have injustices of various kinds). The former can be called a comparative approach. In *The Idea of Justice*, I called the latter approach "transcendental" (since it concentrates on identifying ideal arrangements—or perfect outcomes—that can not be transcended), but the term was perhaps not altogether well chosen. The word "transcendental" has other—pre-established—meanings as well, and it has proved difficult to adopt the word without its pre-existing associations. For this reason, in this chapter let me call the approach by a different term, "perfection-focused."

The dominant theories of justice in the world, including those of Hobbes (who led the approach), Locke, Rousseau, and in our own time, John Rawls, Robert Nozick, Ronald Dworkin, have tended to follow the "perfection-focused" route, confining its attention mainly—often *only*—to the contrast between perfect justice and its absence. Rawls's theory of "justice as fairness" is concerned with identifying principles of justice that pinpoint perfectly just institutions, and this becomes the central exercise in his "theory of justice."

In contrast with this generally Hobbesian approach, a number of other Enlightenment philosophers, who did not present formal theories of justice but commented on issues related to the idea of justice, took a variety of approaches that shared a common interest in making comparisons between different social arrangements and realizations. Many of their arguments were particularly focused on removing cases of manifest injustice, without focusing on the nature of the perfectly just social arrangements. Different versions of such comparative thinking can be found in the works of the Marquis de Condorcet, Adam Smith, Jeremy Bentham, Thomas Jefferson, Mary Wollstonecraft, John Stuart Mill, Karl Marx, among a number of other leaders of new thought in the eighteenth and nineteenth centuries. Even though they proposed very different ways of making comparisons, they were all involved, in one way or another, in making social comparisons that could identify how a society could be improved and terrible injustices removed. It is possible to argue that the focus of the second group of thinkers was on the comparative assessment of the world in terms of the *nyaya* of realizations, whereas the focus of the first group was on the perfection-focused assessment of just arrangements, in the sense of identifying some ideal *niti* of institutions and organizations.

The comparative approach is central to the analytical discipline of "social choice theory," which is a subject in which I have been personally involved over many decades. This takes the form of basing comparative judgments about societies on the relevant individuals' comparative assessments, with various axioms that place demands on how the translation is to be done. In a somewhat ad hoc form (dealing particularly with a class of voting rules), social choice theory was initiated by the Marquis de Condorcet, along with other French mathematicians (such as Jean-Charles de Borda), in the eighteenth century, but it was revived and established in its present form by Kenneth Arrow in the middle of the twentieth century (Arrow 1951). The literature of social choice theory is typically quite technical, and many of the results in the field cannot be established except through fairly extensive mathematical reasoning.[1] As a result, the basic philosophy of practical reason that lies behind the social choice approach has tended to receive relatively little general public attention.

And yet that approach and its underlying reasoning is quite close to commonsense understanding of the nature of reasoned decision-making in a society with many individuals, with a commitment to making reasonable choices, in line—as much as possible—with what people value. Even though Arrow's contribution received gigantic attention through the "impossibility result" that he presented as a young man (and it is indeed an extremely elegant—and unexpected—result), Arrow was also establishing a systematic approach to social decision-making. This approach can be used with different axioms and different informational requirements, which can yield positive possibilities—as well as (often unsuspected) impossibility results—within the broad framework of the comparative analysis.[2] And it is social choice theory in this broader

---

[1] See my critical survey of the literature in Sen 1986.
[2] On this see my Alfred Nobel Lecture in Stockholm in Dec. 1998, later published as Sen (1999). The use of a broad social choice approach to theory of justice is discussed and presented in Sen (2009), particularly in ch. 4.

form that I shall be invoking as background to the analysis of progress in social terms, without, however, going into formal results and theorems.

4

In the perspective of *nyaya*, the use of a comparative approach, we can fruitfully examine the institutional choices and motivational suitabilities that can help to advance what we can recognize as progress—to the extent we can base them on public reasoning (a subject on which Condorcet was extremely keen). We are not trying to look here for a *perfect* combination of institutions, or some *ideal* human motivation, but we have to attempt to understand how different institutions and distinct motivations help in the advancement of societies, judging progress in terms of enhancement of human well-being and freedom.

It is not an embarrassment for this broad approach to recognise that different people may well have rather different views on how exactly well-being may be measured, or human freedoms are to be compared. I have discussed the technical aspects of these variations and their implications for social choice in more formal works[3] than I will here, given the purpose of this chapter and its role in allowing general discussion. It is sufficient to note here that, even when different people do not exactly agree, the shared components in their orderings would generate a partial ordering (formally, an "intersection partial order"), and this would allow us to make many choices with definitiveness, while leaving other choices on which we may continue to disagree.

An understanding of social progress, I would argue, must (1) make room for interindividual variations of priorities, and also (2) accommodate our elements of agreement (formally, non-trivial intersection partial orders), without demanding complete agreement. Through public discussion and better understanding of each other's reasoning—or lack of it—we can hope to expand the domain of (2), through critical discussions on (1). And this is where we invoke the idea of objectivity in ethics and politics in the way Rawls, among others, has argued (as was referred to earlier).

The discipline of arriving at partial agreements through open and critical discussion has a long history, going back many centuries. In fact when the Indian Buddhist emperor Ashoka, in the third century BCE, instituted rules for public dialogue (including the demand that dissenting points of views must be given a respectful hearing), the hope was that by examining each other's arguments, people with differing judgments could arrive at some consensus on priorities. Prince Shotoku in Japan followed a similar strategy in insisting on discussion and consultation as a way of arriving at agreed decisions, which he included in the Constitution of Seventeen Articles in 604 CE (six centuries before the Magna Carta, which also reflected something of a similar

---

[3] See particularly the articles included in my (2002).

approach). In our time, the importance of public reasoning as a way of reaching partial agreements has been discussed and advanced by a number of authors, including Jurgen Habermas, in addition to John Rawls.

5

It is sometimes argued that even if there is some post-discussion agreement *within* a country, there would be no such agreement *between* people of different countries, with their own distinct cultures. This subject comes up often in pointing to the difficulty in arriving at an international consensus on the priorities to be attached to certain recognized "human rights." It is quite often argued that, in a world with much cultural variations and widely diverse practice, there can be no rights that are universally accepted.

Edmund Burke was one of the first to argue along this line in criticizing the French Declaration of the Rights of Man in 1789. Prevailing beliefs do vary in different parts of the world, but what has to be asked is to what extent those variations reflect immovable objects, rather than indicating the absence of exposure to the ideas and arguments in other parts of the world. This is an issue that was clearly analysed by the great economist, Adam Smith, in his first book, *The Theory of Moral Sentiment*, published in 1759 (Smith 1790/2009), which was a major contribution to philosophy that Smith wrote as Professor of Moral Philosophy at Glasgow University, well before writing his more famous *Wealth of Nations*.

Of course, even with fuller exposure there may be no complete agreement on matters of ethics between people in different countries. But there will most probably be no such total agreement on ethical priorities even among people in the same country—inter-country variation may not be the central difficulty here (Barack Obama and Paul Ryan, both from the United States, do not, perhaps, agree more than Obama and François Hollande, the French President, do). The central issue is how extensive a partial ordering, based on limited consensus, we can get through open-minded public reasoning—*within* and *across* countries.

Why is open exposure to ideas from elsewhere important? Adam Smith answered the question thus:

> We can never survey our own sentiments and motives, we can never form any judgment concerning them; unless we remove ourselves, as it were, from our own natural station, and endeavour to view them as at a certain distance from us. But we can do this in no other way than by endeavouring to view them with the eyes of other people, or as other people are likely to view them. (Smith, 1790/2009, III.1.2; p. 110)

The Smithian line of reasoning has three very powerful implications for the theory of human rights. First, the force of a claim for a human right would be seriously undermined if it were possible to show that it is unlikely to survive open public scrutiny. But contrary to a commonly offered reason for scepticism and rejection, the case for human rights cannot be discarded simply by pointing to the fact that in politically and socially repressive regimes, which do not allow open public discussion, many of these human rights do not have much social traction. Uncurbed critical scrutiny is essential for dismissal as well as for defence of claimed human rights.

Second, we have to recognize that what are taken to be "foreign" criticisms often correspond to internal criticisms from non-mainstream groups. If, say, Iranian dissidents are imprisoned by an authoritarian regime because of their heterodoxy, any suggestion that they should be seen as "ambassadors of Western values" rather than as proud "Iranian dissidents" would only add serious insult to manifest injury.

Third, as Adam Smith pointed out, the values that are dominant are often influenced by prevailing practice: he illustrated this with the support that the beastly custom of infanticide received from Athenian intellectuals, even great and humane philosophers, including Plato and Aristotle. As Smith explained this apparent puzzle,

> uninterrupted custom had by this time so thoroughly authorized the practice, that not only the loose maxims of the world tolerated this barbarous prerogative, but even the doctrine of philosophers, which ought to have been more just and accurate, was led away by the established custom, and upon this, as upon many other occasions, instead of censuring, supported the horrible abuse, by far-fetched considerations of public utility. (Smith, 1790/2009)

What was needed was critical examination, with explicit account being taken of how things would look from "a certain distance," in other lands with different practices and different political, social and moral thinking.

Scrutiny from a "distance" may have something to offer today in the assessment of practices as different from each other as the stoning of adulterous women in Taliban-ruled Afghanistan, the selective abortion of female fetuses in China or parts of India, and the plentiful use of capital punishment in China, or for that matter, in parts of the United States. This is the kind of issue that made Smith insist that "the eyes of the rest of mankind" must be invoked to understand whether "a punishment appears equitable" (1982: 104).

What others do, discuss, or defend, are good subject matters for public reasoning: not automatic respect, nor unconsidered rejection, but open-minded examination and scrutiny. Unrestrained and uncensored discussions may not generate complete ethical agreements across the globe, or for that matter within any given country, but what the approach of human rights tries to identify are widespread agreements that may emerge on the importance of certain freedoms and the corresponding social obligations.

The fact that the invoking of the idea of human rights has such social and political effectiveness across the world is itself some evidence in the direction of the possibility of significant consensus on some particular matters through unrestricted public reasoning. Indeed, the fact that dissidents who fight for human rights are strongly feared by authoritarian rulers, who lock them up and try to silence them, is itself a huge tribute to the power of public discussion. And it is on the discipline of public reasoning that the rationale and force of asserting human rights—and indeed other ethical claims—ultimately depend.

6

I turn now to the choice of institutions, including markets and state-based institutions, both of which, as it happens, were strongly backed by Adam Smith, even though he has often been seen just as a great advocate of the pure and unsupplemented market economy. It is certainly true that Smith was particularly pioneering in explaining the rationale of the market economy (Smith 1776/1976). He presented far-reaching discussion of the usefulness and creativity of the market economy, and *why*—and particularly *how*—that dynamism worked. His explication of the rationale of the market economy is central to the understanding of what is now seen as the basic success of capitalism in the modern world. Smith's causal investigation provided an illuminating diagnosis of the principles of the market economy just when that dynamism was powerfully emerging, and the contribution that *The Wealth of Nations* made to the understanding of this part of economics, among others, was absolutely monumental. Smith showed how the freeing of trade can very often be extremely helpful in generating economic prosperity through specialization in production and division of labour and through making good use of economies of large scale.

Those lessons remain crucially relevant even today. Indeed, the economic analyses that followed those early expositions of markets and capitals in the eighteenth century have succeeded in solidly establishing the understanding of the rationale of the market system in the corpus of mainstream economics. Central to Smith's approach to the achievements of the market economy is the critical importance of trade and exchange (departing from the mirage of tradeless prosperity). It is also crucial to Smithian analysis of economic progress—and of development—to understand the importance he attached to the economy of large scale and the formation of human skill and productivity through specialization.

David Ricardo, who was also a great contributor to the world of economic ideas, followed Smith in focusing on the importance of trade, but to a great extent departed from him in explaining the rationale of trade in terms of comparative advantages of different countries—or regions—in the world (Ricardo 1817/2005). In fact, the main thrust of "Ricardian" advocacy of trade lies in the existence in variations in the resource bases of different countries: for example, country A may be richer in iron and country B in agricultural land. They can all benefit through exchanging commodities, the production of which draw on the resources respectively plentiful in the different regions, giving them differential comparative advantages in the production of diverse commodities that can be exchanged with mutual profit.

While Ricardian reasoning and its variations have been central to a great deal of trade theory (and it is certainly of profound importance), the Smithian reasoning, focusing on benefits of specialization, and economies of scale and cultivated skill formation, highlights a huge source of trade opportunities in the world.[4] Even if all countries had the same mixture of resources, they could still greatly benefit from trade through specialization in different types of production. These Smithian lessons, along with Ricardian ones, are very central to understanding the demands of economic progress, and remain as relevant today as they have been over the centuries.

7

If the market economy is so central to progress, why is there any need to look beyond the dynamism of a market-based capitalism? It is interesting to note that Smith never used the term "capitalism," but more importantly, he was not willing to turn into an unqualified admirer of the market. Indeed, even as the positive contributions of market processes and profit motives were being clarified and explicated in a novel way by Adam Smith, its negative sides for social progress were also becoming clear—to Smith himself. The balancing of the power and limitations of the market mechanism is important to understand to appreciate the demands of economic progress in the world.

A number of socialist critics (including Karl Marx and also, to a great extent, John Stuart Mill), in the century following Smith's own writings, would present the case for censuring and ultimately supplanting capitalism. What is, however, particularly interesting is that even to Smith—the trailblazing exponent of the rationale of the market economy—the huge limitations of relying entirely on the market economy and only on the profit motive were clear enough (he sought substantial *supplementation* of the market mechanism, though he would not endorse any proposal to *supplant* it). Even though the so-called "welfare state" that would emerge later on in Europe was far away from ideas current in Smith's own time, he expressed with much clarity, in his various writings, his overwhelming concern—and worry—about the fate of the poor and the disadvantaged, whose needs, he analysed, might not be met even by a very successful market economy.

The most immediate failure of the market mechanism as an engine of progress lies, Smith argued, in *omissions* rather than commissions—the necessary pursuits that the market leaves *undone*. Smith was not only a defender of the role of the state in providing public services, such as education and poverty relief (but with greater freedom for the indigent than the Poor Laws of his day provided), he was deeply concerned about the inequality and poverty that might survive in an otherwise successful market economy.

Lack of clarity about that distinction between omission and commission has been responsible for some misdiagnosis of Smith's assessment of the market mechanism, and the insights on development economics that can be obtained from Smith's work.

---

[4] For modern economic reasoning involving these dynamic aspects of trade, see particularly Krugman (1990). Also Krugman and Helpman (1985), and Roemer (1986).

Consider, for example, Smith's analysis of the need for state action to prevent hunger and famines. Adam Smith's defence of private trade in food grains and criticism of prohibitory restrictions imposed by the state on free trade have often been interpreted as a proposition that state interference can only make hunger and starvation worse. This is, in fact, a complete misinterpretation of Smith's contentions. His defence of private trade, in this context, only took the form of disputing the belief, common among policy-makers at his time, that allowing trade, particularly in food, would tend to produce serious distortions, and through that, an intensification of hunger. Smith strongly contradicted that general belief, and argued that trade can greatly help to relieve shortage in a particular area by bringing in food (e.g. food grains) from other areas, which were not comparably stricken. Similarly, if the income of those who have been pauperized could somehow be enhanced, then the market can help to feed these people.

The problem, however, lies in the fact that the market need not generate any new income to those who have been pauperized for one reason or another, for example, by crop failure, or a collapse of employment through floods or droughts or wars or social disorders. That understanding, which is central to contemporary theories of famine, was seen with unusual clarity by Adam Smith himself. If employment were to go down sharply thanks to bad economic circumstances or bad public policy, the market would not, on its own, recreate the lost incomes of those who are destituted. The newly unemployed "would either starve, or be driven to seek a subsistence either by begging, or by the perpetration perhaps of the greatest enormities," and "want, famine, and mortality would immediately prevail" (Smith 1776: I, I.viii.26/1976: 91).

Smith rejected *market-excluding* intervention, but was in favour of *market-including* interventions aimed at doing the necessary things that the market may leave undone (in particular generating income, for example, through public employment programmes, and then allowing the market to respond by bringing food to meet the newly created demand coming from erstwhile indigents). A combination of market-inclusive but state-dependent policies has been widely used in successful programs of famine prevention both in South Asia (including India) and in Africa in the second half of the twentieth century (see Dreze and Sen 1987).

8

As was mentioned earlier, Adam Smith is not known to have used the term "capitalism," but, in addition, it would also be hard to carve out from his works any theory of the *sufficiency* of the market economy (as opposed to the *necessity* of markets). Smith wanted institutional diversity and motivational variety—not monolithic markets and singular dominance of the profit motive (Rothschild 2001). Markets were seen as doing good work within their context, but they required support from other institutions for viability and success in securing human well-being and freedom.

The reason I am devoting so much time and space to Smith's belief in the need for a multi-institution understanding of the need for social progress, is that his reasoning still remains essentially correct and also critically important for thinking about progress in the contemporary world. Most importantly, Smith saw the task of political economy as the pursuit of "two distinct objects":

> first, to provide a plentiful revenue or subsistence for the people, or more properly to enable them to provide such a revenue or subsistence for themselves; and secondly, to supply the state or commonwealth with a revenue sufficient for the publick services. (1776: I.4. intro. 1; 1976: 428)

Smith's priorities for good economic performance and rapid economic development included, in addition to a well-functioning market economy, the role of the state in making adequate provision of public services.

Unlike Malthus, Smith did not reject the need for—and the rationale behind—the Poor Laws. Rather, he thought the Poor Laws needed reform, particularly by allowing greater liberty of locational movement for the indigent, who receive support, to look for employment elsewhere, rather than tying them down, as the Poor Laws demanded, to a particular region from where their support came. Going beyond his investigation of the demands of a well-functioning market system, Smith was deeply concerned about the deprivations and inequities that might survive in an otherwise successful market economy.

Indeed, even in dealing with regulations that restrain the markets, Smith saw the case for intervention in the interest of the poor and the underdogs of society. At one stage he gives a formula of disarming simplicity (Smith's views would make any "Tea Party" activist in America today deeply upset):

> When the regulation, therefore, is in favour of the workmen, it is always just and equitable; but it is sometimes otherwise when in favour of the masters. (1776: I.I.X. C.61/1976: 157–8)

We could speculate whether Smith meant this rather extreme remark to be taken literally. He was in fact commenting only on a particular class of state interventions. But underlying the plural institutional structure that Smith proposed was not only Smith's skepticism of the reach of the market (important as the market economy, he argued, was), but his attempt to marry the pursuit of the interests of the poor and the deprived involved both good use of the market economy and well-chosen state intervention.

9

There is another feature of Smith's economic analysis that is worth emphasizing in the context of understanding the demands of social progress. He focused particularly on building up human capability both for its direct importance for human living and for its role in enhancing fast and sustained economic expansion. One of the areas of state intervention to which

Smith attached special importance was education in general, and school education in particular. He wanted much greater use of state resources for public education and argued:

> For a very small expence the publick can facilitate, can encourage, and can even impose upon almost the whole body of the people, the necessity of acquiring those most essential parts of education. (1776: I.ii and V.i.f/1976: 27 and 785)

In focusing on the central role of universal education as an essential part of development strategy, Smith was both visionary and prophetic, in the eighteenth-century world of widespread illiteracy in Europe. The experiences of Europe—and of America—bring out most forcefully the pervasive role of education, led typically by governmental initiatives, in facilitating and sustaining economic and social progress.

That understanding also inspired the rising economic powers in Asia. Already in the mid-nineteenth century, the transforming role of school education was seen with remarkable clarity in Japan—the pioneering country to undertake modern economic development in Asia. Shortly after the Meiji restoration, in 1868, Japan adopted the "Fundamental Code of Education" in 1872, affirming an unequivocal public commitment to make sure that there must be "no community with an illiterate family, nor a family with an illiterate person." By 1910 Japan was almost fully literate, and the concentration on education determined, to a large extent, the nature and speed of Japan's extraordinary economic and social progress. Following Japan, South Korea, Taiwan, Singapore, Hong Kong, and of course China followed similar routes and firmly focused on basic education, largely delivered by the state. In explaining the rapid economic progress of East Asia, its willingness to make good use of the global market economy has been rightly emphasized. But that process was greatly helped by the achievements of these countries in public education. Widespread participation in a global economy would have been hard to accomplish if people could not read or write.

The so-called "East Asian strategy" of economic development, combining rapid progress in universal education and widespread use of the global market economy, can perhaps be best understood in terms of the strategy for economic progress and development that Adam Smith was firmly advocating. To the strong advocacy of public education, we can add the need for public health care, necessitated particularly by the presence of asymmetric information as well as extensive externalities in health and medical needs (see particularly Arrow 1963b). This combination is very much in the spirit of Smith's general approach of using a combination of institutions—of the state and the market—to advance human capability and to create conditions that favour social progress.

10

This way of seeing the demands of progress (including giving an adequate role to public education and similarly to public health care, while making powerful use of the market economy) helps us to understand what has gone very deeply wrong in the plans and programs for economic development in a number of countries, of which a prominent example is India. Indeed, while India has come to appreciate the virtues of a market economy, it has missed out the basic lessons of the East Asian development story, which involves balancing the state and the market (Dreze and Sen 2013). India has failed to give sufficient importance to the need for supplementing a vigorous market economy by major efforts in providing a national coverage of public education and public health care (even though the choice of individuals who can afford to have private care need not be eliminated, as indeed they are not in the East Asian—or for that matter—the European approach). There is something of the Smithian wisdom that India has managed to overlook.

India did for a while have the second highest rate of economic growth among the larger economies in the world. But even when India overtook other developing countries in the rate of growth of GDP, and sometime even in terms of absolute size of the GDP per head, it was quite often overtaken by other developing countries in terms of such indicators of living standards as life expectancy, basic health, and basic education. And now even India's fast economic growth rate has slackened. There is an odd lack of general understanding of the demands of economic progress among a vocal part of the Indian business commentators about how critically important it is to have public services, in the way East Asia has done, for enhancing living standards and even for sustaining rapid economic expansion.

There was a time when India had government policies that concentrated on those things that the government is very bad at doing (like running a so-called "license Raj"), while neglecting what it could do very well if it tried (like public education and public health care). That terrible combination needed dual correction. To characterize Indian policy at that time as "socialist," as some commentators chose to describe it, was of course a mistake (no socialist or communist economy—from the old Soviet Union or China to Cuba or Vietnam—had as low public education and public health care as India had), but there can hardly be any serious doubt that the inefficiency and inequity of an over-extended "license Raj" needed to be removed. This India has been doing for some decades now, and there is indeed a strong case for speeding up that still incomplete process.

However, along with that, it is also extremely important for the state to do those positive things that the state should be able to bring about, including much faster expansion of public education and public health care. There is arguably nothing as important for durable and shared economic growth as the enhancement of an educated and healthy labor force.

Even in comparative terms today, China's more successful experience shows that devoting much more public revenue than India does to the education, health care, and nutrition of the people is compatible with—and can indeed be very helpful for—high and sustained economic growth. Comparing India's miserable allocation of 1.2 percent of GDP to governmental expenditure on health with China's much higher figure of 2.7 percent, what is striking is not only the lack of appreciation of the demands of public health in India, but also how limited the understanding of many champions of economic growth in India is of the precise requirements for fast and sustained economic growth.

I am singling out India for illustration in this chapter, but of course the failure to recognize the complementarity between economic growth and human capability expansion applies to many other countries as well. It can be argued, for example, that an unreal presumption of a "disconnect" between public services and economic expansion has plagued the recent European attempts at overcoming its ongoing economic and financial crisis through largely indiscriminate "austerity," without taking adequate account of the far-reaching social and economic consequences of withdrawal of public services and employment-supporting policies, based on isolated financial reasoning—concentrating almost exclusively on cost cutting with little serious note being taken of the positive role of the public services.

11

If Adam Smith's reservations on the market economy about errors of *omission* of the market have tended to be drowned in the stylized representation of Smith as a "free marketeer," the challenge is even greater in understanding that Smith also had much to say—of great interest—about errors of *commission* of the market. It was not only that the market leaves many important tasks undone, but also that the operation of an unregulated market can lead to serious mistakes in the performance of the economy.

This applies particularly to Smith's analysis of the promoters of excessive risk in search of profits, whom he called "prodigals and projectors." Smith's use of these terms was quite pejorative. For example, by "projector" Smith did not mean those who "form a project," but specifically in its derogatory sense, apparently common from 1616 (so it appears from *The Shorter Oxford English Dictionary*); it means "a promoter of bubble companies; a speculator; a cheat." Indeed, Jonathan Swift's unflattering portrayal of "projectors" in *Gulliver's Travels*, published in 1726 (fifty years before the *Wealth of Nations*), corresponds closely enough to Smith's deployment of that word.[5] Unwavering faith in the wisdom of the stand-alone market economy, which has had considerable responsibility in the removal of the established regulations in a number of countries, including the United States, has contributed to making these economies more vulnerable to a crisis, precisely because of the activities of those whom Smith called "prodigals and projectors." There is a strong similarity here between Smith's analysis and the causation of the recent economic crisis of 2008, in which over-speculative financial investment in search of a "quick kill," unrestrained by

---

[5] I am grateful to Giorgio Basevi for drawing my attention to the importance of the similarity of terminology between Smith and Swift.

governmental regulations (which had been gradually relaxed over a sequence of executive regimes, beginning in the days of President Reagan) played a big part.

Smith's reservations about the market economy—not just about its omissions but also about commissions—may seem quite strange to those who see Smith as an unqualified admirer of the pure market mechanism. Interestingly enough, Smith's reservations about the market mechanism were subjects of critical commentary in his own days. In one of the really interesting, if largely forgotten, intellectual debates of the eighteenth century, Jeremy Bentham grumbled about Smith's inability to understand enough about the virtues of the market economy. Indeed, Bentham took Smith to task in a long letter he wrote to Smith suggesting that he—Smith—was unreasonably anti-market. Smith should, Bentham argued, leave the market alone, rather than criticize—and propose to interfere with—the market for its inability to control those whom Smith called "prodigals and projectors," and that Smith should give up (in Bentham's view) supporting state regulation of financial transactions.[6] Bentham may have missed the force of Smith's reasoning on this subject (he certainly did that), but his diagnosis of Smith's skepticism of the market was not really mistaken.

12

I have been concentrating a great deal on institutions and organizations, but the demands of progress also relate closely to the role of human motivation. Even though Smith gave much room for emotions in guiding people's thoughts as well as actions, he did think that even our instinctive attitudes to particular behavior cannot but rely—if only implicitly—on our reasoned understanding of causal connections between conduct and consequences in "a vast variety of instances." Furthermore, first perceptions may also change in response to critical examination, for example on the basis of causal empirical investigation that may show, Smith noted in *The Theory of Moral Sentiments*, that a certain "object is the means of obtaining some other."

Mischaracterization of Smith's analysis of reasons for action has been a rampant feature of twentieth-century economics. Smith has often been seen as a pioneer of what is now called "rational choice theory" in which rationality is identified with intelligently pursuing only one's self-interest. If you do something for anyone else, this can be rational, in this theory, only if you get something from it yourself. There is no room in this characterization of Smith for moral values of various kinds, from altruism to social commitment—values the reasonableness of which Smith discussed in considerable

---

[6] Bentham included this letter in the second of the two prefaces he wrote for the 2nd edn of his combative defense of the market economy against regulations that restrain usury: Bentham (1797).

detail in *The Theory of Moral Sentiments*. Indeed, that book—Smith's first—opens with the following sentence:

> How selfish soever man may be supposed, there are evidently some principles in his nature, which interest him in the fortunes of others, and render their happiness necessary to him, though he derives nothing from it except the pleasure of seeing it. (1790/2009: p. x)

The analysis of plural objectives and a broader understanding of human motivation are further developed by Smith as the book proceeds, and he makes particular use of his thought-experiment of "the Impartial Spectator" as a device for reasoned self-scrutiny, of which, he thought, reasoning human beings are perfectly capable. As Smith put it:

> we either approve or disapprove of our conduct, according as we feel that, when we place ourselves in the situation of another man, and view it, as it were, with his eyes and from his station, we either can or cannot entirely enter into and sympathize with the sentiments or motives which influenced it. We can never survey our own sentiments and motives, we can never form any judgment concerning them; unless we remove ourselves, as it were, from our own natural station, and endeavour to view them as at a certain distance from us. But we can do this in no other way than by endeavouring to view them with the eyes of other people, or as other people are likely to view them. (1790: III.1.2/2009: 133).

Instead of the naïve simplicity of the "as if" Smith's behavioral beliefs, the real Smith distinguishes between the different kinds of reasons people have in taking an interest in the lives of others, separating out "sympathy," "generosity," "public spirit," and other motivations, each of which differs from the others, and yet all of which have the implication of taking people away from purely selfish pursuit of their own interests. Smith discusses how reasoning, which is at the heart of rationality, has a big role in preventing us from being consciously self-centered or unconsciously uncaring.

The fact that profit-seeking is an important part of human motivation is not, of course, in doubt. But the question is whether that is the *only* motivation that can move people—a question that has major implications for our understanding of the demands of progress. In providing incentives for economic activities—from investment to work—economic gain can be a major factor, and a development plan that ignores that elementary connection can do so only at its own peril. And yet there is so much more to people's motivation than can be captured within the limited box of profit maximization. The development of good work habits, spontaneous punctuality, regular diligence, attention to work performance, ability to work cooperatively with others—all this is much aided by broader motivations.

Smith did note that sophisticated reasoning about self-interest can cover a larger ground by taking note of incentives developed in situations that are repeated or paralleled over time. In making use of what in today's terminology of game theory would be called "repeated games," Smith developed his own theory of the rewards of good reputation, including the benefits arising from people having reason to develop "trust" in decent behavior and reliability of each other.

A great deal of the confusion surrounding Smith's presumptions about human motivation and his assessment of the usefulness of different kinds of motives has tended to arise from not distinguishing between (1) people's reasons for seeking trade, and (2) the motivations that make different kinds of economic activities, including trading, successful and stable. It is in answer to the first question that Smith noted the relevance of the motive of self-seeking. He noted that to explain why people seek trade and exchange, we do not have to go beyond the simple pursuit of self-interest. In his most famous and widely quoted passage from the *Wealth of Nations* (very popular in mainstream economics as well as in the specialized discipline that has come to be called "law and economics," and also in so-called "rational choice politics"), Smith wrote:

> It is not from the benevolence of the butcher, the brewer, or the baker that we expect our dinner, but from their regard to their own interest. We address ourselves not to their humanity but to their self-love. (1776/1976)

This is a fine point about motivation for trade—interesting in itself—but it is not a claim about the adequacy of self-seeking for the success of a society or even of the market economy, or even the success and sustainability of trade and exchanges themselves.

Indeed, a market economy demands a variety of values for its success, including mutual trust and confidence, whether derived from the discipline of "repeated games" (when that works) or from reasoning of other kinds. Smith made this basic point with several illustrations. He argued, for example:

> When the people of any particular country have such confidence in the fortune, probity, and prudence of a particular banker, as to believe he is always ready to pay upon demand such of his promissory notes as are likely to be at any time presented to him; those notes come to have the same currency as gold and silver money, from the confidence that such money can at any time be had for them. (1776: I, II.ii.2, 28/ 1976: 292)

Smith discussed why such confidence need not always exist. Even though the champions of baker-brewer-butcher reading of Smith, enshrined in many economic books, may be at a loss about how to understand the recent economic crisis of 2008 (since people—even bakers, brewers, and butchers—still had excellent reason to *seek* more trade even during the crisis, but had far less *opportunity* to sell their wares), the devastating consequences of mistrust and the shattering of mutual confidence that was an important feature of the crisis would not have appeared puzzling to Adam Smith.

Economic practice demands a realistic understanding of the variety of motivations that enter into human behavior, and the institutional demands of economic development have to take note of these variations. On one side, many well-meaning but

overtrusting development initiatives have foundered in the world because of unanticipated self-seeking behavior—e.g. public servants making use of their power to seek
bribes and other personal advantages—and there is need for more realism in setting
up these arrangements. And yet, on the other side, a failure to develop work ethics
and disciplined conduct restricts the feasibility of many institutional arrangements
on which successful development experiences across the world have standardly
depended.

Smith recognized the fallibility of human conduct in moral terms, but emphasized
the possibility both of influence of reasoning on human behavior, and of the formation
of good conduct based on reasoning that might become habitual, even when the
original reasoning does not remain uppermost in people's thinking. As Smith put it:

> Many men behave very decently, and through the whole of their lives avoid any
> considerable degree of blame, and who yet, perhaps, never felt the sentiment upon
> the propriety of which we found our approbation of their conduct, but acted
> merely from a regard to what they saw were the established rules of behaviour.
> (Smith 1790/2009)

In the development of "established rules of behaviour" lies one of the most important
challenges of ensuring social and economic progress. A combination of accountability
and enhancement of new rules of behavior remains as important for development
efforts today—from China and India to Brazil and Mexico—as it was in the development experiences in Smith's own time.

13

Before I end, I must make a few remarks on problems of sustainable development as a
part of social progress. The threat that the environment faces today has rightly been
emphasized in recent discussions, but there is need for clarity in deciding on how to
think about the environmental challenges in the contemporary world. Focusing on
human freedom and on the quality of life can help in this understanding, and throw
light not only on the demands of sustainable development, but also on the content and
relevance of what we can identify as "environmental issues."

The environment is sometimes seen—I believe oversimply—as the "state of nature,"
including such measures as the extent of forest cover, the depth of the ground water
table, the number of living species, and so on. To the extent that it is assumed that this
pre-existing nature will stay fine and right unless we add pollutants or decimate parts of
it, it might appear superficially plausible that environment is best protected if we
interfere with it as little as possible. This understanding is, however, deeply defective
for two important reasons.

First, the environment is not only a matter of passive preservation, but also one
of active pursuit. Even though many human activities that accompany the process of

development may have destructive consequences (and this is very important to see and address), it is also within human power to enhance and improve the environment in which we live. In thinking about the steps that may be taken to halt environmental destruction, we have to include constructive human intervention. Our power to intervene with effectiveness and reasoning can be substantially enhanced by the process of development itself. For example, greater female education and women's employment can help to reduce fertility rates, which in the long run can reduce the pressure on global warming and the increasing destruction of natural habitats. Similarly, the spread of school education and improvements in its quality can make us more environmentally conscious; better communication and a more active and better informed media can make us more aware of the need for environment-oriented thinking. It is easy to find many other examples of interconnection. In general, seeing development in terms of increasing the effective freedom of human beings brings the constructive agency of people in environment-friendly activities directly within the domain of developmental achievements.

Second, the value of environment cannot be just a matter of what there is, but also of what opportunities it actually offers to people. The impact of the environment on human lives must be among the principal considerations in assessing the value of the environment. To take an extreme example, in understanding why the eradication of smallpox is not viewed as an impoverishment of nature (we do not tend to lament: "the environment is decimated since the smallpox virus disappeared"), in the way, say, the destruction of ecologically important forests would be seen, the connection with lives in general and human lives in particular has to be brought into the understanding.

It is, therefore, not surprising that environmental sustainability has typically been defined in terms of preservation and enhancement of the quality of human life. The rightly celebrated Brundtland Report (the Report of the World Commission on Environment and Development, chaired by Gro Brundtland, published in 1987), defined "sustainable development" as "development that meets the needs of the present without compromising the ability of future generations to meet their own needs." Robert Solow (1992) has extended this approach in a powerful way, integrating the sequential roles of different generations in terms of a comprehensive and easily understandable formula. There is a lot of wisdom in this visionary understanding, but we can enrich it further by moving from the valuation of needs-fulfillment to valuing human freedom (taking a broader view of humanity).

14

Consider our responsibility toward the species that are threatened with destruction. We may attach importance to the preservation of these species not merely *because*—nor only to the *extent* that—the presence of these species enhances our own living standards. For example, a person may judge that we ought to do what we can to ensure the preservation of some threatened animal species, say, spotted owls of some specific kind. There would be no contradiction if the person were to say: "My living standards would be largely, indeed completely, unaffected by the presence or absence of spotted owls—I have in fact never even seen one—but I do strongly believe that we should not let those owls become extinct, for reasons that have nothing much to do with human living standards."

This is where Gautama Buddha's argument, presented in *Sutta Nipata*, becomes directly and immediately relevant. He argued that a mother has a responsibility toward her child not merely because she has generated her, but also because she can do many things for the child which the child cannot itself do. It is this "power to make a difference" that must, Buddha argued, generate a corresponding responsibility. Buddha went on from there to argue that human beings similarly have responsibility toward animals precisely because we have such power over their lives.

In the environmental context it can be argued that, since we are enormously more powerful than the other species, we have some responsibility toward these species that links with this asymmetry of power. We can have many reasons for our conservational efforts—not all of which need be parasitic on our own living standards (or need-fulfillment) and some of which turn precisely on our sense of values and on our acknowledgment of our reasons for taking fiduciary responsibility for other creatures on whose lives we can have a powerful influence.

If the importance of human lives lies not merely in our living standards and need-fulfillment, but also in the freedoms that we enjoy, then the idea of sustainable development has to be correspondingly extended. There is cogency in thinking not just about sustaining the fulfillment of our needs, but more broadly about sustaining—or extending—our freedoms (including, of course, the freedom to meet our needs, but with the possibility to go well beyond that). Thus recharacterized, the idea of sustainable freedom can be broadened from the formulations proposed by Brundtland and Solow to encompass the preservation, and when possible expansion, of the substantive freedoms and capabilities of people today without compromising the capability of future generations to have similar—or more—freedoms.

15

Central to the exercise of evaluation of progress is the conception of human beings. The importance of greater fulfillment of people's needs has been rightly emphasized by a number of leading thinkers. Karl Marx's powerful call for progress—much repeated in political dialogues—toward a society where each gets what he or she needs ("from each according to his ability to each according to his needs") has inspired generations of people. It is on that rich tradition that Gro Brundtland has drawn in characterizing sustainable development as "development that meets the needs of the present without compromising the ability of future generations to meet their own needs." This can surely serve as a major basis for assessing human progress. And yet the idea can be further enriched by invoking a fuller concept of humanity.

People do have *needs*, but they also have *values*, and in particular, cherish their ability to choose, act, argue, agree, or disagree—and most importantly, reason alone and reason with others. Seeing people only in terms of their needs may give us, ultimately, a rather meager view of humanity. Giving a fuller role to our ability to reason must be seen as quite central to understanding the demands of human progress. The world tends to progress not just by expanding the achievement of pre-identified needs, or by expanding the fulfillment of antecedent values, but also by progressive assessment—and reassessment—of the values we can defend and the reasons that we can give in support of our priorities: old and new.

Slavery lost its moral grounds in public reasoning more than a century ago, and the tolerance of systematic discrimination against women, unnecessary hunger, or abject poverty, or the absence of medical facilities for impoverished people may be moving toward unacceptability right now (though there is still some way to go for the underlying reasoning to be victorious and effective). The moving force behind these transformations is the possibility, power, and reach of public reasoning in step with the changing nature of the world in which we live.

Even as the world grows more affluent in terms of pre-existing aspirations, the reach of those aspirations is in constant need of scrutiny which our reasoning, in public discussions as well as private reflections, allows us to do. It is in the interplay of reason and accomplishment that the idea of progress has to find its sustainable home.

REFERENCES

Arrow, Kenneth J. (1951). *Social Choice and Individual Values*. New York: Wiley.

Arrow, Kenneth J. (1963a). *Social Choice and Individual Values*. 2nd edn. New York: Wiley.

Arrow, Kenneth J. (1963b). Uncertainty and the Welfare Economics of Medical Care. *American Economic Review*, 53: Vol LIII, Number 5, December 1963, pp. 941–73.

Bentham, Jeremy (1787). *Defence of Usury*. 2nd edn. London: Printed for T. Payne, and Son.

Dreze, Jean, and Amartya Sen (1987). *Hunger and Public Action*. Oxford: Oxford University Press.

Dreze, Jean, and Amartya Sen (2013). *An Uncertain Glory: India and its Contradictions* (London and Delhi: Penguin, and Princeton: Princeton University Press.

Krugman, Paul (1990). *Rethinking International Trade*. Cambridge, MA: MIT Press.

Krugman, Paul, and Elhanan Helpman (1985). *Market Structure and Foreign Trade*. Cambridge, MA: MIT Press.

Rawls, John (1993). *Political Liberalism*. New York: Columbia University Press.

Rawls, John (2001). *Justice as Fairness: A Restatement*, ed. Erin Kelly. Cambridge, MA: Harvard University Press.

Ricardo, David (1817/2005). *On the Principles of Political Economy and Taxation*; reprinted in *The Works and Correspondence of David Ricardo*, ed. Piero Sraffa, with the assistance of Maurice Dobb, vol. i. Cambridge: Cambridge University Press; Indianapolis: Liberty Fund.

Roemer, Paul M. (1986). Increasing Returns and Long Run Growth. *Journal of Political Economy*, Vol. 94, No. 5 (Oct, 1986), pp. 1002–37.

Rothschild, Emma (2001). *Economic Sentiments: Adam Smith, Condorcet and the Enlightenment*. Cambridge, MA: Harvard University Press.

Sen, Amartya (1986). Social Choice Theory. In Kenneth Arrow and Michael Intriligator (eds), *Handbook of Mathematical Economics*. Amsterdam: North-Holland.

Sen, Amartya (1999). The Possibility of Social Choice. *American Economic Review*, Vol. 89, No. 3, pp. 349–78.

Sen, Amartya (2002). *Rationality and Freedom*. Cambridge, MA: Harvard University Press.

Sen, Amartya (2003). Sraffa, Wittgenstein and Gramsci. *Journal of Economic Literature*, Vol. XLI (Dec, 2003), pp. 1240–55.

Sen, Amartya (2009). *The Idea of Justice*. London: Penguin; Cambridge, MA: Harvard University Press.

Smith, Adam (1776/1976). *An Inquiry into the Nature and Causes of the Wealth of Nations*, ed. R. H. Campbell and A. S. Skinner. Oxford: Oxford University Press.

Smith, Adam (1790/2009). *The Theory of Moral Sentiments*. Revised edn (originally publ. 1759), republ. Oxford: Clarendon Press, 1976, and New York: Penguin Books, 2009.

Smith, Adam (1982). *Lectures on Jurisprudence*, ed. R. L. Meek, D. D. Raphael, and P. G. Stein. Indianapolis: Liberty Press.

Solow, Robert (1992). *An Almost Practical Step toward Sustainability*. Washington, DC: Resources for the Future.

CHAPTER 10

AN ENTREPRENEUR'S REFLECTIONS ON PROGRESS

JACK MA

Abstract

This chapter draws on the experience in founding and developing Alibaba in China and discusses whether and how enterprises might contribute to progress, sustainable growth, legitimate and long-term governance, and trust. The importance of information and, increasingly, data technology are underlined. The centrality of the individual in Alibaba's economic and organizational models is also stressed. If we are to think about better models of growth then we must aim not only for industrial progress but also for individual progress. In industrial progress the rules are predefined and people have to fit in. The future is one where enterprises will be better able to integrate individuals with different talents and styles. This is a future in which growth and progress will be more coherent.

In developing this chapter I was urged to reflect on some "big" questions. Is there a form or version of capitalism that might jointly advance efficiency and fairness? Is growth the same as progress? Should and can private companies be agents of progress?

These are broad and difficult questions. Yet, from my view, perhaps as an idealist entrepreneur, I will share some thoughts based on our experience at Alibaba, the internet-enabled infrastructure company that we have been building. This infrastructure includes platforms to help Chinese importers and exporters, platforms for domestic consumption and payment, a logistics network to ensure rural denizens are afforded the same resources as big-city dwellers, and world-class cloud computing services.

Markets, knowledge, and management all exert profound influence on the structure and operation of a society. These factors can be leveraged no matter whether the society in question is socialist or capitalist.

So-called capital markets, the products of capitalist social structures, have already been discovered to have many inherent weaknesses, for example, the tension between short-term orientation of capital markets versus long-term vision needed by companies. Many countries are experimenting with tactics to ameliorate these problems, for example, by allowing the listing of company shares with different voting classes in the US.

Industrial societies place an enormous emphasis on the importance of capital to economic activities, hence the main factors of capitalist production have historically been capital, machines, and labor. This was not always the case: in pre-industrial agricultural societies, land was often the chief factor of production, and by the 1980s, more diversified forms of capital (e.g. social and human capital) began to enter our theories. In practice, however, the most important resources for firms are various monetary forms of capital and machines of many kinds: Marx's formulation of capitalism's alienation of the person still holds true.

We are at the cusp of a transition to the new era of data, where the rules for capitalism will be rewritten. Technology is breaking down barriers to entry in industry after industry, making capital and labor less and less crucial for market success. In this information age, the most important assets for production will be data and creativity, and the main challenges for firms will not be how to amass enormous quantities of capital, but how to enable people to access and unleash their creative potential with technology and data. Put another way, one of the fundamental roles of technological platforms is to allow efficient and fair access to opportunity.

The use of data will be the key determinant of who can succeed in this new socio-economic system. The efficiency of productive activities of an organization will rely more and more on the way and extent that creative ideas and data are integrated. We can think of this new category of organizational relationships as the future of management.

Alibaba's innovations on the level of governance, including our partnership structure, are attempts to experiment with these future modes of management. We are trying to find structures and systems that will allow for long-term, sustainable company development while also insuring the inheritance of culture and continuous innovation.

The changes described are more than a change in economic systems, they also go hand in hand with a new, ecological business logic. The reason we advocate open, cooperative, and transparent business ecosystems (exemplified by our various business platforms) is to experiment with new socio-economic methods of organization and interaction. In the future, the interactions between companies will be more fluid and mobile, and the strict boundaries between companies will even begin to blur as firms begin to exchange data and evolve new forms of cooperation.

These changes are nothing short of a paradigm shift, but even we at the forefront of change need more time to evaluate where these changes will eventually take our society.

Governments have and will continue to play a role in making a better future, as there are certain areas in which private markets are not sufficient. There is however a fundamental role for business enterprise in contributing to progress. Indeed, on a fundamental level, business is a good process of solving social problems. And in a way our own company's mission has been to change industries and societies through our enterprise. Hence we are not a company in the traditional sense of the word. The reason we exist, and our core value, is to solve the problems faced by our community locally and globally.

In the twenty-first century, one must define an organization's mission and reason for existence. In the past century, companies could prosper by simply grabbing one good opportunity. Big companies today must understand this principle: they must solve social problems before solving corporate problems. This is the best (only?) way to achieve long-term development.

Therefore, Alibaba is in the business of solving social problems like innovating traditional business by leveraging the internet. We are no longer simply a company; we are an ecosystem. If we can solve problems through economic development, we will not need conflict and wars to influence people and create change.

We anticipate China's broader transformation and provide what businesses and consumers need the most. We keep seeing opportunities to change not just the way business is done, but more broadly to change our society for the better.

It is also true that the most challenging problems we face are not the problems of business, but the problems of society, for example, how to establish systems of trust and cooperation and how to channel innovation into production and value creation.

Alibaba also views environmental stewardship as a central part of our mission. In 2010, we established the Alibaba Foundation, which is funded every year from 0.3 percent of our income (not profits!). This foundation aims to tackle the hardest problems in Chinese society, from water quality to the support of local philanthropy.

I have mentioned open, cooperative, and prosperous business ecosystems. On one level, this is our business model. But on a deeper level, this is our experiment at social governance in a knowledge economy. These methods of governance rest on sharing, cooperation, and self-organization, and hence are not exactly the same methods a government traditionally uses to govern a society.

We are still experimenting, but we believe that these new modes of governance will become mainstream someday. That is the reason many people are paying attention to the problems Alibaba faces and the methods we use to address them.

I was also asked how I would characterize the idea of progress.

We believe in equality and transparency, which are the essence of the internet. Hopefully these values will lead to the transformation of Chinese society, allowing us to leapfrog in our development of a stronger institutional and social infrastructure.

When we started Alibaba fifteen years ago, we hoped that even a person from a very poor background could launch a business and live a good life through creative ideas and perseverance powered by "e-infrastructure." We wanted to level the playing field for anyone who wants to start a business and to help the small and medium-sized company have a chance to succeed. To date, we've already created some 15 million direct and indirect employment opportunities through our platforms. Many of these jobs go to university graduates, but also the disabled, and young people from the countryside who want to make a living by running small businesses. One huge problem we see is that China's rural areas are far less developed than our cities, and there has been a hollowing out of villages where working adults leave behind children and grandparents in search of jobs in the big cities. Developing online platforms that allow people to make money while staying in their hometowns has moved us toward a more balanced society. Currently, farmers who use our platforms can sell their goods to consumers all over the country, which will become easier as our logistics platform further develops.

We will keep building the infrastructure for commerce in China in the next ten years, bringing our country from an era of IT to an era of DT (data technology) and creating more jobs for the society in this process. We are grateful to live in an era of generational change, because if everything stayed stable, we wouldn't have any opportunities.

Economic growth and development are valuable and necessary especially for bringing people out of poverty. All the same as we have observed growth does not always go hand in hand with progress. Growth may bring more pollution, income inequality, congested urbanization, and other undesirable consequences. In our version of market economy, I think we should and can work to avoid those same mistakes. In other words, we must look for better ways to achieve economic growth—ways that aim for harmony between growth and progress.

As I mentioned earlier, in economically developed societies there is a chronic tension over the short-term orientation of capital markets and the long-term orientation that may be healthy for companies and societies. In this environment it is increasingly difficult to maintain the necessary investments and creativity of industry. To address this problem at Alibaba we are experimenting with an approach that we refer to as the "partner system." This is a form of corporate governance that through special voting rights aims to protect against the short-term orientation. We hope it will safeguard our environment for innovation.

Change is not teleological. It does not stop and it will not wait for you or follow your rules. It will rewrite the rules. By the same logic, society too will evolve as the people that constitute it innovate.

Ecological innovation brings growth and efficiency for the system as a whole. Recently, Chinese taxi app companies have been fighting tooth and nail to intelligently connect taxi drivers to passengers. This smart, data-driven, and moreover natural allocation may mean that we will eventually need fewer cars on the road. These types of innovations may even be able to help us protect the environment. Of course, any ecosystem needs equal access, cooperation, and affordable infrastructure to work properly, for example, cheap and reliable cloud computing and data analytics that anybody can use.

While I believe in the power of technology I must note that technology per se is not a distinct thing. Technology is what influences peoples' mindsets; the way people interact with others; the way people make choices. Compared to the past the technological change we are witnessing seems fundamental. The internet and its applications are based on an open architecture and distributed capabilities. This is different from the assembly lines of the last century. Technology is again going to impact organization but this time it can help unleash peoples' creativity.

If we are to think about better models of growth then we must aim not only for industrial progress but also for *individual* progress. In industrial progress the rules are predefined and people have to fit in. For example, people may need an MBA to succeed in a company and achieve a certain position. The future looks different, one where enterprises will be better able to integrate individuals with different talents, skills, and styles. This will not happen automatically. Enterprises will have to aim to do this and be willing to be organized differently. To me this is a future in which growth and progress can be more coherent.

PROGRESS: DISCUSSION SUMMARY

Tʜɪs short write-up summarizes the discussions that took place around the chapters centered on the theme "Progress." Any prospect of reconciling performance with progress depends on our ability to articulate relevant conceptions of progress. The group directed its attention both to abstract conceptual challenges involved in defining this notion, and to some concrete questions of measurement and implementation.

A large share of the discussion surrounding "Progress" can be usefully characterized in relation to Sen's suggestion—drawing loosely on John Rawls's notion of "public reason"[1]—that the definitive standard of social progress is to be identified through the pursuit of inclusive intersubjective agreement. Echoing this proposal, Kitcher in his chapter emphasizes that any notion of progress must be continuously subject to a democratic process of social evaluation: "critique and appraisal in the light of well-informed, mutually engaged deliberation." Sen noted, in agreement with Kitcher, that the success of deliberation should not be judged only by whether it generates comprehensive and unanimous agreement. Clarification of the reasons for differences (when they survive) is important and, even without comprehensive and wholehearted agreement, it is also very useful to strive for a point at which a large share of us at least find a given proposal reasonable enough to pursue.

The suggestion that we might construct standards through some kind of agreement raised a number of concerns for the participants. For starters, how inclusive is the relevant moral community? As Kitcher observed, social progress in specific parts of the world has often come at significant cost to other parts of the world. Are such cases really instances of progress? We seem to need a framework for thinking about progress on a global or "cosmopolitan" scale. Similarly, following on a comment by Neiman in the discussion of "Problem," Sen emphasized the importance of internationalizing discussion, citing the Copenhagen climate talks as an example of the inadvisability of seeking a shared commitment without adequate dialog on its pros and cons, seen from different perspectives. As Collomb noted, the problem in this case was that it proved so

---

[1] See John Rawls, *Political Liberalism* (New York: Columbia University Press, 1993).

difficult for the Europeans nations to achieve any kind of consensus among themselves that addressing the concerns of other nations became almost impossible.

Collomb's observation about the difficulties of inter-European dialog connects concerns about moral inclusiveness to a second set of challenges, namely those of feasibility. On a skeptical note, Barney thus asked how we are supposed to proceed in light of the disparity between the sort of reciprocal, good-faith discussion that Sen and Kitcher have in mind, and the discouraging reality of contemporary moral discussion. A different kind of concern about practicality attends to the enormous diversity of moral and social perspectives. As Arrow observed, public discussion tends to be much more tractable when the community can be broken down into smaller, more homogeneous groups, as in the example of American federalism.

Part of the answer to this problem, Kitcher and Sen both suggest (in somewhat different ways) in their chapters, is to abandon "teleological" notions of progress, i.e. the idea that progress consists in steadily moving toward some timeless, universally valid, ideal state. Instead, we should think about progress in what Kitcher dubs "pragmatic," terms: progress consists in changes from our present standpoint that are recognizable as improvements to us, given the values, aims, and desires that make us who we are. Progress, as Sen put it, "is about comparative judgment."

A third concern about the model of progress as a function of public reason concerns the status of reasoning itself. As Fuerstein noted, many of the great episodes of moral progress in human history were precipitated by action—protests, civil disobedience, public theater, etc.—as much as rational dialogue. In a similar vein, Appiah noted the importance of sentiments in thinking about progress, pointing to Neiman's example of progress surrounding gay marriage and gay relationships.

Discussion of the public reason model introduced significant concerns associated with diversity within the moral community. Perhaps a more fundamental issue is that of diversity within the standard of progress itself. In his presentation Appiah observed the apparently incommensurable nature of the various goods at stake when we talk about progress: improvement in some domains can often lead to declines in other domains, both within individual persons and across the moral community, and there is no uncontroversial way of aggregating all of this into one coherent metric of social progress.

While Sen's Rawlsian appeal to public reason suggests a kind of methodology for constructing standards of progress, much of the discussion revolved around more concrete proposals for what the standards themselves should encompass. One possibility, suggested by Snabe, would be to at least start our pursuit of progress by focusing on basic human needs, such as food and clean water. That indicates one possible line of response to some of the core concerns about commensurability and global diversity. Another baseline concern is that of inequality. While no one in the group advocated for strong equality of economic outcome, the primary concern seemed to be the various ways in which economic inequalities might undermine the basic social and political capacities of some members of society.

In his presentation, Kitcher suggested that we might think about progress, not only in terms of basic material goods and egalitarian social standing, but also more broadly in terms of the promotion of human capacities to lead a good life, a notion encompassing the ability to make autonomous decisions, the opportunity for meaningful work, and the opportunity to participate in community. Echoing Kitcher, Walsh suggested that we might think about progress as a two-fold notion encompassing, first, our ability to tend to "the vulnerable, the weak, and the infirm" and, second, "the freedom to be." He observed that the latter idea is plausibly modeled in the jobs of professors themselves, who have the opportunity to define their professional role around projects that they find meaningful and that makes a real difference in the world. Perhaps professors might advance progress, not only through their research, but also by inspiring genuine hope among their students? One way of thinking about hope is in terms of an irrational anticipation of positive outcomes. But another, as Pettit suggested, is to "put our credences offline," that is, to make a shared commitment to stick with a project independently of variations in our confidence of its success. Perhaps professors might inspire some such commitment?

Kitcher expressed concern, however, about a deep tension between the kind of expansive notion of progress embodied in the capabilities approach and the imperatives of modern capitalism. If industrial efficiency is to be realized through ever greater technical specialization, then that might very well compete with the forms of development—of imagination, freedom, possibility—that promote the kind of human flourishing embodied in a "freedom to be." As Risse observed, this problem connects with important dynamics in higher education at the moment, where students appear to be increasingly focused on narrowly careerist ambitions at the expense of a broadly humanistic, liberal arts education.

Walsh's emphasis on the significance of hope, and hopefulness, in promoting progress, suggests a broader question: what are the psychological conditions in which progress is likely? A psychological mechanism like hope seems particularly important if, as Frank suggested in reference to climate change, the principal obstacle to progress is not any lack of knowledge about ends or means but, rather, the lack of a will to do what needs to be done. Or perhaps, as Neiman noted, there is a pervasive sense of powerlessness that individuals feel when confronted with the massive scale of the world's problems. Perhaps hope is a kind of psychological antidote to that.

Appiah's chapter focused on the role that an ethos of honor might play in cultivating more pro-social behavior within the business world. For Appiah, the notion of "honor" refers, in effect, to an entitlement to respect among one's peers. Honor is of course a prevalent notion in some traditional cultures, but also plays a crucial role in some professions, such as medicine, where it is particularly easy to get away with doing wrong so far as your "customers" (patients) are concerned. In light of that fact, the desire to be worthy of peer esteem plays a crucial role in motivating ethical behavior. Perhaps, Appiah notes, we might seek ways of inculcating an ethos of honor more broadly across the business world?

What are the conditions under which the spread of a moral ethos—honor-based or otherwise—is most plausible? In responding to Appiah's essay, Meyer observed that norms such as honor are most effective when they are seeded broadly through organizations and not only in their leaders. We should thus be thinking about professional norms on the level of the organization rather than the individual.

Has there been a cultural decline in norms of honor? Jafar mentioned an account he had recently read of the *Titanic*, according to which "few men from first or second class violated the norm of 'women and children first.'" He then asked: "if today we had a *Titanic* of the world's wealthiest, to what extent would those codes still exist? How many would care?" A number of participants observed various features of the modern business environment that might be working against that kind of moral code. Frank noted that reliance on material incentives to induce good behavior can in some cases undermine the effectiveness of moral motivation, particularly in those cases where our ability to detect code violations is weak. On the other hand, as Davis pointed out, contemporary technology has increasingly made the workplace an environment in which individuals are pervasively monitored. Does modern technology mitigate the sort of problem that Frank observed, or make it worse? Anderson mentioned a different sort of force that cuts against a moral ethos in the workplace, namely, the "bureaucratization" of professional services. She noted the contemporary experience of many doctors, for example, in which they are deluged with specific protocols and checklists from above that can often leave little time to devote real care to the patient.

Tiberius observed that, from a basic psychological perspective, there is significant agreement among moral philosophers and developmental psychologists that it is essential to begin inculcating a moral perspective at a young age. Though this issue was not explored further, Tiberius's point dovetails nicely with Walsh's and Risse's observations about higher education to underline the importance of further reflection on the proper role of educational institutions, at all stages, in fostering progress.

PART III

BALANCING AND TRADE-OFFS

CHAPTER 11

THE BUSINESS ENTERPRISE AS AN ETHICAL AGENT

ELIZABETH ANDERSON

Abstract

Many for-profit firms integrate ethical considerations into their operations in ways that go beyond obedience to the law and to the letter of contracts they make with employees, customers, creditors, and suppliers. They recognize that their day-to-day operation and legitimacy depend on relations of reciprocity and trust among internal and external stakeholders in the firm. Reciprocity depends on reasonable, informed expectations that all sides will gain from their relationship. On this understanding, multiple stakeholders commit investments to the firm that it is costly or impossible for them to withdraw. Firms should not exploit those commitments but should conceive of their mission in a positive sense as including the interests of all stakeholders. The firm is not just a nexus of contracts, but a nexus of reciprocal relationships. The implications of this model of ethics for for-profit firms are considered.

ETHICS IN THE CONTEXT OF BUSINESS ENTERPRISE

Let us begin our consideration of the role of ethics in for-profit business enterprises by contrasting two ends of a spectrum. On one end stands the norm set forth by Milton Friedman for publicly held corporations: that they maximize profits, subject only to the constraint that they obey the laws (Friedman 1970). Such an enterprise prioritizes returns to shareholders, and will seek their advantage at the expense of the interests of anyone else interacting with the firm—employees, customers, suppliers, the community—whenever it faces legally permissible trade-offs. On the other end stands the social enterprise, which defines its core mission as promoting some moral value, such as poverty alleviation or environmental improvement, and which expects to make a profit while doing so. Healthpoint Services India, for example, aims to deliver clean water and health services to rural Indian communities, without caste, class, or gender discrimination. Patagonia Sur sells carbon offsets, which it uses for environmental projects such as reforestation. A social enterprise prioritizes the public benefit and will compromise profits when its public mission demands this.

The somewhat amorphous Corporate Social Responsibility (CSR) model occupies the spectrum between these two poles. Closer to the profit-maximization pole lie corporations that engage in philanthropic activity as a minor side-activity disengaged from the day-to-day mission of the firm. They may, for example, sponsor local arts in the communities where they operate. At this end, a firm's CSR activities may function primarily as a public relations campaign which may even aim to deflect criticism away from core business activities that may damage public interests. For example, McDonalds's operation of the independent non-profit Ronald McDonald Houses, which offers housing to families so they can live near their hospitalized children, has been viewed by critics as a way to distract attention from the negative public health impact of its high-fat food offerings.

Somewhat further along the spectrum lies a model analogous to that advanced by Andrew Carnegie (1889). Carnegie argued that great accumulations of wealth should be devoted mainly to the public good, principally by endowing independent non-profit institutions such as schools and libraries open to less advantaged individuals interested in improving their prospects. Carnegie promoted his "Gospel of Wealth" as an ideal for the individual recipients of the distributed profits of enterprises. It can be adapted as a model for enterprises that sincerely want to devote substantial portions of their profit to the public good. United by Blue offers an example: this apparel company removes one pound of trash from waterways for every item it sells. The difference from the McDonald's case concerns both the scale of philanthropy and (possibly) the motive for giving. Yet the Carnegie model, like the McDonald's case, separates the principles driving day-to-day business decisions from the final use of the profits. Carnegie's own business, Carnegie Steel, had antagonistic relations with its workers, and ultimately replaced them with strikebreakers in the notorious 1892 Homestead strike, which originated in a lockout when workers demanded higher wages.

I am interested in exploring the part of the spectrum in which for-profit firms incorporate ethical considerations into their day-to-day operations (not simply as a way of spending their profits), without necessarily defining their core mission either in terms of service to the disadvantaged, or in the production of some public benefits, such as environmental goods, that deliver large positive externalities. Many corporations take such considerations seriously. For example, Apple just announced that it has stopped buying tantalum obtained from regions of armed conflict, and is working on eliminating other conflict minerals from its supply chain, to ensure that its supplies are not obtained by forced labor or other human rights abuses. The interest in these sorts of cases is that they are generalizable to all firms, not just those with a social mission.

A key question one may ask about firms that deeply integrate ethical considerations into their business model (neither as a mere legal side-constraint, nor as an ancillary philanthropic use of profits, nor as their main product, as in social enterprises), is how they should manage trade-offs between ethical goals and profits. Do we have any systematic ways to think about this? I think we do. However, doing so requires that we not frame the question *simply* in terms of trade-offs between shareholder and other stakeholder interests, as if these are inherently opposed, or as if service to other stakeholders amounts to altruistic self-sacrifice on the part of the corporation, its officers, or its shareholders. It is often said that a for-profit firm is not a charity. That is correct. It does not follow that it should define its interest in terms of selfishness, profit-maximization, or service to shareholder interests exclusive of the interests of others. Indeed, I shall argue that the kinds of cooperation and multiparty investment required for corporations to function already contain a broader view of the interests that the for-profit firm serves. Furthermore, the understandings implicit in these kinds of cooperation can help us think about how to balance these interests.

THE FIRM AS A JOINT ENTERPRISE FOUNDED ON RELATIONS OF RECIPROCITY AND TRUST

Let us begin by reflecting on the kinds of problems we can expect for-profit firms to solve. Without pretending to offer an exhaustive account, we can sketch a general idea. For-profit firms interact with people primarily, although not exclusively, by means of contracts and voluntary market exchanges. A fundamental normative presumption of legitimate contracts and market exchanges is that both sides reasonably expect to gain from them. For a large body of such trades, both sides should *expect* to gain ex ante and *actually* gain ex post in *each* transaction considered separately. The vast majority of retail trades operate on this understanding. In other cases, as in installment loans, each party expects to gain net from the sum total of all transactions undertaken in an ongoing relationship with another, with reasonable assurance that the transactions will continue for long enough that both sides will ultimately gain ex post. In other cases, as in insurance contracts and other contracts involving a genuine hedging of risk, both sides can gain even if the buyer does not suffer an insured loss: insurance provides peace of mind, and also makes the insured eligible for other profitable contracts (as e.g. home mortgage loans). The insurer, for its part, might not gain from a particular transaction with a particular buyer who suffers an insured loss, but reasonably expects to gain from the entire pool of insured customers.

In degenerate cases, as in purely speculative stock trades and other pure gambles, the ex post gains to all parties, neglecting transaction costs, are zero-sum. The best that can be said of such trades is that each side expected (reasonably or not) to gain ex ante.

From a social point of view such trades are negative-sum once transaction costs are included, unless the gamblers get entertainment value from the activity. They are negative-sum ex post even from the point of view of the gamblers if, as is common, the losing party loses more welfare from it than the winner gains. This is the source of the morally dubious character of purely speculative trades. I set these cases aside for purposes of this chapter, as it is difficult to see how an enterprise devoted to such trades can be justified from an ethical point of view. This does not entail that such enterprises should be banned. However, if economic activity is increasingly devoted to such trades, this is a sign that the economy is not well-ordered and may call for regulation to direct people's energies to productive work.

So, in general, the sorts of problems for-profit firms can solve are ones that can be solved by means of mutually beneficial, reciprocal exchanges among all the participants. Many problems are not of this sort. Here is a far from exhaustive sample. Everyone is dependent on largely unreciprocated giving during childhood and periods of serious illness and disability. It may be difficult in some circumstances for the destitute to offer assurance of reciprocity to those who might help them. Individuals with a known high risk of incurring loss may be unable to secure insurance against it. The needs of such people, and often of their caregivers as well, are difficult or impossible to provide by purely market means. In addition, provision of public goods, from which it is difficult for producers to make a profit because they cannot cheaply exclude free riders, cannot be left to for-profit firms operating on their own. In such cases the family, the state, or some other non-profit agent is needed either to directly provide the goods in question, or to function as a third-party payer to for-profit firms providing these goods.

Let us propose, then, that we understand the ethical for-profit firm as occupying a zone of thorough-going reciprocity with all stakeholders, including shareholders, creditors, managers, workers, customers, suppliers, and all communities in which the firm does business or on which it has an impact. In general, the firm's interactions with each stakeholder should be reasonably expected to be beneficial ex ante, and (in the normal case) actually be beneficial ex post, to every party that interacts with the firm. Firms in fact propose to interact with others on reciprocal terms, and the legitimation of for-profit firms depends on this expectation being largely fulfilled in practice, allowing for honest failures.

It might be supposed that the reciprocity condition is satisfied by means of law and contracts alone. As long as each party stays within the bounds of the law, and enters contracts voluntarily with their eyes open, then what each owes the other is nothing more than what the contract specifies, and each is free to ruthlessly pursue their own self-interest in negotiating (or, where the party has market power, imposing) terms. I note first off that such an interpretation does not support the view that corporations should maximize shareholder value. Neither directors nor executives have a contractual relationship with shareholders, and the law does not require them to act on behalf of shareholder interests alone. As I shall discuss, directors owe a fiduciary duty to the corporation itself, not to the shareholders exclusively.

More importantly, contracts and law alone do not exhaust the reciprocal under-standings on which the productivity of the firm rests. To explore this point in more detail, let us first distinguish stakeholders internal and external to the firm. Internal stakeholders include everyone who plays a role within the government of the firm. Shareholders elect directors, who are the ultimate governors, who delegate day-to-day managerial authority to executives and managers, who govern the rank-and-file work-ers, who may be represented by labor unions. External stakeholders include suppliers, customers, and the communities in which the corporation does business. Let us consider how noncontractual, extralegal reciprocal understandings pervade the rela-tions among internal and external stakeholders.

Internally, the firm may be represented as an enterprise whose members are jointly committed to team production for the mutual benefit of all. Each party irrevocably contributes some input necessary for production, the coordination of which calls for some kind of centralized authority (Alchian and Demsetz 1972). Authority is needed in part to solve collective action problems that arise within the productive process. In team production, the marginal products of each worker and manager are unobservable. No particular bits of output can be specifically attributed to any particular member of the team. Rather, the whole product is due to everyone working together, in coordin-ated fashion. Under such conditions, some workers may be tempted to shirk and free ride on others' efforts. When outputs cannot be independently measured, someone needs to monitor everyone's inputs to prevent shirking. This is one of the jobs of managers, besides their primary job of coordinating the efforts of different team members.

Yet we cannot suppose that contractual agreements and authority relations are sufficient for high productivity teamwork. It is impossible to contractually specify, to the last detail, all the ways team members need to cooperate for efficient production at low cost. And managers' eyes cannot be everywhere all the time. Moreover, most workers value some degree of autonomy on the job. Excessive monitoring is unlikely to elicit their best efforts. It is hard to be creative or take initiatives when someone is looking over one's shoulder all the time. Excessive monitoring also expresses distrust, which fosters reciprocal distrust from those being monitored. Why put in more than the minimum effort required to avoid getting fired under such conditions? This is why well-managed firms cultivate norms of trust and reciprocity among team members. These norms call for effort beyond legally and contractually specified minimums, in return for which contractually unguaranteed rewards—for example, consideration for promotions and bonuses, decent treatment in the allocation of work hours, tolerance for productivity slowdowns due to family emergencies, and better working conditions—may be offered. To a considerable degree, norms of gift exchange com-plement contracts in well-managed firms (Akerlof 1982). Motivation means more than going through the motions. Team morale, so critical to production, is due not to explicit contracts but to implicit shared understandings of reciprocity and decent treatment, cultivated and fulfilled in the day-to-day interactions of team members.

The boundary between the market and the firm, between external and internal stakeholders, is often defined as that between purely contractual and governance relations (Coarse 1937). While there is something to this idea, even external stake-holders often have more than purely contractual relations with firms, in the sense that the gains from trade with the firm are secured by reciprocal normative understandings beyond any contractual or other legal guarantees. Customers may be attracted to a firm by its reputation, by enduring personal relationships of trust and affiliation with salespeople, by courteous treatment at the hands of customer satisfaction representatives. They may enhance firm productivity by volunteering feedback on the quality of its products and services, and by offering other customers free tips on how to use the firm's products. They may be rewarded for such efforts by contractually unguaranteed discounts, coupons, loyalty programs, early releases, trial products, VIC treatment, and other gifts. Communities typically invest in firms through the provision of public goods—schools to educate workers, utilities, fire service, roads, and other infrastructure—on the noncontractually specified understanding that the firms, in turn, will employ their residents and otherwise enhance community life over the long term. Even creditors trust the firm not to take excessive risks that may enable shareholders and executives to extract short-run gains at the expense of long-run solvency.

The flip side of trust and reliance on legally unenforceable norms of reciprocity is that stakeholders put some investments at risk in relation to the firm. When they enter into a long-term relationship with the firm, exit may be possible, but it is rarely costless. Indeed, a distinctive feature of the corporate form is that it "locks in" investments by multiple stakeholders (Blair and Stout 1999). Shareholders are not entitled to withdraw capital they have invested in the firm, although they may sell their share. Managers and rank-and-file employees invest in firm-specific human capital, which they lose if they quit.

External stakeholders, too, sink investments into firms that they cannot costlessly withdraw. Consumers who purchase durables may commit themselves to purchasing parts and servicing from the original manufacturer. Enterprise software purchasers commit themselves to training their staff to use the software, an investment that usually commits them also to purchasing software upgrades. Similar points can be made for most firm purchases of capital goods from suppliers. Suppliers, for their part, may invest in custom-designed goods for their clients, on the expectation of continuing a long-term supply relationship. Communities build durable infrastructure to serve the needs of a firm and its employees. If the firm leaves, that infrastructure is unlikely to be able to be costlessly rededicated to alternative uses.

Once stakeholders lock in firm-specific investments that cannot be costlessly withdrawn, they become vulnerable to exploitation by others, particularly those with governing power—directorships and executive positions—within the firm. As we have seen, law, explicit contracts, and governance relationships cannot do all the work to ensure that everyone does their part to make the corporation a success. Trust, norms of reciprocity and teamwork, and team morale are also needed to support the best productive uses of the assets dedicated to team production. Without these supracontractual understandings, team members are liable to withhold full effort, take precautions that may undermine production, waste time in rent-seeking, and undermine other team members to protect their own positions.

Thus, we should view the firm not simply as a "nexus of contracts." It is a *joint enterprise* constituted by a nexus of cooperative relationships in which internal stakeholders commit firm-specific assets to relatively long-term team production arrangements, submit to common governance, and repeatedly interact on the basis of norms of trust and reciprocity, all for *mutual and reciprocal benefit*, the terms of which are *not* exhausted by law and contracts. The firm also typically enters into protracted reciprocal relationships with external stakeholders—customers, suppliers, creditors, and communities—which are supported by normative expectations of trust, reciprocity, and mutual gain, not all of which are defined in explicit contracts. The firm, then, is a "nexus of reciprocal relationships" with internal and external stakeholders. Let us now turn to an analysis of the ethical implications of this view.

ETHICAL IMPLICATIONS OF UNDERSTANDING THE FIRM AS A NEXUS OF RECIPROCAL RELATIONSHIPS

The "nexus of reciprocal relationships" view of the firm stands in contrast with a better known account of market relationships, which views them as purely self-interested transactions in which obligations to the other parties are limited solely by the law and explicit contractual agreements. On that view, the rule is not simply "buyer beware" but "everyone beware," as each should act on the presumption that the other party will take maximum advantage of one's ignorance, vulnerabilities, distress, limited options, exit costs, and competitive and first-mover disadvantages, and therefore should try to maximize their own advantage in response. On that view, ethical considerations beyond those limited to following the law and abiding by the letter of contractual agreements appear to call for decision-makers to sacrifice their own self-interest out of altruistic regard for the other parties. This understanding naturally leads one to frame the ethical question as a matter of how far to trade off one's own self-interest for the sake of others.

If the parties instead understand one another to be jointly committed to mutual advantage in enduring cooperative relationships based on trust and norms of reciprocity, we can frame questions of business ethics from the standpoint of the normative understandings embedded in such relationships. John Dewey and James Tufts proposed this perspective in their ethics textbook:

> [N]either egoism nor altruism nor any combination of the two is a satisfactory principle. Selfhood is not something which exists apart from association and intercourse . . . . [R]egard for self and regard for others are both of them secondary phases of a more normal and complete interest: regard for the welfare and integrity of the social groups of which we form a part. (Dewey and Tufts 1981: 298, 299)

From this perspective, what the parties in business relations should ask is what actions would sustain, and promote the constitutive aims of, those relationships:

> From the moral standpoint, the test of an industry is whether it serves the community as a whole, satisfying its needs effectively and fairly, while also providing the means of livelihood and personal development to the individuals who carry it on. This goal could hardly be reached, however, if the business man (a) thought exclusively of furthering his own interests; (b) of acting in a benevolent way toward others; or (c) sought some compromise between the two. In a justly organized social order, the very relations which persons bear to one another demand of the one carrying on a line of business the kind of conduct which meets the needs of others, while they also enable him to express and fulfill the capacities of his own being. (Dewey and Tufts 1981: 299)

Since the production of gains from these relationships is premised on mutual expectations of trust and reciprocal advantage to which the parties have jointly committed themselves, sustaining those relationships involves pursuing the objectives to which team members have committed themselves by following through on those commitments.

A major implication of this way of thinking is that the parties to a business relationship should (1) define their mission or joint enterprise in terms that encompass the mutual advantage of all parties, and (2) thenceforth orient their actions toward their mission and the cooperation needed to achieve it, including compliance with the norms of trust and reciprocity on which all parties rely. *Profit arises as the by-product of the mission and is a sign of success, rather than that which constantly guides every action undertaken within the relationship.*

Why not take profit-maximization as the aim of business? The point is in some ways similar to Henry Sidgwick's "paradox of hedonism" (1982: 48–9). Pleasure is a sign of successful activity, but to focus on maximizing it as an end in itself may be self-defeating. Successful activity is absorbed in itself, in its own aims. People have fun playing tennis by focusing on playing the game, not by asking what plays would yield them more or less pleasure. To focus on pleasure as one's end is to distract oneself from absorption in the game and may lead one to play the game less well and get less pleasure from it. The point extends beyond pleasure. Taking the maximization of test scores as an aim rather than a by-product and sign of learning leads teachers to "teach to the test." This makes scores a less accurate measure of real learning beyond the ability to score highly on tests, and may lead teachers to sacrifice broader learning for the sake of higher scores.

Similarly, taking profits as a systematic guide rather than a by-product and sign of success may lead executives to adopt business models that may not actually work to the reciprocal advantage of all stakeholders, but merely enrich shareholders and executives at the expense of the other parties. Many business models operate in this fashion, betraying the understandings on which the other parties entered them, or otherwise undermining the promise of reciprocity that grounds their justification.

A far from exhaustive list of such reciprocity-violating models includes the following types.

(1) Taking advantage of asymmetrical information. A bank may market complex and risky investments to naïve investors in no position to bear substantial losses or to independently evaluate the product being sold to them.

(2) Taking advantage of desperation, as in "price gouging." A hotel may dramatically hike room rates when a blizzard closes an airport, thereby extracting rents from stranded travelers.

(3) Taking advantage of macroeconomic failure. Under conditions of significant involuntary unemployment, firms can increase their profits by cutting wages even when labor productivity is increasing. Generalized across the entire economy, this behavior can reduce aggregate demand and economic growth, leading firms to accumulate cash without any promising vehicles in which to invest it. While this may enable them to increase share prices, no economic function is served by bidding up the prices of already existing assets while leaving factors of production—workers and capital—idle.

(4) Taking advantage of market power. Most employers enjoy some degree of monopsony power with respect to their employees (Manning 2003). Some use this power to make it difficult for workers to seek alternative employment. For example, some companies, including Starbucks and Subway, require employees to sign noncompete clauses that are enforceable in some states even if the employee is laid off or offered only part-time work. Others use this power to increase the pace of work beyond normative expectations, or to force workers to work under dangerous conditions.

(5) Exploiting small faults to force larger ones. Some mortgage-servicing companies have found it profitable to exploit delinquent loans by charging heavy fees, delaying relief, obstructing refinancing, and rushing to foreclosure even if alternative arrangements would permit the homeowner to keep their home while providing better returns to the investors who own the loans (Goodman 2009). Such business models, in which it is more profitable to "sweat" the distressed borrower with fees and interest, even to the point of forcing default, than to offer terms which could earn a profit while enabling the borrower to pay off the loan, are common in the credit industry, particularly for less creditworthy customers (Mann 2006).

(6) Violating previously established implicit norms of reciprocity. An employer may unilaterally rescind benefits or accommodations upon which workers have long relied, without cause. Or a manufacturer might degrade the durability of its products without notice, taking advantage of customers' reliance on its formerly sound reputation for quality.

(7) Exploiting second-mover advantage. An enterprise software firm may force the purchase of exorbitant upgrades once its customers have made an initial purchase, by refusing to offer routine security patches to its original product.

(8) Shifting risks to other stakeholders to enhance one's own position. Thomas H. Lee, a private equity firm, purchased the heavily indebted Simmons mattress company in 2003 in a leveraged buyout, using $327 million of its own money and $745 million in bonds and loans. After the purchase, THL borrowed even more at up to 10 percent interest to reward its owners with $375 million in special dividends, $77 million in other profits, and millions more in management fees, as the company's ability to withstand market downturns declined. THL's extraction of wealth from Simmons ended in the 2008 recession, when payments to bondholders were suspended, more than a quarter of the workforce laid off, contributions to the pension plan ended, and the firm filed for bankruptcy with $1.3 billion in debt, most of which it could not repay. THL's owners, however, had already awarded themselves millions in profits beyond their original investment, leaving the other stakeholders with devastating losses (Creswell 2009).

Innumerable more types of business model could be listed, in which profits are maximized through arrangements that violate reciprocity by taking unfair advantage of other stakeholders. We can capture some sense of the limits on legitimate profit-taking that this model imposes by adopting a loosely contractualist perspective: would every stakeholder gladly accept the terms of cooperation realized in the relationship, regardless of which position they occupied? In general, terms of cooperation that exploit the vulnerabilities of stakeholders, rescind implicit norms, extract rents by exerting market power, taking advantage of the fact that others cannot costlessly exit the relationship, or exacerbating collective action problems, would be reasonably rejected. Yet we would fail to grasp the ethical implications of understanding the firm as a network of reciprocal relationships if our focus were merely on identifying business models that should *not* be adopted. My point, in listing a small sample of such models, was simply to demonstrate that profit-maximization is not a good guide to business plans that work to everyone's advantage.

Far more important is to consider how the "network of reciprocal relationships" model can guide decision-makers toward business models that positively advance the interests of all stakeholders in reciprocal fashion. For this to work, executives need to ask not "how can I maximize profits?" but "how can everyone who has invested in the company (where investment includes, as I have argued, all stakeholders contributing to its functioning, not just shareholders) gain from a mission aimed at delivering something of genuine value to the firm's customers?" The central issue is to define the mission of the firm from the start in terms that incorporate everyone's advantage, such that everyone gains as the firm and its profits grow. Only then can growing profits be a sign that everyone else is also benefitted by the firm's activities—that the firm's activities add value from a social point of view. Profits are a by-product of sound business practices; the point of a business is its mission, which incorporates the advantage of all internal and external stakeholders, in keeping with a conception of the firm as a nexus of reciprocal relationships in which stakeholders commit themselves to team production for the mutual benefit of themselves and their customers.

Dewey is not alone in advocating this reciprocity-based conception of business ethics. Russell Pearce and Brendan Wilson (2013) advocate a similar conception of business ethics, focused on reciprocity in the social relations that constitute the firm. This conception can even be traced back to the origins of the "doux commerce" debate in the eighteenth century, in particular to the thought of Antonio Genovesi (Bruni and Sugden 2008).

A reciprocity-based conception of the nexus of relationships that constitute the firm and are the basis of its activities is qualitative. No numbers are attached to how the firm should balance the interests of different stakeholders. This is because, as Dewey argues, the point of conceiving of the firm as a joint commitment of stakeholders for mutual benefit is to get beyond the self-interest/altruism dichotomy, and towards a conception of the flourishing of each person as constituted by the flourishing of the social relationships in which each participates—that is, the sustained ability of the individuals in the joint venture to cooperate with good will toward each other, and succeed in realizing a mission they all endorse. The model directs team members to focus on the corporate mission and to follow through on the expectations of trust and reciprocity, as well as contractual obligations, that make efficient achievement of the mission possible. It forbids them from exploiting the commitments and vulnerabilities of others, from mere rent-seeking at the expense of other team members.

Constraints on the Reciprocity Model?

The reciprocity model implies that corporate directors and managers have *duties* to restrain profit-seeking when doing so exploits other stakeholders or exacerbates collective action problems. It also implies that they are *morally permitted* to pursue any business plan that advances the good of all stakeholders, without any special obligation to maximize profits or share prices. Most importantly, it tells directors and managers to guide their decision-making through a conception of the corporate mission that positively aims at the good of consumers and other stakeholders. It rejects the strategy of using profits as a comprehensive guide while leaving it up to all other parties to defend their self-interest as best they can.

It might be objected that the reciprocity model faces grave constraints that undermine its feasibility. Let us consider seven objections of this type.

1. It is alleged that corporate directors have a legally mandated fiduciary duty to shareholders to maximize profits.
2. The market for corporate governance favors takeovers by those who do aim to maximize profits.
3. Firms that fail to maximize profits are liable to face difficulties raising capital.
4. Competitive pressures are liable to drive non-profit-maximizing firms out of business.

5. The governance rules of corporate boards bias them in favor of profit-maximization at the expense of other goals.
6. The structure of compensation biases executives in favor of profit-maximization at the expense of other goals.
7. The norms of esteem among executives bias them in favor of profit-maximization at the expense of other goals.

Fiduciary Duties of Corporate Directors

The common assumption that directors have a fiduciary duty to maximize shareholder value is false. No body of state corporate law in the US imposes a legal requirement on directors to maximize profits or share prices or to concern themselves exclusively with shareholder interests. All 50 states of the US have laws authorizing corporations to make charitable donations at the expense of shareholders, and more than thirty have enacted constituency statutes that explicitly license directors to consider the interests of other stakeholders (Elhauge 2005: 738). Although Delaware, the dominant state of incorporation in the US, is not among the states with a constituency statute, its extensive body of corporate legal doctrine gives directors wide discretion in balancing the interests of different corporate stakeholders. Moreover, although Delaware law permits corporations to institute shareholder primacy in their charters, not a single corporation has done so (Stout 2002: 1207). Directors have a fiduciary duty to the corporation itself, not to shareholders alone. If we understand the corporation as a joint enterprise of stakeholders in a nexus of reciprocal relationships, directors' duty to the corporation is a duty to stakeholders. Given that US law privileges shareholders in corporate governance relative to other international corporate legal systems, such as those of Germany and Japan (Weimer and Pape 2002), the fact that even the US model is highly permissive with respect to board consideration of other stakeholders suggests that the reciprocity model is internationally viable, at least from a legal point of view.

The Market for Corporate Governance

One might object that directors have no choice but to maximize shareholder value, because if they fail to do so, the corporation will be subject to a hostile takeover by someone who can bid more for the shares than their current market value. Under *Revlon v. MacAndrews & Forbes Holdings* directors must accept the maximum bid for a corporation on behalf of shareholders when the sale of a corporation is inevitable. However, *Revlon* holds only for corporations chartered in Delaware. Constituency statutes in the thirty states which have them were explicitly adopted to protect corporations against hostile takeovers, in the interest of other stakeholders. And even Delaware permits directors to adopt many defenses against takeovers. *Paramount Communications, Inc. v. Time* narrowed *Revlon* to just those cases in which the sale of a corporation was initiated by the directors, or the corporation was already going out of business as a distinct entity. Directors have no general duty to authorize the sale of a corporation simply because a bidder offers to buy its shares at higher than market price.

Capital Constraints

Firms that fail to maximize profits may have difficulties raising capital. This objection applies to raising capital from the stock market, and not from other sources such as loans and bonds, where returns are contractually fixed. Given the highly speculative nature of investments in IPOs, it isn't clear how much of a constraint this is except on subsequent issues of stock, or on a firm's cashing in its own holdings. Even in those cases, two considerations may limit the force of this objection. (i) Investors may have other motives besides maximizing returns on their investment. A firm that advertises a meaningful mission may attract socially conscious investors. (ii) Nothing stops executives from choosing to dedicate firm profits to other uses besides their own pay. This point is particularly applicable to firms in the US and UK, where executive pay has skyrocketed in recent years. Since highly successful firms in other countries do not pay their executives nearly as much as US and UK executives receive, it does not appear that extraordinary executive compensation is needed to motivate performance. It stands to reason that a substantial share of profits currently distributed to executives is available for uses that would benefit other stakeholders (at least in the US and UK) without compromising firms' access to capital. It is possible that laws may need to be changed to create the right incentives to open up room to reallocate firm resources to other uses. In particular, taxation of executive compensation may need to change. An objection with greater force than that addressed to capital raised from the stock market is that non-profit-maximizing firms have lower potential to grow by drawing on retained profits. However, to the extent that growth is achieved by exploiting other stakeholders, such growth is not desirable from a social point of view.

Competitive Pressures

One might argue that firms that fail to maximize profits will be driven out of business by more competitive firms. To assess this argument, we must distinguish different ways in which a profit-maximizing firm might make higher profits than a firm focused on comprehensive reciprocity toward all stakeholders. (i) It might exploit market power or informational asymmetries with respect to consumers. Since, in these cases, higher profits are extracted at the expense of consumers, it is hard to see how a firm that treats consumers better will be driven out of business by loss of sales. The latter firms may need to publicize the ways in which they are treating consumers better. Moreover, they may need to support more vigorous antitrust enforcement to block the extension of monopoly power by competing firms. But, in general, treating customers better should enhance the competitiveness of a firm. (ii) A profit-maximizing firm might exploit its market power against suppliers or employees, and thereby deliver products and services at lower prices to consumers. This is a much greater danger to more equitable firms. However, many consumers are willing to pay a premium for goods known to be produced through more equitable practices. Fair trade coffee and chocolate command higher prices. In other cases, where firms make profits through the exercise of some monopoly power, as through use of their own intellectual property or licensing of university logos, they are free to dedicate their profits to uses that benefit other stakeholders. Because market power insulates firms from competition, this undermines the force of the competitive pressure objection. In still other cases, the price increases involved in treating other stakeholders decently are too trifling to make much difference in demand (Pollin et al. 2004). (iii) A profit-maximizing firm may outcompete more socially conscious firms by operating at the expense of external stakeholders—for instance, by polluting. In such cases state regulation may be needed to correct the situation.

Corporate Governance Constraints

Most corporate directors have executive experience, and view firms from the perspective of executives and shareholders. It may be difficult for them to appreciate the interests of other stakeholders. Changes in corporate governance may help correct this problem. Directors could be required to regularly meet with other stakeholders, in fora designed to enhance sustained interaction. Kathleen Hale suggests that directors meet with small groups of stakeholders rather than in the "town hall" format of annual shareholder meetings, which encourages directors to dismiss questions with scripted replies prepared in advance. Having to directly engage the concerns of other stakeholders at length, face-to-face, in small groups where stakeholders can elaborate upon and reinforce their concerns (and perhaps prepare a shared agenda in advance), would reduce the psychological distance between directors and other stakeholders, motivating them to be more responsive to stakeholder concerns, and more informed about the content of those concerns (Hale 2003). More ambitiously, corporate law could be changed to add stakeholder representatives to corporate boards. Germany, which has included labor representatives on its boards for nearly a century, offers a possible model of what this could look like Page 2009).

Executive Compensation

Current US practices of executive compensation, which tie bonuses to share prices, bias executives strongly toward maximizing short-run profits. It is not evident that these practices are good even for shareholders. Short-run profits may be maximized at the expense of investment that may bring higher returns in the long run. Current compensation practices therefore may reward merely speculative investors (who are focused on taking advantage of accidental fluctuations in share prices, or speculative bubbles) at the expense of shareholders who are interested in the long-run performance of firms, and at the expense of recessions for everyone else, when speculative bubbles burst. Nor are current practices even evidently good for executives, as spectacular compensation packages have also been paired with faster turnover of CEOs. This only increases the temporal myopia of executives, inhibiting their ability to base their careers on the pursuit of a meaningful corporate mission beyond short-term profit-maximization. If current compensation practices constrain executives, however, then this is a reason to change them. Current practices were forged only in the 1990s, and can be changed.

Executive Culture

I suspect that the greatest obstacle to realizing a corporate practice based on comprehensive reciprocity is the culture of executives. The ideology of maximizing shareholder value, which had such a great impact on executive compensation practices, caused the norms of esteem among executives to narrow. Of course, money has always been a yardstick of success among executives. But now it overwhelms all other criteria. Today's leading executives are paid so much that the value of their compensation packages is largely detached from the consumption possibilities they enable. Executives are already consuming as much for themselves and their families as they can. Additional pay counts mainly in a positional competition with other executives for esteem from their peers. No wonder executives in the financial sector, which has taken an ever-growing share of corporate profits without demonstrating commensurate value added to the economies of any OECD country, command the highest prestige today. Norms of esteem, once established, are difficult to change. Nevertheless, if current executive culture is the product of ideologically driven compensation practices, different compensation practices embodying different ideals of corporate success can change this culture. The motivational power of money at the top of the income distribution derives not from consumption possibilities but from the prestige of having so much. Suppose, to obtain esteem from their peers and from the wider society, executives had to be able to explain their achievements in terms of success in promoting a corporate mission that includes the reciprocal advantage of all stakeholders? Suppose making money simply by manipulating the rules of the game at everyone else's expense brought disparagement rather than praise on the executives of Goldman Sachs, who engineered an increase in the price of aluminum by uselessly shuffling the metal among warehouses, gratuitously increasing the time of delivery to manufacturers from six weeks to sixteen months (Kocieniewski 2013)? I expect that executives would be more likely to practice reciprocity if doing so was honored among their peers.

Many contributors to this volume, including Arrow, Frank, Fuerstein, Jafar, and Sen, point to the social costs of economic institutions that focus exclusively on individual wealth maximization. Neiman persuasively argues that even the most extreme advocates of laissez-faire capitalism do not find fulfillment in great wealth alone, but rather value it as a sign of virtue and moral desert. What would it take to shift our economic activities beyond sheer wealth accumulation, incorporating conceptions of meaningful projects and ideals pursued on terms of full reciprocity with others? We need to explore more fully how social change occurs. Some instruments of social change, such as regulation, taxation, and private law (e.g. torts) are reasonably well-understood. It seems, however, that these state-based instruments do not fully address what ails us. Neiman is surely right that we are afflicted by a misguided ideology of wealth that does not even track people's larger aspirations. Closely connected to this problem are constricted cultural norms stressing wealth as the most important basis of esteem competition, particularly among the most influential economic actors. If these diagnoses are accurate, the task before us is to explore how to change ideologies and cultural norms within the constraints of respect for human rights and individual freedom.

I have argued that we should conceive of for-profit firms as joint enterprises of internal stakeholders committed to team production in a nexus of relations defined not only by law and contract but by norms of trust and reciprocity. These firms stand in similar reciprocal relations to customers, suppliers, and communities, albeit without bringing them under their governance structures. The public justification of firms relies on their claim to thorough-going reciprocity, and their productivity usually relies on norms of trust and goodwill that promise reciprocity in ways that extend well beyond the requirements of the law and the letter of contracts. These norms help to secure the firm-specific investments of team members, which leave members vulnerable to exploitation if the other stakeholders do not live up to implicit commitments of reciprocity on their part. The firm, regarded as a nexus of reciprocal relationships, is thereby committed to the mutual benefit of all parties. Within this nexus, shareholders have limited privileges as the nominal electors of directors and residual claimants of the firm's assets upon its dissolution through sale or closure. But they are not entitled by law, contract, or implicit commitment to be the sole principals on whose behalf directors and executives should act. Nor is there any moral or economic rationale for advancing shareholder interests at the expense of other stakeholders, who, no less than shareholders, have committed investments to the firm that they cannot costlessly withdraw. The for-profit corporation, considered as an ethical agent, should define its mission in a way that incorporates the positive good of all stakeholders, and focus primarily on achieving that mission by following through on the teamwork and contractual and extracontractual commitments that make that achievement sustainable over time. If it has adopted its mission with due attention to conditions, it will earn profits as a matter of course, and, in a well-ordered culture, earn the esteem of others for living up to the promises that justify its place in the world.

References

Akerlof, George (1982). Labor Contracts as Partial Gift Exchange. *Quarterly Journal of Economics*, 97: 543–69.

Alchian, Armen, and Harold Demsetz (1972). Production, Information Costs, and Economic Organization. *American Economic Review*, 62(5): 777–95.

Blair, Margaret, and Lynn Stout (1999). A Team Production Theory of Corporate Law. *Virginia Law Review*, 85(2): 247–328.

Bruni, Luigino, and Robert Sugden (2008). Fraternity: Why the Market Need Not Be a Morally Free Zone. *Economics and Philosophy*, 24(1): 35–64.

Carnegie, Andrew (1889). Wealth. *North American Review*, 148(391): 653–65.

Coase, Ronald (1937). The Nature of the Firm. *Economica*, 4(16): 386–405.

Creswell, Julie (2009)."Profits for Buyout Firms as Company Debt Soared. *New York Times*, Oct. 4, p. A1.

Dewey, John, and James Tufts (1981). *Ethics*, ed. J. A. Boydston. *The Later Works, 1925–1953*. Carbondale, IL: Southern Illinois University Press.

Elhauge, Einer (2005). Sacrificing Corporate Profits in the Public Interest. *NYU Law Review*, 80(3): 733–869.

Friedman, Milton (1970). The Social Responsibility of Business is to Increase its Profits. *New York Times Magazine*, Sept. 13.

Goodman, Peter (2009). Lucrative Fees May Deter Efforts to Alter Loans. *New York Times*, July 29, p. A1.

Hale, Kathleen (2003). Corporate Law and Stakeholders: Moving Beyond Stakeholder Statutes. *Arizona Law Review*, 45: 823–56.

Kocieniewski, David (2013). A Shuffle of Aluminum, But to Banks, Pure Gold. *New York Times*, July 20.

Mann, Ronald (2006). Bankruptcy Reform and the "Sweat Box" of Credit Card Debt. *University of Illinois Law Review*, 1: 375–403.

Manning, Alan (2003). *Monopsony in Motion: Imperfect Competition in Labor Markets*. Princeton: Princeton University Press.

Page, Rebecca (2009). *Co-determination in Germany: A Beginners' Guide*. Düsseldorf: Hans-Böckler-Stiftung.

Pearce, Russell, and Brendan Wilson (2013). Business Ethics. In Luigino Bruni and Stefano Zamagni (eds), *Handbook on the Economics of Reciprocity and Social Enterprise*. Northampton, MA: Edward Elgar, 49–58.

Piketty, Thomas, EmmanuelSaez, and Stefanie Stantcheva. (2011). *Optimal Taxation of Top Labor Incomes: A Tale of Three Elasticities*. NBER Working Paper, 17616 <http://www.nber.org/papers/w17616>.

Pollin, Robert, Justine Burns, and James Heintz (2004). Global Apparel Production and Sweatshop Labour: Can Raising Retail Prices Finance Living Wages? *Cambridge Journal of Economics*, 28: 153–71.

Sidgwick, Henry (1982). *The Methods of Ethics.* 7th edn. Indianapolis: Hackett.

Stout, Lynn (2002). Bad and Not-So-Bad Arguments for Shareholder Primacy. *Southern California Law Review,* 75: 1189–209.

Weimer, Jeroen, and Joost Pape (2002). A Taxonomy of Systems of Corporate Governance. *Corporate Governance: An International Review,* 7(2): 152–66.

CHAPTER 12

....

SHAREHOLDERS, STAKEHOLDERS, AND STRATEGIC FACTOR MARKETS

....

JAY B. BARNEY

Abstract

Despite calls to integrate a stakeholder perspective into managerial decision-making, the shareholder supremacy model continues to dominate practice. A key assumption of the shareholder supremacy model is that shareholders are the only firm stakeholder with a residual claim on a firm's cash flows. This chapter shows—using strategic factor market theory from the field of strategic management—that if this assumption is correct, then a firm will not have any economic profits to distribute to its shareholders. If, on the other hand, a firm has economic profits to distribute to its residual claimants, then stakeholders besides a firm's shareholders will have a claim on these residual cash flows. The implications of this argument for the role of stakeholder analysis in managerial decision-making are discussed.

Numerous academics, policy-makers, and business leaders have called for integrating a stakeholder perspective into management decision making (Freeman et al. 2010). Some justify this integration on political grounds—for example, political trends in society require managers to be sensitive to the interests of multiple stakeholders if the firms they lead are to survive (Hillman and Keim 2001). Others justify this integration on legal grounds—for example, since the law in most countries does not require managers to focus only on maximizing shareholder wealth, learning how to incorporate the interests of non-shareholding stakeholders in managerial decision-making is central (Stout 2012). Still others justify this integration on moral and ethical grounds, for example, decision-making that does not take a stakeholder view can lead firms to engage in socially irresponsible and immoral actions (Bridoux and Stoelhorst 2014).

Finally, others justify this integration on practical grounds, for example, the best way for firms to maximize shareholder wealth is to make decisions that are consistent with the varied interests of their stakeholders (Jensen 2002).

Despite these numerous calls for integration, shareholder supremacy models of managerial decision-making still dominate many discussions of both how managers make, and ought to make, decisions (Stout 2012). And while even the most strident defenders of the shareholder supremacy model acknowledge some role of stakeholder logic within the shareholder supremacy approach (Jensen 2002), the advantages of the shareholder dominance model—for many observers—simply outweigh any added insights that a stakeholder perspective might generate. After all, the shareholder supremacy view identifies a single objective against which to evaluate managerial decision-making (does a choice increase the wealth of shareholders?); suggests a simple way of valuing a firm (the discounted cash flow model); clarifies the role of corporate governance (to insure managers make decisions consistent with shareholder value maximization); is the foundation of the entire edifice of modern financial theory; and directly links managerial decision-making to social welfare (Jensen 2002). Even if the shareholder dominance model is not a perfect description of how managers make, and ought to make, decisions, its answers to the practical problems facing managers are still very compelling.

This chapter takes the logic underlying the shareholder supremacy model seriously and does so within the context of the strategic management literature. This literature focuses on the conditions that enable firms to gain competitive advantages (Peteraf and Barney 2003). By applying one of the foundational theories within the field of strategic management—strategic factor market theory (Barney 1986)—it is shown that stakeholder theory is not just a convenient (or inconvenient, depending on one's point of view) add-on to the shareholder supremacy model, but is, in fact, a logical consequence of that model. In this sense, by taking the shareholder supremacy logic seriously, one discovers the necessity of stakeholder logic. Put differently, the central conclusion of this chapter is that engaging stakeholder analyses is not a choice shareholder dominance adherents get to make. Rather, it is a logical consequence of shareholder dominance logic.

The chapter begins by briefly reviewing shareholder dominance logic. It then discusses strategic factor market theory. Next, the implications of strategic factor market theory for shareholder dominance logic are explored, and it is shown that stakeholder theory is a logical consequence of shareholder dominance logic. The chapter then discusses some of the theoretical and practical implications of the relationship between shareholder dominance, strategic factor market theory, and stakeholder theory.

THE SHAREHOLDER DOMINANCE MODEL

The central conclusion of the shareholder dominance model of managerial decision-making is that maximizing shareholder's wealth is the only appropriate objective against which to evaluate a manager's decision-making (Friedman, 1970; Jensen, 2002). This does not mean that a firm's stakeholders are irrelevant. However, it does mean that once all the fixed claims on a firm's cash flow from its stakeholders are satisfied, any residual cash—i.e. cash in excess of that required to pay the fixed claims—is distributed to shareholders. In this sense, shareholders are a firm's only residual claimant. Maximizing shareholder wealth not only makes it likely that there will be sufficient cash to pay off these stakeholders, but that there will also be residual cash to distribute to shareholders.

As suggested earlier, the shareholder dominance model has a wide variety of very practical implications for managers and for society as a whole. However, not surprisingly, to derive these implications, the shareholder dominance model has to make a variety of assumptions. One of these assumptions is that a firm's only residual claimant is its shareholders (Zingales 2000). For this assumption to be reasonable, all of a firm's stakeholders—except its shareholders—need to be compensated for making resources available to a firm such that the price paid for these resources equals the value they create for a firm. Assuming that both stakeholders and shareholders are trying to gain maximum economic benefits from their interactions with a firm, any price lower than this would be rejected by stakeholders and any price higher than this would be rejected by shareholders.

To see why the prices of the resources a firm acquires from a stakeholder must equal the value those resources create in order for a shareholder to be a firm's only residual claimant, consider what happens if a stakeholder makes its resources available to a firm for a price that turns out to be less than the value those resources ultimately create. This could happen, for example, if there is some uncertainty about the value that these resources might create. In this setting, a stakeholder would only make its resources available to a firm if there was a way that it could be compensated for any value that this resource might create in the future. Obviously, this stakeholder no longer has just a fixed claim—equal to the known value of the resources made available to the firm—but also a contingent claim—based on any additional value that the resource in question creates. Compensation from this extra value creation makes this stakeholder a residual claimant on a firm's cash flows, much the same as a shareholder. Thus, the only way that shareholders can be a firm's only residual claimant is if all of a firm's other stakeholders are paid for the resources they provide to a firm such that the price of these resources equals their full value when used by a firm.

But when are the prices of resources from stakeholders likely to equal their full value for the firm? Clearly, the answer must be when these resources are provided to a firm through a perfectly competitive market process. Under perfect market competition, multiple stakeholders compete to provide resources to multiple potential firms, and both stakeholders and the firms understand fully the value these resources will create once acquired. In these settings, the price paid for resources will equal the value they create. In this sense, most of the eminently practical conclusions of the shareholder supremacy model depend critically on the assumption that the markets through which firms acquire resources from their stakeholders are perfectly competitive.

STRATEGIC FACTOR MARKET THEORY

Strategic factor market theory, as developed in the field of strategic management, also examines the implications of the process by which firms acquire critical resources. However, instead of examining this process in the context of the shareholder supremacy model, this work focuses directly on the relationship between pricing these resources and the ability of a firm to generate economic profit. In this (Peteraf and Barney 2003) and related (Klein et al. 1978) literatures, an economic profit is defined as a rate of return greater than the cost of all the resources a firm uses to implement its strategies.

Strategic factor market theory was developed when the primary explanation of the ability of a firm to generate an economic profit focused on the firm's exploiting market power to charge higher prices for their product than what would prevail in a more competitive industry. Thus, for example, firms with large market share in their product market may not only enjoy cost advantages (if important economies of scale are operating in an industry) but may also enjoy pricing power based on their quasi-monopolistic position in that market (Porter 1979, 1980).

Strategic factor market theory suggests that returns to a firm do not depend just on a firm's position in its product market, but also on the price of the resources needed to implement the strategies that generated this product market position. For example, a key resource needed to realize economies of scale and pricing power in a product market is market share. Firms can acquire market share in a variety of ways, for example, reducing prices, increasing service quality, and so forth. However, these activities are costly to a firm. The cost of the activities needed to acquire market share can be thought of as the price of market share. Returns to exploiting a firm's quasi-monopolistic position in a product market depend on the value generated by this position and by the cost of creating this position. Only if the value created by the position is greater than the cost of creating this position will a firm's product market strategies actually generate an economic profit (Barney 1986).

Of course, the competitiveness of these strategic factor markets—i.e. the markets where firms acquire the resources necessary to implement their product market strategies—can vary. Barney (1986) shows that when strategic factor markets are perfectly competitive, the price of the resources needed to implement a firm's product market strategies will equal the value that these product market strategies will create, and a firm will not generate an economic profit. This will be the case even if a firm has a very dominant position in its product market.

Of course, not all strategic factor markets are perfectly competitive. Barney (1986) goes on to show that strategic factor markets can be imperfectly competitive in two ways: (1) when those selling and buying resources in a strategic factor market both have inaccurate expectations about the future value of a particular resource and (2) when those buying a resource have more accurate expectations about the future value of that resource than those selling a resource and others buying a resource. Any economic profits created in this first condition are completely attributable to a firm's good luck (Barney 1986). Economic profits created in the second condition usually reflect a firm's ability to combine resources it already controls with resources it is acquiring to create value in ways that other firms either could not identify, or if they could identify them, could not imitate. Thus, ultimately, strategic factor market theory suggests that most economic profits for firms depend on rare and costly to imitate resources controlled by a firm that enable that firm to acquire resources in strategic factor markets for less than the value those resources will ultimately generate (Barney 1991).

While this logic has generated a great deal of research in the field of strategic management, its primary implications for this chapter are: (1) firms that acquire all their resources from perfectly competitive strategic factor markets cannot generate economic profits and (2) firms that acquire at least some of their resources in imperfectly competitive strategic factor markets may be able to generate economic profits.

IMPLICATIONS OF STRATEGIC FACTOR MARKETS FOR SHAREHOLDER DOMINANCE LOGIC

The marriage of strategic factor market logic with shareholder dominance logic creates a logical conundrum for the latter. This conundrum begins by observing that the markets within which firms acquire resources from their various stakeholders are equivalent to the strategic factor markets identified in Barney (1986). If these markets are perfectly competitive, two things follow. First, as suggested earlier, only a firm's shareholders are residual claimants on a firm's cash flow. Second, as suggested by strategic factor market theory, a firm in this setting will not be able to generate any economic profits that it can then distribute to its shareholders. Thus, shareholders may be a firm's sole residual claimant, but in the settings where this is true, there will be nothing for shareholders to claim.

On the other hand, the strategic factor markets within which a firm acquires its critical resources may be imperfectly competitive. In this setting, a firm may be able to generate economic profits which could be distributed to its residual claimants. However, as suggested earlier, shareholder dominance logic suggests that when these factor markets are imperfectly competitive, stakeholders besides a firm's shareholders have a claim on a firm's residual cash flow.

As a matter of theory, it is reasonable to discuss perfectly competitive strategic factor markets. However, in practice, most strategic factor markets are likely to be imperfectly competitive. This is because the actual future value of resources acquired by a firm are often not known with certainty—the first kind of strategic factor market imperfection mentioned earlier—or important information asymmetries exist regarding the value of a particular resource in a particular firm—the second kind of strategic factor market imperfection mentioned.

If most strategic factor markets are, most of the time, imperfectly competitive, then one of the key assumptions of the shareholder superiority model—that shareholders are the only residual claimants on a firm's cash flows—cannot generally hold (Zingales 2000; Blair 1994). Instead, because there are usually multiple residual claimants on a firm's cash flows, firm managers will usually have to find ways to allocate the economic profits that their firm has been able to generate across these multiple stakeholders. This is not an option for managers based on political, legal, or moral grounds, nor because this is the best way to maximize returns to a firm's shareholders. Rather, this is a logical necessity based on the setting within which firms often find themselves—a setting within which several of a firm's stakeholders, including its shareholders, have legitimate claims on a firm's residual cash flow.

An Example with Human Capital

Thus far, the argument about the relationship between stakeholder supremacy logic and strategic factor market theory has been, of necessity, quite abstract. To more clearly see the implications of this argument, consider the implications of how firms acquire access to human capital from their employees (Blair 1994).

As suggested by Becker (1964), human capital can be divided into two categories: general human capital that is valuable in many economic settings and specific human capital that is valuable only in those settings where investments were made to create it. The implications of acquiring access to one particular type of specific human capital— firm-specific human capital or human capital that is valuable only in the firm where it was developed—are discussed here. Examples of general human capital include the ability to read, write, and do arithmetic. Examples of firm-specific human capital include the knowledge an employee develops about how to use a firm's proprietary software or about how to work within a firm's unique bureaucratic structure.

Assuming that both those that are selling access to their human capital and those that are buying this access are trying to improve their economic performance, it is not hard to see that access to general human capital will often take place in reasonably competitive strategic factor markets. Because general human capital is broadly valuable, competition for employing individuals with this capital will typically emerge. Moreover, because of this competition, individuals will have an incentive to invest in general human capital. Finally, because general human capital is so widely valuable, its value, ex ante, can usually be known with reasonable certainty. Large numbers of well-informed profit-seeking buyers and sellers suggest that this strategic factor market will often be reasonably competitive.

These observations have several important implications. For example, strategic factor market theory suggests that general human capital, by itself, will not usually be a source of economic profits, even if a firm uses this capital to create economic value. Put differently, the price of acquiring access to this general human capital will typically rise to equal its value to an acquiring firm—profit-seeking firms will not pay any more than this price and profit-seeking employees will accept no lower price. Also, stakeholder dominance logic suggests that, in this setting, a firm's employees that have only general human capital will have a fixed claim on a firm's cash flows equal to the value of their general human capital.

However, the situation is much different for the case of firm-specific human capital investments. Strategic factor markets for the acquisition of firm-specific human capital are not likely to be competitive even if both those selling access to human capital and those buying this access are trying to improve their economic position. Because firm-specific human capital is not widely valuable, competition for employees that have made firm-specific investments will often not emerge.[1] Also, the full value of firm-specific human capital is often not known when it is created. Rather, this value is only revealed over time, as it is used within a firm. Since it is not widely valued, and since whatever value it creates in a particular firm can only be known with certainty in the future, strategic factor markets for firm-specific human capital are typically not perfectly competitive.

These observations about the markets where firm-specific human capital is acquired have several important implications. For example, it will often be the case that much of the value created by an employee's firm-specific human capital will be appropriated by the firms within which it is developed (Becker 1964; Morris et al. 2014). In other words, firm-specific human capital can be a source of economic profits for a firm. However, fixed compensation contracts cannot be used to incentivize employees to make such investments since, at the time they are made, the value they will create in the future cannot be known with certainty. Employees may think that any fixed compensation in this setting might underestimate the ultimate value their investments generate. Firms may think that any fixed compensation might overestimate the ultimate value of these investments.

Instead of a fixed claim, employees will usually only be willing to accept, and firms only be willing to offer, contracts that compensate an employee for making firm-specific investments from the value those investments create in the future. This compensation can take many forms. For example, employees can be compensated for making firm-specific investments through equity in a firm. The value of that equity in the future will depend, to some extent, on the value that employee-specific investments create for a firm. Also, more senior employees in a firm may receive disproportionately high levels of compensation—compensation that might ultimately be available to less senior employees who make firm-specific investments over long periods of time.

---

[1] Morris et al. (2014) show that, in some circumstances, an employee's firm-specific human capital can be a signal of the willingness and ability to make firm-specific investments. This willingness and ability is a form of general human capital.

Whatever form this compensation takes, it is clear that employees who have made specific investments in a firm can become residual claimants on a firm's future cash flows, and that this can be consistent with the interests of both employees and firms. Moreover, this can be the case even though these employees may have a fixed claim on a firm's current cash flows equal in value to the value of their general human capital.

In summary, when employees make specific investments in a firm, the strategic factor markets within which firms acquire this human capital are imperfectly competitive. Such human capital can be a source of economic profit for a firm. However, employees will be compensated for making these investments from the value they create in the future. This means that these employees become residual claimants on a firm's cash flow. Moreover, their claim on this future cash flow is as legitimate—in this case, contractually specified—as the claims of a firm's shareholders. As suggested earlier, when strategic factor markets are competitively imperfect, firms can generate economic profits, but stakeholders besides shareholders will then have legitimate claims on this residual cash.

DISTRIBUTING RESIDUAL CASH AMONG MULTIPLE STAKEHOLDERS

The conclusion that multiple stakeholders can be residual claimants on a firm's cash flows creates a management challenge that does not exist in the shareholder supremacy model: how to allocate residual cash across multiple competing stakeholders? This issue does not exist in the shareholder supremacy model because in that model there is only one residual claimant—shareholders. However, when strategic factor markets are imperfectly competitive—as they often will be—the economic profits generated by firms will need to be distributed—in some way—to multiple residual claimants.

Stakeholders who provide their resources to firms in imperfectly competitive strategic factor markets will typically be reluctant to provide such resources unless they receive some assurances about compensation for doing so. This is because the provision of resources to a firm in such settings generally creates transaction-specific investments between stakeholders and a firm. Such investments create a real risk of opportunism on the part of the firm vis-à-vis its stakeholders.

For example, suppose a supplier (as an example of a stakeholder) designs a unique technology that will be incorporated into a firm's final product. The final value of this unique technology depends, ultimately, on the sale of this firm's products, and these sales are uncertain, ex ante. Thus, the market where this technology is acquired is an imperfectly competitive strategic factor market. As important, the value of this new technology is much higher if it is included in a firm's final product versus when it is not included in this final product. In this sense, this supplier has made a transaction-specific investment vis-à-vis this firm, i.e. the value of this investment in this particular relationship is much higher than the value of this investment in any other transaction (Williamson 1985).

In this setting, this supplier is at risk of opportunistic actions by the firm it supplies to. This opportunism can take several different forms, including adverse selection (where the firm misrepresents its ability to integrate the technology in question into its products), moral hazard (where the firm can integrate the technology into its products but chooses not to), or hold-up (where the firm insists on a lower price and/or higher level of service to integrate the technology into its products) (Barney and Ouchi 1986). In all these settings, claims by a firm that it will "fairly compensate" its supplier sometime in the future for current transaction-specific investments are simply not credible. Put differently, current promises that this supplier will be a residual claimant on a firm's future cash flows are not reliable.

In order to get its stakeholders to provide resources in these imperfectly competitive factor markets, firms must find ways to credibly commit to these stakeholders that they will be residual claimants on a firm's cash flows. One way to do this is to compensate these stakeholders, ex ante, in a way that assures that they will be residual claimants, ex post. This can be done through compensating stakeholders, ex ante, with equity in the firm or through other equity-like forms of compensation.

Consider, again, the example of an employee who makes her firm-specific human capital available to a firm through an imperfectly competitive strategic factor market. On the one hand, without credible commitments to compensate her for these investments, they are not likely to be forthcoming and the firm will not benefit from these investments. On the other hand, a firm is unlikely to be willing to provide fixed compensation for these investments, since their true future value is not known. In this context, compensating this employee with equity in the firm addresses both the concerns of the employee and the firm. The employee gets a credible commitment that she will be a residual claimant by receiving the same form of compensation as stockholders. The firm gets a flexible compensation package with a value that varies based on how much value the human capital of the firm creates.

Equity-like compensation may also be available to other of a firm's stakeholders. For example, the supplier who is contemplating developing a unique technology for a firm and the firm may create a joint venture. Any profits generated by this joint venture could then be allocated, in predetermined ways, between the supplier and the firm. In many settings, such a joint venture can create a flexible way to compensate suppliers— something the firm wants—but in a credible way—something the supplier wants.

Note that these compensation schemes are designed to not just give stakeholders incentives to behave in the interests of the firm and its shareholders, i.e. to reduce the cost of agency (Jensen and Meckling 1976). They also create incentives for stakeholders to invest in a firm, in a way that may generate economic profits, in the first place.

To establish these compensation schemes, a firm is likely to negotiate with each of its stakeholders who are likely to become residual claimants on its cash flows. Both sellers and buyers of resources in these imperfectly competitive strategic factor markets will have expectations about the future value of the resources in question. These expectations, together with the negotiating skills and bargaining power of the firm and its stakeholders, will ultimately determine how much of a firm's equity will need to be offered in order to induce stakeholders to provide resources to the firm.

Of course, firm management will be intimately involved in these negotiations. If they are not well prepared—with a clear understanding of the expected value of the resources that different stakeholders can provide—these ex ante allocation decisions can ultimately create difficult challenges, once a firm begins generating economic profits to be distributed. For example, if one stakeholder receives compensation that is disproportionate to their actual contributions to a firm's economic profits, costly renegotiations will be required.

Moreover, it is important to recognize that, if a firm is seeking to gain economic profits by acquiring resources in imperfectly competitive factor markets, negotiating residual claims as part of the process of acquiring these resources is virtually assured. Thus, as was suggested earlier, stakeholder analysis is not just politically expedient, moral, or a practical way to maximize returns to a firm's shareholders, but is essential to successfully creating a coalition of residual claimant stakeholders who are providing the resources a firm needs to generate economic profits.

This does not mean that there will not be ongoing challenges in marshalling all the resources needed to create economic profits for a firm. Free riding and other forms of shirking may emerge. The importance of particular resources, ex post, in creating economic profits may have been over- or underestimated. This may require some post hoc negotiations among a firm's residual claimants. In all these settings, a firm's management must again have a complete understanding of the resources controlled by different stakeholders.

The Problem of Externalities

The communities within which a firm operates are often included as stakeholders in current versions of stakeholder theory (Freeman et al. 2010). And indeed, such communities may act as any of the other stakeholders discussed in this chapter. That is, the communities within which a firm operates may make resources available to a firm (e.g. tax breaks, an educated population), the markets within which access to these resources is gained may be imperfectly competitive, and these communities, in this sense, can become residual claimants on the economic profits a firm generates.

However, these communities sometimes bear additional costs in the form of externalities created by a firm's efforts to create economic profits. Externalities exist when the benefits generated by stakeholder resources are appropriated by these stakeholders, but where the costs associated with generating these benefits are not fully borne by stakeholders. A specific example of such externalities might include, for example, where stakeholder's resources create economic profits that have to be allocated among a firm's residual claimants, but where some of the costs of creating those profits—including environmental pollution—are not fully borne by the firm or its residual claimant stakeholders.

Neither non-community stakeholders nor the firms that use the resources made available by these stakeholders to create economic profits have strong economic incentives to incorporate the cost of such externalities in ex ante negotiations with the firm about the distribution of residual cash flows. The reason for this is clear: including the cost of these externalities in these negotiations can adversely affect both the size of the total economic profit created by a firm and the amount of that profit appropriated by a firm's residual claimant non-community stakeholders. It is usually better for these stakeholders if the cost of these externalities is borne by "the community at large."

In the context of the argument developed in this chapter, it is important for all of a firm's stakeholders that can have a significant impact on the ability of a firm to generate economic profits to be involved in ex ante discussions about how those profits, and any associated costs, will be allocated across stakeholders. In a perfect world (i.e. a world without transaction costs), this negotiation would lead to a clear assignment of responsibility to particular stakeholders, and the costs of externalities would be appropriately internalized (Coase 1960). Of course, in the real world, transaction costs are almost always positive in these negotiations and the allocation of the costs associated with externalities must often be done through regulation or other forms of government intervention.

Conclusion

Despite a growing literature on the stakeholder approach to managerial decision-making, the shareholder supremacy model continues to dominate practice. To the extent that stakeholder considerations enter into these discussions, they have a decidedly "add on" flavor, i.e. stakeholder analysis is important assuming that it is consistent with maximizing shareholder wealth or stakeholder analysis is important because it is the means through which shareholder wealth is maximized. However, the key assumption of the shareholder supremacy model—that shareholders are a firm's only residual claimants—remains the de facto operating assumption of many managers in many firms.

This chapter suggests that this assumption is logically inconsistent. A firm might acquire the resources it needs to conduct business in perfectly competitive strategic factor markets, in which case only a firm's shareholders will have a residual claim on a firm's cash flows. However, in this context, a firm will not be able to generate any economic profits, so shareholders cannot expect there to be any residual cash flows to appropriate. More realistically, a firm is likely to acquire the resources it needs to conduct business in imperfectly competitive strategic factor markets. In these settings, a firm can generate economic profits, profits which can be allocated among those with residual claims. However, stakeholders who provide these resources to a firm through imperfectly competitive markets become residual claimants on a firm's cash flows, in addition to any fixed claim they might have, and in addition to the residual claims of a firm's shareholders.

When a firm has multiple residual claimants, management must allocate its residual cash among these claimants. Firms and stakeholders will often find it helpful to make these allocation decisions ex ante, before the value created by these resources is realized. In this context, managers must have a deep understanding of which of their firm's stakeholders have the kinds of resources that are likely to contribute to the creation of economic profits. In this sense, stakeholder analysis is not just an add-on to managerial decision-making designed to maximize shareholder wealth. In an important sense, such analysis actually replaces the shareholder dominance model.

Put differently, instead of the standard conclusion that managers should "maximize shareholders wealth," this analysis suggests that managers should "maximize residual claimants' wealth." To do so requires managers to have a deep understanding of their firm's relationship to all of its stakeholders, an understanding that cannot be realized by focusing only on shareholders.

REFERENCES

Barney, J. B. (1986). Strategic Factor Markets: Expectations, Luck, and Business Strategy. *Management Science*, 32(10): 1231–41.

Barney, J. B. (1991). Firm Resources and Sustained Competitive Advantage. *Journal of Management*, 17(1): 99–120.

Barney, J. B., and W. G. Ouchi (1986). *Organizational Economics*. San Francisco: Jossey-Bass.

Becker, G. S. (1964). *Human Capital*. Chicago: University of Chicago Press.

Blair, M. (1994). *Ownership and Control*. Washington, DC: Brookings Institute Press.

Bridoux, F., and J. W. Stoelhorst (2014). Microfoundations for Stakeholder Theory: Managing Stakeholders with Heterogeneous Motives. *Strategic Management Journal*, 35: 107–25.

Coase, R. (1960). The Problem of Social Cost. *Journal of Law and Economics*, 3: 1–44.

Freeman, E., J. Harrison, A. Wicks, B. Parmar, and S. de Colle (2010). *Stakeholder Theory: The State of the Art*. Cambridge: Cambridge University Press.

Friedman, M. (1970). The Social Responsibility of Business is to Increase Profits. *New York Times*, Sept. 13: 33.

Hillman, A., and J. Keim (2001). Shareholder Value, Stakeholders Management, and Social Issues. *Strategic Management Journal*, 22: 125–39.

Jensen, M. (2002). Value Maximization, Stakeholder Theory, and the Corporate Objective Function. *Business Ethics Quarterly*, 12(2): 235–56.

Jensen, M., and W. Meckling (1976). Theory of the Firm: Managerial Behavior, Agency Costs, and Capital Structure. *Journal of Financial Economics*, 3(4): 305–60.

Klein, B., R. Crawford, and A. Alchian (1978). Vertical Integration, Appropriable Rents, and the Competitive Contracting Process. *Journal of Law and Economics*, 21: 297–326.

Morris, S., S. Alvarez, J. Molloy, and J. Barney (2014). Firm Specific Human Capital as a Signal of General Value. Unpublished manuscript, Department of Entrepreneurship and Strategy, Eccles School of Business, University of Utah.

Peteraf, M., and J. Barney (2003). Unraveling the Resource-Based Tangle. *Managerial and Decision Economics*, 24: 309–23.

Porter, M. (1979). How Competitive Forces Shape Strategy. *Harvard Business Review*, 57: 137–56.

Porter, M. (1980). *Competitive Strategy*. New York: Free Press.

Stout, L. (2012). *The Shareholder Value Myth*. San Francisco: Berrett-Kohler.

Williamson, O. (1985). *The Economic Institutions of Capitalism*. New York: Free Press.

Zingales, L. (2000). In Search of New Foundations. *Journal of Finance*, 55(4): 1623–53.

CHAPTER 13

....

CLIMATE CHANGE, JUSTICE, AND HUMANITY'S COLLECTIVE OWNERSHIP OF THE EARTH

Intergenerational Perspectives

....

MATHIAS RISSE

Abstract

This chapter develops an intergenerational approach to think about responsibilities arising from climate change. The central idea is that the Earth is collectively owned by humanity as a whole, across generations. What needs to be assessed is what this status implies for obligations of earlier generations toward subsequent ones. Humanity's collective ownership of the Earth was the pivotal idea of the political philosophy of the seventeenth century and has since fallen by the wayside. That idea has ramifications for a range of areas, but specifically for climate change/obligations towards future generations it has the theoretical virtue of making the concern with our planet central, and making it a matter of justice. I also discuss alternative approaches to climate change that lack these features.

1

....

My goal is to provide intergenerational perspectives on climate change from a standpoint of justice. The approach I use is that of humanity's collective ownership of the earth, developed in *On Global Justice* (*OGJ*). To be sure, as far as climate change is concerned, our main challenges are political. We must persuade people to accept sacrifices to avert threats that are unlikely to materialize fully during their lifetime.

The philosophical question about how to divide up burdens acquires practical relevance only if we get that far. Nonetheless, as we are reflecting on what justice requires, we must address that question.

Stephen Gardiner's 2011 *Perfect Moral Storm: The Ethical Tragedy of Climate Change* aptly characterizes the challenges we confront when dealing with climate change. A perfect storm involves the unusual intersection of several serious, mutually reinforcing storms. In the case of climate change, three major problems interfere with our ability to behave ethically: the global, intergenerational, and theoretical storms. The global storm concerns our difficulties in reaching any kind of international agreement on measures to combat climate change. It is collectively rational for humanity to reach agreement on how to control emissions. It is nonetheless also rational for each country to exempt itself from regulation hoping that others take the lead. The intergenerational storm consists in the fact that the current generation has asymmetric power over future generations. Earlier generations can affect the prospects of future generations, but not vice versa. Any generation has incentives to generate front-loaded goods, goods that largely benefit the present but for which later generations pay. All goods whose production generates emissions are such goods, given how long some of these gases stay in the atmosphere. The third storm is theoretical: there are no robust general theories to guide us. Existing theories are underdeveloped in many relevant areas, including intergenerational ethics, international justice, scientific uncertainty, and questions about our relationship to animals and the rest of nature.

Before offering my approach to justice in the context of climate change (despite the pessimism created by Gardiner's talk about the theoretical storm), let me briefly introduce John Broome's 2012 *Climate Matters*. As far as justice is concerned, Broome's approach differs substantially from mine. But his approach is sensible on the face of it, and has been broadly discussed. So it will be beneficial to contrast my approach with his. Broome distinguishes obligations of justice from those of goodness. The former are obligations not knowingly to inflict avoidable harm. The latter are obligations to improve the world (i.e. generate more objective and subjective value). He also distinguishes individuals and governments as duty holders.

Finally, Broome distinguishes obligations to current generations from obligations to future generations. Broome believes the "non-identity problem" implies that duties of justice do not apply to future generations. To the extent that current policies determine the composition of future generations, their existence depends on such policies. Thus Broome finds it implausible that such policies can harm future generations. If they cannot harm them, they cannot wrong them. If they cannot wrong them, they cannot treat them unjustly. Nonetheless life can be made better or worse for them. Thus only obligations of goodness hold vis-à-vis future generations.

Improving the lives of future generations (or making sure their lives are not bad) is up to governmental climate policies. Citizens should do their share in getting governments to implement good policies. As consumers they merely have duties of justice because they can do little to make the world better as far as climate is concerned. Both governments and individuals have obligations of justice vis-à-vis current people. For governments the more salient duties are those of goodness. For individuals the only obligations are those of justice. Each person has the duty to offset her emissions to leave zero net greenhouse gas emissions. Net emissions translate into loss of a number of days of healthy life somewhere.

If everybody followed Broome, the injustice not done to present people would also be an injustice not done to future people, were we to regard those as susceptible to injustice. So if we were to argue that future generations are susceptible to injustice, this would be done to a large extent to get our theoretical understanding of the moral dimensions of climate change right. But it would have a practical dimension, to the extent that the occurrence of "more injustice" would presumably have a larger motivating impact on those who care about justice.

I have nothing new to say about the non-identity problem. I enlist a certain way of arguing that we can wrong future generations. That approach was offered by Kumar (2003) drawing on Scanlon (1998). Using this approach I develop an understanding of intergenerational justice with regard to climate change that draws on ideas about humanity's collective ownership of the Earth. That standpoint helps us frame the moral problem posed by the division of burdens from climate change (i.e. burdens that arise if states adopt policies of mitigation or adaptation and thereby deviate from business-as-usual trajectories). Duties to future generations are puzzling because the existence of future people depends on present actions and because relations that usually render principles of justice and demands of reasonable conduct applicable (contracts, cooperation, coercion) do not extend across generations. The ownership approach is not marred by these problems. Its key contribution is to illuminate a moral relationship in which *all* human beings stand (no matter when and where they live) vis-à-vis original resources and spaces. In spite of the intricate theory that is to follow readers should keep in mind that I am trying to capture a straightforward thought: that the preservation of this planet is a matter of justice, and that ruining the environment is an injustice to future generations.

I enlist two kinds of moral considerations that arise for collective ownership. First, there are considerations of justice, defined by their stringency. Justice plays its central role in our lives because its demands are the hardest to overrule. Considerations of *distributive* justice are such stringent considerations that address relative or absolute holdings of something. But I also talk about (mere) reasonable expectations. Those are moral demands that do not rise to the stringency of justice. Something can be right if it is just, but also if it can be reasonably expected. Something can be wrong if it is unjust, but also if it can be reasonably expected that it not be done. Framed in terms of legitimate expectations in relationships, Kumar's account covers both senses of wronging.

2

According to Kumar, wronging "requires that the wrongdoer has, without adequate excuse or justification, violated certain legitimate expectations with which the wronged party was entitled, in virtue of her value as a person, to have expected her to comply" (2003: 107). What can be legitimately expected depends on the relationship. There can be wronging without anybody being harmed in the sense that her interests have been thwarted, as when somebody is oblivious about being threatened by a car over which a drunk driver momentarily loses control. There is something wrong with failing to exercise due diligence even if nobody suffers harm (and even if, unbeknownst to the driver, the pedestrian has waived his right to safety). Or consider a case in Parfit (1984). Somebody born to a 14 year old takes offense at teenage motherhood being criticized. He insists his life is worth living although his first years were hard. This man retrospectively waived any right to being born under different conditions. However, this waiver does not rebut the objection to his mother's giving birth. The objection is that "if she had waited, she could have given to some other child a better start in life" (1984: 365).

What matters for legitimate expectations is not that individuals of a psycho-physical identity (*this* or *that* person) stand in a relationship. What matters is what people of certain "types" do. "Types" are normatively significant sets of characteristics, roles persons play in relationships. A wrongs B if A does not meet legitimate expectations that B has against her within a relationship in which A and B embody certain types. In parent–child relationships one type is that of a parent and one that of a child. In teacher–student relationships one type is that of a teacher and one that of a student. A teacher might have a duty to order books for a course (Baier 1981). If she fails to do so (without adequate excuse), she wrongs her students because her role ("type") required such an act. She commits a wrong regardless of whether it matters to the students if they can get the books in time, regardless even of whether anybody takes the course.

Or suppose parents omitted precautions that would have spared a newborn a handicap. Precautions delay intercourse. So the child's psycho-physical identity would be different. Depending on how one conceives of harm, *that* (handicapped) child would not be harmed because *it* would not exist otherwise. However, it is a legitimate expectation on being a parent to take care of the child's needs, which includes saving her from handicaps at minor costs. We may or may not want to say the child was harmed. The child may or may not regret that it was conceived. But the child was wronged because the parents violated legitimate expectations within parent–child relationships.

Since legitimate expectations are a function of roles individuals occupy, acts that are among the conditions of a person's existence can wrong her. Present behavior and policies can wrong, and inflict injustice on, future generations. For a given relationship, the questions become what the *source* of legitimate expectations is (what generates duties), and what their *contents* are. The source in the parent–child relationship is that children generally exist because of an act of the will of at least one parent. Part of the content of these expectations could be not to let the child suffer serious harm parents can easily prevent. We can utilize this approach to explore the nature of our relationship with future generations understood as a relationship among generations of co-owners and identify source and contents of legitimate expectations they have against us.

3

OGJ offers a foundational theory that aims to makes it plausible that there are multiple grounds of justice and to defend a view of the grounds that I call *internationalism* or *pluralist internationalism*. The grounds I discuss are shared membership in a state, common humanity, shared membership in the global order, shared involvement with the international trading system, and humanity's collective ownership of the Earth.

Collective ownership was pivotal for seventeenth-century political philosophy. Philosophers such as Grotius, Hobbes, Pufendorf, Filmer, and Locke had views on what such ownership amounted to. According to the Old Testament, God had given humanity "dominion over the fish of the sea, and over the fowl of the air, and over the cattle, and over all the earth, and over every creeping thing that creepeth upon the earth" (Genesis 26). The point of thinking about the earth as collectively owned outside of theology is not to establish human despotism. Instead, it is to emphasize that all human beings, no matter when and where they were born, are in some sense symmetrically located with regard to the earth's resources and spaces. It is also to emphasize that humanity increasingly faces problems that concern our use of the earth as such, a point to which I return shortly.

A common objection is that all the work this approach would do could be done in terms of basic needs alone. But not only is the reach of claims drawing on basic needs frustratingly amorphous, it is also readily constrained by considerations of individual and collective responsibility and achievement. It is doubtful that the sheer fact that P badly needs X overrules all other claims people may have to X if P is badly off on account of her failings and X was created from scratch by others. But if X exists without human interference, P's claim would be stronger for the absence of any accomplishment-related competing claims others may have to X.

I make three claims to establish that (and the sense in which) humanity collectively owns the Earth. First of all, the resources and spaces of the Earth are necessary for all human activities to unfold, most importantly for survival. What is meant is not that *all* resources are necessary for *each* human activity to unfold. What is meant is that the Earth is humanity's natural habitat, a closed system of resources everybody needs for survival. If space travel expands humanity's habitat, we may have to reformulate this claim. The second claim is that the satisfaction of basic human needs matters morally, and matters more than any environmental value (such as protecting the biosphere). The satisfaction of basic needs is morally as significant as life itself. The third claim states that, to the extent that resources and spaces have come into existence without human interference, nobody has claims to them based on contributions to their creation. This claim merely states an implication of the nature of the resources whose ownership status is at stake. The matter is nonetheless significant. Since nobody has such claims, nobody can have claims to resources drawing on accomplishments of *others* either, as I may be entitled to an inheritance qua designated beneficiary of somebody's efforts.

Based on those claims all humans have some kind of claims to original resources and spaces that cannot be constrained by reference to what others have done. We should think of the Earth as in some way collectively owned by humanity. Appropriate weight must be given to the moral and aesthetic value of the environment and of non-human life. Humanity's collective ownership captures claims human beings have vis-à-vis each other. Only in this way could it make sense to talk of planetary ownership by a species that has been around only for a minuscule fraction of the planet's lifetime.

Humanity faces problems that concern our use of the planet as such. Climate change is one example, or more generally our duties to future generations. Immigration is another, concerning the distribution of people across the Earth. Therefore it behooves us to theorize about humanity's relationship with the Earth. What is at stake is ownership of, as John Passmore put it, "our sole habitation . . . in which we live and move and have our being" (1974: 3), or in Henry George's words, of "the storehouse upon which [man] must draw for all his needs, and the material to which his labor must be applied for the supply of all his desires" (1871: 27). Or as Hannah Arendt says, "The earth is the very quintessence of the human condition, and earthly nature, for all we know, may be unique in the universe in providing human beings with a habitat in which they can move and breathe without effort and without artifice" (1958: 2).

Ownership at this level of abstraction is connected to ownership in the civil law in much the same way in which Rawls thinks the administration of justice in a legal system is connected to principles of justice: there is a multi-stage sequence in descending order of abstraction where the findings at each stage constrain the next (in Rawls's case, decisions on principle of justice constrain the constitutional stage, the constitution constrains legislation, and legislation constrains the administration of law). That humanity collectively owns the Earth might mean everyone has a claim to an equal share of overall resources; or that a collective process is needed to satisfy each co-owner as far as any use of resources is concerned; or that the Earth as a whole is like the town commons of old, where each co-owner had a right of use within constraints. This latter view is Common Ownership, the view I consider philosophically preferred (see Risse 2012: ch. 6 for details).

According to Common Ownership all co-owners ought to have an equal opportunity to satisfy basic needs to the extent that this turns on collectively owned resources. In Hohfeldian rights terminology, common ownership rights include liberty rights accompanied by what Hart (1982: 171) calls a "protective perimeter" of claim rights. To have a liberty right is to be free of duties to the contrary. Co-owners are under no duty to refrain from using resources. However, were co-ownership reducible to such rights, a Hobbesian state of nature would arise where everybody is allowed to interfere with anything. Common Ownership guarantees minimal access to resources by adding a protective perimeter of claim rights. There might be further-reaching natural rights with respect to these resources, including exclusive rights to bits of the Earth arising from such actions as occupation, consent, and so on.

Property arrangements of the positive law may be conventions where access to resources plays little immediate role for most people. A necessary condition for the acceptability of such conventions is that the core purpose of the original rights is still met. That purpose is to ensure that co-owners have the opportunity to meet basic needs. In Hohfeldian terminology, co-owners are *immune* from living under arrangements that interfere with their having such opportunities. The right involved in common ownership is a disjunctive right to either use (in the narrow sense) resources and spaces to satisfy one's basic needs, or else live in a society that does not deny opportunities to satisfy basic needs that one otherwise could have satisfied through original resources and spaces.

Libertarians have ridiculed the idea of humanity's collective ownership by asking whether, say, a nugget of gold found on the ocean floor belongs to all of humanity, and how we should divide up its value. But none of the aforementioned ways of spelling out collective ownership applies object by object. What matters is that each person has a share in the world's resources. That idea can be developed in different ways. The argument is concerned only with natural conditions and resources. The distinction between what "is just there" and what has been shaped by humans can be blurred. But by and large we understand well enough the idea of something's existing without human interference.

4

So all human beings have some kind of claims to original resources and spaces that cannot be constrained by reference to what others have accomplished. Like the claims leading up to it that view does not mention the temporal status of individuals. To delineate legitimate expectations of future people within the ownership approach, we must inquire how to accommodate the fact that individuals live at different times.

In the view adopted from Kumar, wronging consists in violations of legitimate expectations in relationships. For a given relationship, the question becomes what the *source* of legitimate expectations is (what generates duties), and what their *contents* are. Constitutive of the morally relevant relationship among generations is that they successively occupy the same space to whose creation nobody has contributed more than anybody else. An *asymmetrical capacity to shape the natural world* is the source of future generations' legitimate expectations.

One might say future people need not, or cannot, be taken seriously as owners. There is no X successive generations own *together*. Instead, for each generation j there is an Xj (resources j collectively owns). Xj emerges from Xj-1 through the cumulative impact of generation j-1. But this objection presupposes an erroneous view of what we commonly own. The domain of the ownership relation is not merely a set of materials that can be removed from the common pool so that the next generation owns whatever is left. That domain is the three-dimensional space *within* which humans make a life. Resources and spaces are located, consumed, shaped, left waste, or intact, etc., within this domain. That domain is likely to be left to the next generation in some shape. There *is* something successive generations own together: the Earth, whose ongoing existence for now is necessary for humanity's survival. This might seem trivial, but rebuts one way of thinking about ownership across generations.

Only the living can *exercise* rights. Future people can factor into decision processes *only* as beneficiaries. Thomas Hurka (1993: 36) suggests the ownership standpoint pushes towards mitigating climate change, rather than adaptation, because we must take future people seriously as individuals with claims to resources. However, to that end one must show that the best way to *benefit* future people is to mitigate climate disruption. Perhaps the best way to benefit future people is to adapt to climate change. At least more argument is needed to get to where Hurka wants to go. So we need to assess carefully what to make of the point that future owners can be taken seriously only as beneficiaries.

We have noted three points: none of the reasoning that supported collective ownership mentioned the temporal status of individuals; there is something successive generations own *together*, the Earth itself; and future people can be taken seriously as co-owners only as beneficiaries. Future people are co-owners now, although their status is special in this way. We can now assess how to accommodate the fact that individuals live at different times and determine the source of legitimate expectations of future generations. Humankind spreads over generations, occupying the same three-dimensional space. Except for additional duties regarding the preservation of the cultural world, I submit that *all* that constitutes their moral relationship is that they are humans who successively occupy the Earth; can expect that there are subsequent generations; and that those need resources for survival without having done more than anybody else to create these resources.

What is characteristic of this relationship is an *asymmetrical capacity to shape the Earth*: earlier generations can leave the Earth in the shape in which subsequent ones find it. This capacity is the source of legitimate expectations future generations have against earlier comers (as far as Common Ownership is concerned). It is because of the three points given that it is appropriate to consider this capacity the source of legitimate expectations. The first point forces us to see that there exists a duty-generating relationship among generations. The second reveals a domain with regard to which there can be intergenerational duties. The third shows that we must capture future people's passivity in this relationship. To think of the asymmetrical capacity to shape the Earth as a source of duties is sensible as much as it is sensible to think of the involvement of the parents' will with the existence of children as such a source.

The dependency of later generations on earlier generations for the shape in which the planet is left to them differs from vulnerability, explored by Goodin (1985). Future generations are vulnerable to us in ways in which we are not to them. Perhaps future people can do things for us (as O'Neill 1993 argues), but their deeds benefit us only through our beliefs (e.g. that they will preserve our memory). Asymmetrical capacity captures a broader idea: later generations are vulnerable, but also must be taken seriously as co-owners. One may ask with regard to each ground of justice how to think about future generations. Vulnerability might matter greatly when we discuss future generations with regard to common humanity. But collective ownership allows us to go beyond what we can say based on common humanity alone, and to that extent makes our conclusions more secure.

5

We are developing an account of duties to future generations in terms of legitimate expectations within a relationship. The relevant *relationship* is that among subsequent generations of co-owners. The *source* of expectations is the asymmetrical capacity to shape the Earth. Mine is a deflationary account of duties to future generations, but being able to say this much is no small feat in this difficult terrain. Next I explore the *contents* of these expectations. I first formulate one abstract obligation that captures the contents of these expectations and that then generates two more specific obligations.

The general duty giving contents to legitimate expectations of future generations is that they can expect of earlier generations not to take *undue advantage of this asymmetry*. Since there is a domain successive generations own together; since of any two individuals, no matter when they live, neither has done more to create original resources; and since future generations can only be taken seriously as co-owners in a passive way, we can ask earlier generations not to take undue advantage of this asymmetry. *Undue* advantage-taking occurs, first of all, if earlier comers use resources without trying to make sure future people too can exercise their ownership rights.

To spell out what it means to make sure future people too can exercise ownership rights, I enlist my view of human rights in my 2012 (ch. 7). Human rights are membership rights in the global order, rights we hold in virtue of being subject to the system of states and international organizations that jointly constitute the global order. A defining feature of human rights is that the duty holder in the first instance is the global order as such. Crucially, these membership rights already partly derive from humanity's collective ownership of the Earth. Guaranteeing a certain range of rights is a global responsibility because co-owners are potentially threatened not merely by their state, but also by the ability of other states to refuse entry in case of need.

If there continues to be a global order, individuals continue to have membership rights. Future people can legitimately expect that the current generation leave behind institutions within which they can exercise membership rights, if they are in a position to do so. Various arguments support this duty. First, the current generation ought to ensure that their institutions respect human rights. Second, preserving institutions that realize human rights is a paradigmatic case of a scenario where *cultural accomplishments* of earlier generations ought to be preserved (see my 2012: ch. 9). So the present discussion merely adds support to duties we should recognize anyway.

The second of the two more specific obligations that capture the idea that no undue advantage should be taken is closer to the core of collective ownership, and introduces a new obligation: to the extent that within current institutions plans are made or policies adopted that affect future generations, those generations can expect that such planning makes sure their ability to meet basic needs is preserved, to the extent that this depends on original resources and spaces. There is no such duty if people cannot satisfy their needs; but if they use resources to build a life in which they can do more than merely satisfy basic needs, they ought to enable later comers to do at least as much (that is, satisfy basic needs). We are not merely obligated to leave behind institutions within which this could be done *in the future*, but future concerns must already be integrated now. The prevalence of front-loaded goods makes this a significant obligation.

6

One might wonder why I add "to the extent that this depends on original resources and spaces" to the formulation of the duty just introduced. Since we can take future owners seriously only as beneficiaries, somebody might argue we benefit future people most by finding ways of satisfying needs that do not turn on resources and spaces. So we should add "to the extent that this depends on original resources and spaces *or on substitutions thereof* that have been made better to meet needs that previously were satisfied by access to original resources and spaces."

However, for two reasons we must preserve actual resources and spaces (and thus aim for "strong sustainability"). First, there is the instrumental value of nature. Human life has emerged in its natural environment. The global biological and physical support systems that give us sustenance have made the emergence of our species possible in the first place. We do not know how to do better. E. O. Wilson has developed the theme that humankind cannot flourish apart from the rest of the living world under the name of "biophilia" (Wilson 1984). We do not even know which substances or species might be essential for human life in the future, which is an argument to preserve biodiversity. Wilson (1993: 281) calls biodiversity "our most valuable but least appreciated resource."

The second reason draws on the proper way of valuing nature. Bernard Williams (1995) uses the term "enlightened anthropocentrism" for the view that, although all values must be values to human beings and on a human scale, this does not mean instrumental values or values of human flourishing exhaust their range. Enlightened anthropocentrism (which I think is the correct view of the value of nature) recognizes that answers to environmental questions "must be based on human values, in the sense of values that human beings can make part of their lives and understand themselves as pursuing and respecting" (Williams 1995: 234). This excludes extreme views on environmental ethics that ask us to see ourselves only as part of ecosystems, alongside other species. But it also pushes us to integrate the moral and aesthetic value of nature, especially of other species, into our thinking. Nature is worth preserving for its own sake.

Given the existence of the global order the two obligations stated in the preceding section (like the more abstract one from which I derived them) capture duties that correspond to a principle of justice. That principle states that the distribution of the original resources and spaces of the Earth across different generations is just only if everyone has the opportunity to use them to satisfy their basic needs, or otherwise lives under a property arrangement that provides the opportunity to satisfy basic needs. That principle follows from the pivotal principle associated with humanity's collective ownership as a ground of justice ("The distribution of original resources and spaces of the earth among the global population is just only if everyone has the opportunity to use them to satisfy their basic needs, or otherwise lives under a property arrangement that provides the opportunity to satisfy basic needs," my 2012: ch. 6) once we explain how to take future generations seriously within a theory of justice—which I have done now, albeit in a sketchy manner, and which has led to an account of the source and contents of legitimate expectations of future generations. The obligations we have discussed so far are obligations of justice, not merely of reasonable acceptability.

As far as Common Ownership is concerned, resource depletion is not *unjust* if it is consistent with the obligations stated. One might think justice should require more vis-à-vis future generations. After all, we are dealing with an unknown number of generations, and can safely assume they want to procreate. So if we do not preserve resources, some generation might be unable to procreate who can sustain themselves. However, it would not *now* be *unjust* to exercise one's rights and help bring about a situation where future people ought not to reproduce, as they ought not if their offspring cannot sustain themselves. There is no duty to bring future people into existence.

However, in addition to these considerations of justice we can inquire about how much of what is collectively owned each generation can consume in a way that would be reasonably acceptable to all generations. If we knew how many generations are ahead, we would only have to leave enough for each generation to live above a threshold. But we do not know. So no proposal that captures a demand of reasonable conduct can permit a decrease between generations of the stock of natural resources (for a suitable measure of the stock of natural resources). Intergenerational equality is a sensible response to this situation. However, this reasoning entails only a defeasible commitment to intergenerational equality. One reason for waiving it is if a temporary decline in resources generates improvements for remote generations. Another is if one generation is in an exceptionally good position to transform resources into technological advancements, or finds itself in dire need for resources. But within such limits, intergenerational equality is a demand of reasonable conduct.

My work on collective ownership draws much inspiration from Hugo Grotius. If one makes collective ownership as central as Grotius did, one must assess the moral status of future people eventually. Grotius does so, but dismisses the matter:

> [H]e who is not yet born, can have no right, as that Substance which is not yet in Being has no Accidents. Wherefore if the People (from whose Will the Right of Government is derived) should think fit to alter that will, they cannot be conceived to injure those that are unborn, because they have not as yet obtained any Right. (*De Jure Belli ac Pacis*, 2.4.10.2)

Grotius does not think *successive* generations *collectively* own the Earth. Future people own what is left. The ownership approach as I develop it does not generate strong duties of justice towards future generations. However, it does deliver some, and duties of reasonable acceptability must be added. So here I deviate from Grotius.

A very different view on future generations was offered by Karl Marx. "From the standpoint of a higher economic form of society," Marx wrote in *Capital*,

> private ownership of the globe by single individuals will appear quite as absurd as private ownership of one man by another. Even a whole society, a nation, or even all simultaneously existing societies taken together, are not the owners of the globe. They are only its possessors, its usufructuaries, and, like *boni patres familias*, they must hand it down to succeeding generations in an improved condition. (1972: ch. 46, p. 776)

So according to Marx each generation has a duty to hand down this planet in an improved condition. Whereas Grotius did not take future generations seriously enough, Marx overdoes it. In my view, there is no duty to leave the planet in an improved condition.

What I argued about injustice and unreasonableness vis-à-vis future generations applies at the level of humanity and has no immediate implications for particular countries. But one could inquire about duties to future people with regard to *any* ground of justice—a matter that merits further investigation. Consider shared membership in a state. A helpful reference point is de Shalit (1995: 124), who argues that a person's self is constituted by an intergenerational community. The "self is not totally confined within the barriers of its own physical existence" (p. 124). De Shalit thinks membership in such communities generates duties.

To avoid intergenerational-communitarian commitments, we can recast the fact that our community shapes our selves, and so generates duties to contemporaries in the community, in terms of the profound importance of the basic structure. The community of the future might well continue to live in that same basic structure. Thus people at that time will have duties to each other much like the duties contemporaries have towards each other. By preserving or developing a particular basic structure, rather than another, we shape the basic structure in which future people will find themselves. This point by itself is a source of obligations toward future generations. The basic structure generates attitudes and policies that preserve the environment for future generations. For that reason, my arguments for obligations to future generations *at the level of humanity* also apply at the level of the basic structure *for given countries*. A demand of reasonable conduct is that each generation arrange the basic structure in such a way that it generates environmental policies in accordance with strong sustainability.

7

Collective ownership also helps us frame the moral problem of the division of burdens from climate change. To begin with, we face moral questions about the distribution of these burdens only if actions that trigger climate change constitute a wrong. Otherwise climate change would just be among the events that render independently existing duties applicable (which it *also* is). But the nature of this wrong cannot simply lie in the fact that climate change thwarts people's interests. Competitive markets do so, but no wrong might occur. One way of characterizing the moral wrong done through climate change is to argue that the ownership status of the atmosphere is incompatible with certain patterns of greenhouse gas emissions.

One way of developing that theme, in turn, is to regard the atmosphere, as Peter Singer (2002) does, as a "global sink" whose use must be regulated. Singer thinks of such regulation in terms of an equal per-capita approach: each person has an equal claim to pollute. The distribution of burdens from climate change can then be derived by assessing who has polluted more than they should. However, this way of developing what the ownership approach has to say about burdens from climate change is flawed: we own the Earth *as a whole*, not the atmosphere *in particular*. Common Ownership does not imply that any nugget of gold on the ocean floor must be shared out among all of humanity. But then neither does the atmosphere have to be shared out in that manner. So we must think carefully about what it means for ownership *of the atmosphere* (and thus for the moral assessment of patterns of greenhouse gas emissions) that humanity owns *the Earth*.

Consider an objection to the claim that we should assess the ownership status of the atmosphere to determine the distribution of burdens from climate change. If those burdens arise because of damage to goods in which we have ownership rights, this objector says, we do not need to know who owns the objects used for the interference. Suppose A uses a car to run over B's fence. We need not settle who owns the car to know who must fix the fence. In the case of climate change, we already know who owns, say, the crops that fail because of climate change. Therefore, inquiries about who owns the atmosphere are superfluous.

The car is used for the unmediated infliction of harm. In the climate change scenario, however, climate change affects the crops, but emissions cause the change. Instead of one occurrence, as in the car case, we have two occurrences related as cause and effect: emissions and atmospheric changes. We need not know who owns the car because the fact that it is used to inflict harm is obvious and salient. If the car is intentionally driven into the fence, the wrongness of the harm is clear. But in the climate case, emissions are causally once removed from the harm whose wrongness is at issue. We should inquire about ownership of the atmosphere to see if this way (greenhouse gas emissions, the first occurrence) of affecting the medium that does harm (climate change, the second) is right or wrong. To this inquiry there is no parallel in the car case since there is no relevant distinction between two occurrences. The car case does not contradict the idea that we should investigate the ownership status of the atmosphere.

8

Like no other work in the philosophy of international relations, Grotius's *De Jure Belli ac Pacis,* published in 1625, makes world ownership central to international relations.

Grotius is well-known for his view that the originally collectively owned world falls into two parts: parts that can be appropriated by groups to the exclusion of others, for the sake of founding communities, and parts that cannot be so appropriated. In addition to *De Jure Belli*, he also published *Mare Liberum*. He argues that oceans should remain at everybody's disposal. Grotius's approach reflects a cautious approach to appropriation. Humanity collectively owns the Earth. The presumption is that privatization will occur, but if there is no good reason for it, it should not. As far as the seas are concerned, there was no good reason. Grotius thought so partly because he thought there was no meaningful way of appropriating the seas, and partly because any sensible use of the seas was consistent with everybody making that same use (think of ships sailing through).

In the nineteenth century, Sidgwick realized that Grotius's argument for leaving the seas unappropriated was no longer valid. Fishing, after all, is the kind of sensible use of the seas that, at least in more recent times, is not the sort of thing everybody could do without undermining the activity altogether (2005: 228). Nowadays the seas can be monitored in ways in which they could not in Grotius's day. But while Grotius's case for freedom of the seas no longer applies, we can ask whether within Common Ownership too a distinction is available between parts of the Earth that can be legitimately privatized and parts that cannot. We cannot reproduce such a distinction in terms of justice. Provided everybody's ability to satisfy basic needs is preserved, it is consistent with justice that people try to exclude others from parts of the world. It is equally consistent with justice that those others ignore those attempts and enter. But we can draw some distinctions between parts of the Earth in terms of demands of reasonable conduct. This takes us back to climate change, and illuminates how the ownership approach can help us characterize the moral problem of climate change.

Areas of the Earth may have three different sorts of moral ownership status, capturing different demands of reasonable conduct with respect to privatization. First of all, parts can be owned in accordance with conventions allowing for occupation to the exclusion of others. A straightforward case is the founding of communities, which allows for appropriation to the exclusion of others. Second, parts of the Earth can remain in common ownership, there being a demand of reasonable conduct against attempts to regulate these parts. These two sorts appear in Grotius. But *in addition*, parts of the Earth may be governed by conventions to regulate access to and use of particular elements of the space in question (and there is a demand of reasonable conduct to provide such regulation), but none focusing *on occupation to the exclusion of others*. Such conventions may include different regulations for different goods, and may leave access to some goods unregulated. Like Caesar's Gallia, the Earth is divided into three parts, not two.

Buck (1998: ch. 1), distinguishes among different categories of goods, depending on two criteria: excludability and subtractability. Goods may allow more or less readily for users to exclude others. Moreover, use by some prevents similar use by others to more or less considerable degrees because it subtracts value from the entity in question. Put in these terms, a clear case for leaving areas in common is if: first, the area does not lend itself to the founding of durable communities (presumably because humans cannot easily survive there), and second, the goods this area provides are characterized by low degrees of excludability and subtractability. For such areas, nobody can be expected to respect conventions deviating from common ownership, and there is a demand of reasonable conduct not to try and privatize bits of such areas (or regulate their use).

Technological change may create a situation where the reasons why areas should remain in common no longer apply. That is the case for Grotius's discussion of the seas. Appropriation to the exclusion of others may then be acceptable. Or we may need conventions beyond the original rights without permitting exclusion, if *neither* the clear case for leaving areas in common *nor* a case for the founding of durable communities applies. It would then be unreasonable to expect others to accept occupation. But it would be unreasonable too if unrestricted liberty rights persisted. For such areas, we need different norms of access to the goods provided by that part, depending on their nature.

9

The skies are a paradigmatic case of a part of the Earth for which co-owners could not be reasonably expected to waive their rights in favor of exclusive appropriation. There is no demand of reasonable conduct on people to accept it if others tried to privatize bits of the skies, and there is a demand of reasonable conduct not to do so. Nor would it be reasonable for everybody to retain the unrestricted exercise of their rights.

Different conventions should be adopted for different goods provided by the skies. Before airplanes, the skies played little practical role in human affairs. This invention, however, created a new good: airspace control. Because of the possibility of aerial bombing, such control is precious. It is highly subtractable, and technology has increased possibilities for exclusion. The norm quickly emerged that control of airspace above a country belongs to it. For airspace above the high seas, access is not restricted in this way. Although the skies *as such* should neither be legitimately appropriated to the exclusion of some nor be left in common ownership, this convention pertaining to this particular good is supported, as a demand of reasonable conduct, by whatever arguments support the moral acceptability of states to begin with.

Another good provided by the skies is the *absorptive capacity* of the atmosphere, its ability to absorb greenhouse gases in a manner that preserves basic climate conditions. That capacity is highly subtractable: there are limits to how much greenhouse gas we can emit in total without climate change. Unlike airspace, it is a good of low excludability: greenhouse gases disperse uniformly in the atmosphere. What damage they cause does not depend on where they are emitted.

Absorptive capacity is a peculiar good. Like airspace control, it is provided by the skies, so by a part of the Earth that should neither be legitimately appropriated to the exclusion of some nor be left in common ownership. But there is great moral urgency to regulating access to the absorptive capacity. A collapse of the climate conditions under which human life flourishes may easily make it impossible for individuals to meet basic needs. *That regulation be provided* for this good to make sure individuals can meet basic needs is a requirement of justice associated with collective ownership. Given the nature of the absorptive capacity, this point follows from the obligation introduced earlier that, to the extent that within current institutions plans are made or policies adopted that affect future generations, those generations can expect such planning to make sure their ability to meet basic needs is preserved, to the extent that this depends on original resources and spaces.

Two strands of argument merge here. One is that the absorptive capacity is a good provided by a part of the Earth (the skies) for which co-owners cannot be reasonably expected to accept exclusive appropriation, while at the same time it would also be unreasonable for everybody to retain the unrestricted exercise of their rights. The second strand is that regulating access specifically to the absorptive capacity is required as a matter of justice. Justice requires that access be regulated so as to stop catastrophic damage from climate change. This requirement (thus the second strand of argument) by itself does not preclude, say, privatization of the skies (whatever that might mean for the absorptive capacity).

The first strand raises the question of how we should regulate access to the absorptive capacity. Relevant for assessing how we should regulate this good are the economic importance of emissions and the absorptive capacity's subtractable and non-excludable nature. Nobody can be reasonably expected to accept regulation that permits privatization of this good (whatever that might mean). Nor would it be reasonably acceptable that access be regulated in accordance with bargaining power. Airspace control can legitimately be regulated by norms that respectively exclude some. However, airspace control is a good of high excludability, and there is no parallel to the support for that kind of regulation that arguments for the moral acceptability of states provided. Reasonable conduct requires an appropriate *fair division* scheme.

10

A full solution to this fair division problem is beyond the scope of this chapter (but see Risse 2012: ch. 10). One needs to approach it the old-fashioned way: nominate several criteria that could apply, and argue for or against them to see which criterion is most plausible. Here I focus on how collective ownership helps with intergenerational perspectives on obligations to future generations in the context of climate change. But in conjunction with the approach I just sketched this standpoint generates a full-fledged proposal for how to divide up the burdens from climate change. For completeness,

I attach the full proposal in an appendix. Much of the work required for obtaining it does not draw on the ownership approach. But some of it does. One way in which the ownership approach contributes is by providing an argument against Singer's equal division proposal. Another way is by throwing insights on past emissions.

Did past emitters violate obligations of justice or demands of reasonable conduct that follow from Common Ownership? Again, according to Common Ownership, in addition to areas subject to appropriation by occupation to the exclusion of others, there are areas that should be left in common, or else be governed by conventions that go beyond common ownership without permitting appropriation. The moral ownership status of these areas depends on the available technology, and may change. What changes especially is whether co-owners can be expected to waive liberty rights either because private occupation is appropriate, or because access to the respective parts should be regulated by norms other than those permitting appropriation. In Grotius's day, co-owners could not be expected to waive rights to the seas. But advancements in fishing and seabed exploitation created a situation where they can be expected to accept principles regulating access to these goods. The same is true for the absorptive capacity.

It *now* is a violation of justice for states to leave access to the absorptive capacity unregulated. However, technology at earlier stages was *already* such that justice required a new regime of access. The volume of emissions even then, made possible by new technology, had made the absorptive capacity highly subtractable. Early emitters violated duties of justice when permitting unrestricted emissions. But they could not know about the problematic consequences. We reach a familiar distinction. We often appeal to what individuals, subjectively speaking, had reason to do by way of assessing when to *blame* or *excuse* them. But we think of requirements of justice differently, in terms of what, all things considered, or objectively speaking, people ought to do.

So while it did violate obligations of justice not to adopt conventions of access, a set of conditions of *maximally excusatory force* applies to early emitters. The standpoint from which we can say earlier decision-makers violated justice sets aside their scientific limitations. "[A]ttempts to apply fault-based standards are virtually guaranteed to become embroiled in more or less irresolvable controversy about historical explanations," says Shue (1996: 16). "Yet never to attempt to assess fault is to act as if the world began yesterday." We can assess fault, but although there was wrongdoing in the past, there was no blameworthy fault. The world did not begin yesterday, and this approach in terms of Common Ownership allows us to articulate the thought that what justice requires with regard to the absorptive capacity, and what people could reasonably be expected to know, has evolved.

What is the relevant date such that, before it, emitters should not be blamed for emissions? Gosseries (2004) mentions various sensible dates, among them 1896 (publication of an article by Svante Arrhenius on the greenhouse effect, "the first warning of global warming" (Neumayer 2000: 188)); 1967 (publication of first serious modeling exercise on the matter); 1990, and 1995 (publication of first two IPCC reports). An advocate of historical accountability, Neumayer (2000) thinks it was not before the mid-1980s that the public and decision-makers became aware of the greenhouse effect.

The 1992 UN Framework Convention on Climate Change too sets a plausible date. The years of the publication of the third and fourth IPCC report (2001 and 2007), are also possible, as both added clarity on climate change.

The crucial question is at what time decision-makers could be expected to know, specifically, the dangers of climate change. By this standard, 1990 is the latest sensible date: the 1990 IPCC report already absorbed a body of insights gathered over years. Any choice of date will trigger the objection that, if countries cannot be blamed for emissions prior to Year X, they cannot be blamed for having committed themselves, over generations, to lifestyles that essentially involve massive emissions. Come Year X, they were locked into certain patterns. However, if Year X is fixed as the latest possible year this objection loses its force.

In light of the relevance and visibility of the 1990 IPCC report, and of persistent doubts that a choice of date other than the latest sensible one would inevitably create confusion about what decision-makers may have been expected to consider, 1990 is also a sensible choice, *provided* the proposal for the distribution of burdens acknowledges reasons other than rectification of wrongful past emissions as reasons for which disadvantaged countries can demand aid. The importance of 1990 can then make us neglect the fact that it is the *latest* sensible date. There is a duty to help states realize human rights, and thus help them create conditions under which the realization of these rights is possible, as well as a duty of assistance with building institutions (see Risse 2012: ch. 4). One sensible way of making good on these duties is the sharing of technology and other support to address climate change. It is because of these independently existing duties that also affect the distribution of burdens from climate change that the choice of the latest sensible date before which emissions are not blameworthy is not too worrisome.

Our discussion of historical accountability has reached three conclusions. First, past emitters violated obligations of justice. Second, they cannot be blamed for their emissions. Third, defining past emitters as emitters before 1990 depends on the assumption that the proposal for the distribution of burdens acknowledges reasons other than rectification of blameworthy past emissions as reasons for which disadvantaged countries can demand aid in dealing with climate change. My proposal for the distribution of burdens is informed by these points, and adopts only a highly qualified version of historical accountability. Collective ownership offers a language of "right" and "wrong" with regard to use of parts of the Earth that has entered the reasoning leading to these conclusions.

11

Let me conclude. Governmental policy directed at future generations is a matter of justice. My purpose here has been to formulate one way of giving a bigger role to reflection on justice in the debate about climate change. The results are much less neat than Broome's straightforward prescription for all individuals to offset their green-house gas emissions. The subject of justice for future generations is a messy one. But reflection on the collective ownership status of the Earth allows us to make some progress. I also believe the idea that preserving this planet for future generation as a matter of justice has much intuitive pull. It is that pull to which I have tried to give a philosophical framework.

That thought also contrasts to some extent with another philosophical approach to climate change, namely, to cast the moral problem involved in human-engineered climate change as primarily a human rights violation. That thought is developed in the ongoing work of Simon Caney (e.g. 2009). The human rights paradigm has rightly become prominent, and I myself have contributed to it and used it here. Climate change is *also* a human rights violation, but that characterization falls short of capturing the magnitude of the problem. Its true magnitude becomes clearer if we theorize it in the intergenerational context of collective ownership of the Earth and thus embed human rights concerns into that approach.

To be sure, there is a way of thinking of the scope of human rights talk as broad enough so that human rights of future generations are also affected by climate change, and this is what I have done in this chapter. But the effort of integrating climate change issues into human rights talk also opens it up to the kind of *moral corruption* Gardiner (2011) notes in many applications of moral discourse to climate change. Using a particular kind of moral approach opens up opportunities of favoring some constitu-ents over others. The danger here is that the concerns of contemporaries are over-emphasized because representatives of future generations are necessarily absent. Human rights talk would be susceptible to such corruption. Once the human rights approach is embedded into the collective ownership approach, its intergenerational dimensions become clear. That is how it should be.

Much more work remains to be done. The grounds-of-justice approach has to be scrutinized in more detail. Is this a good approach to justice? Does it identify the right grounds, and are there additional ones? Does it identify the right principles for given grounds? One could ask for any ground how to think about future generations. Here I have done so only for collective ownership. In addition, my idea of revitalizing reflection on humanity's collective ownership should be critic-ally scrutinized, especially as far as my use of that idea for exploring obligations to future generations is concerned. If that idea is found plausible, it should be expanded. Beyond what *OGJ* does, I have recently applied that approach to the question of whether there is a human right to water (Risse 2014). Also, more discussion is needed about whether my approach to climate change in terms of collective ownership (and in that sense, in terms of justice) is superior to the other approaches I mentioned. Not all the proposal for the division of burdens from climate change in the appendix is derived from collective ownership. That proposal will need to receive critical reflection. And then of course there are questions of implementation that this chapter has not even begun to address.

APPENDIX

....

We can sum up my proposal for the division of burdens from climate change as follows. Suppose there is a fixed overall level of acceptable future emissions that keeps climate change to a bearable level.

- Burdens from adaptation
  - *Adaptation that becomes necessary because of emissions after 1990 but prior to conclusion of major climate treaty*: Countries that did not take considerable measures to reduce emissions after 1990, the wealthy ones anyway, have a duty to compensate those that have been harmed because of this, with a priority on the poorer ones. Since it will be impossible to assess specifically which kinds of adaptation become necessary because of these emissions, at the practical level this duty will generate an obligation to transfer money and technological aid to countries that need to adapt.
  - *Adaptation that becomes necessary because of emissions that occurred before 1990 or after the conclusion of a climate treaty*: No action required.
- Burdens from mitigation
  - Must assess which countries need to make how much of a sacrifice, compared to their business-as-usual trajectories so that emissions stay below the overall acceptable level.
  - States that should modify their production are those that, in terms of per-capita wealth, can best afford changes ("ability to pay"), and those that on a per-capita basis emit most ("polluter pays"). The amount of reduction for which a country is responsible, by reducing its emissions or by paying others to do so, is a function of a ranking of countries in terms of a combined index of these criteria (both being weighted equally). A country would be the higher on this ranking the higher its per-capita income, and the higher its per-capita emissions.
  - For roughly equal index levels on this list, countries ought to make more sacrifices if they benefit from past emissions.

This proposal brings into reflective equilibrium the morally relevant considerations for regulating access to the absorptive capacity of the atmosphere.

REFERENCES

Arendt, Hannah (1958). *The Human Condition*. Chicago: University of Chicago Press.

Baier, Annette (1981). The Rights of Past and Future Persons. In Ernest Partridge (ed.), *Responsibilities to Future Generations: Environmental Ethics*. New York: Prometheus Books, 171–83.

Broome, John (2012). *Climate Matters: Ethics in a Warming World*. New York: Norton.

Buck, Susan (1998). *The Global Commons: An Introduction*. Washington, DC: Island Press.

Caney, Simon (2009). Human Rights and Moral Thresholds. In Stephen Humphreys (ed.), *Human Rights and Climate Change*. Cambridge: Cambridge University Press, 69–90.

de-Shalit, Avner (1995). *Why Posterity Matters: Environmental Policies and Future Generations*. London: Routledge.

Gardiner, Stephen (2011). *The Perfect Moral Storm: The Ethical Tragedy of Climate Change*. Oxford: Oxford University Press.

George, Henry (1871). *Progress and Poverty*. New York: Vanguard.

Goodin, Robert (1985). *Protecting the Vulnerable: Reanalyzing our Social Responsibilities*. Chicago: University of Chicago Press.

Gosseries, Axel (2004). Historical Emissions and Free Riding. In Lukas Meyer (ed.), *Justice in Time: Responding to Historical Injustice*. Baden-Baden: Nomos, 355–82.

Hart, H. L. A. (1982). *Essay on Bentham*. Oxford: Oxford University Press.

Hurka, Thomas (1993). Ethical Principles. In Harold Coward and Thomas Hurka (eds), *Ethics and Climate Change: The Green House Effect*. Calgary: Laurier, 23–38.

Kumar, Rahul (2003). Who Can Be Wronged? *Philosophy and Public Affairs*, 31(2): 99–188.

Marx, Karl (1972). *Capital*, iii. London: Lawrence & Wishart.

Neumayer, Eric (2000). In Defense of Historical Accountability for Greenhouse Gas Emissions. *Ecological Economics*, 33: 185–92.

O'Neill, John (1993). Future Generations: Present Harms. *Philosophy*, 68(263): 35–51.

Parfit, Derek (1984). *Reasons and Persons*. New York: Oxford University Press.

Passmore, John (1974). *Man's Responsibility for Nature: Ecological Problems and Western Traditions*. London: Duckworth.

Risse, Mathias (2012). *On Global Justice*. Princeton: Princeton University Press.

Risse, Mathias (2014). The Human Right to Water and Common Ownership of the Earth. *Journal of Political Philosophy*, 22(2): 178–203.

Scanlon, T. M. (1998). *What we Owe to Each Other*. Cambridge, MA: Harvard University Press.

Shue, Henry (1996). Environmental Change and the Varieties of Justice. In Fen Osler Hamilton and Judith Reppy (eds), *Earthly Goods: Environmental Change and Social Justice*. Ithaca, NY: Cornell University Press, 9–29.

Sidgwick, Henry (2005). *The Elements of Politics*. London: Elibron Classics.

Singer, Peter (2002). One Atmosphere. In *One World: The Ethics of Globalization*. New Haven: Yale University Press, ch. 2.

Williams, Bernard (1995). Must a Concern for the Environment Be Centered on Human Beings? In *Making Sense of Humanity and Other Philosophical Essays*. Cambridge: Cambridge University Press, 233–41.

Wilson, Edward O. (1984). *Biophilia*. Cambridge, MA: Harvard University Press.

Wilson, Edward O. (1993). *The Diversity of Life*. New York: Norton.

CHAPTER 14

....

PARADOX OF ABUNDANCE

Automation Anxiety Returns

....

DAVID H. AUTOR

Abstract

Despite sustained increases in material standards of living, fear of the adverse employment consequences of technological advancement has recurred repeatedly. This represents a paradox of abundance: technological change threatens social welfare not because it intensifies scarcity but because it augments abundance. For most citizens of market economies, the primary income-generating asset they possess is their scarce labor. If rapid technological advances were to effectively substitute cheap and abundant capital for (previously) expensive and willful labor, society would be made wealthier, not poorer, in aggregate, but those who own labor but do not own capital might find it increasingly challenging to make a living. This chapter considers why automation anxiety has suddenly become salient in popular and academic discourse. It offers informed conjectures on the potential implications of these developments for employment and earnings.

THE PARADOX OF ABUNDANCE

....

Anxiety about the adverse effects of technological change on employment has a venerable history. In the early nineteenth century, for example, a group of English textile artisans calling themselves the Luddites staged a machine-trashing rebellion. Their brashness earned them a place (rarely positive) in the lexicon. Economists have historically rejected what we call the "lump of labor" fallacy, the supposition that an increase in labor productivity inevitably reduces employment because there is only a finite amount of work to do. While intuitively appealing, this idea is demonstrably false. In 1900, for example, 41 percent of the United States workforce was in agriculture. By 2000, that share had fallen to 2 percent, after the Green Revolution revolutionized crop yields. But the employment-to-population ratio rose over the twentieth century as women moved from home to market, and the unemployment rate fluctuated cyclically, with no long-term increase.

Despite sustained increases in material standards of living, fear of the adverse employment consequences of technological advancement recurred repeatedly in the twentieth century. In his widely discussed Depression-era essay "Economic Possibilities for our Grandchildren," John Maynard Keynes (1930) foresaw that in a century's time, "we may be able to perform all the operations of agriculture, mining, and manufacture with a quarter of the human effort to which we have been accustomed." Keynes viewed these developments as posing short-term challenges, "For the moment the very rapidity of these changes is hurting us and bringing difficult problems to solve. . . . We are being afflicted with a new disease of which some readers may not yet have heard the name, but of which they will hear a great deal in the years to come— namely, *technological unemployment*." But Keynes was sanguine about the long run, opining that "this is only a temporary phase of maladjustment," and predicting that the fifteen-hour workweek (supporting a high standard of living) would be commonplace in a century's time.

Keynes's projection that the maladjustment was "temporary" was a bold one given that he was writing during the Great Depression. But the end of the Second World War seemed to affirm the rising prosperity that Keynes had foreseen. Perhaps more surprising is that "automation anxiety" recurred two decades after the Second World War during what was arguably the height of American economic preeminence. In 1964, President Johnson empaneled a "Blue-Ribbon National Commission on Technology, Automation, and Economic Progress" whose charge was "to identify and assess the past effects and the current and prospective role and pace of technological change; to identify and describe the impact of technological and economic change on production and employment, including new job requirements and the major types of worker displacement, both technologically and economic, which are likely to occur during the next 10 years."

While the commission ultimately concluded that automation did not threaten employment at that time, it recommended, as insurance against this possibility, "a guaranteed minimum income for each family; using the government as the employer of last resort for the hard core jobless; two years of free education in either community or vocational colleges; a fully administered federal employment service, and individual Federal Reserve Bank sponsorship in area economic development free from the Fed's national headquarters" (*The Herald Press* 1966).

The blue-ribbon commission's sanguine conclusions did not entirely allay the concerns of contemporary social critics. In an open letter to President Johnson in 1966, the self-titled Ad Hoc Committee on the Triple Threat, which included Nobel laureates Linus Pauling (chemistry) and Gunnar Myrdal (economics), as well as economic historian Robert Heilbroner, opined that "The traditional link between jobs and incomes is being broken. . . . The economy of abundance can sustain all citizens in comfort and economic security whether or not they engage in what is commonly reckoned as work" (quoted in Akst 2014).[1] Writing separately in the *Public Interest* in 1965, Heilbroner argued that, "the new technology is threatening a whole new group of skills—the sorting, filing, checking, calculating, remembering, comparing, okaying skills—that are the special preserve of the office worker.... In the end, as machines continue to invade society, duplicating greater and greater numbers of social tasks, it is human labor itself—at least, as we now think of 'labor'—that is gradually rendered redundant" (1965: 34–6).

In the five decades since the Ad Hoc Committee penned its open letter to the President, human labor has certainly not been rendered redundant, as these scholars had feared. But automation anxiety has clearly returned. Casual empiricism suggests that economists and public intellectuals have begun to question whether these earlier projections of technological unemployment were in fact flat-out wrong, as had been widely accepted, or whether instead they were simply ahead of their time in anticipating imminent employment challenges that in reality took several additional decades to materialize. For example, in a 2012 *New York Times* column titled "Rise of the Robots," Paul Krugman cites the falling share of payments to labor in US national income as a harbinger of things to come: "If this is the wave of the future, it makes nonsense of just about all the conventional wisdom on reducing inequality. Better education won't do much to reduce inequality if the big rewards simply go to those with the most assets." Krugman is not alone among economists in invoking this concern. The *Economist* (Jan. 18, 2014) reports that

> Larry Summers, a former American treasury secretary [and Clark Medal winner in economics], looked at employment trends among American men between 25 and 54. In the 1960s only one in 20 of those men was not working. According to Mr. Summers's extrapolations, in ten years the number could be one in seven. This is one indication, Mr. Summers says, that technical change is increasingly taking the form of "capital that effectively substitutes for labour."

In a similar vein, MIT scholars Erik Brynjolfsson and Andrew McAfee argue in a 2011 book that humans are in danger of losing the "race against the machine." And in a 2012 working paper, economists Jeffrey D. Sachs and Laurence J. Kotlikoff posit that "smart machines" may threaten us with "long-term misery."[2]

Perhaps most telling is the finding of a recent poll of leading mainstream academic economists conducted by the Chicago Initiative on Global Markets regarding the impact of technology on employment and earnings.[3] Consistent with the canonical

---

[1] The three threats perceived by the ad hoc committee were: the cybernation revolution; the weaponry revolution; and the human rights revolution.

[2] Of course, popular writing on the topic is far less circumspect. Journalist Kevin Drum opined in *Mother Jones* that we are becoming enslaved to our "robot overlords," while Noah Smith laments in *The Atlantic* that we have reached "the end of labor."

[3] The IGM webpage describes the panel members as follows: "Our panel was chosen to include distinguished experts with a keen interest in public policy from the major areas of economics, to be geographically diverse, and to include Democrats, Republicans, and Independents as well as older and younger scholars. The panel members are all senior faculty at the most elite research universities in the United States. The panel includes Nobel Laureates, John Bates Clark Medalists, fellows of the

economic view that technology is, in the memorable phrase of Joel Mokyr, the "lever of riches," a full 88 percent of economists in the poll either agreed or strongly agreed with the statement that "advancing automation has not historically reduced employment in the United States" (see Figure 14.1). Yet, surprisingly, 43 percent of those polled endorsed (i.e. agreed with) the statement that "information technology and automation are a central reason why median wages have been stagnant in the US over the past decade, despite rising productivity." In contrast, only 28 percent disagreed or strongly disagreed.[4] While I know of no comparable survey data from a decade earlier, I find these poll results stunning because they suggest that a plurality of mainstream economists has accepted—at least tentatively—the proposition that a decade of technological advancement has made the median worker no better off, and possibly worse off.

The concern that technological progress may harm a substantial fraction of workers presents a paradox of abundance. The paradox is that the threat to social welfare posed by technological change is the threat of *excess* rather than the threat of *scarcity*. Why is excess threatening? For most citizens of market economies, the primary income-generating asset they possess is their scarce labor. If rapid technological advances were to effectively substitute cheap and abundant capital for scarce and demanding labor, society would be made wealthier, not poorer. But this capital-biased technological progress would create a substantial income distribution problem: those who own labor but who do not own capital might have no means of making an adequate living.[5] This would disrupt our central mechanism for economic organization and dramatically dis-equalize the income distribution, even at current high levels of inequality. Thus, the paradox: abundance threatens social welfare.

How did we reach a point where the robust faith of mainstream economists in the beneficence of technological advancement appears to have become decidedly tentative? And is there now a strong case for concern about the long-term consequences of advancing technologies—computers and robotics specifically—for employment and earnings?

This chapter presents evidence that labor scarcity has declined in rich countries. It then considers the current trajectory of technological advancement and considers why automation anxiety has suddenly become salient in popular and academic discourse. It ends by considering (more accurately, speculating on) implications for employment and earnings.

Econometric Society, past Presidents of both the American Economics Association and American Finance Association, past Democratic and Republican members of the President's Council of Economic Advisors, and past and current editors of the leading journals in the profession." Caveat emptor: the author is also a member of the panel.

[4] Survey results are found at <www.igmchicago.org/igm-economic-experts-panel/poll-results?SurveyID=SV_eKbRnXZWx3jSRBb> (accessed Mar. 2014).

[5] To clarify terminology, capital-biased technological change is a change in production technology that raises capital's share of output.

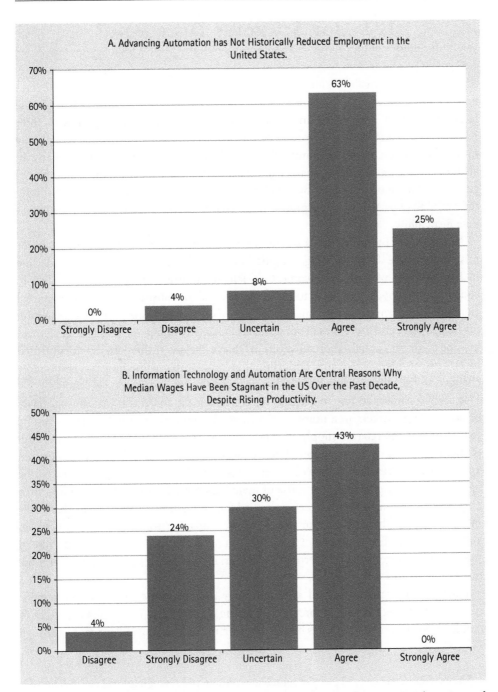

FIGURE 14.1. Chicago Booth IGM Expert Poll: Impact of Automation on Employment and Wages

Notes: Survey date February 25, 2014. Details available at <http://www.igmchicago.org/igm-economic-experts-panel/poll-results?SurveyID=SV_eKbRnXZWx3jSRBb.>

IS LABOR SCARCITY DECLINING?

....

Three salient patterns in US and international data suggest that labor may indeed have become less scarce. A first is that labor's share of national income has declined in the large majority of countries since the early 1980s. Figure 14.2, reproduced from Karabarbounis and Neiman (2014, KN hereafter), documents this trend specifically for the four largest world economies: the United States, Japan, China, and Germany. In all four countries, the labor share—specifically, the share of corporate gross value-added paid to labor—declined by roughly 2 to 4 percentage points per decade during the 1975–2010 period, with the precise time window differing by country according to data availability.

As evidenced by the remarks quoted from Krugman and Summers, many economists find these facts startling. Karabarbounis and Neiman attribute the decline in labor's share of national income to a fall in the price of investment relative to consumption goods—i.e. due to rising capital-labor substitution (a technological change). This form of technological change is of course only one possible explanation for this pattern, and there is as of yet no *direct* evidence linking the falling labor share of income to direct capital-labor substitution.[6] Nevertheless, if the patterns documented by KN prove robustly true and enduring, they suggest that something has profoundly changed in the macro-economy that has reduced the "scarcity" value of labor.

A second pattern adding to the case for concern is the sharp falls in real wage levels of non-college workers in a number of advanced countries in recent decades, despite the *decline* in the relative supply of these workers. In the United States, this is seen particularly in the declining wages of non-college males evident in Figure 14.3. Between 1979 and 2012, real full-time weekly earnings of male high school graduates fell by approximately 15 percent while those of male high school dropouts fell by more than 25 percent. In a similar vein, Green and Sand (2013; Figure 14.1) document sharp falls in real wages in the bottom four deciles of the Canadian wage distribution between 1981 and 1996, while Card et al. (2013; Figure 14.1) document a substantial decline in the real daily wages of West German male workers between 1997 and 2009 from the median on downward.[7]

How economically important are these wage declines? One gauge of their significance is their effect on labor force participation. Figure 14.4, which plots changes in employment-to-population rates between 1979 and 2008 among males ages 25 through

---

[6] KN's model assumes an elasticity of substitution between labor and capital that exceeds one—a necessary condition for a fall in the price of capital goods to raise the capital share. Elsby et al. (2013) closely study the evolution of the US labor share over the period 1948–2013 and corroborate KN's finding of a substantial decline in the labor share from the early 1980s forward. Their correlational evidence suggests, however, that outsourcing of labor-intensive tasks rather than capital-labor substitution is the largest proximate contributor to declining labor shares at the level of industries.

[7] Gregg et al. (2013) report that a similar decline in low earnings has not occurred in the UK.

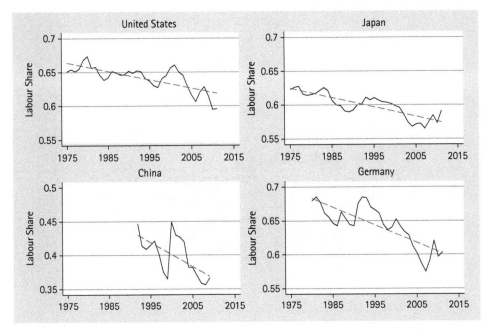

FIGURE 14.2. Trends in the Labor Share in National Income in the Four Largest World Economies

Source: Karabarbounis and Neiman (2014), figure II.

39 by race and education group against changes in their real hourly wages, offers a third major cause for concern. Employment rates have fallen sharply among demographic groups that have seen the large fall in wages over the last three decades.[8] These declines are substantial, ranging from 7 to 10 percentage points among males with high school or lower education, and far greater among black males.

Such employment declines would not necessarily be problematic if they were concentrated among groups with high and rising earnings. This would merely suggest that well-off groups were spending their growing resources on additional leisure—arguably a sign of the rising abundance of leisure that Keynes envisioned in 1930. The fact that employment rates have instead dropped steeply among demographic groups with low and falling earnings suggests that employer demand for less skilled workers has declined—so much so that many are either choosing not to work, or are unable to find gainful employment at prevailing wages.[9] Thus, the combined weight of the

---

[8] As reported in Autor and Wasserman (2013), over the entire 1979–2008 period, a 10% fall in wages for a demographic group is robustly associated with a 5.7 percentage point decline in its employment-to-population rate. The positive correlation between rising (or falling) wages and rising (or falling) employment rates holds in each of the last three decades (1979–89, 1989–99, and 2000–10), as well as before and during the Great Recession (2000–7 and 2007–10). The robust positive relationship between wage and employment changes is detected for all demographic subgroups: both sexes, all race groups, both younger and older workers, and both college and non-college workers.

[9] This latter possibility would suggest that employment is "rationed" among low-skill groups, which cannot occur in a competitive neoclassical labor market setting. Contemporary labor markets are far

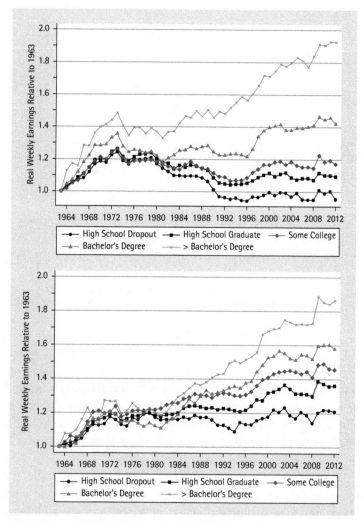

FIGURE **14.3.** Change in Real Wage Levels of Full-Time Male (top) and Female (bottom) Workers by Education, 1963–2012

Notes: Real earnings levels are plotted relative to their 1963 values. Wages are deflated to real 2012 values using the Personal Consumption Expenditure Deflator. Figure uses March CPS data for earnings years 1963–2012. Calculations hold constant labor market experience within each education group.

evidence in Figures 14.2 through 14.4 lends credence to the concern that we have entered a realm where there is a growing surplus of labor—or at least a surplus of less-educated labor. These workers may not be "technologically unemployed" in the sense that scholars including Heilbroner or Myrdal had feared; it is plausible that many could

from the textbook neoclassical model, however. The presence of wage rigidities (such as minimum wages or downward nominal wage rigidities), fixed hiring or firing costs, or significant search frictions, all make involuntary unemployment a plausible possibility.

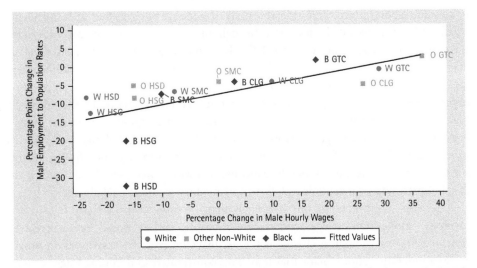

FIGURE 14.4. Changes in Male Employment to Population Rates and Changes in Real Male Hourly Earnings among Males Aged 25–39, 1979–2008

Source: Census IPUMS 5 percent samples for years 1980, 1990, and 2000 and American Community Survey (ACS) 2009. (Reproduced from Autor and Wasserman, 2013: figure 6).

still command a positive market wage. But if a significant fraction of young, less-educated adults has substantially withdrawn from market employment due to falling demand for their skills, this may be operationally equivalent to technological unemployment.

THE PUZZLE OF FALLING WAGES

There is no economic law that says that wages must always rise. Under normal competitive conditions, an increase in the supply of a given skill group will reduce its market wage. The falling wages of low-skill workers could, therefore, reflect nothing more interesting than a rise in their relative supply. Yet, in essentially all advanced economies—and certainly in the US, UK, and Germany—this is not what has occurred; workers with tertiary education have become increasingly abundant in recent decades while workers with secondary or lower education have becoming increasingly rare. Provided that high- and low-skill workers are gross complements (formally, provided that the elasticity of substitution in production between these skill groups exceeds one), an increase in the relative supply of high-skill workers should *reduce* the real wages of high-skill workers and *raise* the wages of low-skill workers (see Acemoglu 2002, and Acemoglu and Autor 2011 for discussion). Neither has occurred.

A second candidate interpretation of these demographic and wage patterns is that there have been "skill-biased" demand shifts that have raised demand for high-relative to low-skill labor. Indeed, a considerable body of evidence suggests that such shifts have occurred both in recent decades and throughout most of the twentieth century (see Katz and Autor 1999; Autor et al. 2008; Goldin and Katz 2008). However, while a skill-biased demand shift will raise the *relative* wages of high- relative to low-skill workers (again assuming the elasticity of substitution exceeds one), such a shift would *not* be expected to reduce real wages of low-skill workers. In fact, the opposite should occur: both high- and low-skill workers should experience an increase in earnings, though high-skill workers should gain by more.[10] The fact that real wages of high-skill workers have risen while those of low-skill workers have fallen in the face of a *falling* relative supply of low-skill workers is therefore inconsistent with *either* a supply-induced rise in the skill premium or a canonical skill-complementary technological change.

What else might be going on? It is likely that the causes for the sharp falls in real earnings among non-college workers are multiple, and it would be incorrect to conclude that technological change is the exclusive or even, necessarily, the primary explanation. One central factor that may have contributed to declining wages of less-educated workers is the globalization of labor markets, seen particularly in the greatly increased US trade integration with developing countries. Globalization has become particularly important for US labor markets since the early 1990s when China began its extremely rapid integration into the world trading system. Between 1987 and 2007, the share of total US spending on Chinese goods rose from under 0.5 percent to close to 5 percent. While the influx of Chinese goods lowered consumer prices, it also fomented a substantial decline in US manufacturing employment, contributing directly to the decline in production worker employment (Autor et al. 2013).

A second factor impinging on the earnings of non-college males is the decline in the penetration and bargaining power of labor unions in the United States. Unions have historically obtained relatively generous wage and benefit packages for blue-collar workers. Over the last three decades, however, US private-sector union density—i.e. the fraction of private-sector workers who belong to labor unions—has fallen by approximately 70 percent, from 24 percent in 1973 to 7 percent in 2011 (Card et al. 2004; Hirsch 2008). While the precise contribution of declining unionization to the evolution of male wage levels and wage inequality is a subject of ongoing debate, a number of studies place this contribution at 20 to 30 percent. Notably, because union membership has been historically quite concentrated among blue-collar workers, the majority of whom are males, the decline in union membership may have differentially affected non-college male earnings.

A third possibility, one which is the focus of this chapter, is that the ongoing substitution of computer-intensive machinery for workers performing routine task-intensive jobs has depressed demand for workers in both blue-collar production and

---

[10] The reason is q-complementarity. A high-skill-labor-augmenting technological change increases the effective supply of high-skill workers. Analogously to an increase in the capital/labor ratio, which increases the marginal product of capital in a standard two-factor production function, a high-skill-labor-augmenting technological change should raise the marginal product of low-skill labor.

white-collar office, clerical, and administrative support positions, and reduced the set of middle-skill career jobs available to non-college workers more generally (Autor et al. 2003; Autor and Dorn 2013). I discuss this possibility in detail next.

It bears emphasis that these three forces—technological change, deunionization, and globalization—work in tandem. Advances in information and communications technologies have directly changed job demands in US workplaces while simultaneously facilitating the globalization of production by making it increasingly feasible and cost-effective for firms to source, monitor, and coordinate complex production processes at disparate locations worldwide. The globalization of production has in turn increased competitive conditions for US manufacturers and US workers, eroding employment at unionized establishments and decreasing the capability of unions to negotiate favorable contracts, attract new members, and penetrate new establishments. This multi-dimensional complementarity among causal factors makes it both conceptually and empirically difficult to isolate the "pure" effect of any one factor.

HOW COMPUTERIZATION CHANGES WORK: A CONCRETE CHARACTERIZATION

Economists frequently speak in abstract terms about capital-skill complementarity and capital-labor substitution—and with some justification, since these terms have precise meanings in the abstract production functions that the economics profession uses to represent economic processes. I find it useful, however, to conceptualize these terms concretely as reflecting distinctive technological phenomena with specific characteristics. Very roughly, one may characterize the recent phases of workplace computerization as undergoing three successive epochs: simulation, communications, and engagement.[11] The first is well understood, the second much less so, and the third reflects the current frontier. Its economic implications are a *terra incognita*.

Simulation

The notion of using computers to simulate (or replicate) codified, repetitive information-processing tasks stretches back to the dawn of the computer era. An early example was the use of punch card-driven computers at the Los Alamos National Laboratory to calculate the physical properties of explosions and implosions during the development

---

[11] This trichotomy is used by my MIT colleague, roboticist Seth Teller. While it is not common parlance in the computer science community, I find it extremely helpful for organizing ideas.

of the first nuclear warheads.[12] But the scope of computer simulation is not limited to simulating *physical* processes. It includes simulating any work process that can be fully specified with an explicit procedure, and hence codified in a computer program. When a computer processes a company's payroll, alphabetizes a list of names, or tabulates the age distribution of residents in each census enumeration district, it is "simulating" a work process that would, in a previous era, have been done by humans.[13]

The implications of computer simulation for work organization are reasonably well captured by the ideas set forth in Autor et al. (2003, ALM hereafter). ALM describe the process whereby computers substitute for workers in performing "routine" codifiable tasks. Routine tasks are characteristic of many middle-skilled cognitive and manual activities, such as bookkeeping, clerical work, and repetitive production tasks. Because the core job tasks of these occupations follow precise, well-understood procedures, they have in recent decades become increasingly codified in computer software and performed by machines. This has led to a substantial decline in employment in clerical, administrative support, and, to a lesser degree, production and operative employment.

But simulation as a computing paradigm has clear boundaries: programmers cannot write a program to simulate a process that they (or the scientific community at large) do not explicitly understand. This constraint is more binding than one might initially surmise because there are many tasks that humans understand tacitly and accomplish effortlessly for which they do not know the explicit "rules" or procedures. In the words of philosopher Michael Polanyi (1966), "We know more than we can tell." When we ride upright on a two-wheeled bicycle, recognize different species of birds based only on a blurry glimpse from afar, write a compelling paragraph, or develop a hypothesis to explain a poorly understood phenomenon, we are engaging in tasks that we only tacitly understand how to perform.

As ALM discuss, the applicability of "simulation" to accomplishing human work tasks is particularly constraining in two broad areas, which they term "abstract" and "manual" tasks. These lie at opposite ends of the occupational skill distribution. Abstract tasks require problem-solving capabilities, intuition, and persuasion. They typically employ workers with high levels of education and analytical capability. The secularly falling price of accomplishing routine tasks using computer capital complements the "abstract" creative, problem-solving, and coordination tasks performed by highly educated workers such as professionals and managers, for whom data analysis is an input into production.

In contrast, manual tasks require situational adaptability, visual and language recognition, and in-person interactions. These tasks are characteristic of the jobs performed by janitors and cleaners, home health aides, construction laborers, security

---

[12] Prior to the Manhattan Project, an even earlier example of industrial-scale simulation was the use of mechanical "tabulators" to enumerate the 1890 Census of Population, which was stored on millions of punched cards.

[13] In many cases, the workers who performed these tasks were given the job title of "computer" (Grier 2005).

personnel, and motor vehicle operators. They demand workers who are physically adept and, in some cases, able to communicate fluently in spoken language. They appear to require little in the way of formal education, however, at least relative to a labor market where most workers have completed high school.

This latter observation (low education and training requirements) applies with particular force to service occupations. Tasks such as food preparation and serving, cleaning and janitorial work, grounds cleaning and maintenance, in-person health assistance by home health aides, and numerous jobs in security and protective services, are highly intensive in non-routine manual tasks. These are not highly skilled activities by human labor standards, but they present daunting challenges for automation. Equally noteworthy is that many of the outputs of these jobs (haircuts, fresh meals, housecleaning) must be produced and performed on-site or in person (at least for now), and hence these tasks are not currently subject to outsourcing. Yet, because these jobs generally do not require formal education or extensive training beyond a high school degree, the potential supply of workers who can perform these jobs is very large—which is likely to mute the potential for rapid wage growth in these occupations even in the face of rising demand.[14]

Since jobs that are intensive in either abstract or manual tasks are generally found at opposite ends of the occupational skill spectrum—in professional, managerial, and technical occupations on the one hand, and in service and laborer occupations on the other—it is natural to suspect that computer "simulation" of routine job tasks has contributed to a "polarization" of employment opportunities. A large body of US and international evidence confirms this intuition: by reducing job opportunities in middle-skilled clerical, administrative, production, and operative occupations, computerization is strongly associated with employment polarization at the level of industries, localities, and national labor markets (Goos and Manning 2007; Autor and Dorn 2013; Michaels et al. 2014; Goos et al. forthcoming).

The implications of this process for employment and earnings are multivalent. For highly educated workers, computerization has almost certainly complemented their skills—raising their productivity and the scale of operations they can command, with attendant increases in relative and real earnings (Autor et al. 1998). For less-educated workers, the implications are ambiguous at best. On the one hand, the displacement of workers from middle-skill clerical, administrative support, production, and operative positions likely leads to downward occupational mobility toward less highly trained service positions. This undoubtedly places downward pressure on wages in these occupations. At the same time, it is possible for the real "value" of the output of

---

[14] Interestingly, employment projections from the US Bureau of Labor Statistics also support the view that low-education service jobs are likely to be a major contributor to US employment growth going forward. The BLS forecasts that employment in service occupations will increase by 4.1 million, or 14%, between 2008 and 2018. The only major occupational category with greater projected growth is professional occupations, which are predicted to add 5.2 million jobs, or 17% (US Bureau of Labor Statistics, Current Employment Statistics, available at <http://www.bls.gov/ces>).

services to rise as societal wealth increases and the scarcity value of machine-produced output falls (e.g. think of large-screen TVs). Thus, while it is *possible* but far from certain for workers at all levels to benefit, the weight of the evidence suggests this has not for the most part occurred, particularly in the last decade.[15] My unproven hunch is that the net effect of the wave of computer "simulation" of workplace tasks has been to depress the earnings, and ultimately the employment, of less-educated workers.

Communications

Starting in the early 1980s, the advancing capabilities of computers in simulation were complemented by advances in telecommunications. Although large organizations such as airlines, banks, and (of course) the military had been harnessing telecommunications to connect computers for decades, price declines and technological advances in the 1980s and 1990s made computer communications ubiquitous and powerful. The commercialization of inexpensive local area networking technologies (Ethernet, specifically) in the early 1980s enabled firms to network computers within a workplace to share data and resources (e.g. file servers and printers). Before long, local area networks were interconnected in "wide area networks" within organizations, allowing the personal, mini, and mainframe computers belonging to a single organization to communicate across disparate locations over dedicated backbones. The opening of the internet to civilian and commercial use in 1995 provided firms with a set of protocols and non-dedicated infrastructure that ultimately enabled any digital device to communicate with any other internet-connected digital device anywhere in the world. Even more recently, the deployment of high-speed mobile networks has enabled digital devices to remain continuously connected to the internet over a large portion of the world's populated land areas (and at sea or in the air via satellites).

How do these enhanced capabilities—ubiquity, high-speed communications, and a limitless set of "online" resources—expand or reshape the simulation paradigm? I do not pretend to have the complete answer to this question, but I see at least two profound consequences.[16] One is that the marriage of computing and communications makes it far easier for computers to take on a coordination or oversight role than was conceivable in the "simulation era"—for example, dispatching trucks, routing packages, orchestrating the flow of parts on an auto assembly line, or dynamically managing

---

[15] Autor and Dorn (2013) present evidence that the complementarity effect dominated the displacement effect on net between 1980 and 2005. But this effect was primarily driven by wage developments in the 1990s when labor markets were extremely tight. After 2000, the expansion of manual task-intensive service occupations accelerated, but wages in these occupations fell.

[16] Papers by Garicano and Rossi-Hansberg (2004, 2006) explore how these two distinct eras of computerization—simulation and communications—may have distinct effects on the organization of knowledge hierarchies within firms.

the layout, restocking, and order retrieval from a warehouse.[17] These examples are all, arguably, simulation tasks in that computers are "simply" calculating, optimizing, and controlling following a procedure set down by a programmer. However, unlike the examples of payroll processing or census enumeration, computers in these applications are interacting in real time with the environment. Sensing and communications technologies give computers the ability to monitor a disparate set of activities in continuous time and issue instructions to coordinate and adapt these activities as new data arrive or conditions change.

One prominent application that builds on these capabilities is online sales. Prior to the communications era of computing, the primary functions of computers in retail sales were to track inventory and assist cashiers in customer checkout. The advent of cheap, ubiquitous computer communications vastly expanded the range of sales-related activities subject to computerization. Contemporary business-to-consumer websites showcase products in virtual electronic malls, recommend alternative or complementary purchases based on the search behavior of the current and past users, verify the buyer's identity, conduct the financial transaction, move the order into the back-end fulfillment system, and notify the purchaser, seller, and shipper of the transaction's status as it unfolds.

One can object that these activities are simply glorified "simulation": online sales systems are, in effect, carrying out the codified steps of tracking inventory, displaying products, transacting purchases, and tracking fulfillment.[18] But this interpretation strikes me as reductive. Fifteen years ago, one might have persuasively argued that computers could not effectively substitute for salespersons because they are unable to showcase products, make product recommendations, offer expertise and advice on product suitability and features, and more generally cannot "get to know" the customer. Those predictions would have been technically correct but substantively wrong. While it remains the case that online storefronts cannot measure your shoe size or help you to lace up a pair of oxfords, the virtues of convenience, broad selection, abundant information, and informative product recommendations (based on the behavior of countless prior buyers) appear in many cases to trump the virtues of in-person sales. Notably, the genesis of these advances is *not* simply that "simulation" has improved. The key enabler is communications: online storefronts serve the customer from any location and at any time, and provide remarkably rich decision-relevant information (photographs, product specifications, user reviews, how-to videos), in many cases exceeding what an expert salesperson could offer.

---

[17] Kiva Robotics, now owned by Amazon, offers a compelling example of how a warehouse can be reconceived as a dynamic filing system, with robotic "turtles" performing the filing—specifically, transporting shelves from location to location on their backs.

[18] Similarly, ubiquitous smartphone-based navigation systems are "nothing more" than digitized maps married to route calculation software, off-the-shelf satellite global positioning circuitry, and real-time traffic and road hazard information. Nevertheless, this virtuous combination of data, calculation, and communication has turned vehicle operators from navigators to helmsmen whose primary function is to steer their vehicles safely through road hazards as the computer calls out routing commands.

Computer communications—and the internet in particular—also enable a set of information-based services that arguably had no close counterpart in the pre-communications area: search engines. Search engines draw on systems of network computers to provide services at zero marginal cost that, until recently, were both time- and resource-intensive to obtain: rapid, accurate search and retrieval of specialized information from encyclopedias, medical reference manuals, travel books, publications databases, and how-to libraries. Search engines have become such an essential tool that a substantial fraction of today's high school students have probably never looked up a historical fact, investigated a medical or recreational drug option, or checked the prevailing spring weather in another country using any tool but a search engine.

Again, one can argue that computers are merely "simulating" what a skilled research librarian would do if she had access to many of the world's best libraries, and also had time to read and memorize their full contents for instant recollection. But the absurdity of the comparison highlights a critical set of differences. The methods that search engines use to "search" for information are so different from how humans search for information (absent computers) that it is inaccurate to characterize computers as "simulating" human search. Humans do not read, memorize, and sort limitless amounts of information for later retrieval. Instead, they catalog where information is likely to be found (using the Dewey decimal system, travel guides, encyclopedias, journal indexes) and make directed, purposive searches within those locations to identify specific pieces of information. Humans have limited information absorption and recall capability, but they can use context and logic to quickly narrow the scope of a search to the logical locations where the information is likely to reside (e.g. to look up the historical population of Manhattan, I would consult old census volumes).

One focal contrast between human and machine search helps to highlight these differences. Human search techniques require prior organization and cataloging of information; attempting to search for a specific fact in a library where all of the books had been randomly distributed across shelves would be fruitless. Such a library would, however, pose no problem for a search engine; in fact, the World Wide Web presents an electronic facsimile of this type of library—a vast repository of disorganized information. Unlike humans, search engines are indiscriminate information collectors—absorbing vast amounts of data without specific organizational principles or explicit understandings of how one piece of information may be connected to another. When a user performs a query, the search engine offers its best guess at what the user is seeking based largely on statistics: what patterns the user's query matches, what similar queries this and other users have posted in the past. Stated compactly, human search is directive—guided by prior knowledge and context. Computer search, by contrast, is statistical and non-directive. And the differences between these approaches are dictated by the distinct information-processing capabilities of people and machines.

The power of online search also highlights the complementarity between successive waves of information technologies—specifically, simulation and communications. Search engines depend fundamentally on computer communications not only for information delivery but also for primary data gathering. Google does not, to a first approximation, *create* the information it serves; it simply aggregates the countless information sources that others have made available through their computer systems. Thus, it is the very existence of computer networks that generates the resources that search engines search over. Search engines, and their close relatives, are meta-technologies that have virtuously—and arguably unexpectedly—emerged from the collective interaction of a vast number of computer systems, many of which are engaged in standard "simulation" tasks.

The power of this "meta" technology is increasingly evident beyond search. Automated "discovery" software reads reams of legal documents disgorged by companies undergoing lawsuits, identifies themes, catalogs contents, and attempts to thread together conversations based on email and paper chains (Markoff 2011). Fraud detection software applies statistical tools to flag suspicious patterns of transactions in real time, and often calls credit card holders to alert them of possible frauds. Recommendation engines suggest music and movies to consumers based on their expressed and revealed tastes, which are aggregated and compared with the browsing and rating tastes of countless other users.

While it would be foolhardy to attempt to infer general labor market implications from these high level observations, it is inarguable that the era of computer communications has substantially expanded the set of tasks beyond that which could be accomplished by computer "simulation." On the one hand, the information presentation and interaction seen in online sales allow computers to accomplish many interactive "manual" tasks that are *not* directly amenable to simulation in the canonical sense, such as order-taking and sales (i.e. the computer does not closely replicate what a human agent would do). On the other hand, the growing sophistication of statistical pattern recognition algorithms enables computers to encroach upon "expert" domains—work that has historically been the province of research librarians, paralegals, travel agents, and teachers.

Engagement

Computerization has recently entered a third era, "machine engagement," in which computers are emerging from their largely passive role as ever-ready information appliances to become increasingly "alert" machines—aware of people and objects, sensitive to contexts, and able to adjust plans accordingly to accomplish useful tasks.[19] One does not have to look hard to find early examples of "engaged" machines:

- Smartphones interpret and respond to voice commands based upon both verbal and contextual clues—where the user is currently located (e.g. home or work),

[19] Note that "alertness" does not mean machine consciousness—only that machines are aware of and responsive to the human environment, and to people in particular.

what events are scheduled on the calendar, what names are present in the address book, and what commands and queries the user has supplied in the past.

- Robotic vacuums (e.g. Neato Botvac) use lasers to scan and map rooms while vacuuming, thus plotting a purposive course over the autonomously mapped cleaning area rather than using the traditional "bump and turn" principle used by earlier generations of self-propelled devices.[20]
- Self-driving cars (e.g. the Google Car) semi-autonomously pilot conventional vehicles (retrofitted with sensors and actuators) along moderately complex sub-urban and urban roads—applying the accelerator, operating the steering wheel, complying with road signs and speed limits, and braking for unexpected hazards. Because robotic vehicles are never distracted, drowsy, or temperamental, it is a certainty that they will ultimately prove safer drivers than human operators.

These recent advances sit atop prior waves of computer simulation and telecommunications (as well as dramatic hardware price declines). Laser sensing and object recognition tools harness "simulation" software for digitizing physical environments. Location and contextual awareness technologies exploit mobile data connections to access digitized maps and search engines.

Distinct from earlier waves of computerization, recent advances in machine "engagement" with humans do *not* rely upon conventional computer simulation. Because these engagement tasks remain, to a substantial extent, unsolved problems in science and engineering, contemporary artificial intelligence has devised an "end run" around the problem. Rather than explicitly codifying such tasks, statistical machine learning algorithms inductively learn these tasks through a process of exposure, training, and reinforcement. This process enables computers to (in some cases) accomplish non-codified problems that, while remarkably mundane for humans, remain daunting challenges for engineering.

As one concrete example of machine learning, consider the challenge of object recognition, specifically the task of visually identifying a chair. Chairs come in innumerable varieties: some of have four legs, some have three, other have none; chairs may or may not have backs, may or may not rotate, swivel, or telescope, may or may not be upholstered, may or may not have arms; chairs may be comprised of any number of materials; and chairs may be highly stylized or unconventional. For example, the 1932 Zig Zag chair, designed by Gerrit Rietveld, is shaped like an upside down letter Z with an extra perpendicular ascender protruding from the top. It lacks distinct legs, arms, or an ergonomic seat or back. Nevertheless, most grade school children would immediately recognize the Zig Zag chair for what it is: a chair. But this is not the case for most object recognition programs. Why not?

---

[20] The Botvac employs a technology called Simultaneous Localization and Mapping (SLAM), where an autonomous machine builds up a map within an unknown environment. As Brynjolfsson and McAfee (2014) discuss, SLAM has been a holy grail of artificial intelligence researchers for decades.

Applying the "simulation" paradigm, a programmer might attempt to specify ex ante what features of an object suggest that it is a chair—it possesses legs, arms, a seat, and a back, for example. One could then program machines to identify objects possessing these features as chairs. But having specified such a feature set, one would immediately discover that many chairs that do not possess all features (e.g. no back, no legs). If one then relaxed the required feature set accordingly (e.g. chair back optional), the included set would clearly encompass many objects that are not chairs (e.g. tables). Thus, the simple "simulation" approach to object recognition—and many more sophisticated variants—would likely have very high misclassification rates.

Why is this ex ante approach unlikely to work? Ultimately, what makes an object a chair is that it is a device purpose-built to facilitate human beings in the act of sitting. Because there are an endless number of ways to accomplish this objective, it is likely almost impossible to pre-specify what attributes an object must possess to be a chair. Accordingly, humans (likely) recognize chairs not (simply) by comparing candidate objects to pre-specified feature sets but, instead, by reasoning about both the attributes of the object and the attributes of the human body to assess whether the candidate object is likely intended to serve as a chair (Grabner et al. 2011). For example, both a toilet and a traffic cone look somewhat like a chair, but a bit of reasoning about their shapes vis-à-vis the human anatomy suggests that a traffic cone is unlikely to make for a good seat. This implies that the problem of object recognition—at least as practiced by the human brain—is far deeper than the problem of determining whether objects have specific attributes; it likely requires reasoning about what an object is "for" and whether it is likely to serve that purpose. One is reminded of Carl Sagan's remark that, "If you wish to make an apple pie from scratch, you must first invent the universe."

Contemporary object recognition programs do *not*, for the most part, take this reasoning-based approach to identifying objects—likely because the task of developing and generalizing the approach to a largest set of objects would be extremely challenging. Could, for example, a machine that recognizes chairs by reasoning about their potential compatibility with human anatomy also be readily reprogrammed to recognize bicycles—or would it require another set of reasoning capabilities to determine whether the object could support a human being in the act of balancing while in motion?

Many contemporary object recognition tools circumvent the reasoning problem by exploiting what some would call "brute force": applying statistical machine learning tools to infer by example what objects are likely to be chairs. Relying on very large databases of so-called "ground truth"—essentially, a vast set of curated examples of labeled objects—computers can be "trained" to recognize chairs (and other objects) by induction; i.e. they statistically infer what attributes of an object make it more or less likely to be designated a chair. This approach does not require either an explicit model of "chairness" or a model of the human anatomy; instead, it relies only on large training databases, substantial processing power, and of course sophisticated software. Machine-learning algorithms do not, at present, perform as well as grade school children in correctly classifying objects. But the underlying technologies—the software, hardware, and training data—are all improving rapidly (Andreopoulos and Tsotsos 2013).

Not surprisingly, the long-term potential of machine learning to circumvent the reasoning problem is a subject of active debate among computer scientists. Some researchers expect that as computing power rises and training databases grow, the brute force machine learning approach will ultimately approach or exceed human capabilities. Others suspect that the machine learning approach will only ever get it right "on average" while missing many of the most important and informative exceptions. In either case, there is little disagreement that, at present, the ability of machines to "engage" in the human world is substantially constrained by (at least) three attributes of the candidate task:

1. *Structure in the environment.* Machine adaptability to variation in environment is, at present, far less complete, less accurate, and less reliable than human adaptability. It is natural, therefore, that the first (and current) primary application of commercial robotics is on production lines, where the environment is radically simplified and there are few variations in task requirements with which machines must contend (often only a handful of distinct operations). In production settings, industrial robots are typically bolted to the floor and surrounded by large cages that serve to protect nearby humans from their potent combination of superhuman speed and near-complete blindness to their environments.

2. *Degrees of freedom in dexterous interactions.* Though robots probably will eventually be able to walk up and down stairs, load and unload dishwashers, and fold towels, robotic dexterity will be far short of human dexterity for many years to come. It is unlikely that robots will cook fresh meals, sand and paint houses, cut hair, or wrap birthday presents anytime soon.

3. *Richness of perceptual information required to support completion of tasks.* Many mundane daily tasks are deeply dependent upon rich perceptual information. To remove, dust, and replace the objects on a shelf, untie a pair of shoes, or pack a set of items in a suitcase, an agent must recognize non-uniform objects, understand and respect their physical properties (e.g. clothes can be folded in a suitcase but shoes cannot), and make fine visual discriminations (e.g. are the shoelaces single or double-knotted?). These perceptual demands are trivial for human actors but are far outside the realm of machine capability at present.

Of course, a fourth constraint on all of these tasks is cost. While it might be technically feasible to build a robotic dishwasher loader/unloader in the near future, it will not be commercially viable to do so until the cost of numerous digital and mechanical components falls considerably.

What do these observations imply about the trajectory of capital-labor substitution? Again, it would be foolhardy to confidently project general equilibrium economic implications from these stylized characterizations. Nevertheless, it seems very likely that the scope of computer substitution into what ALM described as "manual" tasks is poised to greatly expand in the next ten years. I anticipate that we will see fewer housekeepers and janitors, fewer waiters and busboys, fewer vehicle operators, fewer assembly line workers, fewer store stockers and warehouse workers, and fewer salespersons—even in "brick and mortar" shops. At the same time, there will remain core manual task-intensive jobs that are not subject to machine substitution anytime soon: child care, elder care, and health care; food preparation; construction and skilled repair; and numerous dexterous jobs that require high levels of adaptability, precision, and contextual awareness.

While the implications for the *aggregate* labor demand are ambiguous—since these technological advancements both substitute for and complement labor—their implications for *skill* demands appear more readily discerniable. Advances in machine engagement appear poised to have a far greater labor-substituting impact in low education, manual tasks than in high education, abstract tasks. These advances will likely amplify the paradox of abundance: by making low education labor that much less scarce, they will augment inequality even as they generate riches.

CONCLUSIONS

Generations of scholars and pundits have worried about the adverse labor market consequences of technological change. Generations of neoclassical economists have assured these thinkers that their worries are misplaced. Though I consider myself a neoclassical economist, I believe that economists' bland reassurances are becoming less and less convincing. Technological advances have not created the mass unemployment that many feared. But my reading of the evidence is that they have significantly depressed wages among a substantial subset of workers, catalyzing sharp falls in labor force participation. Though declining participation in response to falling wages may be "voluntary," it is definitely not welfare-improving relative to a setting where non-college workers might be drawn back into the labor force by higher wages. While it is dangerous to extrapolate far into the future based on current trends, I foresee the challenge facing non-college workers becoming more severe as "engaged" machinery increasingly subsumes manual tasks.

There will of course be encroachments upward as well: core job tasks of salespersons, educators, attorneys, engineers, and computer programmers will be increasingly subject to automation. I worry less about these worker groups, both because I think the rate of encroachment will be slower, and because these groups have greater resources and skills to adapt accordingly. But the changes will nevertheless be significant.

Some writers would at this point draw an analogy between the economic eclipse of horses by motorized vehicles in the first decades of the twentieth century and the coming obsolescence of human labor. But there is an important difference between these examples: horses do not own capital and people do. Horses were not made wealthier by the availability of machine substitutes for their labor, but people will be (collectively) enriched. Thus, the paradox of abundance is not one of impoverishment but one of maldistribution. If technological advances make human labor substantially less scarce—as many have feared, and as Keynes eagerly anticipated—the challenge will not be finding jobs for people to do, but rather finding a means to distribute our abundant societal riches absent labor scarcity as a primary means of income distribution.

Acknowledgments

I thank Frank Levy, Brendan Price, Subi Rangan, Amartya Sen, Seth Teller, participants in the MIT CSAIL/Economists Lunch Seminar, and contributors to the Inaugural Assembly in London in Apr. 2014 for ideas and feedback that helped to shape the chapter.

References

Acemoglu, Daron (2002). Technical Change, Inequality, and the Labor Market. *Journal of Economic Literature*, 40(1): 7–72.

Acemoglu, Daron, and David Autor (2011). Skills, Tasks and Technologies: Implications for Employment and Earnings. In Orley Ashenfelter and David Card (eds), *Handbook of Labor Economics*, iv/B. Amsterdam: Elsevier, 1043–1171.

Akst, Daniel (2014). What Can we Learn from Past Anxiety over Automation? *Wilson Quarterly* (Summer [online only]).

Andreopoulos, Alexander, and John K. Tsotsos (2013). 50 Years of Object Recognition: Directions Forward. *Computer Vision and Image Understanding*, 117(8), 827–91.

Autor, David H., and David Dorn (2013). The Growth of Low Skill Service Jobs and the Polarization of the US Labor Market. *American Economic Review*, 103(5): 1553–97.

Autor, David H., and Melanie Wasserman (2013). *Wayward Sons: The Emerging Gender Gap in Education and Labor Markets*. Washington, DC: Third Way.

Autor, David H., Lawrence F. Katz, and Alan B. Krueger (1998). Computing Inequality: Have Computers Changed the Labor Market? *Quarterly Journal of Economics*, 113(4): 1169–213.

Autor, David H., Frank Levy, and Richard J. Murnane (2003). The Skill Content of Recent Technological Change: An Empirical Exploration. *Quarterly Journal of Economics*, 118(4): 1279–333.

Autor, David H., Lawrence F. Katz, and Melissa S. Kearney (2008). Trends in US Wage Inequality: Revising the Revisionists. *Review of Economics and Statistics*, 90(2): 300–23.

Autor, David H., David Dorn, and Gordon H. Hanson (2013). The China Syndrome: Local Labor Market Effects of Import Competition in the United States. *American Economic Review*, 103(6): 2121–68.

Brynjolfsson, Erik, and Andrew McAfee (2011). *Race Against the Machine*. New York: Digital Frontier Press.

Brynjolfsson, Erik, and Andrew McAfee (2014). *The Second Machine Age: Work, Progress, and Prosperity in a Time of Brilliant Technologies*. New York: W. W. Norton & Co.

Card, David, Thomas Lemieux, and W. Craig Riddell (2004). Unions and Wage Inequality. *Journal of Labor Research*, 25(4): 519–59.

Card, David, Jörg Heining, and Patrick Kline (2013). Workplace Heterogeneity and the Rise of West German Wage Inequality. *Quarterly Journal of Economics*, 128(3): 967–1015.

Drum, Kevin (2013). Welcome, Robot Overlords. Please Don't Fire Us? *Mother Jones* (May/June [online only]).

Elsby, Michael W. L., Bart Hobijn, and Aysegül Sahin (2013). The Decline of the US Labor Share. *Brookings Papers on Economic Activity* (Fall): 1–52.

Garicano, Luis, and Esteban Rossi-Hansberg (2004). Inequality and the Organization of Knowledge. *American Economic Review*, 94(2): 197–202.

Garicano, Luis, and Esteban Rossi-Hansberg (2006). Organization and Inequality in a Knowledge Economy. *Quarterly Journal of Economics*, 121(4): 1383–435.

Goldin, Claudia, and Lawrence F. Katz (2008). *The Race between Education and Technology*. Cambridge, MA: Harvard University Press.

Goos, Maarten, and Alan Manning (2007). Lousy and Lovely Jobs: The Rising Polarization of Work in Britain. *Review of Economics and Statistics*, 89(1): 118–33.

Goos, Maarten, Alan Manning, and Anna Salomons (forthcoming). Explaining Job Polarization: Routine-Biased Technological Change and Offshoring. *American Economic Review*.

Grabner, Helmut, Juergen Gall, and Luc Van Gool (2011). What Makes a Chair a Chair? In *Computer Vision and Pattern Recognition 2011*. New York: IEEE Press Books, 1529–36.

Green, David A., and Benjamin Sand (2013). *Has the Canadian Labor Market Polarized?* University of British Columbia Working Paper, Nov.

Gregg, Paul, Stephen Machin, and Mariña Fernández-Salgado (2013). *Real Wages and Unemployment in the Big Squeeze*. Centre for Economic Performance Working Paper, Nov.

Grier, David Alan (2005). *When Computers were Human*. Princeton: Princeton University Press.

Heilbroner, Robert (1965). Men and Machines in Perspective. *Public Interest*, 1: 27–36.

Hirsch, Barry T. (2008). Sluggish Institutions in a Dynamic World: Can Unions and Industrial Competition Coexist? *Journal of Economic Perspectives*, 22(1): 153–76. Updated data to 2011 available at <www.unionstats.com>.

Karabarbounis, Loukas, and Brent Neiman (2014). The Global Decline of the Labor Share. *Quarterly Journal of Economics*, 129(1): 61–103.

Katz, Lawrence F., and David H. Autor (1999). Changes in the Wage Structure and Earnings Inequality. In Orley Ashenfelter and David E. Card (eds), *Handbook of Labor Economics*, iii/A. New York: Elsevier, 1463–555.

Keynes, John Maynard (1930). Economic Possibilities for our Grandchildren. In *Essays in Persuasion*. New York: Classic House Books, 358–73.

Krugman, Paul (2012). Rise of the Robots. *New York Times*, Dec. 8.

Markoff, John (2011). Armies of Expensive Lawyers, Replaced by Cheaper Software. *New York Times*, Mar. 4.

Michaels, Guy, Ashwini Natraj, and John Van Reenen (2014). Has ICT Polarized Skill Demand? Evidence from Eleven Countries over 25 Years. *Review of Economics and Statistics*, 96(1): 60–77.

Mokyr, Joel (1990). *The Lever of Riches: Technological Creativity and Economic Progress*. New York: Oxford University Press.

Polanyi, Michael (1966). *The Tacit Dimension*. New York: Doubleday.

Sachs, Jeffrey D., and Lawrence J. Kotlikoff (2012). *Smart Machines and Long-Term Misery*. NBER Working Paper, 18629, Dec.

Smith, Noah (2013). The End of Labor: How to Protect Workers from the Rise of Robots. *The Atlantic*, Jan. 14.

Solow, Robert (1965). Technology and Unemployment. *Public Interest*, 1: 17–26.

The Economist (2014). The Future of Jobs: The Onrushing Wave. Jan. 18.

The Herald Press (1966). Skirting the Automation Question. Feb. 7: p. 2.

CHAPTER 15

··

A UNIQUE OPPORTUNITY

Balance without Trade-offs?

··

JIM HAGEMANN SNABE

Abstract

The traditional capitalist system offers a powerful means for driving betterment and value, but is based on the principles of mass production and labour optimization. During the industrial era companies have largely focused on applying technology to optimize labour productivity and efficiency. As a consequence, the capitalistic system consumes natural resources and produces enormous waste, and often leads to increased unemployment. With the digitization of products and services and the connectivity of billions of people and things, we have a unique opportunity to focus business on meeting individual customer needs more accurately and optimizing value chains. By incentivizing businesses on optimization of scarce resources and elimination of waste instead of labour, we can rethink traditional business models to become more sustainable. In parallel the digitization of products and services offers new opportunities for innovation and employment.

THE CAPITALISTIC SYSTEM: CHASING OPPORTUNITIES, WITH CONSEQUENCES

··

The capitalist system offers a powerful means for driving performance and innovation. As it allows for individual value creation, participants are incentivized to apply extra efforts to chase economic opportunity. Fundamentally it is a decentralized approach, setting the framework centrally and then allowing for individual creativity and innovation. Finally, it is transparent, making success easy to recognize and replicate. By setting such an economic framework, the system allows for enormous innovation, opportunity, and value creation as close to the market as possible.

However, as a result, there is an overall tendency to strive for economic reward while disregarding potentially negative consequences on the surrounding environment. This happens because the one producing the consequences rarely bears the full burden of paying for them. We tax enterprises and people, mainly by way of corporate and labor taxes, to allow the state to compensate for the negative consequences such as pollution, public health issues, resource depletion, and labor arbitrage, etc.

The capitalist system was fueled by the Industrial Revolution when, by today's standards, our rate of consumption was marginal compared to the abundance of natural resources. The system is largely based on the rules of "economies of scale" whereby companies gain a competitive price advantage through mass production. Technology is often applied to optimize labor productivity, driving down costs while increasing production. The automation of labor is maximized in order to minimize the cost of an hour of work, largely by the replacement of human laborers with machines.

By focusing on applying technology to optimize labor productivity, the system produces enormous waste of energy and natural resources, and as a result, often has a highly negative impact on the environment. For example, it is estimated to take 15,000 liters of water to produce just 1 kg of beef, or 8,000 liters of water to produce a single pair of jeans (Hoekstra 2013). This logic was first described in the Environmental Impact Equation, produced by two economists, Paul Ehrlich and John Holdren, in the 1970s (Ehrlich and Holdren 1971).

$$I\,(Impact) = P\,(Population) \times A\,(Affluence) \times T\,(Technology)$$

The equation describes how the human impact on the environment (I) is a result of the size of the population (P) multiplied by the consumption per person (A) multiplied by the technology used to mass produce the products we consume (T).

As the global middle class rapidly expands and there are limited incentives in place to meet consumer demands in more sustainable ways, it is easy to see the rising negative impact on resource consumption and the environment, in particular if we continue to apply technology mainly to optimize labor productivity.

In the capitalist system, where the focus is largely on the taxation of labor, there are few financial incentives for businesses to address these negative impacts. In general, companies are willing to accept undesirable consequences in the trade-off between profit and environmental impact. For example, in Europe the implicit tax rate on labor continues to account for over half of all tax revenues in the euro area (EA17), as reported by the European Commission. This is followed by consumption taxes at roughly one-third and capital taxes at approximately one-fifth. Although it is widely recognized that raising environmental "green" taxes (taxes on transport, energy, pollution, and resources) could give room for reductions in labor tax, green taxes account for only 6 percent of the total weighted average of tax revenues. These are largely taxes on transport and transport fuels. Taxes on pollution and resources are negligible (Eurostat 2013).

The conventional assumption is that we need the goodwill of business leaders to balance business results and negative impacts. Therefore, while the capitalist system is a powerful means to drive performance and innovation, it needs to be guided correctly if we are to manage scarce resources and ensure progress. With the global population surging to 7 billion and increasing levels of unemployment, the critical resource is no longer labor. It is time to rethink our approach and align the system with the current reality.

THE TIPPING POINT: DIGITIZATION INTRODUCES A UNIQUE OPPORTUNITY

It is important to recognize that we are at a unique tipping point where technology is driving new opportunities for transparency, optimization, and individualization that were previously inconceivable. This will radically increase the ability of businesses to optimize business performance and in parallel address resource scarcity, if they are incentivized to apply technology in the right ways and, in doing so, rethink traditional business models.

This digital era is fueled by rapid increases in the availability of affordable and powerful mobile devices, connectivity through high-speed internet and cloud computing, and the digitization of products and services. All around us, we are witness to the resulting dramatic transformation of traditional industries. For the first time in history, we have the opportunity to challenge the assumption that waste is an unavoidable outcome of mass production, and instead to minimize or even eliminate waste by applying technology.

A familiar example is the music industry, one of the first industries to undergo such a highly visible transformation driven by technology. The combination of new mobile devices (mp3 players), the connectivity between people (broadband internet) and the digitization of the product (mp3 file format), drove a radical change by which supply chain costs plummeted while consumers gained unprecedented individualized access through digital services. The mass production, shipment, distribution, and sale of music in physical formats such as records, cassettes or compact discs, which had been the focus of the industry for over sixty years, became largely irrelevant in less than a decade. Opportunities for optimization shifted dramatically from the value chain of the physical product to the digital assets of customer loyalty and data, with a radical reduction of costs and resource consumption as a consequence.

Digitization is now happening in all industries and will drive a similar radical transformation of most businesses. For the first time in history, businesses can have direct interaction with individual consumers at a massive scale, enabling them to understand and cater to individual needs more accurately than ever before. As a result, the fundamental principles of mass production are being challenged. Rather than mass produce and ship generic products in the hope that they will fit a broad market need, businesses can now tailor to individual preferences and track changes in demand in real time. As a consequence, systems can be significantly optimized to deliver better outcomes with much less waste. A recent example, though perhaps extreme, is Amazon's patent on "anticipatory shipment" where future orders are predicted based on the buying history and browsing habits of individual consumers. A precise selection of goods are pre-shipped to a location near the consumer in anticipation that they will be purchased, reducing wait times and shipping costs, and turning traditional retail distribution on its head (Bensigner 2014).

At the same time we are able to create transparency in the environmental impact of entire value chains and optimize for constrained resources like energy and water, instead of optimizing labor productivity. This is especially valuable in resource-intensive industries, such as utilities. Industrialist Ray Anderson claimed that "The cheapest barrel of oil is the one not used." Today with solar panels installed on private homes and integrated to smart grids and smart meters, every household can also become a producer of energy. Using the technology of big data analytics, we can predict demands, predict capacities, and calculate dynamic prices. If we add the electric car to the grid, as a storage mechanism for energy, we have an opportunity to take out the peaks in such a system. It is estimated that, in Europe alone, removing such peaks could reduce the need for raw material in utilities by up to 15 percent without reducing the access to energy. Imagine the impact on the economy and the environment when technology is used to optimize entire supply chains and make energy affordable and clean because it is economically attractive to do so.

For the first time in history we are in a situation where we can digitize products and services and digitize relationships between millions of businesses and billions of people. We have an unprecedented opportunity to apply technology in a completely new way, a way in which we understand and satisfy individual needs not mass needs. We can rethink entire value chains to optimize what is scarce (resources) rather than what is overly abundant (labor). We can even create value chains without any waste, based on cradle to cradle design principles.

Returning to the Environmental Impact Equation, this can be expressed by moving the "T" to the denominator as follows.

$$I \ (Impact) = \frac{P \ (Population) \times A \ (Affluence)}{T \ (Technology)}$$

In such a system, technology is applied to optimize resource productivity, and thus reduce the negative impact, end to end. Suddenly it becomes far more feasible and desirable for businesses to focus on optimizing the consumption of scarce resources and reducing waste, by using innovation and technology to solve relevant problems. For the first time in history we can deliver better business performance and ensure the progress of society at the same time. If we understand the new opportunities and adjust the capitalist system to focus on optimizing the right resources, we may achieve a balance between performance and progress without the traditional trade-offs—and create more sustainable business in all aspects of the word.

REIMAGINING CAPITALISM IN THE DIGITAL ERA

In this digital era, it is possible to completely reimagine traditional industries as value shifts from physical to digital assets. One example is the banking industry. Traditionally, consumer banking centered on brick-and-mortar banks. Customers visited their local bank to deposit and withdraw money. Expansion required investments of capital and resources to build more physical branches and employ staff to operate them. Today, the internet and mobile technology are radically changing the consumer banking experience. In less than one generation, consumers have shifted their behavior to expect a virtual, mobile banking experience. In emerging markets, such as Africa and India, banks are adding thousands of customers a month who have no access to a traditional bank. With little more than a basic mobile phone and ID card, clients can open an account in under ten minutes and transact using mobile payments. The marginal cost of opening a new account is close to nothing. "Banking outlets" in the form of corner grocery stores that can provide basic banking services replace brick-and-mortar banks (SAPEnterpriseMobile 2012). Traditional labor can be redirected to high-value services and the generation of new business and innovation.

A similar transformation is taking place in retail with the rise of e-commerce. In traditional retailing, the products and the shelves were the assets. But retailers are rapidly digitizing the shopping experience. They are becoming digital enterprises, where the assets are now customer loyalty and data. Point of sales data and social sentiment analysis are creating the opportunity to predict future demands, personalize offers in real time, and rethink supply chains, as in the previous example of Amazon. Rather than optimizing the operations of their stores, retailers suddenly have the option to remove physical stores altogether, reducing their environmental footprint, and putting people into new jobs in areas such as transportation and customer support.

Even in industries where products cannot be digitized, alternatives to mass production are emerging. For example, alternative manufacturing methods, such as 3D printing, may eventually allow individualized products to be produced at the price point of mass production at the location of the consumer—no plant or distribution required.

Clearly we are entering a new paradigm, where technologies such as mobile, cloud computing, and big data enable us to radically rethink our approach to resource optimization. For the first time we have an opportunity to optimize businesses and value chains end to end, cradle to cradle. Digitization offers transparency of resource consumption and optimization towards individual needs at the end customers.

Guiding the Capitalist System: Making Sustainable Business Good Business

A commonly proposed means of achieving this is Environmental Tax Reform. In the European Union it has been well recognized for some years that shifting the focus of taxation from labor to environmentally damaging activities (pollution and waste) could incentivize the right behaviors and be a win-win for both environmental and employment issues (European Commission 2007). This is especially relevant in light of an ageing population and globalization. Other market-based instruments could include pricing policies (such as on water usage), subsidies or tradable permits (such as the sale of wetland credits to property developers in the United States).

However, as we have seen with carbon taxation, the implementation can be complex. One study found that in Norway, where carbon taxes are among the highest in the world, the effect on reducing emissions has been surprisingly low. Fossil fuel intensive industries, where the tax would have been most effective, were largely exempt dues to concerns over competitiveness. In industries that were taxed, carbon substitutions were often unavailable (Bruvoll and Larsen 2004). A uniform and fair distribution of the tax burden across industries, across sources of pollution and across geographies is clearly required. Economic incentives to invest in new technologies that reduce or eliminate waste are also recommended.

In addition to market-based instruments such as taxes, there have also been calls for a much higher degree of transparency into environmental impact across the entire value chain of a product. In his paper "Re-engineering the Planet: Three Steps for a Sustainable Free Market Economy," Eckart Wintzen proposes mandatory ecological bookkeeping which "accounts for the ecological burden a product places on the ecosystem throughout its lifecycle." He imagines a future where such information would be listed on packaging, along with nutritional value etc. Such transparency would enable regulators to develop common policies across industries (Wintzen 1994). With modern technology supporting business transactions within and between companies, one could imagine that every product would carry a digital "product passport," which would capture all relevant information associated with the product from its initial design to the moment of recycling—cradle to cradle—including consumption of energy, waste, CO_2 emissions, environmental footprint, etc. This would allow optimization across the entire value chain—and transparency toward the final consumer.

Conclusion

The traditional capitalist system has proven to be very powerful in driving performance and innovation, but is so far based on the principles of mass production and labor optimization—resulting in waste and resource scarcity. Technology is driving new opportunities for transparency, optimization, and individualization that were previously inconceivable. In the rise of the digital era, it is critical that we capture these opportunities by redefining the framework guiding the capitalist system. If we can redirect the capitalist system toward meeting individual market needs more accurately while optimizing constrained resources and minimizing waste, we will enable businesses to do what they do best—optimizing business performance—while at the same time ensuring that the objectives in business are aligned with the objectives of progress in society. If we understand the new opportunities and adjust the capitalist system, we can achieve balance without the traditional trade-offs, and create more sustainable businesses.

The main challenge in shifting the capitalist system will be the short-term redistribution of wealth resulting from the change. A rapid shift is necessary in order to ensure the needed impact on the environment. This is possible given the technology available. However a significant breakthrough can only be achieved through strong collaboration between business, industries, and politics on a global level. Most importantly, we require visionary leadership ready to challenge current assumptions and committed to optimize holistically.

References

Bensigner, Greg (2014). Amazon Wants to Ship your Package Before you Buy it. *Wall Street Journal*, Jan. 17. <http://blogs.wsj.com/digits/2014/01/17/amazon-wants-to-ship-your-package-before-you-buy-it> [Accessed Apr. 2014].

Bruvoll, Annegrete, and Bodil Merethe Larsen (2004). Greenhouse Gas Emissions in Norway: Do Carbon Taxes Work? *Energy Policy*, 32/4: 493–505.

Ehrlich, Paul R., and John P. Holdren (1971). Impact of Population Growth. *Science* (American Association for the Advancement of Science), 171(3977): 1212–17. JSTOR 1731166.

European Commission (2007). *Green Paper on Market-Based Instruments for Environment and Related Policy Purposes*. <http://ec.europa.eu/taxation_customs/common/archive/news/2007/article_3849_en.htm> [Accessed Apr. 2014].

Eurostat (2013). *Taxation Trends in the European Union: Data for the EU Member States, Iceland and Norway*. <http://ec.europa.eu/taxation_customs/taxation/gen_info/economic_analysis/tax_structures/index_en.htm> [Accessed Apr. 2014].

Hoekstra, A. Y. (2013). *The Water Footprint of Modern Consumer Society*. London: Routledge.

SAPEnterpriseMobile (2012). Standard Bank of South Africa is Bringing Banking to the Unbanked. YouTube, Jan. 27. <http://www.youtube.com/watch?v=10XDU5EvPuY> [Accessed Apr. 2014].

Wintzen, Eckart (1994). Re-engineering the Planet: Three Steps to a Sustainable Free Market Economy. Apr. 19. <www.ex-tax.com/knowledge-centre/taxes/wintzen-re-engineering-planet-three-steps-sustainable-free-m> [Accessed Apr. 2014].

CHAPTER 16

···

THE GOAL AND ROLE
OF BUSINESS

···

SAMUEL J. PALMISANO

Abstract

Businesses throughout the world share a goal of creating value—value principally for their customers. But because businesses don't operate in a vacuum they should also create value for society. This is in their interest as they need permission to operate from society. Therefore, business, especially global business, has an obligation to be relevant to the societies in which they are operating and help to advance societal needs and opportunities. This chapter outlines the author's experience as a business leader at IBM and illustrates how this enterprise engaged with and integrated customers, employees, and society. It highlights the significance of values in orienting IBM technology and innovation to this aspiration, and underlines the rising importance of trust in a globally integrated enterprise.

Businesses throughout the world share a goal of creating value—value principally for their customers. But because businesses don't operate in a vacuum they should also create value for society. This is in their interest as they need permission to operate from society. Therefore, business has an obligation to be relevant to the societies in which they are operating and help to advance societal needs and opportunities.

Within this management philosophy, three principles can serve as a framework for enterprises in the world's first true global economy.

- First, businesses have to deliver unique value.

In an integrated global economy, investment, work, and people flow freely. The question is: what will cause them to flow to *us*? The companies that succeed will have clarity about the kind of economic and societal innovation they do uniquely well. They will understand the qualities of their culture, their expertise, their skills base, their business environment, and their infrastructure that make them stand out in a globally competitive market for talent and investment. And they will make choices, strategically targeting investments, incentives, and research relative to those differentiators.

- Second, every enterprise must simultaneously invest in the future *and* improve its competitive muscle tone.

Businesses—particularly those focused on innovation—have to invest in their future, and they have to sustain it in good times and bad. They cannot cost-cut their way to competitiveness. This is something IBM learned decades ago—and the lesson is similar for cities and societies. Winning on a flatter, higher playing field will require *increased* investments in key areas such as infrastructure, disruptive business models, contemporary skills, and deep research.

However, it's not just about investment. There is also a need to adapt policies to nurture and promote an innovation economy. Every country and city, like every start-up or globally integrated enterprise, must be able to tap into global supply chains, talent pools, and collaborative relationships. They must use them to create things of indigenous value, whether products or services. That will require greater flexibility in how one operates.

- Third, companies have to embrace the potential of data.

The convergence of Big Data, social, mobile, and cloud technologies has fundamentally changed the way products and services are created, distributed, and consumed. But this is only the beginning. Consider the potential impact of 3D manufacturing. Not just computerized and intelligent, but radically distributed, it aligns customer with producer in a nearly seamless way. Its model is inherently global, and its economics promises to disrupt those of traditional manufacturing.

What will this do to how the world makes and distributes products and goods? How, for instance, must China respond to a world of radically distributed and less labor-dependent manufacturing?

Or consider energy. There is enormous excitement about the potential of new energy sources—from innovative batteries for electric vehicles, to shale oil, to solar and wind. What is making these new sources possible? Again, it's the availability and accessibility of data.

Data is nothing less than the emergence of a vast new natural resource. There is a saying that data is the new oil—but even that doesn't capture its historic significance. What steam power was to the eighteenth century (spawning the first Industrial Revolution), and what the electromagnetic spectrum was to the nineteenth century (enabling the second Industrial Revolution), and what hydrocarbons were to the twentieth century (making possible the modern age of transportation and energy), the explosion of data will be to the twenty-first.

We can literally see and understand the world as never before. The economic and societal value of that is almost incalculable. But capturing that value will require more than new science and new technology. We need new forms of governance, new kinds of decision-making, new systems of public engagement, and new ways of thinking about crucial issues such as privacy and security.

Achieving Societal Relevance

If companies are going to achieve long-term success they must be relevant to the societies in which they operate. That calls for engaging on a number of issues where there are shared interests between society and markets. Sometimes societies and markets run in parallel, but usually they are linked somehow. Companies need to focus on the linkages and assess the relevance to their business.

The single most important issue will be helping to develop a workforce composed of individuals with high-value skills. That's because the vast majority of the work undertaken by successful companies, and globally integrated enterprises in particular, will require individuals with a strong foundation in key disciplines such as STEM (science, technology, engineering, and mathematics). Enhancing skills will benefit individual workers as well as the performance of national economies. The Organization for Economic Cooperation and Development (OECD), an intergovernmental research organization, has found that more than half of the productivity gains achieved by developed countries over the past decade were a by-product of better skills.

The demand for high-value skills is only going to accelerate and it underscores the need for rigorous education systems. But recognizing that education systems in the United States and elsewhere are often strapped for resources and high-quality instruction, company leaders should partner with governments to help ensure that students develop the skills that are in demand by society and the marketplace. This is in everyone's interests.

For leaders of global companies, engagement in local education initiatives such as the one I know best—P-Tech in New York City—should be complemented by engagement on national and international issues. One such issue is intellectual property protection. Intellectual property (IP) laws were created to enable individuals and institutions to reap the rewards of their inventions, while at the same time making these intellectual assets available for society as a whole.

Within this rather delicate IP framework, however, there are diverging opinions about whose interests should come first. Some believe the best way to provide incentives for innovation is by fiercely protecting the inventor's proprietary interest. Others argue that we should open the doors and give full access to intellectual assets. I believe we need a new path forward, an approach that offers a balance of those two extremes. To ensure the viability of companies—particularly globally integrated enterprises—we must protect the truly new, novel, and useful inventions. But at the same time, we need to protect the interests of innovative communities and creative ecosystems—groups that are not incorporated or chartered but that nonetheless are engaged in genuine (and genuinely important) innovation. In short, we need expanded notions of ownership for the global era, and the leaders of globally integrated enterprises can—and should—play a role in this process.

As a specific reference point of my own, I chose to become personally involved in working to advance innovation soon after I became IBM's CEO. I saw some disturbing trends developing. While the United States had achieved global leadership in innovation during the twentieth century, I saw the country losing its edge at precisely the moment when other countries were becoming more focused on innovation. Skills were eroding and research was declining, with Federal funding for research at only half the level of the 1960s and corporate R&D investment at its lowest level in fifty years. I also had a sense that the nature of innovation was changing, with fewer sole inventors tinkering in garages or garrets. Finally, I felt that business leaders and policy-makers had not fully grasped the implications of global economic integration for companies and for the country. The need for innovation was becoming more critical as the global economy was on course to become more integrated.

To address these challenges, I agreed to co-chair the National Innovation Initiative (NII), which was sponsored by the Council on Competitiveness. I worked closely with my co-chairs, Wayne Clough (the then-President of Georgia Institute of Technology) and Duane Ackerman (the then-Chairman and CEO of BellSouth), and our final report, issued in December 2004, built on input from more than 400 leaders drawn from throughout American industry, government, labor, the non-profit sector, colleges, and universities.

The report emphasized the need for business, government, and academia in the United States to place renewed focus on innovation—not just "inventions" but also the economic value that could be derived from service industries and service models. In all, there were twenty-six recommendations, which included specifics on tax policy, research and development, labor practices, physical sciences, education, intellectual property, and portability of employee benefits (such as health care and pensions).

For me, the experience of co-chairing the innovation initiative deepened my understanding of how the global economy was changing and how the nature of innovation was changing. Both were becoming more multidisciplinary and more collaborative. I saw many similarities between my efforts to ensure IBM's long-term competitiveness and how the dynamics of the global economy were impacting the future resiliency of America.

THE SMARTER PLANET AGENDA

One of IBM's great strengths has been its ability to see future information technology trends and to develop exciting and impactful new technologies. This ability results from a longstanding global business footprint and the tremendous capabilities of the IBM Research Division.

Smarter Planet evolved over a number of years, building on a bold vision of the future. Given the explosion in unstructured data, we saw how this, matched with enhanced computing power (such as the "Watson" computer), had the potential to transform business operations as well as the core functions of society. And this idea underpinned what became our Smarter Planet agenda. Announced in November 2008, it revolved around how the digital and physical infrastructures of the world were converging. With computational power being put into things we wouldn't recognize as computers, we saw how almost anything—any person, any object, any process, or any service, for any organization, large or small—could become digitally aware and networked.

With so much technology and networking abundantly available at such low cost, it became possible to offer new services and new connections, and to unearth new data for exciting new purposes. We saw a need to make our companies, institutions, and industries smarter—not just at moments of widespread shock, but integrated into our day-to-day operations. We recognized that the mundane processes of business, government, and life—which are ultimately the source of those "surprising" crises—were not smart enough to be sustainable. Huge amounts of energy were being wasted, roadways were congested, supply chains were inefficient, health care was inadequate, the planet's water supply was drying up, and financial institutions couldn't track risk. It was obvious, when considering the trajectories of development driving the planet, that the machinery of business and government was going to have to run a lot smarter and more efficiently.

Smarter Planet became the overarching framework for IBM's growth strategy, and it prompted forward-thinking leaders and citizens around the world to consider innovative ideas such as traveler-centric transportation, consumer-centric electric power, and intelligent systems for managing health care, water, public safety, and food.

The IBM Commitment to Africa

In December 2007, IBM announced plans to deepen engagement with Africa. While we had maintained a presence on the continent for more than fifty years, we believed that our people could make a significant difference in accelerating economic progress in Africa, and that doing so would benefit both IBM and the entire planet. To that end, we announced that we would increase our investment by $120 million over the following two years to capitalize on growth in two areas: (1) the number of people with skills and expertise and (2) the investment in IT to modernize African societies and build out their fundamental business infrastructures in areas such as government services, banking, and telecommunications.

The following June, we opened an Africa Innovation Center in Johannesburg. It was the first of its kind on the continent. In addition to cloud computing, the center showcased Web 2.0 technologies, service-oriented architecture (SOA), systems management, next-generation banking systems, and environmentally friendly computing designs as it nurtured information technology skills and addressed business challenges that could be obstacles to the economic growth of Sub-Saharan Africa.

IBM's investment in, and commitment to, Africa has continued. In November 2013, the company opened its first research lab in Africa, at the Catholic University in

Nairobi. And IBM announced in early 2014 that it plans to spend $100 million over the next ten years to bring Watson and other cognitive systems to Africa. To help fuel the cognitive computing market and build an ecosystem around Watson, IBM is also establishing a new pan-African Center of Excellence for Data-Driven Development (CEDD) and is recruiting research partners such as universities, development agencies, start-ups, and clients in Africa and around the world. By joining the initiative, IBM's partners will be able to tap into cloud-delivered cognitive intelligence that will be invaluable for solving the continent's most pressing challenges and creating new business opportunities.

The IBM Commitment to Public Sector Effectiveness

In 1996, IBM launched the IBM Institute for Electronic Government in Washington, DC, which was a predecessor to the Center for the Business of Government. Designed to help guide domestic and international public sector executives who were managing the transformation of their government agencies, ministries, and departments in a rapidly changing world, the Institute grew out of IBM's belief in the transformational power of the internet—in both the private and public sectors. Since the Institute's launch, more than 64,000 visitors from more than 120 countries have engaged in thought leadership discussions on the most important issues facing public sector organizations today. The Institute provided insights and expertise on emerging technology solutions, drawing on IBM researchers, experts in advanced software platforms, and consultants with deep industry knowledge in areas such as government, health care, transportation, social services, public safety, customs and border management, revenue management, defense, logistics, and education.

The IBM Center for the Business of Government helps to draw connections between public management research and practitioners. Started in 1998, it has been focused on helping public sector executives improve the effectiveness of government with practical ideas and original thinking. It sponsors independent research and fosters dialog on public management.

The IBM Focus on Transformation, Leadership, and Values

During my time leading IBM, and in the years leading up to it, my colleagues and I recognized the dramatic change unfolding across the global business landscape. And we knew that while we could *respond* to these changes, the bigger long-term opportunity was in *driving* change and setting a standard that would become a baseline for companies throughout the world. Given our size, we knew that implementing such transformative change would not be easy. Indeed, it would be highly disruptive within the company, and there was no guarantee the changes would succeed. But we also knew that "business as usual" wasn't an option and if we didn't undergo a transformation and do more to distinguish ourselves from our competitors, we would not be positioned for success in the future.

We decided to compete on the basis of expertise and openness, and we moved from a multinational to a globally integrated business and operating model as fast as we could. This wasn't easy. At IBM, as at other companies, people develop an emotional attachment to the sources of their prior successes—businesses and ways of doing business that are well established and very profitable. Proposing to overhaul these businesses—perhaps even sell them off—generated resistance from colleagues, shareholders, and the "chattering classes" of IBM observers. But if companies want to differentiate themselves and compete in this globally integrated environment, they have to be willing to reinvent themselves. Indeed, that has been true as long as there have been businesses—as IBM's history vividly attests. And they have to be willing to tolerate the critics who tell them they're making a big mistake.

GLOBALIZATION

To seize the global opportunity, we as a leadership team committed ourselves to change in a focused and unwavering way. We restructured our operations to enable us to draw more efficiently on our global resources, and to capitalize on opportunities in emerging growth markets.

We began our restructuring in Europe. With the goal of lowering the center of gravity in the company, we eliminated layers of bureaucracy and pressed for more decision-making in local markets and less at IBM headquarters. We also moved managers out into local markets, where they could execute closer to our clients. If our structure was that of a pyramid, we wanted to recreate it as a diamond, with the people at the top of the pyramid moving to the middle of the diamond. We did that by restructuring the financial incentives so that work with clients would be more handsomely rewarded. We found that this leaner management system, coupled with solid execution and a slowly improving business environment, enabled us to compete more effectively in the European markets.

We also took core processes and functions that were once managed regionally, shifted them to a horizontal model, integrated them, and began managing them globally. These changes enabled us to improve responsiveness to our clients through new ways to bring together sales support. We called these "deal hubs," and in the parts of Europe where we tried them out, our win rates improved dramatically.

Illustrative of IBM's global focus, our chief procurement officer, John Paterson, made the decision to relocate from Somers, New York, to Shenzhen, China, in October 2006. He was the first IBM division head to be based outside the United States. The decision to locate in Asia was simple. We already had more than 1,850 procurement and logistics professionals in the region, many of them at our China Procurement Center in Shenzhen. We also had strong and collaborative relationships with nearly 3,000 suppliers across Asia, accounting for about 30 percent of the $40 billion IBM was spending annually on procurement. Just as important, the move to Shenzen made it acceptable for other departments to shift out of Armonk, and before long data center delivery moved to India and intellectual property to the Netherlands.

LEADERSHIP AND VALUES

If I learned one lesson about leadership from my thirty-nine years at IBM, it was that the longer you wait to implement change, the harder it is to implement it—and the less effective it is likely to be. In the global era, the changes are going to come faster, they're going to come from countries—and especially cities—throughout the world, and they're going to be more transformative than in the past. Resisting the change is a recipe for oblivion.

As part of IBM's transformation into a globally integrated enterprise, I recognized that the style of leadership would need to change as well. Effective leadership takes many forms, but one of the keys is a healthy dose of humility. Given the array of cultures, languages, insights, and points of view the GIE deals with, no one person or country will have all the answers. Hierarchical, command-and-control approaches simply do not work anymore. They impede information flows inside companies, hampering the fluid and collaborative nature of work today. Instead, leaders will need to be focused on the success of their teams, which also means rewarding successes of others instead of themselves. Leaders should also take the time to listen to diverse ideas even when the answer seems self-evident. Being much more open and collaborative is, at times, messy and, by definition, uncontrollable. But at IBM we found that listening and treating our people as grown-ups—and having confidence that they will behave in a manner consistent with our values—was a demonstration of trust that enabled us to get support for challenging projects or initiatives.

Today's global economy is driven by integration and transparency. Agility and productivity are premiums that highly determine one's success. At IBM we operated in over 170 countries and with over 300,000 employees. A seminal management question for this business reality is how to manage an organization effectively given these market dynamics?

I knew there was no way to optimize IBM through organizational structure or by management dictates alone. We needed to empower people to make decisions. However, we also needed to ensure that they were making the right calls the right way. And by "right" I mean more than ethics and legal compliance; at IBM those are table stakes. Decisions were needed to support and advance IBM's strategy and brand—decisions that would shape a culture of helping clients.

In a company as diverse and as committed to the "right way" as IBM, values have always been its cultural foundation and daily connective tissue. As a result, values became a cornerstone for decentralized decision-making. It used to be a rule of thumb that "people don't do what you expect; they do what you inspect." It was going to be impossible to inspect everyone. But we could not simply let go of the reins and let people do what they wanted without guidance or context. So we needed to create a management system that would empower people and provide a contemporary basis for decision-making that was consistent with IBM's DNA. Doing this in a top-down controls-based management system was going to be contentious and challenging.

After considerable reflection with a number of colleagues, we chose to refresh a values-based approach that had guided the company. The three values that supported the company—respect for the individual, the best customer service, and the pursuit of excellence—had been laid down in 1914 by Thomas Watson, Sr. Those values served IBM well, but they had evolved into a sense of entitlement. A lot had changed at IBM and throughout the world over the course of nine decades. We wanted to take stock of our values given these changes.

Consequently, I asked key members of our leadership team to begin the process of tapping the wisdom of IBMers around the globe. Jon Iwata, senior vice president for communications at the time, was a key architect of our GIE thinking. He is a master at bringing really hard things into a clear and relatable form. So on July 29, 2003, we launched a "ValuesJam," which was an online, three-day event that allowed any IBMer anywhere in the world to weigh-in on what the company should stand for and how IBMers should operate. It was a free-for-all, which meant that there was a fair share of comments that were far from complimentary. Some of my colleagues thought we should pull the plug on the exercise, but we opted to keep the commentary open, and it gradually became more thoughtful.

We had a team analyze the comments and it was clear that the proposed value statements needed to change to reflect the nuances and emotion people expressed. Drawing on this analysis, along with other employee feedback, we settled on IBM's new corporate values.

The first value was "dedication to every client's success." At one level, that is pretty straightforward: bring together all of IBM's capabilities—in the laboratory, in the field, in the back office, wherever—to help solve difficult problems clients cannot solve themselves. But this is also a lot more than the familiar claim of unstinting customer service. "Client success" isn't just "the customer is always right." It means maintaining a long-term relationship where what happens after the deal is more important than what happens when it's signed. It means a persistent focus on outcomes. And it means being invested in your client's success.

The second value was "innovation that matters—for our company and for the world." When employees discussed how IBM makes a difference in the world, they included more than our work of inventing and building great products. They recalled how their work touches people and society and how we helped improve lives, citing IBM's work with Memorial Sloan Kettering Cancer Center, with America's Apollo program in the 1960s, with mayors and community leaders to create safer and more sustainable cities. This type of innovation enabled us to attract great scientists to build what later became our Smarter Planet agenda. This value also reflected IBM's commitment to continual experimentation. Throughout our company's history, with the exception of one period when we became arrogant and complacent, IBM never stopped questioning assumptions, trying out different models, testing the limits—whether in technology or business or in progressive workforce policies. Employees reminded us that those features mattered as much as new products.

The third value was "trust and personal responsibility in all relationships." Interestingly, the feedback from employees on this value focused on relationships among people at IBM. But we were also talking about the company's relationships with clients, suppliers, investors, governments, and communities. As IBM globalized its operations, trust became an essential ingredient to the success of the GIE.

EARNING TRUST AROUND THE WORLD

Fundamental to companies enjoying the trust of various stakeholders is understanding that trust must be earned, which can only happen through behavior and actions, not through marketing. At IBM, we found that helping a region—or entire country—to advance its standard of living (particularly through education) would help earn the trust of government officials and make it much easier to achieve market access. While at IBM I characterized this as getting "permission to operate," and over time we saw that our identity as an "American" company mattered less than the indigenous value we created in the countries where we were doing business.

The value creation started with generating jobs, making local investments, paying taxes, and bringing high-quality, trustworthy products and services to new buyers. But it went beyond that. We saw that we could create more value—for the society and for IBM—by doing more than entering a market. We would *make* a market, which involved working with leaders in business, government, academia, and community organizations to help advance their national agenda and address their societal needs—whether those needs involved better schools, more robust public safety, more modern infrastructure, or something else altogether. In short, we would strive to build real skills in the local workforce and enable new capabilities among the citizenry. We consciously worked to serve as a force for modernization and progress.

There are multiple explanations for IBM's robust performance over the past decade or so, but I attribute much of it to the company's evolution into a globally integrated enterprise. It made us more efficient, more flexible, faster, and more competitive.

It's easy to look back now and see the wisdom in this transformation. But there were quite a few challenges along the way—both internal and external to the company. Transforming a company of any size is never easy. And the bigger the company, the more difficult the transformation. There are different transformations for different circumstances, of course. If a company is on its back and struggling to survive, there's going to be less resistance—internally and externally—to wholesale change. But sometimes success can be a company's undoing, as it breeds complacency and an unwillingness or inability to institute the reforms needed to sustain the success. And this applies not just to companies—countless countries have fallen into the trap of basking in their past glories rather than positioning themselves for future growth.

I learned an important lesson along the way. *It's not easy to go to the future.* You need to be confident about what you think the future holds. That said, if a business doesn't have a view about the future, it can't allocate resources to position itself to get there.

BALANCING AND TRADE-OFFS: DISCUSSION SUMMARY

A conventional perspective on market logic suggests that any reconciliation of business performance with societal progress will require trade-offs between competing objectives. The theme of "Balancing and Trade-Offs" was devoted to assessing the precise form of those trade-offs, the manner in which they might be made and, indeed, whether trade-offs were required after all.

Much of the discussion suggested that any assumption of a straightforward trade-off between performance and progress was at best based on a crucial oversimplification. Picking up on the theme of "Smithian esteem" discussed earlier, Anderson's chapter offers a notion of "reciprocity" that models the idea of businesses as "ethical agents." Anderson's idea of reciprocity is that businesses should conduct themselves with a motivation to serving the interests of others—customers, workers, suppliers, etc.—on the expectation that others will similarly work to serve their interests. Business thus seeks mutual gain through cooperation first, with profit following as a secondary motive.

One crucial question is whether treating profits as a secondary motive might actually tend, in an odd way, to increase profits. One reason for this might be that, as Anderson pointed out, the effective operation of business depends on a good faith willingness of all parties to go beyond bare contractual stipulations in the name of reasonable adaptation and accommodation. Perhaps businesses that seek to do right by their employees and surrounding community might thereby advance profit?

On the labor side of things, Frank observed that, in general, employees are willing to work at lower wages for a company that has a mission they believe in. Likewise, highlighting Akerlof's work on gift exchange, Autor noted the way in which businesses can often secure advantages in the marketplace through actions that are not "incentive compatible." That is, one can gain the monetary advantages of trust through acts of apparent goodwill that cut against immediate self-interest. And, as Arrow noted, reciprocity entails, not only the willingness to act against immediate self-interest for the sake of cooperative advantages, but also the willingness to punish deviations from cooperative norms. Companies that fail to act in a spirit of good faith cooperation thus may suffer doubly: first in the loss of cooperation itself and, second, in the experience of retaliation from offended parties.

As Autor skeptically noted, treating trust as instrumental to profit effectively collapses an ideal of reciprocity to one of pure self-interest. All too often, he observed, companies that earn trust through apparent acts of mutuality wind up exploiting their gains in reputation at the ultimate expense of stakeholders. And, sounding a theme from his own chapter, Pettit observed that trust is only appropriate between agents who have relative equality of power. From this point of view, even if we are right to demand that businesses put the ethical requirements of reciprocity before profit, we would be naïve to ask employees and customers of large corporations to ground their own behavior in unenforceable assurances: "*trust* me."

However, from Collomb's point of view, the very premise of a trade-off in this context is somewhat misguided. Good companies do not weigh the economic costs of doing right by their stakeholders against the economic benefits. Rather, they treat ethical considerations as an integral part of the value which they are creating. This echoes ideas in March's chapter on the logic of appropriateness.

Perhaps the canonical "egoistic" model of business motivation is the shareholder dominance perspective, according to which the exclusive guiding objective of businesses is to maximize returns to shareholders. Barney's chapter, in effect, offers a formal account of the way in which—at least under certain idealized conditions—the pursuit of profit should lead that firm to promote, in parallel, the interests of those who incur costs or accept risks to make profit possible. Shareholder logic becomes stakeholder logic. But what are the practical implications of the argument? One oddity observed by Anderson is that the behavior of businesses changed dramatically with Friedman's introduction of the shareholder perspective. Why would this have been the case if shareholder logic really implies a concern for stakeholders? Barney declined to answer the historical question but nonetheless observed that there is great heterogeneity in the way that corporations actually pursue the shareholder perspective. Contrary to conventional wisdom, he suggested that such heterogeneity might very well be "a manifestation of good business sense," rather than gaps between managerial and shareholder values.

Drawing on his own experience, Jafar observed the tendency of stakeholder logic to translate principally into "reputation management" and nebulous "add-ons" to the core mission of the company that ultimately conflict with the perspective of shareholders. Without a clear framework for thinking about how to weigh the interests of the broader community of stakeholders against shareholders, perhaps, Jafar suggests, we might do better simply to think in terms of short-term versus long-term profit-maximization? Barney noted that, from an analytical point of view, both short- and long-term perspectives should be the same, but nonetheless agreed with a remark from Pettit that, practically speaking, an eye to longer term returns would push companies toward a stakeholder perspective.

To frame the obligations of businesses in terms of stakeholders inevitably raises the question: who counts as a stakeholder? This problem becomes particularly extreme in light of business practices whose negative consequences are radically distributed in both space and time. Risse's chapter thus focuses on the distinctly thorny question of our obligations to future generations, specifically in the context of the climate change problem. Risse's central contention is that "humanity has collective claims to the earth as a whole," and that this grounds an obligation to bequeath to future generations "[roughly] the same amount of natural stock" that was bequeathed to our own generation. In light of present difficulties achieving meaningful reductions in global carbon emissions, Walsh raised the inevitable question: how can we instill the relevant sense of collective ownership? And, relatedly, what is the role of business in trying to realize the actions that follow from such an ideal? To connect this discussion with the discussion surrounding "Problem": What is the role of rules versus players in this context?

A number of participants objected to Risse's suggestion that collective ownership grounds a requirement to preserve the Earth's natural stock in its present form. Schmidtz, Kitcher, and Sen all made related suggestions that the appropriate aim was one of preserving an equivalent opportunity for flourishing, even if that entails transforming the Earth's "stock" in important respects. As Schmidtz noted, each generation tends to make the next one dramatically better off in spite of the fact that—inevitably—those advances are made possible by denuding the environment in various ways. The advancements themselves create wealth that makes it possible to repair past damages.

Both Kitcher and Sen focused their attention, beyond questions of material resources, on "what kind of life we lead" (Sen), where that entails, not only certain material environmental conditions, but also, as Kitcher suggested, Walsh's notion of a "freedom to be." The danger, Sen cautioned—pointing to the case of nuclear energy—is that we fail adequately to appreciate the great risks that may be involved in sustaining and advancing those opportunities.

Sen's and Schmidtz's response to Risse both highlight the central role that technology must play in any viable route to squaring profit and progress. Snabe's and Autor's chapters highlight both the great promise, and the potential perils, of technology in this context. For Autor, advances in technology make possible a future in which enormous productivity gains are achieved, but at the cost of worsened unemployment within unskilled sectors, where technology will lessen the need for labor. Society over all will be better off, but unskilled laborers will do worse. In response Sen observed that, when products become cheaper in a certain sector, the output of that sector tends to increase in response to demand which, in turn, can in many cases increase employment. Market forces, in effect, tend to reconstitute the composition of demand in ways that ameliorate the labor-displacing effects of technology. Under those conditions, problems such as long-term structural unemployment (noted in a comment by Anderson) are best understood as problems in the social organization of the labor market rather than problems that stem from technology as such.

For Snabe, our prospects for the future hinge on changing the core relationship that has long existed between technology and labor. This view is reflected as well in the

chapter by Palmisano. Overwhelmingly, advances in technology have served principally to optimize labor productivity, sometimes at the expense of a significant waste of
resources. Moving beyond the digital frontier, however, Snabe suggests that we are
moving to an era in which optimizing labor productivity is no longer a necessary
priority. Instead, we should pursue technological innovation that is designed principally to minimize waste.

For Walsh, the basic orientation of Snabe's presentation towards a vision of *doing*, as
opposed to merely *knowing* or thinking, was itself an inspiration. As Mendiola articulated at the outset of the session, one crucial issue looming over the discussion was the
question of how to "land the plane," i.e. how to move from the realm of analysis to
meaningful action. On the note of "doing," Davis thus concluded the session with a
mischievous "homework assignment" for Snabe: "an iPhone workplace democracy app
that turns General Motors into a kibbutz." That is, Davis envisioned the possibility
of technology that facilitates organizational information-sharing, deliberation, and
decision-making in a way that radically expands the possibilities of worker governance.
This suggests a dual promise of technology: first, the promise of reducing costs
associated with furthering social goods and, second, the promise of facilitating communication that enables organizations better to identify and act on those goods. "The
technology is there," Davis suggested, "to take the transaction costs out of democracy."

PART IV

CHOICES AND
PREFERENCES

CHAPTER 17

HOLISTIC CAPITALISM
The Role of Individuals

RAMÓN MENDIOLA

Abstract

An early oversimplified definition of capitalism defines the term as "essentially the investment of money in the expectation of making a profit." In reality, capitalism is an open social and holistic system. Not only is it a mechanism for creating economic growth, but it can also create simultaneously societal and environmental value for multiple stakeholders. Capitalism is capable of advancing progress through innovation more than any other social system in the world. Echoing a fitting metaphor formulated by John Mackey (co-founder and CEO of Whole Foods), the chapter argues that business leaders should transform themselves from "caterpillars" to "butterflies." The author draws on his own recent experience as CEO of Florida Ice and Farm Company to reflect on and illustrate these ideas. He discusses the importance of purpose, the mobilization of employees, the leverage of partnerships, and the consent of the board and owners.

CAPITALISM: AN EARLY OVERSIMPLIFIED DEFINITION

An oversimplified definition of capitalism is as "essentially the investment of money in the expectation of making a profit" (Flucher 2004). When analyzing the limited scope of such a narrow economic definition, it is important to consider that capitalism, in itself, is a relatively new concept and system. Its origin dates back to the 1600s with merchant capitalism and the advent of the English East India Company, a precursor to modern-day companies. It wasn't until 1970, that the neo-liberal model of capitalism became dominant around the world. This recent origin is maybe one of the main reasons why it was originally defined as an economic system only, with certain structure, agents, assumptions, and interconnectivity.

The aforementioned narrow definition was built on a theoretical misconception that people only pursue their self-interest.

> Economists, social critics, and business leaders largely disregarded the second and often more powerful aspect of human nature: the desire and need to care for others and for ideals and causes that transcend one's self-interest. The founding father of modern capitalism, Adam Smith, recognized both of these powerful human motivations. His book *The Theory of Moral Sentiments* preceded his far better-known book, *The Wealth of Nations,* by seventeen years. In the earlier book, he outlined ethics based on our ability to empathize with others and care about their opinions. Smith was far ahead of his time, both in his economic philosophy and ethical system. If the intellectual of the nineteenth century had embraced his economic and ethical philosophies, we might have avoided the extraordinary strife and suffering that occurred in the nineteenth centuries over competing political and economic ideologies. (Mackey 2013)
>
> How selfish soever man may be supposed, there are evidently some principles in his nature, which interest him in the fortunes of others, and render their happiness necessary to him, though he derives nothing from it, except the pleasure of seeing it. Of this kind is pity or compassion, the emotion we feel for the misery of others, when we either see it, or are made to conceive it in a very lively manner. That we often derive sorrow from the sorrows of others, is a matter of fact too obvious to require any instances to prove it; for this sentiment, like all the other original passions of human nature, is by no means confined to the virtuous or the humane, though they perhaps may feel it with the most exquisite sensibility. The greatest ruffian, the most hardened violator of the laws of society, is not altogether without it. (Smith 1759: "Of Simpathy")

An Introduction to Holistic Capitalism

Holism is the idea that natural systems (physical, social, economic, etc.) and their properties and potential, should be viewed as wholes, not as collections of parts. This often includes the view that systems function as wholes and that their functioning cannot be fully understood solely in terms of their component parts. Capitalism is the creation of us, human beings, and mirrors our nature. As individuals, we act simultaneously as different economic and social actors (consumers, investors, employees, opinion leaders, political and social leaders, etc.). A common mistake of our era has been reductionism—a theory stating that a complex open system such as capitalism could be explained by reducing it to its fundamental parts. Social scientist and physician, Nicholas A. Christakis, explains that "for the last few centuries, the Cartesian project in science has broken matter down into ever smaller bits in the pursuit of understanding. And this works, to some extent . . . but putting things back together in order to understand them is harder, and typically comes later in the development of a scientist or in the development of science" (2011).

In reality, capitalism is an open social and holistic system which is more complex and more capable than we can ever imagine. Not only is it a mechanism for creating economic growth. It can also create simultaneously social and environmental value for multiple stakeholders. Capitalism is capable of advancing progress through innovation more than any other social system in the world. Its power lies in its dynamics. When it is in place, it expands very rapidly and fosters relationships among disconnected individuals. It demonstrates conservation of momentum and energy like no other social system. It is imperative to understand capitalism as a holistic system and to evolve it to a model that can create further positive impact in society and the planet, where traditional trade-offs no longer apply.

Freedom to Define Preferences and Make Choices

We hold these truths to be self-evident, that all men are created equal, that they are endowed by their Creator with certain unalienable Rights that among these are Life, Liberty and the pursuit of Happiness.

(United States of America Declaration of Independence,
1776, in Boyd 1950)

Before we explore the sphere of choices and preferences, it is important to consider that both of them rely on the premise of freedom. But are we really free to choose? Let us analyze if every human being has the right to do so given today's conditions. In order to experience the opportunity of establishing our preferences and, ultimately, make choices, our basic needs must be met. One may argue that lack of food, health care, and basic shelter obstructs the entrance to the spheres of aspirations, desires, choices, and preferences, thereby reducing the possibility to even consider the pursuit of a higher purpose in life.

For this reason, the freedom to set preferences and make choices is dependent on a human being's right to survival which should be given to every human being as another unalienable right. In his book, *Equality and Efficiency: The Big Tradeoff*, author Arthur M. Okun refers to the scope of rights and raises an important question: "How and where does society draw the boundary lines between the domain of rights and that of the marketplace? It is tempting to say that rights deal with noneconomic assets while the market handles economic assets" (Okun 1975: 10). However, there are many economic assets such as water and food that are fundamental to survival and are part of the marketplace domain. It is critical to analyze if all human beings in today's world are truly able to make choices and decisions based on their own individual preferences. A new version of capitalism should be created that prioritizes the fulfillment of the right to survival and the eradication of poverty from the world.

FIGURE **17.1.** The Pursuit of Happiness as a Human Growth Process

Abraham Maslow's *Motivation and Personality* (1954) explores the hierarchy of needs as a basis for the pursuit of happiness. Maslow developed his theory of developmental psychology by describing the stages of human growth through the use of terms such as "physiological," "safety," "belongingness and love," "esteem," "self-actualization," and "self-transcendence" to describe the patterns that tend to govern human motivation. If we consider the pursuit of happiness as a human growth process, three main stages can be defined: survival, aspirations, and purpose (Figure 17.1). Survival can be defined as the stage where basic needs are covered. Once this stage has been addressed, an individual can shift his thinking to his aspirations: leisure, pleasure, material security, etc. Most people start and finish their lives by pursuing this stage and once they attain it remain there until the end of their lives. Only a small group advances to a different level of consciousness and develops a deeper interest in exploring transcendental topics such as the reason for their existence (why they were born).

If every individual is able to survive, we can now explore the fundamentals of making choices. According to Aristotle's best known work on ethics, "every individual man and all men in common aim at a certain end which determines what they choose and what they avoid. This end, to summarize it briefly, is happiness and its constituents" (*Nicomachean Ethics*). Therefore, choice is based on the pursuit of happiness as an end or the conditions that lead to happiness (means). Aristotle summarizes the means as follows: a healthy birth, plenty of friends, good friends, independence of life, prosperity, wealth, good children, plenty of children, happy old age, bodily excellence, health, beauty, strength, athletic powers, secure enjoyment of the maximum of pleasure, fame, honor, good luck, and virtue. Each individual defines his preferences based on the probability of attaining the means necessary to pursue happiness. "It is not unreasonable that men should derive their concept of the good and of happiness from the lives which they lead" (*Nicomachean Ethics*).

In the social sciences, "preferences" refer to a set of assumptions related to ordering certain alternatives, based on how they relate to attaining happiness, as a final end and means toward it such as satisfaction, gratification, enjoyment, etc., a process which that results in an optimal "choice" (whether real or theoretical).

In a capitalistic system, choices and preferences are critical, not only for demand analysis (actions of the consumers), but for all other economic stakeholders (investors, employees, decision-makers, opinion leaders, etc.). Ultimately, we are all human beings who define our preferences and choices based on all the roles that we play in our lives. It can be argued that those who have entered the purpose stage in human growth are the ones who should lead the evolution of capitalism to pursue a good society.

VOICE AND DECISION: THE POWER
OF THE INDIVIDUAL

According to the law of human nature, the law of nations, and the law of markets (capitalism), every human being has voice and decision. Individuals can express their preferences and share their points of view about almost any topic in the world, whether or not it is directly related to their lives. One can choose between two types of decisions: direct and indirect. Direct decisions include all the different choices that an individual can make every day. (What to do? Where to work? What to buy? When and what to invest in?) Indirect decisions are those decisions made by someone else whom an individual allows to define preferences and to make choices for him. In his book, *Leviathan,* the seventeenth-century British philosopher, Thomas Hobbes, establishes his doctrine for the foundation of states and legitimizing government authority.

> The final cause, end, or design of men (who naturally love liberty, and dominion over others) in the introduction of that restraint upon themselves, in which we see them live in Commonwealths.
>
> The only way to erect such a common power, as may be able to defend them from the invasion of foreigners, and the injuries of one another, and thereby to secure them in such sort as that by their own industry and by the fruits of the earth they may nourish themselves and live contentedly, is to confer all their power and strength upon one man, or upon one assembly of men, that may reduce all their wills, by plurality of voices, unto one will: which is as much as to say, to appoint one man, or assembly of men, to bear their person; and every one to own and acknowledge himself to be author of whatsoever he that so berate their person shall act, or cause to be acted, in those things which concern the common peace and safety; and therein to submit their wills, everyone to his will, and their judgments to his judgment. This is more than consent, or concord; it is a real unity of them all in one and the same person, made by covenant of every man with every man, in such manner as if every man should say to every man: I authorize and give up my right of governing myself to this man, or to this assembly of men, on this condition; that thou give up, thy right to him, and authorize all his actions in like manner. This done, the multitude so united in one person is called a COMMONWEALTH; in Latin, CIVITAS. This is the generation of that great LEVIATHAN, or rather, to speak more reverently, of that mortal god to which we owe, under the immortal God, our peace and defense. (*Leviathan*, ch. XVII: Of the Causes, Generation, and Definition of a Commonwealth)

Choosing Means versus Ends

Everyone craves meaning and purpose in life and spends their lives trying to find happiness. However, the short-sighted goals and overloaded schedules that permeate our lives prevent individuals from thinking about their higher purpose in life and how to make that a reality. People make quick decisions that may eventually conflict with long-term life goals (welfare of future generations, elimination of poverty and inequality, the environment, etc.). For example, if you ask consumers if they care about the environment and protecting our planet, they generally say "yes." Yet although they may firmly believe that, when they must decide on purchasing a soda in a plastic PET bottle over a glass bottle, most people will buy the PET bottle. The reason is that the plastic bottle provides instant gratification since it is a less expensive, more convenient product in the short term. Choosing the "means" instead of the "ends" is one of the biggest challenges that society must overcome in order to build a good society.

Balance Defines Choices and Preferences: The Four Poles of the Good Society

According to James O'Toole in his book *The Executive's Compass*, there are four polar forces (liberty, equality, efficiency, and community) tugging at all modern decisions by human beings.

The choice between liberty and equality is one of the most fundamental trade-offs facing society. The Communist manifesto refers to the history of class struggles (bourgeois versus proletarians) and argues that the concentration of property and capital in a few hands creates inequality. On the other hand, the implementation of Marx's model which strives for absolute equality, at the cost of liberty and efficiency, has failed around the world and it has been almost universally accepted that individuals should be free to pursue their personal ends and desires.

Another domain of choice emerges between efficiency and equality. "Economists argue that highly progressive rates of taxation reduce incentives to work, welfare transfer payments create bureaucratic waste, that motivation is lost when financial rewards are separated from productive contribution, and entrepreneurial effort diminishes when the size of jackpots from capital gains gets too small." (O'Toole 1993: 102). There is another trade-off between individual desires and the collective good (liberty versus community). Zoning laws, taxes on junk food, and bans on smoking in public areas are examples of society's restrictions on personal freedom in the name of common good.

More than exemplifying all of the trade-offs between the four poles, it is important to notice that there is no right or wrong answer, and that each decision made by an individual favors one value or pole over the other. Such value-based decision-making

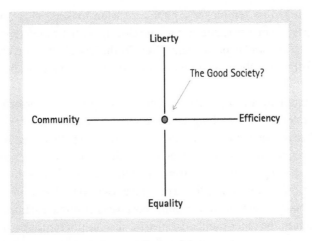

FIGURE **17.2.** Polar Forces (O'Toole)

depends, after all, on individual preference and is never disputed. However, "one process is peculiarly capable of achieving reconciliation among these conflicting values—democracy. The genius of a well-functioning democracy is to be responsive to all of a nation's citizens, constituencies, and interest groups and to serve as a process for balancing their conflicting demands. A good society should not be viewed as a wishy-washy compromise represented by a single point at the very center of the quadrant." (O'Toole, 1993: 106)

As participants in such a dynamic decision process, we face the challenge of developing a new type of capitalism so that it may become a greater social and economic system where "good society" could be represented as an area or a social fabric where the maximum liberty, equality, efficiency, and community can be attained (Figure 17.2).

INFLUENCES

Choices and preferences are influenced by both internal and external factors. It is very difficult to argue which factors (intrinsic versus extrinsic) are more important since they act simultaneously and complement each other in the decision-making process.

Extrinsic Factors

Modern society apparently spends a large amount of time collecting information to make better choices in terms of products and services to buy. Marketing, signaling, and advertising all play important roles in conveying meaningful information to individuals. However, it must be emphasized that individuals, in their different economic roles as consumers, investors, employees, public decision-makers, etc., no longer make decisions in a passive manner, but rather consciously set their preferences and choices to shape their realities and express themselves. In this era of data and communication, almost any information about a company, a product, or service can be found instant-aneously through the internet.

Extrinsic factors play an important role in providing useful information to the con-sumer and investor toward making better choices to build a good society. Through marketing and advertising, a company can share knowledge that is critical to shape the choices and preference of consumers. Companies like Natura and Patagonia, have been very effective in shaping informed consumer preferences and choices through marketing, advertising, and public relations (PR). They have also been able to evolve the rules of competition to incorporate more dimensions (positive environmental impact, added social value) in addition to the other traditional metrics such as price, quality, and availability.

Marketing is a very useful tool to create "custom made experiences" for a product or a service. Its significance is evident, particularly, if we consider that consumers will often reject products that have mass appeal and prefer brands that are "tailored" to reflect their preferences and desires. At the end of the day, products are made in factories while brands are shaped in people's minds and in a marketplace that is becoming overly crowded and overwhelming. Marketing can make a difference in developing an intimate connection with individuals.

Intrinsic Factors and the Notion of "Purpose"

> What are the two most important days of your life? Richard Leider asks this question to every audience he addresses. The first one is obvious: the day you were born. The second is not so obvious. It is not the day you die; that is the end of the story. It is not the day you graduate, get married, or have your first child—all significant milestones, of course, but not life defining for most. Richard's answer: it is the day you realize why you were born. Not everyone experiences that day; many of us don't even know to ask the question. Nevertheless, for those who do, that day becomes a major fulcrum in their lives. Nothing is ever the same once you discover your true purpose, your calling. (Mackey 2013)

I strongly believe that intrinsic factors strongly influence our preferences and choices. Core values are the guiding principles (moral compass) that an individual possesses to differentiate right from wrong and act accordingly. Based on human nature, individ-uals will make choices to pursue happiness and simultaneously "do good." Throughout history, philosophers have believed that when human beings must decide between their own well-being and that of others, they ultimately will choose to "do good." Mencius, the Chinese philosopher (371/390–289/305? BCE) and arguably the most famous Confucian after Confucius himself, for example, argued that human beings are natur-ally good, but could become corrupted by society. His basic assertion states that,

"Everyone has a heart-mind which feels for others." He believed that people only acted badly as a result of neglect or negative influences.

> Human nature is neither disposed to good nor to evil,
> just as water is neither disposed to east nor west.
> However, the tendency of human nature to do good is
> like that of water to flow downward.
>
> (Mencius, "Human Nature," lines 13–16)

According to Mencius, the sense of mercy (humanity) is found in all men as is shame (righteousness), respect (decorum), and the difference between right and wrong (wisdom).

Following this same line of thought, Charles Darwin stated that "of all the differences between man and the lower animals, the moral sense or conscience is by far the most important . . . Man can generally and readily distinguish between the higher and lower moral rules. The higher are found on the social instincts, and relate to the welfare of others. They are supported by the approbation of our fellow-men and by reason." (Darwin 1871: ch. 5).

Consequently, it can be said that human beings have a natural tendency to set preferences and make choices, based on how that decision will impact the wellness of others. This is a very important parameter as well as their own self-interest. By recognizing and responding to the need for meaning that is an essential human condition, we can unlock a vast source of creativity and energy to solve many of the most challenging problems of the world.

Prospects for Societal Progress within a Capitalist System

The Concept of Holistic Capitalism: A Natural Evolution

Individuals, and especially business leaders (investors and managers), need to become conscious about their role in society.

> Consider one of the nature's many small miracles: a caterpillar transforming into a butterfly . . . For its brief existence, a caterpillar does little more than eat; that is seemingly its only purpose . . . When the time is right, certain cells become activated in the caterpillar and it enters the cocoon phase, from which it emerges a few weeks later unrecognizably transformed into a creature of enchanting beauty, one that also serves an invaluable function in nature through its role in the pollination of plants and thus the production of food for others to live by. This analogy can be applied to human beings as well as to . . . institutions . . . We humans can choose to exist at a caterpillar level, consuming all we can, taking as much as possible from the world

and giving little back. We are also capable of evolving to a degree that is no less dramatic than what happens to a caterpillar, transforming ourselves into beings who create value for others and help make the world more beautiful. (Mackey 2013: ch. 2)

I would argue that the traditional definition of capitalism is Newton's approach to it. Considering that capitalism is a relatively new concept (developed 400 years ago), fiercely challenged by Marx, Engels, and their followers in the 1800s, and that the history of capitalism is, in any case, littered with crisis, its definition as "a system to make profits" was approximately correct until the modern era (until we approached the "speed of light" as Einstein explained in the Theory of Relativity). In our era, the analogy to the speed of light is nothing more than the fast pace of globalization, information technology, population growth, and global warming. The "fabric of our capitalistic world" (space-time opportunities) to work towards a better society has no limits and depends on our state of motion and role as participants in the market (consumers, employees, investors), as members of society (son, daughter, sister, brother, father, mother, friend) and inhabitants of our planet. In the words of William Shakespeare:

> All the worlds a stage,
> And all the men and women merely players:
> They have their exits, and their entrances;
> And one man in his time plays many parts.

Until the wave reaches us (using an analogy to Einstein's explanation of gravity to conciliate Newton's theory with his own), and we realize that it is not worth it to live in a society which is "not quite failed," we will not start a new form of capitalism in which individuals set new priorities and make choices towards a good society.

Holistic capitalism reflects Einstein's approach to the theory of capitalism—a holistic view that can analyze the dominant economic model of our era (capitalism) and take it to its next level of effectiveness. Holistic capitalism considers itself a natural system (social, economic, environmental) where its agents should be viewed as whole individuals, not a collection of roles. Therefore, a holistic company has the following characteristics:

- *It has a purpose*: the company has a reason to exist; something that makes it truly unique, a glue that holds the organization together. It evolved from a caterpillar to a butterfly.
- *It is three-dimensional*: it works at the same time and with the same excellence to create economic, social, and environmental value.
- *It makes no trade-offs* between economic and societal prosperity (common good).
- *It is inclusive*: it works to satisfy multiple stakeholders' needs and desires. It does not work as a silo but in partnership with other actors of society (no rigid sectors normally defined as government and civil society and NGOs). It works without artificial barriers to value creation and prosperity; there is no limit to harvesting

progress opportunities. It expands its potential for value creation beyond the walls of the company or its value chain and considers all actors as allies in creating economic, social, and environmental value.

- *It is innovative* in terms of products, services, processes, and business models. Each innovation has an objective linked to the purpose of the company.

John Stuart Mill insisted that he would be a communist if he believed that economic misery and deprivation were inherent in a capitalistic economy. And Mill was right, they are not inherent and they can be eliminated. Indeed, in a democratic capitalism, they must be eliminated. (Okun, 1975: Conclusion)

The Role of Individuals within a Holistic Capitalism System

There is a huge opportunity for societal progress toward constructing a "good society" within the capitalist system, not only since capitalism juxtaposed with democracy has proven to be a feasible and effective economic system so far, but because its "invisible hand" has tremendous power to extend beyond profit-maximization. The key lies in convincing investors, business leaders, and consumers that holistic capitalism both fulfills the profit objective and that of benefitting society as a whole and that it is a win-win decision, in terms of satisfying one's own self-interest and that of others, reconciling performance with progress.

I would like to argue that the most efficient actor to work upon is the investor (the owner of the capital). They are not numerous, normally concentrated and connected to each other. According to the Credit Suisse *Global Wealth Databook* for 2013, the eighty-five richest people in the world have more wealth than that of the poorest 3.5 billion. In fact, 0.7 percent of the population owns 41 percent of the world's wealth.

When considering companies and their control of world wealth, the data are equally amazing. According to an article in *Forbes* magazine,

> Three systems theorists at the Swiss Federal Institute of Technology in Zurich have taken a database listing 37 million companies and investors worldwide and analyzed all 43,060 transnational corporations and share ownerships linking them. They built a model of who owns what and what their revenues are and mapped the whole edifice of economic power. They discovered that global corporate control has a distinct bow-tie shape, with a dominant core of 147 firms radiating out from the middle. Each of these 147 own interlocking stakes of one another ("super connected companies") and together they control 40% of the wealth in the network. A total of 737 companies control 80% of it all. (Upbin 2011)

If we could convince them, and especially the boards of directors of the world's leading companies, that holistic capitalism is the next phase of evolution of our economic system, they could set priorities and make the decisions necessary for the system to move quickly in the right direction.

The Role of Investors: How to Convince them to Move beyond Profits?

Milton Friedman's famous quote, "the business of business is business" (1998: 133) underestimates the power of capitalism as an economic and social system. This theory, repeated often in business school courses, has influenced many CEOs throughout the world and has led business leaders to focus on maximizing profits for shareholders, creating jobs, paying taxes, and, then, once business runs appropriately, worry about writing checks for charitable causes. Great thinkers, such as Albert Einstein, explained this cultural trend rather forebodingly, "perfection of means and confusion of ends seem to characterize our age" (1950: ch. 14)—which showed that such a loss of higher purpose was not an uncommon modern phenomenon.

However, being an optimist myself, I feel that investors and managers have a tremendous opportunity to use the capitalist system to create social and environmental value while continuing to profit economically as it has done since the 1600s. The key is finding a way to convince them to see beyond short-term results and envision a holistic company.

One can argue that fear could be used to convince them. Fear of additional regulation and restrictions, fear of losing their license to operate in a particular community, fear of higher taxes that may reduce profits, fear of losing consumers (who are now more sophisticated and demand more from companies). In short, fear has been the single most prevalent mechanism to foster a Corporate Social Responsibility movement in many regions of the world. Stiglitz noted: "An economy in which most citizens are doing worse year after year is not likely to do well over the long haul" (2012). However, there is another alternative to convincing investors and business leaders to redirect their business practices so that they may continue to create economic value with positive social and environmental repercussions. They need to understand that trade-offs among these three dimensions of value creation are not real. Some people argue that reducing a company's environmental or social footprints could have negative short-term financial effects. For example, if a company is required to build a water treatment plant to reduce its operational water footprint, this investment may have a negative impact on its P&L statement. Another example of the social dimension involves healthy consumption patterns. If a beer company wants to improve consumption patterns, it may have to eliminate volume promotions that are associated with alcohol abuse. Such a decision may have negative repercussions on short-term sales.

In order to overcome this short-sighted perspective, it is important to understand that this is a trade-off that will eventually be replaced by other positive effects, such as consumer preference, stakeholder support, and an overall improved business setting for business operations. Investors and entrepreneurs must feel compelled to follow their moral compasses and realize that, today, companies must have a higher purpose in order to ensure their long-term success. Mackey underscores the need for such a holistic approach and purpose in corporations:

A firm's purpose is the glue that holds the organization together, the amniotic fluid that nourishes the life force of the organization . . . You can also think of it as a magnet that attracts the right people—the right team members, customers, suppliers and investors-to the business and aligns them. A compelling purpose reduces friction within the organization and its ecosystem because it gets everybody pointed in the same direction and moving together in harmony. (Mackey 2013)

Purpose has a stronger power than compensation to appeal to employee ideals and get them motivated to go the extra hundred miles. The great Austrian psychologist Viktor Frankl taught that "people can discover meaning and purpose in their lives in three ways: by doing work that matters, by loving others unconditionally, and by finding meaning in their suffering" (quoted in Mackey 2013). This represents a great opportunity for investors and managers to set a purpose for the company, connect with their employees at a higher level, and unleash their creativity and energy to create value for society as a whole. "The difference in business impact and personal happiness between a team member who is inspired, passionate, and committed and one who merely shows up for a paycheck, is enormous" (Mackey 2013).

The Role of the Business Leader

The role of the business leader has been changing dramatically over the last few decades. Fifty years ago, the main responsibility of a business leader was to maximize profits for his shareholders and, in doing so, generate jobs and pay taxes. With the creation of Corporate Social Responsibility (CSR) in the 1970s, the role of business leaders has evolved to incorporate first philanthropy (caring for society, generally, in the form of monetary gifts) and, afterwards, footprint minimization. Nowadays, executives understand that every company (independent of its economic sector) has environmental and social footprints (use of water and energy use, carbon emissions, solid waste, etc.) and that they have the responsibility to reduce those footprints to the minimum level possible. This stage 1 incorporates the notion of footprint minimization to existing profit criteria. There is a stage 2, where leaders see a business opportunity in producing new products or services that have a positive societal impact and/or benefit the environment. In this stage 2, the company supplements this sustainable innovation with strategic social investment, in which a company invests in social or environmental projects related to its core business. In this manner, the company leverages on its core competencies as well as the expertise and know-how of its employees as volunteers to increase the effectiveness of these initiatives, in addition to money. Finally, there is a stage 3 in which companies become positive agents within an interconnected sustainability ecosystem, also known in the business world as "Triple Bottom Line," which measures a company's long-term success according to its financial, social, and economic performance. In this strategic model, the business leader does not have a business strategy with an additional corporate social responsibility strategy next to it.

> Maximize:
>
> Economic Value + Social Value + Environmental Value

FIGURE 17.3. Triple Bottom Line

On the contrary, there is a merging between the two and the business leader measures the success of the company in three dimensions: economic, social, and environmental simultaneously (Figure 17.3).

While business leaders continue to maximize economic profits, they must simultaneously create social and environmental value with the same excellence and rigor. Social value can be created within the company by promoting the well-being of its employees and that of their families. In addition, the company must work with communities in the countries under the responsibility of the business leader to foster progress and sustainability. In terms of creating environmental value, companies must reduce their environmental impact to the minimum level possible and offset its environmental and social footprint. One theory maintains that companies cannot create social or environmental value and that their only possibility is to reduce footprints or, in the best case scenario, compensate for them by becoming environmentally neutral. This is certainly not true. It is feasible for a company to offset more carbon emissions than necessary to protect biodiversity and natural resources. Yet, in a holistic capitalism system, becoming neutral is not enough. Business leaders must pursue the creation of positive social and environmental value in addition to creation of economic value.

This evolution to holistic capitalism does not imply that philanthropy is wrong. However, companies that embrace the "Triple bottom line" concept run their businesses in a manner which naturally benefits and creates value for all stakeholders (clients, consumers, suppliers, regulators, government, media, academia, communities, etc.) "Every business has stakeholders, whether or not it thinks of them that way" (Mackey 2013). Unfortunately, most managers continue to work under the old premise that their only responsibility is to maximize profits. Research conducted by Mercer and Angus in 1999 showed that 30 percent of general managers interviewed chose "increase profitability" as their first priority (Willard 2002). Such a one-dimensional and narrow perspective could only function if companies and capitalism worked isolated from any external intervention.

Okun noted: "Economy is only one aspect of society." (1975). According to Forest Reinhardt in his book *Down to Earth*:

> Common intuition can make business leaders blind to a triple bottom line approach. In the old mental model, society and the environment were separated entities and worked outside of the economic world in which they had a miniscule importance. In that model, economic, social and environmental priorities competed among each other. The sustainability model is more precise and understands that the global economy is a sector of society. Society, itself, works within a global environment (planet Earth). (2000: 179)

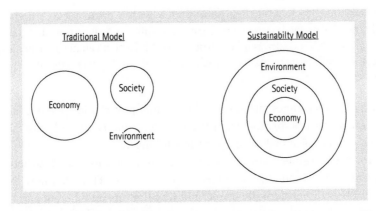

FIGURE **17.4.** Sustainability Model

Table 17.1. Investment Performance of Humanistic Firms versus the S&P 500

Return	Cumulative	Annualized
Firms of Endearment	1,646.1%	21.0%
S&P 500	157.0%	6.5%

This new model shows that there are no trade-offs among dimensions (Figure 17.4). Business leader Stephan Schmidheiny noted that "It's impossible to build successful companies in failed societies."[1]

The paradigm that says that economic success is separate from social wellness and environmental balance has been totally overcome. We have seen direct evidence that social and environmental value creation in a company has a direct positive impact on financial results. In *Firms of Endearment: How World-Class Companies Profit from Passion and Purpose*, Raj Sisodia et al. selected companies on the basis of their so-called humanistic profiles (their sense of purpose; how well they were loved by the customers, team members, suppliers, and communities; their cultures, and their leadership). They found that these companies not only do all those good things, but also deliver extraordinary returns to their investors, outperforming the market by a nine-to-one ratio over ten years (from 1996 to 2006). The authors have updated the data to span a fifteen-year period from 1996 to 2011. Table 17.1 shows how these companies outperformed the S&P 500 index by a factor of 10.5 over that period.

The most successful business leaders of the next decade will be those who understand the three dimensions of the triple bottom line. Our world, capitalism, and companies are and have always been three-dimensional. Our mistake has been to oversimplify them to understand them better and to grasp and manage them easier.

---

[1] Speech at INCAE Business School, 1996.

> Businesses need to look at their performance with a broad set of criteria. They should not be judged purely on financial results...A business that generates financial wealth but destroys other forms of wealth (which can have greater impacts on people's well-being) adds far less value to the world that it is capable of... There are no such things as main effects and side effects. (Mackey 2013)

Considering the challenges ahead (global warming, poverty, inequality), the role of a business leader must be broadened; a triple bottom line is not only desirable but an imperative and a choice that cannot wait much longer.

If a group of business leaders were asked if they care about society and the environment, they would all, undoubtedly, answer "yes." However, how they understand those other dimensions, their role, and why they are an inherent part of business will get thousands of different answers. Some business leaders believe that they are truly philanthropists because their administrative assistants write a check at the end of each month; they fight regulation through lobbying and take care of their employees to escape the negative implications of a high turnover. Only a few are ready to implement a new, sustainability-based business strategy. The challenge that lies ahead is not to decide if this is or is not a good business idea, but to find ways to do it better and faster. As author and anthropologist Carlos Castañeda says, "Things don't change. It is you (the individual) who has to change the way you see the world" (1974: 17). Only visionary business leaders will have a holistic view of the tremendous opportunity that lies in front of them. It is no longer a matter of reducing footprints, but a matter of creating progress and environmental value within the capitalist system.

Perhaps one of the main concerns that some business leaders may have is how to go along with the implementation of a holistic business model. Based on my personal experience, this process involves at least four main steps:

1. Begin with interactive and open continuous dialogue with all stakeholders (customers, consumers, employees, suppliers, shareholders, government officials, NGOs, media, academia, etc.) to gain a better understanding about their general company perception: what are the company's main strengths and footprints in the three dimensions (economic, social, and environmental) as well as their expectations regarding the company's actions.

2. Based on the stakeholder insights and the experience and opinion of the company's executives, a company must define strategic business objectives along the three aforementioned dimensions and set ambitious and concrete goals that reflect its commitment to society. A critical objective of every company should be manufacturing new products or services that will have a positive impact on society and the environment. This entails adapting its products, operations, and processes. Brands must embrace these efforts, given the critical role they play in being in direct contact with consumers. Sustainable innovation is one of the main catalysts to creating a company's competitive advantage.

3. The third step involves the creation of a measurement system to monitor company progress towards its strategic triple-bottom line objectives and link executive compensation to the set objectives and KPIs.

4. Finally, it is crucial to report back to stakeholders and society as a whole (accountability). Results must be openly communicated in order to analyze the main improvements to the three dimensions so far and what are the areas that need further work. This is a virtuous cycle that never ends. Once the company has reported back to society, it is important to start the process all over again.

The Role of Consumers: How to Convince them to Move towards Sustainable Products and Services?

The other critical agent in the capitalistic model is the consumer—the individual who has the final say on which products and services are purchased. However, convincing consumers is time consuming. Also, gaining leverage and momentum to increase prosperity, reduce poverty, strengthen human rights, and create more opportunities through the collective action of consumers, is a challenging goal.

Yet, changing individual preference is a critical initiative to undertake and once it is implemented, it has an ever-expanding ripple effect and it is literally unstoppable. In our technological era, the opportunity to change consumer preferences and choices is easier now that social networks and the Internet allow us to communicate with an immense number of individuals in real time and at a very reasonable cost.

In order to influence consumer behavior towards a more sustainable consumption pattern, it is critical to share information and knowledge with them. Knowledge constitutes a valuable intangible asset and vehicle to change behavior and although the majority of consumers are not ready to pay more for sustainable products, they should be ready to choose those that are more environmentally friendly or socially responsible, if the other decision basic factors (price, quality, and availability) are similar. Demand is becoming more and more sophisticated, asking for more and better at the same price. They don't like trade-offs, "they want it all and on demand."

The other mechanism that should be used to convince individuals and households to choose sustainable products is "attribution." We have to show them that they have the responsibility and the power to transform capitalism into a system that has multiple societal benefits. We have to show them, in a clear and concrete way, the link between what they prefer and what they choose and the effects that those decisions will have in the long term for society and the planet.

Another important initiative to consider is a change in the formal education system to incorporate more information and knowledge about the components of a good society, sustainability, and the role of the individual in fostering progress, while also considering that we all share one planet. Higher education and, specifically, business schools should incorporate a more holistic view of the role of the private sector and allow individuals to recalibrate their worldview and definition of success.

THE ROLE OF GOVERNMENT: PROVIDING
A FERTILE GROUND

It is important for governments to foster and facilitate an improved version of capitalism. From a political perspective, two primary variables play a dominant role in shaping public policy agendas: the type of government intervention used to promote responsible business efforts and the specific issue or action area to be addressed.

Encouraging, sustaining, and enhancing growth and sustainability in a country requires decisive action by the business leaders to complement government investments. In order to be efficient, government must define priorities and action areas (such as education, health, entrepreneurship promotion, etc.) so companies in their specific business (core competencies, knowledge, and know-how) can invest in the "sweet spot" that is formed in the intersection between the priority areas necessary to boost the country's competitiveness and sustainability and the company's specific business (Figure 17.5). This "sweet spot" defines which projects and investment are strategic for both the company and the country where it operates and can lead to sustained higher growth and prosperity over the long term.

In selecting the appropriate types of policy intervention, governments must take into account local socio-economic, political, and cultural contexts as well as the specific problems or action areas in and through which social change is desired. According to United Nations Global Compact, there are at least three types of government intervention that can usefully be distinguished to support responsible businesses.

Awareness-Raising

Awareness-raising instruments represent an important tool for governments in disseminating the idea of sustainability and providing incentives for business to adopt it.

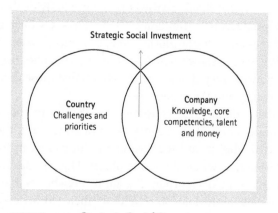

FIGURE 17.5. Strategic Social Investment

Aimed at demonstrating how companies can contribute to sustainable development, these tools are often used to create a common understanding of sustainability among companies and their stakeholders. Raising awareness is an important first step leading to public sector engagement. Specific examples of policy instruments include: tax exemptions for social investments, internet platforms and award schemes that increase the visibility of social and environmental initiatives, training and capacity building for companies, etc.

Partnering

Partnering instruments lie at the heart of the sustainability public policy agenda. It is important to understand that governments do not have all the necessary resources to solve all social, environmental, and economic problems. Partnerships and strategic alliances combine the expertise, competencies, and resources of the public sector with those of business and other societal actors to address action areas within the sustainability agenda, thus creating benefit for all stakeholders. For example, governments can launch multi-stakeholder dialogues, undertake collective action or capacity building efforts, involve various stakeholders in standard-setting procedures, or simply mobilize resources. Numerous alliances have evolved in recent years to tackle issues such as poverty reduction, access to health and safety, and educational infrastructure.

Proactive Soft Interventions

Proactive soft interventions to promote sustainability are non-regulatory interventions (i.e. sustainability guidelines, tax incentives, national action plans, etc.) that can provide a fertile ground for companies to put their innovative capacities to good use, enabling them to be better than the law requires.

It is crucial to consider that holistic capitalism has to be based on the dual reinforcement between capitalism and democracy.

> Life in capitalist democracies is shaped by two systems of governance: democracy and capitalism. These two systems influence each other and can be made to serve the public interest if their potential is understood and adapted accordingly and effectively.
>
> Capitalism, like democracy, is a system of governance, and the institutions of capitalism, are ultimately shaped through political processes. The critical features of capitalism are not so much in the operations of markets as they achieve equilibrium, as in the institutions or legal frameworks supporting and shaping those markets to achieve equilibrium. Moreover, political forces help determine changes to that equilibrium over time, through reform that may or may not promote the long-term development of their societies. (Scott 2011)

A Sense of Urgency

As many world leaders have argued, it is time to take action. It is time for business leaders, government officials, and academics, social, and environmental leaders to work together toward a good society. As Stiglitz has written (2012: 1): "Americans have been watching protests against oppressive regimes that concentrate massive wealth in the hands of an elite few. Yet in our democracy, 1% of the people take nearly a quarter of the nation's income—an inequality even the wealthy will come to regret."

> What is now happening to the people of the East as of the West is like what happens to every individual when he passes from childhood to adolescence and from youth to manhood. He loses what had hitherto guided his life and lives without direction, not having found a new standard suitable to his age, and so he invents all sorts of occupations, cares, distractions, and stupefactions to divert his attention from the misery and senselessness of his life. Such a condition may last a long time. When an individual passes from one period of life to another, a time comes when he cannot go on in senseless activity and excitement as before, but has to understand that although he has outgrown what before used to direct him, this does not mean that he must live without any reasonable guidance, but rather that he must formulate for himself an understanding of life corresponding to his age, and having elucidated it must be guided by it. And in the same way a similar time must come in the growth and development of humanity. I believe that such a time has now arrived. (Tolstoy 1908: ch. VI, line 5)

The Power Lies Within

I believe that this new era of capitalism presents a tremendous opportunity, one that better reflects the current state of our world (environmental and societal challenges) and the intrinsic need of individuals to have a positive impact. It is our responsibility to raise greater awareness among individuals in their respective roles as economic actors (investors, managers, employees, and consumers), and convince them of the holistic role they need to play. Even Adam Smith, the father of capitalism, defined the need for society to progress for the overall common good before proceeding to develop the concepts and theories on which capitalism is based. The challenge lies in convincing business leaders to reconcile performance with progress and accept that there is a better way of doing business—one with no trade-offs and where corporate success is defined holistically. One thing is true, the power lies in each individual to determine preferences and make choices. The critical question that we now face is how to boost the cocoon phase of holistic capitalism so it can be readily embraced by all individuals and especially, by the corporate world.

> The power and capacity of learning exists in the soul already, and that just as the eye was unable to turn from darkness to light without the whole body, so too the

instrument of knowledge can only by the movement of the whole soul be turned from the world of becoming into that of being, and learn by degrees to endure the sight of being, and of the brightest and best of being, or in other words, of the good. (Plato, *The Republic*)

QUESTIONS FOR FUTURE RESEARCH

- Under what circumstances is there a positive correlation between holistic capitalism and financial performance?
- How can we influence business leaders (boards of directors and CEOs) of the leading companies around the world to adopt holistic capitalism?

REFERENCES

Boyd, J. (1950). *The Papers of Thomas Jefferson, i. 1760–1776, The Declaration of Independence as Adopted by Congress*. Princeton: Princeton University Press.

Castañeda, C. (1974). *Una realidad aparte*. Mexico City: Fondo de Cultura Económica México.

Christakis, Nicholas A. (2011). *Shorthand Abstractions and the Cognitive Toolkit*, Edge.

Darwin, C. (1871). *The Descent of Man*. < http://darwin-online.org.uk/EditorialIntroductions/Freeman_TheDescentofMan.html> [Accessed Feb. 2014].

Einstein, Albert (1950). *Out of My Later Years*. New York: New York Philosophical Library.

Flucher, J. (2004). *Capitalism: A Very Short Introduction*. Oxford: Oxford University Press.

Friedman, M. (1998). *Capitalism and Freedom*. Chicago: University of Chicago Press.

Hayek, F. (1944). *The Road to Serfdom*. Chicago: University of Chicago Press.

Ingham, G. (2008). *Capitalism*. Cambridge: Polity Press.

Keller, A., ed. (1913). *The Challenge of Facts and Other Essays*. New Haven: Yale University Press.

Locke, J. (1689). *The Second Treatise of Government*. <www.efm.bris.ac.uk/het/locke/government.pdf> [Accessed Feb. 2014].

Mackey, J., and R. Sisodia (2013). *Liberating the Heroic Spirit of Business: Conscious Capitalism*. Cambridge, MA: Harvard Business Review Press.

Mander, J. (2012). *The Capitalism Papers: Fatal Flows of an Obsolete System*. Berkeley, CA: Counterpoint.

Maslow, Abraham (1954). *Motivation and Personality*. New York: Harper.

Mencius (2013). *Human Nature*, tr. C. Muller. Cambridge, MA: Union of Concerned Scientists.

Normore, A., ed. (2010). *The Social Contract*. Seattle: Pacific Publishing Studio.

Okun, A. (1975). *Equality and Efficiency, the Big Tradeoff*. Cambridge, MA: Brookings Institution Press.

O'Toole, J. (1993). *The Executive Compass: Business and the Good Society*. Oxford: Oxford University Press.

Plato (1892). *The Republic*, tr. B. Jowett. <http://classics.mit.edu/Plato/republic.html>.

Reinhardt, Forest (2000). *Down to Earth: Applying Business Principles to Environmental Management*. Cambridge, MA: Harvard Business School Press.

Scott, B. (2011). *Capitalism: Its Origins and Evolution as a System of Governance*. New York: Springer.

Sisodia, Raj, D. B. Wolfe, and J. N. Sheth (2007). *Firms of Endearment: How World-Class Companies Profit from Passion and Purpose*. Upper Saddle River, NJ: Wharton School Publishing.

Smith, A. (1759). *The Theory of Moral Sentiments*. Cambridge: Cambridge University Press.

Smith, A. (1776). *The Wealth of Nations*. Cambridge: Cambridge University Press.

Stalley, F., ed. (2009). *Politics*. Oxford: Oxford University Press.

Stiglitz, J. (2012). The 1 Percent's Problem. *Vanity Fair*. May 31. <www.vanityfair.com/politics/2012/05/joseph-stiglitz-the-price-on-inequality> [Accessed Feb. 2014].

Tolstoy, L. (1908). *A Letter to a Hindu*. <www.nonresistance.org/docs_pdf/Tolstoy/Correspondence_with_Gandhi.pdf> [Accessed Feb. 2014].

Upbin, Bruce (2011). The 147 Companies that Control Everything. *Forbes*, Oct. 22.

Willard, B. (2002). *The Sustainability Advantage: Seven Business Case Benefits of a Triple Bottom Line*. British Columbia: Friesens.

CHAPTER 18

....

WHITHER THE GOOD FIRM

Quasi-Experiments in Corporate Social Responsibility

....

HARRISON HONG AND INESSA LISKOVICH

Abstract
Several decades of empirical research into the economic role of corporate social responsibility have yielded inconclusive results due to a lack of identification strategies. We propose the use of quasi-experiments to address fundamental questions such as how much of corporate social responsibility spending is agency related and how much is driven by strategic profit considerations. In contrast to field studies or experiments that are open to the critique of extrapolative relevance, we use the 2003 Dividend Tax Cut in a quasi-experiment to identify the portion of corporate goodness that is driven by agency motives. We then isolate a specific channel through which strategic corporate goodness works using the recent enforcement of the Foreign Corrupt Practices Act.

INTRODUCTION

....

Social responsibility is becoming an increasingly important part of corporate strategy. For example, in the mid-2000s, Google initiated its famed 1 percent program, which invested 1 percent of its profits in philanthropic and non-profit interests. In the late 2000s, General Electric spent $160 million on community and employee philanthropic programs and earmarked billions more for the development of eco-friendly products. At the same time, Intel spent $100 million on global education programs and energy conservation. And most recently, CVS Pharmacy announced plans in 2014 to stop selling cigarettes at all retail locations, a move forecasted to cost $2 billion a year in direct sales. (See Hong et al. (2011) and Cheng et al. (2013) for discussions of these figures.) In addition, firms are increasingly switching to greener and more costly production processes or voluntarily choosing to pay living wages to employees.

Yet the value of corporate social responsibility has never been more vague. According to a 2009 McKinsey survey of 300 chief financial officers, investment professionals, and corporate social responsibility practitioners, even as two-thirds of them embraced corporate social responsibility, most agreed that they could not identify, much less quantify, either the financial or social value of their program.

Unfortunately, academics have not been able to quantify these values either. As a matter of fact, the debate on corporate social responsibility in academia has never been more contentious. Milton Friedman (1970), in a biting op-ed for the *New York Times*, declared that the only social responsibility of corporations is to make money. His view regarding spending on corporate social responsibility (CSR) places it alongside agency problems, managerial perks, and pet projects. In other words, managers are doing good with other people's money. This view is shared by Jensen and Meckling (1976) and has become the paradigm in the finance literature and in the classrooms of prestigious business schools. A contrasting view is the business case for corporate goodness, dubbed "doing well by doing good" (see e.g. Benabou and Tirole (2010), Heal (2005), Margolis et al (2009), and Kitzmueller and Shimshack (2012)). Goodness may pay by improving employee efficiency, reducing conflicts among stakeholders, mitigating litigation risk, deterring potential regulation, signaling product quality, and improving investor and consumer relations by preventing product or capital market boycotts by socially responsible consumers or investors.

Despite the many papers that have been written on this topic, it is difficult to draw causal conclusions regarding the motives for corporate goodness spending because of the lack of a clear identification strategy. Notably, the large literature on "doing well by doing good" explores the correlation between firm performance and CSR but not the causation. Evidence from experiments and field studies also suggests that there are potential warm-glow effects from being charitable or good (see e.g. Elfenbein et al. 2012; List 2006). But these studies suffer from an extrapolative critique of being too different from CSR as practiced by large corporations. Moreover, in realistic CSR contexts, the motivation for CSR may not stem from the presence of warm-glow effects. Altruistic managers may invest in CSR to protect stakeholders such as employees or the broader community, in ways that do not directly contribute to shareholder wealth. As Tirole (2001) points out, a stakeholder instead of shareholder maximization paradigm can very quickly lead to mission creep and agency perils.

Despite the lack of consensus regarding CSR, the stakes in this debate have never been higher. Institutional investors are increasingly adopting socially responsible factors, also known as "environmental, social and governance" (ESG) factors, in their portfolio choices. For example, the United Nations Principles of Responsible Investing (UNPRI) has as signatories institutions that manage around $1.5 trillion globally. The ESG movement makes the argument for socially responsible investing on the basis of a combination of the business case for corporate goodness and moral principles.

To make progress on identifying the value of CSR, we argue in this chapter for the use of quasi-experiments to study these issues. This methodology was originally applied by labor economists and has since spread to a wide variety of disciplines.

Quasi-experiments or natural experiments make use of randomization that occurs naturally and that we can use to make causal statements. For example, labor economists have used plausibly exogenous variation as an instrumental variable to estimate the returns to education (see e.g. Angrist and Krueger 1991) and have used randomization in close elections to conduct regression discontinuity analysis estimating the electoral advantage to incumbency (see e.g. Lee 2008).

We make our case in three parts. In section 2, we address whether it is possible to accurately measure corporate social responsibility in the first place, and in particular whether commercial measures produced by "goodness" rating agencies are informative. In section 3, we discuss a recent quasi-experiment that distinguishes between an agency motive and a business case for CSR. In section 4, we provide some ideas and evidence on identifying the channels through which strategic CSR works.

CAN CORPORATE GOODNESS BE ACCURATELY MEASURED?

The most widely used measure of corporate social responsibility is the Kinder, Lydenberg, and Domini (KLD) scores. KLD scores are developed by a for-profit company, akin to a credit rating agency. The scores measure firm-level social responsibility along the lines of community relations, product characteristics, environmental impact, employee relations, and diversity. Beginning in 2010, KLD scores were retooled into what are now known as MSCI ESG scores, after MSCI acquired RiskMetrics in 2009. KLD scans public databases, such as those on employee strikes and Environmental Protection Agency (EPA) violations, and uses a team of analysts to measure these and other social responsibility dimensions of firm decisions. Firms are graded on roughly eighty indicators. Each indicator represents a strength or a concern in one of seven major areas: community, corporate governance, diversity, employee relations, environment, human rights, and product. The total strengths, net of the total concerns, are summed together to calculate a final KLD score.

We begin our discussion by stating the advantages and disadvantages of the KLD score as a measure of firm goodness. The disadvantage is that, like most ratings produced by commercial firms, there is a black-box aspect to the KLD score. Ideally, one would have data on dollar amounts spent on corporate social responsibility. Unlike an extra dollar of charitable donations, it is unclear what exactly an increase in the KLD score represents. As a result, there is skepticism about what exactly these scores capture. One particular concern is that CSR is nothing more than cynical greenwashing with little economic implications. This greenwashing comprises nothing more than some year-end reports about various recycling initiatives or seminars that do not cost very much.

But there is mounting evidence in the literature that the equal-weighted KLD scores are indeed informative of corporate social responsibility. First, Chatterji et al. (2009)

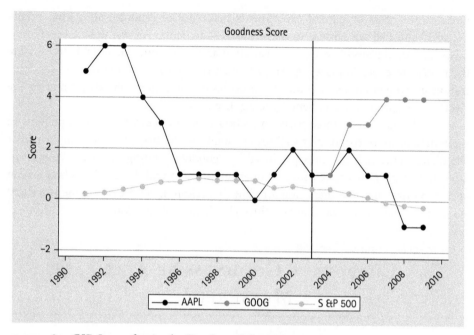

FIGURE 18.1 CSR Scores for Apple, Google, and the S&P 500

Note: This figure plots the KLD score each year for Apple and Google and the average score of S&P 500 firms

find that KLD scores which capture the past environmental performance of firms also forecast the probability of future pollution and environmental regulatory violations reasonably well. Second, Cheng et al. (2013) provide some anecdotal evidence for the effectiveness of KLD scores in picking up the timing of changes in social responsibility. Figure 18.1 plots the development of KLD scores for Apple, Google, and the S&P 500 from 1990 through 2010. In 1996, Apple's KLD score fell dramatically and remained substantially lower than its previous average for most of the remaining sample. This drop coincides with Steve Jobs's return as CEO when he took control of Apple in 1996. The company was also nearing bankruptcy during this period. Steve Jobs famously decided to cut all of Apple's CSR programs. He subscribed to the view that the only responsibility of a corporation is to make and sell great products for society, and presumably earn its shareholders a lot of money in the process (Greenfield 2011). The fact that Apple was near bankruptcy when it cut its programs is indicative that cutting CSR is a drastic move and therefore costly.

Third, Hong et al. (2011) show that a principal components analysis places roughly equal weights across the five dimensions of CSR: community relations, product characteristics, environmental impact, employee relations, and diversity. They show that there is a common component in firm scores. Firms that score well in one dimension (e.g. community) also score well in another (e.g. environment). If the KLD scores only represented greenwashing, we would expect firms with very poor scores in one area to make up for it in another by appearing more environmentally friendly. This does not appear to be the case. Using identification strategies related to the internet bubble of 1996–2000 and the credit crisis of August 2007, they find that corporate goodness is significantly and positively correlated with financial slack, again implying it is costly to implement.

Fourth, Cheng et al. (2013) also gathered donation data from the Chronicles of Philanthropy for approximately 100 large firms each year, chosen from *Fortune* magazine's list of top revenue-producing firms in the US. The sample covers 2000–11. They find that equal-weighted KLD scores predict donations well in annual levels.

Fifth, KLD scores are widely used by socially responsible investment (SRI) funds to screen out irresponsible companies from their indexes. SRI funds typically own stocks with the highest KLD scores within an industry. Additionally, Hong and Kostovetsky (2012) find that money managers of non-SRI funds who have, on net, contributed towards Democratic candidates in elections, and whose political values are thus likely to favor social responsibility, tilt their portfolios toward firms with the highest KLD scores within industries. DiGiuli and Kostovetsky (2011) find that firms with Democratic CEOs are also more likely to have higher KLD scores.

In sum, the preponderance of the evidence establishes KLD as an informative measure of a firm's genuine attempts to address the impact of their production on society.

SEPARATING AGENCY MOTIVATED FROM STRATEGIC CSR

Having established that CSR is informative and is not just greenwashing, it is still not clear what motivates firms to engage in these activities. A broad classification of competing motives is profit versus agency. Are firms engaging in these activities to boost profits? Or does CSR reflect the fact that managers typically own only a small part of public companies and hence have incentives that are not perfectly aligned with profit-maximization?

Cheng et al. (2013) provide a first attempt at identifying whether there is an agency motive for CSR using a quasi-experiment. They test a key prediction of an agency theory in which managers engage in unproductive CSR as a way to enjoy private benefits. The first and most basic prediction is that increasing the ownership stakes of a manager leads to a reduction in firm goodness. Since managerial ownership stakes regulate the degree of agency conflicts between the manager and shareholders, agency models predict that larger stakes lead to less of an agency conflict and lower unproductive CSR spending. Their perspective is that agency problems need not simply manifest themselves as managerial selfish perks, as has traditionally been framed since Jensen and Meckling (1976), but also as managerial altruism or social preferences (see e.g. Fehr and Schimdt 1999; Charness and Rabin 2002).

For the quasi-experiment using the 2003 Dividend Tax Cut, they use data on top-five total executive share ownership from S&P's ExecuComp database, dividend data from the CRSP Monthly File (aggregated to annual frequency), and other firm variables from CRSP and CompuStat. The sample consists of firms that were in the S&P 500 in 2001 or 2002 and have inside share ownership data from ExecuComp. All together, there are 503 firms.

They expand on Chetty and Saez (2005, 2010), who argue that the Jobs and Growth Tax Relief Act of 2003 (commonly known as the 2003 Dividend Tax Cut) raised the effective ownership stakes of shareholders by cutting the highest statutory dividend tax rate from 35 percent to 15 percent. This tax cut had a particularly strong effect on the after-tax ownership of managers because managers are exposed to the maximum statutory tax rate, unlike other large shareholders who can filter ownership through tax-advantaged accounts (Shleifer and Vishny 1986). Chetty and Saez (2005, 2006) argue that the tax cut was largely unanticipated and led to a surge in dividend payouts. These dividend payouts were unlikely to have come from reductions in productive investment, because most corporate investment models predict that productive investment should weakly *increase* following the tax cut (Chetty and Saez 2010). Instead, Chetty and Saez (2005, 2006, 2010) argue that the tax cut led managers to substitute away from perk projects toward dividends after their effective ownership stakes increased. Consistent with their agency perspective, evidence from Poterba (2004) and Auerbach and Hassett (2006, 2007) point to higher equity prices as a result of the tax cut. It is important to highlight that their analysis does not test whether all CSR, or even that undertaken by the average firm, is unproductive. Instead, they test whether the extra marginal dollar spent on CSR is a form of perk spending by exploring how KLD scores change following the tax cut.

In general, the dividend tax cut increases the effective ownership stake of management because each share's claim to after-tax profits increases. If the marginal dollar spent on goodness is unproductive and the result of agency conflicts, then the tax cut should lead to an average decline in goodness. Cheng et al. (2013) find that KLD scores do significantly decline on average after the 2003 dividend tax cut. However, they point out that this is not clear evidence per se of an agency motive for some CSR since there could have been a coincident time trend.

To get more directly at the effect of insider ownership rates and hence agency on CSR, they point out that the dividend tax cut has a very small effect on effective managerial ownership if the ex-ante managerial share ownership is very low. When managers own close to 0 percent of the firm, even a large dividend tax cut will not change their incentives. At the same time, managers with very high levels of ownership are likely to have incentives that are already closely aligned with those of shareholders. These high ownership managers spend very little on inefficient goodness to begin with, so there is little scope to cut agency-motivated goodness following a dividend tax cut. Hence, a canonical agency model predicts that managers with intermediate firm ownership stakes should respond more to a dividend tax cut than managers with very low or very high ownership stakes.

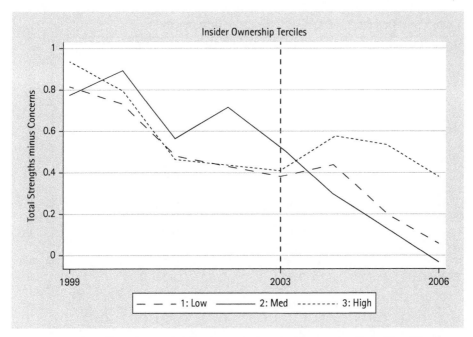

FIGURE **18.2.** The Effect of 2003 Dividend Tax Cut on CSR by Insider Ownership Terciles

Note: This figure plots the average KLD score in each ownership tercile portfolio for each year 1999–2006
for our main sample of firms in the S&P 500 during 2001–2

To test this prediction, they split firms into ownership terciles based on 2001 and
2002 executive ownership data and then employ a differences-in-differences methodology that flexibly allows the effect of the tax cut to vary through time in order to
capture its long-run dynamic effects. The differences in trends across terciles are
graphed in Figure 18.2. Indeed, consistent with their prediction, the KLD scores of
medium ownership firms fall steadily after 2003 whereas the KLD scores of low and
high ownership firms remained somewhat stable right after 2003. From 2003 through
2004, average goodness among the medium ownership firms fell more than that in both
high and low ownership firms.

This result is further confirmed in Table 18.1, which shows that cumulative changes
in KLD from 2003 were significantly negative for medium ownership firms and
significantly different from low and high ownership firms. This analysis, while pin-
pointing that the marginal dollar of CSR spending is agency motivated, also provides a
sense of the size of the agency effect. Relative to low ownership firms, the goodness
scores of medium ownership firms fell by 0.14 standard deviations more, where
standard deviations are calculated from the distribution in 2002. Relative to high
ownership firms, medium ownership firms' goodness scores fell by 0.22 standard
deviations more. These effects are statistically significant at the 10 percent and 1
percent levels, respectively. By the end of 2006, the difference in changes between
medium and high ownership firms widened to 0.29 standard deviations, although the
difference in changes with low ownership firms attenuated to 0.10 standard deviations.

Table 18.1. Dividend Tax Cut Difference-in-Differences

Year t	Year Effects	Interaction Effects	
		Low Own.	High Own.
1999	0.074	0.129	0.336
	(0.47)	(0.68)	(1.90)*
2000	0.312	0.063	0.112
	(2.67)***	(0.41)	(0.79)
2001	−0.03	0.112	0.123
	(−0.34)	(0.99)	(1-33)
2003	−0.183	0.095	0.099
	(−1.88)	(0.73)	(0.85)
2004	−0.405	0.32	0.489
	(−2.88)***	(1.90)*	(3.17)***
2005	−0.736	0.243	0.59
	(−4.35)***	(1.13)	(3.07)***
2006	−0.849	0.227	0.635
	(−4.32)***	(0.93)	(2.86)***
N	3671		
R^2		0.054	
Firms	503		

Note: This table reports the results from a difference-in-differences estimation in the annual panel where the dependent variable is the level of the goodness score. The right-hand side variables are firm-specific fixed effects, year-specific effects, and interaction effects between year effects and indicators for all ownership portfolios. Ownership portfolios are formed based on tercile of average ownership in the two-years prior to the shock year. The omitted category is always the medium ownership portfolio (tercile 2 or quintile 3). We also control for a set of market capitalization portfolio indicators (tercile or quintile) fully interacted with all year effects. The omitted year among market capitalization portfolios is the middle portfolio. The omitted year is 2002, and the coefficients are cumulative changes from the end of 2002 through the end of year t. Standard errors clustered by firm are presented in brackets. */**/*** indicates significant at the 10%, 5%, and 1% levels, respectively.

Finally, notice that while the estimates imply that marginal CSR is due to agency problems, it is still true that a significant part of corporate goodness spending is not agency motivated. Even firms without large agency problems engage in CSR. We can conclude that there is a sizeable but far from overwhelming effect of agency on corporate goodness.

DISTINGUISHING AMONG DIFFERENT STRATEGIC MOTIVATIONS FOR CSR

Having established that spending on goodness is only partly motivated by agency problems, the natural next question is what strategic considerations drive the profit-motivated goodness? According to the 2009 McKinsey Survey cited in the introduction, the only unanimity among those surveyed seemed to be that CSR was good for corporate image. In the example of CVS Pharmacy, their press release suggested that the move was indeed motivated by a desire to improve the company's reputation as a health care provider.

The three leading theories for strategic corporate social responsibility also all revolve around improving corporate image. The first is that CSR is a form of advertising in which the company engages in costly signaling of product market quality (see e.g Milgrom and Roberts 1986). The second is that corporate social responsibility is delegated giving, whereby firms are well-positioned to deliver warm-glow feelings (Becker 1974; Andreoni 1989) to consumers because of complementarities involving goodness in the production function (see e.g. Besley and Ghatak 2005). Here, the channel is not advertising to get consumer recognition but simply a way of bundling a product with delegated giving. The third explanation is that corporate social responsibility generates a halo effect, a cognitive bias long documented by psychologists (see Thorndike 1920; Nisbett and Wilson 1977) in which one's judgments of a person's character can be influenced by one's overall (and usually first) impression of him or her with little actual knowledge of the individual. In other words, consumers (over) extrapolate from a firm's investment in CSR to other firm or product characteristics. For example, they may assume that, just because a firm cares about the Amazon jungle, it also produces great computers.

The literature on "doing well by doing good" has long tried to tease out these various strategic motivations but to no avail (Benabou and Tirole 2010; Heal 2005; Margolis et al. 2009; Kitzmueller and Shimshack 2012). The best studies rely on field experiments to identify a warm-glow effect. For instance, Elfenbein et al. (2012) find that eBay sellers who contribute to an eBay charity program are able to sell their goods for a higher price. They argue that this reflects signaling since small firms are much more likely to do this than established sellers. However, it is difficult to use this result to understand how consumers and third parties react to CSR by large firms.

We have already discussed one reason for why it is hard to pinpoint the rationale for CSR, the lack of an identification strategy. Another major limitation is that all tests of the leading theories of strategic corporate social responsibility, namely advertising, warm-glow, and halo effects, explain the effect of CSR on consumers. Under every theory, consumers will value social responsibility, but for different reasons. Even well identified tests of CSR on consumer preferences cannot differentiate between the three effects. Focusing on the responses of consumers may show that CSR matters but cannot show that any one channel exists.

A more modest and plausible strategy is to focus on prosecutors, who are only susceptible to halo effects. Because they are not consuming the firm's products, prosecutors should not react to advertising or to warm glow. In contrast to the other two channels, the halo effect is present in a wide range of situations and relationships and is not limited to interactions between firms and consumers. In fact, ever since psychologist Edward Thorndike first coined the term "halo effect," researchers have focused on its relation to attractiveness and its bearing on the judicial and educational systems. Given the history of a halo effect in sentencing individuals, a judicial setting is optimal for testing for the halo effect for more attractive corporations. To test for its presence with respect to firms, we study how prosecutors punish crimes by socially responsible corporations.

We focus on a setting in which crimes are easily quantifiable and therefore the differences in sentencing are likely due to judicial bias rather than unobserved variation. For this we choose instances of corporate bribery which violates the Foreign Corrupt Practices Act (FCPA) of 1997. The FCPA was passed in response to the realization that bribery was prevalent and the idea that bribery by some US firms was detrimental to the the reputation of US firms overall. The report to the House of Representatives that initially introduced the FCPA outlined the reasoning behind this legislation. In recent years, more than 400 companies admitted making illegal payments to foreign government officials, 117 of which were in the Fortune 500.[1] These actions undermine the free market system championed by the US and harm foreign policy by lowering its credibility. Not only were these actions judged as harmful, but a survey of corporations cited in the report indicated that bribery was not deemed necessary by companies in a variety of industries and of various sizes. As a result, the FCPA made it illegal for any US issuer, domestic concern, or other person to bribe a foreign official in order to influence his acts or decisions or those of his government or political party.

The number of cases prosecuted under the FPCA has grown rapidly in recent years, prompting Choi and Davis (2013) to name the anti-bribery provisions of the FCPA as the most important rules in the regulation of US business abroad. There were few cases against corporations in the 1990s and early 2000s but the number ballooned in 2007. A total of fifteen cases were brought against corporations in the period 1991–2000 but this rose to 185 in 2001–10. This is partially due to the changing nature of US business involvement. At least 20 percent of the cases in the 2000s took place in Iraq and at least 15 percent took place in China. Regardless of the reasons, this surge in FCPA enforcement allows us to shed light on judicial practices by comparing sanctions for companies with differing levels of corporate social responsibility.

The enforcement approach of the FCPA is detailed in *A Resource Guide to the U.S. Foreign Corrupt Practices Act*, published in the Criminal Division of the US Department of Justice and the Enforcement Division of the US Securities and Exchange Commission. The criminal penalties detailed in this guide explicitly allow for judicial discretion. The initial "offense level" depends on the details of the bribe, such as its level, and the cooperation of the offender. This base is then scaled by a "culpability score" which can reduce the fine to 5 percent of the base or raise it to 400 percent. This culpability score depends on firm characteristics such as the size of the organization and prior misconduct and corporate character. These are exactly the characteristics

[1] <www.justice.gov/criminal/fraud/fcpa/history/1977/houseprt-95-640.pdf>.

Table 18.2. Summary Statistics

	Mean	Median	StDev
Market Cap	29,086	6,420	55,834
KLD	−.915	−1	2.91
US Company	0.859	1	0.35
Sanction	28.9	5.25	83.2
Payments	8.45	2	24.8
Number of Years of Bribery	5.79	5	3.33
Value	230	66.5	734
Related Party Involved	0.521	1	0.503
Foreign Investigation Ongoing	0.127	0	0.335
Multiple Countries	0.408	0	0.495
Involved in Multiple Ongoing Trials	0.366	0	0.485
Repeat Offense	0.239	0	0.43

Note: These are summary statistics for the 71 FCPA cases that we can match to KLD data. Market capitalization, sanction, payments, and value are in millions of dollars.

people may ascribe to socially responsible firms. This discretion makes FCPA sanctions highly susceptible to the halo effect. Although the prosecutor does not consider the company's product when deciding on a sanction, it is quite likely that a firm's reputation for social responsibility would influence his or her opinion of their culpability.

To measure corporate social responsibility, we use the full sample of KLD scores. These scores were first collected in 1991 for 488 firms and coverage grew over the years to include 2,894 firms in 2009. On average roughly 1,486 firms are covered in every year. We start with a sample of 271 cases against corporations from 1991, the first year in which KLD scores are available.[2] In seventy-one of these cases, we can match the defendant's name to a company name in the KLD database. The characteristics of these firms are summarized in Table 18.2. The average firm involved in one of these FCPA cases has a market capitalization of $26 billion, with a median of $5 billion. These are larger than the average firm in the KLD sample, consistent with the fact that multi-national firms are larger and also have more opportunities to bribe. The mean and median KLD scores are around −1. In contrast, the average KLD in the full survey is 0.26 and the median is 0. The majority of these companies, 85 percent, are headquartered in the US, as expected given the jurisdiction of the FCPA.

Table 18.2 also describes the details of the bribes for which the firms are being prosecuted. The median sanction is $5 million. The median bribe involves a payment of $2 million, lasts five years, and results in a $66.5 million gain for the firm. In 52 percent of the FCPA actions, related companies, often subsidiaries, are involved. Many of the cases span multiple countries and jurisdictions; 40 percent take place in more than one country and 13 percent are part of a foreign investigation. The data also imply that the

---

[2] The data on FCPA cases is taken from the website of law firm Shearman & Sterling LLP, <http://fcpa.shearman.com/?s=matter&mode=list&tab=list>.

bribes in question are not usually a one-off offense but relate to a wider pattern of firm bribery: 37 percent of offending firms are involved in multiple FCPA trials at once, and 23 percent of cases stem from a repeat offense by a firm. Tables 18.3 and 18.4 further explore the types of companies and countries involved in these cases. In line with the report to the House of Representatives, offenses are not concentrated in any one industry. However, there is a good deal of disparity across countries, with a majority of bribes taking place in China and Iraq.

Table 18.3. Cases by Industry

Food	7
Oil	9
Apparel	2
Chemicals	2
Consumer Goods	7
Construction	2
Steel	1
Fabricated Products	2
Machinery	12
Transportation	3
Utilities	1
Other	23
Total	71

Note: Industries are defined as the 17 Fama-French industry portfolios.

Table 18.4. Cases by Country

Angola	4
Argentina	6
Brazil	4
China	21
Greece	5
India	6
Indonesia	8
Iraq	11
Nigeria	6
Poland	4
Russia	4
Thailand	8
United Arab Emirates	4
Total	91

Note: For brevity, we only display the countries for which there are more than 3 FCPA cases. The number of observations is larger than 71 because each FCPA case may involve multiple countries.

In order to test for a halo effect from corporate social responsibility, we estimate the relationship

$$p_i = \beta_0 + \beta H KLD_i + \beta BB_i + \beta FX_i + \epsilon_i$$

where the outcome variable pi is the punishment, as measured by the sanction assigned for FCPA case i. The variable KLD_i is the firm's overall *KLD* score in our main specification and the coefficient β_H identifies the halo effect. It represents the change in punishment for bribery offenses for firms with higher corporate social responsibility, holding all else equal. The details of the bribe are captured by B_i and firm characteristics are represented by X_i. In choosing relevant bribe, firm, and country characteristics, we were guided by our reading of the *Resource Guide* and by factors that Choi and Davis (2013) found relevant.[3]

For every bribe we include the amount of bribe payments and the value gained by the firm as a result of the bribe. When these variables are missing, we use the sample mean and include an indicator for missing variables. We also include in Bi the number of years the bribe spans and indicators for whether there are multiple parties involved in the bribe, whether it is being investigated by a foreign entity, whether it occurred in multiple countries, and whether it is a repeat offense by the firm. At the firm level, we control for whether the offender is a US company and also for its market capitalization. To account for the fact that more socially responsible industries may be looked upon more favorably, we also control for the average KLD within the firm's industry. This is an alternative to including industry fixed effects that allows us to lower the number of control variables. Results are similar but understandably less significant when we use industry fixed effects instead.

The results of the regression analysis are presented in Table 18.5. The firm's KLD score, as the independent variable of interest in this regression, we view as being determined by business circumstances as opposed to worries about the FCPA fines. In other words, we can treat the KLD scores as not having a reverse causality interpretation since KLD scores for product, environment, and diversity are clearly motivated by other considerations and not by worries about the FCPA fines themselves.[4]

Due to the small size of our sample, we are highly sensitive to relying on outliers for our result. To assuage this doubt, we show the results for a number of different specifications. Column (1) includes all observations. In column (2), sanction, value, and payments are winsorized at 2.5 percent and 97.5 percent. In column (3), these variables are winsorized at 95 percent. In column (4), we drop the observations that

---

[3] We do not have data on voluntary disclosure, cooperation, and remediation. While it is true that these variables may be correlated with CSR, Choi and Davis (2013) find that none of these variables seem to affect sanction amounts.

[4] The only subcategory that we might plausibly be worried about a reverse causality interpretation is KLD categories having to do with employees, where one might think that treating employees well cuts down on their chances of bribing officials in other countries. But even this interpretation is a stretch since employee scores are mostly driven by outcomes like employee strikes or unrest which seem more to do with whether the firm allows unions or not.

Table 18.5. Effect of CSR on Sanctions

	(1)	(2)	(3)	(4)
	Sanction	Sanction	Sanction	Sanction
KLD	−2.589[+]	−2.802[+]	−2.102[+]	−1.744
	(−1.85)	(−1.88)	(−1.81)	(−1.63)
Payments	2.083*	2.721*	1.072	2.114*
	(2.90)	(5.45)	(1.34)	(4.58)
Value	0.026	0.020	0.046	0.028
	(1.27)	(1.02)	(1.60)	(0.84)
No. of Years of Bribery	0.784	0.672	1.226	0.741
	(0.87)	(0.75)	(1.38)	(1.05)
Related Party Involved	0.338	−0.568	1.294	3.178
	(0.06)	(−0.10)	(0.26)	(0.88)
Foreign Investigation Ongoing	22.331*	25.992*	18.686*	20.363*
	(2.75)	(2.77)	(2.64)	(2.35)
Involved in Multiple Ongoing Trials	−18.000[+]	−20.268[+]	−13.924[+]	−7.518
	(−1.83)	(−1.82)	(−1.68)	(−1.11)
Multiple Countries	7.634	5.767	7.057	8.286[+]
	(1.29)	(0.84)	(1.33)	(1.84)
Repeat Offense	4.001	4.531	2.324	−6.419
	(0.37)	(0.37)	(0.28)	(−1.10)
US Company	−14.102	−13.778	−12.793	1.307
	(−1.34)	(−1.28)	(−1.25)	(0.19)
Market Cap	0.000	0.000	0.000	0.000
	(1.55)	(1.36)	(1.55)	(1.60)
Industry KLD	−2.080	−0.909	−2.427	1.668
	(−0.40)	(−0.17)	(−0.48)	(0.34)
Observations	71	71	71	63
R^2	0.964	0.937	0.687	0.694

Note: All regressions include year fixed effects and indicators for the missingness of payments and value. Market capitalization, sanction, payments, and value are in millions of dollars. Column (1) includes all observations. In column (2), sanction, value, and payments are winsorized at 2.5% and 97.5%. In column (3), these variables are winsorized at 95%. In column (4), the observations that were winsorized in column (3) are dropped. Standard errors are robust. * $p < 0.05$, + $p < 0.10$.

were winsorized in column (3). Our preferred specification is in column (3) because it limits the influence of outliers while still retaining the full sample.

In all four specifications of Table 18.5 firms with higher KLD receive significantly lower sanctions, all else being equal. On average a one point increase in the KLD score results in a reduction in sanction of $2 million. At 38 percent of the median sanction, this is a sizeable change in punishment. Recall that a one point increase in KLD requires a firm to change one corporate social responsibility indicator from a concern to neutral, or from neutral to a strength. Using the "retirement benefits" indicator as an example, a company would need to implement a "notable strong retirement benefits

Table 18.6. Effect of CSR on Sanctions, with Country Variables

	(1)	(2)	(3)	(4)
	Sanction	Sanction	Sanction	Sanction
KLD	−3.840*	−4.278*	−2.677*	−2.684[+]
	(−2.25)	(−2.19)	(−2.48)	(−1.89)
Payments	1.429	2.019*	−0.665	0.699
	(1.63)	(2.73)	(−0.84)	(0.64)
Value	0.037	0.030	0.058*	0.052
	(1.63)	(1.44)	(3.37)	(1.31)
No. of Years of Bribery	1.250	1.026	3.016*	1.959
	(1.06)	(0.80)	(2.59)	(1.48)
Foreign Investigation Ongoing	26.414[+]	32.931[+]	11.342	17.930[+]
	(1.92)	(1.89)	(1.42)	(1.79)
Involved in Multiple Ongoing Trials	24.614[+]	−32.109*	−2.075	−0.600
	(−1.84)	(−2.12)	(−0.23)	(−0.04)
Market Cap	0.000	0.000	0.000	0.000
	(1.08)	(1.21)	(0.72)	(0.76)
Industry KLD	−6.266	−6.657	5.553	6.735
	(−0.53)	(−0.50)	(0.73)	(0.94)
US FDI to Country	−0.000	−0.001	−0.000	0.000
	(−1.04)	(−1.15)	(−0.41)	(0.20)
Government GNI	0.002[+]	0.002[+]	0.001	0.000
	(1.79)	(1.76)	(1.27)	(0.84)
Government Rule of Law	−5.853	−12.945	2.217	5.307
	(−0.27)	(−0.56)	(0.13)	(0.39)
Government Effectiveness	−33.128	−29.216	−33.427[+]	−22.325
	(−1.41)	(−1.18)	(−1.76)	(−0.98)
Observations	56	56	56	49
R^2	0.964	0.918	0.753	0.734

Note: All regressions include year fixed effects and indicators for the missingness of payments and value. Market capitalization, sanction, payments, and value are in millions of dollars. Column (1) includes all observations. In column (2), sanction, value, and payments are winsorized at 2.5% and 97.5%. In column (3), these variables are winsorized at 95%. In column (4), the observations that were winsorized in column (3) are dropped. Standard errors are robust. * $p < 0.05$, + $p < 0.10$.

program." If it had an underfunded or subpar retirement benefits program in place, it would need to improve its funding or increase benefits.

One worry raised by these results is that corporate social responsibility may be correlated with the types of countries in which firms are willing to bribe. Bribery may be punished more harshly when committed in countries less equipped to battle corruption or countries in which the reputation of the US is important. To control for this possibility, we match in a number of country-specific variables for each country in which a bribe takes place. If a FCPA case covers multiple countries, we take the average over all countries involved. We control for the amount of US foreign direct investment (FDI) into the country in investment (FDI) into the country in 2004, the country's GNI, and the Worldwide Governance Indicators (WGI) measures for government effectiveness and rule of law. We are able to match these country-level variables for fifty-six of the cases. If the violations took place in multiple countries, we average over all countries involved. The results of these regressions are displayed in Table 18.6. Even taking into account country characteristics, it is still true that higher KLD firms are punished less for bribery. The point estimate is also very similar, implying a one point increase in KLD decreases sanctions by $3 million. The importance of KLD for the punishment of corporate crime is evidence of the presence of a halo effect for corporate social responsibility.

We more fully measure the halo effect of CSR in Hong and Liskovich (2014). We examine which components of KLD scores (diversity versus environment) affect sentencing outcomes more and whether lagged KLD scores from previous years predict sentencing outcomes (i.e. how persistent is the halo effect?) Finally, we also investigate whether the effect is likely to be rational or illusory by studying the incidence of bribery in high KLD firms and the types of bribes that these firms undertake as well as controlling for the possible influence of political connections and cooperation with the FCPA investigation.

Conclusion

In this chapter, we have argued that CSR is measurable and not simply greenwashing and that quasi-experiments borrowed from various strands of economics can help us understand the economic role of CSR. In contrast to field studies or experiments, which are open to the critique of extrapolative relevance, or panel data studies, which can only capture correlation and not causation, we show that a quasi-experiment using the 2003 dividend tax cut allows us to identify the portion of corporate socially responsibility driven by agency motives. Drawing the focus away from consumers and toward prosecution of the Foreign Corrupt Practices Act allows us to shed further light on the motivation for corporate responsibility by isolating a specific channel through which strategic CSR operates. We view these two sets of results as simply the beginning of a set of exciting inquiry into the increasingly important role of CSR in our society.

References

Andreoni, James (1989). Giving with Impure Altruism: Applications to Charity and Ricardian Equivalence. *Journal of Political Economy*, 97(1): 1447–58.

Angrist, Joshua D., and Alan B. Krueger (1991). Does Compulsory School Attendance Affect Schooling and Earnings? *Quarterly Journal of Economics*, 106(4): 979–1014. <http://ideas.repec.org/a/tpr/qjecon/v106y1991i4p979-1014.html>.

Auerbach, Alan J., and Kevin Hassett (2006). Dividend Taxes and Firm Valuation: New Evidence. *American Economic Review*, 96(2): 119–23.

Auerbach, Alan J., and Kevin Hassett (2007). The 2003 Dividend Tax Cuts and the Value of the Firm: An Event Study. In Alan J. Auerbach, J. Hines, and J. Slemrod (eds), *Taxing Corporate Income in the Twenty-First Century*. Cambridge: Cambridge University Press, 93–126.

Becker, Gary (1974). A Theory of Social Interaction. *Journal of Political Economy*, 82: 1063–93.

Benabou, Roland, and Jean Tirole (2010). Individual and Corporate Social Responsibility. *Economica*, 77: 1–19.

Besley, Tim, and M. Ghatak (2005). Competition and Incentives with Motivated Agents. *American Economic Review*, 95(3): 616–36.

Charness, Gary, and Matthew Rabin (2002). Understanding Social Preferences with Simple Tests. *Quarterly Journal of Economics*, 117(3): 817–69.

Chatterji, Aaron K., David I. Levine, and Michael W. Toffel (2009). How Well do Social Ratings Actually Measure Corporate Social Responsibility? *Journal of Economics and Management Strategy*, 18(1): 125–69.

Cheng, Ing-Haw, Harrison Hong, and Kelly Shue (2013). *Do Managers Do Good with Other People's Money?* Technical report, National Bureau of Economic Research.

Chetty, Raj, and Emmanuel Saez (2005). Dividend Taxes and Corporate Behavior: Evidence from the 2003 Dividend Tax Cut. *Quarterly Journal of Economics*, 120(3): 791–833.

Chetty, Raj, and Emmanuel Saez (2006). The Effects of the 2003 Dividend Tax Cut on Corporate Behavior: Interpreting the Evidence. *American Economic Review*, 96(2): 124–9.

Chetty, Raj, and Emmanuel Saez (2010). Dividend and Corporate Taxation in an Agency Model of the Firm. *American Economic Journal: Economic Policy*, 2(3): 1–31.

Choi, Stephen J., and Kevin E. Davis (2013). *Foreign Affairs and Enforcement of the Foreign Corrupt Practices Act*. Technical report, NYU Law and Economics Research Paper, 12–15; NYU School of Law, Public Law Research Paper, 12-35, Available at SSRN: <http://ssrn.com/abstract=2116487>, Dec.

DiGiuli, Alberta, and Leonard Kostovetsky (2011). *Are Red or Blue Companies More Likely to Go Green? Politics and Corporate Social Responsibility*. SSRN Working Paper, 2084900.

Elfenbein, Daniel W., Ray Fisman, and Brian McManus (2012). Charity as a Substitute for Reputation: Evidence from an Online Marketplace. *Review of Economic Studies*, 79(4): 1441–68.

Fehr, Ernst, and Klaus Schimdt (1999). A Theory of Fairness, Competition and Cooperation. *Quarterly Journal of Economics*, 114(3): 817–68.

Friedman, Milton (1970). The Social Responsibility of Business is to Increase its Profits. *New York Times Magazine*, Sept. 13, 122–6.

Greenfield, Rebecca (2011). Yes, You Can Think Less of Steve Jobs for Not Being a Philanthropist. *The Atlantic Wire*, Aug. <www.theatlanticwire.com/technology/2011/08/yes-you-can-think-less-stevejobs-not-being-philanthropist/41885> [Accessed July 2013].

Heal, Geoffrey (2005). Corporate Social Responsibility—Economic and Financial Perspectives. *Geneva Papers*, 30: 387–409.

Hong, Harrison, and Leonard Kostovetsky (2012). Red and Blue Investing: Values and Finance. *Journal of Financial Economics*, 103(1): 1–19.

Hong, Harrison, Jeffrey D. Kubik, and Jose A. Scheinkman (2011). *Financial Constraints on Corporate Goodness*. Princeton University Working Paper, Feb.

Hong, Harrison, and Inessa Liskovich (2014). *Crime, Punishment and the Halo Effect of Corporate Social Responsibility*. Technical report, Princeton University Working Paper, Mar.

Jensen, Michael C., and William H. Meckling (1976). Theory of the Firm: Managerial Behavior, Agency Costs and Ownership Structure. *Journal of Financial Economics*, 3(4): 305–60.

Kitzmueller, Markus, and Jay Shimshack (2012). Economic Perspectives on Corporate Social Responsibility. *Journal of Economic Literature*, 50(1): 51–84.

Lee, David S. (2008). Randomized Experiments from Non-Random Selection in U.S. House Elections. *Journal of Econometrics*, 142(2): 675–97. <http://ideas.repec.org/a/eee/econom/v142y2008i2p675-697.html>.

List, John A. (2006). The Behavioralist Meets the Market: Measuring Social Preferences and Reputation Effects in Actual Transactions. *Journal of Political Economy*, 114(1): 1–37.

Margolis, Joshua D., Hillary A. Elfeinbein, and James P. Walsh (2009). *Does it Pay to be Good . . . and does it Matter? A Meta-Analysis of the Relationship between Corporate Social and Financial Performance*. SSRN Working Paper, 1866371.

Milgrom, Paul, and John Roberts (1986). Price and Advertising Signals of Product Quality. *Journal of Political Economy*, 796–821.

Nisbett, Richard E., and Timothy D. Wilson (1977). The Halo Effect: Evidence for Unconscious Alteration of Judgments. *Journal of Personality and Social Psychology*, 35(4): 250.

Poterba, James (2004). Taxation and Corporate Payout Policy. *American Economic Review*, 94(2): 171–5.

Shleifer, Andrei, and Robert W. Vishny (1986). Large Shareholders and Corporate Control. *Journal of Political Economy*, 94(3): 461–88.

Thorndike, Edward L. (1920). A Constant Error in Psychological Ratings. *Journal of Applied Psychology*, 4(1): 25–9.

Tirole, Jean (2001). Corporate Governance. *Econometrica*, 69(1): 1–35.

....

CHAPTER 19

POSITIONAL
EXTERNALITIES AS
A SOURCE OF MARKET
FAILURE

....

ROBERT H. FRANK

Abstract

In contrast to many of his modern disciples, Adam Smith never believed that unfettered markets always ensure socially benign outcomes. To him, what was remarkable was that self-interested actions often led to socially benign outcomes. Like Smith, modern progressives tend to attribute the market's failings to conspiracies by powerful corporate actors. This chapter defends the competing view that those shortcomings are rooted in competition among individuals for relative advantage. Discrepancies between individual and collective interest help explain the presence of overtime laws, workplace safety regulations, and many other institutional features of the modern welfare state. These features would be useful even if all consumers were perfectly informed and markets took the perfectly competitive ideal form described in textbooks.

Adam Smith's invisible hand theory was a groundbreaking insight. Many writers before Smith realized that producers generally introduce improved product designs and cost-saving innovations not to help society, but to capture market share and profits from their rivals. In the short run, these steps work just as producers had hoped. But what Smith saw more clearly than earlier writers was that, because rival firms are quick to mimic the innovations, the resulting competition quickly causes prices to fall in line with the new, lower costs. In the end, he argued, consumers are the ultimate beneficiaries of all this churning.

There is indeed little doubt that market forces have done much to alleviate poverty around the globe. But many of Smith's modern disciples believe he made the much bolder claim that markets *always* harness individual self-interest to serve the common good. Our invitation to gather for this meeting presumes widespread disagreement with that premise.

Smith's own account, for that matter, was far more circumspect than that of his modern acolytes. He wrote (2005: 364), for example, that a profit-seeking business owner "intends only his own gain, and he is in this, as in many other cases, led by an invisible hand to promote an end which was no part of his intention. *Nor is it always the worse for the society that it was not part of it* [emphasis added]."

Smith never believed that the invisible hand guaranteed good outcomes in all circumstances. His skepticism was on full display, for example, when he wrote (2005: 111), "People of the same trade seldom meet together, even for merriment and diversion, but the conversation ends in a conspiracy against the public, or in some contrivance to raise prices." To him, what was remarkable was that self-interested actions often led to socially benign outcomes.[1]

Like Smith, modern progressive critics of the market system tend to attribute its failings to conspiracies by powerful actors. In this chapter, I'll attempt to defend the competing view that the market outcomes people worry most about are not rooted primarily in excessive enterprise power. Many firms are indeed large and powerful. But even such firms, for the most part, do what consumers demand of them. That's usually how they got to be large and powerful in the first place, after all, and increasingly it's what's required for them to remain so.

Absent the threat of violence, there are limits on the extent to which people can be manipulated to do what they'd prefer not to. Advertising by powerful tobacco companies, for example, has only a small influence on the smoking rate. Its primary effect is to move existing smokers from one brand to another. Lots of people smoke heavily even in countries in which cigarette are produced by small companies that don't advertise at all.

My main focus here will be on how concerns about relative position give rise to behaviors with harmful, if unintended, side effects—which for short I'll call positional externalities. I'll describe how positional concerns shape individual demands and how those, in turn, influence how enterprises respond. I believe that most of the problems we all worry so much about stem from a fundamental conflict between what it's rational for individuals to want and what we want collectively. It's a simple idea, really. If others are standing to get a better view, it's rational for me to stand, too, even though we'd all be happier if we could remain comfortably seated.

---

[1] For a comprehensive account of how laissez-faire enthusiasts have often misrepresented Adam Smith's positions, see Sen (2009).

A Troubling Feature of the Left's Critique of Capitalism

Much of the modern skepticism about market outcomes was spawned by the work of John Kenneth Galbraith, who died in 2005 at the age of 97. The Nobel Prize in economics is not given posthumously, so Galbraith will never receive one. Yet he was easily the most widely read economist of the twentieth century and was also considered one of the most influential.

There are, of course, many distinguished economists who never receive a Nobel. But the list of winners also includes some whose work has had little lasting impact. Why, then, did the Nobel committee pass on each of its thirty-six opportunities to select Galbraith?

In *The Affluent Society*, published in 1958, he argued that Americans would lead longer, more fulfilling lives if they spent less on private luxuries and more on their external environments. As he memorably put it (1958: 223): "The family which takes its mauve and cerise, air-conditioned, power-steered, and power-braked automobile out for a tour passes through cities that are badly paved, made hideous by litter, blighted buildings, billboards, and posts for wires that should long since have been put underground."

The standards that define luxury consumption have of course escalated considerably since he wrote those words. Yet with 40,000-square-foot mansions springing up all around us even as our government tells us we cannot afford to repair our crumbling roads and bridges, his assessment still resonates. Why, then, wasn't his work more warmly received by his fellow economists?

A succinct answer was offered by Milton Friedman, himself one of the first Nobel laureates in economics and at once Galbraith's longtime friend and passionate intellectual adversary. Interviewed just after Galbraith's death, Friedman characterized his rival's work as "not so much economics as it is sociology."

Although many economists shared Galbraith's skepticism about prevailing spending patterns, they were also skeptical of his explanation of the imbalance. According to standard economic models, consumers scrutinize the list of available goods, then select those that best suit their preferences. But in Galbraith's account, the causal arrow traveled in reverse: firms first decide which goods are most convenient to produce, and then employ marketing wizardry to persuade consumers to buy them.

Most economists readily conceded that firms would gladly exploit consumers in this fashion if they could. Yet most also doubted that firms had much power to do so in the long run. Galbraith's account, they felt, gave short shrift to the inventiveness of greedy rival capitalists.

His critics argued, for example, that if consumers were paying high prices for goods of little intrinsic value, there would be "cash on the table"—the economist's metaphor for unexploited profit opportunities. In today's information-rich environment, rivals could easily identify poorly served consumers and earn easy money by luring them away with slightly cheaper and better offerings. Why, they wondered, shouldn't the same marketing prowess that enabled Galbraith's firms to bamboozle consumers also enable rivals to attract consumers to better options?

These critics had a point. Indeed, Galbraith's explanation for society's spending imbalance suffered from the same deficiency that has plagued arguments of social critics on the left since Karl Marx. Because it implied that greedy capitalists were leaving cash on the table, most economists couldn't accept it. To this day, however, many remain equally skeptical of Milton Friedman's competing claim that unbridled market forces ensure optimal allocation of society's resources.

But those who continue to believe that market failure results primarily from excessive corporate power might do well to reconsider. In an earlier era, limited information and high transport costs enabled firms offering inferior products or exploitative jobs to survive for extended periods. That's much less likely today. If someone is paying too much for a shoddy product, or is being denied a safety device that he values at more than its cost, rival firms can quickly confront that person with a better offer and boost their profits in the process. Markets still aren't the totally frictionless ideal assumed in textbooks, but the most important frictions are much less important than before.

An Equilibrium Explanation of Insufficient Workplace Safety

Galbraith studied at the University of California at Berkeley in the 1930s. Had he received his training decades later, he would have been better equipped to come up with explanations that might have satisfied his critics. For instance, modern game theory, a staple of current economics programs, shows why bad allocations often occur even in highly competitive markets in which well-informed consumers and firms are doing the best they can individually.

Thomas C. Schelling, a pioneering game theorist who won the Nobel Prize in economics in 2005, offered an example that neatly captures the idea. He began with the observation that hockey players, left to their own devices, invariably skate without helmets. Yet when they vote in secret ballots, they almost always favor a rule requiring helmets. Schelling (1978) asked, if helmets are a good idea, why don't players just wear them on their own? Elsewhere (Frank 1985, 2011) I have argued that his answer to that question will eventually transform the way economists think about the relationship between competition and social welfare.

When reward depends primarily on absolute performance—the standard presumption in economics ever since Adam Smith—individual choice does indeed turn out to be remarkably efficient. But when reward depends primarily on relative performance, as in hockey, the invisible hand breaks down. In such situations, unrestricted choices by rational individuals often yield results that no one favors.

To explain why, Schelling observed that, by skating without a helmet, a player increases his team's odds of winning, perhaps because he can see and hear a little better, or more effectively intimidate opponents. The downside is that he also increases his odds of injury. If he values the higher odds of winning more than he values the extra safety, he will discard his helmet. Yet when others inevitably follow suit, the competitive balance is restored—so that while everyone faces more risk, no one benefits. And hence the attraction of helmet rules.

As in hockey, many of the most important outcomes in life depend on relative position. Because a "good" school is an inescapably relative concept, for example, each family's quest to provide a better education for its children has much in common with the athlete's quest for competitive advantage. Families try to buy houses in the best school districts they can afford, yet when all families spend more, the result is merely to bid up the prices of those houses. Half of all children must still attend bottom-half schools.

Schelling's example thus suggests a radical new perspective on the various ways in which societies restrict individual choice. Consider the similarity between helmet rules and workplace safety regulations. Because riskier jobs pay higher wages, workers can gain relative advantage by accepting such jobs. Just as unrestricted hockey players may feel compelled to discard their helmets, workers who are free to trade their safety for higher wages may realize that failure to do so will consign their children to inferior schools. In each case, limiting our options can prevent a mutually disadvantageous race to the bottom.

The logic of Schelling's example also challenges the economist's cherished theory of revealed preference, which holds that we learn more about what people value by watching what they do than by listening to what they say. If someone chooses a risky job paying $1,000 instead of a safer one paying $900, the theory concludes that he must value the extra safety at less than $100. Maybe, but only in the limited sense that a bareheaded hockey player reveals that he values winning above safety. In both cases, we may learn more about what people value by examining the rules they support than by studying their individual choices.

HOURS REGULATION

Adam Smith's modern disciples often denounce the Fair Labor Standards Act, which requires employers to pay overtime premiums for all hours worked in excess of forty each week, noting that many workers would voluntarily work the longer hours that employers would have offered in the absence of premiums. Yet here, too, the incentives confronting workers are much like those confronting hockey players.

Thus, as Schelling's fellow Nobel laureate George A. Akerlof has written (1976), people can often increase their odds of promotion by working longer hours, but when others follow suit, everyone's promotion prospects remain roughly as before. The result is often a rat race in which all must work until 8 o'clock each evening merely to avoid falling behind. As these examples make clear, there can be no presumption that the self-serving choices of rational individuals produce the greatest good for all.

REGULATING FINANCIAL MARKETS

Asset bubbles like the one that caused the most recent economic crisis have long plagued financial markets. But like hurricanes in the Gulf of Mexico, these crises have been occurring more often. If we want to prevent them, we must first understand their causes.

It isn't simply "Wall Street greed," which Senator John McCain quickly blamed for the 2008 crisis. Coming from McCain, a longtime champion of financial industry deregulation, it was a puzzling attribution, one squarely at odds with the cherished belief of free-market enthusiasts everywhere that unbridled pursuit of self-interest promotes the common good. As Smith wrote (2005: 19) in *The Wealth of Nations*, "It is not from the benevolence of the butcher, the brewer, or the baker that we expect our dinner, but from their regard to their own interest."

Greed underlies every market outcome, good or bad. When important conditions are met, greed not only poses no threat to Smith's invisible hand, but is actually an essential part of it.

The forces that produced the current crisis reflect a powerful dynamic that afflicts all kinds of competitive endeavors. This dynamic is again on vivid display in the world of sports.

Consider a sprinter's decision about whether to take anabolic steroids. His reward depends not on how fast he runs in absolute terms, but on how his times compare with those of others. Imagine a new drug that enhances performance by three-tenths of a second in the 100-meter dash. Almost impossible to detect, it also entails a small risk of serious health problems. The sums at stake ensure that many competitors will take the drug, making it all but impossible for a drug-free competitor to win. The net effect is increased health risks for all athletes, but no real gain for society.

This particular type of market failure occurs when two conditions are met. First, people confront a gamble that offers a highly probable small gain with only a very small chance of a significant loss. Second, the rewards received by market participants depend strongly on relative performance.

These conditions, which are met in both the hockey helmet and steroid examples, have caused the invisible hand to break down in many other domains in the market-place. In unregulated housing markets, for example, there are invariably too many dwellings built on flood plains and in earthquake zones. And as noted earlier, workers typically face excessive health and safety risks in unregulated labor markets.

It is no different in unregulated financial markets, where easy credit terms almost always produce an asset bubble. The problem occurs because, just as in sports, an investment fund's success depends less on its absolute rate of return than on how that rate compares with those of rivals.

If one fund posts higher earnings than others, money immediately flows into it. And because managers' pay depends primarily on how much money a fund oversees, managers want to post relatively high returns at every moment.

One way to bolster a fund's return is to invest in slightly riskier assets. (Such investments generally pay higher returns because risk-averse investors would otherwise be unwilling to hold them.) Before the current crisis, once some fund managers started offering higher-paying mortgage-backed securities, others felt growing pressure to follow suit, lest their customers desert them.

Warren Buffett warned about a similar phenomenon during the tech bubble of the late 1990s. Buffett said he wouldn't invest in tech stocks because he didn't understand the business model. Investors knew him to be savvy, yet the relatively poor performance of his Berkshire Hathaway fund during the tech stock run-up persuaded many to move their money elsewhere. Buffett had the personal and financial resources to weather that storm. But most money managers did not, and the tech bubble kept growing.

A similar dynamic precipitated our most recent crisis. The new mortgage-backed securities were catnip for investors, much as steroids are for athletes. Many money managers knew that these securities were risky. As long as housing prices kept rising, however, they also knew that portfolios with high concentrations of the riskier assets would post higher returns, enabling them to attract additional investors. More important, they assumed that, if things went wrong, there would be safety in numbers. An advisor could hardly be blamed for giving the same advice everyone else was giving.

Phil Gramm, the former senator from Texas, and other proponents of financial industry deregulation insisted that market forces would provide ample protection against excessive risk. Lenders obviously don't want to make loans that won't be repaid, and borrowers have clear incentives to shop for favorable terms. And because everyone agrees that financial markets are highly competitive, Gramm's invocation of the invisible-hand theory persuaded many other lawmakers.

But again, all bets regarding the invisible hand are off when rewards depend heavily on relative performance. A high proportion of investors are simply unable to stand idly by while others who appear no smarter or more hardworking than they are nonetheless earn conspicuously higher returns. This simple fact of human nature makes the invisible hand an unreliable shield against excessive financial risk.

Many people respond by advocating greater transparency in the market for poorly understood derivative securities. More stringent disclosure rules would no doubt be desirable for multiple reasons. But they would not prevent future crises, any more than disclosing the relevant health risks would prevent athletes from taking steroids.

The only effective remedy is to change people's incentives. In sports, that means drug rules backed by strict enforcement. In financial markets, asset bubbles cause real trouble when investors can borrow freely to expand their holdings. To prevent such bubbles, we must limit the amounts that people can invest with borrowed money.

Most societies already do that, at least to some extent. And those that embraced such restrictions most fully—Canada, for example—suffered least during the global downturn.

MANDATORY SAVINGS

Before the introduction of the American social security system, a much larger proportion of senior citizens spent their retirement years at or below the poverty line. Much of the resulting discomfort could have been avoided if they had saved more during their working lives.

Social security is not a savings program. Basically it collects tax revenue from workers, which it then transfers to retirees. But from each individual's point of view, it is the functional equivalent of a mandatory savings program. The government takes a portion of your wages, and then makes funds available to you in retirement.

Why did government introduce this program, which libertarians often denounce as a violation of people's right to decide for themselves when and how much to save? One possible answer is that most people lack the discipline to save adequately for retirement. And since humanitarian concerns will predictably prompt government intervention to prevent widespread starvation among retirees, a fairer approach might be to ask people to underwrite such support with additional tax payments during their working years.

Yet many Americans would have had difficulty achieving adequate savings even if they had exceptional self-discipline. The basic incentive problem is captured in the following thought experiment:

> *If you were society's median earner, which option would you prefer?*
> You save enough to support a comfortable standard of living in retirement, but your children attend a school whose students score in the 20th percentile on standardized tests in reading and math;
> *or,*
> You save too little to support a comfortable standard of living in retirement, but your children attend a school whose students score in the 50th percentile on those tests.

It is an unpleasant choice, to be sure, but most people say they would pick the second option.

Again, because the concept of a "good" school is relative, this thought experiment captures an essential element of the savings decision confronting most families.

If others bid for houses in better school districts, failure to do likewise will often consign one's children to inferior schools. But again, no matter how much each family spends, half of all children must attend schools in the bottom half.

The savings decision thus resembles the collective action problem inherent in a military arms race. Each nation knows that it would be better if everyone spent less on arms. Yet if others keep spending, it may be too dangerous not to follow suit. Curtailing an arms race requires an enforceable agreement. Similarly, unless all families can bind themselves to save more, those who do so unilaterally risk having to send their children to inferior schools.

Americans are of course not the only ones who face temptation and collective action problems. Why do people in other countries generally save much more than Americans do? One possible explanation is that both problems are made worse by income disparities, which have widened much faster in the US than elsewhere.

A collective agreement that each family save a portion of its income growth each year would attack both sources of the savings shortfall. Such an agreement might specify that one-third of income growth be diverted into savings until a target savings rate—say, 12 percent of income—was achieved. A family whose income did not rise in a given year would be exempt from the agreement.

Such an agreement would put the magic of compound interest to work for retirement savings, a benefit that the current social security system completely misses. Most of the money currently taken from workers in payroll taxes gathers no interest in the decades before their retirement. Instead, it is paid directly to current retirees, who spend it on rent and food. We have a pay-as-we-go system because the program was started in the Great Depression, when there was simply no money to create a fully financed system.

Many would object that requiring families to save a portion of each year's income growth would be an infringement of individual liberty. Yet it may be the very absence of such a requirement that currently prevents most American families from saving as much as they wish to. Just as nations find it advantageous to restrict their options by signing arms reduction treaties, families may have a similar interest in limiting their freedom to engage in bidding wars for houses in top school districts.

It is clear, in any event, that failure to save entails risks of its own to freedom. America's rapidly rising debt to foreigners now threatens the economic prosperity on which so many of our cherished liberties depend.

PROGRESSIVE TAXATION

Every year at tax time, libertarians mount the stump in high dudgeon, indignantly denouncing government income transfers from rich to poor. Society's income distribution, they argue, should reflect as closely as possible what people would earn in unregulated private markets.

When critics on the left counter that income transfers are required in the name of social justice, libertarians yawn—and the debate goes nowhere.

There may be a more fruitful way to frame this issue. Suppose, for the sake of discussion, that we grant the libertarian premise that private pay systems provide an acceptable ethical template for society's income distribution. As closer scrutiny of that premise will make clear, the libertarian denunciation of income transfers still fails on its own terms.

The main problem is that private pay patterns embody an implicit tax that is actually far more progressive than the Federal income tax. To understand why, first consider some background about the way these patterns work.

Economic theory holds that, in competitive labor markets, workers are paid the market value of what they produce. In actual markets, pay does rise with productivity, but not by much. The most productive carpenter in a framing crew, for example, might produce twice as much as his least productive colleague, but is rarely paid even 30 percent more.

To see the pattern at first hand, consider groups of co-workers who perform similar tasks in your own organization. In one case, suppose that your two most productive co-workers leave the job; in the other, suppose that the three least productive leave. Which group's departure would cause a greater loss of value? Most people would answer that losing the top two would hurt more.

If so, economic theory holds that their combined salaries should be higher than the combined salaries of the bottom three. Yet the typical pattern is the reverse: any three workers in a group performing similar tasks earn substantially more than any other two.

In short, the startling fact is that private businesses typically transfer large amounts of income from the most productive to the least productive workers. Because labor contracts are voluntary under United States law, it would be bizarre to object that these transfers violate anyone's rights.

But they do raise an interesting question: if the most productive workers in a group are paid less than the value of what they produce, why don't rival employers just lure them all away?

One answer is that these employees appear to care, albeit often subconsciously, about things besides pay. The most productive workers in a group, for example, often appear to value their status, perhaps because they enjoy greater self-esteem and respect than the least productive workers. To bid successfully for the high achievers, a rival employer might not only have to increase their pay, but also place them in a group where they continue to enjoy a high ranking.

In a free market, however, no one can be in the top half of any group unless others agree to be in the bottom half. And if people prefer not to occupy low-ranking positions, filling these positions would require extra compensation. The rival's offer, then, would have to resemble the original pay pattern.

The upshot is that the ostensibly underpaid top-ranked workers may have no incentive to leave. The high ranking they enjoy appears to be more than enough to offset their sacrifice in pay. Similarly, their less productive co-workers may find it onerous to be at the bottom of the ladder, but they appear adequately compensated for that fact by their premium wages.

In effect, then, private markets are already applying an implicit progressive tax in the way they pay workers. And in the process, they serve the interests of everyone in the hierarchy. The alternative would be costly social fragmentation.

Can anyone doubt that high rank has value, not just among groups of co-workers but also in society more broadly? For starters, high-ranking members of society, who also tend to have the highest incomes, know they will be able to send their children to the best schools and have access to the best health care. Low-ranking members enjoy no such confidence.

It's much harder, of course, to organize new societies than to start new businesses. But that doesn't mean high-ranking positions in the real world should be available at no cost. They are possible only when others bear the costs associated with a low social ranking.

Tax systems that transfer income from rich to poor, thus mimicking the implicit transfers in virtually every private labor contract, reflect the costs and benefits of different rungs on the social ladder. They help make stable, diverse societies possible.

Enlightened libertarians believe that the best social institutions mimic the agreements people would have negotiated among themselves, if free exchange had been practical. Private pay patterns suggest that our current tax code meets that test.

BETTER STILL: A PROGRESSIVE CONSUMPTION TAX

For more than thirty years now, I have been proposing a progressive tax on consumption. The basic idea is simple. You report your income to the tax authorities as you do now, and you also report how much you saved during the year—as we already do for taxexempt retirement accounts. Your income minus your savings is how much you spent during the year, and that amount minus a large standard deduction (to allow for the people at the bottom who do not save much) is your taxable consumption. Taxes are levied on that amount, with rates that start very low, then rise steadily as taxable consumption rises.

That simple policy change would deflect much of today's luxury consumption into additional investment. Having more investment and fewer mansions and expensive parties will help fuel additional growth. And there is no evidence at all that, if mansion size grew more slowly, the wealthy would be any less happy than before. Beyond some point, across-the-board growth in mansion size serves only to raise the bar that defines how big a mansion the wealthy feel they need.

Similarly, there's no evidence that growth in the amount that American families spend on weddings—almost $30,000 on average now, up from about $10,000 in

1980—has made marrying couples any happier. The main effect has been to raise the standard that defines what families feel they must spend to acknowledge the importance of special occasions. A progressive consumption tax would provide powerful incentives to curtail such arms races.

Growth in certain kinds of consumption threatens the environment, and we need to use available policy levers—such as a tax on carbon emissions—to restrain growth in those areas. But when income grows, many aspects of society that we really value get better. The air gets cleaner, the cures for diseases are discovered more quickly, and so on. Economic growth is a good thing, as long as society is prepared to help direct how it's used.

Many people applaud a progressive consumption tax in principle only to lament that its adoption would be politically impossible. But although tax policy changes are always difficult, support for the progressive consumption tax is surprisingly diverse. A progressive consumption tax was proposed in the US Senate during 1995, for example, under bipartisan sponsorship.

One week after I published an article about this tax in 1997, I received a warm letter from Milton Friedman, who began by saying that he didn't agree with me that the US government should be raising and spending additional revenue (Federal budgets at the time were edging toward surplus). But he quickly added that, if the government did need additional revenue, a progressive consumption tax would be by far the best way to raise it. He enclosed a reprint of his 1943 *American Economic Review* article in which he advocated a progressive consumption tax as the best way to pay for World War II.

More recently, two economists from the American Enterprise Institute, the conservative think tank, have published a book extolling the virtues of a progressive consumption tax (Viard and Carroll 2012).

The progressive consumption tax is, in effect, a Pigovian tax on positional externalities. It's a crude instrument, to be sure. In a world of complete information and perfect government, we could simply set a different tax rate for every good in accordance with the extent to which context shapes its evaluation. The most positional goods would be taxed most heavily, the next-most positional goods would be taxed at slightly lower rates, and so on. But although researchers have begun to estimate the differences in the extent to which context influences demands for specific categories of goods, existing knowledge is far too fragmentary to support such an ambitious approach.

Even if we knew much more about these magnitudes, it would be politically costly to establish a separate tax rate for every good. Lobbyists would inundate legislators with studies purporting to show why their particular client's product or service was nonpositional and therefore entitled to tax-exempt status.

This simpler alternative of a steeply progressive tax on total consumption expenditure rests on the observation that positional concerns are stronger for luxuries than necessities. There are obvious pitfalls in trying to identify specific goods as luxuries. But given that luxury is an inherently context-dependent phenomenon, it's uncontroversial to say that the last dollars spent by those who spend most are most likely to be spent on luxuries. A steeply progressive consumption tax is thus a luxury tax that completely sidesteps the need to identify specific goods as luxuries.

It might seem natural to worry that a tax that limits consumption could lead to recession and unemployment. Under normal economic conditions, however, money that is not spent on consumption would be saved and invested. Many who are now employed to produce consumption goods would instead be employed to produce capital goods. This would increase the economy's productive capacity and growth rate in the long run.

Should a recession occur in the short run, a more powerful fiscal remedy would be available under a consumption tax than is currently available under the income tax. A standard textbook remedy for recession is a temporary income tax cut. One problem, however, is that those who remain employed have a strong incentive to save their tax cuts as a hedge against the possibility of becoming unemployed. A temporary consumption tax cut would sidestep this difficulty, since the only way consumers could benefit from it would be to spend more money now.

Transition problems could be minimized by introducing the program gradually—with phased increases in the amount of savings a family could exempt and phased increases in the highest marginal tax rates.

If a progressive consumption surtax were enacted into law today and scheduled for gradual phase-in once the economy was back at full employment, it would produce immediate, off-budget economic stimulus by giving wealthy families powerful incentives to accelerate future spending. For example, a family that had been planning to build a new wing onto its mansion, or buy a yacht, would want to make those purchases now rather than be taxed on them later.

Stimulating a new luxury spending spree may not seem an ideal way to stimulate the economy. Far better, perhaps, would be for the government to repair dilapidated bridges and build high-speed trains. But continuing political gridlock appears to foreclose those options. Rather than sit idly by, it would be much better to provoke an additional burst of luxury spending than to let high unemployment linger for years.

Concluding Remarks

Smith's invisible hand theory assumes that reward depends only on absolute performance. But as Charles Darwin's theory of evolution by natural selection made abundantly clear, life is graded on the curve. It's not how big or strong or smart you are that matters, it's how you compare on those dimensions with your direct competitors. And for that simple reason, no one should be surprised that concerns about relative position are such a central feature of human preferences.

Yet traditional economic models continue to ignore these concerns. Until we weave the consequences of such concerns into our narrative about government's role in market economies, we'll continue to miss opportunities for substantial mutual gain.

References

Akerlof, George A. (1976). The Economics of Caste and of the Rat Race, and Other Woeful Tales. *Quarterly Journal of Economics*, 90/4: 599–617.

Frank, Robert H. (1985). *Choosing the Right Pond*, New York: Oxford University Press.

Frank, Robert H. (1997). The Frame of Reference as a Public Good. *Economic Journal*, 107 (Nov.): 1832–47.

Frank, Robert H. (2011). *The Darwin Economy*. Princeton: Princeton University Press.

Friedman, Milton (1943). The Expenditure Tax as a Wartime Measure. *American Economic Review*, 33 (Mar.): 50–62.

Galbraith, John Kenneth (1958). *The Affluent Society*. Boston, MA: Houghton Mifflin.

Schelling, Thomas C. (1978). *Micromotives and Macrobehavior*. New York: W. W. Norton.

Sen, Amartya (2009). Introduction to the 250th-Anniversary Edition of Smith's *The Theory of Moral Sentiments*. New York: Penguin.

Smith, Adam (2005). *An Inquiry into the Nature and Causes of the Wealth of Nations*. State College, PA: Penn State University (originally publ. in 1776).

Viard, Alan D., and Robert Carroll (2012). *Progressive Consumption Taxation: The X-Tax Revisited*. Washington, DC, American Enterprise Institute.

....

CHAPTER 20

WELL-BEING, VALUES, AND IMPROVING LIVES

....

VALERIE TIBERIUS

Abstract

While large-scale crises such as global poverty or climate change require large-scale solutions, individual agents—as consumers, activists, voters, and leaders—certainly must play a role. This chapter proposes a theory of individual well-being that affords a strategy for generating reasons to do better by the world that also promote long-term self-interest. The theory defended characterizes well-being in terms of value fulfillment over time, and it holds that a person's current values might be in need of improvement or modification to count as best for the person over time. After an overview and brief defense of the theory, the chapter turns to the question of how a person's values might be modified and improved in ways that benefit both the person and the planet.

With the growth of the global economy and the world population have come a variety of growing pains (or, less euphemistically, problems): climate change, an increasing gap between rich and poor, health consequences associated with the availability of cheap but nutrition-poor food, large-scale economic upheaval, and so on. Of course, there have also been some good consequences of economic growth (a decrease in the percentage of the world's people who are poor, malnourished, or illiterate), but the trajectory of the largest problems is troubling: for example, global climate change threatens to undo much of the progress that has been made and to make certain problems (such as the gap between rich and poor) much worse.

Large-scale problems require large-scale, structural solutions that draw on the resources of governments and institutions. Nevertheless, it is worth thinking about the individual's role in guiding the world toward real progress, if only because the policies that large institutions devise must ultimately act on individual people. Individuals contribute to large-scale problems in at least three ways. First, in the aggregate, individual consumer choices exacerbate problems such as climate change. Second, lack of individual attention to and concern for large-scale problems influences corporate and government policy or allows such policies to go unchecked. The preferences, choices, interests, and votes of individual citizens do play a role in creating and maintaining global problems. Moreover, insofar as institutions or organizations aim to change behavior through regulation, policy, or consumer incentives, they must consider the motives and values of the individual. Third, the institutions and organizations whose policies may have large-scale effects are still led by individual politicians, policy-makers, and businesspeople. As this volume attests, corporate leaders with the right values can make a difference on a large scale.

One way to frame the problem of the individual's role in furthering solutions to global problems that will be familiar to philosophers is as the problem "why be moral?" Think of it this way: there are various actions that individuals could take (using public transportation, for example) that are such that, were everyone to take these actions, some large-scale problems (climate disrupting carbon emissions) would be reduced. From the point of view of self-interest, individuals prefer the convenience of driving alone in their cars. There is a moral reason to sacrifice convenience for the sake of avoiding global catastrophe, but this moral reason does not move many of us. Hence the question: why be moral? Or, in other words, why care about the moral reasons that there are to sacrifice our own interests? This brief description grossly oversimplifies, of course. It's not actually clear what we have moral reason to do in cases of collective action problems, for instance. But I think the basic conflict between self-interested and moral reasons can be found in many cases of individual contribution to global problems. Even if the coordination problems could be solved so that individuals would know that their actions were not in vain, there would still be people who would not want to sacrifice their own comfort, convenience, or money for the sake of the greater good.

Solutions to the "why be moral?" problem have ranged across two extremes. The Hobbesian response takes self-interest in its narrowest sense (self-interest as survival and desire satisfaction) and holds that our reasons to act morally depend on an enforcement mechanism that makes it worth our while in this narrow sense. The Kantian response, on the other hand, rejects the demand for self-interested reasons to be moral: the moral law imposes rational requirements on us and these imperatives give us reasons independently of our self-interested desires.

There have also been responses in the middle that weave self-interest and morality together so that moral reasons and self-interested reasons are not so starkly distinguished. In this chapter I explore the resources of one such middle path. I take the goal here to be to articulate an ideal of a good human life that locates moral reasons in the overall pursuit of well-being for an individual in a way that is constrained by psychological reality. The middle path is attractive insofar as it characterizes an ethical life in such a way that it doesn't demand so much of us that there's no hope for it.

This is a very large goal, obviously, and I can only make incremental progress in a single essay. The bulk of the chapter is devoted to presenting an overview of a theory of well-being as value fulfillment. I will not be able to argue conclusively for the view, which would require defending it against the alternatives; rather, I'll just explain what it is and why it is attractive. One of the things that I think is promising about the theory is the way it leads us to think about personal transformation or improvement, where making changes in one's life in response to global moral crises is one example. I'll turn to an explanation of this promise in the second part of the chapter. Here, I'll consider how well-being as value fulfillment creates opportunities for critical evaluation and development of one's own preferences in ways that would, for example, contribute to the moral challenges we face—opportunities, to echo a metaphor mentioned by Ramón Mendiola (Chapter 17), to change from a caterpillar to a butterfly.

WELL-BEING AS VALUE FULFILLMENT

Overview

The big challenge for theories of well-being is to explain both why well-being is good and why it is good for the creature whose well-being it is. In other words, to use some philosophical jargon, the best theory must capture both the subjectivity and the normativity of well-being.[1] Theories that define well-being in terms of people's psychological states such as their desires or feeling of satisfaction have a ready explanation for the subjectivity of well-being, but have a more difficult time explaining why it gives us good reasons to do things. Theories that define well-being in terms of objective values do better at explaining why well-being is supposed to generate good reasons, but they have a greater challenge explaining the special connection to the individual subject. I think that the way to meet the challenge is to define well-being in terms of psychological features of individual people that are subject to improvement toward an ideal. In particular, I think we should define well-being in terms of individual *values* (rather than our desires or our satisfaction with life) where achieving or fulfilling our values constitutes an ideal in a sense that helps confer reason-giving status. The idea of a "value-full" life (the adjective I've coined to correspond to the noun value fulfillment), I will argue, does constitute an ideal and one that is sensibly identified with well-being.

Following this strategy leads us to the value fulfillment theory of well-being (VFT), which says that a person's life goes well to the extent that she pursues and fulfills or realizes things that she values.[2] The best life for a person is the one in which she gets the most value fulfillment she can, given her circumstances, and what is good for a person now is to do what contributes to some specification of the best, value-full life. In short,

---

[1] In philosophy, "normative" refers to what *ought* to be, or what we have good reason to do, as opposed to the purely descriptive matter of what *is*. "Normative" has quite a different meaning in philosophy than it has in the social sciences, so I will avoid it in what follows.

[2] For a similar approach to the relationship between values and well-being see Raibley 2010. For an earlier but more detailed discussion of my own view see Tiberius 2008.

we live well when we realize what matters to us. This includes achieving certain states of affairs (such as career goals) and also maintaining the positive affective orientation that comprises valuing something. If your values include your own enjoyment, relationships with family and friends, accomplishing something in your career, and contributing to certain morally worthwhile projects, then your life goes well for you insofar as you have good relationships and career success, make a moral contribution, and enjoy what you're doing, as these continue to be the things you care about. A value-full life is an ideal in at least two respects. First, we value many things and some values are more "fulfillable" than others: for example, values that do not suit our talents or circumstances are not easy to achieve and tend to produce frustration. Second, because pursuing what we value is something we do over time, some combinations or arrangements of values are better than others: some values frustrate the pursuit of others, for example. Further, a value-full life is an ideal that is relative to the individual subject insofar as the values that are included in the ideal are a person's own values and may differ from person to person. In the remainder of this section, I'll explain in more detail some of the key elements of the theory.

Values and Valuing

To value something (in the sense that is significant for well-being) is to care about it in a special way. We take our values to give us reasons to do things and we take our values to be the standards for how well our lives are going. For example, if you ask someone how her life is going, she may reflect briefly on the important domains in her life (family, work, health) and consider how she is doing in terms of these important ends.[3] Values, then, are well suited to play a central role in a theory of well-being because they are the very thing that people take to make their lives go well.[4]

I take a person's values in the relevant sense to be comprised of patterns of relatively robust attitudes (such as emotions and desires) that we take to generate reasons for action.[5] For example, if you value your job, then you will be disposed to enjoy what you

---

[3] Indeed, overall life-satisfaction is highly correlated with domain satisfaction (Schimmack and Oishi 2005).

[4] Mere desires are not like this; people can have desires that are trivial or even unworthy of satisfaction from their own point of view. This is not to say that the satisfaction of our trivial desires is worthless according to the value fulfillment theory. VFT can say that the satisfaction of even fairly trivial desires (e.g. for a beer this afternoon) is relevant to overall well-being when it contributes to something the person values such as enjoyment, relaxation, or health.

[5] We can also use the word "values" to refer to the objects of our valuing attitudes, i.e. to what is valued. For a more detailed version of the account of valuing and values see Tiberius 2000, 2008. For sympathetic treatments see Raibley 2010, Schmuck and Sheldon 2001, and Anderson 1995. These are specialized notions of valuing and value. These terms are not perfect, but they seem to me better than the alternatives. Many values (in my sense) are like "goals," but it seems odd to describe a friendship as a goal. "Personal projects" comes closest, but I think it's stylistically awkward and also conveys something more intentional than necessary. We can value something in the sense I mean (e.g. health and happiness)

do, to feel proud when you get promoted, and disappointed when you don't do your best work; when you reflect on how your life is going you will tend to think about how you are doing in your work as relevant to this question and you'll tend to take your job into account when you're making plans for the future. Valuing, therefore, has both an affective and a cognitive dimension—it involves our emotions and our judgment. We should be inclusive about what counts: people can value activities, relationships, broad aims, ideals, principles, particular goals that serve these more general ends, and so on. This characterization of valuing has features that make it compelling on its own as an account of valuing (as opposed to wanting or desiring). It also comports better with psychological research on values than philosophical theories that identify valuing with either a belief or a desire (Smith 1995; Dorsey 2012; Lewis 1989; Tiberius 2008). Below I'll discuss in more detail four distinctive features of values and valuing that are relevant to well-being and then I'll turn to the question of why it makes sense for a theory of well-being to focus on valuing in this sense.

First, to value something is to care about it in a particular way, and to care about something is, at least in part, to have some positive affective orientation toward it.[6] Other things equal, we are *motivated* to pursue or promote the values to which we are committed and we are disposed to react emotionally when these values are helped or threatened. For example, a mother who values being a parent is relatively robustly disposed to enjoy spending time with her child, to feel proud when he tells her she's a great mom, to be ashamed when she forgets to pick him up from school, and so on. Further, she takes her being a parent to justify certain decisions and plans she makes for her life, including decisions that require sacrificing other things she wants, and she takes "being a good parent" to be highly relevant to how well her life is going.

Second, because of the role they play in deliberation, planning, and action, values are "robust" in the sense that they are relatively stable and do not evaporate under moderate reflection. A person might *like* something or think that it is valuable, but do so only very briefly, or in a casual, unreflective manner that would disappear under the merest scrutiny, or in a way that plays virtually no role in her psychic economy. Such capricious attitudes do not plausibly reflect what a person genuinely cares about, who she is, where she stands, or what she thinks it is to live well. This feature of the view should not be taken to imply that our values can't change. It's unlikely (though not impossible) for the most basic values (e.g. health and happiness) to change, but change in instrumental values and how values are specified is likely to be a necessary feature of most normal lives. What kinds of changes in our values are recommended is a difficult practical problem, one facet of which we'll take up in section 2.

---

without making it our personal project. I do think, though, that many values are instantiated in personal projects and goals that are intended to fulfill them.

[6] For an illuminating discussion of caring see Jaworska 2007. I agree with Jaworska that caring does not have to involve reflectiveness (one of the main theses she defends in this article), but I do not take caring and valuing to be quite the same thing, as will become clear.

Third, to value something, and not merely to want it, is to see it as the kind of thing that generates *reasons* for you—as tending to justify responding in certain ways to it, and limiting how you might reasonably respond to it. Again, this feature of valuing has to do with the role that values play in our lives. Our values structure our choices and our assessments of how we're doing, and this is just another way of saying that we take them to give us practical reasons.

Fourth, on this view of values, we can see that (for most people) values themselves will exhibit certain patterns of mutual reinforcement and coherence. Some values will be more "core" than others, in the sense that they are used more often in explanations of the importance of other values. For example, the value of (psychological) happiness is likely to be a core value for many because it will be appealed to in explaining what is important about other values such as sports, hobbies, and friendships. I do not assume that values occupy a rigid hierarchy (though they may for some people); rather, values are more likely to be arranged in a web of mutual support with some values more centrally located than others. Notice another feature of this web: the centrality or "core-ness" of a value does not necessarily track its motivational strength, since there is more to valuing than having the relevant motivations. Notice also that some values will be merely instrumental (the value of money is usually like this), but even intrinsic values can vary in degrees of centrality; happiness may explain the value of more instrumental values than, say, a particular friendship, though both are valued (in part) for their own sakes. Further, the means–end relationship is not the only way in which values are related to each other, as we'll see in the next section.

Given these four features of values, we can see that a person's values (in the sense relevant to her well-being) are not necessarily identical with what she would report her values to be (say, on a values survey). Values, in the sense relevant to the value fulfillment theory, are complex psychological states that come in degrees (some may be more emotionally entrenched than others, for instance); they may not always be recognized for what they are by the person who has them. For example, most people value health and happiness, but it isn't necessarily the case that people would put these at the top of their list if you asked them to enumerate their values. Nevertheless, if a pattern of emotional dispositions exists to promote health and happiness, and these ends play an important and stable role in decision-making, they are values. Furthermore, these four features of values imply that values can be refined and improved. Each of us starts out with certain very basic proto-values that develop in normal human infants: typically these include comfort and the attention of our parents. As our values develop, they are shaped by our surroundings and personalities, and more are added as we experience the world: we add values that are instrumental to comfort and parental attention, we add new interpretations of how our basic intrinsic values can be realized, and we even add new intrinsic values over time (likely by a process of association). But the sets of values we develop could almost always be better—that is, they could be more emotionally suited to us, better justified, more stable, or more coherent. Values (unlike mere preferences) have built in standards for improvement.

With this account of values in hand, we can ask why a theory of well-being should focus on values rather than desires.[7]

First, because values do have constitutive standards for improvement, the appeal to values better explains how well-being constitutes a good goal or a goal we have good reason to try to achieve. Many of the unintuitive implications of desire theories stem from the fact that we do not take all of our desires to give us reasons that justify action. But values just are those patterns of attitudes that we take to be reason-giving, and our taking them to be so is reinforced by the fact that values are held to standards of improvement. Further, values have both a cognitive and an affective aspect, which gives a value-based theory an advantage in explaining two different ways in which we can assess whether or not something is good for us. First, we sometimes challenge or change our view about what is good for us in the light of judgments about what is worth valuing. For instance, a person who discovers she cannot conceive a child might reconsider how important biological connection is to the real value of being a mother and she might decide that it would be best for her to adopt. Second, we sometimes challenge our judgment of what is good for us on the basis of our emotional responses. We sometimes realize just how much something matters to us because we notice that we feel down when it is taken away from us, or elated when it comes back into our lives (Stocker 1990). When this happens we learn from our feelings that there are things about our well-being of which we were not aware. Because values have these two dimensions, they are well suited to explain how both manners of change constitute improvements to our views about what is good for us.

Second, values are especially related to subjects, unlike mere desires: people identify themselves in terms of their values and values are, by definition, of particular importance to people from their own point of view. Values have special relevance to well-being, then, insofar as well-being is a good that has a special relationship to the subject.

Value Fulfillment

What it is for a value to be fulfilled or realized and what it means to say that one life has more value fulfillment than another are obviously very important for VFT. Values, like desires, bring with them standards for success, and living up to these standards is part of value fulfillment. In the example discussed above, it's easy to see how valuing one's job entails standards of success or fulfillment: whatever counts as doing well at your job fulfills that value. But standards for values are not always so obvious. Some values are such that we succeed in their terms by having the right attitudes or being a certain kind

---

[7] One might think of values as a special subset of preferences that has a particular role in our deliberation, planning, and assessment of how our lives are going. In this way of thinking, the VFT is not fundamentally different from standard preference satisfaction theories of well-being; it is, rather, a variant of such theories.

of person. Nevertheless, there are standards for values in the sense that there are ways of responding appropriately or inappropriately given the nature of what is valued (Anderson 1995). Moreover, most values encompass standards that are objective in the sense that whether or not we fulfill them is not a matter of whether we believe we are fulfilling them. There is something to meeting the standards that our values impose that goes beyond our subjective experience. In this respect, value fulfillment is similar to desire satisfaction: you may fail to get what you want without knowing it (say, if you are seriously deluded), and you may fail to fulfill your values, though you believe otherwise. Finally, if we are going to achieve what matters to us, it is not only success in terms of what is valued that matters, but also the valuing attitudes themselves. We require some stability in our valuing attitudes if we are going to succeed by the standards we think are important. Value fulfillment, then, is succeeding by the standards of that value while continuing to think that these standards are important to how well your life goes.

Assessing *total* value fulfillment requires attending to the relationships between values. People's values are typically complex. We value some things largely as a means to others (e.g. you might value running marathons as a means to the values of health and fitness), but (as I have mentioned) values are interrelated in other ways besides as means to ends. Some values are expressions of other, more abstractly described values. A person who values music may value playing the piano as a way of valuing music. In this case playing the piano is valued intrinsically, not as a means to appreciating music; the piano player does not value a distinct musical good that is brought about by playing the piano. Some values impose constraints on other values. For example, a person who values honesty will be constrained in how she pursues her career goals. For most people who value honesty, it is not just another desirable in the hopper, rather, the virtue of honesty acts as a limiting condition on what sorts of means to other ends are permissible. Considerations about the various ways in which values can be related to each must be taken into account when we evaluate total value fulfillment and we ask whether choosing one path over another promises more overall value fulfillment.

Value-Full Lives

The complexity of systems of values and the fact that values themselves are open to interpretation mean that there will be no single, well-defined best life for a person overall or even at a particular time. This is in part because there aren't precisely defined units of value fulfillment and in part because there are different ways that values can be successfully organized even for a single person. If the units of fulfillment were precise, we could rank possible lives in terms of minute gains and losses. If there were only one way for a particular set of values to be realized together, then there would be a clear sense in which there is a best life for a person. But this is not how values are. Instead, the value fulfillment approach tells us that the good life for a person overall is one of the lives in a set of roughly equivalently value-full lives that constitutes a model of a good life for a person.[8] Like a model home with no clothes in the closets or a model airplane with no functioning toilet, the model of well-being simplifies real life: none of the best lives that comprise the model include every detail (what shampoo the person uses, how many holiday cards she sends); rather, they include the relatively large, important features of a life. As with other models that have a practical purpose, the model of a good life shows us which aspects of reality are relevant to the practical purpose at hand, which in this case is to make decisions about how to live or how to help others; in other words, its simplification is tailored to the purpose for which we are using it. Further, the model of well-being allows that a person might live an equally good life pursuing somewhat different values to different degrees, especially at an early point in the person's life. We can represent this by thinking of the model as a set of simplified best lives.

People achieve well-being, then, to the extent that they live a life like one of the lives in the set of best lives. What is good for a person to do is what will contribute to one of the best lives that is currently available to her, or to what will contribute to one best way of realizing the model, given her circumstances. Contributions come in degrees, as does the goodness of an action or decision for a person. The value fulfillment theory defines well-being in terms of a model of a good life for a person that must be brought to life by translating the important features into actual decisions and actions.

This way of thinking about well-being moves a lot of the action to the application of the theory. When we apply a theory of well-being we do so for some practical purpose. For example, we might be interested in making a decision about our own lives, helping someone we know, helping strangers on the other side of the world, or making policy that will improve the well-being of current citizens of a town or future generations of a nation. There are different points of view one can take on the question of what it is to live a good human life for these different practical purposes. At the highest level of abstraction from the particular details of people's lives we can imagine paradigmatically good lives that include successful valuing and pursuit of values that most people have and that fit together well: meaningful work, close personal relationships, health, and enjoyment, for example. This perspective is appropriate when our goal is to improve the lives of a large population of people. As our eyes move down from the abstraction to a specific person whose life we want to improve, the model must be brought to life by filling in the details of how these values are to be instantiated and how they will function together over time. This is an appropriate perspective for making ordinary decisions about one's own life or for helping a friend or relative.

---

[8] Raibley (2012) uses the notion of a "paradigm" where I prefer to talk about a model. I think it is just as useful and perhaps a bit more precise to think about a set of best lives for a person that is a model of well-being.

An analogy might help to explain this way of thinking about applying a model of a good life. Think of the model of well-being as like an AAA vacation trip-tik.[9] It gives you rough guidelines for how to have a good road trip, given certain parameters that you assume at the outset (e.g. do you prefer country roads or highways, do you want to stop for certain tourist attractions or take the most direct route to a specific destination?). The trip-tik does not tell you exactly where to stop for gas, which restaurant to go to, or how long to stop. You have to make decisions at this level of detail as you go. Further, if you change your mind as you're driving, or if something goes wrong, you might need to improvise and pick up the map again later or revise the map. Similarly, the theory of well-being tells us the rough outlines of a good life and it explains why this life is good for one person while a different life is good for someone else. But the theory does not identify a good life in detail; this is something that must be done through the practice of living by engaging in reflection, planning, gaining experience, observing the effects of these experiences, and so on. The value fulfillment theory, like the trip-tik, plots a good trip in general, but leave the details open for negotiation. We negotiate the gap between real and ideal as we try to improve our lives or the lives of others.

Further, exactly how you use the map will depend on your purposes, just as the way that the model of a value-full life will guide decision-making and ethical practice depends on your purposes. If you are using the trip-tik to calculate how much you'll spend on gas, you don't need much specification: the distances will be roughly the same no matter whether you stop to eat at a truck stop or a local diner. But if you want to use the trip-tik to plan a meeting with some friends, you'll have to get much more specific. Similarly, there are different uses to which we could put a theory of well-being and how much the model of well-being must be specified in detail depends on what question we're trying to answer and what we're trying to achieve. For example, if you are making policy for a large population, you will want to think about good human lives in general terms, leaving the model fairly unspecified. On the other hand, if you want to help a friend decide whether to quit her job and join the circus, you'll need a much more detailed conception of what a good life is for her.

To summarize the discussion of this section, here are the main features of the value fulfillment theory:

- Values are relatively stable, emotionally entrenched, reason-giving patterns of attitudes.
- A good life for a person is one in which she pursues and fulfills what she values over time where those values are emotionally suitable and seen by the person to make her life go well.
- The best life for a person is the one in which she gets the most value fulfillment she can, given her personality and environment.

---

[9] The American Automobile Association (AAA) trip-tik was a customized paper map, usually used as a vacation planner.

- Because what counts as fulfillment of values is imprecise, we cannot define the best life for a person in fine detail. Rather, for any person there is a broadly characterized model of a good life or set of good lives that can be specified in different ways.
- How the model should be specified depends on what question you're trying to answer and what you're trying to accomplish by applying the theory of well-being.
- What is good for you now is to do what contributes to some specification of one of the most value-full lives.

It is worth addressing one glaring objection to this theory, before we move on to the next section. One might think that *values* are too inclusive to be at the heart of individual well-being. In particular, since people have *moral* values, defining well-being in terms of values seems to collapse the divide between self-interest and morality too easily and to make it impossible for a person to sacrifice her well-being for her moral values. Notice that this is also a problem for preference satisfaction theories (often called the problem of self-sacrifice; Heathwood 2011).[10] The answer to this problem for the value fulfillment theory is that the values that are relevant to our well-being are those we take to provide standards for how well our lives are going for us. This leaves room for distance between a person's moral values and the values that constitute her well-being. A person who has no other values besides her moral values will not be capable of sacrificing her welfare for morality, but this isn't so obviously unintuitive.

Changing Values and Improving Lives

The value fulfillment theory recognizes that we are concerned to shape our lives in response to what we value, and that while our values do have a psychological basis they also pull us out of our own heads toward objective and inter-subjective standards of success. Some values do this more than others, of course, and some people do value idiosyncratic things in idiosyncratic ways. But most people have some values with standards of success that go beyond how they feel about them. These standards of success afford one mechanism for criticizing the status quo, that is, for assessing how one's life is currently going and imagining how it might go better.

This mechanism is an instrumental one: the basic values are taken as given and one asks how well one is doing at living up to these values. Does the value fulfillment theory provide a mechanism for asking about the intrinsic worth of one's values; in other

---

[10] The VFT is also inclusive in the sense that it does not put moral constraints on what a person may value; individuals may have immoral values, just as they may have immoral preferences. This fact means that increasing aggregate well-being will sometimes require trade-offs, just as for preference satisfaction theories.

words, for asking whether "one's ladder is up against the right wall"? I think it does provide such a mechanism, in virtue of the long-term perspective that VFT takes. I'll explain how this works in the next section.

Value Fulfillment and Holism

In the overview, I said that what's good for a person to do *now* is what will contribute to a good life overall. This makes it seem like the value fulfillment theory privileges the long term and discounts what we might call momentary well-being. This is true, and VFT is holistic in the sense that it takes the worth of welfare segments to depend in part on their role in larger sections of a life. Of course, in application the theory cannot follow a top-down approach: because we do not know how an entire life (or a long segment of it) will go, we must pay attention to the quality of smaller segments and the short term. I think holism of this sort is a very plausible view about the well-being in the relevant sense: well-being as a central aim of human deliberation, planning, and decision-making about how to live one's own life and how to help other people.[11] We do not tend to deliberate separately about what is good for us at this moment and what is good for us overall. We deliberate about what is good for us with a concern for the short term and an eye to the future.

Furthermore, holism is suited to the value fulfillment view, because values are relatively stable patterns of attitudes that are not typically the kinds of things we can fulfill in the moment. One can satisfy a desire for gustatory pleasure in an instant, but a person who *values* gustatory pleasure must organize her life so that she has opportunities for it that fit with the other things she does and the importance of some of this organizing will only be detectable from a bird's eye point of view. Of course what happens in the moment is important to many values too: you won't fulfill the value of gustatory pleasure if you turn down every opportunity to eat something tasty in the moment and, in general, momentary experiences of pleasure contribute to a pleasant life overall. The point is that a certain priority to the long term, and to the overall shape of a life, is built in to a theory that focuses on values.

As a holistic theory, the value fulfillment theory gives in principle priority to the model of a value-full overall life. (The priority in practice is constrained by our epistemological limits—the fact that we don't have the bird's eye point of view.) This feature of VFT provides a needed critical perspective on our *current* values, goals, and desires. That we need some critical perspective on our current values is clear from the observation that these can have bad long-term consequences for our lives overall. The point of view of one's whole life provides a critical perspective on our current values for

---

[11] I don't mean to rule out the possibility that there is another sense of well-being—well-being at a time—that is distinct from what it is to be doing well overall (Velleman 2000). I have been persuaded by Anna Alexandrova (2013) that the assumption that there is just one notion of well-being worthy of our attention is probably not tenable.

which there is a natural rationale. After all, we are interested in living good overall lives and this interest motivates us when we think about well-being.

So, VFT allows us to critically evaluate our desires and values by assessing them in relation to each other, and as to whether they will contribute to living one of the best overall lives we could live. You might think that this is still a means–end evaluation: the goal is a value-full overall life and individual values are assessed for their instrumental value. But this appearance is misleading. When our focus is on values rather than desires, we see that how the fulfillment of one value affects the fulfillment of another is not always a question about an instrumental relationship. Certainly, some of the important relationships between values in a system are instrumental. But not all intrinsic values are created equally; different values function in different ways in people's psychic economies. In particular, there are certain moral values, and values that define one's self-identity more generally, that function as constraints even on the pursuit of other intrinsic desires. Consider: Jane has an intrinsic desire for her own pleasure and comfort; she also intrinsically values being a morally decent person. Being a morally decent person, according to Jane (and, indeed, many of us) means not even considering harming others for the sake of our own comfort. Deliberating about the satisfaction of which intrinsic value would bring more satisfaction or fulfillment overall would be what Bernard Williams has called "one thought too many" (Williams 1981). For this reason, too, some intrinsic desires can be bad for us in ways that are not reducible to means–end failures. Having desires that cause Jane to ponder whether she ought to buy a fur coat or exploit her cheap labor source (if these are things she's morally against) can be bad for her because they undermine her identity as a morally decent person. A desire or value can affect others in the system by instrumentally preventing their fulfillment, but it can also affect them by its mere presence: the existence of the desire can undermine the identity that is partly constructed by the intrinsic value in question.

Holism, together with the focus on values, gives the value fulfillment theory a way of assessing the merit of certain values that is not instrumental. Rather than asking whether a particular value is a means to a given end (e.g. as we might ask whether a certain activity is a means to pleasure or life satisfaction), we ask what values fit together into a life that succeeds according to the standards imposed by these values over time. This standard of assessment is coherentist, not instrumental, because there is no fully specified description of the end to which individual values are a means.

Applying the Theory: Individual Change and Global Crises

With a theory of well-being in hand, we can return to the question with which we began and ask what it is to improve one's life, and where the demands of morality (as imposed by global crises, for example) might be included in this improvement. This part of the chapter will be, unavoidably, rather programmatic. The aim here is to point to the questions and research that are made salient by the value fulfillment approach.

In general, according to VFT, we can assess how a life is going and how it might go better by asking three kinds of questions:

1) Given a person's values, their relative strengths, and standards for success, how well is the person doing at fulfilling them, or succeeding in terms of them?
   a. Is the person taking ineffective means to ultimate values?
   b. Are there more effective means to ultimate values that the person isn't currently taking?
2) To what extent are these values and these standards of success the right ones, given the overarching goal of a value-full life?
   a. Are there some values the person would be better off without?
   b. Could some values be reinterpreted with different standards of success?
3) Are there values that the person does not have currently but which would make her better off in terms of value fulfillment?

So far, the theory I've described is quite abstract. It posits the ideal of a value-full life, but does not say anything about what these values are or how they are prioritized. To get from the general to the particular we need to know how various common human values can be pursued successfully over time. More specifically, we need to know what normal human values are, how people tend to define success in terms of them, what particular plans or projects conduce to this success, what psychologically tenable options there are for changing these values or their associated standards (either rejecting them completely or redefining them), what obstacles people tend to confront when they try to change their values, and what kinds of commitments tend to foster value fulfillment over time.

Answering these questions requires a great deal of empirical information. One source for the relevant empirical information is the work that has been done in positive psychology. Particularly useful for our purposes are studies on the well-being effects of materialistic values and of personal projects. Typically, in positive psychology, well-being is measured by assessing global life satisfaction, domain satisfaction, and/or positive and negative affect. These measures are taken to constitute what Ed Diener (1984; Diener et al. 2003) calls "subjective well-being" and they have become central to much of the work that is done by psychologists (including even psychologists who have different conceptions of well-being[12]). I believe that VFT recommends taking this research seriously for the following reason: people do tend to value their own subjective well-being (SWB) as psychologists have defined that notion, and the value of SWB is likely to be part of a value-full life in the long term. Indeed, the fact that these hedonistic measures of well-being are taken to be a kind of default in psychology is

---

[12] Even eudaimonist psychologists very often take themselves to have the burden of establishing that their constructs are correlated with SWB defined in terms of positive affect or life satisfaction (Waterman 2013).

some evidence that these values are deeply entrenched, at least at this moment in history. Further, there is a great deal of evidence that SWB is at least correlated with other near-universal values such as health and intimate relationships (Tiberius and Plakias 2010).

The value fulfillment theory gives us direction as we confront the vast body of literature on the psychology of well-being with the aim of thinking about improving lives. I think the right approach is to start with a set of near-universal, fairly uncontroversial, general ultimate values that are likely to be part of a value-full life over time. Life satisfaction and emotional happiness are two of these, and we could add health, intimate relationships, and the welfare of one's friends and family. Taking these as our presumptive starting points, we should then look for evidence of what sorts of projects, goals, and specific values produce success in terms of the presumptive values; evidence for projects, goals, and specific values that are incompatible with success in terms of these presumptive values; and evidence for the human capacity to change or modify the ways in which we characterize and pursue these (and other) values.

Personal projects analysis, a research program founded by psychologist Brian Little, is a particularly promising source of the requisite information, because of the way personal projects are defined and the kinds of research questions that have been central to this program. Personal projects are defined as "extended sets of personally salient action in context" and they tend to be nested in hierarchical structures with more ultimate goals or values occasioning specific tasks. One of the things that psychologists who study personal projects are interested in discovering is which projects (or features of projects) are conducive to happiness and flourishing. Researchers are discovering that "individuals experience well-being [SWB] to the extent that they are engaged in personal projects that they appraise as estimable, meaningful undertakings that are manageable, both supported by and redound to the benefit of others, and positive and rewarding" (Little et al. 2007: 40). Meaningfulness and manageability turn out to be often at cross purposes, so one challenge for choosing good projects is to strike a balance between what is important and what you can actually do. This is precisely the kind of empirical information that VFT calls for, particularly if our ultimate purpose is to use the theory to think about how people's values and projects could be changed for the better.

Once we have a way to think about improving lives, we can ask how this framework could be used to make the case for personal change that is instrumental to solving global crises. As a first step, what I will do in the remainder of the chapter is to articulate the questions that would need to be answered in order to find a path away from "consumerism," that is, an argument for transforming one's life—or one's business—into one that is less resource-intensive (where this could mean a life in which one advocates for better large-scale policy regarding the consumption of resources).

First, what ultimate values are served by consumerism? In other words, what are consumerist values a means to, or what ultimate values do they instantiate? The answer to this question will be different for different people, of course, but some generalizations seem warranted. Material goods are often a means to pleasure, enjoyment, friendship, love, and security. They might also be, for some, constitutive of status or power.

Second, does consumerist behavior serve the ends it is meant to serve? Does it make us happy, increase the quality of our friendships, and so on? There is evidence that people with materialist values (people who care a lot about having consumer goods, money, and fame) are less subjectively happy than people with less material-istic values (Kasser 2002). But it is important to observe that consumption may serve some values very well in the *short* term, and this reveals a pervasive obstacle to non-consumerist changes in values. This obstacle is the urgency of the short-term perspective and its inevitable conflicts with the long term. To live a life that we are happy with, we can't just do what we want at every moment. We have to have standards for what it means to live well, and we have to meet these standards, which requires making some short-term sacrifices. At the same time, we can't just ignore the short term, since ultimately a whole life is made up of experiences that happen in the moment, and since there's always uncertainty about the future. It won't do to deny the urgency of the short term and yet if we want to live good lives overall, we must put it in perspective. Insofar as opting to consume less means denying short-term enjoyment, acknowledging this pervasive obstacle is important as we think about improving lives.

Third, insofar as having material goods is constitutive of a more ultimate or intrinsic value, is this ultimate value (say, status, reputation, or comfort) one that is part of a value-full life? If it is, could that ultimate value be interpreted or specified in a different way? The value of fame or status might be difficult to maintain in the long term, since these values are necessarily comparative and one's relative merit in these terms is highly likely to fluctuate over time; these might be values that one is better off without, even if they are intrinsically valued. Comfort seems on better footing as a component of a value-full life, but one could argue here that, while having certain material goods signifies comfort in many cultures, we could reinterpret this values so that our notion of its fulfillment does not rely on using up a lot of scarce resources.

Fourth, are there other values that people already have that could be used to anchor a reduction in consumerism? How could these values be specified or interpreted to best promote value fulfillment over time in such a way that would help with our problems? Values that come to mind include peace of mind, lack of stress, financial security, the well-being of one's children, being a good parent, being a decent person, and virtues such as thrift, justice, or compassion. These are widespread values at varying levels of abstraction that could be used to build a case for individual changes in consumption, charitable giving, or advocacy for policy responses to global crises. As already dis-cussed, traits of character might be especially useful values to think about in this context insofar as they impose limits or constraints on behavior. For example, someone who identifies herself as a thrifty person might have various policies that comprise this virtue—always fix small appliances rather than throwing them away, always turn down the thermostat overnight—such that following these policies has a kind of priority over satisfying other desires.

Fifth, are there values that it would be good for people to have (values not currently in play that would contribute to greater value fulfillment) that could anchor a reduction in consumerism? For those who do not have the values mentioned, or those for whom these values do not play a significant role in their decision-making, there is an argument to be made for the importance of at least some of them. For example, lack of stress has significant positive consequences for mental and physical health, and for the health of one's intimate relationships. Trying to keep up with the Joneses is stressful and living more simply might promote a less stressful life. It might also be possible to make a case for something like the value of sustainability itself. Consider some of the literature on consumerism that has attempted to brand materialistic values as a disease called "affluenza." The positive counterpart to this strategy is to promote the value of a sustainable lifestyle as a value that fits well into a good life over time. Of course, the promotion of a sustainable lifestyle as an ideal or virtuous way of living has not been effective so far, and it might be that efforts to introduce new values are less likely to be successful than efforts to reinterpret or to promote more effective means to already existing values.

If we want a deep understanding of how people can improve their own lives in ways that will make a greater contribution to solving global problems (rather than exacerbating them), these are the questions it makes sense to ask. Earlier I said that we require different things from a model of well-being depending on our purposes. What that means in this context is that a serious attempt to answer these questions would take a different form depending on whether we are asking as policy-makers or activists trying to change populations, as individuals trying to change our own lives or the lives of our friends and families, as corporate leaders aiming to change business practices that will profoundly affect employees and consumers, or as educators who are trying to help students navigate the various demands of trying to live a successful life. Large-scale efforts must proceed on the basis of our best information about what the target population is like in general, the kinds of values they have, and how they are able to succeed in terms of them. Individual efforts require a more reflective and imaginative process. This too requires information, but it also requires that one try to imagine how else one could live one's life by reflecting on what matters most.

CONCLUSION

According to the value fulfillment theory of well-being, a good life is a life in which you succeed in terms of the set of values that suit you emotionally, that you take to make your life go well, and that are mutually achievable over time. The theory is not fundamentally different from familiar desire satisfaction theories. It still makes the individual the ultimate standard for her own well-being and it takes very seriously subjective concerns and interests. Unlike desire satisfaction theories, however, the value fulfillment theory does make room for evaluating one's values, goals, projects, and desires that goes beyond the assessment of means–end efficiency. In other words,

VFT makes some room for thinking about whether one's ladder is up against the right wall. It does so by positing an ideal of a good life that puts the things we care about together in a coherent way, and by paying attention to the subtle ways in which some values function differently from mere desires.

There is also, of course, a direct moral appeal to be made. Insofar as the opportunity for everyone to achieve a value-full life is a morally compelling goal, the value fulfillment theory would support an argument that we are morally obliged to respond to global crises that hamper people's ability to live this kind of life. But the special contribution of the value fulfillment theory, in my view, would be that it finds a place for reasons to care about and respond to global crises in the overall pursuit of well-being for an individual. It finds a place for the critical evaluation of our values and personal projects that respects the psychological reality that we are creatures who care most about ourselves and those we love.

ACKNOWLEDGMENTS

I would like to thank the participants of the Inaugural Assembly on the Evolution of Capitalism for helpful and informative discussion. Particular thanks to Subi Rangan, Elizabeth Anderson, Philip Pettit, and Amartya Sen for their questions.

REFERENCES

Alexandrova, A. (2013). Doing Well in the Circumstances. *Journal of Moral Philosophy*, 10/3: 307–28.

Anderson, E. (1995). *Value in Ethics and Economics.* Cambridge, MA: Harvard University Press.

Diener, E. (1984). Subjective Well-Being. *Psychological Bulletin*, 95/3: 542–75.

Diener, E., C. Napa Scollon, and R. E. Lucas (2003). The Evolving Concept of Subjective Well-Being: The Multifaceted Nature of Happiness. *Advances in Cell Aging and Gerontology*, 15: 187–219.

Dorsey, D. (2012). Subjectivism Without Desire. *Philosophical Review*, 121/3: 407–42.

Heathwood, C. (2011). Preferentism and Self-Sacrifice. *Pacific Philosophical Quarterly*, 92/1: 18–38.

Jaworska, A. (2007). Caring and Internality. *Philosophy and Phenomenological Research*, 74/3: 529–68.

Kasser, T. (2002). *The High Price of Materialism.* Cambridge, MA: MIT Press.

Lewis, D. (1989). Dispositional Theories of Value. *Proceedings of the Aristotelian Society*, supplementary volume, 63: 113–37.

Little, B. R., K. E. Salmela-Aro, and S. D. Phillips (2007). *Personal Project Pursuit: Goals, Action, and Human Flourishing.* Hillside, NJ: Lawrence Erlbaum Associates.

Raibley, J. (2010). Well-Being and the Priority of Values. *Social Theory and Practice*, 36/4: 593–620.

Raibley, J. R. (2012). Welfare over Time and the Case for Holism. *Philosophical Papers*, 41/2: 239–65.

Schimmack, U., and S. Oishi (2005). The Influence of Chronically and Temporarily Accessible Information on Life Satisfaction Judgments. *Journal of Personality and Social Psychology*, 89/3: 395–406.

Schmuck, P. E., and K. M. Sheldon (2001). *Life Goals and Well-Being: Towards a Positive Psychology of Human Striving*. Seattle, WA: Hogrefe & Huber Publishers.

Smith, M. (1995). *The Moral Problem*. Oxford: Blackwell.

Stocker, M. (1990). *Plural and Conflicting Values*. Oxford: Clarendon Press.

Tiberius, V. (2000). Humean Heroism: Value Commitments and the Source of Normativity. *Pacific Philosophical Quarterly*, 81(4): 426–46.

Tiberius, V. (2008). *The Reflective Life: Living Wisely with our Limits*. New York: Oxford University Press.

Tiberius, V., and A. Plakias (2010). Well-Being. In J. Doris (ed.), *The Moral Psychology Handbook*. Oxford: Oxford University Press, 402–32.

Velleman, J. D. (2000). Well-Being and Time. In *The Possibility of Practical Reason*. Oxford: Oxford University Press, 56–84.

Waterman, A. S. (2013). *The Best within us: Positive Psychology Perspectives on Eudaimonia*. Washington, DC: American Psychological Association.

Williams, B. (1981). Persons, Character, and Morality. In his *Moral Luck*. Cambridge: Cambridge University Press, 1–19.

CHAPTER 21

....

IDEAS OF REASON

....

SUSAN NEIMAN

Abstract

The 2001 terrorist attacks on New York and Washington were, among other things, an attack on a particular notion of rationality. The contempt of the attackers for that notion connects them to members of the US Tea Party and right-wing nationalist groups currently opposing the EU. Such groups have in common a rejection of *Homo economicus,* the human being considered "solely as a being who desires wealth, and who is capable of judging the comparative efficiency of means for obtaining that end" (John Stuart Mill). A notion of reason based on Kant is introduced which should serve as an alternative. The major question for further research remains: given that the *Homo economicus* model of human motivation has been undermined by recent research in primatology, psychology, neurobiology, and even by many economists, why does it continue to exercise such a hold on us?

The 2001 terrorist attacks on New York and Washington led to a wave of nostalgia for something whose demise had been celebrated just a decade before: the Cold War.[1] Frightening though it had been to contemplate a nuclear arsenal large enough to extinguish life on earth several times over, there had always been comfort in the thought that the men controlling the buttons acted according to principles that could be easily analyzed by game theorists working for the Rand Corporation. As Lorraine Daston (2013) has observed, "It was an article of faith that the Soviet enemy was coolly calculating its strategic interests in exactly the same terms as the Americans, the adversaries conceived as mirror images of each other." Even those who knew nothing about game theory or the Rand Corporation were acquainted with the apt anagram MAD. However deeply they were opposed to each other, a nuclear war would surely lead to the destruction of both, a prospect so inimical to each power's self-interest they would have to be crazy to start one. And indeed, the carefully calculated arms race

---

[1] I write this at a moment when such nostalgia has temporarily receded in view of recent events in the Ukraine, but those events, whatever the outcome, do not affect my central claim.

succeeded in bankrupting the Soviet Union and preventing the mutually assured destruction that both leaders and citizens of the superpowers feared. Movies like *Dr Strangelove* and *Failsafe* kept alive fears that the strategy could fail, and at several moments during the Cold War, nuclear war was more narrowly averted than most of us knew. But those moments turned on errors like that of the Soviet commander who mistook a Norwegian weather balloon for an American missile, and the cinematic nightmares concerned individuals who had one way or another gone mad. Confrontations like the Cuban Missile Crisis actually served to confirm our trust in a model of rationality that would keep the world turning. Americans and Russians depicted each other in demonic terms, but they were terms that rested on commitment to a shared conception of rationality that made life negotiable. Small wonder 9/11 left many nostalgic. How could one negotiate with enemies who not only commanded scores of fighters cheerfully seeking their own doom but, as it emerged, were perfectly willing to contemplate devastation on a scale that had horrified both superpowers?

Al Qaeda's disregard of the rational considerations that kept the Cold War in balance is not an accident. In the following I'll consider Al Qaeda's attack on Wall Street and the Pentagon as, among other things, an attack on a particular notion of rationality itself. This also allows us to consider what members of Al Qaeda have in common with members of the US Tea Party and even their moderate European cousins, members of right-wing nationalist groups currently opposing the EU. It's important to emphasize that I am not accusing these diverse groups of irrationality, though there is plenty of that in plain view. The first two reject scientific evidence for everything from evolution to climate change. The latter groups may be less hostile to arguments from the natural sciences, but seem impervious to the overwhelming evidence that, without a strong EU, every nation that belongs to it will be globally irrelevant in a matter of decades (Cohn-Bendit and Verhofstadt 2012).[2] Those who wish to mock such groups will have no trouble finding examples of beliefs and behavior that violate minimal standards of scientific and instrumental reasoning. If our interest is not in mocking but understanding them, we should view each as a helpless, often twisted, but effective way not of violating standard canons of rationality but of defying them.

For all the differences between such groups, they are united by a rejection of *Homo economicus,* the human being considered "solely as a being who desires wealth, and who is capable of judging the comparative efficiency of means for obtaining that end" (Mill 1968: 137). John Stuart Mill, whose work engendered the term, emphasized that it "is an arbitrary definition of man, as a being who inevitably does that by which he may obtain the greatest amount of necessaries, conveniences, and luxuries, with the smallest quantity of labor and physical self-denial with which they can be obtained" (Mill 1968: 137). In response to critics he quickly added that no political economist "was ever so

---

[2] Although Cohn-Bendit and Verhofstadt call that vision "plausibly utopian," the arguments on which it rests could be taken from Hobbes.

absurd as to suppose that mankind are really thus constituted" (Mill 1968: 137). Mill's caveats were ignored, and many economists and policy-makers found his arbitrary definition convenient, although many criticized it for failing to describe us. Crucially, most of the criticism concerned the ways in which we *fall short of this model* of rationality, focusing on the ways in which passions and perceptual distortions routinely prevent us from maximizing utility in the ways the model demands.[3] Too little of the criticism addresses the ways in which this model *falls short of us*, and hence is liable to outrage those who refuse to view reason as reducible to a means of maximizing self-interest, or value as reducible to market value.

Al Qaeda's rejection of *Homo economicus* is the most explicit, reflected in the images of Osama bin Laden on t-shirts and bath towels sold throughout the developing world. Doubtless some of the admiration they expressed was for the man who first attacked and then eluded the world's largest military power, but what was most often esteemed was the fact that he gave up a massive fortune in order to do so. Bin Laden spurned a lifestyle of luxury available only to a handful of the Earth's inhabitants in order to live in a cave. A more concise disdain for *Homo economicus* would be hard to find. The years that followed 9/11 witnessed a flurry of research which showed that bin Laden was no exception. Contrary to what (both neo-liberal and Marxist) materialism might have predicted, those drawn to terrorism were not the wretched of the Earth. Anthropologist Scott Atran (2004) summarized:

> In fact, study after study finds suicide terrorists and supporters to be more educated and economically well-off than surrounding populations. They also tend to be well-adjusted in their families, liked by their peers, and—according to interrogators—sincerely compassionate to those they see themselves as helping.

After interviewing hundreds of supporters of jihadism in a study for the US Department of Defense, Atran (2006b: 128) concluded that the jihadi mission is more likely to appeal to "bright and idealist Muslim youth" than "the marginalized and dispossessed."[4] Nor will it do to dismiss that idealism as fueled by fantastic visions of post-mortem gain. As Atran quotes one jihadi leader, "If someone came to me wanting to join the jihad in order to gain virgins in paradise I would slam the door in his face" (2006a). Suicide terrorists are not concerned with maximizing utility in this or any other world. Nor are they acting from ignorance. On the whole, they've had more exposure to the Sirens of Western culture than their countryfolk. They simply don't like the song.

The Tea Partiers do not share the jihadis' most destructive methods, but their rage is directed toward many of the same targets. While both the Islamist movement and America's religious right are sexist and puritanical, you need not be either to feel distaste for the ways in which sexuality has become so commodified that only its most

---

[3] See, for instance, the very different work of Stephen Holmes, Daniel Kahnemann, and Dan Ariely.

[4] See also the recent studies of terrorists by Hans Juergensmayer, Louise Richardson, and Jessica Stern.

grotesque or explicit versions still receive any comment. It is easy to ridicule the Tea Party's contempt for fact and analysis, but not so easy to dismiss their unease with a world controlled by the technocratic expertise embodied by the finance industry and apparently devoid of ideology. (The Tea Party's embrace of free market absolutism ignores the ways in which that absolutism, and the resulting deregulation of the finance industry, created the financial crisis that enraged them, but that's what happens to those who disregard fact and analysis.) In Thomas Frank's words, "[T]he newest Right has met its goals not by deception alone—although there has been a great deal of this— but by offering an idealism so powerful that it clouds its partisans' perceptions of reality" (2012: 12).[5] He concludes:

> Now, constructing an alternative reality would normally put a worldly political movement at a profound disadvantage. But this case is different. The reborn Right has succeeded *because* of its idealism, not in spite of it; because idealism in the grand sense is precisely what our fallen economic world calls for. (Ibid.)

Of course neither Frank nor I hold the Tea Party's idealism to be the kind that is called for or can do anything but more harm at the present moment. Yet in describing its roots not in deception or stupidity but in idealism, he has pointed to something important.

The right-wing nationalists currently organizing to undermine the EU are different again from the first two groups mentioned. Comparatively moderate, they avoid the extreme contempt for fact and argument that marks the others. What should give pause are the ways in which right-wing nationalist groups make common cause, forming far more extensive and active networks than their internationalist opponents. At first glance this presents a paradox: what unites nationalist parties whose *raison d'être* is the primacy of their own tribe? I submit they are united at least in part by reaction to what has been called the post-heroic age. The pro-European narrative often looks like this: let us celebrate the end of the glorification of great men and the wars they led us into, and rejoice in the fact that we now trade with our neighbors instead of running them through. It is not a narrative that can inspire. Wilders and LePen may be racists and demagogues, but they win followers who want to glorify *something*, and there's nothing disreputable about that desire. They are repelled by the idea that the only human bonds are bonds of trade, the only human aspirations a heap of goods. The nationalists may not offer much, but they offer a vision of something beyond the helpless instrumental rationality on which the defenders of Europe rest their case. For a variety of reasons, the EU has failed to present an ideal of Europe, and its efforts to promote support for the Union rely on lame lists of utilitarian benefits that move no one.

Why suggest that the three groups here mentioned are rejecting a particular concept of rationality rather than rejecting reason altogether? Whatever they call it, no group

[5] Thomas Frank, *Pity the Billionaire: The Unlikely Comeback of the American Right* (New York: Vintage 2012), 12.

that seeks to recruit others can do without some form of persuasion that seeks to create trust and establish legitimacy. (Otherwise they could limit themselves to the use of guns and howls.) At a time when reason is under attack from most quarters it's easy to forget that it is a fluid concept whose variations have little more in common than some connection or other to thinking, and a normative tone. The considerable efforts modern philosophy made to define it may not inspire confidence, but they should at least make clear that the concept cannot be taken for granted. Kant, the philosopher whose efforts were the greatest, is usually the object of caricature. While this is not the place to review his conception of reason, a brief sketch of its main components will be important for understanding a central example.[6]

Kant decisively rejected the classical rationalist conception of reason as instrumental and mechanical, not only because it was unable to explain what we do in the world but because it cannot foster freedom. For that is its central task, which it carries out by formulating ends of action in scientific inquiry as well as moral behavior. The task of reason is not to oppose nature, as the romantics complained, but to oppose authority, which defends its power by restricting the right to think to a small elite group. (In his time this would have been the clergy; today we might consider the role of economists in convincing us that the forces that determine the world are too complex for the rest of us to understand.) Even more importantly, where reason was opposed to nature it was in the interest of questioning conventions that tradition insisted were natural. Consider some of the things generally held to be natural at the start of the eighteenth century: poverty, slavery, subjection of women, feudal hierarchies, and most forms of illness. (As late as the nineteenth, some members of the British clergy opposed relief efforts during the Irish famine with the argument that such efforts disturbed the order of nature.) What is natural is contested. As the Enlightenment realized, you cannot abolish slavery, overthrow existing hierarchies, or cure illness unless you can show that they are not necessarily part of the way the world is. Kant was well aware that reason has limits; he simply wasn't prepared to let the state be the one to draw them. Instead he encouraged us to think for ourselves: any peasant can do it, just as any professor can fail. Reason is neither limited to calculation nor opposed to the passions. The embodiment of Kant's conception of reason is not the rule-obsessed technocrat but Mozart's self-assured Figaro, who used his own reason against the aristocracy precisely in order to realize his passion.

Admirable as they are, most of Figaro's exploits fall under what Kant calls the hypothetical use of reason, which has the form "If I want x, I should do y and z." If he wants Susannah to himself, Figaro must outwit the count, contain Cherubino, avoid Marcella, and solve several other problems on the way. Though Kant would encourage independent thinking on this as in every other matter, this sort of reasoning is very much secondary to what he calls the real use of reason. This is the activity of setting ends, the highest form of which occurs in moral choice. What he means by this is often

---

[6] For more, see chapter 5 of my (2011). I present a much more detailed account in my (1994).

obscured by attention to examples in his *Groundwork of the Metaphysics of Morals,* the shortest of his works on ethics, but his *Critique of Practical Reason* contains a far more powerful example.

There Kant asks us to imagine a man who claims to be overwhelmed by temptation every time he passes "a certain house." (The eighteenth century was more discrete than our own.) He'd like to be prudent, perhaps even faithful, but whenever he reaches the whorehouse he feels compelled to enter. Were he told, however, that he would be executed upon exiting—with a gallows installed before the entrance to grab his attention—he would suddenly be able to resist temptation very well indeed. This is a matter of the simplest instrumental reasoning: any ordinary desire fades before the desire to go on living, which is the condition on fulfilling any of the others. Now imagine that the same man were summoned before an unjust ruler and given a choice: either he must sign a denunciation that will lead to an innocent man's execution, or be executed himself.

Kant always insisted on the limits of our knowledge, and one thing we never know for certain is the content of our souls. No one is so righteous as to be certain she would withstand threats of death or torture; most of us do not. Yet unlike the first case, where the choice between death and brothel is easy, we are not sure how we would choose between death and justice, and our wavering counts. We know what we *should* do— refuse to denounce an innocent though it cost our own lives—and we know that we *could,* though most of us would falter in the end. In that moment of uncertainty we recognize our own freedom: not the desire for pleasure but the desire for justice can lead us to action that overcomes the most basic of human desires, the preservation of life itself.

Kant wrote that this thought experiment is simple enough to be grasped by "businessmen, women and ten year old schoolboys." Having used it in many different settings, sometimes with variations, I'm convinced he is right. While I've met students who claimed to be cowards who'd sign anything, even they placed some limits on what injustice they'd be prepared to commit in order to stay alive. And all of them had one hero, in history or in fiction, who was ready to defy death to do what was right. Kant's ethics are usually distorted as a matter of following rules. In fact, he believed that ethics should be taught by using such examples, because only they reveal a sense of human freedom and dignity that move us all. "Here virtue is worth so much because it costs so much" (Kant 1996: 265). We have moral needs that go beyond reward.

We know this is true. Even animals have been known to risk their lives to save others (De Waal 2009), and human beings do it regularly. Not only that: we regularly admire them for doing so, even as we fear we could not emulate them, for they realize deep human desires to transcend the world of natural necessity. In my own experience, only evolutionary psychologists will deny it. A particularly vivid example of the lengths to which they're prepared to go occurred at a recent Harvard conference on Darwin and morality. Eager to examine cases in which people risk their lives for reasons that have no discernible adaptive advantage, I mentioned Wesley Autrey, the construction worker who threw himself under a New York City subway train in January 2007 to save the life of a stranger. The fact that Autrey was a 51-year-old working-class black man accompanying his young daughters to school while the man he saved was a 20-year-old white student underlines the difficulty of any explanation referring to membership in any group smaller than the human race as a whole. Autrey's spontaneous heroism attracted a good deal of official attention and, perhaps more importantly, the immediate fascination of people all over the world, as evidenced by over two million Google entries about this hitherto quiet man two days after his deed. Steven Pinker argued that the admiration millions felt for Autrey was not sheer admiration for his courage and character—awe and wonder before someone able to overcome our natural interest in self-preservation in order to save another life—but something entirely different. Our admiration for Autrey, Pinker argued, had nothing to do with the wish that we might ourselves be capable of similarly heroic deeds, but the wish that someone would be there to do them for us, should we be so unlucky as to fall into the path of an oncoming train.

Our discussion was long and inconclusive, not only because it's unclear what sort of argument would count as conclusive here, but because of the difference in the concepts of reason from which we began. For evolutionary psychologists such as Pinker, an instrumental notion of rationality appears self-evident: we act rationally when we maximize our chances of (individual or species) preservation. Any action that cannot be ultimately explained as a function of that interest is paradoxical or irrational. A good example of these assumptions was provided by Pinker (2008):

> Community, the very different emotion that prompts people to sacrifice without an expectation of *payback*, may be rooted in nepotistic altruism, the empathy and solidarity we feel toward our relatives which evolved because any gene that pushed an organism to aid a relative would have helped copies of itself sitting inside that relative. In human societies, of course, communal feelings can be lavished on non-relatives as well. Sometimes it *pays* people (in an evolutionary sense) to love their companions because their interests are yoked, like spouses with common children, in-laws with common relatives, friends with common tastes or allies with common enemies. And sometimes it doesn't *pay* them at all, but their kinship-detectors have been tricked into treating their group-mates as if they were relatives by tactics like kinship metaphors (blood brothers, fraternities, the fatherland), origin myths, communal meals and other bonding rituals.

While the presence of the subjunctive signals the speculative nature of Pinker's claims, the tone continually suggests that they are the only rational explanation for community-directed behavior. I have added italics to underline the fact that evolutionary psychology's use of the *Homo economicus* model of human motivation is not even implicit: it is blithely and repeatedly expressed. Like those behavioral economists who criticize the model because we often fall short of its conception of rationality, evolutionary psychology, which frames altruism as a problem, acknowledges deviations from the model as functions of being tricked. Yet we know how often it's the other way around: this model, as Mill knew when formulating it, falls short of who we are.

I introduced Kant to show that you needn't be a romantic, a suicide bomber, or a nationalist to find the instrumental model of reason both false and repulsive. Cases of those who prefer death to injustice make this explicit; Kant's own favorite was Thomas More. But even without offering their lives, millions of people sacrifice considerable bits of them daily, spending time and energy and money on things that bring them no advantage, adaptive or otherwise. Our ordinary experience is rife with elements that defy the *Homo economicus* model. As Debra Satz has pointed out, someone who offers to buy your friendship does not understand what it means to be or have a friend (2010: 80). Even the strongest defenders of neo-liberalism never find it sufficient to appeal to self-interest; they need and deploy strong moral claims about responsibility in order to maintain supporters. Nor did the best-known advocate of selfishness rest her case with an appeal to *Homo economicus*. Ayn Rand's novels win followers not through their Dostoevskyan plot twists, still less by their tediously long speeches, but because their leading characters represent freedom, dignity, courage, and passion in a world full of meanness and envy. For all their talk about selfishness, Rand's men and women are always depicted as great and noble souls engaged in battle against small-mindedness. The Tea Partiers may be the only adults who read them, but many of your most creative friends were reading them as teenagers, whatever their politics then or today. (Any casual survey will be illuminating.) Rand's heroes are nothing like Mill's beings who inevitably do whatever they can to obtain the greatest amount of goods with the smallest amount of labor and self-denial; such people are precisely the villains of her stories. On the contrary, whether designing homes or inventing metals, they work as creators who embody human freedom. As surely as any abstract laborer imagined by Marx or Hegel, their labor—not the goods it may bring—is the truest expression of their humanity, and the act that gives them a claim to something meant to replace the divine.

If the *Homo economicus* model of human motivation doesn't even work in the places we would expect to find it, how did it become the dominant one? Reductionism and simplicity appeal to many, and even those who prefer complexity may be dismayed by the company that a rejection of the model seems to require them to keep. Anyone who wants to reject the irrationality of jihadis, Tea Partiers, and the likes of Marine LePen will be unlikely to see it as not just a failure but a protest. Those committed to accepting standards of scientific rationality may feel bound to accept the conclusions of Adam Smith and Charles Darwin, who created modernity's most substantive sciences of human behavior, whatever the consequences.

But it doesn't take much study to learn that both thinkers held views that were not only far more complex than but almost entirely opposed to the ones generally ascribed to them. Far from believing that maximizing self-interest always led to the best results for society as a whole, Adam Smith found it noteworthy that it sometimes did. Charles Darwin was never a Social Darwinist but a thinker who wrote, "Any animal whatever, endowed with well-marked social instincts . . . would inevitably acquire a moral sense or conscience as soon as its intellectual powers had become as well developed, or nearly as well developed, as in man" (Darwin 1981: 71–2). Nor did he hold this acquisition to be a matter of calculating "payback" for social behavior. Like other higher mammals, we seek status and territory, but like other higher mammals, we also regularly act in ways that have nothing to do with maximizing self-interest. Rousseau noted the existence of compassion and pity in the ordinary higher animals he saw around him, which furthered his view that compassion and pity are natural to humankind. After confirming such observations with decades of careful experiments, primatologist Frans de Waal (2009: 7) concludes that we need

> a complete overhaul of assumptions about human nature. Too many economists and politicians model human society on the perpetual struggle they believe exists in nature, but which is a mere projection. Like magicians, they first throw their ideological prejudices into the hat of nature, then pull them out by their very ears to show how much nature agrees with them. It's a trick we have fallen for too long.[7]

The trick is as familiar as it is often successful: project your worldview onto the state of nature, then argue that your worldview is the only natural one. In fact we have no access to an original state of nature, and what we now know about our origins supports Rousseau's account as much as it does that of Hobbes. Presented with these alternatives, what accounts for our inclination to choose the worst of Hobbes's view of what moves us is no less (and no more) speculative than Rousseau's, but the sheer number of positions which begin from it gives it an appearance of weight.

This is a fact about contemporary culture that doubtless has more than one explanation, but one is surely that Hobbes's view of human nature is part of a long and dismal tradition that seems to make us feel at home. Many committed atheists hold fast to one of the more problematic elements of Christianity, the doctrine of original sin. Christianity has made that doctrine very familiar, but I don't believe it is the source of it. Original sin, in its many variations, doesn't feel comfortable because Christianity cultivated it; Christianity cultivated it because it's a useful way of understanding the problem of evil, which I understand as the point where most thinking begins: why is there such a gap between the way the world is and the way that it should be? The doctrine of original sin may give us the blame for the existence of evil, but it also offers consolation, for it offers a reason for all the evils we experience. Our inclination to believe the very worst about human nature gains at least as much support from faith as from fact.

De Waal offers another explanation of why Social Darwinism, with its Hobbesian picture of human nature as "red in tooth and claw," gained such traction after the Industrial Revolution created wealth that was unconnected to aristocracy. For earlier feudal society, divisions of wealth were dependent on class structure that seemed part of a fixed natural order. The newly rich of the nineteenth century could have no such illusions.

---

[7] We have indeed been falling for this trick too long; in a letter from 1875 Friedrich Engels wrote: "The whole Darwinian teaching of the struggle for existence is simply a transference from society to living nature of Hobbes's doctrine of *bellum omnia contra omnes* ... When this conjuror's trick has been performed ... the same theories are transferred back again from organic nature into history and it is now claimed that their validity as eternal *laws* of human society has been proved." Quoted in Sahlins 1976: 54.

Many of them had belonged to the lower class only a few generations before. They evidently were of the same blood. So shouldn't they share their wealth? They were reluctant to do so, though, and were thrilled to hear that there was nothing wrong with ignoring those who worked for them, that it was perfectly honorable to climb the ladder of success without looking back. This is how nature works, Spencer assured them, thus removing any pangs of conscience the rich might feel. (De Waal 2009: 31)

And indeed John D. Rockefeller argued that unconstrained and ruthless corporations were "merely the working out of a law of nature," as a few decades later, German generals would support World War I with the claim that war was the best way to decide who is fittest to survive.

But few complicated matters admit of monocausal explanation, and the widespread acceptance of the *Homo economicus* model surely has more than one cause. Albert Hirschmann's account of the ways in which the self-interest model was developed as an alternative to the more destructive passions is important and illuminating.[8] Less well known is sociologist Eva Illouz's discussion of the massive efforts made to convince people to act upon self-interest. Early in the twentieth century, the attitudes that now seem self-evident were encouraged by psychologists to cultivate the qualities that corporate capitalism requires. After examining training manuals and self-help books she concluded that psychologists not only codified emotional conduct inside the workplace but more importantly made self-interest, efficiency, and instrumentality into valid cultural repertoires. Under the aegis of therapeutic discourse, emotional life became imbued with the metaphors and rationality of economics. Illouz's conclusions may seem extreme until one recalls that dueling was a social practice that persisted into the twentieth century. To be a man was to draw a weapon if you were insulted—not to exercise emotional control in pursuit of your self-interest. Recalling a world driven by ideas of honor is not, of course, to plead for a return to dueling, but it is a demand to consider how many views that now seem self-evident are both products of history, and of very particular interests.

Robert Frank describes an important phenomenon that is less of a cause than an effect of the predominance of the self-interest model, but it contributes to its ongoing support.

> The flint-eyed researcher fears no greater humiliation than to have called some action altruistic, only to have a more sophisticated colleague later demonstrate that it was self-serving. This fear surely helps account for the extraordinary volume of ink behavioral scientists have spent trying to unearth selfish motives for seemingly self-sacrificing acts. (Frank 1988: 2)[9]

---

[8] See Hirschmann (1976) as well as Holmes (1995).
[9] It's interesting to note that this is, after all, the search for a kind of honor that earlier ages tested with dueling.

Frank's description of the fear of humiliation should remind us how pervasively those fears dominate not simply the behavioral sciences, but contemporary Western culture. They are less fears of being actually tricked—by one's "kinship detectors" or anything else—than about being seen to be vulnerable to trickery. Of all the hopes and fears which may be inextricably bound with our views of human nature, fear of embarrassment ought to be the most embarrassing. Shouldn't we abandon the desire to appear cool in the eyes of a group that is itself desperate to appear cool by late adolescence, at the latest? How human beings evolved, in one short century, from fear of the shame of being insufficiently moral to fear of the shame of seeming insufficiently self-serving deserves serious investigation.

Consider discussions of human motivation in Smith's or Darwin's own times. No reader of Tolstoy or Eliot can imagine that the nineteenth century was naïve about what moves us, or the complex mixture of self-interest and other motives that most of our actions reveal. The difference is that, until quite recently, motives were assumed to be mixed. It seemed self-evident that people are inspired by desires to behave according to certain standards, swayed by passion, driven by greed. No one of these elements, nor any of the other beliefs and desires that lead us to action, was seen to require deconstruction to another. In one short century we have moved from a norm that assumes morally driven behavior as the standard of rationality, then explained derivations by reference to greed, passion, weakness, or misperception, to a norm that assumes maximizing self-interest as the standard of rationality, then works to explain deviations like the so-called problem of altruism. No doubt some things needed deconstructing: World War I, at the least, showed the deadly brute competition that lay behind high-flown rhetoric about honor and glory. Still we should consider: is the assumption that genuine explanations of human behavior penetrate grandiose description to reveal the self-interested motivation behind them *itself* a twentieth-century cultural construction?

I believe that it is, though a great deal of further work would be needed to show it. I'd like to close by raising a related question. The last few decades have not only seen a wealth of data from fields as diverse as primatology, child psychology, and neurobiology which decisively undermine the *Homo economicus* model of motivation; even many distinguished economists have argued against it.

> Why should it be *uniquely* rational to pursue one's own self-interest to the exclusion of everything else? It may not, of course, be at all absurd to claim that maximization of self-interest is not irrational, at least not necessarily so, but to argue that anything other than maximizing self-interest must be irrational seems altogether extraordinary. (Sen 1987: 15)

Yet the increasing evidence that the model is altogether extraordinary, as Sen so elegantly puts it, has had little effect on popular culture, which continues to blast the same mangled message attributed to Smith and Darwin.[10] One can bemoan the fact

---

[10] I am thinking e.g. of the editorial or magazine sections of the *New York Times,* which might count as high popular culture.

that complex theories are often misunderstood; knowledge doesn't trickle down any more simply than wealth does. But it cannot be entirely accidental that the end of the Cold War, and the accompanying triumphalism of neo-liberalism, created a climate in which *Homo economicus,* bolstered by an evolutionary theory that predicates constant competition as the natural form of action, would come to feel at home.[11]

Perhaps because I have long lived in Germany, whose deep social democratic framework has survived any number of conservative governments, I do not think we yet know what the fall of the Berlin Wall has proved. The jury will be out for quite some time. For the record, I hold Marxist theory, with its materialist explanation of behavior, to be as much responsible for the failure of real existing socialism as the practices. Memories are short enough for readers to swallow the standard claim that 1989 showed the folly of Marx's view of human motivation: people want consumer goods more than cooperative lifestyles. But there's very little difference between the late Marx's use of *Homo economicus* and that of the neo-liberals; Kantian socialists like Eduard Bernstein lost the arguments over what Marxists called bourgeois morality (see Neiman 2011: ch. 2).

It is certainly not an accident that religious fundamentalism exploded at the same moment when market fundamentalism became the leading global ideology, though it is a tragedy that it has become the most popular alternative to it. The winners of the Cold War were certain that other ideologies would be replaced by their own version of neo-liberalism, in which the bottom line is the measure of all value. Against such predictions, the past decades have witnessed various forms of rage in rejection of the idea that material needs are what move us, and everything else is expendable fluff. That idea was succinctly attacked by Marx long ago:

> The bourgeois drowned the most heavenly ecstasies of religious fervor in the icy water of egotistical calculation. It has resolved personal worth into exchange value, and in place of the numberless indefeasible chartered freedoms has set up that single, unconscionable freedom—free trade. All that is solid, melts into air, all that is holy is profaned.

But at a time when every promise of Marxism seemed undermined by the failures of real existing socialism, the shortest road to idealism is traditional religion. It already has, after all, a long tradition of opposing profanation of the holy.

Fundamentalism has been on the rise in all major religions, for it seems to offer something of value that cannot be bought or sold. Even where it does not lead to violence, its tragedy is its inability to offer the kind of dignity it seeks. But what alternatives do we offer? A world in which former mayor Rudy Giulani's idea of an

---

[11] The convergence of neoliberalism and evolutionary psychology is a question that deserves further study, which would begin by noting that what was originally called sociobiology had undergone such criticism in the 1970s and 1980s that it had to change its name to avoid the disrepute attached to the original one.

uplifting—no, heroic—response to the terrorist attack on New York was to tell its citizens to go shopping, is a world that has incorporated a slogan once meant to be ironic: *whoever dies with the most toys wins.* A culture that cannot provide its citizens with the sense that life within it has more meaning than increasing their collection of playthings should not be surprised when its rejection takes explosive and twisted forms.

Any interesting phenomenon has more than one cause; it would be silly to reduce the motivation of the groups here discussed to their rejection of *Homo economicus.* There are important differences between the three groups I've lumped together, and many factors have contributed to their growth. But one factor we can actually influence is this one, and one thing we can do is to reject with whole hearts and unembarrassed voices the model of human meaning and motivation that leaves us childish and brutish—and cannot even do justice to children and brutes.

REFERENCES

Atran, Scott (2004). Soft Power and the Psychology of Suicide Bombing. *Terrorism Monitor,* 2/11.   <www.jamestown.org/programs/tm/single/?tx_ttnews[tt_news]=26613&tx_ttnews [backPid]=179&no_cache=1#.U6BicKi46Iw> [Accessed June 2014].

Atran, Scott (2006a). An Edge Discussion of Beyond Belief: Science, Religion, Reason and Survival. *Edge,* Nov. 29. <http://edge.org/discourse/bb.html>.

Atran, Scott (2006b). The Moral Logic and Growth of Suicide Terrorism. *Washington Quarterly,* 29: 128.

Cohn-Bendit, Daniel, and Guy Verhofstadt (2012). *For Europe! Manifesto for a Postnational Revolution in Europe.* CreateSpace.

Darwin, Charles (1981). *Descent of Man.* Princeton: Princeton University Press.

Daston, Lorraine (2013). The Paradoxes of Self-Interest. Lecture, Einstein Forum, Why Do We Believe in Self-Interest?, Potsdam, June 13–15.

De Waal, Frans (2009). *The Age of Empathy: Nature's Lessons for a Kinder Society.* New York: Harmony Books.

Frank, Robert (1988). *Passions within Reason: The Strategic Role of the Emotions.* New York: W. W. Norton.

Frank, Thomas (2012). *Pity the Billionaire: The Unlikely Comeback of the American Right.* New York: Vintage.

Hirschmann, Albert (1976). *The Passions and the Interests.* Princeton: Princeton University Press.

Holmes, Stephen (1995). *Passions and Constraint.* Chicago: University of Chicago Press.

Kant, Immanuel (1996). *Critique of Practical Reason,* in Immanuel Kant, *Practical Philosophy,* tr. Mary J. Gregor. Cambridge: Cambridge University Press.

Marx, Karl, and Engels, Fredrich (1848). The Communist Manifesto, in Eugene Kamenka, ed., The Portable Karl Marx, p. 206.

Mill, John Stuart (1968). *Essays on Some Unsettled Questions of Political Economy.* New York: Augustus M. Kelley.

Neiman, Susan (1994). *The Unity of Reason: Rereading Kant.* Oxford: Oxford University Press.

Neiman, Susan (2011). *Moral Clarity: A Guide for Grown-Up Idealists.* London: Vintage.

Pinker, Steven (2008). The Moral Instinct. *New York Times Magazine,* Jan. 13. <www.nytimes.com/2008/01/13/magazine/13Psychology-t.html?pagewanted=all>.

Sahlins, Marshall David (1976). *The Use and Abuse of Biology: An Anthropological Critique of Sociobiology.* Ann Arbor: University of Michigan Press.

Satz, Debra (2010). *Why Some Things Should Not Be for Sale.* Oxford: Oxford University Press.

Sen, Amartya (1987). *On Ethics and Economics.* Malden, MA: Blackwell.

CHOICES AND PREFERENCES: DISCUSSION SUMMARY

THE societal consequences of market capitalism depend significantly on the constitution of preferences and, relatedly, the manner in which choices are made, at the level of individuals as consumers, employees, and investors. For the theme of "Choices and Preferences" the group turned to reflect on this cluster of issues.

Mendiola's presentation began the discussion by drawing on a metaphor from John Mackey (CEO and co-founder of Whole Foods): how can business leaders transform themselves from mere "caterpillars," focused narrowly on enriching themselves and shareholders, to "butterflies" who "pollinate" the world by creating value that is broadly shared? Drawing on his own experience, he suggested that companies must be guided by a "higher purpose" that establishes a "moral compass" as the bottom line in guiding action. Mendiola's reference to a higher purpose was indicative of a broader theme that ran through much of the discussion: that the prospects of reconciling performance with progress hinge crucially on fundamental ideals of a valuable or meaningful life.

If progress depends on the establishment of a moral compass within business, one crucial challenge, as Tiberius noted, is how to "scale" that kind of psychological shift. One question here concerns the extent to which economic and social objectives converge. Do we really need a "higher purpose" or do we just need to recognize the true relationship between progress and profit? Thus Battilana asked, in reference to Mendiola's enterprise, "is it that this kind of firm makes no trade-offs, or is it that this kind of firm has learned how to deal with those trade-offs?" Snabe suggested that, once the "knowledge problem" was solved, there were in fact no trade-offs. For SAP, the choice to reduce waste, for example, was easier to make once they realized how profitable it was: "*green* is the color of the money we save." This potential alignment of progress and profit might be further aligned, Abouchakra (of the Abu Dhabi Crown Prince Court) suggested, through taxes and regulations that help "fence off greed" as a motivation. For Anderson, Mendiola's case suggested the enormous power that a small number of individuals might have in changing business practice, particularly by helping to advance ideological shifts (re Neiman) that change our cultural "esteem hierarchy" (re Appiah).

The chapter by Hong and Liskovich offered a more systematic empirical take on the underlying motivations of management in weighing progress versus profit. Summing up his results, he suggested that available data give evidence that CSR (corporate social responsibility) spending is driven significantly but not wholly by "agency" issues, i.e. managerial objectives that are at odds with immediate shareholder interests. At the same time, he notes, CSR spending does yield meaningful benefits to shareholders in the form of gentler treatment within the legal/regulatory system.

As Davis observed, Hong's argument seems to support the view that CSR is promoted by insulating management from shareholders. Mendiola, meanwhile, suggested that we ought to think broadly about the possible motivations behind CSR: to what extent might the "intrinsic" motivations associated with a moral compass be playing a role? As Jafar noted, this issue might be studied by comparing the CSR tendencies of family-owned versus publicly traded firms. While Hong's results suggest some possible moral benefits to managerial autonomy, Pettit noted that this might have a darker anti-democratic aspect if it translates into disproportionate political influence through donations.

Hong observed that, in general, CSR behavior tends to decline under difficult economic conditions, as pressure from shareholders mounts in favor of immediate financial concerns. Perhaps, Barney suggested, CSR is caused by financial performance and not the other way around?

Frank's chapter tackles the question of choice and preference from the consumer side of things. He notes that a large share of consumption spending goes towards goods that perpetuate social competition—in house size or wedding lavishness, for example— without necessarily promoting anyone's well-being. On his view, the case of positional goods reveals a certain kind of perversity in markets: everyone can be made worse off by the collection of individual choices that are economically rational. As a solution, he proposes that we tax consumption rather than income.

In response to Frank's presentation, Risse observed that "there are kinds of consumption that are problematic and there are other kinds that are not." Perhaps a general consumption tax risked "overkill?" A number of other participants picked up on this theme. Referring back to Autor's chapter on technology and unemployment, Pettit suggested that the continual pursuit of status among the wealthy might in fact serve as a crucial driver of demand for unskilled labor. Likewise, Autor noted that a great deal of social competition in fact drives social improvements in cases such as schools, for example. The crucial issue, he suggested, is "whether the additional investment causes the good to be supplied elastically." Chiming in on this point, Sen suggested that the relative value of consumption versus saving was a contextual matter. In China, he noted, one crucial objective at present is to increase domestic consumption.

A number of the participants also commented on the complexities of taxation itself. As Snabe observed, taxation itself is often an imperfect and complicated instrument. A large tax on cars in his native Denmark, for example, has created incentives for people to hold on to old, heavily polluting vehicles. On the other hand, Appiah wondered whether, as a positive side-effect, consumption taxes might help induce a kind of analog for the "potlatch" ritual practiced among some indigenous communities within Canada and the United States, in which the wealthy give away a substantial portion of their riches to society. Perhaps the well-off would rather give to charity than to the government? Following on Snabe's and Appiah's points, one possibility playfully suggested by Kitcher would be to try to "compute taxes in such a way that represents *all* the social costs of *all* of the things that people do." That might sometimes yield consumption taxes, but would presumably yield different possibilities on a case-by-case basis depending on what sort of behavior is in fact the source of relevant social costs.

As Autor noted, in thinking about the value of social competition, one must attend to the crucial distinction between whether we are satisfied with some set of conditions and whether those conditions are actually good for us. Climbing some ladder of competition in life expectancy, for example, might not make us more satisfied even if, nonetheless, we are in fact better off. Autor's distinction brings us back to the central theme—what makes for a valuable or meaningful life? Climbing a ladder of competition is one thing; but what does it mean, as Rangan put it (citing an Irish CEO whom he had met), for our ladder to be "up against the right wall?"

Tiberius's chapter takes that particular question head on, articulating a conception of well-being as the ideal of a "value-full life" in which we are able to live up to a cohesive and reflectively endorsed set of values over time. Applying her view to the case of business, Tiberius wondered whether much of the dysfunction observed in consumer and business behavior might be diagnosed as a tendency to give too little weight to a reflective, "whole-life"—as opposed to short-term—perspective in assessing what we value.

In response, Rangan observed that, as the influence of traditional institutions (such as religious institutions) has waned in some corners of society, the gap thereby created has been filled by influences within the marketplace itself and, in particular, the enormous influence of marketing. Tiberius's ideal of the "whole-life" perspective, Rangan noted, highlighted the crucial connection of value to a reflectively conceived sense of self, i.e. our identity.

Meyer, however, drew the group's attention to a substantial body of empirical work illustrating a "disjunction between values and action." Valuing academic productivity greatly, for example, often correlates very badly with sitting down to write an essay. This sort of example suggests that a conception of value could only provide a partial diagnosis of some of the problematic behavior observed in the marketplace.

Highlighting another complication in this domain, Sen observed the crucial distinction between valuing something because it will make us personally better off (e.g. getting a pay rise) and valuing something for other reasons, whether or not it makes us better off (e.g. the welfare of one's children or living in a society without terrible deprivation). The importance of this distinction, Sen suggested, not only requires preserving some conceptual separation between well-being and value-fulfillment, but also requires resisting the temptation to treat the increase in one's well-being, whenever it occurs, as the reason why one values a change. We may value living in a society without famines, for example; but while that might make us happier as well, it is not one's own happiness that one is seeking in trying to prevent famines.[1]

A number of participants raised issues that concern the social realization of Tiberius's conception of well-being. While Tiberius characterized the crucial defect of valuation within the marketplace in terms of a short-term versus "whole-life" perspective, Fuerstein, highlighting Anderson's chapter, suggested that we should also be thinking in terms of an individualist versus social perspective. From an individualist point of view, we think about what is valuable in relation to our own well-being whereas, from a social point of view, we think about value in a way that also encompasses the good of others. Pettit noted that in moving from individual welfare to aggregate social welfare, we run into difficulties when we must reconcile incompatible valuations, such as those which attach to positional goods. Perhaps social aggregate welfare should only encompass those values which satisfy a "compossibility" constraint? Frank, however, suggested that, rather than introducing such a constraint, we ought to pursue institutional solutions that manage the consequences of positional competition.

While Tiberius's conception of well-being is subjective—in the sense that it takes the point of view of the agent as primary—Risse wondered aloud whether the preoccupation with subjective welfare, and with happiness in particular, was a narrowly British tradition. In the case of Nietzsche, for example, well-being "is about creating a beautiful soul, a noble soul, a great personality with certain accomplishments." Risse's comment served in effect to question some of the most fundamental motivational premises involved in the rationalization of markets, i.e. that people are driven principally by the desire to achieve happiness or satisfaction, and that achieving these things is a substantial aspect of what makes a life go well.

In her essay, Neiman develops a related point, arguing that we ought to question whether the central *Homo economicus* presumption of economic analysis—that people are driven principally by the logic of self-interest—is merely an artifact of a particular, culture-bound market ideology. She suggests that groups like Al Qaeda, the Tea Party, and right-wing nationalist groups in Europe represent a kind of rejection of that model as what some thinkers have called a post-heroic ideal, in which the only human bonds are those of trade.

Neiman's argument inspired significant reflection among the group about the precise nature of the *Homo economicus* view. Arrow argued that, on a standard economist's interpretation, the point was simply that "ends are arbitrary and all we say is they are going to be achieved efficiently." From this point of view, all economic behavior can be seen as self-interested, but only in the sense that all such behavior is directed at the fulfillment of an agent's desires, whether they involve self-destruction, personal happiness, or the good of others. In response, Neiman clarified that she was

---

[1] Sen cited Thomas Nagel's discussion of this distinction in *The Possibility of Altruism* (Princeton: Princeton University Press, 1979).

referring to a particular conception of *Homo economicus* characterized in J. S. Mill's work, where the primary driving end of individuals is wealth "by the simplest means and with very little exertion." On this point, Frank cited Sen's well-known suggestion in print that *Homo economicus* is, in effect, a "social moron."[2]

Chiming in, Anderson once again brought Adam Smith into the conversation, citing his own take on the Millian *Homo economicus*: "The tendency to admire and even to worship the rich and powerful is the single greatest source of the corruption of moral sentiments." For Smith, Anderson suggested, we should admire people with virtue irrespective of wealth. Nonetheless, on Smith's view, there are both "calm" and "heroic" virtues and there might, Anderson noted, be good reason to prefer a society in which the calmer virtues dominate. At the same time, Arrow noted, heroic ideas might serve a crucial social function in inspiring solidarity and cooperation. From that point of view, they might ultimately be analyzed in terms of their survival value from an evolutionary point of view. But, he suggested, there is "nothing degrading" in that possibility. Sen likewise noted the crucial role that self-interest might play in guiding us away from a "world where people are minding everybody else's business rather than your business." From that perspective, one crucial value of the *Homo economicus* model is instrumental in deterring us from senseless acts of war, for example. Another possibility noted by Sen is that the model aims, not to represent what is true in the world, but only to provide a certain theoretical simplification for the sake of certain kinds of problem-solving.

---

[2] "Rational Fools: A Critique of the Behavioral Foundations of Economic Theory," *Philosophy and Public Affairs*, 6 (1977), 336.

PART V

POWER AND TRUST

CHAPTER 22

TWO FALLACIES ABOUT CORPORATIONS

PHILIP PETTIT

Abstract

One of the most important challenges for political theory is to identify the extent to which corporations should be facilitated and restricted in law. By way of background to that challenge, we need to develop a view about the nature and the potential of corporations and indeed of corporate bodies in general. This chapter discusses two fallacies that we should avoid in this exercise. One, a claim popular among economists, that corporate bodies are not really agents at all. The other, a claim associated with US jurisprudence, that not only are they agents, they are persons whose rights call in the same way as the rights of individual persons for legal recognition and protection.

INTRODUCTION

We are moving towards a world in which more and more people live their working lives as the employees of corporations, and more and more corporations are part of large multinational conglomerates. This development is probably inevitable in a world of global markets, where economies of scale, efficiencies of location, and the attractions of greater market control converge in support of ever more intense incorporation. There are many challenges that we face in looking for ways in which to organize our lives on this planet over the coming decades and centuries but one of the major issues is: how are we to cope with this growing corporatization of our world?

Corporatization is as likely to have economic advantages as it is to generate economic problems and I see the challenge that it raises as one of a more political kind. As things stand in most countries, corporations are not only economically well-resourced, they are also legally privileged, politically powerful, and democratically uncontrolled (Galanter 2006). Such titans raise a challenge for us as individuals insofar as we coexist with them in our neighborhoods, seek employment by them in their workplaces, purchase the goods and services they provide, compete with them in open markets, and deal with them as plaintiffs or defendants in the courts. And they raise a challenge for us as communities insofar as they often have a stranglehold over our politicians, whether by virtue of the permanent threat of moving elsewhere or by dint of the capacity to exercise electoral patronage and extract payback.

The political challenge of corporations is hard to underestimate. In the competition for corporate advantage—say, the maximization of shareholder income and wealth—corporations are bound to use their muscle to seek concessions from governments that are likely to make the lives of ordinary people worse off. They will seek to preserve and even enhance the existing infrastructure of their influence: their legal privilege, their political power, and the absence of democratic control over their operations. And putting that infrastructure to work, they will push for more business-friendly arrangements: less unionization, fewer worker rights, weaker consumer organizations, looser environmental constraints, lighter regulatory controls, and, of course, a lower level of corporate taxation.

From my point of view, the prospect of that world is a specter to shrink from. Consider the possible consequences under a worst-case scenario. In the absence of unions or workplace restrictions, we would depend on the whim of a manager for being kept in corporate employment. In the absence of consumer organizations, we would lose important checks on the quality of our food and other purchases. In the absence of environmental constraints, we would be in danger of a serious decline in the quality of public health. In the absence of equality in legal power, we would have little or no chance of using our day in court to call corporations to book. In the absence of independent regulations, we would be in danger of corporate risk-taking and another disaster like the GFC. In the absence of control over corporate boardrooms we would find it hard to know what was going on in the first place. And in the absence of political equality with corporations, we would have almost no hope of getting government to impose our shared, democratic will on larger corporate bodies. We would live in a condition of corporate domination, not a condition of freedom and independence (Pettit 2014b).

It may be said against the picture I have offered that in the past decade or so corporations have begun to shrink in size, choosing to outsource a large range of their activity, productive and otherwise (Davis 2013). But while this is a very interesting development, and needs to be carefully tracked, I do not see it as a source of consolation. As a corporation shrinks to a board and a management that operate in the interest of shareholders, outsourcing production, distribution, marketing, and other functions, that threatens to concentrate progressively the power of those at the top, making them less responsive to the ever more replaceable bodies of workers that they employ. There is little or no possibility of unions serving as countervailing forces, for example, if a corporation can switch the production of the goods it sells from one body of workers to another.

I may have painted an excessively lurid description of an excessively pessimistic vision. I put it on the table to try to muster agreement that whatever differences divide us on matters of detail, we can all agree that this image of a fully corporatized world—this image of Earth Inc—is not attractive, and not even tolerable. And if we agree on that, then the questions we ought to be facing bear on what our different governments ought to be doing, individually and in collaboration, in order to guard against it.

Unfortunately, I cannot begin to deal with those questions here; limitations of space and skill make it impossible. What I propose to do instead is to identify and criticize two fallacies or mistakes that might dull our sense of dismay at the scenario of a fully corporatized world, weakening our commitment to guard against it. They would each mislead us, although in different ways, about the power of corporations.

The first fallacy is that corporations are dense sites of market-like activity and not entities of the kind that raise concerns of the type illustrated. They are networks of individual-to-individual, relatively enduring arrangements, so the idea goes, and they exist because of serving the contracting parties better than more regular, episodic contracts (Williamson 1989). The mistake or fallacy here is the assumption, quite common in economics circles, that there is no literal sense in which corporations constitute agents like you and me.

The second fallacy is common within legal rather than economic traditions of thought and involves an error of exactly the opposite kind. It holds that corporations are indeed agents like you and me, not just impersonal contractual arrangements. But it maintains that they are personal agents and that they have a just claim to the rights that our constitutions give to natural persons like you and me. They may not have the capacity to exercise all the rights that we routinely enjoy but where they have appropriate abilities, they should not be denied the corresponding rights.[1]

The two fallacies I describe are not just misleading in relation to commercial bodies. They mislead us with any familiar sort of corporate body, whether that be a voluntary association, a political party, an ecclesiastical organization, or even a social movement. In the discussion that follows, therefore, I shall often speak of corporate bodies in general, focusing only as appropriate on corporations in particular. I do not suggest that all corporate bodies should be granted the same rights, only that the fallacies I consider are misleading in relation to all.

AGAINST THE CLAIM THAT CORPORATE BODIES ARE NOT REAL AGENTS

Corporate Bodies are Representable as Agents

When people incorporate for any purpose or purposes they form a body that acts through its members as if it were an individual agent (List and Pettit 2011). They

---

[1] My argument on both fronts is heavily indebted to joint work with Christian List (2011).

embrace or at least acquiesce in relevant purposes, and perhaps in a mode of revising or extending those purposes. They endorse a method of forming common judgments that can direct them in the pursuit of those ends; these judgments will identify the opportunities for advancing the ends, the relative costs and benefits of different options, the best overall means for realizing their ends, and so on. And they act as their purposes require, according to their judgments; they may act as a whole in some cases but in most they will authorize one or another member or subgroup to act in their name.

In order to be effective in the manner of an individual agent, such an incorporated group has to organize itself so as to be more or less reliable on two fronts. First, it must be evidentially reliable in the judgments that it forms. That is, it must follow some procedure for generating representations of opportunities, costs, benefits, and means that are supported by the evidence available via its members to the group as a whole. And second, it must be executively reliable in the actions it sponsors. That is, it must generally adopt those actions or initiatives that promise to advance its purposes according to its judgments; it must not stall in its decisions, dither about what to do, or misidentify the right path. Like individuals, corporate bodies may often fall away from these evidential and executive standards but they cannot fall too far or too frequently without losing any claim to mimic individuals.

There are many corporate bodies in this sense: organizations of individuals that operate as evidentially and executively reliable centers of decision and action. Any voluntary association that recruits its members effectively in furthering some cause counts as a corporate agent of that kind. So too does any political party that gets behind a set of policies or initiatives and organizes itself for the purposes of achieving democratic power. So does the church that mobilizes its members in confessional unity and recruits them to act in support of ecclesiastical community, evangelization, and social or political action. And so of course does the corporation or business that marshals its management and workforce in pursuit of the means laid down by its board for maximizing the profits accruing to its shareholders.

These corporate bodies all function under the laws of the state or states in whose territories they operate. And each state of that kind is itself a corporate body, albeit one that imposes itself coercively within its territory. It operates or claims to operate on behalf of its membership or citizenry, however they are defined. It is organized via subgroups of elected or unelected officials, legislative, administrative, and judicial, whose activities are coordinated under a written or unwritten constitution. And while its judgments over means and other matters may shift with electoral or other changes in the body of governing officials, it acts or claims to act for the benefit of its members, both in domestic and international contexts.

The striking thing about corporate bodies, as these examples illustrate, is that they come in many different sizes and, more important, assume many different styles. The small-scale voluntary association—say, the small association you and some friends form for the pursuit of environmental goals—may operate in a wholly egalitarian way, with every member exercising a vote in determination of overall general purposes and judgments and with different members rotating in the exercise of special offices. But most parties and churches and corporations and states are very different from this. They are much larger in scale, they operate under hierarchical rules, and they often distribute purpose-shaping and judgment-making functions across different, coordinated sub-bodies (Hess 2014). All corporate bodies have to establish a corporate internal decision-making structure—a CID, as Peter French (1984) calls it—but those structures may vary enormously across different organizations.

To the extent that corporate bodies pursue certain purposes in an executively reliable way according to evidentially reliable judgments, they are representable as agents in a straightforward manner. Their behavior allows us to identify independently plausible purposes and judgments such that in general they can be seen as oriented toward the promotion of those purposes under the guidance of those judgments. We can sensibly adopt the intentional stance, as Daniel Dennett (1987) has long called it, in seeking to make sense of the steps a corporate body takes in the actual situation and to predict what it is likely to do under different scenarios (Tollefsen 2002). We can treat it as we treat other animals, or at least other more or less complex animals, when we look on them as centers of purpose, judgment, and agency.

Corporate Bodies Represent themselves as Agents

But in one important respect corporate bodies are different from other animals and more akin to human agents. Not only are they representable as acting reliably, in accordance with more or less reliable judgments, for the promotion of certain purposes. They actively represent themselves in that light too. They speak for themselves, whether through an authorized spokesperson or, more typically, a coordinated network of authorized spokespersons, each operating in a different domain. Those spokespersons announce the purposes adopted by the corporate body and the judgments it makes about relevant opportunities, means, and the like, inviting their own members, other individuals, and indeed other bodies to judge them for how far they act for those purposes, in fidelity to those judgments: inviting them, in effect, to take an intentional stance and view them from that perspective.

In representing themselves in this way, corporate bodies operate in the fashion of human beings like you and me. For not only do we constitute agents who pursue our purposes, according to our judgments, as many animals do. We also speak for ourselves in a distinctive manner. We declare that this or that is the case, or that we will do such and such, avowing the corresponding belief or intention. And in doing this we foreclose the possibility of excusing a failure to live up to those attitudes by claiming that we misread the evidence on our own minds. Moreover, we promise that we will take this or that action, foreclosing the possibility of excusing a failure to live up to those words, not just by claiming that we misread our minds, but also by claiming that we changed our minds since uttering those words.

With both avowals of attitude and promises of action, we do not just report on how we think or what we will do, since reports allow of mind-misreading and mind-changing excuses. We put ourselves on the line, making it reputationally costly to fail to live up to our words; we commit ourselves to thinking and acting as the words indicate.

What we do in these respects, every corporate body can do also. Each body will have an incentive, shared by its members, to endorse only purposes and judgments—for short, only attitudes—that it can live up to and, given the attitudes it endorses, to take all the actions that its attitudes require. If it fails to perform in that way, then it will not act effectively for the purposes shared among the membership. And if it fails to perform in that way—if it fails to live up to its word—then it cannot hope to attract others to cooperate with it: say, to take it at its word and establish contractual relations in one or another domain.

The members of any corporate body can be expected, in view of this incentive, to fall in line with the purposes or judgments announced by an authorized spokesperson. And of course the spokesperson can be expected to endorse only such purposes and judgments as the members authorize them to endorse in the name of the organization. Since this is going to be manifest to all, that means that the announcement of such an attitude commits the corporate body in such a way that the group cannot excuse a failure to live up to the words uttered on the grounds that the spokesperson misread the mind of the group. A similar lesson applies when a spokesperson makes a promise on behalf of the group, committing the group to an action rather than just an attitude. In this case the spokesperson commits it in such a way that the group cannot excuse a failure to act appropriately either by claiming that the spokesperson misread the group mind or by claiming that it changed its mind since the promise was given.

There is a salient and important distinction between agents like mute animals that cannot speak for themselves and agents like us, who can. A traditional way of marking that distinction is to describe the latter sorts of agents as persons: agents that can speak for themselves, give their word in explicit or implicit commitment to others, and be held responsible for whether or not they keep their word. Persons in this sense are distinguished by how they can function, not by how they are composed. And in that functional sense, we can now see that not only do we individual human beings count as persons, so do the group agents that we constitute.[2]

The idea that corporate bodies can represent themselves appropriately, and therefore count as persons, appears in the high Middle Ages. In a papal bull of 1246, Pope Innocent IV agreed that a corporate body is a *persona* or person in arguing, more specifically, that because it is a *persona ficta*—a fabricated person—it cannot be excommunicated. While theologians often took this qualification to mean that it was a fictional rather than a real person, the lawyers took it to imply that it was an artificial person: a real person, to be sure, but not a natural person like you and me (Eschmann

---

[2] While this conception of a person has its roots in medieval, legal usage (Duff 1938), it is developed in different forms by Hobbes (1994), as I note in the text, and also by Locke (1975); see Rovane (1997) and List and Pettit (2011).

1946; Canning 1980; Kantorowicz 1997). And with this development the recognition of corporate bodies as full-scale persons became a centerpiece of Western thought.

The theme reappears in the writings of Thomas Hobbes in the seventeenth century, for example, although modified to suit the purposes of his political philosophy (Pettit 2008). He makes representation or "personation," as he also calls it, central to the possibility of a group's creating and enacting a single mind. "A multitude of men are made one person, when they are by one man, or one person, represented." Where does the unity come from? From the fact that the representing individual—or body—will speak with one voice, thereby testifying to one mind in the group: "it is the unity of the representer, not the unity of the represented, that maketh the person one" (Hobbes 1994: 16.13).

Against the First Fallacy

The claims I have just defended run directly counter to the tradition in economic circles of claiming that group agents are expressive fictions and that in the words of John Austin (1869: 364), the nineteenth-century jurist, they can be cast as subjects or agents "only by figment, and for the sake of brevity of discussion." Anthony Quinton (1975: 17) sums up the view in the following passage: "We do, of course, speak freely of the mental properties and acts of a group in the way we do of individual people. Groups are said to have beliefs, emotions, and attitudes and to take decisions and make promises. But these ways of speaking are plainly metaphorical. To ascribe mental predicates to a group is always an indirect way of ascribing such predicates to its members."

I hope that my remarks about corporate bodies already makes clear that this view is utterly at odds with how we ordinarily think. It is certainly true that we sometimes speak in a figurative way of the things that certain groups think and do, not giving it any literal significance. We may say in this key that the electorate has opted for dividing power among different parties, or that the markets have made a harsh judgment on the government's policies, or indeed that the working class are resistant to anti-trade union laws. But this sort of talk is clearly intended to be figurative, since the groups in question lack the organization that would enable them to form attitudes and abide by them in action. With the groups envisaged in our examples, however, there is more than enough organization to allow us speak in quite a literal way of what they seek and think and do.

The reductionist line espoused by Austin and Quinton often makes an appearance in the economic literature in the observation any would-be group agent is constituted by a framework of relations among its members—"a nexus of contracts," in the favored phrase—and that this means it cannot be an agent in any literal sense. On this approach, as one commentator puts it (Grantham 1998: 579), it is taken as obvious that a corporation or group agent is just "a collective noun for the web of contracts that link the various participants."

The suggestion behind this reductionism makes little sense. It is true that the existence of contractual arrangements between individuals does not ensure in itself that the group they constitute is an agent; otherwise every market, for example, would be an agent. But that does not mean that that no sorts of contractual arrangements are capable of making a group into an agent. Consider the argument envisaged in the nexus-of-contracts line of thought: "Markets and corporations are both built out of contracts; but markets are not agents; and so neither can corporations be agents." That the argument is invalid should be obvious from the clear invalidity of the parallel argument: "Trees and human beings are both built out of cells; but trees are not agents; and so neither can human beings be agents."

As the cellular structure of human beings enables them to be agents, unlike the cellular structure of trees, so the contractual structure of corporate bodies enables them to be agents, unlike the contractual structure of markets. It makes it possible for them to be representable as agents and indeed to self-represent as agents. Contractual or quasi-contractual arrangements among members will give rise to a corporate agent if they are designed to ensure that overall the group meets the conditions for being self-representable in that way.

There is more to say in support of the agential status of corporate bodies, since the fact that they are not fictions of the kind that Quinton has in mind does not mean that they are not fictions in a distinct sense: for example, in a sense that someone like Hobbes might have endorsed (Skinner 2010). But that possibility need not detain us; the considerations rehearsed ought to be sufficient for current purposes (Pettit 2014a).

Against the Claim that Corporate Agents Have Autonomous Rights

Some Legal History

The medieval tradition that began with Innocent IV was continuous with a long line of legal thought, already found in the compendium of Roman law, compiled under the Emperor Justinian in Constantinople in the 6th century CE. The *Digest*, which is a central part of that compendium, quotes the eminent second-century jurist, Ulpian, with approval on the crucial idea: "if anything is owed to a group agent (*universitas*), it is not owed to the individual members (*singuli*); nor do the individual members owe that which the group agent owes" (Duff 1938: 37). This idea meant that the group, acting as such, has to be treated as enjoying an important autonomy relative to the individuals who make it up. It can enjoy rights and duties in its own name and these are distinct from the rights and duties of any individual in its ranks.

The medieval tradition built on the Roman in dignifying any such corporate body with the name of a *persona* or person, as we saw. The legal tradition in particular took it to signify just that the corporate body is an artificial person. It is a person as real as you and me, albeit one constructed by institutional rather than biological means: that is, as they would have thought, by human rather than divine hands.

The legal tradition of the fourteenth century already made much of the idea of the corporate person. Thus Bartolus of Sassoferrato, who was a Professor of Law at the University of Perugia, used it to great effect in maintaining that a city republic like Perugia was a self-governing entity (Woolf 1913; Canning 1983; Ryan 1999). At the time the Holy Roman Emperor was treated in the common law the Roman law, rediscovered at the end of the eleventh century, that formed the basis of civil and canon law—as *dominus mundi*, lord of the world. This gave him great legal powers of interference in the states that belonged within the Holy Roman Empire—in effect, within Germany and Italy—at least insofar as they did not have rulers of their own. It was accepted that, if a city or state had a king or prince of its own, then that person represented the Emperor within local boundaries and the Emperor could not interfere within those boundaries. The principle was that the king in his own realm is the Emperor of that realm: *rex in suo regno est imperator sui regni*.

A city republic like Perugia was in obvious difficulty insofar as it did not have a king or prince—a *rex* or *princeps*—of its own. But Bartolus used the new doctrine of the corporate person to great effect in arguing that this difficulty was only apparent. He pointed out that a city republic organized its business like any familiar corporate body such as a guild or monastic order: it was ruled by a council that citizens elected and on which they took turns in serving. Thus he argued on this basis that the *civitas*—the state or citizenry—was itself a corporate body or *universitas*. But if it was a corporate body, it was a *persona* or person, albeit a *persona ficta*, an artificial person. And if it was a person, then in virtue of its role in governing its members, it counted as a *princeps* or prince. In words long quoted after Bartolus's death, it was a *sibi princeps*, a prince unto itself.

The political use of the idea of the corporate person went hand in hand over the following centuries with its use in characterizing other corporate bodies, in particular corporations. Thus in the 1640s Hobbes (1998: 5.10) could claim that just as a company of merchants counts as a corporate person, so too does any commonwealth count as a civil person. While the use of the image of the corporate person in describing states declined in the eighteenth century—a great exception, however, is Rousseau's (1973) *Social Contract*—its use in relation to corporate bodies, in particular corporations, greatly increased. Thus in his classic *Commentaries on the Laws of England*, published in the 1760s, William Blackstone (1978: bk 1, ch. 1, §123) could write: "Persons also are divided by the law into either natural persons, or artificial. Natural persons are such as the God of nature formed us; artificial are such as are created and devised by human laws for the purposes of society and government, which are called corporations or bodies politic."

This traditional way of thinking about corporations was given a firm place in American law in a famous case decided by the Supreme Court in 1819, *Dartmouth College v Woodward*. The court decided that the Constitution protected the contractually based constitution of Dartmouth College from interference by the legislature. And in the course of the hearing Chief Justice Marshall summed up the court's position in asserting that by means of incorporation "a perpetual succession of individuals are capable of acting for the promotion of the particular object, like one immortal being."

What rights did corporate bodies enjoy under the law? Blackstone (bk 1, ch. 7, §§272–3) held that when they incorporate with the permission of the King, "a number of private persons are united and knit together, and enjoy many liberties, powers, and immunities in their politic capacity, which they were utterly incapable of in their natural." More specifically, so he argued (bk 1, ch. 17, §§475–6), the bodies thereby formed enjoy five rights: first, to continue indefinitely in existence, enjoying "perpetual succession"; second, "to sue or be sued, implead or be impleaded, grant or receive, by its corporate name"; third, "to purchase lands, and hold them"; fourth, to "manifest its intentions," as when it "acts and speaks . . . by its common seal": i.e. via an authorized spokesperson; and fifth, to "make by-laws or private statutes for the better government of the corporation; which are binding upon themselves, unless contrary to the laws of the land."

Blackstone was writing at a time when the rights of corporations proper were limited under the South Sea Bubble Act of 1720, which had prohibited the formation of commercial corporations not authorized by royal charter or Act of Parliament. And so it is unsurprising that he puts the following qualification on the fifth right: "But no trading company is with us allowed to make by-laws which may affect the king's prerogative, or the common profit of the people . . . unless they be approved by the chancellor, treasurer, and chief justices, or the judges of assize in their circuits; and, even though they be so approved, still, if contrary to law, they are void."

The South Sea Bubble Act was repealed in 1825 and over the following few decades, corporations gained enormously in the rights they were given both in Britain, in Europe more generally, and in the United States. They could be formed by recourse to a notary or lawyer; they could operate across the land, not just in a specific territory; they could change their sphere of activity at will; they could own and be owned by other corporations; and their shareholders could enjoy the right of limited liability, which had been implicit at best up to the mid-nineteenth century (Horwitz 1977). This growth in the rights of corporations went along with the ever more important economic role that they played in industrial development, particularly in the construction of canals and railroads.

At the height of this development, the question arose in the United States as to the constitutional standing of corporations and of corporate bodies more generally. With a written constitution in place, and with lots of issues to settle about the status of corporations, it was inevitable that sooner or later the Supreme Court would have to decide what rights accrue to corporations. And, given the focus of the Constitution on individuals, it was inevitable in particular that it would have to make a judgment on whether the articles and amendments of the document that articulated the rights for individuals established the same rights for corporate persons.

The issue finally came to a head in a case heard in 1886, *Santa Clara County v Southern Pacific Railroad*. The Court had to decide in that case whether the Railroad was required to pay taxes on the wooden fences that bordered the track it used in Santa Clara County. In its defense the Railroad made a number of points: at the more mundane end, that it did not actually own the fence; at the more elevated, that it was protected against the allegedly unfair treatment by the County under the Fourteenth Amendment to the Constitution, which had been passed in 1868. The relevant part of the first section of that amendment reads: "No State shall make or enforce any law which shall abridge the privileges or immunities of citizens of the United States; nor shall any State deprive any person of life, liberty, or property, without due process of law; nor deny to any person within its jurisdiction the equal protection of the laws." The claim made by the Railroad was that the County proposed to breach its claims as a person under the last equal protection clause.

The Court found for the Railroad on the grounds of its not actually owning the fence on which the County wished to tax it. But the court report cited the Chief Justice at the time—he died before the report actually appeared—as offering an important aside, or *obiter dictum*, on the constitutional defense. "The court does not wish to hear argument on the question whether the provision in the Fourteenth Amendment to the Constitution, which forbids a State to deny to any person within its jurisdiction the equal protection of the laws, applies to these corporations. We are all of opinion that it does" (Horwitz 1987: 13).

This remark had important ramifications. Supported in a long line of judgments, the Court was able to maintain in 1909, in its judgment on *Southern Railway Co. v Greene*: "That the corporation is a person, within the meaning of the Fourteenth Amendment, is no longer open to discussion" (Schane 1987). This judgment has always been contentious in US jurisprudence, since the Fourteenth Amendment was one of the Reconstruction Amendments designed to establish the civic status of emancipated slaves in the wake of the Civil War. But time and again it has played a role in judgments that invoked the Constitution to argue for corporate rights. These included the right to search and seizure protection under the Fourth Amendment (1906); the right to jury trial in criminal cases under the Sixth Amendment; the right to jury trial in civil cases under the Seventh Amendment; and, on the grounds that money is speech, the same right as individuals to independent political expenditures under the First Amendment (2010).

This jurisprudential tradition, particularly the finding in 2010 in the case *Citizens United v Federal Election Commission*, has given life to the second of our two fallacies. This is the claim that corporate bodies have the same claim as individuals to be given certain rights under law. We naturally think that individuals have a claim to be given rights under law on the basis of their having natural, pre-legal rights of a certain kind or on the basis of their having certain needs or preferences. In either case we hold that they have a claim to autonomous rights in law: a claim that is based on their own interests, whether they are construed as pre-existing rights or needs or preferences, and not on the interests of other entities. According to second of our fallacies, corporate persons have a claim of a parallel kind to autonomous legal rights: a claim that is based on their own interests as corporate persons. I think that this claim is just as mistaken as the earlier claim we considered.

Against the Second Fallacy

When a number of people form to create a corporate person, they exercise the right of association that they are likely to enjoy under any reasonable dispensation and they do so, presumably, because that answers to certain shared interests, commercial or otherwise. But our shared interests as members of a presumptively equal community lead us to impose legal limits on how people should associate in any of a range of areas: for example, in conspiring to commit crime, or in forming a cartel to fix prices. And there is every reason, by analogy with such interventions, why our shared, communal interests might lead us to put legal limits on how people may associate in forming corporate bodies. There is every reason, in other words, why those interests should lead us to restrict the range of rights that the artificial persons created by incorporation should be able to enjoy. After all, corporate or artificial persons, as Blackstone says, "are created and devised by human laws for the purposes of society and government."

This argument, spelled out a little more carefully, runs as follows:

- To give any rights to corporate agents is to give corresponding rights of association to their members; thus to give a right of changing its sphere of activity to a corporate body is to give its members the right to associate in a way that enables them to alter the sphere in which they act together.
- The rights of association that ought to be given to individual agents should be fixed by a consideration of the interests of individuals in the community: the interests of those associating and, in an egalitarian spirit, the interests of others too.
- Hence the rights that ought to be given to corporate agents should be fixed by the egalitarian consideration of the interests of the individuals associating and the individuals affected; they ought not to be determined by reference to the interests of the corporate entities themselves.

The first proposition asserts that the rights of corporate persons are determined by the rights of individuals, in particular their rights of association; the second holds that the rights of individuals to associate with one another ought to be restricted to fit with the interests of all individuals in the community; and the third draws the conclusion that the corresponding corporate rights ought therefore to be restricted in the same way.

This argument presupposes, plausibly, that the interests of all individuals in the community, more or less equally balanced, ought to determine the rights accorded to any individuals, in particular the rights of association that we establish. It shows that if we are to stick with this principle—a principle of equal individual interests, as we may call it—then we must be prepared to limit the rights that we establish for the corporate bodies that individuals form, taking account of their effect on the interests of individuals.

If we grant rights to corporate bodies on the basis of the interests of those bodies themselves—if we grant them rights on a parallel basis to that on which we grant rights to individuals—then we are very likely to breach that principle. And insofar as that is possible, the principle of equal individual interests requires us to deny that corporate bodies should have autonomous rights in law; they should only have such rights as answer equally to the interests of individuals. The cost of granting corporate agents rights on an independent basis—that is, other than by reference to the principle of equal individual interests—is that the law might no longer treat individuals as equals; it might give some of those who associate in various corporate forms insider benefits that would impose intuitively unfair costs on those outside such groups or perhaps on other members.

It may be said that these costs ought not to matter if all individuals are given the same legal right to associate in a self-serving way. But that is scarcely a consoling thought. It suggests that giving corporate bodies rights on an independent basis would provide an incentive for individuals to compete in a free-for-all attempt to gain advantages in relation to one another. And since there is no prospect of equal gains in such a zero-sum game, it would mean that some individuals are bound to end up in a position of serious disadvantage in relation to others: that is, in a position where their interests do not count for as much as the interests of others.

Suppose, as is currently the case in the United States, that corporate bodies are given the same legal rights to make independent political expenditures as individuals. That means that those incorporated for collateral reasons—say, as a business or union—can exercise their clout under the corporate form in a way that may swamp the enterprise and the confidence of the unincorporated. Indeed it means in many of these cases that those at the helm of such organizations, who will often be subject to little discipline in the exercise of patronage—think of the CEOs of corporations—will be super-empowered individuals in the political sphere. They will be in a position to disburse corporate funds more or less at will to the causes, and in effect the candidates, of their choosing. The principle of equal individual interests argues against giving any corporate bodies rights that would have such an adverse effect on the interests of some individuals.

Is the principle of equal individual interests sufficiently compelling to support the rejection of our second fallacy? It may not seem so to those who think of the corporate bodies we individuals construct on an analogy with the children we procreate as parents. Just as we do not think that the interests of parents ought to determine the rights that we establish for children so, it may be suggested, we ought not to think that the interests of individuals ought to determine the rights that we establish for corporate bodies. Children have interests of their own, distinct from those of their parents, and the idea here is that corporate bodies also have interests of their own, distinct from those of their creators.

This idea is not persuasive for the simple reason that, while parents produce children that grow up to function without parental support and to have interests that are distinct from their parents, corporate bodies are quite different. They remain completely dependent on their members for being sustained in existence and activity, and their interests remain firmly tied, therefore, to the interests of those members. Whatever interests are ascribed to corporate bodies, they are not just interests of their own, unlike the interests of children; they inevitably reflect the interests of some or all of the members who sustain them. To give independent attention and concern to those interests, then, would be to discriminate in favor of the interests of such individuals.

It is certainly true that, if we establish corporate bodies, then we must give some rights to them; otherwise they would not have a defined space within which to act and would not be able to play their role as agents among agents. It may even be true that if those corporate bodies are to have any useful function, then the rights we give them must include rights like those listed by Blackstone. But that just means that it would make no sense for the law to deny corporate bodies access to such rights—this would be to outlaw corporate bodies, period—and that it would make no sense, the law permitting, for individuals to refuse to allow their corporate creations the enjoyment of such rights. It does not mean that, once created, corporate persons have interests that call for the protection of legal rights in the way that children have such interests. And it does not mean that the law ought to take account of such interests in determining the rights that should accrue to those bodies.

The upshot of these considerations is that we can allow corporate bodies to have autonomous rights only if we are prepared to reject the idea that the law should treat people as equals in determining what rights—in particular, what rights of association—they are to enjoy. The principle of equal individual interests seems unquestionable, however, and is respected in almost every contemporary philosophy of the state. Thus the cost of allowing corporate bodies to have autonomous rights is just too heavy for the proposal to have any appeal.

There are four different areas in which an assignment of corporate rights might offend against the principle. It might favor some members disproportionately over others in the private or the political benefits of membership: in the rate of recompense for effort and talent, for example, or in the degree of power that some enjoy over others. And it might favor at least some members over outsiders in the private or political benefits ensured: in the greater chances it gives them of winning in legal cases, for example, or in their greater capacities to exercise influence over government. The principle of equal interests calls for a normative inquiry into the rights that ought to be given to different corporate entities: say, to churches or NGOs or corporations. But such an inquiry would carry us well beyond the brief of this chapter.

CONCLUSION

We have looked at two sharply opposed views of corporate bodies, each with a firm place in contemporary thinking, and argued that they are both mistaken. One maintains that such bodies have no more claim to the status of agents than markets, the other that they have a claim, not just to the status of agents, but to the status and rights of persons like you and me.

As against the first position, we have argued that corporate bodies are agents—agents indeed that have capacities characteristic of natural persons—and that they do raise a challenge for us as citizens who have to make our lives in their company. And as against the second, we have argued that, on pain of betraying the ideal of individual equality, we should only give corporate bodies the rights that it is in the interest of the community of natural persons to bestow; they do not have any independent claims in their own name.

That two such opposed views each have a place in our thinking reflects a failure on the part of our academic and public culture to bring economic and legal traditions of analysis together in charting corporate reality. And that they are each subject to ready criticism, as I hope the foregoing may suggest, reflects a failure to take that thinking to any depth. We face the prospect in this century of having to come to political terms with an ever more corporatized world, as I suggested in the Introduction. The first prerequisite of doing so is that we put behind us the shoddy thinking that these rival positions exemplify.

ACKNOWLEDGMENTS

I benefitted enormously from the discussion of this and other papers at a meeting in the Royal Society, London, in Apr. 2014, organized by Professor Subramanian Rangan. And equally I benefitted from a thorough discussion of the paper at an event in Paris, Sept. 2014, which was organized jointly by Gloria Origgi of the Institut Jean Nicod in Paris and Astrid Von Busekist of the Institut d'Etudes Politiques de Paris (Sciences Po).

REFERENCES

Austin, J. (1869). *Lectures on Jurisprudence, or the Philosophy of Positive Law*. London.

Blackstone, W. (1978). *Commentaries on the Laws of England*. New York: Garland.

Canning, J. P. (1980). The Corporation in the Political Thought of the Italians Jurists of the Thirteenth and Fourteenth Century. *History of Political Thought*, 1: 9–32.

Canning, J. P. (1983). Ideas of the State in Thirteenth and Fourteenth Century Commentators on the Roman Law. *Transactions of the Royal Historical Society*, 33: 1–27.

Davis, G. F. (2013). After the Corporation. *Politics and Society*, 41: 283–308.

Dennett, D. (1987). *The Intentional Stance*. Cambridge, MA: MIT Press.

Duff, P. W. (1938). *Personality in Roman Private Law*. Cambridge: Cambridge University Press.

Eschmann, T. (1946). Studies on the Notion of Society in St Thomas Aquinas, 1. St Thomas and the Decretal of Innocent IV Romana Ecclesia: Ceterum. *Medieval Studies*, 8: 1–42.

French, P. A. (1984). *Collective and Corporate Responsibility*. New York: Columbia University Press.

Galanter, M. (2006). Planet of the APs: Reflections on the Scale of Law and its Users. *Buffalo Law Review*, 53: 1369–417.

Grantham, R. (1998). The Doctrinal Basis of the Rights of Company Shareholders. *Cambridge Law Journal*, 57: 554–88.

Hess, K. M. (2014). The Free Will of Corporations (and Other Collectives). *Philosophical Studies*, 168: 241–60.

Hobbes, T. (1994). *Leviathan*, ed. E. Curley. Indianapolis: Hackett.

Hobbes, T. (1998). *On the Citizen*, ed and tr. R. Tuck and M. Silverthorne. Cambridge: Cambridge University Press.

Horwitz, M. J. (1977). *The Transformation of American Law 1780–1860*. Cambridge, MA: Harvard University Press.

Horwitz, M. J. (1987). Santa Clara Revisited: The Development of Corporate Theory. In W. J. Samuels and A. S. Miller (eds), *Corporations and Society*. New York: Greenwood Press, 13–63.

Kantorowicz, E. H. (1997). *The King's Two Bodies: A Study in Mediaeval Political Theology*. Princeton: Princeton University Press.

List, C., and P. Pettit (2011). *Group Agency: The Possibility, Design and Status of Corporate Agents*. Oxford: Oxford University Press.

Locke, J. (1975). *An Essay Concerning Human Understanding*. Oxford: Oxford University Press.

Pettit, P. (2008). *Made with Words: Hobbes on Language, Mind and Politics*. Princeton: Princeton University Press.

Pettit, P. (2014a). Group Agents are Not Expressive, Pragmatic or Theoretical Fictions. *Erkenntnis*, 79: 1641–62.

Pettit, P. (2014b). *Just Freedom: A Moral Compass for a Complex World*. New York: W. W. Norton & Co.

Quinton, A. (1975). Social Objects. *Proceedings of the Aristotelian Society*, 75: 1–27.

Rousseau, J.-J. (1973). *The Social Contract and Discourses*. London: J. M. Dent & Sons.

Rovane, C. (1997). *The Bounds of Agency: An Essay in Revisionary Metaphysics*. Princeton: Princeton University Press.

Ryan, M. (1999). Bartolus of Sassoferrato and Free Cities. *Transactions of the Royal Historical Society*, 6: 65–89.

Schane, S. A. (1987). The Corporation is a Person: The Language of a Legal Fiction. *Tulane Law Review*, 61: 563–609.

Skinner, Q. (2010). *A Genealogy of the Modern State*. London: British Academy.

Tollefsen, D. (2002). Organizations as True Believers. *Journal of Social Philosophy*, 33: 395–410.

Williamson, O. E. (1989). Transaction Cost Economics. In R. Schmalensee and R. Willig (eds), *Handbook of Industrial Organisation*, i. Amsterdam: North Holland: 135–82.

Woolf, C. N. S. (1913). *Bartolus of Sassoferrato*. Cambridge: Cambridge University Press.

CHAPTER 23

CORPORATE POWER IN THE TWENTY-FIRST CENTURY

GERALD F. DAVIS

Abstract

Corporations in the twentieth century were generally premised on economies of scale. Control of assets and employment was centripetal, becoming more concentrated over time, while ownership was centrifugal, becoming more dispersed. Corporate power was vested in the executives and boards at the tops of corporate hierarchies, whose control of economic resources could often translate into political influence. Since the 1980s, these two trends have reversed: control of assets is more dispersed, while ownership is more concentrated in the hands of a few financial institutions. The ability to rent rather than buy productive capacity means that pop-up businesses are replacing large incumbents in many industries. This chapter describes some of the consequences of these recent developments for power and trust around the corporation.

In an era of eight-figure CEO salaries and a democracy increasingly controlled by corporate money, few seriously question that corporations dominate American society. Who can doubt the majestic power of Goldman Sachs, Walmart, and Google? Who can observe bailouts of businesses deemed too big to fail, tax policies tilted toward the wealthy, and the revolving door between government and Wall Street and not conclude that business is firmly in control?

In this chapter I survey ideas of corporate power as they have played out in the United States over the past 100 years. I describe the rise of the public corporation as the dominant institution in the economy in the first decades of the twentieth century. Corporations were seen as unavoidable due to economies of scale—they were a necessary evil that required a vigilant centralized state to rein them in and orient them toward social benefit, and to limit the influence of financiers over their operations. By the 1930s, American corporations had taken on their familiar shape: vertically integrated, run by growth-oriented professional managers, and insulated from the demands of their dispersed owners. Their executives were regarded as powerful but generally benign, with a penchant for good works; their shareholders were regarded as irrelevant. This model was a fairly accurate description until the 1980s.

The bust-up takeovers of the 1980s, the new ideology of shareholder value and the compensation practices it brought, and the outsourcing movement of the 1990s created pressures favoring the lean-and-mean corporation. The new model looked like Nike: small in assets and employment, but big in revenues and market capitalization, relying on external contractors for formerly essential tasks. By the 2000s, Nikefication had diffused across many industries, from mobile phones and PCs to pet food to pharmaceuticals, leading the corporation to resemble the nexus-of-contracts described by financial economists. It also provided a model for the Federal government itself to become, in effect, a nexus of contractors.

One surprising result is that, since the turn of the twenty-first century, corporations are increasingly irrelevant. The number of public corporations in the US has declined by more than half since 1997 and dropped every year but one since then, as stalwarts like Westinghouse and Eastman Kodak disappear and are briefly replaced by pop-up enterprises that can rent broadly available modular resources. As a result, corporate power is a conundrum. Where control of corporate resources was widely regarded as a key source of power during the twentieth century, corporate power today is an increasingly puzzling construct.

What is Corporate Power?

It is worth probing what we mean when we talk about "corporate power." The traditional view holds that corporate executives are powerful due to their control over corporate resources. Through decisions about where to locate plants, which charities to support, whom to employ and promote, and how to participate in politics, corporate executives wield great power. At the onset of the Great Depression, Berle and Means (1932: 46) wrote that "The economic power in the hands of the few persons who control a giant corporation is a tremendous force which can harm or benefit a multitude of individuals, affect whole districts, shift the currents of trade, bring ruin to one community and prosperity to another." They concluded that "The rise of the modern corporation has brought a concentration of economic power which can compete on equal terms with the modern state" (313).

In an economy dominated by a few dozen oligopolistic corporations, economic power translated readily into political power. *Fortune* magazine wrote in 1952 that "Any President who wants to run a prosperous country depends on the corporation at least as much as—probably more than—the corporation depends on him. His dependence is not unlike that of King John on the landed barons of Runnymede, where Magna Carta was born."

And how would this power be exercised? Harvard economist Carl Kaysen (1957: 313) wrote that the corporation owed a debt to society: "Its responsibilities to the general public are widespread: leadership in local charitable enterprises, concern with factory architecture and landscaping, provision of support for higher education, and even research in pure science, to name a few." Thankfully the new "soulful corporation" was run by benevolent executives who could safely ignore their distant investors and shepherd their oligopoly profits for public benefit. "No longer the agent of proprietorship seeking to maximize return on investment, management sees itself as responsible to stockholders, employees, customers, the general public, and, perhaps most important, the firm itself as an institution" (314).

Not everyone was convinced of the noblesse oblige of the managerial class. C. Wright Mills (1956), for one, noted that the web of connections among those at the top of hierarchies in business, government, and the military gave inordinate influence to an elite inner circle. It was not a conspiracy but simply a reality of human nature that, when powerful people congregate, decisions can be made that are outside the purview of democracy. The old joke had it that when the president of GE ordered a coffee, one of his over-eager underlings proceeded to buy Colombia. (The history of ITT in Chile suggests that this might not be entirely fanciful.) Whatever their motivations, top corporate executives constituted an unelected power elite.

Defining power for contemporary corporations is far more difficult, if not entirely intractable. For most of the twentieth century, corporate power came from large size and holding an oligopoly or monopoly position in industry. Yet corporate power today, in a globalized economy, is far more ambiguous.

Consider three corporations that many would consider to be obviously powerful: Goldman Sachs, Walmart, and Google. Goldman Sachs must be powerful because it pays huge salaries to its Ivy-educated employees, many of whom go off to influential positions in government. Goldman's power is exercised by the high fees it charges to corporate clients and high net worth individuals, and through incomprehensible trading strategies that it enables or engages in. It has direct contact with only a tiny fraction of the public, yet evidently exercises a pervasive and shadowy influence.

Walmart must be powerful because it is able to pay very low wages to its high-turnover workforce, few of whom go on to powerful positions in government. Walmart's power is realized in part by forcing major corporations like Procter & Gamble, Pepsi, Kraft, Tyson, and General Mills to charge it low prices, which enables it to sell things really inexpensively to consumers, which include a large majority of the American population.

Google is powerful because its flagship products (Google search and the Chrome browser), although given away for free, are indispensably useful and allow Google to collect extremely invasive and detailed information from the (non-paying) consumers who love it and rely on it, which include virtually everyone who uses a computer.

These three fit uneasily with the account of the power of traditional corporations. Researchers might ask what the common metric is that could apply across these three. Certainly, questions of plant location, factory architecture, or support for science are muted at best. How, exactly, are these corporations "powerful"? For the moment, we will leave "corporate power" undefined, but are likely to end up agreeing with Jim March that "On the whole, power is a disappointing concept."

CORPORATE POWER IN THE TWENTIETH CENTURY

Observing the world in April 1914, one might well have concluded that both political and corporate power had an inherent centripetal tendency, becoming more concentrated and centralized over time. Europe had experienced a century of relative peace following the end of the Napoleonic Wars. There was good reason to be an optimist, if not downright Hegelian. A map of Eurasia would show the young states of Italy and Germany and expansive empires that encompassed many formerly independent nations: the Austro-Hungarian Empire, the Ottoman Empire, and the Russian Empire (which included Ukraine, Finland, and the part of Poland not controlled by Germany). Most of Northern Africa was occupied by France, Italy, and Great Britain (which then included Ireland). A map of North America would show that the US had completed its expansion from Atlantic to Pacific.

The same tendency toward concentrated control held in much of the business world. In the US, mergers around the turn of the twentieth century turned scores of regional companies into a handful of national-scale behemoths. US Steel was formed as America's first billion-dollar corporation in 1901, enveloping much of the nation's steel-building capacity. Within a single generation, business empires were created that would span most of the twentieth century: General Electric, Westinghouse, AT&T, General Motors, Bethlehem Steel, Woolworth, Sears, and several regional Standard Oil progeny (Roy 1997).

The business empires turned out to have far more staying power than the political empires. Business historians, most notably Alfred Chandler (1977), explained that the massive new corporations serving continent-sized integrated markets made economic sense, particularly in North America. Technologies for producing goods (such as emerging mass production methods), delivering goods (such as continent-spanning railroads), communicating (such as the telephone), and social technologies for management (the bureaucracy) meant that bigger was cheaper. Corporations had "economies of scale."

In the US, the massive and seemingly unnatural new aggregations of economic power aroused anxiety and political backlash. The dangers of monopolistic railroads were well-understood, but what could we expect of the giant new phone company, or the giant new steel company? Would they use their resources to undermine democracy and control the government? In his "New Nationalism" speech in 1910, Theodore Roosevelt stated that

The citizens of the United States must effectively control the mighty commercial forces which they have called into being. There can be no effective control of corporations while their political activity remains ... It is necessary that laws should be passed to prohibit the use of corporate funds directly or indirectly for political purposes ... Corporate expenditures for political purposes ... have supplied one of the principal sources of corruption in our political affairs.[1]

Roosevelt did not advocate dismantling corporations or preventing their growth, however, because he recognized their economic efficiency: "Combinations in industry are the result of an imperative economic law which cannot be repealed by political legislation. The effort at prohibiting all combination has substantially failed. The way out lies, not in attempting to prevent such combinations, but in completely controlling them in the interest of the public welfare."

What about the 1 percent? "We grudge no man a fortune in civil life if it is honorably obtained and well used ... [But] We should permit it to be gained only so long as the gaining represents benefit to the community. This, I know, implies a policy of a far more active governmental interference with social and economic conditions in this country than we have yet had, but I think we have got to face the fact that such an increase in governmental control is now necessary."

This was, in short, a manifesto for the creation of a progressive centralized government powerful enough to act as a counterweight to the new national corporations and the dynastic fortunes they were creating. To fund this state expansion, Roosevelt advocated a steeply progressive income tax—the US had no income tax at the time, and the miniscule Federal government was largely funded by customs and taxes on alcohol and tobacco—and a confiscatory inheritance tax to prevent the creation of an economic aristocracy.

The tendency toward consolidation in industry was complemented by a tendency toward consolidation in finance, according to some contemporary observers. In *Other People's Money*, Louis Brandeis described how a few bankers in New York, led by J. P. Morgan, had accumulated vast influence over the industrial economy. The bankers controlled the flow of new funds required by the new industrial behemoths and thus held the whip hand. Moreover, Brandeis reported that executives at the top three banks collectively served on dozens of corporate boards, often including competitors in the same industry (e.g. Westinghouse and GE). George F. Baker of First National (predecessor of today's Citigroup) personally served on twenty-two corporate boards, and Morgan's partners held "72 directorships in 47 of the largest corporations of the country." Through ownership, control of access to debt, and a network of board positions, members of this so-called "money trust" had "joined forces to control the business of the country, and 'divide the spoils'" (Brandeis 1914: 27).

V. I. Lenin reported much the same tendency in other advanced industrial economies: as industry becomes concentrated, a few financial institutions gain a position at

[1] <www.whitehouse.gov/blog/2011/12/06/archives-president-teddy-roosevelts-new-nationalism-speech>.

the commanding heights of the industrial economy. In pre-war Germany, for instance, "a very close personal union is established between the banks and the biggest industrial commercial enterprises . . . through the acquisition of shares, through the appointment of bank directors to the Supervisory Boards (or Boards of Directors) of industrial and commercial enterprises, and vice versa" (Lenin 1939/1916: 41–2). Of course, this could prove convenient if one had plans for centralized state control of the economy.

In the US, populists, progressives, and their allies implemented a series of reforms to limit concentrated economic power, and particularly to limit the power of finance (Roe 1994). Antitrust regulations prohibited substantial intra-industry concentration and eventually extended to include constraints on vertical integration. This approach was in contrast to Germany, in part because German industry produced with an eye toward exports (where "national champions" are useful), while American industry was largely oriented toward a domestic market (where monopoly power harms consumers).

Limitations on the power of finance were more severe. Within a year of Brandeis's reporting, bankers resigned board positions en masse, and by the end of the First World War "finance capitalism" was dead in the US (DeLong 1991). Commercial banks were limited to operating within a single state until the late 1980s and were forbidden from owning corporate shares directly. Depression-era reforms separated commercial and investment banking until 1999. For most of the twentieth century, with brief exceptions, Wall Street was approximately as sexy and powerful as the electric utility industry, a refuge for less-ambitious WASPS with Dartmouth degrees.

A singular work by a lawyer and an economist published in 1932 provided a surprisingly durable portrait of the American corporate economy of the twentieth century. *The Modern Corporation and Private Property*, by Adolph Berle and Gardiner Means, assembled data about the 200 largest American corporations and concluded that the US had entered a new phase of capitalism that was analogous to feudalism, but where the manors were corporations and the new landed aristocracy were the professional executives who ran them. Due to economies of scale, corporate control was centripetal: after the merger waves at the turn of the century and during the 1920s, a few dozen corporations controlled half the assets of industry, and if trends continued they would control it all by 1960. Yet corporate ownership was centrifugal, becoming more and more dispersed among the broad public so that by 1930 nearly half of the largest corporations did not have even a single shareholder owning as much as 5 percent. AT&T had over half-a-million shareholders, and the largest held less than 1 percent of its shares. Similar figures held for US Steel, which was the largest steel company, and the Pennsylvania Railroad, the largest transportation company.

By some accounts, this system was not even true "capitalism" any more, but something different. Many corporations no longer sought to maximize profit, given the essential powerlessness of their shareholders, but pursued ends such as growth and stability, which satisfied the desires of corporate managers and employees. Sociologist Ralf Dahrendorf wrote that "Never has the imputation of a profit motive been further from the real motives of men than it is for modern bureaucratic managers" (1959: 46).

Post-war scholars, including critics of the corporation, did not dispute this basic diagnosis but instead sought to analyze the new shape of power. C. Wright Mills described a "power elite" that mingled corporate, government, and military executives through various institutions that helped form a common view, from the country club to shared service on corporate and non-profit boards. Finance was notably irrelevant. Mills stated that "Not 'Wall Street financiers' or bankers, but large owners and executives in their self-financing corporations hold the keys of economic power" (Mills 1956: 125). Indeed, Peter Drucker wrote in 1949 that "Where only twenty years ago the bright graduate of the Harvard Business School aimed at a job with a New York Stock Exchange house, he now seeks employment with a steel, oil, or automobile company."

This basic account—that economic power came from control of corporations, which was primarily held by executives and not financiers—held with little dispute from the 1930s through the 1980s.

The Collapse of Corporate Power in the Twenty-First Century

It is somewhat unnerving to read about the near-irrelevance of shareholders and Wall Street to twentieth-century American corporations because this is such a stark contrast to contemporary experience. Corporate executives and directors today vow their undying allegiance to "creating shareholder value," on display in every corporate mission statement, and a recent article in the *Wall Street Journal* stated that "one can't underestimate the threat from shareholder activists, who now patrol the market like prison guards with billy clubs" (Berman 2014). What happened?

By 1980, after several years of economic stagnation, the diversified conglomerates that were built during the 1960s and 1970s were heavily undervalued by the stock market. Meanwhile, new theories were being promulgated by financial economists asserting that the corporation was nothing more than a "nexus of contracts" that existed to create shareholder value (Jensen and Meckling 1976). In 1982, three things happened that enabled this contradiction to be resolved and that ushered in a new era of financial capitalism in the US. First, the Justice Department changed its merger guidelines to create a more forgiving environment for intra-industry mergers. Second, the Supreme Court struck down most state laws that protected domestic corporations from unwanted outside takeovers. In combination, these two factors unleashed a massive wave of bust-up takeovers that threatened any company that failed to work for shareholder value. Nearly one-third of the Fortune 500 were acquired or merged between 1980 and 1990; counterintuitively, the takeover wave and the divestitures it inspired actually reduced corporate concentration, as targets were often split up and sold to related acquirers (Davis et al. 1994). Third, major corporations began to adopt

401(k) plans and to abandon defined benefit pensions. During the subsequent two decades, the proportion of households invested in the stock market increased from 20 percent to 50 percent, creating a popular constituency for shareholder-friendly policies at the corporate level and at the national level. (During the G. W. Bush administration, this was labeled the "Ownership Society.")

In a relatively brief period, the concept of the corporation as a social institution with obligations to various "stakeholders," which held for most of the post-war era, was abandoned in favor of the theology of shareholder value (Davis 2009: ch. 3).

During the 1920s, corporate ownership had grown more and more dispersed through popular participation in the financial markets, enabled in part by the brokerage networks created to sell war bonds. During the 1980s and 1990s, however, widespread participation in the stock market led to a reconcentration of corporation ownership under the control of financial institutions. A handful of brand-name mutual funds found themselves flooded with 401(k) money and then retail investment after 1982, leading them to hold relatively concentrated positions of ownership. By 1995, Fidelity was the largest shareholder of several hundred American corporations, often holding 10–15 percent stakes in competitors in the same industry (Davis 2008). With the advent of the exchange-traded fund (ETF) in 1993, new players also grew, albeit below the radar screen of the public.

Today, BlackRock—which owns the vast iShares ETF business—manages $4.7 trillion in assets and is the single largest shareholder of almost every major bank (JP Morgan Chase, Citigroup, Bank of America), energy company (Exxon, Chevron, Marathon, Philips), telecom (AT&T), and consumer company (Apple, GE) in the US. Its holdings far outstrip those of any previous financial institution in American history, including JP Morgan at the turn of the twentieth century (Davis 2013a). The shibboleth that the typical American corporation has dispersed ownership is now outdated. Contrary to the situation described by Berle and Means, ownership is now centripetal.

NIKEFICATION AND THE DISPERSAL
OF PRODUCTION

Conversely, corporate control of assets and employment is now centrifugal.

The advent of the theology of shareholder value has had a raft of (often corrosive) consequences for the economy and the culture. We now reflexively use terms like "social capital" to refer to our family, friends, and communities, and "human capital" to refer to our talents and education, not as an ironic critique of finance run amok, but as an obviously sensible way to talk about the social world.

The effect of this new theology on corporate structures and operations has been especially striking. One way to summarize it is "Nikefication." Nike pioneered a model in which the company owning the brand focuses on the high-value tasks of design and marketing, and contracts out the production and distribution of its goods. This approach to "vertical dis-integration" has been common in the garment industry for years, but spread widely across industries in the 1990s and 2000s, due in large part to pressures on firms to create shareholder value.

Those who ran firms came to believe that Wall Street rewards companies that maintain the lightest possible base of tangible assets and employment. Put simply, one can increase return on assets either by increasing returns (profits) or reducing assets, and the latter is far easier in general. This "de-verticalization" originally took the form of outsourcing peripheral functions (e.g. payroll management) but subsequently came to absorb what had traditionally been core functions.

Nike represents this model in a relatively pure form: the company focuses on design and marketing from its Oregon headquarters while contracting out manufacturing to producers in East Asia. Similarly, Apple designs products in California that are assembled in Shenzhen by Foxconn and others. In electronics, there is a large sector of firms you have never heard of that enable this model (e.g. Flextronics, Sanmina, Jabil Circuit, known broadly as "electronics manufacturing services"), serving as essentially generic manufacturers for the broad electronics sector.

One result of Nikefication in electronics is that American employment in this industry has largely collapsed, shedding 750,000 jobs (over 40 percent) since the turn of the twenty-first century. Moreover, much the same process has occurred across American industry, from mobile phones and computers to pet food (where over 100 competing brands of dog and cat chow were manufactured by Menu Foods from the same ingredients in the same facility in Ontario) to pharmaceuticals (where 40 percent of generic and over-the-counter medications in the US are manufactured in India in facilities generally beyond the purview of the FDA).[2] In many industries, it is surprisingly difficult to locate products actually produced by the company whose name is on the label. As the tragic factory collapse in Dhaka, Bangladesh, in 2013 revealed, even the central node in the nexus often has no idea where its products are created (Davis 2013c).

Vertical disintegration is not limited to business. Since Clinton signed the FAIR Act (Federal Activities Inventory Reform) in 1998 as part of his administration's "re-inventing government" initiative, vast parts of the Federal government have been outsourced, from food service in the Capitol to the protection of diplomats in Iraq to the intelligence gathering of the NSA. Indeed, one reason Edward Snowden's employment as an NSA contractor raised no red flags was that the contractor hired to do security clearances on a piece rate was negligent.[3] (As it happens, oversight and investigation of contractors is also done by contractors.) Total Federal employment

---

[2] <www.nytimes.com/2014/02/15/world/asia/medicines-made-in-india-set-off-safety-worries.html?_r=0>.

[3] <www.nytimes.com/2014/01/23/us/security-check-firm-said-to-have-defrauded-us.html>.

declined by 800,000 during the Clinton years and has risen only slightly since then, while spending on contractors doubled during the Bush years. By 2007, Lockheed Martin received more government funds annually than the Energy Department and Justice Department combined (see Davis 2009: ch. 5 on the Nikefication of government).

THE IMPACT OF NIKEFICATION ON THE CORPORATE FORM

Two results of widespread Nikefication are that (1) corporations employ many fewer people directly than they used to, with the exception of retailers; and (2) new entrants can rapidly scale up or down by using the existing base of generic producers, thus eroding the advantages of large incumbents.

First, the largest employers from the 1930s through the early 1990s were manufacturers (GM, GE, Ford), oil companies, AT&T, and Sears. They provided relatively high wages, stable employment, and expansive benefits; most had career ladders with pathways for advancement. These were the corporations contemplated by post-war scholars of the corporation. Today, 9 of the 12 largest US employers are in retail, with Walmart by far the biggest. Retailers in general have low wages, high turnover, minimal benefits, and limited opportunities for advancement (Davis 2009).

Second, contemporary enterprises can rapidly grow to be large in revenues and market capitalization with only minimal assets and employment, by "renting" capacity. Nike and Apple exemplify this possibility. (Apple has relatively few people designing products in Cupertino; the majority of its workers are low-wage employees of its retail outlets.) Newer entrants are even more radically tiny, in spite of being household names: as of the start of 2015, Facebook has 9,199 employees, Twitter has 3,638, and DropBox has only 971 employees.

An underappreciated implication of this situation is that the cost of entry can be very low because the elements of a business can be rented rather than bought, and thus employment is optional. The biggest-selling brand of LCD television in the US in 2010 was Vizio, with a mere 200 employees in Irvine, California. The best-selling portable video camera was Flip, with 100 employees. Meanwhile, Sony, with 150,000 employees, persistently loses money in its electronics business, which it subsidizes with its (highly profitable) life insurance subsidiary. (Sony recently announced that it would sell its computer business and park its television business in a subsidiary.)

In other words, it is possible to become the largest player in an industry segment, at least briefly, with minimal investments in capital and personnel. Conversely, incumbent firms are often weighed down by their large investments. Ten years ago, Blockbuster operated 9,000 physical stores staffed by 80,000 employees, which required substantial capital. Netflix, on the other hand, rents the computing power for its streaming video from Amazon, and employs just 2,000 people.[4] The economies of scale that characterized the American corporate economy for most of the twentieth century have in some cases flipped into dis-economies. Small is beautiful, or at least economical.

A recent widely read article in the *New Yorker* described this new dynamic:

> Once, an entrepreneur would go to a venture capitalist for an initial five-million-dollar funding round—money that was necessary for hardware costs, software costs, marketing, distribution, customer service, sales, and so on. Now there are online alternatives. "In 2005, the whole thing exploded," [an informant] told me. "Hardware? No, now you just put it on Amazon or Rackspace. Software? It's all open-source. Distribution? It's the App Store, it's Facebook. Customer service? It's Twitter—just respond to your best customers on Twitter and Get Satisfaction. Sales and marketing? It's Google AdWords, AdSense. So the cost to build and launch a product went from five million"—his marker skidded across the whiteboard—"to one million"—more arrows—"to five hundred thousand"—he made a circle—"and it's now to fifty thousand." (Heller 2013)

The article went on to note that venture capitalists are increasingly irrelevant for such ventures. "Going public" serves no clear purpose, particularly if the enterprise has a brief expected lifespan, such as the Flip camera, which survived only four years.

Perhaps the most profound implication of Nikefication is that, in an increasing number of sectors, the public corporation is largely obsolete as an economic vehicle.

The rationale for the public corporation was that resources were needed on a large scale for an extended period, which required a special kind of entity to raise capital. Railroads needed land and tracks; integrated manufacturers needed big factories; retail chains needed warehouses and stores. Companies raised capital because they actually needed capital for at least a few years. Today, a credit card and a web connection to Alibaba.com are enough to set in motion production on a large scale by renting rather than buying capacity, for however long it is needed. (Of course some sectors, such as energy, aerospace, and transportation still generally require large fixed investment.)

The profit motive is now optional for creating highly competitive, industry-dominant products, as Linux and Wikipedia have shown. Mozilla, the open-source non-profit, has created an operating system for phones and recently announced an open design for a small smartphone that would cost only $25.[5] Just as Sony is finding it difficult to survive challenges from low-cost nimble competitors who sell televisions, cameras, computers, and phones at much lower prices than it can, it is easy to foresee situations in which Apple would be unable to continue collecting the margins that it does in the face of low-cost open-source competitors.

The machinery of Wall Street and Sand Hill Road are still in place, and there are strong embedded interests in maintaining the system of public corporations. (Investment banks, public accountancies, and business schools have strong attachments to

---

[4] <http://online.wsj.com/news/articles/SB10001424052702304868404579194353031011652>.
[5] <www.wired.co.uk/news/archive/2014-02-26/firefox-os-25>.

this way of organizing business. And future retirees need to put their savings some-where.) But the numbers are stark: there are fewer than half as many listed companies today as there were in 1997, and the number declines every year, as Eastman Kodak, Dell, Circuit City, and Borders disappear from the market and are briefly replaced by Zynga and Twitter (Davis 2013a).

Moreover, firms going public in recent years routinely flout established standards of corporate governance by giving founders exceptional voting rights that effectively guarantee their ongoing control. Mark Zuckerberg, for instance, controls an absolute majority of Facebook voting shares (similar to the founders of Google, Zynga, Groupon, Zillow, and others). The most compelling rationale for Facebook's IPO was not that it needed capital—it stated explicitly in its prospectus that it had no foreseeable use for the money it was raising—but to pay off early investors and to be able to use its shares as currency for acquisitions. This may be a convincing reason for Facebook to sell shares, but it is hardly a compelling reason to buy. In short, it is difficult to foresee this system being sustained into the future (Davis 2013a).

The Collapse of the Corporate Elite

The collapse of the public corporation has been accompanied by the disappearance of the "inner circle" of elites who oversee it. From the early years of the twentieth century to the early years of the twenty-first century, corporate boards have shared directors, creating a relatively dense network of mutually acquainted individuals holding central positions at the apex of the corporate hierarchy.

In 1974 there were ninety individuals who served on five or more corporate boards, eighty-nine of them white and all of the male. Analyses show that most of them either saw each other regularly on shared boards or had "friends" in common. In 1994 there were seventy-five directors serving on five or more boards, and their number now included several well-connected women and people of color. By 2014, there was only one individual left who served on five major (S&P 500) corporate boards in the US: Shirley Ann Jackson, physicist and president of Renselear Polytechnic Institute. As boards began to shun well-connected directors beginning around 2003, the inner circle disappeared, and with it one of the most visible indications of collective corporate influence (Chu and Davis 2013).

The Post-Nike Corporation

Where are we now? Central institutions of the twentieth-century economy in the US have been de-constructed back into a primordial soup of component parts. Just as the Austro-Hungarian, Ottoman, and Russian Empires were disassembled into Poland,

Yugoslavia, Turkey, and others, the Westinghouses, ITTs, and Sara Lees are now transformed, retrenched, scattered, or disappeared. (Occasionally their brand names and logos live on, to be appropriated by "hermit crab" businesses who rent the use of the old firm's brand equity, such as "Memorex" or "RCA.")

It is not just specific corporations that are retrenching or disappearing, but the public corporation as a vehicle for aggregating economic power. At some point the costs of being a public corporation—detailed public disclosures and the scrutiny they bring for things like executive salaries; corporate governance regulations; demands from herds of analysts and activist investors; shareholder lawsuits premised on misguided notions of "fraud on the market"—outweigh the possible benefits. This is why companies like Dell and dozens of others have gone private, perhaps never to re-emerge as public companies. Meanwhile, one hundred S&P500 companies have bought back roughly $1 trillion of their own shares since 2008, presumably because alternative investments—say, in products or facilities—were less attractive. The *Wall Street Journal* reported that "In 1993, IBM had 2.3 billion shares outstanding. Today it has 1.1 billion, shrinking at more than 1% per quarter over the past few years. At that pace, there will be no more publicly traded IBM shares left by 2034" (Berman 2014).

We have effectively closed the book on the twentieth-century corporate economy described by Berle and Means, and now face something rather different.

There are, of course, temporary counter-examples. Who can doubt the eternal power of Apple? But open-source designs for physical products, coupled with increasingly low-cost CNC production equipment and 3D printing to enable distributed manufacturing on a local level, suggest that such dominance will not last. When the $25 open-source Mozilla smartphone becomes widely available, the $500 Apple version becomes less appealing (although Apple's inevitable "cranial implant" phone for trendier consumers might stave off the inevitable). Those old enough to remember Nokia and Blackberry can appreciate the fleeting nature of market dominance in this sector.

The present moment may simply be an interstitial period as we move toward a new system of economic power, but it is worth analyzing the dynamics of our situation. Two distinctive features of our new system are (1) the scale that can be achieved rapidly by participants and (2) the instability of positions of dominance.

In terms of *scale*, I have mentioned several examples of enterprises that were tiny on one scale (e.g. employment) but enormous on others (e.g. sales). Vizio was the best-selling brand of television in the US in 2010, with 200 employees. Flip was the best-selling portable video camera in 2009, with a 22 percent market share, and only 100 employees. DropBox has 500 million users and only 971 employees.

Market capitalization provides the most extreme examples of this disconnect. The grocery chain Kroger—America's second-largest private employer, with 400,000 (mostly unionized) workers and well over $100 billion in revenues—had a market capitalization of roughly $35 billion as of April 2015. Twitter, with 3,638 employees, $1.4 billion in revenues, and $578 million in losses, has a market value of $33 billion.

General Motors, America's largest manufacturer, which employs 200,000 people and sold 9.5 million cars around the world in 2013, is worth $58 billion. Tesla, which employs 6,000 workers and sold 23,000 vehicles in 2013—far less than GM's Silverado truck sold in February 2014—is valued at $31 billion.

The meaning of size is increasingly ambiguous today, and if corporate size is a source of power, then the notion of power is problematic. How powerful is Vizio, exactly? Or Kroger? Certainly, there are executives who engage in recognizable power tactics. A class action lawsuit settled in 2014 alleged that Steve Jobs personally orchestrated a gentleman's agreement among Apple, Google, Intel, and other Silicon Valley heavy-weights to limit employee poaching (i.e. what the rest of us might call "mobility"). When the new CEO of Palm, Inc. refused to comply, Jobs allegedly threatened to turn loose Apple's patent attorneys on the firm (Streitfeld 2014). But it is not obvious what measure of size converts readily into power.

In terms of *instability*, recent years have witnessed a seemingly endless series of large corporations brought low. The past six years were marked by the bankruptcies, liquidations, or effective government seizures of American's largest insurance company (AIG), mortgage company (Fannie Mae), bank (Citigroup), savings and loan (Washington Mutual), manufacturer (General Motors), and more. Other major cor-porations are on death watch (e.g. Sears/Kmart, Eastman Kodak), and still others are gone forever (e.g. Circuit City, Blockbuster). This is not just "creative destruction," as the destruction is not nearly matched by the creation, particularly when it comes to employment. The 1,200 companies that have gone public in the US since 2000 have created fewer than 800,000 jobs globally—about what the US lost in March 2009 alone (Davis 2013b).

A recent analysis found that the five Fortune 500 firms at which employees had the longest tenure on average (Eastman Kodak, Aleris Rolled Products, United Continen-tal, Visteon, and GM)—termed those with the "most loyal" workforces—had all gone through bankruptcy in recent years.[6] Conversely, America's largest employer by far, Walmart, experiences an annual turnover estimated at 60 percent.

It appears that the rewards go to the pop-up companies and those with fleeting attachments. WhatsApp, a company with fifty-six employees and $20 million in revenue, recently sold itself to Facebook for $19 billion. Similar stories are endemic to the contemporary Silicon Valley mythology.

In this context, exercise of "corporate power" can be complex.

In a capitalist economy, ownership of capital is supposed to be the source of economic control; this is why the Berle and Means corporation was anomalous. But corporate ownership today is hard to square with any traditional notion of power.

BlackRock is the world's largest shareholder by far, overseeing $4.7 trillion in assets. (JP Morgan Chase, Bank of America, and Citibank—the three largest US banks, each of whose largest shareholder is BlackRock—had combined total assets of about $4.7 trillion at the end of 2013. Vanguard, Fidelity, and Capital Group—the three largest mutual fund families—collectively have about $5.1 trillion in assets under

---

[6] <www.payscale.com/data-packages/employee-loyalty>.

management.) Yet BlackRock is nearly anonymous, having grown quite rapidly, and few outside Wall Street can name its CEO.

What is even more distinctive is that for much of its assets under management, BlackRock lacks one of the most essential elements of owner power: the discretion to buy and sell shares. Much of its assets consist of "exchange traded funds" that respond to investor demand on a minute-by-minute basis. Unlike Fidelity, BlackRock did not choose to become the largest shareholder of, say, Apple. Rather, investors poured money into BlackRock-managed ETFs that include Apple. BlackRock chooses how to vote at the annual meeting, but it does not have discretion over what it buys. To the best of my knowledge, this is entirely unprecedented.

THE NEW POWERBALL ECONOMY

In broad outlines, we can think of our current situation as a PowerBall economy. PowerBall is a large lottery in the US that often has a small number of very large prizewinners, and many millions of non-winners.

Inequality has vastly increased in the US in the past generation, as the 1 percent pull ever farther away from the 99 percent. Many explanations have been offered for this; empirically, I have found that inequality is strongly linked to the shape of the corporate economy, and specifically to the size of the largest employers relative to the size of the labor force. Countries with very high inequality, like Colombia, tend to have tiny enterprises. Countries with low inequality, like Denmark, often have very large enterprises. Within the US, the correlation over time between the size of corporate employers (relative to the size of the labor force) and inequality is remarkably large, about -0.9. The relation is arguably causal. Bigger employers lowered inequality, and the US reached its lowest level of inequality around 1970, when big companies reached their apex in employment and about 10 percent of the private labor force worked for just twenty-five companies. When corporations were split up in the 1980s and outsourcing took hold in the 1990s, inequality greatly increased. And as Nikefication has taken hold since the turn of the century, inequality has grown far worse (Davis and Cobb 2010).

Although highly paid corporate CEOs are often taken as emblems of societal inequality, the most extreme levels of inequality are generated *outside* the corporate sphere. By the late 2000s, the five highest-paid hedge fund managers collectively earned about as much as all the CEOs of the S&P 500 *combined* (Kaplan and Rauh 2007). Yet nobody in the press calculates the ratio of a hedge fund CEO's pay to the average salary of his or her five employees. And nobody compares the compensation of the temps who work at Amazon's vast network of anonymous warehouses to that of Jeff Bezos— after all, they don't work for Amazon, but for a staffing agency.

In the twentieth-century corporate economy, large, hierarchical organizations provided a straightforward pathway to economic mobility. A post-college career at Eastman Kodak was likely to be stable, remunerative, and even intellectually rewarding, ending with a company pension and health insurance in retirement. But in the twenty-first century, careers can look more like PowerBall. Lots of people write more or less equivalent apps for taking photos and sharing them on a mobile phone. For effectively random reasons, one becomes popular, and the company's founder(s) become fabulously wealthy; the other apps and their founders are quickly obsolete. Instagram had thirteen employees when Facebook bought it for $1 billion. Its founders now serve as exemplars of the riches available in the new economy if you work hard and follow your passion. The founders of the other apps move on, now counting themselves as "serial entrepreneurs." (For calibration purposes, Apple recently announced that is has over one million apps on its app store, although it did not mention how many of their creators had become billionaires.)

CORPORATE POWER TODAY

"Power" in this context is perplexing. Monopoly power at the corporate level was easy to see and understand. Individual power derived from control of corporate resources makes sense. Family wealth is also straightforward. Discretionary control of cash can be very empowering. But wealth derived from seemingly random processes—PowerBall wealth—is a conundrum. Would Theodore Roosevelt have recommended a "lottery tax" to prevent these nouveaux riches from using their wealth to ill effect? And BlackRock's power as an investor comes largely from how it votes in (mostly ceremonial) annual elections; its discretion over buying and selling shares is limited.

To the extent that there is corporate power in a PowerBall economy, it is likely to be highly unstable. Consider an example.

Until now, telecoms have held a traditional form of corporate power for over a century, either as natural monopolies (for landlines) or oligopolies (for cellular service). Yet this position is challenged by applications that allow low-cost communication via the internet. Skype (Microsoft), Hangout (Google), and Facetime (Apple) offer largely interchangeable means of video calling for free. Moreover, there are countless free or cheap apps that allow text and video messaging without use of the cellular network, including WhatsApp, Facebook's recent $19 billion acquisition. With ubiquitous WiFi delivered to open-source smartphones via community-owned ISPs, we may not need the phone company (or its collaborators in the NSA).

We may not need Apple, Google, or Facebook either. Kids in dormrooms around the world are writing open-source apps that can do most of the same things, but without the ads or the Orwellian monitoring. A business or application that experiences brief success can often be easily copied; indeed, rapid copycat businesses transplanted to new markets is the entire premise behind Germany's Rocket Internet.[7]

---

[7] <www.nytimes.com/2014/02/28/technology/copycat-business-model-generates-genuine-global-success-for-start-up-incubator.html>.

There are, of course, exceptions. Oil companies are not going away any time soon. A few corporations may have unique value specifically as public corporations (perhaps GE, Berkshire Hathaway, IBM, Amazon, and a few others). But it's easy to imagine that in a couple of years we will look back on Facebook as AOL redux, and Google as old-school AT&T.

Conclusion and Future Research

My chapter has been US-centric, speculative, and occasionally digressive. Let me emphasize three points in conclusion.

First, the data suggest that the corporations we have today do not fit the stylized facts that guided our thinking about the corporation during the twentieth century. They are smaller in employment, less integrated, less interconnected at the top, and have more concentrated ownership than the companies described by Berle and Means and other scholars. They also don't last as long.

Second, the kind of power accorded to those who own or manage the new enterprises is likely to be fleeting at best. Even the largest non-governmental shareholder the world has ever known, BlackRock, has at best a fitful form of control with respect to the corporations it nominally owns.

Third, there are reasons to believe that the economies of scale that provided the foundation for the public corporation are eroding in many sectors, opening possibilities for non-corporate alternatives.

Researchers and theorists have much to learn about this new system. Two issues stand out as especially pressing. First, we are used to thinking of the corporation as a body (corpus) comprised of members, a collective actor with boundaries and goals and mechanisms for collective decision-making. This imagery made sense when the characteristic problem of the corporation was gathering large groups of people under common management to accomplish collective tasks—that is, when we lived in the world of the Berle and Means corporation. The other chapters in this volume reflect this corporate ontology. In aiming to theorize the business enterprise as an ethical agent, Elizabeth Anderson describes the firm as a "nexus of reciprocal relationships" with a relatively long time horizon. She argues that firms can manage the prospective trade-off between ethics and profits by defining the firm's mission in terms of mutual advantage, and projects that profits will follow. Phillip Pettit describes the growing corporatization of our world, in which "more and more people live their working lives as the employees of corporations," and those corporate bodies act with shared purpose, speaking with one voice. As such, they can be considered agents and held responsible.

Yet today, enterprises are increasingly provisional and short-lived, resembling the nexus of contracts described by financial economists. They are less like an organism or body than they are like a web page, which requires a rather different corporate ontology. (Web pages appear seamless and coherent on your browser, but behind the scenes they generally consist of a set of calls to other web pages and databases where content such as text and images are stored; these calls are typically contingent on when and where and on what device you call up the page.) It is trivially easy to incorporate; if you have a credit card, you can create a Liberian corporation (or flag a ship) right now at <www.liscr.com/liscr>. With the same credit card and a web connection, you can hire programmers, manufacturers, distributors, and a billing service without leaving your seat. Such an enterprise can accomplish collective feats, but without shared purpose, collective decision-making, or speaking with a single voice.

This webpage ontology creates conundrums about corporate responsibility. Is Apple responsible for the labor practices of Foxconn? Or for the provenance of the minerals that go into its processors? The responsibility paradox (Davis et al. 2008) is that we expect to attribute responsibility to collective actors, yet we are faced with networks of shifting boundaries that no longer resemble collective actors with mutually regarding members. If we want better labor and environmental practices, we need a better understanding of supply chains and their points of accountability. Social research needs to explore in much greater detail the nature and dynamics of contemporary supply chains.

Second, it is difficult to reconcile the picture of labile corporations with their evident political influence. There really are ideologically driven billionaires throwing tens of millions of dollars at elections and often taking elaborate steps to hide their tracks, and corporations evade all efforts at rendering their political activities transparent. Teddy Roosevelt would surely gasp in horror at the *Citizens United* decision and subsequent court cases that eliminate constraints on corporations' ability to shape the democratic process.

But I hope this chapter has made clear that the term "corporate power" conveys an impression of coherence that is not backed up by clear definitions or argumentation. "Power" is often invoked to explain things when we lack the energy to lay out the mechanisms involved. In decades past, we could imagine stating that power is proportional to corporate size. Yet "size" is no longer a coherent construct: corporations can be large in revenues and employment but small in market capitalization (e.g. Kroger), and vice versa (e.g. Facebook); indeed, correlations among these variables have declined precipitously since the advent of Nikefication. If corporations derive their power from their ability to create (or reallocate) jobs, then is Facebook weak (because almost no one actually works for Facebook), while Kroger is strong (because it is a massive employer)? Clearly, if we want to gain traction on corporate power in the twenty-first century, we need greater conceptual clarity, and relying on twentieth-century models will not serve us well.

In his commentary on this chapter, Phillip Kitcher suggested that power may depend on the circumstances of its exercise. That is, rather than corporate power corresponding to an unvarying feature of a corporation (such as its size), it might be at crucial junctures that power is revealed. Bacteria are small and short-lived, yet their influence can be benign or devastating, and perhaps this is true as well of contemporary enterprises. He also wondered whether the power of those left behind (e.g. oil companies) was enhanced by the retrenchment of other corporate sectors. Both of these ideas suggest pathways for future research on the nature of corporate power.

Finally, I would note that our conceptions of power need to adjust to new formats and platforms for collective action, as suggested by Jim Snabe. Corporate power now faces new forms of resistance, as employees, customers, and other stakeholders are increasingly able to join together to make their voices heard. When Mozilla appointed a new CEO in March 2014, employees were displeased because he had donated $1,000 to a campaign against gay marriage six years earlier, and they took to Facebook and Twitter to express themselves en masse. An online dating site suggested to customers using Mozilla's web browser to revisit the site using a different browser. Within two weeks, the new CEO had moved on. When the Susan G. Komen Foundation cut off funds for breast cancer screenings to Planned Parenthood in January 2012, hundreds of thousands of Facebook and Twitter users joined together to express their opposition, and many vowed to end their support of the Foundation. Within three days, Komen had reversed course and reinstated the funding. Similar events are becoming a regular occurrence, and suggest that the trajectory of corporate power may not as consistent as critics suggest. The need for new understandings of the dynamics of corporate power (and its constraints) has never been greater.

References

Berle, Adolf A., and Gardiner C. Means (1932). *The Modern Corporation and Private Property* (modern reprint, 1991 edn). New Brunswick, NJ: Transaction.

Berman, Dennis K. (2014). Does IBM Love or Hate itself? *Wall Street Journal*, Jan. 21.

Brandeis, Louis D. (1914). *Other People's Money: And How the Bankers Use it*. New York: Frederick A. Stokes Co.

Chandler, Alfred D. (1977). *The Visible Hand: The Managerial Revolution in American Business*. Cambridge, MA: Belknap Press.

Chu, Johan, and Gerald F. Davis (2013). Who Killed the Inner Circle? The Collapse of the American Corporate Interlock Network. Unpublished, University of Michigan.

Dahrendorf, Ralf (1959). *Class and Class Conflict in Industrial Society*. Stanford, CA: Stanford University Press.

Davis, Gerald F. (2008). A Few Finance Capitalism? Mutual Funds and Ownership Re-concentration in the United States. *European Management Review*, 5: 11–21.

Davis, Gerald F. (2009). *Managed by the Markets: How Finance Reshaped America*. Oxford: Oxford University Press.

Davis, Gerald F. (2013a). After the Corporation. *Politics and Society*, 41: 280–305.

Davis, Gerald F. (2013b). Shareholder Value and the Jobs Crisis. *Perspectives on Work* (Summer 2013/Winter 2014): 47–50.

Davis, Gerald F. (2013c). Can Global Supply Chains Be Accountable? YaleGlobal Online, <http://yaleglobal.yale.edu/content/can-global-supply-chains-be-accountable>.

Davis, Gerald F., and J. Adam Cobb (2010). Corporations and Economic Inequality around the World: The Paradox of Hierarchy. *Research in Organizational Behavior*, 30: 35–53.

Davis, Gerald F., Kristina A. Diekmann, and Catherine H. Tinsley (1994). The Decline and Fall of the Conglomerate Firm in the 1980s: The Deinstitutionalization of an Organizational Form. *American Sociological Review*, 59: 547–70.

Davis, Gerald F., Marina N. Whitman, and Mayer N. Zald (2008). The Responsibility Paradox. *Stanford Social Innovation Review*, 6: 30–7.

DeLong, J. Bradford (1991). Did JP Morgan's Men Add Value? An Economist's Perspective on Financial Capitalism. In Peter Temin (ed.), *Inside the Business Enterprise: Historical Perspectives on the Use of Information*. Chicago: University of Chicago, 205–36.

Drucker, Peter F. (1949). The New Society I: Revolution by Mass Production. *Harper's Magazine* (Sept.): 21–30.

Heller, Nathan (2013). Bay Watched: How San Francisco's New Entrepreneurial Culture is Changing the Country. *The New Yorker*, Oct. 14.

Jensen, Michael C., and William H. Meckling (1976). Theory of the Firm: Managerial Behavior, Agency Cost and Ownership Structure. *Journal of Financial Economics*, 3: 305–60.

Kaplan, Steven N., and Joshua Rauh (2007). *Wall Street and Main Street: What Contributes to the Rise in the Highest Incomes?* Cambridge, MA: National Bureau of Economic Research.

Kaysen, Carl (1957). The Social Significance of the Modern Corporation. *American Economic Review (Papers and Proceedings)*, 47: 311–19.

Lenin, V. I. (1939 [orig. 1916]). *Imperialism: The Highest Stage of Capitalism*. New York: International Publishers.

Mills, C. Wright (1956). *The Power Elite*. New York: Oxford University Press.

Roe, Mark J. (1994). *Strong Managers, Weak Owners: The Political Roots of American Corporate Finance*. Princeton: Princeton University Press.

Roy, William G. (1997). *Socializing Capital: The Rise of the Large Industrial Corporation in America*. Princeton: Princeton University Press.

Streitfeld, Davis (2014). Engineers Allege Hiring Collusion in Silicon Valley. *The New York Times*, Feb. 28.

....

CHAPTER 24

CONTESTING THE MARKET

An Assessment of Capitalism's Threat to Democracy

....

MICHAEL FUERSTEIN

Abstract

The chapter argues that capitalism presents a threat to "democratic contestation": the egalitarian, socially distributed capacity to affect how, why, and whether power is used. Markets are not susceptible to mechanisms of accountability, nor are they bearers of intentions in the way that political power-holders are. This makes them resistant to the kind of rational, intentional oversight that constitutes one of democracy's social virtues. Four social costs are associated with this problem: the vulnerability of citizens to arbitrary interference, the insensitivity of markets to relevant interests, failures of trust in the market system, and the inhibition of social deliberation about matters of public concern. Two suggestions are made: (1) the reconceptualization of business activity as participation in larger group actions; (2) the development of deliberative bodies that bring together business actors, policy experts, and diverse citizens to better characterize the public values for business.

INTRODUCTION

....

Whether or not capitalism is ultimately compatible with democracy, there are at least very powerful tensions running between these two forms of social organization. There is a grand intellectual tradition running through Aristotle, Tocqueville, Marx, and many others observing the various ways in which economic inequalities translate into broader inequalities of social participation, access, and influence that present deep challenges to democracy. Capitalism also tends to reorder social attitudes and relationships in ways that undermine the kind of public ethos that democracy requires (Bowles and Gintis 1986; Dryzek 1996).

Here I am to identify and size up a different kind of threat that capitalism presents to democracy, one that has not received due attention in the traditional dialectic of inequality. I will argue that, independently of the concerns identified above, capitalism threatens the ideal of what—drawing on the work of Philip Pettit (1997, 2012)—I shall call "democratic contestation": the particular manner in which democracy structures decision-making about matters of social significance. Markets are by nature resistant to the kind of rational, intentional oversight that constitutes one of democracy's social virtues. As I will try to show, there are social harms associated with failures of this oversight even under conditions of optimal democratic equality and public-spiritedness. My primary objective will therefore be diagnostic: I hope to illuminate the distinctive nature of the challenges we confront in reconciling capitalist markets with democracy. As a secondary aim, I will make some suggestions towards the end of the chapter about what might be involved in responding to the challenges identified.

THE THREAT OF MARKET POWER

At a minimum, the ideal of democratic governance involves the broad and equitable distribution of basic political powers on terms of freedom. Following Philip Pettit's rich work on republicanism (I discuss Pettit in more detail later on), my suggestion is that we can usefully characterize this arrangement as the institutional realization of the egalitarian social contestation of power. By *contestation*, I mean a process in which the contesting agents, either collectively or individually, have some significant capacity to affect how, why, and whether power is used (Pettit 1997, 2012). By *egalitarian*, I mean that the relevant capacity is to be equally distributed to the greatest extent possible within relevant practical and moral constraints, and beyond some minimal threshold of sufficiency for all individuals. So *democratic contestation* is egalitarian social contestation. Under the right conditions, the egalitarian social contestation of power tends to realize the goods of freedom and equality, and that provides at least one of the core motivations for democratic procedures and institutional structures.

My central contention is that capitalism presents a threat to democratic contestation, and that this is something we have significant reason to worry about. To begin, then, I'd like to bring into view five examples of the distinctive manner in which this threat is expressed:

(1) The widespread, unanticipated loss of employment following the 2008 financial crisis.
(2) The existence of "food deserts," i.e. areas in which citizens confront significant obstacles to accessing healthy foods.
(3) The fact that racial minorities in the United States are far more likely than whites to live close to environmental hazards (Maantay 2002).

(4) The fact that "malaria, pneumonia, diarrhea, and tuberculosis combined constitute 21% of the global disease burden, but receive .31% of all health research funding" (Reiss and Kitcher 2009).

(5) The fact that we continue to increase our global consumption of fossil fuels at a rapid pace in spite of clear evidence of its catastrophic consequences, and in spite of the fact that there are means readily available for significantly reducing such consumption.

Case (1)—the example of the 2008 financial crisis—illustrates the most obvious respect in which capitalist markets play a vital causal role in the determination of human welfare and its distribution: our wealth and opportunities rise and fall with the value of goods and services that the market determines. Cases (2) and (4) both illustrate the way in which the incentives created by market forces frequently tend to produce gross inequalities—and inadequacies—in the accessibility of vital goods and services across different segments of the population. Case (3) also illustrates this phenomenon, though it is complicated by the role of those who are disadvantaged by the phenomenon in its own creation. The fact that racial minorities are disproportionately burdened by environmental hazards in the United States is in part a consequence of the economically motivated choices they make about where to live. Case (5) illustrates the way in which the inexorable logic of capitalist markets can prove enormously difficult to overcome, even when it brings about outcomes that are extremely bad for everyone.

So these cases all illustrate, at a minimum, the vital causal role that capitalist markets play in morally and socially significant states of affairs. By *capitalist markets* (or simply *markets* for short) I refer to systems in which goods and services are freely exchanged according to the norms established by some conventional notion of property rights. But I want to suggest that, beyond the causal role that markets play, they also manifest through their causal role something very much like an exercise of power. In the moral and political context, conceptions of power typically make essential reference to notions like will, goal-directedness, and other essential tokens of human agency.[1] In this respect, the sense in which markets themselves wield power is unclear, since markets do not have minds or manifest intentions in the way that managers, political representatives, corporations, or political parties seem to manifest intentions. Intentions can plausibly be attributed to groups, but only under conditions in which the individuals who constitute them form the relevant kinds of joint intentions (Gilbert 2000). Markets are distinct from groups in this respect because what markets do is an unintended and, indeed, often unforeseen by-product of individual actions whose intentions are directed at other ends. Nonetheless, like the process of natural selection, the behavior of markets under the right conditions mimics intentional or goal-directed action. This is the point of Smith's elegant "invisible hand" conceit: the aggregative consequence of individuals making local decisions directed at their self-interest is

---

[1] Thus e.g. on Robert Dahl's (1957) proposal "A has power over B to the extent that he can get B to do something that B would not otherwise do."

patterns of production and distribution that are dynamically responsive to social aims not held in mind. Thus, the motivation for talking about markets as power-wielders derives from the explanatory role of market-talk in accounting for economic phenomena that are (imperfectly) responsive to important social values (though the values to which they are responsive are not all good). Markets reflect the *as-if* agency of Smith's invisible hand. In my usage, *market power* is constituted by the distinctive causal role that markets play in (a) bringing about socially significant events and states of affairs and (b) doing so in a manner that is dynamically responsive to at least some socially valuable aims.

With these preliminaries out of the way, let us proceed with the primary line of argument. The suggestion that market power poses a distinctive threat to democratic contestation proceeds from two observations. The first concerns the massive significance of market power in its bearing on human interests around the world, as cases (1)–(5) all illustrate.[2] The increasing globalization of markets has only made their power more significant in recent years as, for example, national economic and social policies are influenced by the threat of capital flight (Dryzek 1996), consumer behavior is shaped by the expansion of international corporations into new markets, and indigenous cultures confront economically driven pressures on their ability to sustain traditional ways of life.

The second observation regarding the threat of market power to democratic contestation concerns the peculiar nature of market power itself. In the political context, genuine contestation is possible in virtue of two features of government institutions:

(i) Political agents and institutions are *accountable*. That is, they are susceptible, via institutional design, to meaningful influence by those over whom they exercise power. Political agents can be subjected to public evaluation and review, can be removed through the power of the ballot, and can be placed within a bureaucratic management structure that fosters meaningful (if imperfect) accountability for the service of public goals.

(ii) Relatedly, the operation of political agents and institutions is *intentional*. It typically reflects, to some meaningful degree, the operation of goal-directed agency, though this is often only on the scale of a large bureaucratic organization rather than the individual. The making and enforcement of laws, the operation of political organizations, and the movements of individual political officials are normally manifestations of intentions to do what is done (though this does not exclude the inevitability of unforeseen consequences of those actions).

Accountability is indispensable to the prospect of contestation because the capacity to affect the use of political power requires some institutional mechanisms through which influence is to be exercised. Intentionality is indispensable to the prospect of

---

[2] This statement is not intended to overlook the fact that markets also bear very significantly on non-human interests. But this fact does not bear on its threat to democratic contestation, at least in this context.

contestation because intentionality makes possible the intelligent adjustment of activities in response to concerns and preferences. Market power, however, lacks both of these properties. Though, like intentional agents, markets display a dynamic sensitivity to at least some social goals, that sensitivity arises as a by-product of aggregate individual intentions directed at other concerns. Indeed the relevant point is even stronger than this since—on the logic of the invisible hand—the sensitivity of markets to social goals is at least partly dependent on the fact that the individuals involved do not directly aim at serving those goals. Service of those goals is in this sense not merely a by-product, but rather what Jon Elster (1983) calls an "essential byproduct." The most significant consequence of this fact is that, while markets are dynamically sensitive in their behavior to matters of supply and demand, their as-if intentionality breaks down when considerations not already represented in the price signal are introduced. Thus when markets perpetuate patterns of racial disadvantage, devastating environmental damage, or a catastrophic decline in the value of real estate, there is no apparent route to converting those concerns into modifications of market behavior, except by proceeding via forces (such as political regulation), external to the market's operation.

Markets also lack accountability, or at least present important challenges to accountability. They lack accountability in part as a consequence of their lack of intentionality. When a system is not dynamically responsive to external goals—goals not already represented in the normal operation of the system—the usual mechanisms of accountability with respect to those goals fail. One cannot shame the market into changing course with respect to environmental racism, nor can one appeal to the market by explaining why racism is morally bad. But the market's lack of intentionality is not the only cause of its lack of accountability. There are two other features of markets that are relevant in this respect.

First is a point closely related to, but distinct from, the fact that markets lack intentionality. This is the fact that market behaviors are *radically distributed* phenomena. They are vast collections of individual and smaller-group behaviors which are themselves not coordinated in any intentional way. Calling markets to account therefore requires calling to account a vast, and vastly distributed, group of independent agents whose activities lack agency or responsibility with respect to the phenomena in question. Individual firms and actors are of course responsible for all sorts of things within the boundaries of the market. Companies that pollute the air, mistreat their workers, or create new jobs are responsible for what they do. But there is no particular person or firm responsible for food deserts, environmental racism, or the under-representation of the developing world's needs in the scientific research agenda.

In response one might note that, though firms may lack individual responsibility for the global distribution of scientific research efforts or the exposure of American minorities to greater levels of pollution, they bear responsibility for their individual contributions to these phenomena. I think there is some promise in this observation, and will return to pursue it later in the chapter. But for now this point only underscores the peculiar difficulty created by the vast distribution of market phenomena across individual agents. Though we can surely call individuals and individual firms to account for their contribution to market phenomena, creating accountability for the phenomena as a whole would require calling the vast, and vastly distributed, set of individuals and firms to account in a systematic way.

Complicating matters is once again the peculiar gap between the local goals that motivate individual actors and firms, and the larger-scale social consequences of the aggregation of those behaviors. The primary cause of food deserts is not that grocers are biased against certain neighborhoods.[3] They arise because grocery chain owners are trying to make money and certain geographic areas, for familiar reasons, tend to have difficulty sustaining profitable enterprises that sell healthy food. On top of this, according to the conventional logic of market economics, a firm that sets aside the primary question of profit in order to address questions of social justice and progress will at best suffer a competitive disadvantage in the struggle for growth, capital, and survival. Moreover, as the problematic history of nationalized industry suggests, attempts to treat public values as a priority often introduce ambiguities in managerial aims that foster malfeasance and incompetence (Heath and Norman 2004). Finally, diverting one's efforts to some social value other than profit can often be ineffectual or even counter-productive without the coordination of other actors. Thus, for example, when musical artists set ticket prices at below-market rates as a token of goodwill towards their fans, the result is typically the creation of incentives for scalpers to buy those tickets and then resell them at whatever the market will bear for a neat profit. The only beneficiary of the musician's goodwill is the scalper.

For all of these reasons, holding individual firms accountable for their contribution to the realization of social values rather than profit is at best problematic. Alleviating these problems would require mechanisms that hold entire industries (and perhaps even entire economies more broadly) accountable in a simultaneous and coordinated fashion. Later in this chapter, I explore what that might mean. For now, I want simply to mark this as a significant challenge for democratic contestation with respect to market behavior.

Thus one consideration telling against the accountability of markets is the broad distribution of individual responsibility for market phenomena across discrete individuals and groups, motivated by diverse goals. Whereas political responsibility can be attached to clearly identifiable individuals and groups of individuals, market responsibility seems to be borne by everyone and no one. A second consideration telling against market accountability concerns the *privacy* of its constitutive activities. Systems of free exchange are defined as such in virtue of private property rights that protect the ability of actors to buy, sell, and use the things they own as they wish, though within some reasonable set of moral and legal constraints. Such property rights are private only insofar as they can be exercised at the discretion of individual owners.

To the extent that free markets are properly conceived as systems of private exchange, there is an obvious tension with the imperatives of accountability in both moral and institutional respects. From an institutional standpoint, the privacy of

---

[3] Though, admittedly, one shouldn't be surprised if some such bias played a role in this dynamic. At a minimum, the relevant point is that such bias is not the dominant causal factor in play.

property rights entails the reasonable entitlement, barring the violation of established legal constraints, to keep secret one's records and the motivations for one's actions. It entails that one's institutional obligations to publicly explain one's actions and hear out objections to them are limited. A company that illegally dumps toxins in a river, exploits child labor, or engages in racial discrimination violates moral and legal constraints and will normally incur legal punishment and moral disapprobation. But failing to build a supermarket in a poor neighborhood, consuming large amounts of fossil fuel that one has fairly purchased, or devoting one's research budget to pills that alleviate sexual dysfunction rather than the effective treatment of malaria are all activities that fail to violate conventional moral and legal constraints on the use of private property, and thus require no explanation to the public. The legal and moral constraints that apply to markets are oriented principally towards the identifiable harms of individual actors within the market. But the causally significant behavior of markets, taken as a whole, is often constituted by individual behaviors which are themselves not causally or morally significant.

So market power is by nature resistant to the model of accountability required by democratic contestation. Such contestation, as I have noted, is premised on the existence of institutional mechanisms that facilitate challenges to the use of power, and an institutional ethos that fosters at least some measure of responsiveness to those challenges from public officials. Relatedly, it is premised on the exercise of genuine agency among power holders who direct their activities toward service of government's characteristic aims. Markets thus present additional challenges to accountability in virtue of the way in which agency is radically distributed across individual actors. Market power also lacks intentionality and thus proves difficult to reconcile with the kind of adaptation to diverse objectives that democracy requires.

THE DISTINCTIVE VALUE OF CONTESTATION

I have been arguing that markets present distinctive challenges to the ideal of democratic contestation. I turn now to examine more carefully why we should regard these challenges as problematic. The first step in that project is getting clear about why the ideal of social contestation is good in the first place, and why we should think it appropriate to extend that ideal to markets.

There is of course a well-established strain of classical liberalism which holds that private markets are valuable precisely because they provide us with the means to manage matters of essential human concern without engaging in coercive interference in the lives of individuals. In support of that tradition Hayek (1945) argued that, independently of any moral imperatives to respect private property rights, markets alone were capable of solving the epistemological problems associated with efficient production and distribution on a mass scale. Given the enormous range of considerations bearing on these aims, central planners lacked the means to gather, synthesize, and react to dynamically evolving economic conditions. On this logic, the market solves problems best when left free of governmental interference.

Hayek's perspective essentially supports the general argument that I have been pursuing. Market power is wielded in a way that is radically distributed across individual agents whose activities are not intentionally directed toward the net social consequences to which they contribute. Making it socially contestable in the way that political decisions are socially contestable would seem to undermine precisely the thing that makes markets successful in organizing social behavior. One hears echoes of this argument in the anti-government zeal of some American conservatives on economic matters. If the government subsidizes a start-up industry like solar energy, for example, it is prematurely "picking winners." On this logic, if there is real social value in solar energy, then it will eventually be represented in the price signal, which will facilitate any needed investment. I will shortly consider some of the problems with this perspective. But the point for the moment is that, even if social contestation is a good thing in the context of political decisions, we should proceed carefully before making the assumption that it is a good thing across the board. What is it about social contestation that is desirable, exactly, and why should we worry about a lack of social contestation in the economic context? This question must be approached from a number of different angles, which together constitute most of the core rationale for democracy.

Vulnerability to Arbitrary Interference

In *Republicanism* and a series of related works, Philip Pettit defends a republican conception of freedom as "non-domination." One is dominated, on Pettit's view, insofar as one may be subjected to the "arbitrary" will of another, i.e. when another has the capacity to interfere with one's choices in a manner, and on terms, that one cannot control. One is free when one has the capacity to contest the way in which one is subject to power, and Pettit thus conceptualizes democracy as a set of institutions which enable social contestation (1997, 2012). The conception of democracy that I employ in this chapter is therefore essentially Pettit's.

The dialectic that Pettit employs in support of this conception of freedom is directed principally in opposition to the conventional liberal understanding of freedom as non-interference. From that point of view, we are free to the extent that our choices are not subjected to interference by another's will. Pettit observes, however, that the mere absence of actual interference is not sufficient to secure an attractive form of freedom. That is because the absence of actual interference is compatible with the capacity to interfere arbitrarily, and the capacity to interfere arbitrarily can, in certain domains, create forms of abject vulnerability. Thus, whether or not poor, unskilled workers are able to hold on to their jobs on the basis of their merit as workers, they must typically live with the knowledge that, were their manager to decide to fire them, they would suffer extreme hardship as a result.

This sort of dynamic is problematic in at least two ways. It is problematic, first, insofar as workers must bear the psychological and material costs associated with the unknown prospects of material privation. The point in this case is that, even if one does not suffer from material privation, one must plan and act around that possibility, thus foregoing valuable opportunities and typically dealing with some degree of resultant anxiety. The dynamic between unskilled workers and managers is problematic, second, insofar as workers must adopt a strategy of abject servility in an attempt to avoid incurring the disfavor (whether appropriate or not) of their manager. Under such circumstances, their agency and ability to represent themselves with meaningful integrity is sharply reduced, even if their manager always treats them justly. It is the capacity of the manager to terminate their position without good reason, rather than the exercise of that capacity, which is enough to undermine an attractive form of freedom.

It is not hard to see how this sort of logic can be pursued to make an argument for democratic contestation: citizens are free to the extent that they are not subjected to the arbitrary will of their rulers, and arbitrariness is eliminated through procedural mechanisms and institutions that provide citizens with a meaningful power to participate in control over how political power is used (Pettit 1997, 2012). One of the distinctive goods of social contestation, then, concerns its capacity to mitigate or eliminate the harms associated with being subjected to the arbitrary will of others.

One of the concerns about the capacity for arbitrary interference extends to market power. The other does not. Non-domination shields individuals from the humiliating interpersonal dynamics associated with vulnerability to another's will. But since markets do not themselves have a will, and since they are not agents in either the corporate or personal sense, this concern does not appear to apply in this context. One cannot suffer from servility to a market in the way that one can suffer from servility to an individual manager or firm. This is one respect in which the distinction between market power and will-based notions of power is significant.

But markets do nonetheless expose individuals to the psychological and material costs associated with substantial uncertainty as concerns their basic interests. As the example of the 2008 financial crisis illustrates, people who occupy the bottom rungs of the economic ladder are subject to the same kinds of economic and psychological costs as our worker confronts in the hypothetical case just described. The point in that case is that the fear of such a crisis would itself be a significant hardship for workers, independently of its actual occurrence. Particularly in nations where the social safety net is weaker, the uncertainty associated with this kind of economic vulnerability is a considerable burden. Likewise, to choose a different sort of example, the citizens of Bangladesh and other low-lying parts of the world must live with a greater or lesser (these days: greater) vulnerability to extreme flooding as a consequence of trends in the world market for oil. That kind of vulnerability is not only bad for individual citizens, it is also bad for the nation collectively in its ability to attract and efficiently deploy investment capital.

Of course, no economic or political system can comprehensively eliminate every form of harmful uncertainty. Risk is a fact of life. But some sources of risk are artifacts of human institutions and some are not. Weather patterns as such are not sufficiently subject to human control, and are not artifacts of human institutions. In contrast, markets are entities that we create, and adherence to their logic reflects choices we make about social organization.

In any case, the point at the moment is not that we should reject markets because they introduce forms of uncertainty that are harmful to human flourishing. The point is to represent this uncertainty as a significant cost, one that we have been able to mitigate in the domain of governance.

Insensitivity to Relevant Interests

There is a more obvious respect, however, in which social contestation is desirable. As John Stuart Mill observed in "Considerations on Representative Government" (1991), the likelihood that the ruling class will serve the interests of the ruled is rather low except in circumstances where the ruled have some meaningful opportunity to give expression to their interests, and where there are institutional mechanisms that hold the ruling class accountable to them. Social contestation, in short, is an obvious and necessary measure for ensuring that power is used in a way that tracks the interests of those affected by it. There are at least two reasons for this. One concerns the tendency of power-holders to serve their own interests at the expense of those over whom they hold power. Social contestation provides a mechanism that at least mitigates this tendency by creating incentives to put the public interest first, and by creating mechanisms that allow for the removal of self-serving officials. Social contestation has a *motivational* benefit in this regard. Social contestation also has an *epistemic* benefit. As Mill also observed, even the most benevolent dictator will be confronted by insuperable difficulties in gathering and assimilating the enormous body of information required to serve the interests of a large, diverse public (Fuerstein 2008; Mill 1991).

In the case of market power, there are analogs for both the epistemic and motivational problems that obtain in the case of political power. From an epistemic point of view, a Hayekian perspective implies that the epistemological problems associated with production and distribution are solved—not created—via the radically distributed nature of economic activity. Insofar as increasing contestation requires centralizing economic decision-making in intentional actors, it would seem to reintroduce the very epistemological problems that markets are good at solving. But one way of interpreting cases like (1)–(5) is to point out that, while markets very efficiently manage the particular variety of informational inputs that go into buying and selling, they are blind to a great deal of information that properly bears on the social "actions" that they bring about. Markets create robust incentives for killing elephants in order to harvest their tusks; no one thinks this fact reveals that poaching elephants is a permissible or desirable social activity. Likewise, if markets do not sustain much-needed investment in malaria research, that does not show that we would not do better to increase such investment.

Some familiar observations in this domain: though market demand reflects the existence of some measure of social desire for some good, desires can be founded on all manner of ignorance and selfishness. At the same time, the desires reflected in price signals are reflections of a willingness to pay rather than all things considered judgments about desirability as such. To return to the food deserts example: the fact that there is low economic demand for healthy, ethically sourced food in poor neighborhoods may simply reflect the fact that poor people cannot afford healthy, ethically sourced food, rather than the fact that they do not have a strong desire for such food. Finally, as the climate change example illustrates with devastating clarity, market prices fail to reflect costs that arise as externalities. In light of these observations, one way of understanding the failures of market power to track social interests is in terms of an epistemic failure. Markets do a bad job of pooling and assimilating certain kinds of information that bear essentially on service of the social good.

The motivational problem that contestation solves in the political domain seems obscure in the case of market power given that, as I have repeatedly emphasized, markets lacks minds or intentions. Nonetheless, it is worth bringing back into view the individual producers and consumers—especially large global firms—whose activities collectively constitute market behavior. Milton Friedman's (1970) famous (notorious?) suggestion that firms' defining aim should be the maximization of shareholder value captures a significant moral and organizational consequence associated with market behavior. Market power effects significant social outcomes as a by-product of behavior directed principally at non-social aims. But to the extent that markets fail in achieving socially desirable byproducts, we ought to consider whether the asocial motivational structure proposed by Friedman (and captured in the invisible hand analogy) needs rethinking. The social failures of markets suggest that, even if we cannot motivate markets as such through contestation, we might look for ways of altering the motivations of individual market actors via the contestatory model.

Trust in Markets

Whereas Hobbes (1996) rejects democracy by appealing to the dangers of social instability associated with freedom, Locke (1988) observes that those who have the opportunity to authorize and control their government's activities are far less likely to be a source of civil unrest. Freedom achieves social stability, not through fear, but through mechanisms that tend to induce sufficient approval of social and political conditions. Locke effectively identifies the way in which democratic governments succeed, not only through the primary good of fairly promoting citizens' interests, but also through the secondary good of being publicly seen to fairly promote citizens' interests. In this case there is a kind of virtuous feedback loop that arises through the interaction among these two goods: governments that are seen to be fair and competent tend to enjoy benefits of approval and compliance that better facilitate the achievement of fairness and competence (Fuerstein 2013). At the same time, under the right conditions, the superior achievement of fairness and competence should tend to promote the greater (justified) perception of fairness and competence. Democratic governments achieve these complementary goods, not only through egalitarian voting over representatives, but also through the broad spectrum of civic and political activities that allow citizens to wield some measure of influence over political officials.

Of course, one should not indulge in idealistic fantasies about the state of public confidence in democratic governments. Most contemporary democracies illustrate some non-negligible measure of distrust and disaffection toward their public institutions, for both valid and invalid reasons (Pharr and Putnam 2000). The point, however, is simply to highlight the way in which social contestation supports at least a basic measure of confidence in political institutions, such that those who are on the losing end of political battles nonetheless retain the willingness to comply with the law and continue to fight those battles in good faith within the system.[4]

In the economic context, one can see a variety of contemporary manifestations of public alienation from capitalist institutions, most notably the Occupy Wall Street movement in the United States, and the sometimes violent social unrest that has accompanied Greece's recent conflicts with the IMF. While the causes of such opposition are complicated they both embody not only an opposition to the way in which wealth is distributed, but also a general sense of distrust of capitalist institutions themselves. While that distrust at present does not seem to present any real threat to the global economic order, the tendency of the capitalist system to serve diverse interests depends significantly on the extent to which the public is invested in its success. The general belief that large capitalist actors and institutions are all corrupt and that the economic game is rigged threatens a kind of populist backlash that is likely to be bad both for business and social progress itself. Capitalism is far more likely to serve the full spectrum of social interests under conditions in which it secures the justified confidence of the public in its capacity to serve those interests. Contestation serves that aim in essential ways.

The Deliberative Constitution of Public Value

There is a familiar line of criticism extending back to Plato according to which democratic citizens are hopelessly incompetent on matters of public policy, and that

---

[4] Of course democracies are hardly immune to problems in this regard, as recent obstructionism in the American political system, for example, illustrates.

their beliefs about government are vulnerable to manipulation by elites (Plato 1992; Schumpeter 1942).

In response to such cynicism, John Dewey argued in *The Public and its Problems* (1954) that such cynicism was the consequence of a flawed conception of democracy rather than an essential feature of the democratic public itself. On Dewey's view, insofar as we conceive of democracy principally as a matter of selecting officials to implement the public good, citizens will tend to be passive bystanders to the diverse factors that bear on their good. Without some commitment to cultivating a refined collective conception of the public good, the basic procedural mechanisms of democracy will be inadequate to achieve desirable forms of self-governance. Democracy thus must be understood as a "way of life" and not only a mechanism for selecting officials who will do the work of governance. Specifically, it must be understood to involve a broader spectrum of social norms and institutions so that the public's consciousness of its values, and the challenges that confront those values, can be nourished. Democracy can be thought of as a kind of virtuous feedback loop, in which the values and interests that democracy serves are themselves positively transformed via the practice of democracy itself.

By way of example, consider the case of the environmental movement. The enormous significance that the value of the natural environment has come to assume in policy debates is essentially the consequence of twentieth-century moral innovations, combined with an explosion in relevant scientific theories. Those moral innovations have been forged through a large-scale process of deliberation, one extended over several decades, about how and why the natural environment should be valued by human beings. The recognition of the natural environment's value has been in part a recognition of imperatives related to our own survival, but has also involved the transformation of human desires and goals, including our understanding of wild places, beauty, and our particular place in the cosmos. In this respect the essential collective interest that we have in respecting the natural environment is a product of the democratic process in two ways: first, it is a consequence of collective inquiry that led to the recognition of the relationship between the natural environment and essential goods (e.g. clean water) whose value we already recognized; second, it is a consequence of transformations in our conception of what sorts of things are worth valuing, and how they should be valued. The development of an environmental consciousness is also illustrative of the distinctive value of public institutions that facilitate vigorous, egalitarian involvement in managing affairs of common concern. The development of a public environmental consciousness is a consequence in this respect of institutions of democratic contestation. And the development of that consciousness, at the same time, is a condition that enables more effective and informed democratic governance.

So democratic contestation achieves the goals of public governance in part by creating conditions in which the animating values of public governance, and the conditions that bear on it, can be better identified and progressively transformed. I have engaged in this digression on environmentalism in order to highlight a particular kind of problem that arises when matters of essential public concern—such as the distribution of scientific research funds, the availability of healthy food, the placement of environmental hazards, etc.—are handled and conceptualized as by-products of private activities. When activities are conceptualized as private, they are not subject to procedural mechanisms that foster healthy public dialog, and they are seen as falling outside the full scope of moral and legal responsibility for the service of public aims.

One salient example of this phenomenon is the movement in the United States to privatize many of the most basic functions of the welfare state, including the financial security of the elderly (social security), access to quality health care, and the quality of the educational system. When care for the vulnerable members of our society is conceptualized as a government function, responsibility for their welfare is channeled through government agents, and a public debate about our collective obligations to the vulnerable takes the shape of a debate about public policy that entails some measure of responsibility for all citizens. When charity is a private function, however, the responsibility to care for the needy exists everywhere and nowhere. There are no particular agents to be held accountable for collective failures to serve the needy, and public dialog on questions of social justice is transformed into scattered private conversations about how much of the family budget should go to charity. Dewey's insight about democracy, however, was that, when the problems we confront are consequences of collective patterns of behavior, it is essential that we engage in an attempt to forge some common understanding of what in fact the problem is and how to approach it.

PROSPECTS FOR AMELIORATING THE THREAT

I have argued that market power is distinctly resistant to the democratic model of social contestation and I have tried to identify some crucial problems that arise from this resistance. The question of how best to deal with this problem hinges on complex matters of law, economic policy, and institutional design that cannot be adequately addressed in the remaining space (nor by the author, who lacks sufficient expertise in these areas). I have tried to offer a diagnosis of some of the ills associated with contemporary capitalism that I hope might at least provide the basis for further inquiry. I will nonetheless conclude by bringing into view the most notable analytical implications so far, and then turning to consider in general form some ameliorative possibilities.

At the chapter's outset, I suggested that there are some widely appreciated threats that capitalism presents to the democratic ideal. Capitalism threatens democracy directly and indirectly through its tendency to produce significant economic and social inequalities. Capitalism also threatens democracy by undermining the kind of public ethos that is essential to the healthy functioning of many democratic institutions.

The arguments show that democratic contestation would be threatened by market power independently of these issues. Specifically, I have argued that the incontestability of markets (a) subjects individuals to arbitrary effects on essential aspects of their lives, (b) reduces the responsiveness of large-scale social institutions to the full spectrum of essential human interests, (c) undermines warranted trust in economic institutions, and (d) undermines deliberative processes that sustain the identification and positive transformation of public values. In thinking about how to ameliorate the social ills associated with capitalism, we must therefore think structurally about its relationship to the very prospect of social choice and self-determination, independently of matters of inequality and public-spiritedness.

Our diagnosis of the distinctive threat that market power presents to democracy has some more specific implications for theoretical approaches to business ethics. Most conceptions of corporate social responsibility (CSR) introduce some form of obligation to the broader community of "stakeholders," or individuals who are affected by commercial activities. But while an adequate theory of CSR is undoubtedly essential to the amelioration of various problems associated with market power, the model of contestation calls for genuine mechanisms by which control is to be exercised, above and beyond an articulation of moral requirements. Thus, in discussing J. S. Mill's rationale for democracy, I noted his observation that the tendency of political officials to serve the interests of the public depends essentially on the extent to which the public has mechanisms at its disposal to create appropriate incentives and share relevant information. Likewise, aligning the behavior of markets with social aims will require causal mechanisms that facilitate both (a) the transfer of information to firms about how their activities in the marketplace contribute to collective outcomes that bear on public values and (b) some measure of meaningful motivation to serve those values through their contribution to collective market activities. So it is important that our reflection on the morality of individual market behavior is developed in tandem with a conception of institutional and procedural mechanisms that facilitate genuine friction between the public articulation of values and the behavior of firms participating in market activities.

I turn now to consider the practical implications of our discussion: what might be done about all of this? Part of the answer to this question presumably involves democratically governed regulatory structures. Regulatory structures are the definitive institutional device mediating between public expressions of value and the mass patterns of commercial activity that constitute market behavior. Better realizing the ideal of contestation through those structures entails, on the one hand, reforms in the behavior and self-conception of the firms being regulated and, on the other, democratic reforms that better enable effective public oversight of market behavior.

Regarding the behavior and self-conception of firms, I noted that the invisible hand model of economic activity creates problems for the ideal of contestation. The difficulty is that, to the extent that social progress is a by-product of something else, there is no intentional organization linking the behavior of markets and market actors to progress. My suggestion, then, is that we need to work out a conception of behavior within markets that reintroduces such organization. Since markets are aggregates of individual behavior, the relevant intentions in this case would be some form of joint intention, i.e. intentions to contribute through one's individual action to goals that are realized through the group as a whole (Gilbert 2000). From this point of view, the normal profit-seeking activities of firms within the market would be justifiable just so long as the collective consequences of those activities can be recognized to contribute properly to the achievement of social goods. This ideal is somewhat distinct from standard conceptions of corporate social responsibility insofar as it focuses, not on the individual consequences of business behavior (though one should not ignore that either), but on the way in which those consequences fit into broader social patterns. Firms are to be held accountable and are to hold themselves accountable by reference to a broader conception of how markets serve social goals.

As a practical matter, taking this kind of accountability seriously would entail more vigorous and less strategic participation in deliberative institutions that serve to articulate and transmit public goals. Such deliberative institutions (I will say more about this) might include formal legislative and economic forums, interactions within commercial organizations and alliances, exchanges with shareholders, and engagement with the broader community. The defining objective in such engagement would be, not the strategic pursuit of individual business interests but, rather, an informed conception of how those profit-seeking activities might contribute to broader social concerns. One suggestive model for what business might look like on these terms is the growing body of "hybrid" firms that seek explicitly to advance socially vital goods through profit-seeking enterprise. Perhaps the most prominent example of this has been the rise of micro-credit organizations that provide small-scale loans to the poor on profitable terms, but there is a now a broad spectrum of organizations that employ the hybrid model in advancing environmental, legal, civic, medical, and other vital goods (Battilana et al. 2012, Mair et al. 2012).

Hybrids, however, do not provide the only model for the conception of profit-seeking activity that I have in mind. One of the crucial obstacles to the alignment of profit-seeking activity with social objectives is that, as part of the conventional logic of market behavior, business firms tend to adopt a deliberately oppositional stance when it comes to regulation. A firm committed to the ideal of collective intentionality would be proactive in facilitating the pro-social regulation of its own activities alongside the activities of its competitors. An oil company committed to social progress might commit individually to sacrificing some measure of its own profits for the sake of environmental goods. But as a participant in the collective activities of the market, it should endorse gasoline taxes on the presumption that they represent a shared commitment within the industry—and therefore a shared cost as well—to environmental goods that compete with profits. Likewise a pharmaceutical company might take on the individual responsibility of sponsoring unprofitable research that serves the needs of the world's poor. But to conceive of itself as a participant in broader market trends would be to support policy measures that sustain this kind of research across the industry in a coordinated, long-term manner. So improving the democratic contestation of markets seems to entail the reconceptualization of the goals and responsibility of individual firms in a way that introduces some meaningful degree of collective agency to market behavior. To the extent that firms see themselves, and are seen, as intentional participants in collective endeavors, the public will be in a better position to bring them to account through the regulatory system.

But the capacity of the public to wield more effective control over the behavior of markets also implies improvements in our civic and democratic institutions. At present, so much of our economic policy is a consequence of deliberation among policy elites, subject mainly to contestation by organized interest groups whose principal aim is the service of narrow private concerns. To the extent that the public participates in the regulation of markets, it arises too often via paroxysms of populist anger about high taxes, wage inequality, or overseas outsourcing. While such anger is often legitimate, it tends to be at best clumsy and overreaching, and that is likely because of well-documented failures of public knowledge about basic economic ideas among other things (Caplan 2007).

The challenge in this context is of course not unique to questions of economics. Scientific regulatory practice is similarly subject to populist misunderstandings about the risks and potential rewards associated with technological innovations. Likewise, our policy debates surrounding issues such as vaccination and climate change are (particularly in the United States) too often overwhelmed by fallacious conceptions of scientific practice and unwarranted distrust of scientific institutions (Kitcher 2011; Specter 2009). Much as these challenges suggest the need for a reinvigoration and reconceptualization of science education (Kitcher 2011), any improvement in the democratic contestation of markets is likely to entail measures that improve the grasp of ordinary citizens on at least the basics of economic theory and its relationship to policy. But a general comprehension of economic issues will not be sufficient to improve democratic contestation without institutional measures that facilitate a more vigorous mutual exchange between the business community and the general public. In particular, we should seek expansions and improvements of deliberative forums in which the public has the opportunity to interact with businesses and policy-makers.

At present, a large portion of such deliberative interaction arises (in the United States anyway) via the communal review of specific proposed commercial endeavors, such as the construction of new housing developments or changes in economic zoning regulations, or tax breaks designed to attract new business. A better model would afford citizens and businesses deliberative opportunities to assess the relationship between businesses and public values in a broader sense, and to think about the threats and prospects presented by more long-term commercial trends (Scherer and Palazzo 2007). James Fishkin's promising experiments with deliberative polling—in which citizens are convened in a carefully designed deliberative forum to address vital issues of public concern—provides one general rubric for this sort of thing (Fishkin 2009). There are also a broad range of initiatives under way in Europe at the moment—such as the National Institute for Health and Care Excellence in the UK or "Publiforums" in Switzerland—which are designed to bring policy elites, stakeholders, and a diverse body of lay citizens into dialogue on public matters such as food, healthcare policy, and environmental policy.[5] While these initiatives are still very much works in progress, they suggest a general framework for creating a more substantive dialog between business firms, policy elites, and the public about ongoing issues of value as they arise in the economic forum.[6]

Earlier, I suggested that regulation served as a crucial intermediary between the behavior of the market and public expressions of value. In this respect, it would be natural to organize the sorts of deliberative efforts just described around the production of government regulatory measures. But it is also worth emphasizing the inevitable limitations of working through the government.[7] Government activity is constrained by the distinctive dynamics of political maneuvering, bureaucratic inertia, special interest pandering, and other familiar social maladies. At the outset of the chapter, I characterized democracy as the egalitarian social contestation of power. But so long as effective contestation requires more than the conventional powers and procedures associated with political rights, the democratic ideal ought to encompass a broader spectrum of norms and institutions. In Dewey's words, democracy is a "way of life" in the sense that it entails a broad spectrum of participation in civic life that allows each citizen to realize a fair controlling stake in the social terms of her existence. Although progress in labor conditions, gender and race relations, and the natural environment, for example, has relied in crucial respects on government action, such progress has been just as dependent on the mobilization of public opinion in other forms: consumer pressure, petitioning, journalistic exposure, and worker and shareholder activism, for example. Such mechanisms provide expressions of public consciousness that can be effective even without government intervention, if only because they present a convincing threat to companies' bottom line.

In this respect, it is important to observe that at least some of the kinds of problems exemplified in cases (1)–(5) are consequences of economic disempowerment. There presumably would not be food deserts, for example, if the consumers who occupied the relevant neighborhoods had sufficient resources to pay for healthy food. One way of improving the public contestation of market power, therefore, is to pursue measures that improve the economic standing of those who lack sufficient resources to express their values in the marketplace.[8] That is a form of democratization, but one that proceeds independently of political rights and duties. On the business side of things, ethically oriented trade bodies—such as the Fair Labor Association—international organizations that standardize codes of ethical conduct—such as the International Organization for Standardization—and the plethora of socially responsible investment

---

[5] See Hagendijk and Irwin 2006 for a useful overview of these kinds of initiatives. For an illuminating discussion of NICE in particular see Lever 2012.

[6] On the promise, problems, and complexity of deliberative interactions between experts and non-experts on technical policy matters, see Jasanoff 2005. Jasanoff's focus is on scientific policy, but there are obvious parallels with economic issues.

[7] I thank David Schmidtz and the students in his Philosophy, Politics, and Economics seminar at the University of Arizona for helping me to see the importance of this point.

[8] I am grateful to Elizabeth Anderson for this point.

funds now available, all provide models for mobilization apart from government regulation. Though (inevitably) imperfect, such institutions illustrate what the voluntary cultivation of a public consciousness might look like in the business world.

As I have already emphasized, these are only very general suggestions that require much more development. And even under the most optimistic of scenarios, the implementation of participatory democratic initiatives is likely to introduce problems of its own. While Dewey's response to the democratic cynics was a clarion call to reinvigorate rather than abandon the democratic ideal, he was probably too optimistic about the consequences of sustained and responsible citizen engagement with the workings of policy. In response, we must continue to experiment with models of institutional design and, where appropriate, consider measures that are less dependent on broad citizen engagement (perhaps through more elitist deliberative bodies, for example).

In any case, whatever the promise of the suggestions recently put forward, it is important to emphasize that the problem in question, by nature, admits of no tidy or obvious solutions. That is, first, because the claim that failures of democratic contestation introduce significant social harms does not show that democratic contestation is the sole aim which ought to guide social organization. I take it for granted, at least for the present purposes of argument, that free markets are the overarching economic framework within which we have the greatest prospects for innovation, prosperity, and the creation of value in the long term. And I assume that there is no way for markets to advance those prospects without retaining some of the features that collide with democratic contestation. So the question of "what to do?" with respect to contestation is not the question of how to comprehensively realize the democratic ideal within the economic domain. It is the question of how to achieve meaningful improvements in our contestation of markets while preserving their distinctive capacity, under the right circumstances, to do the world quite a lot of good.

References

Battilana, Julie, Matthew Lee, John Walker, et al. (2012). In Search of the Hybrid Ideal. *Stanford Social Innovation Review*, 51–5.

Bowles, Samuel, and Herbert Gintis (1986). *Democracy and Capitalism: Property, Community, and the Contradictions of Modern Social Thought*. New York: Basic Books.

Caplan, Bryan (2007). *The Myth of the Rational Voter: Why Democracies Choose Bad Policies*, Princeton: Princeton University Press.

Dahl, Robert Alan (1957). The Concept of Power. *Behavioral Science*, 2: 201.

Dewey, John (1954). *The Public and its Problems*. Chicago: Swallow Press.

Dryzek, John S. (1996). *Democracy in Capitalist Times: Ideals, Limits, and Struggles*. New York: Oxford University Press.

Elster, Jon (1983). *Sour Grapes: Studies in the Subversion of Rationality*. Cambridge: Cambridge University Press.

Fishkin, James S. (2009). *When the People Speak: Deliberative Democracy and Public Consultation*. Oxford: Oxford University Press.

Friedman, Milton (1970). The Social Responsibility of Business is to Increase its Profits. *New York Times Magazine*, Sept. 13.

Fuerstein, Michael (2008). Epistemic Democracy and the Social Character of Knowledge. *Episteme*, 5(1): 74.

Fuerstein, Michael (2013). Epistemic Trust and Liberal Justification. *Journal of Political Philosophy*, 21(2): 179.

Gilbert, Margaret (2000). *Sociality and Responsibility: New Essays in Plural Subject Theory*. Lanham, MD: Rowman & Littlefield.

Hagendijk, Rob, and Alan Irwin (2006). Public Deliberation and Governance: Engaging with Science and Technology in Contemporary Europe. *Minerva*, 44: 167.

Hayek, Friedrich A. (1945). The Use of Knowledge in Society. *American Economic Review*, 35: 519.

Heath, Joseph, and Wayne Norman (2004). Stakeholder Theory, Corporate Governance and Public Management: What can the History of State-Run Enterprises Teach us in the Post-Enron Era? *Journal of Business Ethics*, 53(3): 247.

Hobbes, Thomas (1996). *Leviathan*, ed. Richard Tuck. Cambridge: Cambridge University Press.

Jasanoff, Sheila (2005). *Designs on Nature: Science and Democracy in Europe and the United States*. Princeton: Princeton University Press.

Kitcher, Philip (2011). *Science in a Democratic Society*. Amherst, MA: Prometheus Books.

Lever, Annabelle (2012). Democracy, Deliberation, and Public Service Reform. In Henry Kippin and Gary Stoker (eds), *Public Services: A New Reform Agenda*. New York: Bloomsbury Academic, 91–106.

Locke, John (1988). The Second Treatise of Government. In *Two Treatises of Government*, ed. Peter Laslett, Cambridge: Cambridge University Press.

Maantay, Juliana (2002). Mapping Environmental Injustices: Pitfalls and Potential of Geographic Information Systems in Assessing Health Quality. *Environmental Health Perspectives*, 110(suppl. 2): 161.

Mair, Johanna, Julie Battilana, and Julian Cardenas (2012). Organizing for Society: A Typology of Social Entrepreneurship Models. *Journal of Business Ethics*, 111(3): 353.

Mill, John Stuart (1991). Considerations on Representative Government. In *On Liberty and Other Essays*, ed. John Gray. Oxford: Oxford University Press.

Pettit, Philip (1997). *Republicanism: A Theory of Freedom and Government*. Oxford: Oxford University Press.

Pettit, Philip (2012). *On the People's Terms: A Republican Theory and Model of Democracy*. Cambridge: Cambridge University Press.

Plato (1992). *The Republic*, tr. G. M. A. Grube, rev. C. D. C. Reeve Indianapolis: Hackett.

Pharr, Susan J., and Robert Putnam, eds (2000). *Disaffected Democracies: What's Troubling the Trilateral Countries?* Princeton: Princeton University Press.

Reiss, Julian, and Philip Kitcher (2009). Biomedical Research, Neglected Diseases, and Well-Ordered Science. *Theoria*, 24(3): 263.

Scherer, Andreas Georg, and Guido Palazzo (2007). Toward a Political Conception of Corporate Responsibility: Business and Society Seen from a Habermasian Perspective. *Academy of Management Review*, 32(4): 1096.

Schumpeter, Joseph (1942). *Capitalism, Socialism, and Democracy*. New York: Harper.

Specter, Michael (2009). *Denialism: How Irrational Thinking Hinders Scientific Progress, Harms the Planet, and Threatens our Lives*. New York: Penguin Press.

CHAPTER 25

....

RECASTING THE CORPORATE MODEL

What Can Be Learned from Social Enterprise?

....

JULIE BATTILANA

Abstract

Social enterprises are hybrid organizations that combine business and charity at their core. This chapter argues that hybrid organizing, the activities, structures, processes, and meanings by which social enterprises make sense of and combine business and charity at their core, deserves more scholarly attention. Are social enterprises sustainable, and if so, how can they achieve high levels of both social and economic performance? Understanding how social enterprises can be successful has implications for organizations beyond social enterprises, as an increasing proportion of corporations try to integrate corporate social responsibility activities into their strategy. In closing, it is argued that hybrid organizing has the potential to reshape capitalism through the creation of organizations that pursue both social and economic objectives, and are held accountable for doing so.

INTRODUCTION

....

The history of capitalism is associated with remarkable improvements in global health and wealth, as well as with persistent, and in some parts of the world, increasing inequalities (Deaton 2013). Today, almost half of the world's wealth is concentrated in the hands of 1 percent of the global population (Fuentes-Nieva and Galasso 2014; Keating et al. 2013). The financial crisis that began upsetting the world economy in late 2007 has made the inequalities between the wealthiest 1 percent and the rest of the population even more salient (Stiglitz 2012). This has led to a global crisis of confidence in the financial sector, and more broadly in the corporate sector. Trust in banks and big corporations, viewed by many as central actors in the crisis, has significantly eroded.[1] Currently, public trust in multinational companies remains at a much lower level than trust in NGOs.[2] Confidence in the financial service industries is particularly low, lagging behind all other sectors. This profound lack of trust in the financial system and in corporations indicates a fundamental problem, as trust plays a central role in ensuring the functioning of the economy. Indeed research in social sciences suggests that trust is a necessary condition for an economic system to prosper, as it allows individuals and/or organizations to transact with each other on the basis of shared and tacit assumptions about conduct (Arrow 1972; Gibbons and Henderson 2012; Sen 1999; Tonkiss 2009).

Restoring trust requires addressing the demands for reform of the capitalist system from people all over the world. In the aftermath of the financial crisis, debates have emerged in both the public and academic spheres as to the future of capitalism. While necessary changes in market regulation have duly occupied center stage, the search for promising alternative corporate approaches has focused increased attention from the media, public authorities, public opinion, and investors alike, on social enterprises. Social enterprises are organizations that pursue a social mission while simultaneously engaging in commercial activities in order to sustain their operations (Dees 2001; Mair 2010). These organizations, of which microfinance organizations, work integration social enterprises, and organizations that sell fair trade products are well-studied examples, differ from typical corporations by pursuing a social mission that is either their primary objective, or at least as important an objective as generating profit. They also differ from typical not-for-profits by relying on commercially generated revenues to sustain their operations, rather than charitable donations or subsidies. As such, social enterprises are hybrid organizations that combine aspects of both business and charity at their core (Haveman and Rao 2006; Galaskiewicz and Barringer 2012; Besharov and Smith 2014).

While social enterprises have existed for a long time in certain sectors such as education and health care, they have recently been spreading globally across other sectors, including financial intermediation, retail, apparel, consumer products, food processing, and software development (Billis 2010; Boyd 2009; Dorado 2006; Hoffman et al. 2012). Microfinance organizations, which aim to provide loans to impoverished entrepreneurs who lack access to banking and related services, are well-known examples of social enterprises. The increasing importance of social enterprises in modern economies has led observers to speculate about the rise of a fourth sector that is distinct from the traditional for-profit, not-for-profit, and public sectors (Sabeti

---

[1] Author's calculation using GlobeScan survey data. The results are the average of thirteen countries: US, Canada, UK, France, Germany, Spain, Turkey, Russia, Brazil, Mexico, China, India, and Nigeria between 2001 and 2012.

[2] Edelman's 2014 Trust Barometer, *Annual Global Study*. <www.edelman.com/insights/intellectual-property/2014-edelman-trust-barometer> (accessed Mar. 2014) and GlobeScan's 2013 *Global Public Opinion Report on the State of Sustainable Development: The Regeneration Roadmap*.

2011). In the meantime, a community of investors interested in funding social enterprises, referred to as social impact investors, has emerged (Bugg-Levine and Emerson 2011). The size of social impact investing is estimated to reach $1 trillion of invested capital by the year 2020 (O'Donahoe et al. 2010).

At a time when capitalism and one of its building blocks, corporations, are in question, social enterprises have appeared as a promising alternative to create both social and economic value. However, many observers have voiced concerns about hybrid organizations' ability to sustainably combine aspects of market and charity at their core and to achieve high levels of both commercial and social performance. The main problem is that they run the risk of "mission drift," meaning that they stray from their original goals, usually by focusing on profits to the detriment of social good, but sometimes vice versa (Christen and Drake 2002; Weisbrod 2004; Jones 2007; Mersland and Strøm 2010; Haight 2011; Ben-Ner 2002). Research in the sociology of organizations has long established the risk of organizations losing sight of their social mission in the quest for organizational survival and efficiency (Selznick 1949). Recent examples of microfinance organizations that have drifted away from their social mission of helping the poor, thereby becoming regular corporations, have contributed to rising doubts as to social enterprises' ability to sustainably maintain their hybrid nature. The key questions remain. Are social enterprises truly sustainable? And if so, under what conditions can they realize high levels of both social and economic performance?

Hybrid organizing, which in the case of social enterprises includes the activities, structures, processes, and meanings by which organizations make sense of and combine business and charity at their core, is particularly challenging (Battilana and Lee 2014). Research in the field of organization studies points to the unique external and internal challenges that social enterprises face due to their hybrid nature. Because they straddle the well-established categories of business and charity, social enterprises face legitimacy challenges and, as a result, are likely to be discounted by external constituencies such as investors and clients (Hsu et al. 2009; Zuckerman 1999; Ruef and Patterson 2009). Social enterprises are also likely to face internal challenges, as their dual—social and commercial—identities may be a source of conflict among organizational members, who can have differing opinions of the relative importance of these organization's activities (Glynn 2000; Pratt and Foreman 2000; Fiol et al. 2009).

Understanding how social enterprises can overcome these challenges through hybrid organizing is critical for two main reasons. First, before claiming that the so-called fourth sector has the potential to create additional social and economic value for society, we need to examine the extent to which organizations that constitute this sector are sustainable, and if they can indeed achieve high levels of both social and economic performance. Second, from an organizational standpoint, understanding how some social enterprises manage to sustainably combine business and charity at their core has implications for organizations beyond social enterprises. An ever-increasing proportion of corporations are engaging in corporate social responsibility (CSR) policies with the objective of having a positive social impact (Margolis and

Walsh 2003; Kanter 2009). Since the financial crisis, corporations have faced increased pressures from the public to engage in CSR activities (Porter and Kramer 2011). As they try to figure out how to better integrate CSR activities into their core strategy, corporations may learn from the experience of social enterprises. As such, social enterprises can be seen as a laboratory to explore new corporate models that hybridize business and charity to different extents (Billis 2010).

In this chapter, I first explain how the financial crisis that started in late 2007 has called into question large corporations and the logic of shareholder value maximization that has guided them over the last three decades. I argue that the global crisis of confidence that ensued has opened the window for alternative corporate models. Second, I focus on one of these alternative models, namely social enterprises, and document their global rise across sectors. Third, I describe the unique challenges that social enterprises face and call for research to further explore the conditions under which they are sustainable and can achieve high levels of both social and economic performance. Finally, I discuss the implications of research on social enterprises for corporations and society in general. I argue that we have now entered an era of increased hybridization of the economy and that the challenge for corporations in restoring trust is to balance economic and social imperatives.

CORPORATIONS IN QUESTION

The Dominance of Shareholder Value Capitalism

Over the last century, corporations and markets have been critical building blocks of capitalism. To illustrate their relative importance to the capitalist system, Simon (1991) cleverly imagined what a visitor from Mars approaching the Earth would see with a telescope. Depicting corporations as solid green areas and market transactions as red lines connecting them, the green areas would dominate the landscape, according to Simon. In imagining the alien's report back home Simon (1991, 27) famously wrote that the message "would speak of 'large green areas interconnected by red lines.' It would not likely speak of 'a network of red lines connecting green spots.'"

The green areas still occupy a large part of the economic landscape today, but markets have played an increasingly important role over the last forty years as capital has been increasingly allocated through stock and bond markets (Davis 2009). Although corporations continue to be building blocks of capitalism, they have thus increasingly revolved around markets and their signals. Studying the evolution of American corporations, Fligstein (1993) documented how the finance conception of corporate control became dominant in the 1960s. Since then this conception, which relies on financial criteria to evaluate the consequences of courses of corporate action, has continued to dominate. One might even argue that the locus of corporate control in large corporations went from inside the organization to the outside, as stock prices and the logic of shareholder value maximization increasingly drove firms' strategic decisions. The dominance of this logic is not specific to American corporations, as it has come to guide the operations of public corporations in most countries, with local variations in how corporations enact the logic (e.g. Fiss and Zajac 2004; Lok 2010; Meyer and Höllerer 2010).

The legitimization and subsequent diffusion of the shareholder value maximization logic has rested on two central assumptions: if one assumes that firms maximize social welfare by maximizing profits (Friedman 1962, 1970; Jensen 2002) and that, as suggested by the efficient market hypothesis, share prices provide the best estimate of the economic value of assets being traded based on available information and thereby provide the best estimate of a firm's ability to generate future profits, then maximizing shareholder value can be viewed as a legitimate end for corporations (Davis 2009). However, the financial crisis has highlighted both the limits and the dangers of the logic of shareholder value maximization for society.

A Global Crisis of Confidence

The financial crisis challenged the legitimacy of the shareholder value maximization logic on multiple grounds. It first reminded us that, far from being perfectly efficient, financial markets are fallible (Fligstein 2001; Shiller 2005). Second, the crisis revealed the ethical dangers associated with the pursuit of shareholder value maximization as a single objective. By focusing executives' attention on share prices, this logic has led to an escalation process in which executives feel pressured to report ever better results to market analysts. Such pressure has opened the door to corporate malfeasance. In fact, research shows that companies whose performance exceeded the expectations of the market were more likely to engage in illegal practices, as their directors wanted to maintain high levels of performance at all costs in order to continue receiving the praise of market analysts (Mishina et al. 2010).

Finally, the financial crisis demonstrated that the blind pursuit of shareholder value maximization, far from always helping to increase social welfare, could actually have negative social consequences. With its grim by-product of home foreclosures, massive unemployment, and lost pensions, the crisis made the gap between the wealthiest 1 percent and the rest of the population wider. As inequalities grew, they threatened upward social mobility in some countries, including the United States. The "American dream" of starting with nothing and moving up in the world through hard work and determination just does not seem possible any more to many in the 99 percent (Stiglitz 2012).

Overall, the financial crisis revealed the instability of the financial system, the cracks in the discourse used to legitimize the logic of shareholder value maximization, and the increased inequalities among the population. Thus all three conditions that prompt low-power actors to attempt to change a system that subordinates them were fulfilled by the crisis, namely lower perceived stability, lower perceived legitimacy, and lower perceived possibility for upward social mobility (Martorana et al. 2005). In 2011, these conditions led to the rise of the "Occupy Wall Street" movement, which harnessed the disgruntlement of the 99 percent and voiced global distrust in the financial system and, more broadly, the corporate world.

Following the crisis, people all over the globe have been asking for change. Yet, having been embedded in a system of shareholder capitalism for decades, all the key actors of our current economic system (including corporations, investors, public authorities, and the public) are having a hard time envisioning an alternative system. That the current system has to be reformed is now broadly accepted, but how and to what extent it needs to be changed are questions still open for debate.

The Search for Alternative Corporate Models

Ever since the financial crisis began, a flurry of academic articles and books in the various fields of social sciences have examined its interrelated and complex causes, including: the housing bubble (e.g. Shiller 2008; Baker 2008; Abolafia 2010), excessive leverage throughout the financial system (e.g. Acharya and Schnabl 2009), predatory lending practices (e.g. Admati and Hellwig 2013; Rajan 2011), devotion to the efficient market hypothesis (e.g. Lounsbury and Hirsch 2010), executive compensation systems favoring the pursuit of short-term gains (e.g. Dobbin and Jung 2010), the failure of rating agencies (e.g. Rona-Tas and Hiss 2010; Carruthers 2010), and lax financial regulation (e.g. Friedman and Kraus 2011; Reinhart and Rogoff 2009). Some have also proposed solutions as to how to fix the system. A lot of thinking has rightly focused on the role of public authorities in regulating the financial system and preventing the problems that led to the crisis (e.g. Blinder 2013).

Although regulatory authorities play a critical role in overseeing the market and thereby setting the tone for enforcing reform, ultimately it is up to all stakeholders to change their behavior if trust in our economic system is to be restored. Corporations, in particular, are facing increased pressures from public authorities and consumers alike to create new corporate models (Bower et al. 2011). Even before the financial crisis began, calls were being made for corporations to better integrate social considerations into their strategy (Margolis and Walsh 2003). The crisis, in further eroding the public's trust in corporations, has no doubt made the need for change more acute. In the aftermath of the crisis, many stakeholders have alerted companies to the necessity of adopting new corporate models that break away from maximizing value for the benefit of shareholders alone. For example, Porter and Kramer (2011) recognized the failure of past corporate models to adequately take into account the social environment of companies. Most commentators agree that the days when corporations could appear to only care about their financial performance are gone. In order to restore public trust, corporations will have to systematically take into account not only the financial implications of their strategic choices, but also their social impact, which requires recasting their corporate model.

THE RISE AND SPREAD OF SOCIAL ENTERPRISES

A Brief History of Social Enterprises

As the quest for new corporate models ensuring sustainable economic and social value creation has intensified, social enterprises have attracted increased attention from a diverse set of players including the media, public authorities, the public, and investors. The term "social enterprise" first appeared in the 1980s to describe organizations that have both a charity and business mission at their core. Though the terminology is relatively new, examples of these kinds of organizations have existed for generations. Some examples are universities (e.g. Meyer and Rowan 2006), museums (e.g. DiMaggio 1991), hospitals (e.g. Kimberly and Evanisko 1981; Ruef and Scott 1998), and mutual associations and co-operatives (Cornforth 2004; Paton 2003; Schneiberg et al. 2008; Schneiberg 2011). Although research had studied these types of organizations over the years, they were not necessarily thought of as having much in common until the label "social enterprise" emerged. The term quickly gained traction and came into popular use with entrepreneurs the world over seeking to bill their ventures as social enterprises (Moizer and Tracey 2010).

A number of factors contributed to the rise of social enterprises in the 1970s and 1980s, unstable economic conditions were lighting a fire of experimentation under entrepreneurs, who were looking for ways to fill gaps in the economy. For example, some countries in Europe had to deal with high unemployment, which catalyzed the creation of work integration social enterprises (WISEs). These new organizations served the long-term unemployed by providing them with job training, social counseling, and housing programs (Kerlin 2006; Defourny and Nyssens 2006). In the US the government cut funding for non-profits, which made those organizations tap into alternative sources of funding, including commercially generated revenues (Kerlin 2006; Defourny and Nyssens 2006). These experiments led to the founding of more organizations that combined both business and charity at their core.

These types of organizations, which came to be known as "social enterprises," were created all over the world. Nobel laureate Muhammed Yunus was an early pioneer, creating the microfinance organization Grameen Bank in Bangladesh in 1976 (Yunus et al. 2010). In Egypt in 1977 the social enterprise SEKEM took on the challenge of creating farmland out of 70 hectares of Egyptian desert (Seelos and Mair 2004). The Bolivian commercial microfinance organizations BancoSol and Los Andes were likewise early players in the social enterprise arena in South America (Battilana and Dorado 2010). The stories behind all these organizations played well with the media, which relayed the work of social enterprises to the general public. The number of articles published on social enterprises in print journalism took off, going from 37 in 1997, to 529 in 2000, to 14,264 in 2012 (Battilana and Lee 2014).

The Contemporary Spread of Social Enterprises

In the past ten years, the number of social enterprise organizations has increased worldwide and expanded into new sectors of the economy, including financial intermediation, retailing, consumer products, apparel, food processing, and software development (Billis 2010; Boyd 2009; Dorado 2006; Hoffman et al. 2012). This trend is a global one. Although statistics about social enterprises are still hard to collect, as they straddle the well-established organizational and legal categories of for-profits and not-for-profits, multiple efforts have been spearheaded, predominantly in Europe, with the objective of trying to better assess the size of the social enterprise sector. According to recent reports, in the European Union the social economy engages over 14.5 million paid employees representing more than 6 percent of total employment (European Commission 2013). In the UK, recent government estimates suggest that there are 70,000 social enterprises, employing around a million people (3 percent of total employment) and generating total turnover of £46.6 billion (Lomax 2013). In France the social economy represents nearly 10 percent of jobs (2.3 million salaried workers) and jobs in this sector increased by 23 percent between 2000 and 2010.

On the other side of the Atlantic, the United States also witnessed a steady growth in the number of social enterprises launched each year within the past decade.[3] The expansion of the social enterprise sector goes beyond the Western world as social enterprises also play an increasingly important role in Asia and Africa. Mirroring this global growth, an increasing number of social enterprise networks have been established to bring together social entrepreneurs and promote mutual support (Severino 2012).

Other efforts to assess the size of the social enterprise sector have focused on estimating the size of "social impact investing," which refers to investment that is made with the intention of generating positive social impact as well as some financial returns (ranging from below market to market rates). The global assets allocated to impact investment doubled between 2011 and 2012 and accumulated to $36 billion by year 2012 (Saltuk et al. 2011, 2013).

Finally, the creation of social enterprise courses and initiatives in universities all over the world is a testament to its increasing popularity, especially among the younger "millennial generation" that is frequently described as more civic-minded and demanding of meaning at work (Mangold 2007; Sweeney 2005). According to the Aspen Institute, in 2007 63 percent of business schools in the United States offered courses on social enterprise or other aspects of the nexus between environmental, social, and ethical considerations with business decisions (Shapiro 2013).

---

[3] National Social Enterprise Field Study, conducted by the Center for the Advancement of Social Entrepreneurship, Community Wealth Ventures, and Social Enterprise Alliance, Sept. 15, 2008.

A Delicate Balance

Although social enterprises are considered a promising way to create both social and economic value (Sabeti 2011), they have to walk a fine line, pursuing commercial goals while not losing sight of their social goals. At the same time, they also need to make sure that their focus on social goals does not prevent them from generating the commercial revenues that are necessary for their survival. It is a precarious path. If they lose sight of their social mission, they fail, and if they do not generate enough revenues to sustain their operations, they also fail.

Because of the delicate balance social enterprises need to maintain in addressing the often opposing demands of their business and charity sides, concerns have been raised about their sustainability (Strom 2010; Weisbrod 2004). Of particular concern is that profit-maximization considerations will come to dominate at the expense of the organization's mission (Minkoff and Powell 2006; Hwang and Powell 2009). This concern echoes a long tradition of research in organization studies that has highlighted the risk for organizations in their quest for organizational survival and efficiency to lose sight of their values and purpose (Selznick 1949). As Selznick (1957: 135) put it: "The cult of efficiency in administrative theory and practice is a modern way of overstressing means and neglecting ends." Can social enterprises avoid this trap and be sustainable as hybrid organizations? If so, under what conditions can they achieve high levels of social and commercial performance? Answering these questions requires a better understanding of hybrid organizing in social enterprises.

A ROADMAP FOR RESEARCH ON HYBRID ORGANIZING IN SOCIAL ENTERPRISES

Hybridizing Tensions Facing Social Enterprises

Because of their unusual positioning between the charity and commercial sectors, social enterprises experience tensions that are a source of unique challenges. These tensions express themselves both externally, in managing relations with outside constituents in an environment that is still structured around the traditional for-profit and not-for-profit sectors, and internally, in managing organizational identity and resource allocation.

External Challenges

Because social enterprises transcend the boundaries between the well-established for-profit and not-for-profit sectors, they are different from both. Straddling two categories creates challenges in managing interactions with their external environment, meaning funders and other organizations. Organization research suggests that social enterprises, as a new breed of organization, will struggle to establish legitimacy in the eyes of external constituents. Indeed, in addition to the normal challenges all new organizations face in securing the attention and approval of resource providers (Freeman et al. 1983; Haveman and Rao 2006; Ruef and Scott 1998; Stinchcombe 1965), social enterprises face further challenges because they violate the established social boundaries of business and charity models (Zuckerman 1999; Ruef and Patterson 2009). As such, they do not have the built-in advantages of organizations that fit institutionalized expectations, which are often rewarded with resources on this basis (Kraatz and Block 2008). This raises a series of challenges for social enterprises, especially when it comes to legal incorporation and fund raising.

The decision to incorporate as either for-profit or not-for-profit is a problematic one for hybrid entrepreneurs, as neither legal status is truly applicable to their hybrid nature. Non-profits are allowed to receive tax-free charitable donations (Anheier and Salamon 1997) but only if they do not distribute retained earnings (Simon et al. 2006), which keeps them from expanding funding streams into equity markets. On the other hand, corporations are allowed to raise financial capital through the sale of equity, but they cannot receive donations. Thus, organizations are rewarded by regulatory regimes for corresponding to categories from which social enterprises diverge (Kennedy and Haigh 2013).

Because they combine both charity and commercial forms, social enterprises also often have trouble acquiring resources, such as funding, both at founding and later on when they scale up their operations. There is a well-established infrastructure for traditional businesses that want to get a bank loan, or seek equity funding, or a combination of both. Venture capital funds exist to provide not just capital, but advice for the organizations they fund. Non-profits have a similar support structure in place, with funding available for organizations at various stages of development, and for certain types of social programs, through national or community foundations. Social enterprises are outsiders to this system, being neither a typical for-profit nor a typical not-for-profit entity. They are therefore likely to be undervalued by external evaluators, such as funders, who base their assessments on the institutionalized categories that they are familiar with (Hsu et al. 2009; Zuckerman 1999). Social enterprises may be seen as a risky investment because of the high uncertainty of predicting their future behavior. Investors may also worry that these organizations will face demands that may conflict with their own interests. For example, a potential investor who is seeking profit may balk at the prospect of a social enterprise putting its social imperative ahead of its commercial goals. Recent research is finding that, for these reasons, social enterprises may be less successful at securing external funding than traditional charities (Lee 2014).

Internal Challenges

Social enterprises also have the cards stacked against them when it comes to the inside workings of the organization. Internal conflict can jeopardize the very survival of a social enterprise. Research has shown that having multiple identities, as hybrids often do, may lead to internal clashes and ultimately even unsustainability (Pratt and

Foreman 2000; Fiol et al. 2009). Further research reveals that creating a common identity in an organization that combines charity and business at its core is especially difficult (Battilana and Dorado 2010). Individuals within the organization may strongly self-identify with either the social or the business goals of the venture. If they perceive an increase in demands from the "opposing" side, they can feel threatened and underlying differences can escalate into interpersonal conflict (Glynn 2000).

Because social enterprises fuse both business and charity forms, the allocation of resources, which are often limited, is also fraught with the potential for internal skirmishes between competing factions advocating for either social or commercial activities (Moizer and Tracey 2010). Likewise there can be internal competition for management attention. Such internal tensions and competition may create difficult trade-offs, which can exacerbate interpersonal conflict to the point of intractability, thereby further compromising the functioning of the organization (Fiol et al. 2009). Furthermore, disagreement as to how to resolve these trade-offs can lead to decision-making gridlock between members of the organization who adhere to different logics (Pache and Santos 2010).

As time progresses, the methods that organizations use to resolve these conflicts can become embedded in the routine functioning of the group (Feldman 2003). If the resolution regularly favors one group's goals over the other's, the organization is in danger of goal displacement (Christen and Drake 2002; Weisbrod 2004; Jones 2007; Mersland and Strøm 2010; Haight 2011; Ben-Ner 2002). When this is the case, it becomes difficult for a social enterprise to be true to its hybrid nature, as one aspect, either commercial or social, is liable to dominate the other over time (Scott and Meyer 1991). Developments in the field of commercial microfinance illustrate this risk, as some commercial microfinance institutions have been criticized for focusing excessively on profits at the expense of outreach to poorer customers (Carrick-Cagna and Santos 2009; Christen and Drake 2002; Dichter and Harper 2007).

All of the external and internal challenges that presented here are potential land mines for social enterprises, and can make them susceptible to goal displacement and drift to the more known and established organizational forms (Scott 1967; Simons and Ingram 1997). While drift may help the organization navigate through these challenges in the short run, over time the hybrid nature of the social enterprise may be irreparably compromised. Much has been documented about the challenges that social enterprises face as they attempt to combine social and business forms into their core. Less is known about how they can sustainably overcome these obstacles.

Hybrid Organizing

Organization studies have long accounted for the complex nature of organizations that are not unified entities, but rather coalitions of individuals who engage in different activities and often have different interests, values, and objectives that may come into conflict in decision-making (Cyert and March 1963). Building on these insights, subsequent research has explored how organizations can handle the tensions that stem from this multiplicity of organizational members and activities (e.g. Lawrence and Lorsch 1967; March 1991; Tushman and O'Reilly 1996; Smith and Tushman 2005). However, most of these studies have been conducted within the established organizational forms of corporations or not-for-profits. In contrast, social enterprises combine aspects of both forms at their core, which makes the tensions they face even more acute.

Many of the components that allow a traditional corporation or non-profit to be successful may not apply to social enterprises. This is why I argue that there is a great need for further research on hybrid organizing. Recent research suggests that hybrid organizing can be broken down into five major categories: organizational activities, workforce composition, organization design, inter-organizational relationships, and organizational culture (Battilana and Lee 2014). For each of these dimensions, the social and commercial aspects of the social enterprise's endeavors can be more or less integrated (Figure 25.1). Building on the agenda for future research on hybrid organizing outlined by Battilana and Lee (2014), I will call for more research examining these categories not only independently, but also, and maybe more importantly, in relation to each other, as taken together they may constitute different configurations of hybrid organizing. Future research will need to examine the antecedents and effects of these different configurations in terms of economic and social outcomes.

Organizational Activities

Some hybrids pursue their social and commercial goals through one set of activities while others engage in social and commercial activities that are separate from each other. Research has found that the more the two sets of activities are integrated, the easier it is to avoid tensions. This is because there is less competition for internal resources when team members are engaging in activities that are meant to accomplish both social and economic objectives (Nielsen 1986). This integrated approach also has an added benefit of making the organization appear more attractive to outside resource providers, such as investors (Lee 2014). Microfinance organizations are a good example of social enterprises in which social and commercial activities are integrated, as providing loans to the poor also generates commercial revenue.

For many other social enterprises, the social and commercial activities of the organization cannot be integrated to the same extent. An example of this type is work integration social enterprises (WISEs), which hire long-term unemployed people with the objective of training them to reintegrate into the workforce (Garrow and Hasenfeld 2012; Pache and Santos 2013; Teasdale 2012). During their time working for the WISE, beneficiaries produce and sell products and services to outside customers,

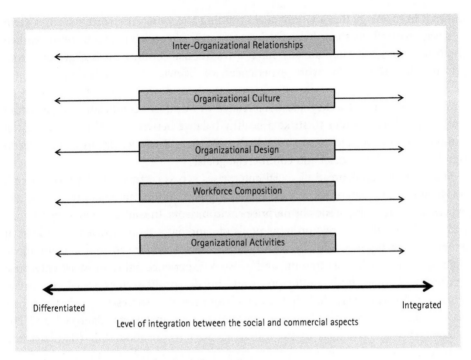

FIGURE 25.1 Dimensions of Hybrid Organizing
Reproduced from Battilana and Lee (2014) in the *Annals of the Academy of Management*

but they also receive social counseling and other non-commercial services provided by the WISE. Because of this, WISEs often face trade-offs allotting beneficiaries' time spent in social training versus working on the production line (Battilana et al. forthcoming).

The level of integration of a social enterprise's social and commercial activities may have consequences for the long-term sustainability of the organization. Future research will need to explore the effect of the level of integration between commercial and social activities on mission drift, and how such drift can be circumvented. It may be that, depending on the level of integration between commercial and social activities, social enterprises need to adopt different approaches in order to sustain their hybrid nature. Accordingly, future research will also need to examine the extent to which different levels of activity integration call for different kinds of workforce composition, organization design, inter-organizational relationships, and organizational culture in order for social enterprises to be sustainable and achieve high levels of both social and commercial performance.

Workforce Composition

Another key area of hybrid organizing in social enterprises is workforce composition and, more specifically, the background and mindset of its employees. We know from research in sociology that an individual's training and work experience socializes them in a way that reflects the values of the organizations in which they previously worked (Bourdieu 1977). If they already have a traditional commercial background from previous training and/or work experiences, or likewise a social background, new hires will bring that approach with them to the hybrid organization they join. Social enterprises thus face two key questions related to workforce composition. One, whom should they hire in order to strike a healthy balance between social mission and the commercial bottom line? And two, what's the best way to socialize them in order to stay focused on both social and commercial goals?

Since the rise and spread of social enterprises across sectors is still a recent trend, social enterprises cannot yet rely on an existing pool of job candidates with extensive experience or training in social enterprise environments. In contrast, both corporations and not-for-profits can rely on large pools of candidates with experience working in either type of organization. Because it is still relatively rare to find a ready-made "hybrid worker" who has training and/or work experience either in social enterprise environments or in both the for-profit and not-for-profit sectors, social enterprises often need to create ways to help their staff work together successfully, whatever their backgrounds may be. The Bolivian microfinance organizations, BancoSol and Los Andes, are good examples of two different ways to go about this (Battilana and Dorado 2010). These two organizations were founded in the 1990s to provide loans to the poor and are hybrids of a bank and a social development organization. When hiring staff, BancoSol and Los Andes found that the people applying for positions as loan officers often had either banking experience or social development experience, but not both. Those with banking experience tended to pay more attention to the profit motives of making loans, and those with social backgrounds were more concerned with the welfare of the borrower.

Although the two organizations faced the same problem, they came up with different solutions. BancoSol hired individuals with either banking or social backgrounds and hoped that their commitment to the overall social mission of the organization would help them transcend their previous training. Los Andes hired university graduates with no previous work experience and, through socialization and training focused on the attainment of operational excellence, turned them into the hybrid employees they sought. The Los Andes approach was more successful, as BancoSol was soon bogged down by disagreements between bankers and social workers and eventually espoused the Los Andes hiring appraoch. The experience of BancoSol cautions us that some characteristics of previous workplaces that employees bring with them may be deeply entrenched and even endanger the functioning of social enterprises.

Future research will need to more systematically examine the influence of different hiring strategies on social enterprises' functioning. As in the case of organizational activities, the workforce of social enterprises can exhibit different levels of integration between the commercial and social realms, ranging from a fully integrated workforce made up of workers with training and/or experience in social enterprise, to a more differentiated one in which they have experience and/or training either in commercial or social sectors. Future research should also examine whether and, if so, how social enterprises will change as a new generation of young people with specific training and experience in the world of social enterprises populate the job market.

Finally, as suggested by the study of BancoSol and Los Andes, once hired, new organizational members need to be socialized into the organization. The process of socialization, whereby individuals come to understand the values and work practices essential to assuming an organizational role and participating as an organizational member, provides an opportunity for organizations to instill in new hires their desired values and associated work practices (Van Maanen and Schein 1979; Louis 1980; Bauer et al. 1998; Cable and Parsons 2001). Future research should thus explore the different combinations of hiring and socialization approaches that social enterprises may adopt and their performance implications. Doing so requires examining the influence of workforce composition not in isolation but rather in conjunction with organization design.

Organization Design

The way the organization is formally structured influences where internal tensions between social and commercial objectives are likely to surface and where they will be resolved (Smith and Tushman 2005; Smith and Lewis 2011). Are both charity and commercial goals going to be pursued by the same individuals or departments in an integrated way? Or will the business and social arms of the enterprise be kept separate? The risk for social enterprises that adopt a structurally differentiated approach, assigning responsibility for social and commercial activities to different units or groups within the organization, is that intergroup conflict will emerge and/or that one group will come to dominate the other, thereby threatening the hybrid nature of the organization. Overcoming this challenge requires social enterprises to be able to ensure coordination between structurally differentiated units (Lawrence and Lorsch 1967). Recent research has indicated that smooth coordination between commercial and social goals may be facilitated by the design of "spaces of negotiation." These are areas of interaction that allow staff members to discuss and come to an agreement on how to handle the daily trade-offs they encounter across social and economic activities (Kellogg 2009; Battilana et al. forthcoming). These spaces of negotiation enable the maintenance of a productive tension between social and commercial objectives (Murray 2010).

Besides the formal structure of the organization, incentives and control systems are another design factor that will influence the functioning of hybrids. Incentive systems can be used to encourage desired behaviors and values in order to align members further with the organizational goals (Feldman 1976, 2002; Gómez 2009; Jones 1986; Saks and Ashforth 1997). Coupled with a system to measure performance on both commercial and social aspects of the social enterprise's activities, incentives play a key role in socializing organizational members and ensuring that the organization does not systematically prioritize the attainment of either social or commercial objectives (Nicholls 2009). With the current public debate about what constitutes fair levels of compensation for executives, and how to redesign corporate incentives in order to avoid the abuses that led to the financial crisis (Dobbin and Jung 2010; Blinder 2013), examining the incentive and control systems used by social enterprises and their effects on economic and social performance will have implications not only for social enterprises, but also for corporations in general.

Finally, social enterprises have governance challenges that are different from typical for-profits and non-profits, because they are accountable for both social and commercial goals. Without effective governance, hybrids can veer off course and drift toward one objective at the expense of the other. Research has shown that governing boards play a key role in avoiding this common pitfall and that the kind of monitoring in which they need to engage in order to avoid drifting varies depending on the level of integration between their commercial and social activities (Ebrahim et al. 2014).

Future research will need to further explore the influence of design factors, including formal organizational structure, incentives and control systems, and governance, on the functioning of social enterprises. In doing so, it will need to pay particular attention to the issue of social and economic performance measurement in social enterprises, as it is an important lever for incentivizing staff and monitoring the balance between social and economic objectives. While financial performance is relatively easy to assess based on commonly accepted methods, there are no set standards of measurement for social performance (DiMaggio 2002; Ebrahim and Rangan 2010; Paton 2003; Trelstad 2008; Battilana and Norris 2015). Although there have been recent efforts to evaluate and quantify the social performance of organizations, and some standards-setting bodies have appeared on the scene, consensus has yet to be reached as to how to measure social performance (Ebrahim and Rangan 2010; Kanter and Summers 1994). As a result, financial data remain much easier to standardize and audit than social data. One problem with evaluating social performance is the need for a longer time range to gauge success. Financial reporting is typically assessed in quarterly or annual reports, but social programs may need several years to see measurable results (Edwards and Hulme 1996; Lindenberg and Bryant 2001; Rogers 2007). This may have an effect on decision-making in social enterprises as it is possible that a social enterprise may focus more on aspects of the organization that it can audit and quantify rather than the vaguer realm of social performance. If this is the case, what are the implications for social change? More research is thus needed to explore how social enterprises construct tools to assess their social performance, how they use them, and how they subsequently communicate their social performance to outside audiences. Finally, research will need to study how these social performance metrics are perceived and used by these audiences, including investors.

Inter-Organizational Relationships

Another crucial dimension of hybrid organizing is managing the relationships that social enterprises forge with outside organizations, such as funders, suppliers, and other kinds of partners. These relationships are not well understood, but it is likely that they have an effect on social enterprises' functioning and ability to achieve their goals (Austin and Leonard 2008). Further research is needed to understand the way a hybrid is affected by the organizational makeup of its funders and partners. For example, does being funded by social impact investors—who themselves have a hybrid approach as they make investments with the objective of positive social impact—change the way a social enterprise behaves? Would the behavior and values of the organization be influenced in the same way if they were funded by a traditional business or charity source? What are the consequences of combining different sources of funding for social enterprises and do these consequences vary depending on social enterprises' stage of development? Furthermore, do social enterprises that have more connections with for-profit partners differ from those that have more connections with not-for-profit organizations and from those that have more connections with other social enterprises? If so, how?

Besides the influences that social enterprises may experience through their relationships with funders and partners, social enterprises themselves may shape their institutional environment and thereby influence other organizations. The effort to have social enterprises recognized as a fourth sector of the economy, along with for-profits, non-profits, and the public sector, is an example of this (Sabeti 2011). One important development has been the recent creation of new legal statuses that better fit the needs of organizations that are neither typical for-profits nor typical not-for-profits. Some of these new forms are benefit corporations, Low-profit Limited Liability Corporations (L3Cs) and Flexible-Purpose Corporations in the United States, Community Contribution Companies in Canada, and Community Interest Companies (CICs) in the United Kingdom (see Murray 2012; Brakman Reiser 2013). However, these legal innovations are still in the early stages of development and lack broad acceptance and awareness. It thus has yet to be seen if they will make things easier for social enterprises to overcome the internal and external tensions highlighted earlier. Future research will need to examine the trajectory of social enterprises that adopt these new legal statuses and to draw comparisons across types of legal status. In particular, it will be interesting to analyze the role of these new legal statuses in preventing social enterprises from drifting away from their social mission. What kinds of legal dispositions are more helpful in ensuring that social enterprises maintain their hybridity?

Organizational Culture

A final important element of hybrid organizing is the culture of the organization that develops over time. Organizational culture can be defined as the pattern of shared behaviors and values that is cultivated by the members of the organization as they perform their work (Schein 2006). Together with the other organizational factors mentioned above (i.e. organizational activities, workforce composition, organization design, and inter-organizational relationships), leadership plays a key tole in defining an organization's culture (Selznick 1957; Kraatz 2009). Leaders of social enterprises have the unique challenge of trying to create a shared culture among members of an organization that encompasses multiple values, as it tries to combine and perform both charity and commercial goals. Leaders of social enterprises thus face an extreme challenge of leadership because of the combination of the organizational forms that they are trying to reconcile.

At the early stages, social entrepreneurs' commitment to both the social mission and effective operations organically attracts like-minded employees and sets the tone for how the organization will operate. Long-standing research suggests that founders' intentions and inclinations at the time of launch have a lasting influence on an organization's functioning and its resulting culture (Eisenhardt and Schoonhoven 1990; Baron et al. 1999; Beckman and Burton 2008; Marquis and Tilcsik 2013). However, as organizations grow, the influence of the founding entrepreneurs on new members becomes less direct and powerful. At that point contemporary leaders, together with the board of the social enterprise, are likely to play a key role in ensuring that the organization remains on target. Indeed we know from previous research that leaders play a critical role in defending, and if necessary, reinterpreting and renewing, the mission of their organizations (Selznick 1957). Future research should examine the influence leadership has on social enterprises' culture and performance. It should also examine the influence of leaders' background on their leadership style in social enterprises. Are leaders with experience in both business and social sectors more likely to be able to understand the nuance and perspective of both sides, and effectively lead a social enterprise?

All of the research questions that I present here will require new scholarly work, as one cannot assume that what we have learned about the functioning of typical corporations and charities applies to social enterprises. In the case of corporations, most scholarly research has so far used mainly economic performance as the key dependent variable. It may be that some of the factors that have been identified as having a positive impact on economic performance in corporations have a detrimental one on social performance in social enterprises and vice versa. Similarly, the findings related to charities may not apply to social enterprises that need to financially sustain their operations.

CONCLUDING REMARKS: TOWARDS AN INCREASED HYBRIDIZATION OF THE ECONOMY

More than a century ago, Max Weber (1952), one of the founding fathers of the field of sociology of organizations, was concerned that modern capitalist organizations, which were increasingly driven by the quest for efficiency, would become an "iron cage" for humanity that would trap and confine our creative spirit and diminish possibilities for a meaningful life. Following his line of thinking, a number of social scientists have likewise worried that the quest for efficiency would lead modern organizations to lose sight of their values and purpose (e.g. Selznick 1957). Shareholder capitalism, with its exclusive focus on the maximization of shareholder value, has certainly promoted quite a narrow view of organizational performance. This view has been called into question by the financial crisis, which revealed its negative social and economic repercussions.

Today, more than seven years after the beginning of the crisis, the world economy has begun to recover, but remains unsteady (Blinder 2013). There are calls from around the world for economic reform, especially among young people, who see a future of deep-seated inequality, marginal job prospects, and rising debt. The youth are especially dismayed by the current capitalist system that no longer offers them a chance of becoming upwardly mobile (Stiglitz 2012). Social entrepreneurs are a voice among those answering the call for reform. By creating hybrid organizations, they are forging a path for social and economic value creation at the intersection of the commercial and charity sectors.

In the meantime, academic research in social sciences is still structured in a rather dichotomous way, with some scholars focusing on corporations and others focusing on not-for-profit organizations. As entrepreneurs increasingly transcend these boundaries, scholars need to do the same and advance research on hybrid organizing. This is important not only to further our understanding of the factors that contribute to the sustainability and performance of this rising fourth sector, but also because more and more corporations are hybridizing characteristics of business and charity into their own operations. It is no longer the case that a corporation's social responsibility and philanthropic endeavors are necessarily distinct from its business arm. More and more corporations are integrating these activities into their commercial core. They may not be hybridizing as much as a social enterprise does, but they are doing so at least to some extent. Because of this trend, research into hybrid organizations like social enterprises will resonate with a wide array of organizations, and the economy at large.

While I believe that we have a lot to learn from social enterprises as we think about how to recast corporate models, we should not fool ourselves into thinking of them as the panacea. The idea is not for social enterprises to replace corporations, charities, and/or public organizations, but rather to complement them and provide an alternative source of economic and value creation to society. The rise and growth of these alternative organizational forms may well represent a historical transition toward more organizationally diverse capitalism (Schneiberg 2011; Davis and Kim 2013) where hybrid organizing becomes the norm rather than the exception. This trend raises another question for social scientists: what is the best mix of corporations, charities, social enterprises, and public organizations for society? In trying to answer this question, it is important that future generations of scholars do not focus only on economic value but also account for social value creation.

In closing, at a time like this when restoring the trust in corporations and markets is critical to ensuring the continuing recovery of the economy, public authorities have a central role to play in developing new regulations that will help restore trust. However, government-led initiatives will be of little use if market players, including corporations, investors, analysts, and rating agencies, do not change their approach as well. In this chapter, I have focused on the role that the growing sector of social enterprises may play both as a complementary source of value creation, and as an inspiration for corporate actors in recasting their organizational model in the aftermath of the financial crisis. While the divide between the commercial and charity sectors has formed the structure of our economic and social life over the last century, hybrid organizing has the potential to reshape capitalism through the creation of organizations that pursue both social and economic objectives, and are held accountable for doing so.

Acknowledgments

I am grateful to Thomas D'Aunno, Victoria Ivashina, Joshua Margolis, Julie Mirocha, and Lakshmi Ramarajan for their comments on earlier versions of this chapter. I also thank Ting Wang and Emma Caldwell for excellent research assistance.

References

Abolafia, M. (2010). The Institutional Embeddedness of Market Failure: Why Speculative Bubbles Still Occur. In M. Lounsbury and P. M. Hirsch (eds), *Markets on Trial: The Economic Sociology of the US Financial Crisis*. Bingley, Yorks: Emerald Group Publishing, 177–200.

Acharya, V. V., and P. Schnabl (2009). How Banks Played the Leverage Game. In V. Acharya and M. Richardson (eds), *Financial Markets, Institutions and Instruments*. New York: John Wiley & Sons, 144–5.

Admati, A. R., and M. F. Hellwig (2013). *The Bankers' New Clothes: What's Wrong with Banking and What to Do about it*. Princeton: Princeton University Press.

Anheier, H. K., and L. M. Salamon (1997). *Defining the Nonprofit Sector: A Cross-National Analysis*. Manchester: Manchester University Press.

Arrow, K. (1972). Gifts and Exchanges. *Philosophy and Public Affairs*, 1(4): 343–62.

Austin, J., and H. Leonard (2008). Can the Virtuous Mouse and the Wealthy Elephant Live Happily Ever After? *California Management Review*, 51(1): 77–102.

Baker, D. (2008). The Housing Bubble and the Financial Crisis. *Real World Economic Review*, 46: 73–81.

Baron, J. N., M. T. Hannan, and M. D. Burton (1999). Building the Iron Cage: Determinants of Managerial Intensity in the Early Years of Organizations. *American Sociological Review*, 64: 527–47.

Battilana, J., and S. Dorado (2010). Building Sustainable Hybrid Organizations: The Case of Commercial Microfinance Organizations. *Academy of Management Journal*, 53(6): 1419–40.

Battilana, J., and M. Lee (2014). Advancing Research on Hybrid Organizing: Insights from the Study of Social Enterprises. *Academy of Management Annals*, 8(1): 397–441.

Battilana, J., and Norris, M. (2015). *The Sustainability Accounting Standards Board*, Harvard Business School case, 414–78.

Battilana, J., M. Sengul, A.-C. Pache, and J. Model (In press). Harnessing Productive Tensions in Hybrid Organizations: The Case of Work Integration Social Enterprises. *Academy of Management Journal*.

Bauer, T. N., E. W. Morrison, and R. R. Callister (1998). Organizational Socialization: A Review and Directions for Future Research. In G. R. Feris (ed.), *Research in Personnel and Human Resource Management*. Stamford, CT: JAI Press, 149–214.

Beckman, C. M., and M. D. Burton (2008). Founding the Future: Path Dependence in the Evolution of Top Management Teams from Founding to IPO. *Organization Science*, 19(1): 3–24.

Besharov, M., and W. Smith (2014). Multiple Logics in Organizations: Explaining their Varied Nature and Implications. *Academy of Management Review*, 39(3): 364–81.

Ben-Ner, A. (2002). The Shifting Boundaries of the Mixed Economy and the Future of the Nonprofit Sector. *Annals of Public and Cooperative Economics*, 73(1): 5–40.

Billis, D. (2010). *Hybrid Organizations and the Third Sector: Challenges for Practice, Theory and Policy*. Basingstoke: Palgrave Macmillan.

Blinder, A. (2013). *After the Music Stopped: The Financial Crisis, the Response, and the Work Ahead*. New York: Penguin Press HC.

Bourdieu, P. (1977). *Outline of a Theory of Practice*. Cambridge: Cambridge University Press.

Bower, J. L., H. B. Leonard, and L. S. Paine (2011). Global Capitalism at Risk: What are you Doing about it? *Harvard Business Review*, 89(9): 104–12.

Boyd, B. (2009). *Hybrid Organizations: New Business Models for Environmental Leadership*. Sheffield: Greenleaf Publishing.

Brakman Reiser, D. (2013). Theorizing Forms for Social Enterprise. *Emory Law Review*, 62(4): 681–739.

Bugg-Levine, A., and J. Emerson (2011). *Impact Investing: Transforming How we Make Money While Making a Difference*. San Francisco: Jossey-Bass.

Cable, D. M., and C. K. Parsons (2001). Socialization Tactics and Person-Organization Fit. *Personnel Psychology*, 54(1): 1–23.

Carrick-Cagna, A. M., and F. Santos (2009). *Kiva Versus Myc4: Business Model Innovation in Social Lending*. INSEAD Social Innovation Center Case, 6: 2009–5595. Fontainebleau: INSEAD.

Carruthers, B. (2010). Knowledge and Liquidity: Institutional and Cognitive Foundations of the Subprime Crisis. In M. Lounsbury and P. Hirsch (eds), *Markets on Trial: The Economic Sociology of the US Financial Crisis*. Bingley, Yorks: Emerald.

Christen, R. P., and D. Drake (2002). Commercialization. The New Reality of Microfinance. In D. Drake, and E. Rhyne (eds), *The Commercialization of Microfinance, Balancing Business and Development*. Bloomfield, CT: Kumarian Press.

Cornforth, C. (2004). *Governance and Participation Development Toolkit*. Manchester: Co-operatives UK.

Cyert, R., and J. March (1963). *A Behavioral Theory of the Firm*. Cambridge, MA: Blackwell Business.

Davis, G. (2009). *Managed by the Markets: How Finance Reshaped America*. Oxford: Oxford University Press.

Davis, G., and S. Kim (2013). Organizationally Diverse Capitalism: Exploring Alternatives to Twentieth-Century Public Corporations. Symposium proposal submitted to 2013 Academy of Management meeting.

Deaton, A. (2013). *The Great Escape: Health, Wealth, and the Origins of Inequality*. Princeton: Princeton University Press.

Dees, G. J. (2001). Mobilizing Resources. In G. J. Dees, J. Emerson, and P. Economy (eds), *Enterprising Nonprofits*. New York: John Wiley & Sons, 63–102.

Defourny, J., and M. Nyssens (2006). *Social Enterprise: At the Crossroads of Market, Public Policies and Civil Society*. London: Routledge.

Dichter, T. W., and M. Harper (2007). *What's Wrong with Microfinance?* Rugby: Practical Action Publishing.

DiMaggio, P. J. (1991). Constructing an Organizational Field as a Professional Project: US Art Museums, 1920–1940. In W. W. Powell and P. J. DiMaggio (eds), *The New Institutionalism in Organizational Analysis*. Chicago: University of Chicago Press, 267–92.

DiMaggio, P. J. (2002). Measuring the Impact of the Nonprofit Sector on Society is Probably Impossible But Possibly Useful: A Sociological Perspective. In P. Flynn and V. Hodgkinson (eds), *Measuring the Impact of the Private Nonprofit Sector on Society*. New York: Kluwer Academic, 249–72.

Dobbin, F., and J. Jung (2010). The Misapplication of Mr. Micheal Jensen: How Agency Theory Brought Down the Economy and Why it Might Again. In M. Lounsbury and P. M. Hirsch (eds), *Markets on Trial: The Economic Sociology of the US Financial Crisis*. Bingley, Yorks: Emerald Group, 29–64.

Dorado, S. (2006). Social Entrepreneurial Ventures: Different Values So Different Process of Creation, No? *Journal of Developmental Entrepreneurship*, 11(4): 1–24.

Ebrahim, A., Battilana, J., and Mair, J. (2014)."The governance of social enterprises: Mission drift and accountability challenges in hybrid organizations." *Research in Organizational Behavior* 34: 81–100.

Ebrahim, A. S., and V. K. Rangan (2010). *The Limits of Nonprofit Impact: A Contingency Framework for Measuring Social Performance*. Cambridge, MA: Harvard Business School General Management Unit Working Paper, 10-099.

Edwards, M., and D. Hulme (1996). Too Close for Comfort? The Impact of Official Aid on Nongovernmental Organizations. *World Development*, 24(6): 961–73.

Eisenhardt, K. M., and C. B. Schoonhoven (1990). Organizational Growth: Linking Founding Team, Strategy, Environment, and Growth among US Semiconductor Ventures, 1978–1988. *Administrative Science Quarterly*, 35(3): 504–29.

European Commission (2013). *Social Europe Guide*, iv. Brussels: European Commission.

Feldman, D. C. (1976). A Contingency Theory of Socialization. *Administrative Science Quarterly*, 21(3): 433–52.

Feldman, D. C. (2002). When You Come to a Fork in the Road, Take it: Career Indecision and Vocational Choices of Teenagers and Young Adults. In D. C. Feldman (ed.), *Work Careers: A Development Perspective*. San Francisco: Jossey Bass, 93–125.

Feldman, M. S. (2003). A Performative Perspective on Stability and Change in Organizational Routines. *Industrial and Corporate Change*, 12(4): 727–52.

Fiol, C. M., M. G. Pratt, and E. J. O'Connor (2009). Managing Intractable Identity Conflicts. *Academy of Management Review*, 34(1): 32–55.

Fiss, P., and E. Zajac (2004). The Diffusion of Ideas over Contested Terrain: The (Non) Adoption of a Shareholder Value Orientation among German Firms. *Administrative Science Quarterly*, 49(4): 501–34.

Fligstein, N. (1993). *The Transformation of Corporate Control*. Cambridge, MA: Harvard University Press.

Fligstein, N. (2001). *The Architecture of Markets*. Princeton: Princeton University Press.

Freeman, J., G. R. Carroll, and M. T. Hannan (1983). The Liability of Newness: Age Dependence in Organizational Death Rates. *American Sociological Review*, 48(5): 692–710.

Friedman, M. (1962). *Capitalism and Freedom*. Chicago: University of Chicago Press.

Friedman, M. (1970). The Social Responsibility of Business is to Increase its Profits. *New York Times Magazine*, Sept. 13.

Friedman, J., and W. Kraus (2011). *Engineering the Financial Crisis: Systemic Risk and the Failure of Regulation*. Philadelphia: University of Pennsylvania Press.

Fuentes-Nieva, R., and N. Galasso (2014). Working for the Few: Political Capture and Economic Inequality. *Oxfam International*, Jan. 20. <www.oxfam.org/sites/www.oxfam. org/files/bp-working-for-few-political-capture-economic-inequality-200114-summ-en.pdf>.

Galaskiewicz, J., and S. Barringer (2012). Social Enterprises and Social Categories. In B. Gidron and Y. Hasenfeld (eds), *Social Enterprises: An Organizational Perspective*. Basingstoke: Palgrave Macmillan, 47–70.

Garrow, E., and Y. Hasenfeld (2012). Managing Conflicting Institutional Logics: Social Service vs. Market. In B. Gidron and Y. Hasenfeld (eds), *Social Enterprises: An Organizational Perspective*. Basingstoke: Palgrave Macmillan, 121–43.

Gibbons, R., and R. Henderson (2012). Relational Contracts and Organizational Capabilities. *Organization Science*, 23(5): 1350–64.

Glynn, M. A. (2000). When Cymbals Become Symbols: Conflict over Organizational Identity within a Symphony Orchestra. *Organization Science*, 11(3): 285–98.

Gómez, L. (2009). Time to Socialize. *Journal of Business Communication*, 46(2): 179–207.

Haight, C. (2011). The Problem with Fair Trade Coffee. *Stanford Social Innovation Review*, 9(3): 74–9.

Haveman, H. A., and H. Rao (2006). Hybrid Forms and the Evolution of Thrifts. *American Behavioral Scientist*, 49(7): 974–86.

Hoffman, A., K. Badiane, and N. Haigh (2012). Hybrid Organizations as Agents of Positive Social Change: Bridging the For-Profit and Non-Profit Divide. In K. Golden-Biddle and J. Dutton (eds), *Using a Positive Lens to Explore Social Change and Organizations: Building a Theoretical and Research Foundation*. Oxford: Routledge, 131–53.

Hsu, G., M. T. Hannan, and Ö. Koçak, (2009). Multiple Category Memberships in Markets: An Integrative Theory and Two Empirical Tests. *American Sociological Review*, 74(1): 150–69.

Hwang, H., and W. W. Powell (2009). The Rationalization of Charity: The Influences of Professionalism in the Nonprofit Sector. *Administrative Science Quarterly*, 54(2): 268–98.

Jensen, M. (2002). Value Maximization, Stakeholder Theory, and the Corporate Objective Function. *Business Ethics Quarterly*, 12: 235–56.

Jones, G. (1986). Socialization Tactics, Self-Efficacy, and Newcomers' Adjustments to Organizations. *Academy of Management Journal*, 29(2): 262–79.

Jones, M. B. (2007). The Multiple Sources of Mission Drift. *Nonprofit and Voluntary Sector Quarterly*, 36: 299–307.

Kanter, R. M. (2009). *Supercorp: How Vanguard Companies Create Innovation, Profits, Growth, and Social Good*. New York: Crown Business.

Kanter, R., and D. Summers (1994). Doing Well While Doing Good: Dilemmas of Performance Management in Nonprofit Organizations and the Need for Multiple-Constituency Approach. In D. McKevitt and A. Lawton (eds), *Public Sector Management: Theory, Critique and Practice*. London: SAGE, 220–36.

Keating, G., M. O'Sullivan, A. Shorrocks, J. Davies, R. Lluberas, and A. Koutsoukis (2013). *Global Wealth Report*. Research Institute of Credit Suisse. <http://images.smh.com.au/file/2013/10/09/4815797/cs_global_wealth_report_2013_WEB_low%2520pdf.pdf?rand=1381288140715>.

Kellogg, K. C. (2009). Operating Room: Relational Spaces and Microinstitutional Change in Surgery. *American Journal of Sociology*, 115: 657–711.

Kennedy, E. D., and N. Haigh (2013). *Path to Hybridization: Offensive and Defensive Changes to Legal Registration*. Working paper. Boston: University of Massachusetts.

Kerlin, J. A. (2006). Social Enterprise in the United States and Europe: Understanding and Learning from the Differences. *Voluntas*, 17(3): 246–62.

Kimberly, J. R., and M. J. Evanisko (1981). Organizational Innovation: The Influence of Individual Organizational, and Contextual Factors on Hospital Adoption of Technological and Administrative Innovations. *Academy of Management Journal*, 24(4): 689–713.

Kraatz, M. S. (2009). Leadership as Institutional Work: A Bridge to the Other Side. In T. B. Lawrence, R. Suddaby, and B. Leca (eds), *Institutional Work: Actors and Agency in Institutional Studies of Organizations*.Cambridge: Cambridge University Press, 59–91.

Kraatz, M. S., and E. S. Block (2008). Organizational Implications of Institutional Pluralism. In R. Greenwood, C. Oliver, R. Suddaby, and K. Sahlin-Anderson (eds), *The Sage Handbook of Organizational Institutionalism*. London: SAGE, 243–75.

Lawrence, P. R., and J. W. Lorsch (1967). Differentiation and Integration in Complex Organizations. *Administrative Science Quarterly*, 12(1): 1–47.

Lee, M. (2014). *Mission and Markets? The Organizational Viability of Hybrid Social Ventures*. Cambridge, MA: Harvard Business School Working Paper.

Lindenberg, M., and C. Bryant (2001). *Going Global: Transforming Relief and Development NGOs*. Bloomfield, CT: Kumarian Press.

Lok, J. (2010). Institutional Logics as Identity Projects. *Academy of Management Journal*, 53(8): 1305–35.

Lomax, S. (2013). Social Enterprise: Market Trends Based upon the Small Business Survey 2012. *BMG Research*. <https://www.gov.uk/government/uploads/system/uploads/attachment_data/file/205291/Social_Enterprises_Market_Trends_-_report_v1.pdf>.

Louis, M. R. (1980). Surprise and Sense Making: What Newcomers Experience in Entering Unfamiliar Organizational Settings. *Administrative Science Quarterly*, 25: 226–51.

Lounsbury, M., and P. M. Hirsch (2010). *Markets on Trial: The Economic Sociology of the US Financial Crisis*. London: Emerald Group.

Mair, J. (2010). Social Entrepreneurship: Taking Stock and Looking Ahead. In A. Fayolle and H. Matlay (eds), *Handbook of Research and Social Entrepreneurship*. Cheltenham: Edward Elgar, 15–28.

Mangold, K. (2007). Educating a New Generation: Teaching Baby Boomer Faculty about Millennial Students. *Nurse Educator*, 3(1): 21–3.

March, J. G. (1991). Exploration and Exploitation in Organizational Learning. *Organization Science*, 2(1): 71–87.

Margolis, J. D., and J. P. Walsh (2003). Misery Loves Companies: Rethinking Social Initiatives by Business. *Administrative Science Quarterly*, 48(2): 268–305.

Marquis, C., and A. Tilcsik (2013). Imprinting: Toward a Multilevel Theory. *Academy of Management Annals*, 7(1): 195–245.

Martorana, P. V., A. D. Galinsky, and H. Rao (2005). From System Justification to System Condemnation: Antecedents of Attempts to Change Power Hierarchies. *Research on Managing Groups and Teams*, 7: 283–313.

Mersland, R., and R. Ø. Strøm (2010). Microfinance Mission Drift? *World Development*, 38: 28–36.

Meyer, H.-D., and B. Rowan (2006). *The New Institutionalism in Education.* New York: SUNY Press.

Meyer, R., and M. Höllerer (2010). Meaning Structures in a Contested Issue Field: A Topographic Map of Shareholder Value in Austria. *Academy of Management Journal,* 53(6): 1241–62.

Minkoff, D. C., and W. Powell (2006). Nonprofit Mission: Constancy, Responsiveness, or Deflection? In W. W. Powell and R. Steinberg (eds), *The Non-Profit Sector: A Research Handbook.* New Haven, CT: Yale University Press, 591–611.

Mishina, Y., B. J. Dykes, E. S. Block, and T. G. Pollock (2010). Why "Good" Firms Do Bad Things: The Effects of High Aspirations, High Expectations, and Prominence on the Incidence of Corporate Illegality. *Academy of Management Journal,* 53(4): 701–22.

Moizer, J., and P. Tracey (2010). Strategy Making in Social Enterprise: The Role of Resource Allocation and its Effects on Organizational Sustainability. *Systems Research and Behavioral Science,* 27(3): 252–66.

Murray, F. (2010). The Oncomouse that Roared: Hybrid Exchange Strategies as a Source of Distinction at the Boundary of Overlapping Institutions. *American Journal of Sociology,* 116(2): 341–88.

Murray, J. H. (2012). Choose your own Master: Social Enterprise, Certifications, and Benefit Corporation Statutes. *American University Business Law Review,* 2(2): 1–53.

Nicholls, A. (2009). We Do Good Things, don't we? Blended Value Accounting in Social Entrepreneurship. *Accounting, Organizations and Society,* 34(6): 755–69.

Nielsen, R. P. (1986). Piggybacking Strategies for Nonprofits: A Shared Costs Approach. *Strategic Management Journal,* 7(3): 201–15.

O'Donahoe, N., C. Leijonhufvud, and Y. Saltuk (2010). Impact Investments: An Emerging Asset Class. *J. P. Morgan Global Research,* Nov. 29. <www.rockefellerfoundation.org/uploads/files/2b053b2b-8feb-46ea-adbd-f89068d59785-impact.pdf>.

Pache, A. C., and F. Santos (2010). When Worlds Collide: The Internal Dynamics of Organizational Responses to Conflicting Institutional Demands. *Academy of Management Review,* 35(3): 455–76.

Pache, A.-C., and F. Santos (2013). Inside the Hybrid Organization: Selective Coupling as a Response to Conflicting Institutional Logics. *Academy of Management Journal,* 56(4): 972–1001.

Paton, R. (2003). *Managing and Measuring Social Enterprises.* Thousand Oaks, CA: SAGE.

Porter, M. E., and M. R. Kramer (2011). Creating Shared Value: How to Reinvent Capitalism and Unleash a Wave of Innovation and Growth. *Harvard Business Review,* 89: 62–77.

Pratt, M. G., and P. O. Foreman (2000). Classifying Managerial Responses to Multiple Organizational Identities. *Academy of Management Review,* 25(1): 18–42.

Rajan, R. G. (2011). *Fault Lines: How Hidden Fractures Still Threaten the World Economy.* Princeton: Princeton University Press.

Reinhart, C. M., and K. Rogoff (2009). *This Time is Different: Eight Centuries of Financial Folly.* Princeton: Princeton University Press.

Rogers, P. J. (2007). Theory-Based Evaluation: Reflections Ten Years on. *New Directions for Evaluation,* 114: 63–7.

Rona-Tas, A., and S. Hiss (2010). The Role of Ratings in the Subprime Mortgage Crisis: The Art of Corporate and the Science for Consumer Credit Rating. In M. Lounsbury and P. M. Hirsch (eds), *Markets on Trial: The Economic Sociology of the US Financial Crisis.* Bingley, Yorks: Emerald Group, 115–55.

Ruef, M., and K. Patterson (2009). Credit and Classification: The Impact of Industry Boundaries in Nineteenth Century America. *Administrative Science Quarterly*, 54(3): 486–520.

Ruef, M., and W. R. Scott (1998). A Multidimensional Model of Organizational Legitimacy: Hospital Survival in Changing Institutional Environments. *Administrative Science Quarterly*, 43(4): 877–904.

Sabeti, H. (2011). The For-Benefit Enterprise. *Harvard Business Review*, 89(11): 99–103.

Saltuk, Y., A. Bouri, and G. Leung (2011). Insight into the Impact: An In-depth Analysis of Investor Perspectives and over 2,200 Transactions. *J. P. Morgan. GIIN*, Dec. 14. <www.thegiin.org/cgi-bin/iowa/download?row=334andfield=gated_download_1>.

Saltuk, Y., A. Bouri, A. Mudaliar, and M. Pease (2013). Perspectives on Progress: The Impact Investor Survey. *J. P. Morgan. GIIN*, Jan. 7. <www.thegiin.org/cgi-bin/iowa/download?row=489&field=gated_download_1>.

Saks, A. M., and B. E. Ashforth (1997). A Longitudinal Investigation of the Relationships between Job Information Sources, Applicant Perceptions of Fit, and Work Outcomes. *Personnel Psychology*, 50(2): 395–426.

Schein, E. (2006). *Organizational Culture and Leadership*. Malden, MA: John Wiley & Sons.

Schneiberg, M. (2011). Toward an Organizationally Diverse American Capitalism? Cooperative, Mutual, and Local, State-Owned Enterprise. *Seattle University Law Review*, 34: 1409–34.

Schneiberg, M., M. King, and T. Smith (2008). Social Movements and Organizational Form: Cooperative Alternatives to Corporations in the American Insurance, Dairy and Grain Industries. *American Sociological Review*, 73(4): 635–67.

Scott, R. A. (1967). The Factory as a Social Service Organization: Goal Displacement in Workshops for the Blind. *Social Problems*, 15(2): 160–75.

Scott, W. R., and J. W. Meyer (1991). The Organization of Societal Sectors: Propositions and Early Evidence. In P. J. DiMaggio and W. Powell (eds), *The New Institutionalism in Organizational Analysis*. Chicago: University of Chicago Press, 108–40.

Seelos, C., and J. Mair (2004). *Social Entrepreneurship: The Contribution of Individual Entrepreneurs to Sustainable Development*. Working Paper 553. Barcelona: University Of Navarra, IESE Business School.

Selznick, P. (1949). *TVA and the Grass Roots*. Berkeley, CA: University of California Press.

Selznick, P. (1957). *Leadership in Administration: A Sociological Interpretation*. Evanston, IL: Pew, Peterson, & Co.

Sen, A. (1999). *Development as Freedom*. Cambridge: Oxford University Press; New York: Anchor Books).

Severino, J. (2012). Barometer of Social Entrepreneurship in France and Worldwide. *Convergence 2015 Report*. <www.convergences2015.org/Content/biblio/BES%20C2015_2012_ENG_web.pdf>.

Shapiro, E. (2013). Social Entrepreneurship: A Fundamental Game Changer. *Skoll World Forum*. <www.forbes.com/sites/skollworldforum/2013/01/07/social-entrepreneurship-a-fundamental-game-changer>.

Shiller, R. (2005). *Irrational Exuberance*. New York: Random House LLC.

Shiller, R. (2008). *The Subprime Solution: How Today's Global Financial Crisis Happened and What to Do about it*. Princeton: Princeton University Press.

Simon, H. A. (1991). Organizations and Markets. *Journal of Economic Perspectives*, 5(2): 25–44.

Simon, J., H. Dale, and L. Chisolm (2006). The Federal Tax Treatment of Charitable Organizations. In W. Powell (ed.), *The Nonprofit Sector: A Research Handbook*. New Haven: Yale University Press, 267–306.

Simons, T., and P. Ingram (1997). Organization and Ideology: Kibbutzim and Hired Labor, 1951–1965. *Administrative Science Quarterly*, 42 (4): 784–813.

Smith, W. K., and M. W. Lewis (2011). Toward a Theory of Paradox: A Dynamic Equilibrium Model of Organizing. *Academy of Management Review*, 36(2): 381–403.

Smith, W. K., and M. L. Tushman (2005). Managing Strategic Contradictions: A Top Management Model for Managing Innovation Streams. *Organization Science*, 16(5): 522.

Stiglitz, J. (2012). *The Price of Inequality: How Today's Divided Society Endangers our Future*. New York: W. W. Norton & Co.

Stinchcombe, A. (1965). Social Structure and Organizations. In J. March (ed.), *Handbook of Organizations*. Chicago: Rand McNally, 153–93.

Strom, S. (2010). The Nonprofit Hybrid Model: A Marriage of Differing Missions. *New York Times: Business Day*, Oct. 20: B1, B8.

Sweeney, R. (2005). Reinventing Library Buildings and Services for the Millennial Generation. *Library Leadership and Management*, 19(4): 165–75.

Teasdale, S. (2012). Negotiating Tensions: How do Social Enterprises in the Homelessness Field Balance Social and Commercial Considerations? *Housing Studies*, 27(4): 514–32.

Tonkiss, F. (2009). Trust, Confidence and Economic Crisis. *Intereconomics*, 44(4): 196–202.

Trelstad, B. (2008). Simple Measures for Social Enterprise. *Innovations*, 3(3): 105–18.

Tushman, M. L., and C. A. O'Reilly (1996). Ambidextrous Organizations: Managing Evolutionary and Revolutionary Change. *California Management Review*, 38(4): 8–30.

Van Maanen, J., and E. H. Schein (1979). Towards a Theory of Organizational Socialization. In B. M. Staw (ed.), *Research in Organizational Behavior*. Greenwich, CT: JAI Press, 209–64.

Weber, M. (1952). *The Protestant Ethic and the Spirit of Capitalism*. New York: Scribner.

Weisbrod, B. (2004). The Pitfalls of Profits. *Stanford Social Innovation Review*, 2: 40–7.

Yunus, M., B. Moingeon, and L. Lehmann-Ortega (2010). Building Social Business Models: Lessons from the Grameen Experience. *Long Range Planning*, 43(2): 308–25.

Zuckerman, E. (1999). The Categorical Imperative: Securities Analysts and the Illegitimacy Discount. *American Journal of Sociology*, 104(5): 1398–438.

CHAPTER 26

....

TRUST AND POWER

....

BERTRAND COLLOMB

Abstract

Trust is essential to the exchanges in a free market economy. Personal trust between individual players becomes institutional trust in a larger, more complex and globalized economy. The last thirty years have seen a strong decline, in all countries, of trust in all types of institutions, including companies. To protect their reputation and image, companies tend to develop policies and compliance mechanisms, like regulation is developed to restore trust at the macro-economic level. But a compliance culture will not promote individual trust, and regulation alone will not restore public trust. Trust can only be base on ethics. A responsible behavior from business based on ethical standards, not legal compliance, is already developing and should become the norm, and the need and value of individual ethical behavior should be more widely taught and recognized.

The importance of trust as the basis of any economic system and even more of a free market economy has long been recognized by the economists, and by the societies which have chosen to enable such systems to flourish.

Trust is Critical to a Free Market Economy
....

While a state-led "command and control" economy can proceed from decisions enforced by the power of the state, a free market economy is based on autonomous decisions by the players to exchange between themselves, with some confidence that some rules of the exchange game or some professional standards are being adhered to by the participants. There is of course a legal system to enforce legal rules and punish abuse of confidence, but it can be used only in limited circumstances. And examples exist of groups, like diamond merchants, where the exchange is only based on trust, without even the legal apparatus (such as signed contracts) required to allow any legal enforcement.

Trust is easily given, and tested, in closely knit groups where the solidarity of the group is assumed to be stronger than any other external incentive. This is the case in families—and the Mafia has extended the concept of family with its associated trust assumption—or small ethnic groups, tribes, or villages, or even among craftsmen engaged in the same trade. When there is more distance between the players, like among merchants of different cities in the ancient time, trust is even more important, as international enforcement mechanisms have long been, and are still today, difficult and not always effective.

The importance of trust—versus power-enforced legal rules—also varies among different cultures. One Japanese industrialist, educated at Cambridge and considered in Japan as a "modern" manager, faced with a distributor who was obviously useless, told me once "Yes, I know we should do without him, but my grandfather sold through his grandfather, and my father through his father. How could I do that?"

In the US, oral testimony is key in judicial proceedings, it is assumed every witness will tell the truth and lying—especially under oath—is considered one of the worst offenses. In continental Europe, to the contrary, very limited trust is placed in verbal statements, and proof must be found in written documents. As it is assumed that the family (including servants) is the focus of trust relationships, and that lying to protect family members is the preferred ethical behavior, the French law does not allow a witness to testify under oath when a member of his family is involved, so that he will not be "obliged" to give a false testimony and to commit perjury.

Another example of cultural differences in the manner trust is granted pertains to written contracts: most American contracts are tens or even hundreds pages long, but they are only signed by the parties on the last page, and often on a detachable "signature page," which is sometimes circulated among the signatories without the full text. In France, where trust is placed in written text, to avoid any alteration of this text every page must be initialled by the signatories! It would be interesting to know whether there are more forgery attempts in the US than in France!

THE PROMOTION OF INSTITUTIONAL TRUST

But the trust issue, as the basis of economic relationship; is completely different when exchanges are conducted between people who have no reason to know each other. The "société anonyme," the French version of the modern corporation, is not an "anonymous" company and has a name, but its shareholders are anonymous, and there is no need and no obligation—with some exceptions—to identify them.

In those situations, personal trust cannot exist between the partners, and it has to be replaced by a different kind of trust, institutional trust. One could trust the promoter of that company, or the banker which sells its shares, or the journalist of the newspaper which has described the excellent prospects of the company, or the rating agency which has given it a good rating.

Experience however shows quickly the limits of the trust you can give to the parties who have an interest—financial or other—in the transaction being considered. This is especially true in the times of rapid economic expansion, where new technological developments or the opening of new markets create a collective excitement.

After a few scandals when worthless shares in new companies were sold to a gullible public, the Securities Exchange Commission was created in 1934, and empowered to authorize and regulate public offering of securities. The institutional trust in this agency is supposed to allow people to buy shares even though they have only limited information on the company, and no personal trust relationship with its promoters or the other shareholders.

Once a public institution is established to protect trust in some category of transaction, there is a choice for its mode of operation. Will it have the power to evaluate the quality of the instrument being offered, and authorize only those it deems to be trustworthy? Or will it only make sure that the appropriate disclosures are made, and that all the relevant information is being given? Or will it call the attention of the buyers on the risks, or even—like the rating agencies—grade the instruments by levels of risk?

In a world of little change and of established practices, it was relatively easy to determine what was a trustworthy practice, and not to allow much deviation from the time-honored standards. That is the way the craft guilds controlled the practice of their craft in medieval cities, by a precise definition of acceptable practices. This obviously did not promote innovation, and had become so unbearable to the craftsmen themselves that at the French Revolution the very existence of these guilds became forbidden by law.

But because business situations are now complex and changing, and nobody wants to stifle the innovation process, the trend has been towards the disclosure approach, at least when it is not obvious that the instrument proposed is fraudulent.

Disclosures have become more and more extensive, and prospectuses longer and longer. At the end the buyer has little chance of making an informed judgement, as too much information kills information. And his only recourse is to trust the professionals who are supposed to be knowledgeable on the issue—analysts or rating agencies. As they often have themselves conflicts of interest, which they dutifully disclose in long formal sentences, the real impact of which is difficult to evaluate, the situation becomes even muddier!

The outcome was clearly visible in the 2008 crisis, where a collective blindness prevented the obvious fallacy of the so-called "subprime loans" from being exposed. Anybody who had trusted the financial system was to be very disappointed!

Is Trust Disappearing in our Societies?

Even before the crisis, a significant development of the last thirty years has been the erosion of institutional trust. No institution has been immune from this trend.

It applies to political institutions, to elected officials, civil servants, but also to established churches, to schools, as well as scientists or so-called "experts," and to business organizations and companies. Not only has any institutional discourse become suspect, but a deep mistrust has developed against the elites of any kind: the feeling often expressed is that these elites have distanced themselves from the problems of the real people, and are entrenched in positions of power and privilege.

This phenomenon may be slightly different in different countries—for example, the American public trusts the Federal Drug Agency somewhat more than the Europeans do its European counterparts. But the evolution is basically the same in all the Western democratic countries.

The origin of this distrust is probably the increasing complexity of the issues, and the difficulties experienced by most people in a world of competition and systemic interrelationship. When the situation is more tense, when the issues are difficult to explain and understand, with often counterintuitive conclusions—like the idea that making firing people easier leads to more job creation!—and when more educated citizens have, with internet and the like, their own "independent" information channels, it becomes difficult to trust the powers that be.

In addition the political process, at least in democratic countries, discourages political leaders from actually "leading" and explaining things that are difficult and unpleasant. They find it much easier to surf on any media wave, and avoid dealing directly with the difficult issues.

Business people, who were seen for some time as more legitimate because they were in an "action" mode, justified by the success of their company, have also lost the public trust, because they could not protect employees in the down cycles, and also because their levels of compensation were deemed, not without reason, to be excessive, and were putting them, in effect, in a different world than the common man. The trust in financial people, so critical to the success of their business, was even more strongly eroded by the circumstances of the financial crisis and the abuse of public trust—and public money—it revealed.

At the same time, we have seen the development of trust in the best international brands. By buying their products, often without a pressing need, consumers show they trust the quality, and the uniqueness, of these brands—and indirectly the companies behind them. Similarly there has been—and there is probably still—too much trust in the ratings given by various agencies. One can look for example to the Shanghai ranking of worldwide universities: its biases and limitations are clear, but it has had an enormous importance in the way people see universities, and the way they see themselves.

More interestingly, there has been a flurry of private ratings on the internet. To plan our vacation, many of us go to Tripadvisor, where we look at the judgment expressed on different hotels, without any guarantee that the experiences described are even real, or reflect a balanced evaluation. But it looks like it is better to trust the judgment of our (supposed) peers than to rely on possibly conflicted experts.

POWER WITHOUT TRUST CANNOT RUN A COMPANY

If trust is essential to economic dealings within society, it is also an important concept within companies themselves. A company is a group of people working together to achieve a common purpose: the effective production of goods and services, so that the value of them for society is higher than the value of the inputs used in the production. This is what used to be called the creation of wealth, and is now called "value creation." The relationships between people within a company can be described with an economic vocabulary: exchange of services, transaction costs, alignment of interests, incentives to work,... But at the end, people in a company do not work only as *Homo economicus*, they work with their guts, their hearts, and the emotional relationships they build between themselves and with the company as a group.

Power relationships are important, as a company is not a democratic institution, and allows the bosses to have significant power, with only limited checks. But people who work only by constraint, because they are obliged to, are not likely to be the most productive and innovative people. Anybody with any business experience can testify that trust is an essential element of success.

Trust is necessary at very different levels: trust in the future of the company allows you to see your own future within its framework; trust in the soundness of its strategy and the competence of its leadership make your efforts meaningful and rewarding; trust in your own boss breeds acceptance of his decisions; trust in your fellow workers is indispensable for any practical work.

And this trust is much more than only the delivering your part of the contract with the company; it is an emotional commitment—sometimes even contrary to your own interest or to the rational evidence—which leads teams to do great things.

To create and maintain an effective climate of trust is easier in small teams, where there is an immediate relationship between team members, and when the relationship with the customers or the outside world is also direct. It is more difficult in larger organizations where people are further apart, objectives are complex and conflicting, and the effectiveness of the process for the delivery of a value-creating product is more remote.

The large companies which developed during the Industrial Revolution often dealt with this difficulty by organizing themselves in a decentralized way, where smaller units could be managed as small companies. General Motors epitomized that approach in the 1930s, and McKinsey succeeded in the 1960s in developing the decentralized organization model. Not coincidentally, it has always been the officially preferred organization model of the Catholic Church, under the name of "subsidiarity," because it recognizes the freedom and the dignity of man by allowing decisions to be taken as low as possible in the organization. Unfortunately it was discovered later that organizing a very large company as a sum of small companies does not enable achieving the best economies of scale, and taking advantage of the size of the company, while it cannot avoid its drawbacks: complexity, slowness,...

The development of information technologies made it possible to locate the various elements of the production process in different places, and to disconnect the handling of information from the people and the places it was generated from. More and more organizations have been changed in order to pool together staff functions, shorten the hierarchical lines, and segment the working process, so that the information and the skills necessary to solve a particular problem are now spread within the whole organization. In these organizations, for example, a manager can be managing, for a product, a "profit center," with a bottom line responsibility, but without managing either the plants, which are multiproduct and report to an industrial department, or the salespeople, organized by geography or sector in the sales department, or the research/development that is in a separate organization.

That type of network organization is undoubtedly, as experience has shown, better in terms of cost reduction and effectiveness. But it is also more demanding on the people who find themselves in the nodes of the networks, and can only discharge their responsibilities through the contribution of other people, over whom they have no power. They need to rely on others, to trust them much more than in traditional decentralized organizations.

THE DEVELOPMENT OF A COMPLIANCE CULTURE

At the same time, companies have felt obliged to replace the autonomy of a decentralized manager by "policies," prescriptive ways to operate, or "best practices," proven effective ways, to make sure that operators in different departments and different geographies effectively converging to achieve the company's objectives. This has been reinforced by the pressure of investors, media, and civil society groups (NGOs). They want to know more about what the company is doing, and to make sure it meets their requirements.

In an internet and media-driven world, anything happening, even in a tiny and remote part of the company, can have an enormous impact on its image or its legal standing. The old statistical (or commonsense) approach, defining a company by the average of what it is doing, and recognizing there has to be some variation around the average, is not acceptable anymore. The company's management, and even its board, are expected to fully guarantee the quality of the company practices, much beyond what was the norm previously.

This has led to a system of "compliance" where managers at all levels must certify time and again that they have not violated company policies, accounting rules, and a myriad of other rules they are supposed to follow. That is clearly the opposite of a culture of trust and empowerment; and managers may feel they are not only subject to contradictory pressures, but also under the suspicion of not following the rules.

The way an organization reacts to that emphasis on policies and compliance mechanisms varies depending on the cultural environment. In North America, where work is seen as delivering on a contract, following detailed rules and processes is relatively well accepted. Being admitted recently to an American hospital for a minor surgery, I had to recite a dozen times my name and date of birth and the reason I was there, as each new player checked for possible identity mistakes, and I also needed to sign fifteen forms! And when I was discharged, although perfectly able to walk, I had to be taken to my car in a wheelchair, according to policy! It was in a sense reassuring to see how safety procedures were taken seriously, but my trust in the hospital was more based on the quality of its medical and nursing staff. All of them, despite this "mechanical" adherence to rules, managed to display a cheerful, enthusiastic, and professional attitude.

But in France, where, as shown by Philippe d'Iribarne (1989), work is related to status and the worker's dignity lies in his freedom to define the content of his work, such a compliance approach is more difficult to implement. And the contradiction with an attitude of trust is more often pointed out.

Naturally, even in the best company, with the best procedures, something is bound to go wrong somewhere at some time! Mechanically, this will result in another control layer, supposedly to avoid repetition of the mistake. The search to establish institutional trust for the benefit of the company risks eliminating personal trust within the company.

The Incredible Power of Trust

These disturbing evolutions are happening even though the importance of trust in the performance of companies has never been more apparent. More specifically, we see more and more clearly that people who feel trusted by the organization can, and will, often react to crises or difficult situations in ways that a rational observer would not have expected.

In my personal business experience, I have witnessed several examples supporting that conclusion. I remember a case where restructuring of the sales organization was taking place after the merger of three companies into a single one. Instead of asking a consultant to draw up the best new organization, we decided to ask the existing sales managers, operating for the three combined companies in the given region, to work as a group, with a facilitator, and come up with a proposal. There were five of them, and after a couple of weeks, much to my surprise, they came up with a much "leaner" proposal than I would have expected, with only two subregional managers. They knew that at least three of them would lose their job in the new design, but they had been trusted to find the best proposal for the company, and this was the best proposal for the company! Of course, they also trusted the company to consider them for other positions, and, in the case of redundancy, to deal with them fairly. This was a striking illustration of the power of trust, as an incentive to go beyond the ordinary and elicit the heroic, to get the best out of people, and even more in tough situations.

Another example is the recent story of a company, Poclain Hydraulics, bought back from Case by members of the Bataille family who had once owned Poclain, a crane and construction equipment company. Poclain Hydraulics specializes in hydraulic engines for these big pieces of equipment, and operates on an international scope. In 2009, due to the crisis, its market shrank all of a sudden by 60 percent! The normal reaction would have been to shed a similar percentage of the workforce, but management felt this would destroy the company. They succeeded instead in concluding agreements with the unions in ten countries, providing that salaries would be cut on average by 30 percent (less at the bottom and of course more at the top), with some future repayments if and when the company recovered. In France, where individual employees are protected against any involuntary reduction of wages, even collectively agreed, all the employees also needed to sign up individually, and 96 percent of the employees did sign!

As there was not enough production demand to occupy the workforce, the company assigned the majority of the employees, during 2009, to special projects, involving innovation, new product development, marketing research, or the like. When the market came back in 2010 (and even though 2011 and 2012 were still not easy years) the company could restore the salaries back, and was a stronger company, with new products and new approaches to the market that increased its market share.

The point is that such an approach, especially in a French-based company, could not have been developed and accepted if there had not been already, before the crisis hit, a good level of trust within the company. Trust from management that the employees could deal with the challenge, trust from the employees that they were not being tricked into a disingenuous scheme benefitting only to the shareholders of the company.

THE LIMITS OF RESTORING TRUST
THROUGH REGULATION

So it is clear that power itself cannot bring economic success, both at the macro-level and at the micro-business level. At the same time actual trust has been eroded and processes are at work that are likely to continue this deterioration. But trust is an essential ingredient of a successful business, or of a harmonious society. How can the necessary level of trust be restored?

In the aftermath of the 2008 crisis, where trust in the financial system was betrayed, the main effort to restore trust is in financial regulation. Regulation by government or public authorities is an attempt to use the power of the state to restore trust. Can it work? Institutional trust may actually be restored if stronger regulation shows its effectiveness over time. After a period where genetic engineering was widely opposed in the US, the FDA was able to regulate this sector in a way that created enough trust for business to enjoy in the US a reasonably peaceful environment to operate in—while the opposite evolution took place in Europe.

However regulation has its own pitfalls. When it is, like often in the US, based on detailed rules legalistically interpreted, it opens the way to an innovative search for loopholes. That is most likely going to be the case in the financial sector, where the potential for innovation—good and bad—has been demonstrated and where monetary incentives are large!

When regulation is based—as was the tradition in Europe—on general principles, it can prohibit any kind of scheme that is not consistent with the regulation principles, however cleverly crafted. But there is always a margin of judgment in the application of principles, which critics say is creating legal uncertainty and can hurt business confidence!

And beyond these cultural differences, in a globalized world, effective regulation should be worldwide. This challenge is difficult to meet, as evidenced by the difficulty of implementing the guidelines agreed in principle in 2009 by the G20 in the financial area. More importantly, regulation addresses only the institutional trust issue. It may be useful for that purpose, but regulation will not favour innovation, will not create enthusiasm, and underestimates the intuitive trust we need to have in everything that is really important.[1]

So I do not believe trust will ever be achieved by regulation enforcement alone, if the players are not willing to participate in the trust-building exercise. Business players have a strong incentive to do so, when they want to protect the trust in their brands, which, as we have seen, is still a powerful driver of consumer behavior. Being seen as a "responsible" or an "ethical" company is becoming for the large international companies a prerequisite of successful development. And the definition of what is ethical is being enlarged every day. Who could have believed ten years ago that large apparel distributors would be under attack, not only because some of their subcontractors were mistreating their workers, or employing children, but because the building where these subcontractors were working had collapsed?

From a legal perspective, it is clear that these firms had no responsibility in the bad construction quality of a building in Bangladesh. But they are now obliged, to protect their reputation and their public image, to take responsibility for situations linked with their activity, even if they are apparently outside of their direct control.

The ethical responsibility of a company now goes far beyond the quality and the security of its operations and of its products. It covers all aspects of its social impact, where the company is expected to promote, or even impose, the same concern for quality, security, and more generally responsiveness.

This can seem frustrating, or even scandalous, to some CEOs, but it is probably a positive evolution to help rebuild institutional trust, and mark a difference between companies that can be trusted and the others. And I believe business should welcome this extension of its responsibility, even if it will certainly lead to abuses here and there.

---

[1] I draw here on the work of a research group of College des Bernardins (2013)

A TRUST BASED ON ETHICS

Not every company sells products with international brands, and we need ways to regain trust more widely in the economy. What about rebuilding trust for investment bankers, or heavy equipment manufacturers, or cement companies?

I believe that trust for any economic player will be based on the perception that it is useful for society, that its economic success is a plus for the common good, and that its success can be achieved without abusing people, inside and outside the organization, and without being unethical.

The concept of ethics is a difficult one, as it is less well defined than the concept of legality. But limiting unacceptable behavior to illegal behavior will not be sufficient. And the business world, both at the collective and individual level, has to face the issue of ethics. Many companies have a code of ethics, or even board committee on ethics. But the definition of ethical behavior needs sometimes to be revisited. Recent examples show how new ethical issues may appear:

Tax haven countries have been around for a long time. It could be argued that they play a useful role when they allow escape from excessive tax rates or an excessive regulatory burden imposed by some countries. Sometimes using them is the only way to avoid double taxation created by the lack of international coordination between national tax regimes. But in other cases they allow illegal actions to be concealed, or the avoidance of any taxation at all.

Tax havens have been attacked by citizens groups, and criticized by "legitimate" states for a long time. But it was only after the 2008 financial crisis that an international movement to curb their practices started, at the G20 meeting in London. Some regulatory constraints have been established, especially in the US and Europe. And a campaign has been started to "name and shame" the companies—especially the banks—which have subsidiaries in these countries. Companies have been obliged to clarify their attitude in that area, sometimes deciding to close any subsidiary that was not linked to effective and "legitimate" operations in the country.

Going one step further, the behavior of companies—like Apple and Google—which had succeeded in locating, in a perfectly legal way, a significant part of their profits in Ireland, where they were not taxed, has been questioned. Will the time come where, independently of the legality of the system, it will be deemed to be "unethical" for an international company not to pay—globally, in its different countries of operations—a minimum rate of tax? And what will be this minimum?

More generally, will a "trustworthy" company be required to avoid anything which could be considered "unethical," even if it is perfectly legal? This would be a big change from the Milton Friedman's approach to the role of business! Some years ago, in a debate with a French philosopher, he argued that a company needed not to have any moral standards. According to him, if I, as CEO of a listed company, could do something that was legal and was profitable for my shareholders, I had to do it, even if it looked immoral to me. I disagreed: I did not see why my shareholders, who were ultimately men and women who had moral standards, would expect me, as CEO of the company, to do something they would not accept to do themselves.

This debate is still going on, and is integral part of the trust issue in our economic liberal system. But we can assume, without being excessively idealistic, that the trend will be to extend the ethical responsibility of business rather than reduce it.

TRUSTING PEOPLE, AND NOT ONLY INSTITUTIONS

This brings us to the individual responsibility to restore trust.

A lot of debate took place, after the financial crisis and the ensuing banking collapse, on whether the crisis was due to failing systems, blindfolded regulators, bad governance of the banks, or unethical behavior of individuals. It is tempting to answer: all of the above, but it is interesting to discuss individual behavior.

Economists have developed, especially since the 1980s, a view of people as being mainly determined by economic objectives and incentives. Under their influence were developed, in the financial world and later in the rest of the business world, compensation schemes with huge "incentives" to push executives to achieve high and fast profits for their organization. It is not very surprising then that this system led people into so much temptation that some ethical breaches were observed.

However the real ethical issues have been more pervasive that the cases where people did things that they knew were against the rules, and the laws. The Enron or Madoff stories, or even the manipulation of Libor rates by unscrupulous traders, were only the tip of the iceberg.

What came to be the real problem was the faith developed by many participants in the financial game that the game itself was a justification of everything. Because the free market system was the best global economic system, as became clear after the fall of communism, and because that system was obviously based on the pursuit by each player of its own self-interest, this pursuit, however egotistic, was justified by the global system.

The Milton Friedman assumption became a reason to abolish any moral judgment: if anything was increasing the liquidity of the market, reducing transaction costs, or favouring more trades, it had to be good, regardless of the circumstances.

As an example, when Goldman Sachs bundled dubious subprime credits at the request of an investor who wanted to play against them, and found other investors to buy them, his specialists were probably thinking in terms of developing opportunities and improving the effectiveness of the market, but they were forgetting commonsense and ordinary ethical principles. The faith in the theory, and the techniques developed from it, may have replaced or obliterated any moral judgment.

In another example, I was shocked when, at the height of the internet bubble, the head of a reputable investment bank told me that, for start-up companies, the main thing was to know when to bail out! It was a far cry from my concept of entrepreneurship, and from the idea of creating value by innovation development. And indeed a number of pseudo-entrepreneurs, who had astutely marketed an idea, bailed out at the peak, and became rich before their companies collapsed, are still respected in Wall Street as successful people!

TRUST AND ETHICS IN BUSINESS SCHOOLS

How can we bridge the gap between "technical" and "ethical" behavior? Of course working on the rules, making clear that some principles are more important than the "perfection" of the market, and punishing the most erratic behaviors will be helpful. But it is also necessary for the collective mindset to evolve. How is it possible, and is it likely to happen?

The evolution of the last thirty years was due to the mix of theoretical work by the Chicago economists, pressure from institutional investors, and the implementation of short-minded incentives. The ethical rules developed by professional associations, or by bodies like the City of London, were increasingly seen as obsolete, even if they were not openly challenged. Anything obviously not illegal came to be permissible. And the regulators themselves became persuaded that regulation was bad, and that self-regulation of markets should become the preferred way.

Business schools played a role in teaching their students the unlimited power of financial innovation, and the idea that furthering market power could not be bad. Is it possible to orchestrate an evolution in the opposite direction, which would emphasize the role of ethical standards in every transaction? Fining major banks billions of dollars should get their attention. Regulating away some of the most egregious abuses (like high speed trading, which organizes dissymmetry of information) could help. "Responsible companies," who put value on displaying ethical behavior, may help create a standard that other companies will be afraid not to follow. Civil society watch groups or NGOs can exercise pressure, balancing that of financial players. And the capping of bonuses—however arbitrary and artificial it can look—may reduce the incentives to go too far.

This can only be a long-term effort, and the outcome remains uncertain at this time. The role of business schools could be essential, and some schools have recognized it. So did some of their students, if one judges by the MBA Oath, developed at Harvard Business School. This oath is quite remarkable, as it encompasses all the main aspects of what ethical behavior should be for business people, and recognizes the need to regain the trust of the people, within companies as well as on Main Street. It ends: "I recognize that my behavior must set an example of integrity, eliciting trust and esteem from those I serve; I will remain accountable to my peers and to society for my actions and for upholding these standards."

I realize that the cynics—or simply the realists—will smile at the idea that MBA students, groomed to be members of this elite which has disproportionately benefitted from the success of the globalized economy, would want to constraint their future by committing seriously to ethical objectives. But I believe that many managers, young and old, at all levels in the business world, are not satisfied by a system that, although highly effective in the production of goods, seems sometimes to have lost its compass. There is, in business like in society, a demand to make the purpose of business actions more visible, and to come back to the "moral sentiments" from the first book of Adam Smith.

At the same time, and unfortunately, I am not sure that this oath is still alive in many business schools today! This could be a matter of a more comprehensive study, to see in which directions the business school community is going.

Conclusion

Democracy and a free market economic system, the two great concepts that Western societies inherited from the Enlightenment, are both based on trust that individual freedom can be harnessed to lead to the common good.

It is a fact that the level of trust in our societies has greatly diminished over the recent decades. I have focused here on the economic aspects of this trust deficit, but it is also obvious in the political field.

We are painfully trying to restore that trust, but the main approach is currently through regulation, which may, by favouring a culture of formal compliance, have perverse effects on individual trust.

At the same time phenomena are at work, the consequences of which are not at all clear: the development of limitless instantaneous communications with the internet and social networks, the growing influence of "civil society," the entry, into the developed world, of countries with quite different cultures and traditions, as well as growing migratory movements which are changing the make-up of our societies.

International companies can testify that modern globalization does create a level of exchange and interaction between people never experienced before. The development of NGOs and the commitment of more people to common good issues are obviously happening everywhere. A "collective consciousness" is in the making, even though nationalistic or religious hatreds have never been more visible.

Optimists, or believers who follow the vision of the French Jesuit Teilhard de Chardin (1955), with his *Noosphere* concept, would bet that the interaction of these different cultures and philosophies will lead to a less mechanistic approach of economic phenomena, and a resurgence of trust, implemented by ethical behavior and not only by regulation.

Pessimists, on the contrary, looking for example at the evolution of China, could conclude that the only common denominator of differing civilizations will be an approach that is both materialistic (making money is the ultimate yardstick) and legalistic (everything not illegal is fine).

What is sure is that developing trust, individual trust and not only institutional trust, will require something more than what is currently in the works. Our Assembly in London may have opened some new avenues!

APPENDIX

....

THE MBA OATH

As a business leader I recognize my role in society.

- My purpose is to lead people and manage resources to create value that no single individual can create alone.
- My decisions affect the well-being of individuals inside and outside my enterprise, today and tomorrow.

Therefore, I promise that:

- I will manage my enterprise with loyalty and care, and will not advance my personal interests at the expense of my enterprise or society.
- I will understand and uphold, in letter and spirit, the laws and contracts governing my conduct and that of my enterprise.
- I will refrain from corruption, unfair competition, or business practices harmful to society.
- I will protect the human rights and dignity of all people affected by my enterprise, and I will oppose discrimination and exploitation.
- I will protect the right of future generations to advance their standard of living and enjoy a healthy planet.
- I will report the performance and risks of my enterprise accurately and honestly.
- I will invest in developing myself and others, helping the management profession continue to advance and create sustainable and inclusive prosperity.

In exercising my professional duties according to these principles, I recognize that my behavior must set an example of integrity, eliciting trust and esteem from those I serve. I will remain accountable to my peers and to society for my actions and for upholding these standards.

This oath I make freely, and upon my honor.

REFERENCES

College des Bernardins (2013). *Agir pour la confiance: un choix, un investissement*. Paris: College des Bernardins.

D'Iribarne, Philippe (1989). *La Logique de l'honneur*. Paris: Seuil.

Teilhard de Chardin, Pierre (1955). *Le Phénomène humain*. Paris: Seuil.

POWER AND TRUST:
DISCUSSION SUMMARY

THE consequences of business for societal progress are in part a function of the relationships that are realized through activity in the economic marketplace. For the theme of "power and trust," the group considered two of the most significant such relationships. What kind of power is created in the private marketplace and how can it best be managed? In what ways do businesses depend on trust for their success, and to what extent do they promote socially valuable forms of trust?

Collomb began the discussion by arguing for the fundamental importance of trust in business and society, but noted that large companies confront a dilemma: in seeking to take advantage of their scale, they must establish policies for effective and safe operations. And yet, in doing so, they tend to foster a "culture of compliance" that sends a message of distrust. The challenge, Collomb suggested, is to cultivate an "ethical culture" that does not depend on compliance mechanisms. Such a challenge is exacerbated both, as Snabe observed, by the shortening lifespan of the average company (which reduces long-term incentives) and, as Walsh observed, by the increasingly disparate, transnational structure of corporate governance (which reduces the kind of organizational cohesion that tends to foster trust).

In response, Neiman—noting Collomb's reference to economic models of human behavior—suggested the great power of ideology to shape the way in which we act. Perhaps ethical culture requires an ideological revolution of sorts? On that note, both Barney and Frank pointed to ways in which the public might serve as an impetus for ideological change. For Barney, public pressure takes the form of market demand for investment. From a market point of view "we get the level of corporate social responsibility in our economy that we demand . . . Just what people are willing to pay for." For Frank, judgments of corporate responsibility are relative. Perhaps, he suggested, a strong public conception of corporate responsibility might induce a "race to the top" in which companies compete to achieve escalating standards of public approval.

In support of compliance strictures, however, Risse noted that in contexts involving complex tasks and diverse actors, a framework of explicit rules has an important role to play. As an example, he noted that recent attempts to incorporate multinational corporations into the human rights framework had been stymied in part by the ambiguous articulation of roles and responsibilities.

In his presentation, Pettit sounded a strong note of skepticism about the prospects for building trustworthy corporations. While trust might serve as the basis for relationships within corporations, Pettit argues that corporations are defined by structural dynamics that tend to place the internal imperatives of the organization outside concerns. That makes them poorly suited to serve as proper objects of trust.

In response, both Collomb and Autor expressed doubt that corporations were, in general, any less trustworthy than individuals. For Autor, the issue of trust is integrally related to the issue of reputation, and there are many circumstances in which the imperatives of reputation are quite strong. For Collomb, though, there is one crucial differentiating feature of corporations: whereas an individual may willingly sacrifice himself for a noble cause, the leaders of corporations confront extreme pressures against allowing their organization "to die" in order to avoid doing wrong. Meyer likewise suggested that to talk about corporations in general was to paint with too broad a brush. Non-profits, he observed, are the most rapidly growing portion of the corporate sector, and these are infused with a very different set of "meanings" governing their behavior.

This last point suggests important connections between our behavioral models of corporations and the role of "ideology" observed by Neiman. Meyer's point about the heterogeneity of corporate organizations, meanwhile, spoke directly to the subject of Davis's chapter, which concerns the recent trend toward a radical dispersion of corporate assets and employment, i.e. what he playfully dubs "Nikefication." Davis noted the irony that, as ever more corporate tasks are outsourced around the globe, the corporation itself "becomes obsolete as a vehicle," since the primary rationale for corporations is to limit liability in order to promote investment in large, "long-lived" assets. Davis thus speculated about a possible future in which technology enables democratic, human-scale, low-cost local production. Snabe cited the example of peer-to-peer music distribution as an example of the way in which technology might facilitate improvements for consumers through decentralized networks.

As Pettit observed, Davis's account of this organizational revolution suggests a future in which the economic power of corporations is considerably diminished. Still, as Davis noted, there will be important exceptions to this trend, such as oil companies. Thus, Pettit asked, is this really a future of diminished corporate power, or merely one in which that power rests in fewer hands? And what are the implications of that possibility for the political system? As Neiman also observed, while decentralization might diminish power, it also promises to reduce accountability in important respects: why shouldn't we regard these multiple layers of ownership simply as "obfuscation in an attempt at deniability?"

For Schmidtz, Nikefication reintroduces some of the themes that arose in Kitcher's discussion of the relationship between progress within the market system and meaningful work. Does the organizational diffusion of the corporation exacerbate a form of alienated labor in which we work anonymously and without creative control? "Are we becoming a world of Dilbert?"[1]

Finally, anticipating some central themes in Battilana's chapter, Barney asked whether the radical changes captured in the notion of Nikefication required rethinking our basic understanding of what a business organization is, i.e. the theory of the firm itself.

Fuerstein's chapter offered a distinctive development of Neiman's worry about the post-Nikefication prospects for holding corporations accountable. In his presentation, he noted the peculiar way in which markets produce profound consequences for human societies, but only as a by-product of large collections of individual activities aimed at local purposes. The result is a system that, in effect, wields power without agency and that therefore cannot be democratically "contested," i.e. subjected to meaningful public control.

Fuerstein suggested that an important part of the solution must run through the regulatory action of governments, but a number of participants pointed to alternative possibilities. For Hong, the solution effectively lay with markets themselves, which are capable of enormous ingenuity in solving social problems. By way of example, he noted that markets have proven enormously effective in distributing access to loans in ways that governments could not possibly replicate, though he emphasized the essential role of proper regulation in channeling market behavior towards the public good. Frank, however, was less sanguine about the role of markets in this regard. Citing the predatory loan industry, he noted that the only effective solution in such cases is to impose government measures that, in effect, make the market smaller and limit consumer choice by capping loans at a certain rate.

In different ways, Schmidtz, Anderson, and Davis all suggested that markets might be effectively contested through the consumer market itself. As Schmidtz put it: "we contest by surfing among a world of providers not limited by economies of scale." Likewise, citing the example of food deserts from Fuerstein's chapter, Anderson noted that one way of responding to the problematic operation of markets is to improve the economic standing of those subjected to their effects, thus enabling them to exercise influence through consumer behavior. Finally, as Davis observed, the public was able exert sufficient pressure on Mozilla to fire its new CEO after discovering that he had donated money to the anti-same-sex-marriage cause.

Battilana's presentation offered an overview of her research on "hybrid" organizations which are explicitly devoted to pursuing a social mission of some sort, but which sustain themselves through profitable enterprise. Such organizations have introduced a new kind of hope to the world of business, she suggested, but are also still relatively poorly understood. What forms of such organization are optimal, she asks, in creating value for society?

Like Davis's speculations about a post-Nikefication future, Battilana's take on hybrid organization provoked the group to a range of reflection on the fundamental form and

---

[1] Dilbert is a popular American comic strip which satirizes the drudgery of office life.

purpose of business organization. Both Snabe and Appiah posed the question of what had given rise to these kinds of organizations in the first place. For Snabe, the fundamental issue was, in effect, the basic premise of the entire conference, namely, that social and corporate goals had become decoupled. In response, Battilana drew on her own experience as a business professor, noting that, over the past eight years, she had seen a dramatic increase in students looking for "meaning" at work. From this point of view, hybrid organizations constitute a kind of response to some of the emptiness—discussed earlier by Kitcher, Schmidtz, and others—in the modern capitalist workplace. Mendiola emphasized, however, the importance of reforming the existing model in addition to creating new ones. We could go a long way, he suggested, simply by nudging profit-seeking companies towards a stakeholder perspective on value creation.

Sounding a note of caution, however, Jafar suggested that there must ultimately be a dividing line between "for-profits" and "non-profits" because businesses will ultimately have conflicts between their "for-profit objectives and the social mission." Ironically, he noted, the high-impact investing in social missions tends to come from foundations—like the Gates Foundation—whose funds derive from fortunes in the for-profit sector. Likewise, Hong suggested that the fundamental question is whether there are effective "complementarities" that rationalize uniting social and for-profit objectives. Turning to the example of Google and some of its social ventures, he suggested that this is typically not the case. In contrast, on the "Buffett-Gates model," we leave businesses to doing what they do best and non-profits to do what they do best.

Schmidtz, however, suggested that there might be more relevant diversity within organizations than the simple profit/non-profit distinction could allow. Perhaps, he suggested, "the fundamental difference might not be so much for-profit or not, as something like . . . what counts as a profit, or is there such a thing as enough profit—or is profit a means to an end?" Similarly, Davis observed the fact that the profit/non-profit distinction is itself an artifact of somewhat arbitrary tax categories. Large research universities, for example, are ultimately indistinguishable in vital respects from multinational corporations.

For the final comment of the gathering, Hong pulled the discussion back toward reflection on the role of those assembled, and on economists in particular, in fostering the ideology that Neiman targets. From Hong's point of view, economists are "getting way too much credit" as the force behind the ideal of wealth maximization. Economists, he argued, were simply "trying to catch up with reality," namely, a reality established by the behavior of corporations themselves.

Index of Names

INDEX OF SUBJECTS